TAKE ARMS AGAINST
A SEA OF TROUBLES

TAKE ARMS AGAINST A SEA OF TROUBLES

The POWER *of the* READER'S MIND *over a* UNIVERSE *of* DEATH

———

HAROLD BLOOM

———

Yale
UNIVERSITY PRESS
New Haven & London

Published with support from the Fund established in memory of
Oliver Baty Cunningham, a distinguished graduate of the Class of
1917, Yale College, Captain, 15th United States Field Artillery, born
in Chicago September 17, 1894, and killed while on active duty near
Thiaucourt, France, September 17, 1918, the twenty-fourth
anniversary of his birth.

Published with assistance from the foundation established in memory
of Philip Hamilton McMillan of the Class of 1894, Yale College.

Yale University Press books may be purchased in quantity for
educational, business, or promotional use. For information, please
e-mail sales.press@yale.edu (U.S. office) or sales@yaleup.co.uk
(U.K. office).

Set in Janson type by Westchester Publishing Services.
Printed in the United States of America.

Library of Congress Control Number: 2020933182
ISBN 978-0-300-24728-2 (hardcover : alk. paper)

A catalogue record for this book is available from the British Library.

This paper meets the requirements of ANSI/NISO Z39.48-1992
(Permanence of Paper).

10 9 8 7 6 5 4 3 2 1

Contents

PRELUDE   Reading to Stay Alive—Poetic Thinking   1

INTRODUCTION   The Rhetoric of Poetic Thinking   14

1. William Shakespeare and John Milton: In Every Deep,
   a Lower Deep   38

2. Milton: The Shakespearean Epic   83

3. Milton and William Blake: The Human Form Divine   110

4. William Wordsworth and John Keats: Something
   Evermore About to Be   159

5. Wordsworth: The Myth of Memory   170

6. Percy Bysshe Shelley and George Gordon,
   Lord Byron: Serpent and Eagle   180

7. Keats: They Seek No Wonder but the Human Face   297

8. Robert Browning: What in the Midst Lay but the
   Tower Itself?   333

9. Alfred, Lord Tennyson: Lest One Good Custom
   Should Corrupt the World   356

10. Walt Whitman: I Stop Somewhere Waiting for You 379

11. Robert Frost: Drink and Be Whole Again
     beyond Confusion 409

12. Wallace Stevens: The Hum of Thoughts Evaded
     in the Mind 422

13. William Butler Yeats and D. H. Lawrence: Start
     with the Shadow 460

14. Hart Crane: The Unknown God 500

15. Sigismund Schlomo Freud: Speculation and Wisdom 559

16. Dante/Center and Shakespeare/Circumference 577

Credits 629
Index 631

TAKE ARMS AGAINST A SEA OF TROUBLES

Prelude
Reading to Stay Alive—Poetic Thinking

*Deep Reading and Dr. Samuel Johnson. Angus Fletcher. Poetic Think-
ing and Poetic Awareness. William Blake's "Idiot Questioner." Milton's Satan and Hamlet. Poetic Thinking: Nietzsche and Vico.*

IN WHAT SENSE DOES deep reading augment life? Can it render
death only another hoyden? Most literary representations of death
do not portray her as being particularly boisterous. Why "her"? Is
it the long cavalcade associating death and the mother?

I have learned from Epicurus and Lucretius what Epicurus stated
so pungently in his letter to Menoceus (late fourth century BCE):

> So death, the most terrifying of ills, is nothing to us, since
> so long as we exist, death is not with us; but when death
> comes, then we do not exist. It does not then concern either
> the living or the dead, since for the former it is not, and the
> latter are no more.

That does not abate my sorrow for the beloved dead, or requite
my loneliness for my many departed friends, yet it holds off any fears
about my own vanishing. I do not want to fall yet once more and
break another hip or leg, or even a rib, but a Keatsian ceasing on the
midnight with no pain would not trouble me. When I say to myself
and to others that reading helps in staying alive, I am aware that I

am being metaphorical. Returning to Dante or Milton will not prolong my existence by a single minute, whereas endless exercise almost certainly will. But if life is to be more than breathing, it needs enhancement by knowledge or by the kind of love that is a form of knowledge.

My model for reading is always Samuel Johnson, who devoured books as he did his meat, possibly remembering his early years of privation in London, when he walked the streets with the poet Richard Savage, neither of them knowing where the next meal or bed or book was to be found. There is a marvelous passage in Boswell where, before dinner, the Grand Cham seizes a book on a recent Swedish revolution and devours it.

When a book arrives in the mail, I emulate Johnson as best I can and devour it instantly. When I was a child I had no money to buy books, and now, in advanced old age, my wife gently complains that a deluge of volumes has taken over our house. Order, despite her best efforts, has been so disrupted that I cannot locate the book I need at just this point: Angus Fletcher's *Colors of the Mind* (1991), his conjectures on thinking in literature. Angus taught me that staying alive is augmented by thinking in metaphors, as Dante, Milton, and, above all, Shakespeare think. For Fletcher, as for W. B. Yeats, the imagination was a holy fire, from which sages emerged to be the singing-masters of our souls.

Angus was descended from Highland Scottish nobility, and he loved the vistas of the Highlands. We were never there together, but I recall taking a phone call from him one early autumn when I was staying at Inverness. It was in the late 1970s and I had lectured on Walt Whitman at Inverness College, which I think is now part of the University of the Highlands and Islands. The students were receptive and the small city seemed a happy place, the horizon appearing endless. After I took Angus's call—he had a tendency to speak at length over the phone—I brooded about what it means to think metaphorically before I fell asleep.

That brooding has continued these last forty years and I think I approach some resolution. That is the concern of the introduction that follows, but here I need to make a central observation on poetic thinking. In a seminal essay, "Dramatic Monologue and the Overhearing of Lyric" (1985), Herbert F. Tucker finds a proper balance between the now-archaic New Critical emphasis on all poetry as being essentially dramatic in nature and the now-receding textualism of Franco-Heideggerianism:

> Renewed stress upon textuality as the basis for the Western written character is a beginning as important to the study of poetry now as it has been for over a century to the writing of dramatic monologues and to the modern tradition they can illuminate in both backward and forward direction. But textuality is only the beginning.

That seems to me critical wisdom. Poetic thinking about poetry denies the illusiveness of character, shrugs off epistemology even as it does metaphysics, and brings together the figures that make up poetic tradition. Those tropes emerge from a matrix of complex relations, historical and psychic, linguistic and imagistic, that work together so as to manifest a raw power that is now difficult to locate elsewhere, whether in theology or in philosophy.

I wish I could believe that the study of poetic thinking might alleviate the technological vicissitudes that multiply weekly. But of course they cannot. Literature, however sublime, cannot heal. What it can do is raise the level of awareness. But is that not Shakespeare's greatest achievement: to make us more aware?

You can argue that Homer, Virgil, Dante, Chaucer, Milton, Goethe, Wordsworth, Pushkin, Victor Hugo, and all the other major Western poets increase our awareness, yet somehow Shakespeare differs in kind rather than just in degree. Cognitive power allied to the creation of personalities and phrased inevitably is Shakespeare's almost consistent hallmark. Perhaps Chaucer comes closest to him in that regard. But there is also an otherness to Shakespeare, difficult to describe or define. Call it the creation of presence, a being at hand, a secular equivalent of the real presence of Christ in the Eucharist.

I emphasize again *secular*. Shakespeare had the artistic wisdom to evade the Incarnation, which is impossibly large for literary representation. Divinity in Shakespeare harrows us throughout *King Lear*, where we are persuaded by all the positive characters for whom

Lear is the emblem of fathership, royal authority, and the possibility of divine justice. But he fails as father, abdicates kingship, dies in total loss of his beloved Cordelia, and perhaps hallucinates her resurrection just as he departs.

For many years I rebelled against Nietzsche's implication (pain being more memorable than pleasure) that aesthetic delight is accomplished by realizing pain itself as the meaning. An involuntary memorizer from childhood on, that gave me the quandary of aesthetic eminence seeming to depend on the quality and quantity of pain, and not the release from suffering. I reread and teach *King Lear* and *Othello* every semester, and confront more pain in my response than I can accommodate.

Poetic imagination at its limits in Dante and in Shakespeare performs like a burning lake or a horizon on fire. Is that trope or is it something else? D. H. Lawrence said that the novel was the one bright book of life, but then extended the novel to Shakespeare and the Bible. One could add Homer, Lucretius, Virgil, Dante, Chaucer, Montaigne, and so many more.

What is poetic awareness? Is it a warning cry that our chase had a beast in view? Are all quests meaningless? Does the seeker invariably discover that she is the subject and object of her own quest?

William Blake excoriated the Idiot Questioner in his poem *Milton* (1804–1810):

> To cast off the idiot Questioner who is always questioning,
> But never capable of answering, who sits with a sly grin
> Silent plotting when to question like a thief in a cave:
> Who publishes doubt & calls it knowledge: whose Science
>   is Despair:
> Whose pretence to knowledge is Envy: whose whole
>   Science is
> To destroy the wisdom of ages to gratify ravenous Envy,
> That rages round him like a Wolf day & night without rest.
> He smiles with condescension: he talks of Benevolence & Virtue:
> And those who act with Benevolence & Virtue they murder
>   time on time.

> [Plate 41]

By now an ancient Blakean, I would abhor becoming an Idiot Questioner. I take it that the God of the Book of Job, when he speaks out of the whirlwind with aggressive rhetorical questions, is exactly such a Questioner. Still, at its most profound, the literature of the Sublime has to risk such equivocal queries. The criticism of that literature faces the same hazard.

Some great poets know far too well exactly what they are doing. But some find freedom by falling back upon the daemon and allowing that force to form purpose, design, and destination. Dante seems to me free of the major theologians, Augustine to Aquinas, who provide him with concepts and images. But my view is a minority one, at least in North America.

Had Shakespeare never written, John Milton would have been one of the freest of poets. Shakespeare, by the time he composed *Hamlet*, had become his own precursor.

What is it when you find your earlier self to be your only pragmatic forerunner? Magnanimity, Shakespeare's prime characteristic, etymologically stems from the Latin for "great soul." I reread or recite Shakespeare to myself, day and night, because he gives me voices lost and found. His generous abundance is the perpetual harvest of voice.

To have made a heterocosm that has turned into our world is also to prop up that world. It is not too much to say that Shakespeare keeps many of us going.

In their very different ways Samuel Johnson and Ralph Waldo Emerson wanted more from Shakespeare. Dr. Johnson desired moral clarity and was offended by Cordelia's murder. Emerson wanted, not a master of the revels to mankind, but a poet-prophet. Nietzsche, who identified himself with Shakespeare, is a better guide than Johnson or Emerson. What we think of as the Nietzschean genealogy of morals and Nietzschean perspectivism were Shakespeare's well before Nietzsche. Desiring to *be* Shakespeare, Nietzsche instead became a Shakespearean tragic protagonist.

John Milton knew he could not be Shakespeare. When he was young he thought of composing his own *Macbeth*. He gave up after writing down the title. What became *Paradise Lost* was originally intended to be a drama, *Adam Unparadised*.

Milton's Satan is a version of Hamlet. Iago, Macbeth, and others get into the mix, but the scope of consciousness recalls the Prince of Denmark. Satan cannot stop thinking, while Hamlet *is* thinking.

Unless you think that there will be universal salvation, along with the vigorous Eastern Orthodox theologian David Bentley Hart in his new book, *That All Shall Be Saved* (2019), then you wonder, what would become of Satan or Hamlet in a next world? Milton rather nastily reduces Satan and his host to so many serpents attempting to ingest inedible fruit on the Dead Sea floor. I would not say that Shakespeare is fully responsible for Hamlet's nihilizing death; by then Hamlet is his own author.

Nietzsche went mad and died at fifty-five. He attempted to live his life as a poem and followed his own counsel: just take one step more and forgive yourself everything. Then the entire drama of fall and redemption will work itself through in your own soul.

Poetic thinking for Nietzsche granted him aesthetic success and personal disaster. One wishes he had been more in the mode of Giambattista Vico, the eighteenth-century inaugurator of the genealogical method in history, poetic speculation, and morals. Vico exalted the act of writing and envisioned it as moving toward poetry, which alone could return us to the wisdom of the ancients:

> The order of ideas must follow the order of institutions. This was the order of human institutions: first the forests, after that the huts, next the cities, and finally the academies. This axiom is a great principle of etymology, for this sequence of human institutions sets the pattern for the histories of words in the various native languages. Thus we observe in the Latin language that almost the whole corpus of its words had sylvan or rustic origins. For example, *lex*. First it must have meant a collection of acorns. Thence we believe is derived *ilex*, as it were *illex*, the oak (as certainly *aquilex* means collection of waters); for the oak produces the acorns by which the swine are drawn together. *Lex* was next a collection of vegetables, from which the latter were called *legumina*. Later on, at a time when the vulgar letters had not yet been invented for writing down the laws, *lex* by a necessity of civil nature must have meant a collection of citizens, or the public

parliament, so that the presence of the people was the *lex*, or "law," that solemnized the wills that were made *calatis comitiis*, in the presence of the assembled *comitia*. Finally, collecting letters, and making, as it were, a sheaf of them for each word, was called *legere*, reading.

> [*The New Science* (1744), translated
> by T. G. Bergin and M. H. Fisch]

Agata Bielik-Robson, Polish-English authority on modern Jewish studies, in her response to my book *Possessed by Memory* (2019), perceived my reliance on the dialectical position of the Hebrew stem called *Niphal*, which founds the paradigmatic Jewish wisdom, explained in my own paraphrase of Rabbi Tarphon: "We are not required to complete the work, but neither are we free to desist from it." *Niphal*, the transitive mode of in-between, perfectly defines the role of the particular ring in the "chain of tradition," granted a middle voice between activity and passivity, "doing and suffering," but also—perhaps most importantly—between mortality and immortality.

In the classical tradition of the excluded middle, this in-between is an impossible position: we may have to choose between the Nietzschean tragic religion of finitude and the Pauline promise of personal infinity. My sense of *Niphal* is precisely the refusal to think about this in the simplistic terms of either/or. *Niphal* can be active doing or passive suffering. Yet the word is ambiguous: Does it tell us that doing and suffering are the same? Does it also imply that immortality and mortality together form a child's spinning top or *dreidel*, but one that never will stop spinning, so that we cannot know our destiny and destination?

What can literary criticism, of whatever variety, tell us about such dark matters of speculation as immortality, resurrection, and redemption? Wittgenstein firmly believed that religious truths could not be expressed in language. St. John of the Cross might have agreed, and yet we have his great devotional lyrics and his brilliant prose commentaries upon them.

Wittgenstein dismissed Freud's work as a speculation and as a powerful mythology. I could not disagree with that. But of course Christianity is a speculation and powerful mythology. So, alas, is Judaism.

From early childhood until now I have ransacked Tanakh, the Hebrew Bible, and have found in it nothing about immortality. The concept reached the Jews through Plato, who in the *Phaedo* gave four proofs for immortality. Currents from Zoroastrianism and (who knows?) perhaps even Indic religions seem to have flowed into their consciousness. I was raised Orthodox Jewish and was never taught immortality or resurrection, and it was understood that redemption would come to the people of Israel all together.

I am puzzled that Wittgenstein once told a Christian friend that he regarded his own thinking as Hebraic. Three of his four grand-parents had been Jewish, but the philosopher was a baptized Roman Catholic and died as one. He remarked somewhere that only holy men, prophets or sages, among the Jews could be considered as pos-sessing genius. To himself he granted talent. I suppose that Gershom Scholem was, for me, prophet and sage, though he could hardly have been considered holy in any sense.

What are the frontiers of literary criticism? Immortality and res-urrection are being taken over by Silicon Valley, whose High Tech High Priests really do intend to go on living forever. Good fortune to them. I find that prospect awful. Yes, it would be good to have another three or four years, if I could stay healthy enough. But lit-eral immortality seems to me a horror. One of my cardiologists whimsically said to me that my brain could live on and keep its mem-ory after I have gone into the Great Perhaps. I gently said to him, No thanks.

I would think one function of literary criticism at this time is to explore the figurations we term immortality, resurrection, and re-demption. Now, in 2019, for many of the most literate among us, these can only be tropes. Their status as commonplaces or topoi has evanesced. Since trope is a substitute formation, we need to ask: For what? The answer is that so few secular intellectuals re-gard these three terms as antique delusions.

It seems accurate to observe that immortality is a trope for longing.

Is resurrection a substitute for not coming alive in this our life? As for "redemption," the term seems to belong to high finance. One wryly observes that the archaic meaning was to purchase one's freedom.

Remove from the Kantian triad God and immortality and what remains is freedom, if it can find you. Vico argued that human freedom mirrors divine freedom. Providence decreed that we could begin again almost as gods. This ambitious sense of freedom was seen as poetic wisdom, the endowment of the first Gentile poets.

Emerson, in "The Poet" (1844), is our strongest authority on the freedom of poetry:

> If the imagination intoxicates the poet, it is not inactive in other men. The metamorphosis excites in the beholder an emotion of joy. The use of symbols has a certain power of emancipation and exhilaration for all men. We seem to be touched by a wand, which makes us dance and run about happily, like children. We are like persons who come out of a cave or cellar into the open air. This is the effect on us of tropes, fables, oracles, and all poetic forms. Poets are thus liberating gods. Men have really got a new sense, and found within their world, another world, or nest of worlds; for, the metamorphosis once seen, we divine that it does not stop.
>
> The poets are thus liberating gods. The ancient British bards had for the title of their order, "Those who are free throughout the world." They are free, and they make free.

That is the optative mood raised to sublimity: unbounded desire for what is not. A devout Emersonian since 1965, I cannot in loyalty demur. Still, at ninety, only Homer and Shakespeare seem really free, and even they cannot make me free. We do not know upon which lost bards Homer battened, but there is rich speculation in a remarkable study by my former student Andrew Ford, *Homer and the Poetry of the Past* (1992). Shakespeare the magpie took what he wanted wherever he found it and outdid the alchemists in changing lead to gold, or if it was Chaucer or Marlowe, "gold to airy thinness beat."

At certain moments, perhaps illusions, particular personalities in Shakespeare grant me respites from anxieties and self-communings. They work upon me as old friends would do, if they were still here, and they are not.

I do not think of our father Walt Whitman as having been free. What freedom he enjoyed he wrested for himself by prodigious imaginings. I more or less know Shakespeare through a hundred personalities he brought forth. What I know of Whitman are his three psychic components: myself ("Walt Whitman, one of the roughs, an American"), the soul (night, death, the mother, and the sea), and the "real me," or "me myself" (what Wallace Stevens was to call "the interior paramour").

I never stop learning from Whitman. My neighbor on Linden Street, whose garden I see through my window, has a lilac bush now beautifully in bloom. As I age I love flowers more, roses in particular, but only lilacs move me almost to tears. They were Walt Whitman's tally, the trope for his image of voice. In the threnody for Abraham Lincoln, Whitman places a sprig of lilac on the martyr's coffin as it passes in procession:

> Coffin that passes through lanes and streets,
> Through day and night with the great cloud darkening the
>   land,
> With the pomp of the inloop'd flags with the cities draped in
>   black,
> With the show of the States themselves as of crape-veil'd
>   women standing,
> With processions long and winding and the flambeaus of the
>   night,
> With the countless torches lit, with the silent sea of faces and
>   the unbared heads,
> With the waiting depot, the arriving coffin, and the sombre
>   faces,
> With dirges through the night, with the thousand voices rising
>   strong and solemn,
> With all the mournful voices of the dirges pour'd around the
>   coffin,
> The dim-lit churches and the shuddering organs—where amid
>   these you journey,
> With the tolling tolling bells' perpetual clang,
> Here, coffin that slowly passes,
> I give you my sprig of lilac.
>   ["When Lilacs Last in the Dooryard Bloom'd" (1865)]

What is the reader's freedom? In 2019 she or he confronts an unstable cosmos in some ways drifting toward chaos. Climate change is more than real: it presages a reality more oppressive than our own. Thomas Henry Huxley, in his speech welcoming the foundation of Johns Hopkins University (September 12, 1876), warned all of us: "A man's worst difficulties begin when he is able to do as he likes."

Secular and disenchanted readers in time may well confront something like the chaos through which Milton's Satan heroically voyaged, named by the poet: "a universe of death." How shall such readers augment the power of mind to sustain their own voyage?

I lack the authority to speak for anyone but myself. What you read and how deeply you read matters almost as much as how you love, work, exercise, vote, practice charity, strive for social justice, cultivate kindness and courtesy, and worship if you are capable of worship. The mind is an activity and will decay into dark inertia if not sustained by the sustenance of reading.

The work of reading does not exclude delight. Energy is the only delight, as William Blake told us. We should read as Don Quixote sallies forth, eager to challenge whatever comes.

The Knight of the Woeful Countenance is frequently battered, and poor Sancho Panza has to sustain innumerable blows, yet the Knight knows who he is and who he might be, should he desire it. Sancho Panza eventually becomes governor of his own island, enjoys the sublime travesties of rule, but is very glad to go back to Don Quixote. The Talmud warns against so reading Tanakh that we find ourselves reflected in it. It is tempting to see myself mirrored also in Don Quixote. Due to age and temperament, that is the danger to be overcome whenever I read.

Two-thirds of a century as a teacher, here and abroad, have burned away a quantity of mere narcissism and taught me some of the uses of silence. How do you teach yourself and others to internalize the essential poems without confusing them with one another? How can you avoid false identifications with poems?

Thomas Hardy's poem "We Are Getting to the End" is a pitiless retreat from the idealism he had learned from Shelley. Like larks in cages, Hardy writes, "We ply spasmodically our pleasuring," while nations make unceasing war: "Ah! We are getting to the end of dreams!"

Hardy is at his best in "Neutral Tones" (1898, written 1867):

We stood by a pond that winter day,
And the sun was white, as though chidden of God,
And a few leaves lay on the starving sod;
—They had fallen from an ash, and were gray.

Your eyes on me were as eyes that rove
Over tedious riddles of years ago;
And some words played between us to and fro
On which lost the more by our love.

The smile on your mouth was the deadest thing
Alive enough to have strength to die;
And a grin of bitterness swept thereby
Like an ominous bird a-wing. . . .

Since then, keen lessons that love deceives,
And wrings with wrong, have shaped to me
Your face, and the God curst sun, and a tree,
And a pond edged with grayish leaves.

Thomas Hardy's first marriage was to Emma Lavinia Gifford, who never permitted him to forget her social eminence. It may not be the unhappiest marriage among the major poets, but it was indeed rather dreadful. After her death, Hardy saluted her in several guilty poems, marked by nostalgia for a time that had never existed.

Eliot's *After Strange Gods* (1934) denounces Hardy and Lawrence where it could have chosen John Milton, William Blake, Percy Bysshe Shelley, and their followers:

The point is that Lawrence started life wholly free from any restriction of tradition or institution, that he had no guidance except the Inner Light, the most untrustworthy and deceitful guide that ever offered itself to wandering humanity.

Eliot surpasses himself in vehement dogmatism. He could have been John Calvin burning Michael Servetus at the stake in Geneva on October 27, 1553, the ground of controversy having been the

Trinity. A master of hyperbole, Eliot dismisses the Inner Light, and with it the major Post-Enlightenment movement of the human spirit that we once called Romanticism. Turn Eliot's prose inside out, and you may shake Shelley loose. Turn Eliot's verse every which way and its idiosyncratic development of late Romanticism is palpable.

The great poems, plays, novels, and stories teach us how to go on living, even when submerged under forty fathoms of bother and distress. If you live ninety years you will be a battered survivor. Your own mistakes, accidents, and failures at otherness beat you down. Rise up at dawn and read something that matters as soon as you can.

Introduction
The Rhetoric of Poetic Thinking

THE UNACKNOWLEDGED PHILOSOPHER OF modern poetry is the Neapolitan rhetorician Giambattista Vico, who died in 1744, the same year as the poet Alexander Pope. In his *New Science*, Vico strikingly de-idealized the origin and purpose of poetry. Vico believed that the life of our primitive ancestors was itself what he termed "a severe poem." Here is my own description of the ancestral powers that Vico imagined:

> These giants, through the force of a cruel imagination, defended themselves against nature, the gods, and one another by metaphoric language, with which they "divinated," that is, at once they sought to become immortal gods and also to ward off potential and future dangers from their own lives. For them, the function of poetry was not to liberate, but to define, limit, and so defend the self against everything that might destroy it.

I recall this paragraph from my article called "The Uses of Poetry," published in the *New York Times* in 1975. That was the year my rejoinder to Paul de Man's critique of my *The Anxiety of Influence* (1973) came forth as *A Map of Misreading*, dedicated to Paul in much the same spirit that I had dedicated *Anxiety* to my fierce teacher William K. Wimsatt. That spirit might be called agonistic affection or admiring irony.

Viconian poetic thinking after the death of Pope becomes more drastic as it moves from William Collins and Thomas Gray through William Cowper and William Blake on to William Wordsworth and all his progeny: Shelley, Keats, Tennyson, Browning, Thomas Hardy, D. H. Lawrence, W. B. Yeats, and so many others. Emerson, as much the American Vico as the American Nietzsche, animated his nation's poetry from Walt Whitman and Emily Dickinson to Edwin Arlington Robinson, Robert Frost, Wallace Stevens, Marianne Moore, W. C. Williams, T. S. Eliot, Hart Crane, and the poets I knew best in my own time: Elizabeth Bishop, May Swenson, James Merrill, A. R. Ammons, John Ashbery.

I think I evaded my debt to Vico for some time but have returned to him in my old age. He teaches me that what I call "poetic influence" is a trope for his kind of cognitive rhetoric. You cannot take up an interpretive stance to any great work of imaginative literature in which that stance will not rely upon a trope, whether it be the irony of Friedrich Schlegel, J. Hillis Miller, and Paul de Man, or the transumption of Angus Fletcher and John Hollander. Only in a limited sense is irony the condition of literary language. Tropes are not so much figures of knowing as they are figures of becoming and of action.

Here is John Hollander in his seminal study *The Figure of Echo* (1981):

> Formal structures . . . are recreated metaleptically. So are genres. Classical rhetoric was a system for enforcing direct persuasion by force of words. The Renaissance interpreted this figuratively as psychogogic for poetic truth. All taxonomies of the rhetorical figure have in fact been themselves interpretive.

Emotional stimulation and poetic truth-telling can be linked only through figuration. But there is a curious duality in the history of rhetoric. Is it a mode of persuasion or is it a panoply of tropes? All systems of tropes defend against other systems. Defense, however, in the Freudian sense, can be a very aggressive process. Nietzsche seems to have had no defense against Shakespeare, who inundated him. His perspectivism is Shakespearean. It could be argued that Shakespeare, and Prince Hamlet in particular, became Nietzsche's shield against the onslaught of nihilism. Hamlet, after his return from the sea, in effect forgives himself everything, and so the entire drama of fall and redemption is enacted in his own psyche.

Nietzsche learned self-forgiveness from Hamlet and from Shelley. Though he saw himself as philosophizing with a hammer, in retrospect his force appears more affirmative than not. There are of course a myriad of Nietzsches and I can never hold him stable for very long. My late friend Richard Rorty taught me to approach Nietzsche through the difficult notion of contingency.

The word "contingency" has many shades of meaning. Richard Rorty is astringent, severely expounding Nietzsche, in disputing Emerson's notion that the poets are liberating gods:

> This needed corrective to Nietzsche's attempt to divinize the poet, this dependence of even the strongest poet on others, is summed up by Bloom as follows [in *Kabbalah and Criticism* (1975)]:
>
> The sad truth is that poems *don't have* presence, unity, form or meaning. . . . What then does a poem possess or create? Alas, a poem *has* nothing and *creates* nothing. Its presence is a promise, part of the substance of things hoped for, the evidence of things not seen. Its unity is in the good will of the reader. . . . Its meaning is just that there is, or rather *was*, another poem.
>
> In this passage Bloom de-divinises the poem, and thereby the poet, in the same way in which Nietzsche de-divinised truth and in which Freud de-divinised conscience. He does for romanticism what Freud did for moralism. The strategy is the same in all these cases: it is to substitute a tissue of contingent relations, a web which stretches backward and forward through past and future time, for a formed, unified, present, self-contained substance, something capable of being seen steadily and whole. Bloom reminds us that just as even the strongest poet is parasitic on her precursors, just as even she can give

birth only to a small part of herself, so she is dependent on the kindness of all those strangers out there in the future.

[*Contingency, Irony, and Solidarity* (1989)]

Rorty's citation of my work takes me back forty-five years, half a lifetime ago. I would not phrase it that way any longer. It is not that my understanding of contingency is less ominous but the anxiety of influence now seems to me literary love tempered by ambivalence, as all love is. Nietzsche ambivalently derived from Schopenhauer. Could there have been a Nietzsche without Schopenhauer, or a Freud without Schopenhauer? I am not a philosopher, yet Wittgenstein's aphorisms sometimes seem as close to Schopenhauer's as were those of Tolstoy or Thomas Hardy. Famously Wittgenstein characterized Schopenhauer's mind as quite crude, that is to say dumb. Granted that almost anyone's mind falls short of Wittgenstein's, that seems ungracious.

As a literary reader of Schopenhauer I am impressed by the urgency and cold rancor of the drive he calls the will to live. There is a famous anecdote that Schopenhauer's mother, a literary bluestocking with aspirations, pushed her son down a flight of stairs when she felt that he was outdoing her in notoriety.

The metaphysics of sexual love in Schopenhauer constitutes a dismal present time and an unenviable future. Thomas Hardy's *Tess of the d'Urbervilles* (1891) and *Jude the Obscure* (1895) are better reading than Schopenhauer but hardly more cheerful.

The terror of Nietzsche is that he tried to live his life as though it were a poem. He saw himself as one of the corrupted strong poets, but is not that kind of corruption a further strength? When I read Nietzsche, am I being offered any insights that do not stem from his own profound literary culture? He asserted that he was wiser than the poets, but all I can find in him is what Vico called poetic wisdom. When you term what we call reality "the primordial poem of mankind," composed by all of us, you can sound rather like Shelley, but this is the Nietzsche of the late aphorisms gathered together as *The Will to Power* in 1901, the year after his death:

One must understand the artistic basic phenomenon that is called "life"—the building spirit that builds under the most unfavorable conditions, in the slowest manner—a demonstration of all its combinations must first be produced afresh: it preserves itself.

[translated by Walter Kaufmann and R. J. Hollingdale]

Book 2 of Vico's *New Science* is called "Poetic Wisdom." It is pithily summarized by Thomas Goddard Bergin and Max Harold Fisch, modern editors of Vico:

In such fashion the first men of the gentile nations, children of nascent mankind, created things according to their own ideas. But this creation was infinitely different from that of God. For God, in his purest intelligence, knows things, and, by knowing them, creates them; but they, in their robust ignorance, did it by virtue of a wholly corporeal imagination. And because it was quite corporeal, they did it with marvelous sublimity, a sublimity such and so great that it excessively perturbed the very persons who by imagining did the creating, for which they were called "poets," which is Greek for "creators."

Vico is aware that he sides with Homer against Plato. I would suggest that the Orphic element in the Neapolitan Professor of Eloquence sides with the fallen angels against John Milton. That marvelous sublimity is purchased by loss, but that is as it should be. When we recite the title, the emphasis should be: Paradise *Lost*. William Blake plays upon that loss in the name he gives to his prophetic artificer Los.

If there is a Dantesque poet in the English language, it has to be Shelley:

> ". . . —I among the multitude
> Was swept; me sweetest flowers delayed not long,
>   Me not the shadow nor the solitude,
>
> "Me not the falling stream's Lethean song,
>   Me, not the phantom of that early form
> Which moved upon its motion,—but among

"The thickest billows of the living storm
I plunged, and bared my bosom to the clime
    Of that cold light, whose airs too soon deform.—

"Before the chariot had begun to climb
    The opposing steep of that mysterious dell,
Behold a wonder worthy of the rhyme

    "Of him whom from the lowest depths of Hell
Through every Paradise & through all glory
    Love led serene, and who returned to tell

"In words of hate and awe the wondrous story
    How all things are transfigured, except Love;
For deaf as is a sea which wrath makes hoary

    "The world can hear not the sweet notes that move
The sphere whose light is melody to lovers—
    A wonder worthy of his rhyme . . ."
                    [*The Triumph of Life* (1822), ll. 460–480]

I once agreed with William Hazlitt that *The Triumph of Life* was a fragment of an *Inferno*. Now, at ninety, it seems almost as much a *Purgatorio*. I do not regard it as unfinished but as abandoned. Paul Valéry can serve as my authority:

A work is never completed except by some accident such as weariness, satisfaction, the need to deliver, or death: for, in relation to who or what is making it, it can only be one stage in a series of inner transformations.
                    ["Recollection" from *Mélange* (1939),
                    translated by David Paul]

Only in glimmers can I find traces in Shelley's last poem of the Promethean revolutionary of his life's work. In one of our many peripatetic disputes about Shelley, Paul de Man fell back on his affectionate refrain: "The trouble with you, Harold, is that you do not believe in de troot" (Paul's Flemish pronunciation). The truth for Paul, as for Heidegger, was death. Who wants to worship death? De Man legitimately caught and exemplified Shelley's epistemological rigor but at the expense of the poet's residual hope that the good time might yet come.

Paul de Man's Shelley is an ironist who teaches himself that disfiguration annihilates meaning or drives it off into wandering exile. But that is also de Man's Rousseau, Wordsworth, Proust, Yeats, or what you will. The alternation of presence and absence suits Yahweh, but human ironies become mere repetitions, and no fresh meanings can be started. To begin again is to revise, and the ultimate trope of revision is what the Greeks termed metalepsis and the Romans called transumption.

I want now to go beyond my previous understanding of transumption. A trope that revises earlier figurations so as to make them seem belated, and itself as possessing priority, is no longer a synchronic phenomenon but takes us into the realm of a diachronic rhetoric. Such a rhetoric remains to be fully formulated. Part of the problem with Saussure's conception of the linguistic sign is that, applied to poetry, connotation vanishes. Nuances, implicit or hidden possible meanings, associations, and echoings depart together. I get no help from a bar between the signifier and the signified, if the linguist cannot tell me on which side of the bar to find connotation. A synchronic rhetoric is all but unimaginable in such a situation. The result is a series of inaccurate accounts of a rhetoric that changes through history.

I regret that one of the inaccurate accounts is that of Paul de Man, who insisted that the pastness of trope itself is illusive, due to what he called the aporia, "the impassable" by etymology, between rhetoric as a system of tropes and rhetoric as persuasion. My disagreement is profound. Tropes are not so much figures of knowledge as they are urgings or willings. I read aporias as negative moments—breakthroughs into the Sublime—that make poems *poems* and not epistemological snapshots.

I have learned that poetry is a mosaic of relationships framed by the act of voicing. Poetry is not just language; "language is fossil poetry," said Emerson in "The Poet." Paul de Man, for many reasons (some of them hidden and personal), had a total skepticism in regard to history, whether individual or aggregate. For Paul, tropes had no history. But the history of rhetoric renders every trope a victim of its own history. It is not just that the irony of one age can become the noble synecdoche of another; it is that all tropes historically are subject to transumption. Belated poets, if they are as strong as Dante or Milton, present themselves as dawnings and not as evensong.

Sometimes I wonder if Wittgenstein's deprecation of Shakespeare did not rise out of his own sense of our being so enclosed by language that we cannot get outside it. This is akin to my own realization that we are inside Shakespeare even as Jonah was within the large fish that swallowed him. We cannot achieve a perspective on Shakespeare that he has not taught us. He is always ahead, and we labor in his wake. I am haunted perpetually by a passage from *Measure for Measure* that also possessed Samuel Johnson:

> Thou hast nor youth nor age,
> But, as it were, an after-dinner's sleep,
> Dreaming on both . . .
>
> [3.1.32–34]

Johnson thought this indicated our inability to live in the present moment. I think that is part of it, but the metaphor is richer. Shakespeare's dinner is our lunch. More than ever, in old age I nod off quite suddenly for a few seconds and start up again, wondering where I am back in my own past. Shakespeare's metaphor implies that our entire existence is, as it were, just a nap after lunch. We are torpid, all but numb, possessing nothing, possessed by memory.

John Keats was capable of taking Edgar's "Ripeness is all" and transuming it by "And fill all fruit with ripeness to the core":

> Season of mists and mellow fruitfulness,
>   Close bosom-friend of the maturing sun;
> Conspiring with him how to load and bless
>   With fruit the vines that round the thatch-eves run;
> To bend with apples the moss'd cottage-trees,
>   And fill all fruit with ripeness to the core;
>   To swell the gourd, and plump the hazel shells
>   With a sweet kernel; to set budding more,
> And still more, later flowers for the bees,
> Until they think warm days will never cease,
>   For summer has o'er-brimm'd their clammy cells.
>
> [(1820, written 1819)]

Keats transumes also his own sonnet written earlier that same year:

> Leave melodizing on this wintry day,
> Shut up thine olden pages, and be mute:
> Adieu! for once again the fierce dispute,
>   Betwixt damnation and impassion'd clay
>   Must I burn through; once more humbly essay
> The bitter-sweet of this Shakespearean fruit.
>
> > ["On Sitting Down to Read King
> > Lear Once Again" (written 1818)]

Even Keats at his most powerful could not fully unpack "Ripeness is all."

> *Edgar:* Away, old man, give me thy hand, away!
>   King Lear hath lost, he and his daughter ta'en.
>   Give me thy hand; come on.
> *Gloucester:* No further, sir, a man may rot even here.
> *Edgar:* What, in ill thoughts again? Men must endure
>   Their going hence even as their coming hither,
>   Ripeness is all. Come on.
> *Gloucester:* And that's true too.
>
> > [*King Lear*, 5.2.6–12]

Gloucester's comment is apt. I hardly mean that it is suitable for this situation, but that no reaction could be adequate to this "fierce dispute, / betwixt damnation and impassion'd clay." I teach *King Lear* every year to very sensitive and informed students and never know how to comment on "Ripeness is all." I seem all but alone in my conviction that Edgar is a heroic and altogether admirable figure, but I have to admit that suffering has darkened him.

One problem of a transumptive or diachronic rhetoric is this: Can you conclude a poem without darkening it? For me, this remains one of my problems with Eliot's *The Waste Land*, which perhaps should be termed the Eliot–Pound *Waste Land*. Anyone consulting Valerie Eliot's facsimile version of *The Waste Land* manuscript confronts two poems, Eliot's sprawling original and the received text so forcefully edited by Ezra Pound. I do not quarrel with the consensus that Pound improved the poem. What remains seems to me as much an indeliberate American baroque defeat as Wallace Stevens's *The Comedian as the Letter C* is a deliberate one.

The Waste Land (1922) is an inverted pastoral elegy for Eliot's close friend Jean Verdenal (1890–1915), who died heroically at Gallipoli, tending wounded soldiers. Eliot and Verdenal met at the Sorbonne, where they shared an enthusiasm for Laforgue. There was some sort of deep attachment between the two young poets, and certainly the memory of Verdenal lingered throughout Eliot's life. This far on in time, I do not know why we should care whether or not they were homoerotic partners. It is enough that they loved one another, and that this may have been the great love of Eliot's life until his second marriage.

Eliot relies upon Indic metaphysics for his attempt at a transumptive close. This works well insofar as *The Waste Land* can be viewed primarily as a revision of Walt Whitman's "Lilacs" elegy, which in one sense it most certainly is. Evidently the Indic conclusion came to Eliot in a vision while he was under treatment for an emotional breakdown. The Sanskrit chant is an invitation to further figuration:

These fragments I have shored against my ruins
Why then Ile fit you. Hieronymo's mad againe.
Datta. Dayadhvam. Damyata.
        Shantih   shantih   shantih

[ll. 430–433]

That first line is Whitmanian in mode; the next is Thomas Kyd's; the next two are Sanskrit for "Give. Sympathize. Control" followed by three invocations of a peace beyond all understanding. Is that peace earned? What has Eliot given? Perhaps the apex of his life before 1922: a momentary union with Jean Verdenal that must be masked from future readers, granted archaic prejudices only now pretty well dissolved. With whom, besides himself and the dead Verdenal, has he sympathized? The control was partly Pound's, partly a Romantic tradition that could not be repudiated.

Eliot at the close of his life, evidently happy in his second marriage, may have known peace, and who could begrudge it? But are these the accents that close off further figuration? Weary as I am of polemicizing against Eliot, I am compelled to remember one of his curious judgments: "Dante made great poetry out of a great philosophy of life; and Shakespeare made equally great poetry out of an inferior and muddled philosophy of life." This seems to mean that Shakespeare did not regard the Incarnation as a fit subject for drama and perhaps also that Shakespeare celebrated the possibilities as well as the hazards of human nature. Eliot did not like Montaigne and preferred Pascal, which is rather like exalting Marlowe or Ben Jonson over Shakespeare. We do not know when Shakespeare first read Montaigne, and doubtless Montaigne made a difference to the later Shakespeare, but Shakespeare did his own thinking. Since he was averse to solving problems, you would be a weak reader if you attempted to take your philosophy of life from the greatest of writers.

Eliot said that he preferred Dante to Shakespeare, but Shakespeare is everywhere in Eliot's poetry, a voice that could not be stilled. It is now nearly a century since *The Waste Land* was composed in 1921. That makes the poem as archaic as the "Lilacs" elegy or John Milton. Insofar as Eliot's poetry seems permanent, he is now another ancient and no more or less a modernist than Callimachus (third century BCE), a scholar and poet who worked at the Great Library in Alexandria.

I think the time will come when more readers will realize that *The Waste Land* essentially is an elegy both for Jean Verdenal and for Eliot himself. Indeed, it is a Shelleyan lament whose model may well be a fusion of *Alastor* (1816) and *Adonais* (1821).

Critical opinion is now very various on the achievement of Eliot's *Four Quartets* (1943). I must rely on my own experience of rereading the sequence. Not much in *Burnt Norton* or in *East Coker* achieves inevitable phrasing: a singsong prosiness prevails. *The Dry Salvages*, though oddly regarded by some exegetes of Eliot as being parodistic, has some remarkably eloquent passages. *Little Gidding* is the most ambitious and, in at least one section, the most accomplished of the *Quartets*. That is the chant beginning, "Let me disclose the gifts reserved for age," where Eliot confronts a composite precursor in direct imitation of Dante's encounter with Brunetto Latini.

Components of that composite include Irving Babbitt, one of Eliot's teachers at Harvard, and a remarkable consort of poets: Dante, Swift, Shelley, Walt Whitman, Mallarmé, and most overtly and surprisingly, Yeats. Eliot was highly equivocal in regard to Yeats; a devout Anglo-Catholic had to be uneasy with a syncretic occultist. Yet Eliot, like Yeats, believed in the daemon, the god within who speaks the poem, frequently in opposition to the poet's own desires. Yeats is present as Eliot's dark double, a shadow self. Eliot was too good a reader not to know that Yeats was the far greater poet of the two. Both of them stemmed from what Shelley called "the fire for which all thirst," Yeats's Condition of Fire.

In 1998 I introduced the late Geoffrey Hill at a poetry reading at the 92nd Street Y. I had to catch a limousine to get back to New Haven so as to teach the next day. The poet and I had never met before and were never to meet again. I apologized to him that I had to leave before the reading. His new long poem *The Triumph of Love* had just appeared and I admired it greatly. We talked for only a few minutes in the green room and then I went onstage to introduce him. I had a prepared text but on a sudden impulse spoke spontaneously. Hill's salient quality for me was his extraordinary capacity for experiencing the sufferings of others, at least in his poems. I ended my brief remarks with a sentence that suddenly slipped out of me: "Geoffrey Hill is the great Gentile poet of the Jewish diaspora." Many years later I read an interview with him in which he said those words had moved him.

I think back to the anguished poet Delmore Schwartz, whom I knew and liked during the early 1960s. I remember several discussions at the White Horse Tavern in Greenwich Village in which generally we were in agreement, but never on Eliot, who seemed with Joyce to be the god of Schwartz's idolatry. Sixty years later, I know only a few living laggards who continue to worship the poet-critic who lived the myth of the GREAT WESTERN BUTTERSLIDE. I take the phrase from Northrop Frye's review of Allen Tate's essays, where it is applied to the Pound–Eliot myth of a great slab of classical, Christian, neo-Fascist butter (whether salted or not) enshrined in Dante and then sliding down the chute of the Renaissance, the Enlightenment, and Romanticism to coalesce at last in the Pound–Eliot *Waste*

Land (the second version is from the first draft; italics indicate words removed or revised):

> *Datta:* what have we given?
> My friend, blood shaking my heart
> The awful daring of a moment's surrender
> Which an age of prudence can never retract
> By this, and this only, we have existed
> Which is not to be found in our obituaries
> Or in memories draped by the beneficent spider
> Or under seals broken by the lean solicitor
> In our empty rooms
>
> [ll. 401–409]

> Datta. *my brother,* what have we given!
> My friend, *my friend, beating in* my heart
> The awful daring of a moment's surrender
> Which an age of prudence *cannot* retract—
> By this, and this only, we have existed,
> Which is not to be found in our obituaries,
> *Nor* in memories *which will busy* beneficent spiders
> Nor *in documents eaten* by the lean solicitor
> In our empty rooms

Eliot allowed himself one public moment in memory of Jean Verdenal:

> My own retrospect [of the Paris of 1910–1911] is touched by a sentimental sunset, the memory of a friend coming across the Luxembourg Gardens in the late afternoon, waving a branch of lilac, a friend who was later (so far as I could find out) to be mixed with the mud of Gallipoli.
>
> [*Criterion*, "Commentary" (1934)]

I tend to struggle against being moved by Eliot, having battled all my life against his influence on our decaying academies. Here I am very touched by that branch of lilac, which Verdenal and Eliot knew was Whitman's tally in the "Lilacs" elegy. The sprig of lilac that Whitman places on the passing coffin of Abraham Lincoln is an image of the poet's Orphic voice.

In Walt Whitman's poetry the sprig of lilac is called a "tally," an image of voice conceived as a sacrifice to Orpheus, who suffered a tearing-apart by the Maenads, fierce and intoxicated women worshippers of Dionysus. Jean Verdenal is Eliot's Orphic sacrifice, scattered and mixed with the mud of Gallipoli.

I require a comparison of another American long poem composed just after *The Waste Land* by Wallace Stevens: *The Comedian as the Letter C* (1923, written 1922). Here is its conclusion:

Or if the music sticks, if the anecdote
Is false, if Crispin is a profitless
Philosopher, beginning with green brag,
Concluding fadedly, if as a man
Prone to distemper he abates in taste,
Fickle and fumbling, variable, obscure,
Glozing his life with after-shining flicks,
Illuminating, from a fancy gorged
By apparition, plain and common things,
Sequestering the fluster from the year,
Making gulped potions from obstreperous drops,
And so distorting, proving what he proves
Is nothing, what can all this matter since
The relation comes, benignly, to its end?

So may the relation of each man be clipped.

That certainly clipped the poetry of Wallace Stevens for almost a decade, until it came to life again in 1931. It is not so much that Stevens is rejecting his marvelous first book, *Harmonium*, but that he has reached an impasse and is mired. If he is only going to go on being the Snow Man, then let the relation go benignly to nothingness. That is not what happened. But we have the advantages of retrospect if we have read and enjoyed the more affirmative Stevens of his major phase, of which the masterpieces are *Notes toward a Supreme Fiction* (1942), *The Auroras of Autumn*, and *An Ordinary Evening in New Haven* (both 1950).

Is it possible to calibrate the power of a reader's mind over what Milton called "the universe of Death" or what Genesis termed *tohu wa-bohu*, "void and formless"? Even Samuel Johnson could not have accomplished that. You have to *be* Prince Hamlet or Shakespeare himself, and even then your intimations will be tenuous. Dictating this on February 25, 2019, from a hospital chair, I breathe as best I can and seek answerable words.

My late friend Frank Kermode (1919–2010) was given to writing mischievous reviews of my books. I found these generally entertaining, and I refrained from reviewing Frank. We shared early enthusiasms for Wallace Stevens and D. H. Lawrence and agreed to disagree on T. S. Eliot. Through the years we exchanged so many views on the trope of the poet's mind *over* a universe of death that I can no longer be certain whether my ideas are his or my own. A key text for both of us was Stevens's "The Idea of Order at Key West" (1934). "She sang beyond the genius of the sea," Stevens begins. "Beyond" is the signature of the farther shore. Wordsworth's "The Solitary Reaper" (1807) helps establish that signature:

> Whate'er the theme, the Maiden sang
> As if her song could have no ending;
> I saw her singing at her work,
> And o'er the sickle bending; —
> I listened, motionless and still;
> And, as I mounted up the hill,
> The music in my heart I bore,
> Long after it was heard no more.

She is singing Erse, the Gaelic of the Scottish Highlands, and the song ends only to begin again. Wordsworth has made this a lyric masterpiece: the unknowable song of the Highland maiden is beyond comprehension, but it stirs Wordsworth to imaginative surmise. The cyclic nature of her song evokes a memorial of a moment that may never be lost.

Though "The Idea of Order at Key West" has moments of zestful recognition of the sublime, clearly it is not an unflawed success like "The Solitary Reaper." Stevens is in the awkward position of simultaneously accepting a natural sublime while deprecating it as meaningless in comparison to the unknown words of the singing woman at Key West. These intense affirmations are Shelleyan but seem not quite available to Stevens. His tone is perilously hyperbolical as he chants her supremacy. Stevens resolves his poem partly by evading his dilemmas.

Stevens insisted that Ramon Fernandez, mentioned in "The Idea of Order at Key West," was no one in particular. It seems now a sound enough judgment that the actual Parisian literary critic and journalist (1899–1944) might be called a Gallic Allen Tate or Richard P. Blackmur, one more anti-Romantic interpreter swept away by the harsh waters of time. Fernandez cannot tell us or Stevens why the lingering memory of the girl's song has the effect of "Arranging, deepening, enchanting night."

Stevens catches fire at the close by opposing Ramon's blessed or wounded rage *for* order to the maker's rage *to* order words of the sea (Walt Whitman once entitled "Out of the Cradle Endlessly Rocking" "A Word Out of the Sea"); and the Keatsian words of portals opening on fairy worlds forlorn; and again Whitmanian words of ourselves and of our origins—all these in ghostly demarcations, keener sounds.

The later course of Stevens's poetry works more successfully at rendering poetic horizons less substantial and subverting them by a rhetoric of acuter resonances. Let me propose a formula of ways by which Stevens evades forerunners and yet returns to them at the end. The final belief according to Stevens is to believe in the supremacy of the fictive while maintaining the nicer knowledge of belief: that what one believes in is not true.

Stevens is in many ways close to Shelley, Keats, Whitman, and, in a broader sense, Wordsworth, who was, beyond question, the poet who ended the tradition that had gone from Homer through Goethe, and began anew, as Hazlitt said, upon a *tabula rasa* of poetry. His early work seems a kind of American pre-Raphaelitism, akin to some of the lovely but forgotten poems of Trumbull Stickney (1874–1904). Stickney died quite suddenly, and sometimes I think he could have come close to Wallace Stevens in achievement had the Fates permitted it. Here is one of my favorite poems, "Mnemosyne":

It's autumn in the country I remember.

How warm a wind blew here about the ways!
And shadows on the hillside lay to slumber
During the long sun-sweetened summer-days.

It's cold abroad the country I remember.

The swallows veering skimmed the golden grain
At midday with a wing aslant and limber;
And yellow cattle browsed upon the plain.

It's empty down the country I remember.

I had a sister lovely in my sight:
Her hair was dark, her eyes were very sombre;
We sang together in the woods at night.

It's lonely in the country I remember.

The babble of our children fills my ears,
And on our hearth I stare the perished ember
To flames that show all starry thro' my tears.

It's dark about the country I remember.

There are the mountains where I lived. The path
Is slushed with cattle-tracks and fallen timber,
The stumps are twisted by the tempests' wrath.

But that I knew these places are my own,
I'd ask how came such wretchedness to cumber
The earth, and I to people it alone.

It rains across the country I remember.

[1902]

I have never been able to get this lyric out of my head. Some-times I recite it to myself and do not immediately know who wrote it. Anyone who has survived siblings, as I have my three older sisters, has to be haunted by:

I had a sister lovely in my sight:
Her hair was dark, her eyes were very sombre;
We sang together in the woods at night.

Something of Trumbull Stickney's sense of a belatedness he could never hope to reverse gives a measured pacing to another of these sonnets of desolation:

These are my murmur-laden shells that keep
A fresh voice tho' the years be very gray.
The wave that washed their lips and tuned their lay
Is gone, gone with the faded ocean sweep,
The royal tide, gray ebb and sunken neap
And purple midday,—gone! To this hot clay
Must sing my shells, where yet the primal day,
Its roar and rhythm and splendour will not sleep.
What hand shall join them to their proper sea
If all be gone? Shall they forever feel
Glories undone and world that cannot be?—
'Twere mercy to stamp out this aged wrong,
Dash them to earth and crunch them with the heel
And make a dust of their seraphic song.

["On Some Shells Found Inland,"1902]

Trumbull Stickney was thinking of the dream of the Arab in
Wordsworth's *Prelude* (1805, 1850), where stone and seashell must be
saved so as to rescue poetry itself from the great flood.

I find my stones and seashells in the major poets who are neglected by the tides of fashion. An interviewer the other day asked
me who was the best living American poet. Since John Ashbery and
his generation have departed, without hesitation I replied: Jay Wright.
The interviewer had heard nothing of him.

In 1971 I picked up a small volume of poems at the old Yale
Co-op, *The Homecoming Singer*, by Jay Wright. I was caught instantly
by the title poem. The transfiguration of the girl into an angelic
singer—a homecoming singer in the fullest sense—is the first of
many transfigurations that mark and make glorious the poetry of Jay
Wright. "The Homecoming Singer" delays its meanings, though
they are accumulated by the inflections of the narrating voice. The
garishness of Nashville on football Homecoming Weekend is set
against the authentic homecoming where the angel strokes the
poet's hair as he kneels before her, and her singing brings up "the
jailed, / the condemned, all that had been forgotten / on this night of
homecomings . . ."

That wry realization of the otherness of black history is a foundation stone of Jay Wright's ambitious edifice. The central figuration

in his poetry is creation-by-twinning, a myth of divine creation in West African Dogon mythology. Amma the creator-god twins himself as a new Adam called Nommo, a John the Baptist kind of forerunner for the coming Black Son of God.

Jay Wright ingeniously turns this story into a mode where a true poem becomes a limbo dance, and thus a gateway out of the Middle Passage of the slave trade, and so a logbook, a release for passage.

The limbo we know is a West Indian dance under a gradually lowering bar, so that the dancer becomes a spider-man, his arms and legs spread-eagled. In the Middle Passage the slaves were jammed into such little space that they had to contort themselves as if they were spiders.

In his early poem "The Albuquerque Graveyard" (1976), Wright went back to where some of his friends were buried: "I am going back / to the Black limbo, / an unwritten history / of our own tensions." This is Wright's *logos*, structure of his enterprise. Dante haunts Jay Wright, and so the very different limbo of the *Commedia*, unique place neither inferno, purgatory, norparadiso, is where he stations himself.

As a poet, Jay Wright is a limbo dancer, contorted by history but with no desire to end it. As poet he uncovers the weave, a labor that acknowledges how many different and incompatible stitches render black history a universal history, even against its wishes. In a 1983 interview Wright said,

A young man, hearing me read some of my poems, said that I seemed to be trying to weave together a lot of different things. My answer was that they are already woven, I'm just trying to uncover the weave. People have never been that removed from each other and wherever you find black people in history, you're going to find black people acting in history. One of our tasks is to recall the forgetful to this fundamental truth. That is why my poetry looks for the basic human connections in experience and why it is one which includes many voices.

["The Unraveling of the Egg: An Interview with Jay Wright," *Callaloo*, Autumn 1983]

But I want to leap into his major mode, his own modification of the Pindaric ode. Here is "The Cradle Logic of Autumn" (1994): "By moving, I can stand where the light eases / me into the river's feathered arms . . ."

Turning sixty, Jay Wright discovers the cradle light of the season we call both autumn and fall. What begins again in the emblematic blue light is a perpetual possibility of poetic failure, a diminished voice. He would like to confront celestial birds, Toltec turtledoves, but instead he beholds "a bird almost incarnadine."

> Whence is that knocking?
> How is't with me, when every noise appalls me?
> What hands are here? ha! they pluck out mine eyes.
> Will all great Neptune's ocean wash this blood
> Clean from my hand? No, this my hand will rather
> The multitudinous seas incarnadine,
> Making the green one red.
>
> [*Macbeth*, 2.2.56–62]

Inevitably Jay Wright invokes Macbeth's unusual word "incarnadine," bloodiness that makes all things red. Wright's agon is to repudiate the cradle logic of autumn, since that vision of fall has no space for the persistence of desire that will lift the red flower of winter into the wind. There is poetic self-sacrifice here, since Wright yields up the celebratory gusto of "a Twelfth-night / gone awry" (in "The Cradle Logic of Autumn").

Jay Wright is a difficult poet, like Geoffrey Hill or Hart Crane or William Blake. Those are four different kinds of difficulty. Blake tells a story of his own with invented personages, who are both human and more than human. Hart Crane pitches his tone so high that the reader can be left behind, unable to keep up with the leap of a "logic of metaphor" storming the heights of the Unapparent. Geoffrey Hill is either gnomic or garrulous, and moves capriciously from formal construction to the rapping of his boundless gnostic harangue. Jay Wright has a nobly lucid style, but it is dense with allusion, and quite deliberately brings together African mythology (mostly Dogon), the Spanish poetry of the Americas, Dante, U.S.

poetic tradition from Emerson and Whitman to T. S. Eliot and Hart
Crane. In one of his greater odes, "Desire's Persistence" (1986), Jay
Wright commences with Náhuatl or Aztec poetry:

> Yo ave del agua floreciente duro en fiesta.
> —"Deseo de persistencia," Poesía Náhuatl

> . . .

> Once, I wreathed around a king,
> became a fishing net, a maze
>   "a deadly wealth of robe."
> Mothers who have heard me sing take heart;
> I always prick them into power.

The speaker is song's weaver and celebrates the persistence of desire. Is it only the desire of the centaur Nessus, mortally wounded by
Heracles for attempting to rape Deianira? The revenge of Nessus
destroys Heracles most horribly, when the deluded Deianira unwit-
tingly carries out the centaur's plot by wrapping her husband in the
infected shirt, ostensibly to turn Heracles away from other women.

> **2**
> Y vengo alzando al viento la roja flor de invierno.
> (I lift the red flower of winter into the wind.)
>   —Poesía Náhuatl

> I
> Out of the ninth circle,
> a Phoenician boat rocks upward into light
> and the warmth of a name—given to heaven—
> that arises in the ninth realm.
> Earth's realm discloses the Egyptian
> on the point of invention,
>   deprived of life and death,
> heart deep in the soul's hawk,
> a thymos shadow knapping the tombed body.
> Some one or thing is always heaven bound.
> Some flowered log doubles my bones.

> The spirit of Toltec turtledoves escapes.
> A sharp, metaphorical cry sends me
>   into the adorned sepulchre,
> and the thing that decays learns
>   how to speak its name.

There is an intricate blend of T. S. Eliot and Hart Crane in this. "A thymos shadow knapping the tombed body" refers to the ancient Greek word for the vitalistic drive that keeps us going, *thymos*, already crucial in Homer. One hears Eliot and Crane fused in the remarkable trope of a "shadow knapping" (archaic meaning: strike with a hard brief sound) "the tombed body." Something elegantly personal is heard in learning to speak one's name even as one decays, a gesture of poetic survival.

> I am the arcane body,
> raised at the ninth hour,
> to be welcomed by the moonlight
>   of such spirited air.
> I am the Dane of degrees
> who realizes how the spirit glows
>   even as it descends.

Jay Wright transmogrifies into the arcane, astral body resurrected at the appropriately Dantesque ninth hour. As such he takes on the identity of Hamlet, uniquely the ambiguous spirit that kindles even as it goes down and out.

Red
> The heart, catalectic though it be, does glow,
> responds to every midnight bell within you.
> This is a discourse on reading heat,
> the flushed char of burned moments one sees
> after the sexton's lamp flows
> over the body's dark book.
> There is suspicion
> here that violet
> traces of

sacrifice
stand
bare.

If the poet's heart is catalectic, then, following prosody, it lacks a final beat. What is it to write a discourse on reading heat? Slyly vulnerable, Wright's stance wavers humanly and metrically.

We have come to an imagined line,
                    celestial,
that binds us to the burr of a sheltered thing
and rings us with a fire that will not dance,
                    in a horn that will not sound.
We have learned, like these birds,
to publish our decline,
when over knotted apples and straw-crisp leaves,
the slanted sun welcomes us once again
to the arrested music in the earth's divided embrace.

This seems to me one of Wright's most beautiful gestures. A static fire, a silent horn are emblems of "our decline" as well as the year's. That the music should be arrested, the earth's embrace divided, shadows marriage as it does nature.

The harmattan is a dry wind on Africa's west coast, December through February. A woman shaman, taking on the power of the dog star Sirius, brightest of the constellation Canis Major, prophesies her rebirth to a new dawn in a better clime. But such transmogrification is ambiguous, and she will vanish. What remains is the song of the old women saluting her, and placing her on a bed of yellow roses. Their culture is finished, but the poet and his readers will find that their hearts are made perfect, that is, complete.

I shall go away, I shall disappear,
I shall be stretched on a bed of yellow roses
and the old women will cry for me.
So the Toltecas wrote: their books are finished,
but your heart has become perfect.

In what sense has Jay Wright celebrated the persistence of desire, and what is the object of what he calls desire? At eighty-four he continues obsessively to compose poems and poetic dramas, though his readership remains modest. Robert Hayden, who died at sixty-six in 1980, and I had several conversations in Ann Arbor, Michigan, and Washington, D.C., about Jay Wright's achievement. There is now a vibrant new generation of African American poets, and perhaps one or two of them will find a place with Hayden and Wright among the best American poets of whatever origin or complexion. Hayden and I shared a passion for Jay Wright's poetry. It will not vanish.

CHAPTER ONE

William Shakespeare and John Milton
In Every Deep, a Lower Deep

I T MAY SEEM A leap from the contemporary poet Jay Wright to John Milton. Yet Shelley in his *Defence of Poetry* anticipated Borges in speaking of one great poem that contains all others:

> They may have perceived the beauty of those immortal compositions, simply as fragments and isolated portions: those who are more finely organised, or born in a happier age, may recognize them as episodes to that great poem, which all poets, like the co-operating thoughts of one great mind, have built up since the beginning of the world.
>
> [1840, written 1821]

John Milton—the poet-narrator of *Paradise Lost* (1667, 1674)—and his hero-villain Satan are both Shakespearean personalities. It is quite certain that Milton would not have accepted that characterization. I propose to clarify, if I can, what is for me the central enigma of *Paradise Lost*: Why does the strongest English epic exclude all mention of Lucifer, Satan's name before he fell, and of the altogether relevant myth of Prometheus?

I have been unable to find any lucid and compelling account of the Shakespearean shadow that falls across all of Milton's poetry, and in particular darkens *Paradise Lost*. This has been for me a lifelong obsession. I want to build and improve upon the chapter called "Milton's Hamlet" in my book *The Anatomy of Influence* (2011).

The man Milton provokes very different reactions depending upon your perspective. I remember with mixed pleasure and distaste two novels that distort him. Robert Graves, good lyric poet and bad historian, in 1943 published *Wife to Mr. Milton*, spoken by Marie (Mary) Powell, the poet's sixteen-year-old first wife, whose family was Royalist and Catholic. It is fair to say that Milton married her for the dowry, which he did not receive. Almost twenty years older than Mary Powell, the poet treated her so badly that she fled back to her parents after a month. She returned three years later, but only because of the bad situation for Catholic Royalists after the beginning of the Civil War. After bearing him four children, she died from complications of childbirth in 1652, at age twenty-seven. Their only son, John, died a little more than a year old. The three daughters survived; there was never much love between them and their father.

Far more exuberant than Graves, *Milton in America* infuriates even as it entertains. Peter Ackroyd, a skilled literary biographer and adventuresome novelist, goes rather too far in limning a John Milton so demonic that he approximates the horrible Satan given us by the merely Christian C. S. Lewis. Ackroyd's Milton delights in slaughter and rapine, he evidently has his sight restored by bumbuggery, and a puissant plethora of humbuggery ensues.

My perspective is decidedly not Christian, yet wondrous is it that pious scholars discover an eminently orthodox Milton in *Paradise Lost*. John P. Rumrich and Stephen B. Dobranski, students of Milton's heresies, are happily blunt on this:

> It is distinctly paradoxical that John Milton—who opposed infant baptism, supported regicide, defended divorce, and approved of polygamy—should be heard as a voice of orthodoxy.
>
> [*Milton and Heresy* (2009)]

Always I find myself baffled—and wickedly delighted—that anyone should derive aesthetic satisfaction from the depiction of God in *Paradise Lost*. Rather than argue with scholars who seem to me arbitrary or equivocal, I will turn to Samuel Taylor Coleridge. As a lover of his prose as well as his poetry, I still share Walter Pater's apprehension that Coleridge lost much that was crucial when he grounded himself upon the organic analogue, oddly inherited from David Hume.

Still, I am moved by Coleridge, who in his 1818 course of lectures remarked that in *Paradise Lost*, "the very grandeur of his subject ministered a difficulty to Milton. The statement of a being of high intellect, warring against the supreme Being, seems to contradict the idea of a supreme Being."

Coleridge is not altogether right; there are other passages in which Milton's God is all too human. I sympathize with the Sage of Highgate's anxiety. Scripture afforded Milton at least two very different versions of the Hebrew God. One is the Yahweh of the J writer; the other is the Elohim of the Priestly writer. Milton shied away from the theomorphic patriarchs and anthropomorphic Yahweh of J. We could wish that he had not portrayed God at all. Milton read and contended against Dante, whose God in *Paradiso* is a light show, a flare of sublimity. Shakespeare, as we would expect, avoided representing God except in his *Cymbeline*, which I can read only as a self-parody. What else could this be?

Jupiter descends in thunder and lightning, sitting upon an eagle: he throws a thunderbolt. The Apparitions fall on their knees.

That marvelous stage direction might as well be Aristophanes. What follows it is absurd enough to be funny:

No more, you petty spirits of region low,
Offend our hearing; hush! How dare you ghosts
Accuse the thunderer, whose bolt, you know,
Sky-planted batters all rebelling coasts?
Poor shadows of Elysium, hence, and rest
Upon your never-withering banks of flowers:
Be not with mortal accidents opprest;
No care of yours it is; you know 'tis ours.
Whom best I love I cross; to make my gift,
The more delay'd, delighted.

[5.4.62–72]

Quoted out of context, who could believe this to be Shakespeare? The sadder question is, is *this* really John Milton? Or is it an elaborate screen for the inner workings of Miltonic mind that will culminate in this God's abdication?

> Only-begotten Son, seest thou what rage
> Transports our Adversary? whom no bounds
> Prescribed, no bars of Hell, nor all the chains
> Heaped on him there, nor yet the main abyss
> Wide interrupt can hold; so bent he seems
> On desperate revenge, that shall redound
> Upon his own rebellious head. And now,
> Through all restraint broke loose, he wings his way
> Not far off Heaven, in the precincts of light,
> Directly towards the new created World,
> And Man there placed, with purpose to assay
> If him by force he can destroy, or, worse,
> By some false guile pervert. And shall pervert;
> For man will hearken to his glozing lies,
> And easily transgress the sole command,
> Sole pledge of his obedience: so will fall
> He and his faithless progeny. Whose fault?
> Whose but his own? Ingrate, he had of me
> All he could have. . . .
>
> [*Paradise Lost*, 3.80–98]

"It must give pleasure." That maxim of Wallace Stevens is an essential requirement for poetry. Does this rant of self-justification award pleasure or irritation? Contrast it to this:

> Yet not for those,
> Nor what the potent Victor in his rage
> Can else inflict, do I repent, or change,
> Though changed in outward lustre, that fixed mind,
> And high disdain from sense of injured merit,
> That with the Mightiest raised me to contend,
> And to the fierce contention brought along
> Innumerable force of Spirits armed,

That durst dislike his reign, and, me preferring,
His utmost power with adverse power opposed
In dubious battle on the plains of Heaven,
And shook his throne. What though the field be lost?
All is not lost—the unconquerable will,
And study of revenge, immortal hate,
And courage never to submit or yield;
And what is else not to be overcome?

[*Paradise Lost*, 1.94–109]

William Blake explained this disjunction between Satanic heroism and divine vengefulness in *The Marriage of Heaven and Hell*
(1790):

Those who restrain desire, do so because theirs is weak
enough to be restrained; and the restrainer or reason usurps
its place & governs the unwilling.
   And being restrain'd it by degrees becomes passive till it
is only the shadow of desire.
   The history of this is written in Paradise Lost, & the
Governor or Reason is call'd Messiah. And the original Archangel, or possessor of the command of the heavenly host, is
call'd the Devil or Satan, and his children are call'd Sin &
Death.
   But in the Book of Job Miltons Messiah is call'd Satan.
For this history has been adopted by both parties.
   It indeed appear'd to Reason as if Desire was cast out,
but the Devil's account is, that the Messiah fell, & formed a
heaven of what he stole from the Abyss.
   This is shown in the Gospel, where he prays to the Father
to send the comforter, or Desire, that Reason may have Ideas
to build on, the Jehovah of the Bible being no other than he
who dwells in flaming fire.
   Know that after Christ's death, he became Jehovah.
   But in Milton; the Father is Destiny, the Son, a Ratio of
the five senses, & the Holy-ghost, Vacuum!
Note: The reason Milton wrote in fetters when he wrote of
Angels & God, and at liberty when of Devils & Hell, is

because he was a true Poet and of the Devil's party without knowing it.

Blake offers an aesthetic criticism of *Paradise Lost*, not a reading of Milton's intentions. If, with C. S. Lewis, one believes that Milton's intentions (surmised from Lewis's own Anglican orthodoxy) are precisely realized in the poem, then Blake must seem irrelevant or misguided. But Blake is not alone in his reading, both in his own time and in ours. What Blake traces is the declining movement of creative energy in *Paradise Lost* from the active of the early books to the passive of the poem's conclusion, where all initiatives not a withdrawn God's own are implicitly condemned. More simply, Blake posits a split in Milton between the moral philosopher or theologian and the poet. From this split ensues what Blake claims is a falsification *in the poem* of the relation between human desire and the idea of holiness. Milton's Satan overtly embodies human desire, and Milton's Messiah is too exclusively the representation of a minimal and constraining kind of reason. Satan, in the Book of Job, is a moral accuser who torments man with the trial of physical pain. In *Paradise Lost* the wrathful fire of the Messiah is instrumental in creating Hell as a moral punishment involving physical torment. It follows, then, for Blake, that "in the Book of Job Miltons Messiah is call'd Satan." In declaring for the Devil's party, and also insisting that Milton was unknowingly of it, Blake is not inverting conventional categories of moral good and evil (as Milton's Satan does on Mount Niphates). Instead, he is insisting that poetic imagination and the energy of human desire are near allied, and that for a poet *as poet* the ordinary moral categories are contained within a more limited context than the larger world of poetry makes available to him. Blake deliberately complicates this point with his ironic vocabulary and its persuasive redefinition of such orthodox counters as Angels, Devils, Heaven, and Hell. The Gospel reference is probably to John 14:16–17, so that Blake is interpreting "the Spirit of Truth" as Desire.

With a few changes, I wrote this commentary in 1962 when I was thirty-two, fifty-six years ago. I return to it here because I cannot improve upon it. The intricate dialectic of *The Marriage of Heaven and Hell* cannot be unpacked because it is sinuous and labyrinthine. William Blake loved Milton above all other poets and wanted to see himself as a fulfillment of Milton, not as a corrective. Blake's younger contemporary Shelley took up an even more complex stance toward the visionary of *Paradise Lost*, subtly indicating the "pernicious casuistry" by which we calculate Satan's faults against God's wrongs, and excuse the faults on that basis. Extraordinary literary critic that he was, Shelley sees and meditates upon Milton's exclusion of any mention of Prometheus in *Paradise Lost*:

> The only imaginary being resembling in any degree Prometheus, is Satan; and Prometheus is, in my judgment, a more poetical character than Satan, because, in addition to courage, and majesty, and firm and patient opposition to omnipotent force, he is susceptible of being described as exempt from the taints of ambition, envy, revenge, and a desire for personal aggrandizement, which, in the Hero of *Paradise Lost*, interfere with the interest. The character of Satan engenders in the mind a pernicious casuistry which leads us to weigh his faults with his wrongs, and to excuse the former because the latter exceed all measure. In the minds of those who consider that magnificent fiction with a religious feeling it engenders something worse.
>   [Preface to *Prometheus Unbound* (1820, written 1819)]

Shelley, a subtle and skeptical intellect, is careful not to over-praise the Satan of *Paradise Lost*. The crucial phrases here are "interfere with the interest," a dry but keen stroke, and "a pernicious casuistry," an undoing of both the Satanist and anti-Satanist arguments. Two years later, in his *Defence of Poetry*, Shelley was even more forceful. He rightly observed that nothing in life or literature could exceed the magnificence and energy of Milton's Satan. With mordant wit, the revolutionary Shelley intimates that Milton created in his Devil a character morally superior to Milton's God. It follows from this that Shelley declares Milton's freedom from commonplace notions of moral virtue:

> Milton's poem contains within itself a philosophical refutation of that system, of which, by a strange and natural antithesis, it has been a chief popular support. Nothing can

exceed the energy and magnificence of the character of Satan as expressed in *Paradise Lost*. It is a mistake to suppose that he could ever have been intended for the popular personification of evil. Implacable hate, patient cunning, and a sleepless refinement of device to inflict the extremist anguish on an enemy, these things are evil; and, although venial in a slave, are not to be forgiven in a tyrant; although redeemed by much that ennobles his defeat in one subdued, are marked by all that dishonors his conquest in the victor. Milton's Devil as a moral being is as far superior to his God, as one who perseveres in some purpose which he has conceived to be excellent in spite of adversity and torture, is to one who in the cold security of undoubted triumph inflicts the most horrible revenge upon his enemy, not from any mistaken notion of inducing him to repent of a perseverance in enmity, but with the alleged design of exasperating him to deserve new torments. Milton has so far violated the popular creed (if this shall be judged to be a violation) as to have alleged no superiority of moral virtue to his God over his Devil. And this bold neglect of a direct moral purpose is the most decisive proof of the supremacy of Milton's genius.

After Shelley drowned in 1822, the *Times* of London crowed: "Shelley the Atheist is dead. Now he knows whether there is a God or not." "As to the Devil, he owes everything to Milton," Shelley observed in his unpublished "Essay on the Devil and Devils" (1819–1820).

My late friend Frank Kermode, in his essay "Adam Unparadised" (1960), carefully endorsed a central concern in the admiring polemic Blake and Shelley waged on Satan's side: namely, that Blake and Shelley were not misreading the character of Satan out of ignorance. Instead, Kermode argues that their reading of Satan "show[s] us a truth about *Paradise Lost* which later commentary, however learned, has made less and less accessible."

This is consonant with an eloquent sentence of Kermode's: "*Paradise Lost* is a poem about death, and about pleasure and its impairment." Romantic readers of Milton, who include a minority still among us, tend to agree with William Empson that Satan is so attractive because Milton's God is so dreadful. Satan at least suffers the process of thinking. God gives us pronunciamentos. As I will trace in some detail, Satan stems from Hamlet, Iago, Edmund, and Macbeth, while God might as well be King Claudius. Dubious as Claudius is, he is not capable of this outrage:

> Hear, all ye Angels, Progeny of Light,
> Thrones, Dominations, Princedoms, Virtues, Powers,
> Hear my Decree, which unrevoked shall stand!
> This day I have begot whom I declare
> My only Son, and on this holy hill
> Him have anointed, whom ye now behold
> At my right hand. Your head I him appoint,
> And by my self have sworn to him shall bow
> All knees in Heaven, and shall confess him Lord.
> Under his great vicegerent reign abide,
> United as one individual soul
> For ever happy. Him who disobeys
> Me disobeys, breaks union, and, that day
> Cast out from God and blessed vision, falls
> Into utter darkness, deep engulfed, his place
> Ordained without redemption, without end.
> [*Paradise Lost*, 5.600–615]

One question is: what can God mean when he bellows:

> This day I have begot whom I declare
> My only Son . . .

In what sense can the Son have been begotten on *this* day? What does "begot" mean? Most interesting, at least to me, is why one of the greatest of all poets dug a sand trap for himself. Is Milton's Heaven a prelude to a delusional President's golf course?

Like his greatest disciple, William Wordsworth, John Milton is not a comic writer. Neo-orthodox scholars somehow find Milton's Satan laughable. Clearly Milton did not. But I am uncertain as to the precise status and function of the Son in *Paradise Lost*. Many suggest that he is an improvement upon the heroes of classical epic. Thus, he is a statesman loyal to the Crown, and a victorious warrior who rides the flaming Chariot of Paternal Deity against the rebel angels and throws them out of Heaven. The divine flame ignites the fallen demons, and their impact upon Chaos creates Hell. William Blake is therefore justified in saying that the Son performs the same work given to Satan by the Book of Job.

However you feel about so bellicose a Son, you may have some difficulty in associating him with Jesus the Nazarene. Milton had to be very uncomfortable about this. Notoriously, he gets Christ off the cross in six words divided by an enjambment: "so he dies, / But soon revives."

The passage is hardly a poetic splendor:

Seized on by force, judged, and to death condemnd,
A shameful and accursed, nailed to the cross
By his own nation, slain for bringing life;
But to the cross he nails thy enemies—
The Law that is against thee, and the sins
Of all mankind, with him there crucified,
Never to hurt them more who rightly trust
In this his satisfaction. So he dies,
But soon revives; Death over him no power
Shall long usurp. Ere the third dawning light
Return, the stars of morn shall see him rise
Out of his grave, fresh as the dawning light . . .
                                    [*Paradise Lost*, 12.412–423]

It is not just Milton's Arianism that figures here; the Incarnation and Crucifixion have little place in his religion of poetry. Here is the famous formulation from his *Of Education* (1644):

Logic therefore so much as is useful, is to be referred to this due place with all her well couched heads and topics, until to be time to open her contracted palm into a graceful and ornate rhetoric taught out of the rule of Plato, Aristotle, Phalereus, Cicero, Hermogenes, Longinus. To which poetry would be made subsequent, or indeed rather precedent, as being less subtle and fine, but more simple, sensuous and passionate. I mean not here the prosody of a verse, which they could not have hit on before among the rudiments of grammar; but that sublime art which in Aristotle's *Poetics*, in Horace, and the Italian commentaries of Castelvetro, Tasso, Mazzoni, and others, teaches what the laws are of a true epic poem, what of a dramatic, what of a lyric, what decorum is, which is the grand masterpiece to observe.

Whatever stance Milton might take toward the Incarnation and the Crucifixion, he was incapable of finding them "more simple, sensuous and passionate." Spirit and energy were talismans for the monistic Milton; Satan possessed and fused them; the Son could not.

Dante, Milton, and Blake all apotheosize freedom, yet these are three freedoms and not one. The *Commedia*'s privilege remains under God. Milton's freedom was Christian Liberty, the Inner Light by which each Protestant could read Scripture for himself. Blake's compass was what he called the Human Form Divine, God in each one of us.

The Marxist historian Christopher Hill wondered to what extent John Milton could be considered a Christian writer, arguing that his lack of emphasis on conversion, Atonement, and the Incarnation and Resurrection of the New Testament revealed his worldview to be more secular than Christian.

Doubtless this is flavored by Hill's political stance, yet it is true enough. It is unlikely that John Milton would have agreed with any distinction between an art of control and one of liberation. Certainly he would have rejected A. D. Nuttall's notion that he, Eve, and Adam join Satan in a Promethean poetry of movement away from the light into a realm of divergences. Blake's Milton descends from a heaven where he feels estranged and incomplete. He goes down to gather his sixfold emanation from the deep. I assume they are sixfold because he had three wives and three daughters, though Blake may intend the body of Milton's writings. Shelley's Prometheus is bound to his rock until Demogorgon, named by Boccaccio as the "Father of the Gentile gods," intervenes and overthrows Jupiter, tyrant of the sky-gods.

Of all the Milton studies that present him as a Christian humanist, the strongest is David Quint's *Inside "Paradise Lost"* (2014). Quint's learning is profound and precise. No one else has been so compendious in charting the labyrinthine ways of Miltonic allusion. Still, is not *Paradise Lost* much more than an epic closure? It seems unlikely to me that David Quint has not heard the rhetorical vapidity of Milton's God. Nor is it sufficient to dismiss Milton's Satan as being trapped in a circular existence. Doubtless Milton intended Abdiel to be more memorable than Satan, but he is not. Quint's flaw, in my judgment, is his inability to see that Shakespeare subverts *Paradise Lost* because Milton *cannot* exclude him. The four invocations and all the other soliloquies—whether Satan's, Adam's, or Eve's—are Shakespearean. Hamlet the Black Prince pragmatically counts for more in the poem than does the sublime prig Aeneas. How can you transume Hamlet? Since Macbeth and Iago also get into the mix, the voices of Shakespearean personality impinge incessantly on John Milton's narrative voice.

The only *thinking* personality in *Paradise Lost* is Satan's. Like Hamlet, he thinks by relentless self-questioning. Nietzsche teaches a poetics of pain in his *On the Genealogy of Morals* (1887). Suffering is far more memorable than pleasure. In Satan, as in Hamlet, thinking is suffering.

Is *Paradise Lost* more an epic *commedia* or an epic tragedy? David Quint argues for the first, but did the poem ever abandon being *Adam Unparadised?* The burden of Hamlet, Othello, Lear, Macbeth, Antony and Cleopatra, and Coriolanus is loss. It is the second word in Milton's title that should be emphasized: *Lost*. Wallace Stevens thought that the death of Satan was a tragedy for the imagination. I would say, rather, in the spirit of Stevens, that Milton's degradation of his Satan in the later books of *Paradise Lost* was a travesty *of* the imagination. Even there, it is not a travesty like John Dryden's libretto for an opera fortunately never staged, in which the voice of Lucifer declaims:

> Is this the seat our conqueror has given?
> And this the climate we must change for heaven?
> These regions and this realm my wars have got;
> This mournful empire is the loser's lott;
> In liquid burnings, or on dry to dwell,
> Is all the sad variety of hell.
>
> [*The State of Innocence* (1676), ll. 1–6]

One wants W. S. Gilbert and Arthur Sullivan to have adapted this for a sardonic operetta. I recall also Christopher Fry's ghastly libretto for Penderecki's dreadful opera *Paradise Lost* (1978), directed by Sam Wanamaker with Arnold Moss as narrator. Clearly Milton's more-than-formidable epic should remain untouched by silliness.

Satan thinks in images and he is capable of imagining new concepts, even though they turn out to be Sin and Death. At its core, Miltonic epic is Shakespearean, though it *wants* to be Virgilian-Homeric, biblical-Dantesque, Tasso-Spenserian. John Milton's hidden agon is with Shakespeare, who is not to be overcome. The man Milton had the courage never to submit or yield, but was overcome by his own heart alone, which neither age nor infamy could temper to its object. The poet Milton received an immortal wound from Shakespeare. Was he aware of it? We do not know. What I hope to investigate in much of what follows is why his Shakespearean allusions, whether deliberate or indeliberate, mostly do not follow his ambitious and successful ventures in transuming all his other precursors.

What you cannot transume crowds you out. Hamlet pushes Lucifer out of the poem and usurps Satan, since Hamlet is also his own Iago. Macbeth invests the shadow of Satan, whose imagination thus is diseased. Lear and Yahweh shove *Paradise Lost*'s God into a scolding shouter, like William Blake's Tiriel.

Ultimately all of *Paradise Lost* is John Milton's vast soliloquy, wounded to wonder by Hamlet and Macbeth. *Paradise Lost* is a dream of firstness, of the regained earliness of epic poetry. Satan dreams Milton into Adamic being, and Eve awakens Milton to the real.

Dante Alighieri, in his letter to Can Grande (1319) concerning the structure of the *Commedia*, describes his mode of treatment as "poetic, fictive, descriptive, digressive, transumptive." Milton's major transumption of Homer, Virgil, Ovid, Dante, Tasso, Spenser, and the Bible is in what Wallace Stevens memorably called "the fiction of the leaves," which has a long history in Western tradition. He tropes on Job, Isaiah, Homer, Virgil, and Dante. Satan's fallen hosts, poignantly still called "angel forms," most directly allude to a prophetic outcry of Isaiah:

And all the host of heaven shall be dissolved, and the heavens shall be rolled together as a scroll; and all their host shall

fall down, as the leaf falleth off from the vine, and as a falling fig from the fig tree.

[Isaiah (KJV) 34:4]

Shrewdly, Milton evades this, and transumes instead Homer,
Virgil, Dante:

Like leaves on trees the race of man is found,
Now green in youth, now withering on the ground;
Another race the following spring supplies,
They fall successive, and successive rise;
So generations in their course decay,
So flourish these, when those are past away.

[Homer, *Iliad* 6, translated by Alexander Pope]

Thick as the leaves in autumn strow the woods,
Or fowls, by winter forced, forsake the floods,
And wing their hasty flight to happier lands;
Such, and so thick, the shivering army stands,
And press for passage with extended hands.
Now these, now those, the surly boatman bore:
The rest he drove to distance from the shore.

[Virgil, *Aeneid* 6, translated by John Dryden]

Thereafter all together they drew back,
    Bitterly weeping, to the accursed shore,
    Which waiteth every man who fears not God.

Charon the demon, with the eyes of glede,
    Beckoning to them, collects them all together,
    Beats with his oar whoever lags behind.

As in the sutumn-time the leaves fall off,
    First one and then another, till the branch
    Unto the earth surrenders all its spoils;

In similar wise the evil seed of Adam
    Throw themselves from that margin one by one,
    At signals, as a bird unto its lure.

[Dante, *Inferno* 3, translated
by Henry Wadsworth Longfellow]

Homer accepts what must be. Virgil acquiesces with sorrowful splendor, in his vision of those who stretch forth their hands out of love for the farther shore. Dante is grim; the evil seed of Adam goes down with the falling leaves. John Milton remembers when he stood in the woods at Vallombrosa, before his blindness, and saw the leaves of autumn strewing the brooks. His metonymy of shades for words puns on Virgil's and Dante's images of the shades that gather for Charon the boatman. Transumptively Milton carries Dante and Virgil back to their beginnings in Homer. The forerunners become belated, and Milton joins himself to Isaiah. The leaves come down from the trees, the generations of men die, only because a third of the Heavenly Host came falling down. Milton stands in a present that is nothing but loss. He will watch no more billowing down of autumnal leaves. Yet his art has seen fully what the precursors saw only in part or merely as reflections in the glass of nature.

Moving to the "scattered sedge" of the Red Sea, Milton alludes again to Virgil, fusing two passages on Orion, one from the *Aeneid*'s Book 1 where stormy Orion crashes Aeneas's ships and this one, from Book 3:

> Then wakeful Palinurus rose, to spy
> The face of heaven, and the nocturnal sky;
> And listened every breath of air to try;
> Observes the stars, and notes their sliding course,
> The Pleiads, Hyads, and their watery force;
> And both the Bears is careful to behold,
> And bright Orion, armed with burnished gold.

Alastair Fowler notes the contrast to the parallel biblical allusions:

> He is wise in heart, and mighty in strength: who hath hardened himself against him, and hath prospered? . . . Which alone spreadeth out the heavens, and treadeth upon the waves of the sea. Which maketh Arcturus, Orion, and Pleiades, and the chambers of the south.
>
> [Job (KJV) 9:4, 8–9]

Seek him that maketh the seven stars and Orion, and tur-
neth the shadow of death into the morning, and maketh the
day dark with night: that calleth for the waters of the sea,
and poureth them out upon the face of the earth: The LORD
is his name.

[Amos (KJV) 5:8]

In Virgil, the rising of Orion preludes the storm season. But in
the Bible, all the stars, Orion included, are no longer powers but
merely signs. When Milton writes "half vexed," he indicates that the
system of signs endures in his own broken day, though he adds
"o'erthrew" to demonstrate that the Satanic stars and the Pharaoh
Bursiris's hosts collapse forever, with Bursiris taken as a type of Satan. Even the beloved Virgil, trapped in an outworn vision of Orion
as potency, is again transumed into just another sign of error.

I have modified this interpretive scheme of transumption from
my much earlier *A Map of Misreading*. Milton's figurations cancel his
obligations to all precursors (save Shakespeare) since he has stationed
them between the truth of *Paradise Lost* (close enough to the Bible's
truth) and the darkness in which he dwells. You could hazard that
transumption sets time aside by troping upon tropes. Word consciousness replaces fallen history. John Milton accomplishes what
Francis Bacon only hoped he could do. Milton becomes the true ancient, while the tradition of poets from Homer through Spenser are
reduced to so many belated moderns. Certainly the living moment
is sacrificed, but the meanings of *Paradise Lost* shed the burden of
the anterior, and Milton prophetically sees himself as being at one
with the future.

In some ways that prophecy was fulfilled. Among all poets who
have written in English, Milton is overmatched only by Chaucer and
by Shakespeare, since they forged human personalities. The hidden
god throughout Milton's career was William Shakespeare. In 1632, the
young Milton, not yet twenty-two, published his first poem in English
as another tribute collected in the Second Folio of Shakespeare's plays:

What needs my Shakespeare for his honored bones,
The labor of an age in pilèd stones,

Or that his hallowed relics should be hid
Under a star-ypointing pyramid?
Dear son of Memory, great heir of fame,
What need'st thou such weak witness of thy name?
Thou in our wonder and astonishment
Hast built thyself a live-long monument.
For whilst to th' shame of slow-endeavoring art,
Thy easy numbers flow, and that each heart
Hath from the leaves of thy unvalued book
Those Delphic lines with deep impression took,
Then thou, our fancy of itself bereaving,
Dost make us marble with too much conceiving;
And so sepúlchred in such pomp dost lie,
That kings for such a tomb would wish to die.

> ["On Shakespeare" (written 1630)]

It is a strange poem, sixteen lines in wavering couplets, and more impressive in its rugged ambivalence than in its irregular eloquence. "Unvalued" takes its obsolete meaning of "invaluable." "My Shakespeare" is fiercely possessive yet unearned, and Milton knows this. The "slow-endeavoring art" is accurate and defensive; the "easy numbers" takes a hint from Ben Jonson. The two crucial lines are:

Then thou, our fancy of itself bereaving,
Dost make us marble with too much conceiving . . .

The young Milton's imagination fears deprivation when confronting Shakespeare's overwhelming inventiveness. Is he to be only another scion, a shoot or twig, not even a branch, of this most fecund Tree of Life?

Kenneth Gross, in a letter to me, suggests that "too much conceiving" that can "make us marble" could belong both to Shakespeare's dramas and to Milton's mind responding to them. He speculates further that these two spaces of "conceiving" are in an agon, being different varieties of "too much," and so each in its own way an answer to the opening query as to what Shakespeare *needs*. That opens up a new vista in Milton's ambivalence.

One could say that a poem's memory of itself can be a defense against remembering a poem by another poet. Milton's fondness for self-echoing constitutes a key element in his baroque shaping of Adam and Eve, and of Satan, into forms intended to evade Shakespearean personalities, evasions so intricate that even their tenuous success testifies to ambivalence. Milton desires and does not desire to be Shakespeare. He created our thoughts, our feelings, our personalities, and sorrowfully some of our prejudices.

I turn back, as I so frequently do, to the great authority of Ernst Robert Curtius in his unmatchable *European Literature and the Latin Middle Ages* (1948; translated into English by Willard R. Trask, 1963):

> We may regard it as certain that Christ too was a poet since, by divine inspiration, he was master of all sciences and arts. This sounds strange to a modern reader. But it is in harmony both with the church's general dogma and with the particular dogma of the *sapientia Christi*. It is part of the permanent stock of Catholic theology.

John Milton knew most of this, since he knew almost everything. He is the most learned of all poets in the English language. Shakespeare knew only what he wished to know. His references to the cormorant, a bird fabled for its insatiable appetite, all involve human gluttony. Milton has Satan disguise himself as a cormorant when he enters Eden to feast his eyes greedily upon Eve. I doubt that Milton would have flinched from acknowledging Satan as a poet. He would have disagreed with Blake and Shelley in their conviction that Milton the poet and his poem of Satan were one. The history of poetry from Milton to the present argues more for the Romantic stance than the Miltonic recalcitrance.

Christopher Marlowe's *Doctor Faustus* (1592) was overt enough that Milton could transume it with no difficulty. Marlowe's scamp Mephistophilis is lively and rather charming, but he is a mere minion of the great Lucifer, who would not be pleased by the language of his loyal but elaborately wistful follower. The hints that Milton took from Marlowe are plain enough, but even the sublimity of the Miltonic Satan of the early books of *Paradise Lost* does not allow for anything quite like the epigrammatic snap of the justly famous "Why, this is hell, nor am I out of it," the most Gnostic statement in the drama. Harry Levin rather strangely compared Mephistophilis to Dostoevsky's Porfiry, the examining magistrate in *Crime and Punishment*. But Porfiry is a good man; Mephistophilis, I venture, is Marlowe's version of the Accuser, the Satan who appears at the opening of the Book of Job. Blake, in a Gnostic insight, called the Accuser the God of this world. Mephistophilis has no such pretensions and is closer to the biblical Book of Job's Accuser because he functions as what Saul Bellow rather nastily calls a Reality Instructor. Mephistophilis has uncanny insight into Faustus; indeed he seems to be the Daemon or Genius of Faustus, perhaps the spiritual form that Faustus will take on in hell.

Jorge Luis Borges remarked: "Reading and rereading Wilde throughout the years, I noticed something that his panegyrists had not, it seems, suspected: namely the verifiable, elementary fact that Wilde was virtually always right" ("On Oscar Wilde" [1952]). In *De Profundis* (1897), Oscar Wilde suggested that Jesus was both a poet and a poem:

> Indeed, that is the charm about Christ, when all is said: he is just like a work of art. He does not really teach one anything, but by being brought into his presence one becomes something.

No two scholars, readers, believers, skeptics ever agree about Jesus. Whoever or whatever he was, he is not the Son in *Paradise Lost*. William Blake called Milton's God Nobodaddy:

> Why art thou silent and invisible,
> Father of Jealousy?
> Why dost thou hide thyself in clouds
> From every searching eye?
>
> Why darkness and obscurity
> In all thy words and laws,
> That none dare eat the fruit but from
> The wily Serpent's jaws?
> Or is it because Secresy gains females' loud applause?
> ["To Nobodaddy"]

The two final lines may sound misogynistic, but Blake intends something very different. When William Blake speaks of the "Human Form Divine," he means both women and men, or an androgyne. What he calls "the Female Will" applies to men and women alike. "The selfish virtues of the natural heart" are melted down when the selfhood, which is Satan, voluntarily enters the furnace of the awakened imagination.

William Wordsworth, in a renowned passage concerning "spots of time" in *The Prelude* (1805), formulated what has been an enabling motto for all great poetry after him, the lordship and mastery of the adverting mind over outward sense:

> A virtue, by which pleasure is enhanced,
> That penetrates, enables us to mount,
> When high, more high, and lifts us up when fallen.
> This efficacious spirit chiefly lurks
> Among those passages of life that give
> Profoundest knowledge to what point, and how,
> The mind is lord and master—outward sense
> The obedient servant of her will. Such moments
> Are scattered everywhere, taking their date
> From our first childhood.
>
> [(1850), 12.216–225]

Frank Kermode, in his brief book *Wallace Stevens* (1960), said of "The Idea of Order at Key West" that it "may stand as a great, perhaps belated, climax to a whole age of poetry that begins with Coleridge and Wordsworth; it celebrates the power of the mind over what they called 'a universe of death.'" Kermode's debt, as he realized, was to Coleridge's poem "To William Wordsworth" (1807), in which the Sage of Highgate gives his reaction to the endless night in which Wordsworth read aloud his "poem to Coleridge," the thirteen-book *Prelude*, in 1807.

> Of tides obedient to external force,
> And currents self-determined, as might seem,
> Or by some inner Power; of moments awful,
> Now in thy inner life, and now abroad,

When power streamed from thee, and thy soul received
The light reflected, as a light bestow'd—
> ["To William Wordsworth," ll. 15–20]

More in this poem than in any other, Coleridge captures the Miltonic sound, though only as an effusion from the Miltonic Wordsworth. I yield to no one in acknowledging that Wordsworth is the first and greatest truly modern poet, even as Goethe is the final representative of the long tradition of the classic that began with Homer. Before Wordsworth, poems had subjects. After him, they have only subjectivity. I recall not altogether playful arguments with my close friend Geoffrey Hartman, the best of Wordsworth critics, in which I maintained that Wordsworth all but destroyed Coleridge, at least as a poet. Like Dante and Milton, Wordsworth is not very lovable. The sorrow of Coleridge is that "The Rime of the Ancient Mariner" is his only completed large-scale poem. "Christabel" consists of four wonderful fragments, and "Kubla Khan" seems to be the only relic of Coleridge's early desire to write an epic on the fall of Jerusalem to the Romans.

Coleridge had a mind of extraordinary range but limited it by his incessant need to find the *Logos* to be the governing agent of all things. Though he was a great literary critic, who realized the importance of comprehending character in each Shakespearean protagonist, he got Hamlet quite wrong. Even if you are Coleridge, it is unwise to underestimate Hamlet. I recall once writing that Milton's Satan was indebted to Iago for his sense of injured merit, to Macbeth for proleptic anxiety, to Edmund of *King Lear* for daring to stand up on behalf of bastards. More than any of these, Hamlet gave to Satan what mattered most, a selfhood of inward-turning torment in the prison house of introspection.

Angus Fletcher knew, and said, that Hamlet was the congener of Milton's Satan, and indeed his inimitable precursor. In my particular favorite among all of Wallace Stevens's poems, "The Poems of Our Climate," the final stanza begins: "There would still remain the never-resting mind," a mind that wants to "escape, come back / To what had been so long composed."

What "had been so long composed" is what Nietzsche meant by his aphorism: "The whole perceptual and sensual world is the primordial poem of mankind." William Blake would have agreed, but with the proviso that a more imaginative mankind, awakened from the nightmare of history, could regain enlarged and more numerous senses to behold a cosmos far beyond that primordial poem. Hamlet's never-resting mind strains at its limits to achieve that infinitude. Satan, Hamlet's bastard child, seethes within his limits and knows he is doomed never to transcend them again. Fletcher's formulation holds firm:

> Throughout his career Milton remained interested in and deeply impassioned by all aspects of thought, not least in its Satanic bent toward isolation and negation. He wrote of the speed of thought, of its lightness, of its tendency to error, of its ordering through logic, of its relation to language and public utterance, of its culminating redemption through prophetic insight.
>
> [*Colors of the Mind* (1991)]

This is what Fletcher terms "the tragedy of mind." I remember many conversations between us on the relation between Hamlet and Satan, two of the West's principal protagonists at play in the theater of mind. Angus and I shared an admiration for William Empson's *Milton's God* (1961), a book I first read in October of the year of its publication. I reread it in 1967, when I began *The Anxiety of Influence*. Returning to it now in 2018, I hear Empson's voice and remember our conversations when he visited Yale. When we were introduced, he said, "You are the man who wrote that dotty book on influence. I like dotty books." I expressed my admiration for his work as a critic and for his sparse but splendid achievement as a poet. He had been reading Hart Crane and wanted to talk about the *Voyages*, where we found deep agreement. Sharing his championship of Shelley, we went on to an exchange on the relationship between Crane and Shelley.

There are many pleasures for me in Empson's *Milton's God*, but this one in particular stays with me:

> Shelley remarked that no man of honour could go to Heaven, because the more he reverenced the Son who endured the more he must execrate the Father who was satisfied by his

pain. But this is only the basic moral objection to the religion, which had been found obvious since its beginning; the ground for an even more severe one had been added during the first centuries. With the additional doctrine, which at least appears to be logically necessary and, as we have seen, is at least not always rejected by modern Christians, the objection becomes hard to express sufficiently strongly. The Christian God the Father, the God of Tertullian, Augustine and Aquinas, is the wickedest thing yet invented by the black heart of man.

The fires of Smithfield were lit by "Bloody Mary," Queen Mary I, Tudor monarch married to Phillip II of Spain. Roughly 280 women and men, Protestant heretics, were burned alive in Smithfield, part of the City of London. Many of them were tortured before incineration.

Bloody Mary and her inquisitors were literalizing a text that is equivocal:

For the Lord thy God is a consuming fire.

[Deuteronomy (KJV) 4:24]

For our God is a consuming fire.

[Hebrews (KJV) 12:29]

John Milton in the opening words of *Lycidas* (1637) ("Yet once more") alludes to the larger passage in Hebrews 12 that culminates in this fierce trope. Though *Lycidas* is probably the best poem of moderate length in the language, I wonder always why its opening stroke suggests apocalypse, rather out of place in a pastoral elegy. It is very likely that Milton would have pondered the image of Yahweh as a consuming fire.

Empson seems to me both reasonable and humane. Can we say the same of John Milton? He approved of Oliver Cromwell's massacre of the Irish and British Royalists at Drogheda in 1649, describing the resistance as "a mixed rabble, part papists, part fugitives, and part savages." Even though *Areopagitica* (1644) is now widely regarded as a defense of the freedom to publish, Milton intended that such liberty was to be granted only to Protestant sectarians. It does not diminish Milton's splendor as a poet that he served Cromwell not just as Secretary for Foreign Tongues to the Council of State for a decade but also as a censor.

The Satan of *Paradise Lost* may seem a kind of papist, each time Milton yields to denigrating him. Is that not also a kind of censorship? Satan initially is a strong poet but he wanes because he cannot transume his forerunners: Hamlet, Iago, Macbeth. Milton as a poet commences and concludes with strength because he transumes the entire tradition from Homer to Spenser. Milton's flaws—God and the Son—are generated by the shadow of Shakespeare. To employ William Blake's terms, the Limits of Contraction and Opacity that prevent Adam from manifesting Chaucerian or Shakespearean personality are Milton's inability to represent otherness. Eve strives for personality, achieves it briefly, and then falls back into Adamic childishness. The tragedy of Satan is Milton's tragedy: Shakespeare became the Covering Cherub who blocked Milton from the creation of voices not his own.

Like John Milton, Satan falls because Macbethian ambition overcomes him. This Fall is from character into personality. Is that a fall or a rising? One puzzle is, why does John Milton evade the J writer's Yahweh, whose personality is so immense? Or indeed, why does Milton circumvent the Gospel of Mark's Jesus, who is so strange and unique a personality?

On May 27, 2001, I traveled with my wife, Jeanne, to the University of Coimbra in Portugal to receive an honorary degree. It was presented to me by my friend, the novelist José Saramago (1922–2010). I continue to be an intense admirer of his work, particularly of *The Gospel According to Jesus Christ* (1991), which I recall reviewing in 2001.

The four personalities who matter in Saramago's *Gospel* are God, Pastor (who is Satan), Jesus, and Mary Magdalene, who become carnal lovers. Saramago's God is a moral nightmare and an aesthetic delight. Here he addresses the innocent victim whom he will choose as his son:

For the last four thousand and four years I have been the God of the Jews, a quarrelsome and difficult race by nature, but on the whole I have got along fairly well with them, they now take Me seriously and are likely to go on doing so for the foreseeable future. So, You are satisfied, said Jesus. I am and I am not, or rather, I would be were it not for this restless heart of Mine, which is forever telling Me, Well now, a fine destiny you've arranged after four thousand years of trial and tribulation that no amount of sacrifice on altars will ever be able to repay, for You continue to be the god of a tiny population that occupies a minute part of this world You created with everything that's on it, so tell Me, My son, if I should be satisfied with this depressing situation. Never having created a world, I'm in no position to judge, replied Jesus. True, you cannot judge, but you could help. Help in what way. To spread My word, to help Me become the god of more people. I don't understand. If you play your part, that is to say, the part I have reserved for you in My plan, I have every confidence that within the next six centuries or so, despite all the struggles and obstacles ahead of us, I will pass from being God of the Jews to being God of those whom we will call Catholics, from the Greek. And what is this part You have reserved for me in Your plan. That of martyr, My son, that of victim.

[translated by Giovanni Pontiero]

I once remarked to Saramago that this God was the greatest of Jewish jokes. For all his sardonic intensity, the novelist was not pleased. I think Kafka, James Joyce, Beckett, Thomas Mann, and Thomas Bernhard might have been cheerful enough, not to mention Philip Roth and Joshua Cohen.

The God of Saramago's *Gospel* is first and foremost time, not truth, the other attribute he asserts. Saramago, an eccentric Marxist and avowed atheist, subverts St. Augustine on the theodicy of time. If time is God, then God cannot be forgiven, and who would seek to forgive him? But then, the *Gospel*'s God is not even slightly interested in forgiveness: he forgives no one, not even Jesus, and he refuses to forgive Pastor, even when the devil makes an honest offer of obedience. God's sole interest is power, and the sacrifice of Jesus employs the prospect of forgiveness of our sins only as an advertisement. God makes clear that all are guilty, and that he prefers to keep it that way. Jesus is no atonement: his crucifixion is merely a device by which God ceases to be Jewish and becomes Catholic, a *converso* rather than a *marrano*. That is superb irony, and Saramago makes it high art, though to thus reduce it critically is to invite a Catholic onslaught. Of all fictive representations of God since the Yahwist's, I vote for Saramago's: he is at once the most comical and the most chilling, in the mode of the Shakespearean hero-villains: Richard III, Iago, Edmund in *King Lear*.

Let us venture to compare Milton's God to Saramago's. Any sense of outrage at Milton's God evanesces in that juxtaposition. In contrast to this Catholic God who was so exuberantly bloodthirsty, quite in the vein of Blake's Nobodaddy, the God of *Paradise Lost* is, alas, a pompous boor. Where Saramago cannot match Milton is in rival devils. Satan is High Romantic, though uneasy, while poor Pastor is stoic at the absurdity of his position:

> Certainly if God exists, He must be only one, but it would be better if He were two, then there would be a god for the wolf and one for the sheep, a god for the victim and one for the assassin, a god for the condemned man and one for the executioner.

This is said to Jesus, who trusts that "the Lord alone is God," a Judaic declaration. But Pastor, like God, is Catholic.

Jacob Burckhardt (1818–1897) was a superbly disenchanted spirit: "Alongside all swindlers the state now stands there as swindler-in-chief." Is that not the United States of America at just this moment? Nietzsche and Burckhardt were colleagues, both profound students of ancient Greek culture and of the Renaissance and its aftereffects. They agreed on Nietzsche's dialectic of Dionysius and Apollo as alternating in Greek tragedy, and on Burckhardt's emphasis on agon, the contest for the foremost place, in Athenian society, literature, and art. Otherwise Burckhardt kept himself a little remote from his younger colleague, despite their warm friendship.

Since he came out of a family of Swiss Calvinists, Burckhardt in his youth considered the ministry but turned strongly against Christian belief and joined himself to the culture of ancient Athens and Renaissance Italy. It is most accurate to describe him as a humanist free of Christianity. With Nietzsche, this would have to be put rather more violently.

John Milton, as a learned and moneyed young Englishman at the brink of thirty, toured extensively in Italy, particularly in Florence, Rome, and Spanish-controlled Naples. Outspoken in his disdain for papism, nevertheless he was widely hosted and acclaimed for his palpable poetic and scholarly gifts.

Could Milton be described as a Christian humanist poet? Or even as a Protestant humanist? Christianity and humanism should not be linked too casually. If Athens is Plato, and First Isaiah is Jerusalem, are they compatible? Here are the closing five challenges made by William Blake in his drawing and engraving of "The Laocoön":

> Is not every Vice possible to Man described in the Bible
>   openly
> All is not Sin that Satan calls so all the Loves & Graces of
>   Eternity
> If Morality was Christianity Socrates was the Saviour
> Art can never exist without Naked Beauty displayed
> No Secresy in Art
>
> [1826–1827]

> When I have bent Judah for me, filled the bow with Ephraim, and raised up thy sons, O Zion, against thy sons, O Greece, and made thee as the sword of a mighty man.
>
> [Zechariah (KJV) 9:13]

The voices of the prophets must finally scatter the dialectics of the scholars and the philosophers. Here is Hegel in his early *The Spirit of Christianity and Its Fate* (1799):

> The fate of the Jewish people is the fate of Macbeth who stepped out of nature itself, clung to alien Beings, and so in their service had to trample and slay everything holy in human nature, had at last to be forsaken by his gods (since these were objects and he their slave) and be dashed to pieces on his faith itself.

In my advanced old age, having just published a brief book, *Macbeth: A Dagger of the Mind* (2019), I must confess I never considered Macbeth to be anything of a Jewish personage. As a reader of Shakespeare I am indebted to Hegel, who made the marvelous statement that Shakespeare's tragic protagonists are free artists of themselves. Glumly, I reflect that even Shakespeare did grave and permanent harm in his creation of Shylock, but Hegel was more ruinous. Can the Hebrew Bible be read with just a bit of accuracy and still be interpreted as presenting the people of Abraham, Jacob, and Moses as trampling everything holy in human nature? I suffer the same fury I receive when, with great reluctance, I glance again at the writings of Simone Weil.

John Milton was far wiser about the Hebrew Bible than Hegel could be. *Samson Agonistes*, probably his last major work (1671), seems to me the most Hebraic poem in the English language, surpassing William Blake's many efforts to render the Bible into "the Great Code of Art." Blake had taught himself some Hebrew, but Milton had been tutored extensively in the language and perhaps even in Aramaic. Many men and women in Milton's circle were highly proficient in Hebrew, not only reading Tanakh in the original but even corresponding with one another in the ancient language. As one might expect from a blind poet of exquisite sensibility, Milton had an extraordinarily acute ear for poetry in many languages, Hebrew included.

Each time I reread or recite *Samson Agonistes* to myself, I wonder at the total absence of Christianity from this drama. Milton had certainly read the Samson saga of Judges 13–16 in the Hebrew original. Like Shakespeare, he had absorbed the Geneva Bible, with its rugged Protestant commentaries. At moments in *Samson Agonistes* as in *King Lear*, I hear the accents of William Tyndale (1494–1536), martyred father of the English Bible, strangled to death and then burned at the stake in Brabant before he had time to finish his work on the Old Testament, as he and Milton called it. Myles Coverdale (1488–1569) finished Tyndale's work even though Coverdale lacked Hebrew and Greek. He was, however, an eloquent translator who caught the accent of Hebrew, and with Tyndale created biblical English.

There is no Miltonic compunction as to the heroic act of Samson in the final action of *Samson Agonistes*, rather weirdly termed "terrorism" by a current Miltonist. It is very much in the spirit of Judges 5, whose high point for me is the Song of Deborah:

> Then sang Deborah and Barak the son of Abinoam on that day, saying,
> Praise ye the Lord for the avenging of Israel, when the people willingly offered themselves.
>
> [Judges (KJV) 5:1–2]

John Milton himself speaks, partly through the voice of Manoa, Samson's father, and partly through the Chorus:

> *Semi-Chorus:* But he, though blind of sight,
> Despised, and thought extinguished quite,
> With inward eyes illuminated,
> His fiery virtue roused
> From under ashes into sudden flame,
> And as an evening dragon came,
> Assailant on the perched roosts
> And nests in order ranged
> Of tame villatic fowl, but as an eagle
> His cloudless thunder bolted on their heads.
> So Virtue, given for lost,
> Depressed and overthrown, as seemed,
> Like that self-begotten bird
> In the Arabian woods embost,
> That no second knows nor third,
> And lay erewhile a holocaust,
> From out her ashy womb now teemed
> Revives, reflourishes, then vigorous most
> When most unactive deemed;
> And, though her body die, her fame survives,
> A secular bird, ages of lives.
>
> [ll. 1687–1707]

Kenneth Gross rightly indicates that the Chorus's vision of Samson's fiery, self-destructive "virtue" strongly echoes Coriolanus's speech to his mother, Volumnia:

My mother, you wot well
My hazards still have been your solace: and
Believe't not lightly—though I go alone,
Like to a lonely dragon, that his fen
Makes fear'd and talk'd of more than seen—your son
Will or exceed the common or be caught . . .

[4.1.29–34]

That "lonely dragon" gave Milton "an evening dragon." To see Samson at his close as a Coriolanus is to enhance his splendor. Frank Kermode and Kenneth Gross both accurately hear the accents of Shakespeare's "The Phoenix and the Turtle" in the "self-begotten bird."

I have a great passion for *Samson Agonistes* (1671), to me second only to *Paradise Lost* in Milton's canon. A student of Pindar since my youth, the choruses have a very strong effect upon me. It seems evident to me that *Samson Agonistes* is not Christian. Is it even theist? Plainly Samson himself, his father, Manoa, and the Chorus would seem to affirm the Hebrew God. And yet the imagery and the metaphoric argument of the dramatic poem point elsewhere. The best account I have read of *Samson Agonistes* is by John Rogers:

As critics have noted, the "rousing motions" behind Samson's inscrutable change of heart are felt again when Milton writes of Samson, "His fiery virtue rous'd / From under ashes into sudden flame." Looking ahead to the image of the phoenix, Milton's loaded verb "rous'd" can be seem to retain a strong element of its original meaning, which was "to shake the feathers" or "to ruffle." But while Milton's verb does gesture ahead to the imminent figure of the phoenix, it is first and foremost the verb that names Samson's own action in his final moments at the temple: "but he though blind of sight . . . / His fiery virtue rous'd." In this more proximate alliance, the verb *rouse* here activates a closely related variant of its original meaning, which, when used intransitively of hair, meant "to stand on end."

["The Secret of *Samson Agonistes*" (1997)]

Milton's Phoenix carries the proud appellation made by Satan:

> Like that self-begotten bird
> In the Arabian woods embost . . .

"Self-begotten" echoes Satan's fierce reply to Abdiel:

> So spake the fervent Angel; but his zeale
> None seconded, as out of season judged,
> Or singular and rash. Whereat rejoiced
> The Apostate, and, more haughty, thus replied:—
> That we were formed, then, sayest thou? and the work
> Of secondary hands, by task transferred
> From Father to his Son? Strange point and new!
> Doctrine which we would know whence learned! Who saw
> When this creation was? Remember'st thou
> Thy making, while the Maker gave thee being?
> We know no time when we were not as now;
> Know none before us, self-begot, self-raised
> By our own quickening power when fatal course
> Had circled his full orb, the birth mature
> Of this our native Heaven, Ethereal Sons.
> Our puissance is our own; our own right hand
> Shall teach us highest deeds, by proof to try
> Who is our equal. Then thou shalt behold
> Whether by supplication we intend
> Address, and to begirt the Almighty Throne
> Beseeching or besieging. This report,
> These tidings, carry to the Anointed King;
> And fly, ere evil intercept thy flight.
>
> [5.849–871]

Here Satan speaks for every strong poet by contending:

> We know no time when we were not as now;
> Know none before us, self-begot, self-raised
> By our own quickening power . . .

On the borders of Milton's consciousness, there may be a recollection of King Henry VIII prophesying the grand career of his daughter Elizabeth I and of her successor James I, in Shakespeare and Fletcher's *King Henry VIII* (1613):

> Nor shall this peace sleep with her; but as when
> The bird of wonder dies, the maiden phoenix,
> Her ashes new create another heir
> As great in admiration as herself . . .
>
> [5.4.39–42]

Milton's monism, allied with his passion for Christian Liberty, and for the Inner Light by which he interprets the Bible for himself, has taken him to the frontier where theism is difficult to distinguish from "self-esteem," his own coinage. Shakespeare's term for the ego was "the self-same." William Blake's Milton cries out:

> I in my Selfhood am that Satan: I am that Evil One!
> He is my Spectre! in my obedience to loose him from my Hells,
> To claim the Hells, my Furnaces, I go to Eternal Death.
>   [*Milton* (1804–1821), plate 14]

Blake, like Meister Eckhart, like Jacob Boehme, desired the Selfhood to be cast out into the refiner's fire of Christian love. John Milton would have dismissed that as spiritual sophistry. Nearing the close of a long life, I surprise myself by agreeing with him. Sigmund Freud argued that thought could be freed from its sexual past, by submitting to the rigors of his myth of psychoanalysis. Eckhart and Boehme, Blake and Freud, all were great spirits; Milton was greater.

There are no accurate measurements for the human spirit. Yet good readers know what they mean when Tolstoy is preferred above Dostoevsky; Victor Hugo over Flaubert; Dante over Petrarch; Chaucer over Spenser; Goethe over Schiller; Shakespeare over Milton. The poet of *Paradise Lost* and of *Samson Agonistes* will always remain the sublime of the English language, but Shakespeare is something else.

John Milton understood that he could not write stage tragedy because of Shakespeare. At one moment he seems to have considered writing his own *Macbeth* but stopped after jotting down the title. The best poets of my time have departed. Had I ever suggested to my closer friends among them—John Ashbery, A. R. Ammons, Mark Strand, William Merwin—that they compose a *Macbeth*, they would have been properly incredulous. Ashbery and Merwin wrote some stage works, as did James Merrill and Richard Wilbur (as translator), yet they knew Shakespeare could not guide them.

With a mind like Milton's it becomes very difficult to surmise how aware he was of the Shakespearean shadow. In a prose work he sneers at King Charles I for cherishing Shakespeare as his favorite author, and nastily assimilates the martyred king to the brutal Richard III of Shakespeare's play. Milton's equivocal tribute, "On Shakespeare," like his overt compliment in "L'Allegro" (1645, written 1632), does not necessarily refer to Shakespearean dramas:

> If Jonson's learned sock be on,
> Or sweetest Shakespeare, Fancy's child,
> Warble his native wood-notes wild.
>
> ["L'Allegro," ll. 132–134]

One would not say that in *Hamlet, Othello, Macbeth* we hear (or overhear) the warbling of native wood-notes wild. But how can a sensitive and faithful reader exploring the grand pleasures of *Paradise Lost* not overhear the accents of Hamlet, Iago, and Macbeth, among many other Shakespearean protagonists?

Milton's puissance is his own, his self-esteem is prodigal, yet his epic's personae are not self-begotten. In perhaps the early 1640s, Milton sketched what would have been a stage work, *Adam Unparadised*. Lucifer, not Satan, would have been the villain, Eve and Adam his tragic victims, and Michael or Moses the effectual leader of the heavenly host. Tragic drama was replaced by the major Western epic after Homer, Virgil, and Dante. Something in Milton compelled him to write and then revise as his final work *Samson Agonistes*, a tragedy as dramatic poem.

There is no Lucifer or unfallen Satan in *Paradise Lost*. Milton needed to exclude so Promethean a figure from his epic. Hamlet's idiom of suffering and negative thinking might have been even more evident in that absent Lucifer. Iago's rebellious sense of injured merit,

Macbeth's powerlessness to halt his inundation by the nightworld, Edmund's standing up for bastardy against legitimacy: all these find home in Satan.

An inspired conversationalist, Coleridge interpreted Satan as an aspect of Milton (and of Coleridge), so that Satan also is a revelation of spirit:

> In the Paradise Lost—indeed, in every one of his poems—it is Milton himself whom you see; his Satan, his Adam, his Raphael, almost his Eve—all are John Milton; and it is a sense of this intense egotism that gives me the greatest pleasure in reading Milton's works. The egotism of such a man is a revelation of spirit.
>
> [*Table Talk* (August 18, 1833)]

Turning the leaves of *Paradise Lost* I find that Milton is the poem, the icon, and the man; redeeming what can be redeemed, wrestling with the angels of blindness and of death, while knowing always that his fiction must keep changing in order to give pleasure. Shakespeare in spirit is a profoundly Ovidian poet. Milton is not. And yet, in praxis he is.

The new meanings I seek to find in Milton are those enigmatic and labyrinthine ways by which he could both fend off Shakespeare and yet employ the plenitude of Shakespearean personality. I have to start with Satan since his troubled and troubling cogitations are so subtly quarried out of Prince Hamlet's.

Milton's Satan may or may not entertain mere illusions of the inward light of cognition, but who among us—even a Wittgenstein—earns the right to call the Black Prince of Denmark's inwardness and power of thought, restless and wavering as it be, in any way illusive? Nietzsche is the authority for reminding us that Hamlet thinks much too well and so thinks himself into the truth, and so into the silent abyss of rest.

Shakespeare, much more than Marlowe or Ben Jonson, bequeathed the soliloquy to Milton. Our word "soliloquy" comes from the Latin *solus* for "alone" and *loqui* "to speak." Should you speak to yourself out loud, you are soliloquizing. Though William Hazlitt said, "It is we who are Hamlet," we are and are not. How fully can we find ourselves in the most famous soliloquy in the English language:

> To be, or not to be, that is the question,
> Whether 'tis nobler in the mind to suffer
> The slings and arrows of outrageous fortune,
> Or to take arms against a sea of troubles,
> And by opposing end them?
>
> [3.1.1–5]

If you think your way carefully through this, phrase by phrase, word by word, it will soon abandon its air of excessive familiarity. Instead it is undiscovered country and we will never come to the end of it. Even Kierkegaard, who in his life and work played the part of Hamlet, and who gave us the admonition that in every utterance of the Black Prince we should listen for the resonance of the opposite, never completed the work of listening. I speculate that John Milton, not altogether knowingly, came close to completing that work. Hamlet is the Promethean Lucifer, who was not permitted by Milton to enter *Paradise Lost*.

The word "question" occurs seventeen times in *Hamlet*, not to mention "questionable" and other variants. Prince Hamlet is an answer without a question, a question without an answer. Satan knows he has no answers to the question of his future. Try the thought-experiment of Satan delivering the "To be, or not to be" soliloquy. Hamlet scarcely contemplates suicide: he broods rather on the question of being. Yahweh says: "I will be [that] I will be." Punning on his own name with *ehyeh* ("I will be"), he tells Moses that as God he will be present when he wills to be present, and absent whenever it suits him. Satan knows that his presence, like his absence, lies not in his own will. Hamlet can assert autonomy with the merest shrug; Satan desperately wants to establish autonomy yet knows he cannot do it.

Hamlet has two fathers: King Hamlet and King Claudius. The Prince does not know how far back the adulterous, incestuous relationship between Gertrude and Claudius reached. As intellectual as Montaigne, Hamlet shows no traits in common either with the Warrior King or with the usurping Machiavel. His true father was his playfellow Yorick. Satan, when he was the unfallen Lucifer, ranked highest in the heavenly hierarchy after God himself. When God declares that on this day he has brought forth Messias, his only-begotten son, Satan copies Iago's Sense of Injured Merit and so commences to fall.

As Wallace Stevens enjoyed telling us: "That things go round and again go round / Has rather a classical sound." Does one wish Milton's God and Satan to have experienced more of the pleasures of merely circulating? Here I return to Hamlet's most profound soliloquy and to the question of soliloquy itself.

The poet John Milton's own soliloquies are the four invocations to *Paradise Lost:* to Books 1, 3, 7, and 9. Let us try the somewhat outrageous experiment of asking, Who might seem more at home in delivering the "to be or not to be" meditation, the poet Milton or his Satan? Who has more power of mind over the sea of troubles, Milton or Satan? The sea of mothering night, primal abyss, forefather and foremother, pragmatically manifests as death, the end to consciousness, for which Hamlet's term is "conscience." Satan heroically sails that sea, voyaging to the new world of Eden, garden of Eve and Adam. Yet Milton portrays himself as heroic, risking his own heavenly ascents and sudden descents to our earth. Hamlet anticipates Cuchulain, the great hero of the Ulster cycle, the Irish Achilles as it were. William Butler Yeats achieves greatness in two of his five Cuchulain plays: *At the Hawk's Well* (1917) and *The Only Jealousy of Emer* (1919), modeled on what Yeats knew of the Japanese Noh dance-dramas. Closer to Hamlet's most famous soliloquy is Yeats's early poem "Cuchulain's Fight with the Sea" (1892), in which the hero vainly turns his sword on the sea after unknowingly slaying his own son. I find unpleasant Yeats's drama *The Death of Cuchulain* (1939), but the Anglo-Irish archpoet redeemed himself with the astonishing poem "Cuchulain Comforted" (1939), in which the slain hero in the afterlife finds himself in the company of cowards and joins them in their song.

In Hamlet's soliloquy there is an agon between this mortal coil, to be shuffled off, and the undiscovered country, from which no traveler returns. John Milton can join that agon, but Satan is sadly immortal. Prince Hamlet has set the odds by which Milton and those who come after him, from Wordsworth through Whitman to Wallace Stevens, can ascertain the limits of their own power over the universe of death. Satan begets Death upon Sin and has to suffer a fearful mix of immortality and powerlessness.

Is the ghost of King Hamlet the Devil? Robert Burton, in his grand *The Anatomy of Melancholy* (first edition 1621), is the ultimate authority for judging melancholia to be Satanic. Though Prince Hamlet decides otherwise, a spirit whose entire enterprise is to convert the most capacious consciousness ever represented in literature into a mere dagger of vengeance is most certainly diabolical. I can think of no higher praise for John Milton, man and poet, than that he never yielded to melancholy, except in the playful "Il Penseroso," which could have been composed as early as 1631. Think of yourself as totally blind, some of your writings burned by the public hangman, and imprisoned in the Tower of London for perhaps three months, not knowing when you would be released or even have to confront execution. We have very little information about that ordeal. But Milton's grateful readers can surmise that he refused to yield to melancholy. Doubtless he worked by dictation. Like his own Satan, he had the courage never to submit or yield, and could have asked the proud rhetorical question: "And what is else, not to be overcome?"

Paradise Lost's Satan has been maligned by a long, bad tradition from Joseph Addison down to the pious Clive Staples Lewis and even beyond. Hamlet, Milton, Satan: all of them have a touch of Farinata's *gran dispitto*. Guido Cavalcanti's father-in-law stands upright in his tomb, "as if of Hell he had a great disdain." Shelley phrased that as "this deep scorn" in his last, unfinished poem, "The Triumph of Life" (1822). Hamlet, grappling with Laertes at the grave of Ophelia, cries out: "This is I, / Hamlet the Dane." Milton, in the invocation to Book 1 of *Paradise Lost*, proclaims his legitimate pride as a poet:

> I thence
> Invoke thy aid to my adventrous song
> That with no middle flight intends to soar
> Above the Aonian mount, while it pursues
> Things unattempted yet in prose or rhyme.
> And chiefly Thou, O Spirit, that dost prefer
> Before all temples the upright heart and pure
> Instruct me, for Thou know'st . . .

> [1.12–19]

Satan, superbly addressing his ruined lover Beelzebub, is as proud as Hamlet, Milton, Dante, and Farinata, upright though in Hell:

> yet not for those,
> Nor what the potent Victor in his rage
> Can else inflict do I repent, or change,
> Though changed in outward lustre, that fixed mind,
> And high disdain from sense of injured merit,
> That with the mightiest raised me to contend . . .
>
> [1.94–99]

That high disdain is Farinata's; that sense of injured merit is Iago's. That change in outward luster is both Satan's and John Milton's, once so fair that he was known as "the Lady of Christ's," Christ's College, Cambridge. Composing *Paradise Lost*, his face has become longer, shadowed, hollow-eyed. His fierce desire for women has never left him. It enchants me that he is so taken with women's hair. Milton would have been happiest as a polygamist, hardly a desire that Western society will tolerate.

Returning to the first invocation, we encounter the strange, apparently Hermetic androgynous image of the Spirit that moved over the face of the waters and brought forth something vitally new:

> Thou from the first
> Wast present, and, with mighty wings outspread,
> Dove-like sat'st brooding on the vast Abyss,
> And mad'st it pregnant: what in me is dark
> Illumine, what is low raise and support;
> That, to the highth of this great Argument
> I may assert Eternal Providence,
> And justify the ways of God to men.
>
> [3.19–26]

Alastair Fowler, an erudite and acute editor of Milton, wishes to see that strange spirit as an image out of Nicholas of Cusa. Fowler also praises Milton's God as a universal father figure. I rather doubt that the senior John Milton, talented composer and successful scrivener, in any way resembled the God of *Paradise Lost*. Nor did his son

John Milton, most eminent of English poets after Shakespeare and Chaucer. Certainly my late father, a silent, stoical man, gently loving his wife and his five children, did not at all resemble Milton's God. I go with William Blake: Nobodaddy.

What impelled Milton to create that androgynous, dovelike spirit? It is not orthodox Christian but Miltonic. It *seems* Hermetic but is not. And I cannot locate it in Nicholas of Cusa. Herbert Marks, in his Norton Critical Edition of *The English Bible* (2012), finds it accurately in an ancient version of the Genesis text, in which "moved" can also be translated "hovered," "swept," or even "brooded."

A close attention to the veritable text of Tanakh, of which Herbert Marks is a master, puts close to Alastair Fowler and Nicholas of Cusa, or the Hermetic Corpus for that matter. John Milton had splendid Hebrew and Aramaic and read Scripture deeply by the inward light of his own spirit. Illumined, raised, and supported by his Protestant Liberty to interpret, blind Milton could abide in light.

The later Victorian Samuel Butler, in his notebooks, has a reflection akin to Blake's and to Shelley's: "Man must always be a consuming fire, or be consumed. As for Hell, we are in a burning fiery furnace all our lives—for what is life but a process of combustion?" (*Notebooks*, edited by G. Keynes and B. Hill, 202).

Samuel Butler had a forerunner in the eloquence of Sir Thomas Browne: "I feel sometimes a hell within myself; Lucifer keeps his court in my breast; Legion is revived in me" (*Religio Medici*). "Life is a pure flame, and we live by an invisible sun within us. A small fire sufficeth for life; great flames seemed too little after death" ("Hydriotaphia, or Urn-Burial").

The play where this flame is most evident is Shakespeare's *Measure for Measure* (1604), which is not just dark or problematic; it is beyond belief and virtually beyond interpretation. Claudio is an ordinary young man, bewildered and fearful. But Isabella is something of a case history. Aside from the masochism, she has a father fixation, and since he is deceased, she hears his voice from the grave. She interprets that voice as saying that incest and coition are the same. There is a brilliant study of *Measure for Measure* by Marc Shell, *The End of Kinship: "Measure for Measure," Incest, and the Ideal of Universal Siblinghood* (1988), that attributes Isabella's obsessiveness to fundamental confusions about monasticism, belief, and incest in Western history and society. I admire

Shell, but I again stress that Shakespeare is interested in personality, and Isabella is a very interesting personality indeed. She readily consents to Duke Vincentio's, disguised as a friar, use of the bed-trick (in the dark they are all alike) by which the monstrous Angelo will ravish Mariana, his spurned and abandoned betrothed, thinking he is enjoying Isabella.

The ex-friar is Duke Vincentio, perpetual trickster, who concludes the play by proposing marriage to Isabella. Evidently she silently consents. What has happened to her strong desire to be a nun? If Shakespeare knows, he will not tell us. *Measure for Measure* is something of a madhouse. It is extraordinarily eloquent, but the eloquence is hollow. We are persuaded that all the characters possess inwardness, and yet we and they scarcely can know it. They are opaque to themselves, to one another, and to us, Shakespeare's auditors and readers. This gives the odd effect throughout that exists also in *All's Well That Ends Well* and *Troilus and Cressida*. The great speeches and exchanges stand by themselves, and we are left puzzled how they could emanate from such closed personalities.

Like Rossiter, I find the classical essay on *Measure for Measure* to be by Walter Pater:

> The old "moralities" exemplified most often some rough and ready lesson. Here the very intricacy and subtlety of the moral world itself, the difficulty of seizing the true relations of so complex a material, the difficulty of just judgement, of judgement that shall not be unjust, are the lessons conveyed.
>
> ["A Fragment on *Measure for Measure*" (1874)]

Pater catches the problem that Shakespeare presents us with, and he knows that Shakespeare is anything but a problem-solver. Intricate the play certainly is, and perhaps it is over-subtle, yet I think Shakespeare wanted it and us to abide in confusion. Let us listen to Shakespeare and ponder, as clearly—if rather reluctantly—as John Milton did:

ISABELLA: O, I do fear thee, Claudio; and I quake,
Lest thou a feverous life shouldst entertain,
And six or seven winters more respect

Than a perpetual honour. Darest thou die?
The sense of death is most in apprehension;
And the poor beetle, that we tread upon,
In corporal sufferance finds a pang as great
As when a giant dies.

CLAUDIO: Why give you me this shame?
Think you I can a resolution fetch
From flowery tenderness? If I must die,
I will encounter darkness as a bride,
And hug it in mine arms.

ISABELLA: There spake my brother; there my father's grave
Did utter forth a voice. Yes, thou must die:
Thou art too noble to conserve a life
In base appliances.

[3.1.83–99]

The reader or playgoer rightly shudders at Isabella's ghostly attribution of her father's grave uttering the noble but false lines of Claudio's mock-heroic.

ISABELLA: O, 'tis the cunning livery of hell,
The damned'st body to invest and cover
In prenzie guards! Dost thou think, Claudio?
If I would yield him my virginity,
Thou mightst be freed.

CLAUDIO: O heavens, it cannot be.

ISABELLA: Yes, he would give't thee, from this rank offense,
So to offend him still. This night's the time
That I should do what I abhor to name,
Or else thou diest tomorrow.

CLAUDIO: Thou shalt not do't.

ISABELLA: O, were it but my life,
I'd throw it down for your deliverance
As frankly as a pin.

CLAUDIO: Thanks, dear Isabel.

ISABELLA: Be ready, Claudio, for your death tomorrow.

CLAUDIO: Yes. Has he affections in him,
That thus can make him bite the law by th' nose,
When he would force it? Sure, it is no sin,
Or of the deadly seven it is the least.

ISABELLA: Which is the least?

CLAUDIO: If it were damnable, he being so wise,
Why would he for the momentary trick
Be perdurably fined? O Isabel!

ISABELLA: What says my brother?

CLAUDIO: Death is a fearful thing.

ISABELLA: And shamèd life a hateful.

[3.1.106–132]

Claudio is at his best in his stirring:

If I must die,
I will encounter darkness as a bride,
And hug it in mine arms.

He sounds there rather Herculean, like another Antony, but of course he does not believe it. Here is the real Claudio, and from him we will pass to Belial in the Pandemonium debate, and thence to Wordsworth and Keats:

Ay, but to die, and go we know not where;
To lie in cold obstruction and to rot;
This sensible warm motion to become
A kneaded clod; and the delighted spirit
To bathe in fiery floods, or to reside
In thrilling region of thick-ribbed ice;
To be imprison'd in the viewless winds,
And blown with restless violence round about
The pendent world; or to be worse than worst

Of those that lawless and incertain thought
Imagine howling: 'tis too horrible!
The weariest and most loathèd worldly life
That age, ache, penury and imprisonment
Can lay on nature is a paradise
To what we fear of death.

[3.1.133–147]

Why did Claudio's desperate appeal to Isabella find a deep recess in Milton's memory? We find *Measure for Measure* outrageous enough; could John Milton have read it without a kind of fury? He was too acute a reader to regard Duke Vincentio as an allegory of God, and I would think he would have rebelled even at the strange play's New Testament title. And why does he make Belial, whom he despises, a kind of Claudio?

One has to go far back to Milton at the age of twenty-two, when he published his poem "To Shakespeare," and when he wrote an abortive, quite bad poem, "The Passion," always a matter upon which he remained uneasy. It concludes with a first trial at the Merkabah or chariot of celestial light in Ezekiel's vision:

VI

See, see the chariot, and those rushing wheels,
That whirled the Prophet up at Chebar flood;
My spirit some transporting Cherub feels,
To bear me where the towers of Salem stood,
Once glorious towers, now sunk in guiltless blood;
There doth my soul in holy vision sit,
In pensive trance, and anguish, and ecstatick fit.

VII

Mine eye hath found that sad sepulchral rock
That was the casket of Heaven's richest store,
And here through grief my feeble hands up lock,
Yet on the softened quarry would I score
My plaining verse as lively as before;
For sure so well instructed are my tears,
That they would fitly fall in ordered characters.

VIII

Or should I thence hurried on *viewless wing*
Take up a weeping on the mountains wild,
The gentle neighbourhood of grove and spring
Would soon unbosom all their echoes mild;
And I (for grief is easily beguil'd)
Might think the infection of my sorrows loud
Had got a race of mourners on some pregnant cloud.

This subject the author finding to be above the years he had, when he
wrote it, and nothing satisfied with what was begun, left it unfinished.

[ll. 36–56]

Milton's wisdom in abandoning "The Passion" was admirable. I
am interested in the phrase I have italicized: "viewless wing," which
goes back to Claudio's "viewless winds" in his vision of death. In
doing so I follow John Hollander again as well as Eleanor Cook, another prodigious student of poetic allusion. In 1630 the young Milton possibly was not aware of how deeply *Measure for Measure* had
contaminated his own fears of dying before his great ambitions could
be accomplished. In time, he transferred his guilt of indebtedness
to Belial:

On the other side up rose
Belial, in act more graceful and humane.
A fairer person lost not Heaven; he seemed
For dignity composed, and high exploit.
But all was false and hollow; though his tongue
Dropt manna, and could make the worse appear
The better reason, to perplex and dash
Maturest counsels: for his thoughts were low—
To vice industrious, but to nobler deeds
Timorous and slothful. Yet he pleased the ear,
And with persuasive accent thus began:—

[2.108–118]

Edward Hyde, First Earl of Clarendon (1609–1674), might well
have been Milton's model for Belial. Though eventually exiled by

Charles II, he was a central actor in the Restoration, and one of the
targets of Milton's *Eikonoklastes* (1649). Reading Clarendon's *The History
of the Rebellion* (1702–1704), I cannot recognize him in Milton's
jaundiced view of Belial, who is no more a sophist than anyone else
in the poem, and no more given to vice or to sloth than most among
us, since I believe we are all fallen angels. Belial's eloquence, echoing
Claudio's, assumes the accents of Prince Hamlet, fiercely pained
and most intellectual of beings:

> And that must end us; that must be our cure—
> To be no more. Sad cure! for who would lose,
> Though full of pain, this intellectual being,
> Those thoughts that wander through eternity,
> To perish rather, swallowed up and lost
> In the wide womb of uncreated Night,
> Devoid of sense and motion?
>
> . . .
>
> Thus Belial, with words clothed in reason's garb,
> Counselled ignoble ease and peaceful sloth,
> Not peace . . .
>
> [2.145–151, 226–28]

Elizabethan rhetorician George Puttenham called transumption
or metalepsis "the farre-fetcher," and the chain of allusions here indeed
fetches from afar and will go on until it will find resting places
in Wallace Stevens. Yet Milton is my concern here, or rather Satan
is, which is to say the post-Shakespearean poet, who must live in the
aura of Hamlet and of his kindred personalities in Shakespeare. The
last thing John Milton would have wanted to hear is the maxim:
"Without Shakespeare, no Milton."

CHAPTER TWO

Milton

The Shakespearean Epic

P ERHAPS DANTE AMONG THE poets before Milton is the
one who intended his great work as the Third Testament, a
new Bible for humankind. After Milton there came Blake
and Wordsworth, who had Scriptural ambitions, though
Wordsworth would not acknowledge this. Since then there was
Walt Whitman, who intended *Leaves of Grass* to be the new Bible for
Americans. Finally (and this does seem final) came Marcel Proust
and James Joyce, to give us the Bible of literary art. There had been
Victor Hugo, massive and deluded genius, who saw himself as God.

Milton would never acknowledge it but his ambitions were unbounded and he wanted more than literary fame, though certainly
he desired that:

> Alas! what boots it with incessant care
> To tend the homely, slighted shepherd's trade,
> And strictly meditate the thankless Muse?
> Were it not better done, as others use,
> To sport with Amaryllis in the shade,
> Or with the tangles of Neæra's hair?
> Fame is the spur that the clear spirit doth raise
> (That last infirmity of noble mind)

To scorn delights and live laborious days;
But the fair guerdon when we hope to find,
And think to burst out into sudden blaze,
Comes the blind Fury with th'abhorred shears,
And slits the thin-spun life.

[*Lycidas*, ll. 64–76]

Lycidas admits that fame is the spur, but the poet invoking the holy light to begin Book 3 of *Paradise Lost* intends to transume the Gospel of John, and he succeeds:

Hail, holy Light, offspring of Heaven first-born!
Or of the Eternal coeternal beam
May I express thee unblamed? since God is light,
And never but in unapproachèd light
Dwelt from eternity—dwelt then in thee,
Bright effluence of bright essence increate!
Or hear'st thou rather pure Ethereal stream,
Whose fountain who shall tell? Before the Sun,
Before the Heavens thou wert, and at the voice
Of God, as with a mantle, didst invest
The rising World of waters dark and deep,
Won from the void and formless infinite!

[3.1–12]

The Priestly author of what is now the opening of Genesis in Tanakh distinctly tells us God created the light. Milton instead gives us various options. Perhaps the light is the offspring of Heaven. Or perhaps the light was never created and existed with God from the first or the light mysteriously flows from an unknown fountain.

This invocation is certainly Milton at his most personal, most poignant, and least Satanic, that is to say least Shakespearean. Viewlessness has yielded to rendering the invisible luminously manifest. It is unclear to me precisely how Milton interpreted the opening of the Gospel of John. He knew it fully both in the Greek original and in the Geneva Bible, where William Tyndale's New Testament is dominant. On the New Testament I tend to accept the authority of David Bentley Hart, whose 2017 translation is masterful. Hart frankly tells us that the prologue of John's Gospel is an exemplary case of the untranslatable. Here is his version of the opening:

> In the origin there was the Logos, and the Logos was present with God, and the Logos was god; This one was present with God in the origin. All things came to be through him, and without him came to be not a single thing that has come to be. In him was life, and this life was the light of men. And the light shines in the darkness, and the darkness did not conquer it.

Contrast this with the Geneva Bible:

> In the beginning was that Word, and that Word was with God, and that Word was God. This same was in the beginning with God. All things were made by it, and without it was made nothing that was made. In it was life, and that life was the light of men. And that light shineth in the wilderness, and the darkness comprehendeth it not.

Hart, following closely the Greek, does not tell us that the Logos was God, but only *a* god, some kind of divine being. Coming to be is not quite making, and the light cannot be overcome by the darkness; nothing is said about whether the darkness comprehended the light or not.

Milton's invocation is not of the Logos or Word, but of the Light, which he catches in the astonishing:

> Bright effluence of bright essence increate!

The blind epic poet is concerned not only with his inward vision but also with the jeopardy of having voyaged through Heaven, Hell, and Chaos in the first two books of his poem. He is well aware that the Virgilian descent to Hell is easy, but the reascent to Earth is arduous. By taking the Satanic predicament upon himself, he has

risked destruction by elements in his own being. In this, as in so
much else, he remains ahead of his critics:

> nor sometimes forget
> Those other two equalled with me in fate,
> So were I equalled with them in renown,
> Blind Thamyris and blind Mæonides,
> And Tiresias and Phineus, prophets old.
>
> [3.32–36]

Milton's hope has been fulfilled in his renown, rightly associating him with blind Maeonides (Homer) and Thamyris, the bard
blinded by the Muses and deprived also of song and lyre for daring
to compete with them. Tiresias, made by T. S. Eliot into the visionary of *The Waste Land*, lived life both as a woman and a man, and
was made blind as a punishment for telling the secret that women
enjoyed more sexual pleasure than men. Phineus was a Thracian
king gifted with clairvoyance, punished with blindness for having
allowed their stepmother to blind his sons. Except for Homer, the
other blind seers must have induced ambivalence in Milton. There
is something dismal in citing them. The advent of Eve, when it takes
place, will return me to that equivocation.

Dexterously Milton then swerves into a pure exquisiteness:

> Then feed on thoughts that voluntary move
> Harmonious numbers; as the wakeful bird
> Sings darkling, and, in shadiest covert hid,
> Tunes her nocturnal note.
>
> [3.37–40]

The blind poet is an English nightingale chanting in the dark,
preluding John Keats in *his* ecstasy:

> Darkling I listen; and, for many a time
> I have been half in love with easeful Death,
> Call'd him soft names in many a mused rhyme,
> To take into the air my quiet breath;

Now more than ever seems it rich to die,
   To cease upon the midnight with no pain,
      While thou art pouring forth thy soul abroad
      In such an ecstasy!
   Still wouldst thou sing, and I have ears in vain—
   To thy high requiem become a sod.

                         ["Ode to a Nightingale" (1819)]

One feels that Keats has taken more than the song from Milton. The accents of Moneta in *The Fall of Hyperion* (1819), admonishing the young poet on the difference between a visionary and a true poet, derived from this invocation. Of those true poets, Moneta says: "They seek no wonder but the human face." Milton's "human face divine" will issue also in Blake's "human form divine," and will haunt the final section of Wallace Stevens's "Esthétique du Mal" (1945).

I do not share David Quint's moral and aesthetic appreciation of the Son's offer to atone for humankind:

The faith that the blind poet asserts in things unseen in the invocation is doubled *inside* the fiction by the Son's faith in the most unseen of all things in which the Christian believes. His heroic volunteering to die to save humanity is followed by a confident declaration.

          on me let thine anger fall;
   Account me Man; I for his sake will leave
   Thy bosom, and this glory next to thee
   Freely put off, and for him lastly die
   Well pleased; on me let Death wreck all his rage.
   Under his gloomy power I shall not long
   Lie vanquished. Thou hast given me to possess
   Life in my self for ever; by thee I live;
   Though now to Death I yield, and am his due,
   All that of me can die, yet, that debt paid,
   Thou wilt not leave me in the loathsome grave
   His prey, nor suffer my unspotted soul

For ever with corruption there to dwell;
But I shall rise victorious, and subdue
My vanquisher, spoiled of his vaunted spoile.

[3.237–51]

There is no more moving passage in *Paradise Lost* than this
one, whose tone Milton so superbly controls. The Son is
confident, and it turns out he has reason to be. He knows
that he has already twice triumphed in glory, after the War
in Heaven and after the Creation—as he will triumph again
when these events that correspond typologically to the Son's
Passion are repeated at the apocalyptic end of history.

[*Inside "Paradise Lost"*]

Reading David Quint's assertion that this is the most moving passage in *Paradise Lost*, and possesses superbly controlled tone, my reactions are complex. Quint has ten times my learning, he is a good friend,
and he is no more a believer in Christianity than I am. But in the margins of his book, at this point I scribbled, "NO! in thunder." Tonality is
frequently disputable, but I hear—David Quint, forgive me—a certain
smugness in the Son's inflection. I think this reflects a Miltonic unease, as the Atonement by crucifixion was hardly his favorite doctrine.
The most moving passages in *Paradise Lost* are spoken by Satan, by
Milton, by Eve, by Adam, and all are animated because they are spoken by Shakespearean personalities. Still, though indebted to Shakespeare, Belial contributes vitally to Wordsworth and to Keats.

There is no single way of describing Milton's poetry. Its range
of allusion is unprecedented. To call him a Christian humanist makes
little sense to me. Jerusalem and Athens may not be antithetical, particularly at this dreadful time, and yet Christian humanism remains
an oxymoron. My late student and friend Thomas Weiskel, in his
book *The Romantic Sublime* (1976), remarked that "A humanistic Sublime is an oxymoron." *Paradise Lost* and *Samson Agonistes* redefine
sublimity and it makes little sense to me to term either a humanistic
poem. *Samson Agonistes* is in no way Christian, and I doubt increasingly that *Paradise Lost* is fundamentally a Christian epic. During the
last four centuries, everyone rewrites *Hamlet*, whether they want to

or not. Milton might have wanted to rework *Macbeth* but not *Hamlet*. Like a whirligig, I spin round again and wonder how he could have failed to note the recognition scene that he keeps staging with Satan or Eve encountering the Black Prince of Denmark.

Ursula K. Le Guin, a substantial poet as well as a master of prose fantasy, composed a brief lay for her fictional planet Gethen or Winter. She writes, "Light is the left hand of darkness, / and darkness the right hand of light," so that light and darkness together resemble lovers in kemmer.

"Kemmer" is Le Guin's term for the coition of the androgynous people of Winter. I wonder sometimes how John Milton might have reacted to reading *The Left Hand of Darkness*. Le Guin's religion was her anarchist version of Daoism, in which darkness or death is the right hand of light and life, and light is the left hand of darkness. Milton's angels, fallen and unfallen, are androgynous, and his particular Holy Spirit has an androgynous aspect also. *Is Milton the left hand of Satan, and Satan the right hand of Milton?*

William Blake would have answered, "In Equivocal Worlds Up & Down are Equivocal." I quote a young expositor, Harold Bloom, as he was fifty-five years ago, in his critical commentary to *The Complete Poetry and Prose of William Blake* (edited by David V. Erdman, 1965):

> In his notes on the *Illustrations to Dante*, Blake comments on a diagram of Hell's Circles that "In Equivocal Worlds Up & Down are Equivocal." This is Urizen's desperate discovery; his solution, heroic but mistaken, is in the arbitrariness of 73:14: "Here I will fix my foot & here rebuild." There is a compass image in "fix my foot," as though Blake were thinking of his own frontispiece to *Europe*, "The Ancient of Days Striking the First Circle of the Earth."

Is Milton himself the compass of his sea of troubles? If I now think not, then I am belated in agreeing with Geoffrey Hartman in *The Fate of Reading* (1975):

> We may eventually decide that [Bloom's] preference of Milton to Shakespeare is prejudicial, and reflects a swerve from the haunting image of female Generation into the Gnostic

view that Regeneration (or all true creativity) is a second birth, "of the Father." Yet in doing so we will only have continued Bloom's mode of analysis and begun to make sense of the perplexing yet persistent link between poetry and negative theology, or fiction and the liberties of myth.

I wish I could tell Hartman that he has now persuaded me, but alas, he died on March 14, 2016. Contemporary publishing will not allow substantial revisions, only reprintings. One purpose of this book *is* to substitute Shakespeare for Milton as the ineluctable "beginning" for a theory of poetic influence. I held back from "the haunting image of female Generation" because half a century ago I was still totally mesmerized by William Blake. Shakespeare has subsumed Blake and nearly every other strong writer for me, with the possible exception of Walt Whitman. Macduff, ripped from his mother's womb, is a strong antidote to the Satanic Macbeth. I think John Milton did believe that Regeneration had to be a second birth "of the Father." William Kerrigan shrewdly read Milton's relation to his father as obedience in all things *except as a poet.*

Even the greatest poets have to lie against time and so against origins. John Dryden reported Milton saying to him that Edmund Spenser was his great original. I cannot conceive Milton saying that of Shakespeare. The Eve of *Paradise Lost* manifests both Spenserian and Shakespearean graces, yet she tends to speak in the idiom of Shakespeare's heroines. From Juliet to Cleopatra is an immense expanse, but erotic power is as intense in the thirteen-year-old tragic protagonist as in the thirty-nine-year-old serpent of old Nile. We cannot speak of Eve's age or of Adam's, and yet Milton very nearly rivals Shakespeare by intimations of Eve's sexual potential.

Ancient theurgy was a praxis by which a god or gods could be summoned, maintained, and even created. There is an element of theurgy in much great poetry, and Milton shares in it, though he might have protested otherwise. *When he calls down the Holy Spirit, it comes as a divinity, as what is best and oldest in the poet Milton's own spirit.* If you cut God and the Son out of *Paradise Lost*, in my judgment the poem would be improved. Milton achieves poetic authority by augmenting the foundations. Virgil, Ovid, Horace, Lucan are invoked allusively to help maintain the god Milton, a phrase that might have outraged him. Poetic theurgy transcends all limits in the second half of *Paradise Lost*, from the Creation in Book 7 down to the expulsion from Eden. A new God is created by Milton, almost as though the first one had abdicated.

The invocation to Book 7 calls upon the heavenly muse Urania, even while questioning the appropriateness of the name, "the meaning, not the Name I call":

Descend from Heaven, Urania, by that name
If rightly thou art called, whose voice divine
Following, above the Olympian Hill I soar,
Above the flight of Pegasean wing!
The meaning, not the name, I call; for thou
Nor of the Muses nine, nor on the top
Of old Olympus dwell'st; but, heavenly-born,
Before the Hills appeared or fountain flowed,
Thou with Eternal Wisdom didst converse,
Wisdom thy sister, and with her didst play
In presence of the Almighty Father, pleased
With thy celestial song. Up led by thee
Into the Heaven of Heavens I have presumed,
An earthly guest, and drawn empyreal air,
Thy tempering. With like safety guided down,
Return me to my native element . . .

                                        [7.1–16]

Chanting this aloud to myself at night, I am bewildered with admiration. In his own mode, Milton is a miracle. Unlike Chaucer and Shakespeare, and rather like Dante, he seems cut off from otherness, though his biographers rightly would disagree. But I speak of Milton the poet and not John Milton the man: how telling is his portrait of himself "in darkness, and with dangers compassed round, / And solitude, yet not alone, while thou / Visitst my slumbers nightly . . ." (7.27–29). For Urania, properly named, is the Wisdom of the Book of Proverbs:

Before the mountains were settled, before the hills was I brought forth:

While as yet he had not made the earth, nor the fields, nor the highest part of the dust of the world. When he prepared the heavens, I was there: when he set a compass upon the face of the depth:
When he established the clouds above: when he strengthened the fountains of the deep:
When he gave to the sea his decree, that the waters should not pass his commandment: when he appointed the foundations of the earth:
Then I was by him, as one brought up with him: and I was daily his delight, rejoicing always before him.

[Proverbs (KJV) 8:25–30]

Despite the celestial patroness Wisdom, Milton has two authentic fears. He thinks back to Bellerophon, who dared to fly, mounted upon Pegasus, up to Olympus. Zeus punished Bellerophon for his temerity by dispatching a gadfly to sting Pegasus and cause his rider to fall and smash into the Aleian Field, where his face hit a thorn bush that blinded him. The other apprehension returns Milton to *Lycidas* and to the dread of an Orphic ripping apart, though now at the hands of drunken Cavaliers roistering outside his windows.

I find even darker Milton's dismissal of the Muse as an empty dream. The master soliloquizer, confronting the sleep of death, apprehends dreams that puzzle the will with a dread of unknown and unknowable thoughts to come. Hamlet hopes for the rest of silence, yet his never-resting intellect is preternatural. Will he go on thinking throughout eternity, thinking through, much too well, and desiring endlessly for an end that will not come? Belial would be content with that. If the Muse be only an empty dream, what will be the fate of the poet Milton in an afterlife? The feeling-tone of Hamlet's voice never quite abandons the voice of Milton in the invocations.

I need to brood further on the question of allusion. My masters in this—Angus Fletcher and John Hollander—taught me the uses of transumption, of making the dead return wearing one's own colors. John Milton may be the only poet since Dante to triumph consistently in that mode. Yet there is something that I might name: "unruly allusion." Whenever it appears in Milton, the antecedent is Shakespeare, who is irrepressible.

You cannot talk about Shakespeare in terms of doctrine and discipline. He will flow away from you. He seems to care neither for problems nor for resolutions. Everything changes. Hamlet changes every time he speaks. Does Satan? Here he is, in sight of Eden:

> With what delight could I have walked thee round,
> If I could joy in aught—sweet interchange
> Of hill and valley, rivers, woods, and plains,
> Now land, now sea, and shores with forest crowned,
> Rocks, dens, and caves! but I in none of these
> Find place or refuge . . .
>
> [9.114–119]

More than a half century ago I wrote an introduction to Mary Shelley's *Frankenstein, or The Modern Prometheus* (1818) in which I located the center of the book in the dreadful relationship between Victor Frankenstein and his daemon, who laments to the scientist: "Remember that I am thy creature; I ought to be thy Adam, but I am rather the fallen angel, whom thou drivest from joy for no misdeed." For the novel's epigraph, Mary Shelley chose Adam's complaint to God:

> Did I request thee, Maker, from my clay
> To mould me Man? Did I solicit thee
> From darkness to promote me . . . ?
>
> [10.743–745]

Shrewdly Mary Shelley made the daemon or "monster" an immensely sympathetic and indeed poetic sensibility in contrast to the irresponsible Victor Frankenstein. Very subtly, the novel is a critique of the two men its author loved best, her husband, the great lyric poet Percy Bysshe Shelley, and her father, William Godwin, theorist of social revolution. In some sense it may also be a confrontation with her mother, who died giving birth to her, the extraordinary Mary Wollstonecraft Godwin.

Mary Shelley went on to write other novels, yet she could have said of *Frankenstein, or The Modern Prometheus* what Ludovico cries out at the close of John Webster's *The White Devil* (1612):

          I do glory yet
That I can call this act mine own. For my part,
The rack, the gallows, and the torturing wheel,
Shall be but sound sleeps to me: here's my rest;
I limned this night-piece, and it was my best.
            [5.6.293–297]

Satan has a touch of John Webster's deathly sensibility, itself a
fascinating distortion of Shakespeare's hero-villains, but severely in-
tellectualized by the inescapable consciousness of Prince Hamlet:

      and the more I see
Pleasures about me, so much more I feel
Torment within me, as from the hateful siege
Of contraries; all good to me becomes
Bane, and in Heaven much worse would be my state.
           [9.119–123]

Imagine an earlier Hamlet, gazing lovingly upon Ophelia, yet
experiencing the hateful siege of contraries, where "siege" takes its
meaning from a prolonged vastation of mishaps.

Contrast this with Milton's invocation to Book 9:

      Sad task! yet argument
Not less but more Heroic then the wrauth
Of stern Achilles on his foe pursued
Thrice fugitive about Troy wall; or rage
Of Turnus for Lavinia disespoused,
Or Neptune's ire, or Juno's, that so long
Perplex'd the Greek, and Cytherea's Son;
If answerable style I can obtain
Of my celestial Patroness, who deigns
Her nightly visitation unimplored,
And dictates to me slumbering, or inspires
Easy my unpremeditated verse,
Since first this subject for heroic song
Pleased me, long choosing and beginning late
           [9.13–26]

Milton's justified pride achieves a kind of ebullience here, and it is hurtful to feel ambivalence in regard to him. Still, I bridle at his judgment on the Fall:

> foul distrust, and breach
> Disloyal, on the part of man, revolt
> And disobedience; On the part of Heaven,
> Now alienated, distance and distaste,
> Anger and just rebuke, and judgment given,
> That brought into this World a world of woe,
> Sinne and her shadow Death, and Misery,
> Death's harbinger . . .
>
> [9.6–13]

"Heaven" is Milton's God at his sublime worst. Many years ago I wrote a commentary on the Yahwist strand in Torah and remember saying that the misfortune of Eve and of Adam is akin to remarking: "When we were children, we were terribly punished for being children." Milton would not have cared for that; Blake and Shelley might have approved. Why should we accept the word "foul" for the mischance of our first parents? Is that truly what Milton meant?

"Distrust," "distance and distaste" is a wonderful wordplay. As one might expect, *Hamlet* features "distrust"; *Macbeth, Othello, Measure for Measure* manifest "distance"; *King Lear, Othello, Troilus and Cressida* disclose "distaste." Milton had an enormous vocabulary, as one might expect from a man who could read nine or ten languages. Shakespeare could read Latin, but preferred English translations wherever he could find them. His French seems rather dubious. But his vocabulary is incredible: he uses more than thirty-one thousand different words, of which about fourteen thousand occur just once. I do not know whether to trust statistical surmises, but some argue that Shakespeare also knew more than thirty thousand words he did not bother to use. It is unclear how many words Shakespeare coined, but there are perhaps four hundred still in common use. Still, Milton is credited with creating more words than any other English writer, with Ben Jonson second, John Donne third, and Shakespeare fourth.

When Wittgenstein, with some distaste, dismissed Shakespeare as "a creator of language," he could have extended that to Milton,

Jonson, Donne. What Wittgenstein would not accept was the pragmatic truth: like Chaucer, Shakespeare was a maker of personalities.
Milton was termed "incorruptible" by the Austrian-English philosopher. It has been suggested that what Wittgenstein meant was that
his encounter with Shakespeare demonstrated to him the limits of
his own personality. I confess my bafflement at all this. Plato began
or perhaps continued the ancient argument between philosophy and
poetry, and that dispute (if it is one) may never end.

I return to my notion of unruly allusion. By the time he had finished composing *Paradise Lost*, Milton might well have believed he
had exorcised Shakespeare. The evidence goes against this. But I
want here to shift from one foot to the other and pass momentarily
to Eve. Her name in Hebrew is *Chava*, related to the word for "life,"
chai. She breathes and lives and has her being belatedly, since Yahweh forms her out of Adam, whom he molded first out of the *ada-
mah*, red clay of earth. One might suggest that Eve, like Milton and
Satan, rebels against a sense of belatedness. Milton treasures *firstness*, and his lifelong agon with Shakespeare was part of his drive to
achieve autonomy and earliness.

The Fall of Eve is only partly caused by Satan's seductiveness.
John Milton palpably was not a misogynist. His three literary triumphs were Eve, Satan, Samson, unless you want to add Milton the
narrative voice and invoker of *Paradise Lost*. John Milton would have
been very unhappy if I were to term *Paradise Lost* the Shakespearean epic. Yet that is what it is. Satan's perspectivism could be that of
Troilus: "what is aught but as 'tis valued"?

Perspectivism necessarily evokes Nietzsche in a pungent apothegm from his late speculations:

> In so far as the word "knowledge" has any meaning, the
> world is knowable; but it is interpretable otherwise, it has no
> meaning behind it, but countless meanings. — "Perspectiv-
> ism." It is our needs that interpret the world; our drives and
> their For and Against. Every drive is a kind of lust to rule;
> each one has its perspective that it would like to compel all
> the other drives to accept as a norm.
>
> [*The Will to Power* (1901), translated
> by Walter Kaufmann and R. J. Hollingdale]

I recall brooding on perspectivism in my early book *A Map of Misreading* (1975), where, more in the spirit of Protagoras than of Plato, I stressed the limitations of metaphor as sharing the blindness of all inside/outside relationships. I still think that the greatest perspectivist in all of poetry is Milton's Satan, since his bewildering perspectivism causes the dissolution of all knowledge, and of any way to choose truth over the lie. Satan's perspectivism is self-contradictory, but that does not weaken its aesthetic power.

I desire to clarify my understanding of the relationship between Shakespeare and Milton. In no way do I deprecate the fecundity, power, originality of Milton's creative mind. He could have protected himself by forming a barrier against Shakespearean influx, but instead exemplified what became Nietzsche's praise of aesthetic greatness as a susceptibility by which power welcomed power. I delight in a remark by Kenneth Gross, sent to me via email:

> No doubt Milton might have been enraged to hear his epic was Shakespeare's, not his own but rather somehow a part of the Shakespearean whole. Yet that way of seeing the poem, that way of placing its debt to Shakespeare, seems to me just now to expand it from within, to open it out to other strengths.

When someone's life seems to run right, she can have the sense that she opens it out by expanding it from within. That sense can become rarer as she enters old age, and suffers the anxiety of preclusion. One wonders: Can even the most ambitious of poems—the *Commedia* or *Paradise Lost*—yield to an anxiety of preclusion?

Shakespeare is anything but a devotional poet or dramatist. His universality would be diminished had he been sectarian in any way whatsoever. Here, as elsewhere, Milton cannot transume Shakespeare, but then who could? In the raising of that great edifice Pandemonium, Milton deliberately tropes against Virgil and Ovid and yet yields an unruly allusion evoking the dissimilar cosmos of *A Midsummer Night's Dream:*

> Mammon led them on—
> Mammon, the least erected Spirit that fell
> From Heaven; for even in heaven his looks and thoughts

Were always downward bent, admiring more
The riches of Heaven's pavement, trodden gold,
Than aught divine or holy else enjoyed
In vision beatific. By him first
Men also, and by his suggestion taught,
Ransacked the Centre, and with impious hands
Rifled the bowels of their mother Earth
For treasures better hid. Soon had his crew
Opened into the hill a spacious wound,
And digged out ribs of gold. Let none admire
That riches grow in Hell; that soil may best
Deserve the precious bane.

[1.678–692]

This passage hurts even more than Milton intended. The great
oxymoron "precious bane" refers to the archaic sense in which bane
is poison. One might want to ask why the pavement of heaven displays such divine ostentation. Riches may grow in Hell, yet they
seem very much at home in Heaven.

The diabolic architect Mulciber, Vulcan to the Latins, Hephaes-
tus to the ancient Greeks, inspires Milton to a curious treatment, a
display of his own burning pride:

Nor was his name unheard or unadored
In ancient Greece; and in Ausonian land
Men called him Mulciber; and how he fell
From Heaven they fabled, thrown by angry Jove
Sheer o'er the crystal battlements: from morn
To noon he fell, from noon to dewy eve,
A summer's day, and with the setting sun
Dropt from the zenith, like a falling star,
On Lemnos, the Ægaean isle. Thus they relate,
Erring; for he with this rebellious rout
Fell long before; nor aught availed him now
To have built in Heaven high towers; nor did he scape
By all his engines, but was headlong sent,
With his industrious crew, to build in Hell.

[1.738–751]

That "Erring" is fierce and not to be disputed. Yet further on, a trouble enters:

> or faery elves,
> Whose midnight revels, by a forest-side
> Or fountain some belated Peasant sees,
> Or dreams he sees, while over-head the Moon
> Sits arbitress, and nearer to the Earth
> Wheels her pale course: they, on their mirth and dance
> Intent, with jocund music charm his ear;
> At once with joy and fear his heart rebounds.
> Thus incorporeal Spirits to smallest forms
> Reduced their shapes immense, and were at large,
> Though without number still amidst the hall
> Of that infernal court.
>
> [1.781–792]

Hartman's strong argument is that *Paradise Lost* has a counter-plot, in which divine knowledge of the Creation must outlast sin and death, and guarantee the defeat of Satan, even though he seduces Eve to rebellion. Geoffrey Hartman, for almost two-thirds of a century, was an older brother to me, and remains a daily presence. We never quite agreed on *Paradise Lost*, because Hartman trusted in the Covenant of the Jewish people with Yahweh, and I could not. I think that such divine knowledge belongs to Tanakh and not to *Paradise Lost*, and that Geoffrey moved too deftly from one to the other.

Paradise Lost is a vast midrash on the Hebrew Bible. Its relationship to the Greek New Testament seems to me a more difficult matter. Like Dante, Milton expected us to accept his supreme fiction as being truth. William Blake, though he was something of a parodist, also would have insisted that his engraved poems *Milton* and *Jerusalem* (ca. 1804–1820) gloried in truth-telling. You can ask: In what sense can a poem be true? If you read, as I do, the Bible essentially as you read Dante, Milton, and Blake, is the Bible true? Plato exiled Homer because, in Plato's judgment, the *Iliad* lied.

The world's history scarcely demonstrates that divine knowledge outlasts death and defeats Satan. It would be banal yet veracious to echo Christopher Marlowe's Mephistophilis:

FAUSTUS: How comes it, then, that thou art out of hell?

MEPHISTOPHILIS: Why, this is hell, nor am I out of it.
> [*The Tragedie of Doctor Faustus* (B Text)
> (1616, written 1588–1592), 1.3.301–302]

Milton's Satan improved on Marlowe: "myself am Hell" (4.75). The Satan of *Paradise Lost* is a spiritual being whose idiom of self-begetting could be taken in a purely literary sense. Robert Hollander, in 2011, wrote an essay, "Milton's Elusive Response to Dante's *Comedy* in *Paradise Lost*." I might modify that to "evasive response," since Dante was a danger to Milton. "Things unattempted yet in prose or rhyme" parodies Ariosto but it was Dante who captured the classical past, Christian theology, and the vernacular mode urged upon him by his best friend, Guido Cavalcanti, a great poet who died in exile, at just forty-five.

Milton must have pondered the *Commedia* and was too keen a literary sensitivity not to apprehend Dante's incredible achievement, which very nearly stands with Shakespeare. Chaucer had a direct and acknowledged debt to Dante (and a larger, unacknowledged relationship to Boccaccio). So sly is Chaucer that reading him close unveils a considerable critique of Dante. I would not say that Dante daunted Milton, as Shakespeare clearly did, but there is considerable evasiveness in regard to the Catholic poet who also asserted direct inspiration by the Holy Spirit.

Famously Malcolm X read *Paradise Lost* in prison and identified his own cause with Satan's. That seems to me an accurate judgment. In my youthful commentary for Erdman's Blake (1965) I wrote that

> the dominion of Edom means, in Blake's terms, that the red figure coming menacingly out of France, the "Devil" called Orc in Blake's *America* and later poems, is truly a savior, however awful he may appear to the "Angels" of Pitt's England.

The reference is to Blake's *The Marriage of Heaven and Hell*, which prophesies "The dominion of Edom, & the return of Adam into Paradise." Blake was writing in 1790, when the prime minister William Pitt the Younger rallied the British ruling classes against the French Revolution and oppressed the English Jacobins with a vast network of spies. Soon afterward, he suspended the chartered rights of Englishmen.

Daniel Isaac Eaton was prosecuted by Pitt's government for publishing remarks by his fellow radical John Thelwall in 1793. Convicted, he served three months. Finally brought to trial, he was acquitted. In 1812 the revolutionary poet and agitator Percy Bysshe Shelley published an essay, "A Letter to Lord Ellenborough," taking up Eaton's cause and demanding freedom of publication.

Malcolm X was in good company: William Blake, Shelley, William Hazlitt. They also understood that Satan's rebellion against the tyranny of Heaven had been reenacted in the French Revolution and in their own aspirations for a better humankind.

I think the issue of *Paradise Lost*'s Satan must finally be resolved by considering the influence of the mind of the poet John Milton upon itself. One of my constant endeavors is to surmise the influence of Shakespeare's mind upon itself by speculating upon the influence of *Hamlet* on its poet-playwright. Prince Hamlet and the poem unlimited *Hamlet* made possible *Othello*, *King Lear*, *Macbeth*, and *Antony and Cleopatra*. Falstaff and the two *Henry IV* plays made Shakespeare possible by making him popular. But with John Milton I experience greater difficulty at surmising his poetic mind's influence upon his indwelling spirit, or the deep effect of completing *Paradise Lost* upon its poet. Shakespeare had his audience at the Globe. Milton did find fit audience though fewer. Falstaff and Hamlet perform in the theater of mind. So do Satan and Eve. But the mind has many mansions, and only Shakespeare could dwell in all of them at once. Milton has a vast reach, yet his epic has to accept limits. Where are the limits of Sir John Falstaff or of Prince Hamlet?

How does John Milton's pride differ from that of *Paradise Lost*'s Satan? Milton asserted that he had found "a better way" than Shakespeare's freedom of nature, a way that would allow the representation of Heaven as well as Hell. No sensitive reader prefers Milton's Heaven to Dante's paradiso. If there is a paradise in Shakespeare, it would have to be the forest of Arden. Whatever the enchantments of *The Tempest*, its time scheme is merciless and Prospero nearly misses his cue.

Would not Milton have said that he knew no time when he was not as now? He felt that his puissance was his own. As a poet he believed himself to be self-begotten. The Holy Spirit embedded in him went back before the Creation and so was the earliest element in his poetic mind.

The Freudian drive beyond the pleasure principle is close enough to Satan's trajectory that ends on the Dead Sea shore. Satanic darkness and salt reply to Christ in the Gospel of Matthew:

> Ye are the salt of the earth: but if the salt have lost his savour, wherewith shall it be salted? It is thenceforth good for nothing, but to be cast out, and to be trodden under foot of men. Ye are the light of the world. A city that is set on an hill cannot be hid.
>
> [Matthew (KJV) 5:13–14]

It may be that I mistake some matters in Milton. Yet I never make the error of underestimating him. In some regards he is always out ahead of you, whoever you are. Something in him may have wanted light without fire. He certainly desired a myth excluding both Lucifer and Prometheus. Beyond question, he made his myth work. Here he gives us Eve as Narcissus, idealized human marriage, and Satan's lustful torment:

> and laid me downe
> On the green bank, to look into the clear
> Smooth lake, that to me seemed another sky.
> As I bent down to look, just opposite
> A shape within the watery gleam appeared,
> Bending to look on me. I started back
> It started back; but pleased I soon returned,
> Pleased it returned as soon with answering looks
> Of sympathy and love.
>
> [4.457–465]

> aside the Devil turned
> For envy, yet with jealous leer malign
> Eyed them askance, and to himself thus plained:
> Sight hateful, sight tormenting! thus these two,

Imparadised in one another's arms,
The happier Eden, shall enjoy their fill
Of bliss on bliss; while I to Hell am thrust,
Where neither joy nor love, but fierce desire,
Among our other torments not the least,
Still unfulfilled, with pain of longing pines!

[4.502–511]

By any measure this is a Miltonic triumph of juxtaposition and of precise pathos. Satan laments a peculiarly Miltonic consequence of the angelic Fall: Hell allows lust but no fulfillment. What is lost is conveyed later by the affable and blushing Archangel Raphael, in response to Adam's question:

To whom the Angel, with a smile that glowed
Celestial rosy-red, Love's proper hue,
Answered:— Let it suffice thee that thou know'st
Us happy, and without Love no happiness.
Whatever pure thou in the body enjoy'st
(And pure thou wert created) we enjoy
In eminence, and obstacle find none
Of membrane, joint, or limb, exclusive bars.
Easier than air with air, if Spirits embrace,
Total they mix, union of pure with pure
Desiring, nor restrained conveyance need
As flesh to mix with flesh, or soul with soul.

[8.618–629]

This inspired William Blake to his vision of a sexual Eternity in *Jerusalem:*

Embraces are Cominglings: from the Head even to the Feet;
And not a pompous High Priest entering by a Secret Place.

[Plate 69]

John Keats famously equated the sympathetic imagination with the dream of Adam in *Paradise Lost:*

> The Imagination may be compared to Adam's dream—he
> awoke and found it truth.
> > [Letter to Benjamin Bailey (November 22, 1817)]

Adam has two dreams. In the first, a Divine presence shows him his first sight of Eden. In the second, Eve is created from his rib and becomes his wife. I have always assumed that Keats compounded the two dreams. It is all the more poignant because his authentic love for Fanny Brawne was never consummated, so far as can be known. It is difficult for me to believe that Keats went to his death with no sexual experience: there is speculation that he was compelled to turn to prostitutes. When he said of Milton that "life to him would be death to me" (letter to Joshua Reynolds [September 22, 1819]), his explanation for abandoning the first *Hyperion* in May 1819, he seems to have meant that he wanted a less Latinate English than Milton's in *Paradise Lost*. Keats had so Shakespearean a sensibility and intellect that probably much more than language was involved. He credited Wordsworth with more knowledge of the human heart than Milton manifested, but his true divinity was Shakespeare.

Keats devoted Sundays to reading and meditating on Shakespeare rather than the Bible. His deep need led him to *King Lear* more often than to *Hamlet*. The great odes and sonnets, *The Fall of Hyperion* and some late fragments, are Shakespearean to the core. In a kind of rare alchemy, Keats Shakespeareanizes Spenser, Milton, and Wordsworth, an observation worked out more fully by William Flesch.

Sometimes I wonder why Keats did not take Eve's dream as his vision of the sympathetic imagination. I think he was negating his own sympathetic nature despite his wonderment at so compelling a vision of female narcissism as Eve's in Book 4 of *Paradise Lost:*

> A shape within the watery gleam appeared,
> Bending to look on me. I started back
> It started back; but pleased I soon returned,
> Pleased it returned as soon with answering looks
> Of sympathy and love. There I had fixed
> Mine eyes till now, and pined with vain desire,
> Had not a voice thus warned me: "What thou seest,

"What there thou seest, fair Creature, is thyself;
"With thee it came and goes: but follow me,
"And I will bring thee where no shadow stays
"Thy coming . . ."

[4.461–471]

Freud loved Milton, but it is just as well he never commented on this remarkable passage. Narcissism is a very mixed concept in Freud and his followers and revisionists. The delicate balance between narcissistic object-choice and narcissistic self-esteem was never quite maintained, even when Freud himself revised his vista of narcissism. Milton keeps the balance. He must have known that by increasing her inwardness, he heightened her aesthetic appeal. Eve's dream augments consciousness. Even though she speaks this to Adam, it works as soliloquy. To become more Shakespearean is to move toward our common fall, the autumn gathering toward the evening.

For in much wisdom *is* much grief: and he that increaseth knowledge increaseth sorrow.
[Ecclesiastes (KJV) 1:18]

Sorrow need not be sin. Does Milton impale himself on the thorns of life? I cannot reread *Paradise Lost* without an enlargement of knowledge. The Fall is not so much fortunate as fortuitous. I am delighted when William Tyndale gives us: "And the LORde was with Ioseph and he was a luckie felowe . . ." (Genesis 39:2). Milton's God was not with us and Milton's Adam is not a lucky fellow. Nor is Eve, since she suffers expulsion from the Garden, the pangs of childbirth, and the murder of Abel by Cain. If disobedience is so dreadful a sin, are we to think of the man John Milton as a pillar of obedience? His normative scholars fall back on his supposed obedience to the Holy Spirit who preferred his pure and upright heart to all temples, whether established or independent. Milton's indwelling spirit is what Wallace Stevens called "the interior paramour": "We say God and the imagination are one . . . / How high that highest candle lights the dark" ("Final Soliloquy of the Interior Paramour" [1955]).

You don't get a candle to see the sun rise.
                              [Emerson, *Journals*, October 1832]

How high does even the highest candle light the dark? Milton read the Book of Proverbs in Hebrew and also in the Geneva version:

The light of the Lord is the breath of man, and searcheth all the bowels of the belly.
                              [Proverbs 20:27, Geneva Bible]

The same line is given in the King James as "The spirit of man is the candle of the LORD, searching all the inward parts of the belly."

As a sect of one, John Milton identified the Holy Spirit as his personal muse and employed the candle of the Lord as the Inner Light by which he read Scripture for himself. The followers of the delightfully named Ludowicke Muggleton (1609–1698), fierce exponents of the Inner Light, went so far as to see the Fall as Eve's actual sexual seduction by Satan. There are ancient rabbinic anecdotes in which a fallen angel begets Cain upon Eve. Milton was careful to avoid staining his marvelous Eve with such lascivious scandal since a naughty mother of all living would have marred the high decorum of his epic.

I would remark that it turns upon the perspective you bring to seduction. Must it be the flagrant persuasion to the act, or is temptation on whatever level of consciousness sufficient? The daemon or genius of Milton is to show us that only Eve seduces Eve. Her splendid narcissism is aesthetically accurate: she is the most beautiful harbor of the entire Creation. Pragmatically her own spirit says: She for herself only / He for the goddess in her.

Whose poem is it anyway: Satan's, Eve's, Milton's, the Holy Spirit's, or the reader's? By aesthetic criteria, it is not God's, the Son's, and, rather sadly, not Adam's. Would I rather Milton have given me another speech or two by Belial or by Adam? We have to go with eloquence, cognition, longing, *over* piety, conformity, obedience. Dr. Samuel Johnson, an admirer of *Paradise Lost* but not of John Milton, whom famously he described as "an acrimonious and surly republican," said of the greatest English epic: "*Paradise Lost* is one of the books which the reader admires and puts down, and forgets to take up again. None ever wished it longer than it is" (*Lives of the Poets*).

I endlessly revere Johnson but do not share his ambivalence. It might indeed be better if Milton had composed an account of Eve and Adam and their progeny after the cruel expulsion. I join Shelley and the late A. D. Nuttall in wondering if Milton, like Blake, Walt Whitman, Herman Melville, Emily Dickinson, and some other great visionaries, had become a sect of one. It is a paradoxical possibility that *Paradise Lost* is a Protestant epic yet not a Christian poem.

George Santayana's *Interpretations of Poetry and Religion* (1900) shows an accurate wisdom as to Shakespeare's pragmatic remembering to forget Christianity in his plays and poems:

> In our day, with our wide and conscientious historical sympathies, it may be possible for us to find in other rites and doctrines than those of our ancestors an expression of some ultimate truth. But for Shakespeare, in the matter of religion, the choice lay between Christianity or nothing. He chose nothing; he chose to leave his heroes and himself in the presence of life and of death with no other philosophy than that which the profane world can suggest and understand.
>
> ["The Absence of Religion in Shakespeare"]

If I am right in suggesting that Shakespeare is the hidden God in the heterocosm created by John Milton (with the exception of *Paradise Regained* [1671]), can we surmise that Milton also chose nothing? The voices of the great invocations, Satan, Eve, Adam: all confront life and death as we do in our necessarily secular existence.

When Milton, like the unlimited God of rabbinic tradition, goes within himself, he creates by contraction, at some psychic expense. Perhaps, whether with Milton or God, this is not so much a withdrawal as a concentration upon a point, a sort of intensification as you take a step inside. This concentration is a strengthening that allows a more exuberant creation. I think that Shakespeare and John Keats after him perform exactly the reverse movement. They commence *ab extra*, as Coleridge in his marginalia said of Shakespeare:

Drawn from the . . . faculties of the human mind, the idea always *a priori*, tho' incarnated by observation *a posteriori et ab extra*.

I supervised Thomas Weiskel, both graduate and undergraduate. He stands with David Bromwich, Leslie Brisman, the late Barbara Packer, and Camille Paglia among my most gifted students. Weiskel, who lived down the street from my house, came by every Thursday late afternoon to meditate upon our mutual teaching and writing. He would have written several more books as valuable as *The Romantic Sublime* (1976), published posthumously, edited by Leslie Brisman, and with a somber introduction by his grieving teacher.

Neither Weiskel nor I believed that Milton's Satan found his mind to be continuous with Chaos. Incredible eloquence, searing pathos, self-serving anguish, despair fused with the courage never to submit or yield: there are chaotic elements, but there is also what may be judged an increment in consciousness.

The burden of Shakespeare for Milton is Hamlet's capacious consciousness, still without rival in Western literature. The word "consciousness" retains the aura of its Latin origin: knowing, being aware of—almost in the heraldic sense of "cognizance." The mind of John Milton has few limits until it touches the contingency of human otherness. It is there that Milton falls far short of Chaucer and of Shakespeare.

We know what we mean when we speak of the personality of the Wife of Bath or of Sir John Falstaff. There are no personalities in Milton's poetry. Adam, Eve, Satan are something more and less than personalities. Shakespeare invented a hundred major personalities and a thousand minor ones. Amidst all these, Hamlet is unique. His consciousness seems to tear loose of all limits and breaks out of the revenge tragedy so hopelessly inadequate to his power of being and range of awareness.

I teach, read, and write to increase my sense of otherness and to fight against self-consciousness. But always there is the sadness of apprehension, a foreboding as to how much increased consciousness I can sustain. When we pick up the morning newspaper and read of massacres, terrorist bombings, tornadoes, infant starvation, murders, suicide, Trump, we have to close ourselves down to get through breakfast. It is not as T. S. Eliot once trumpeted: mankind cannot bear very much reality. Of necessity it endures whatever does not crush it. But I at least, at ninety, cannot solace myself that it has been often thus. Cruelty is cruelty, evil is evil, the suffering of others can be absorbed only to a particular point. After that, one may as well not go on since one is neither saint nor sage.

William Wordsworth was not saintly (few poets are) and he seems to me unwise. It does not matter. He remains the originator of modern poetry. Ernst Robert Curtius rightly maintained that from Homer through Dante and Shakespeare on to Goethe, European literature was a continuity. Wordsworth ended that cavalcade. William Hazlitt acutely recognized the radical newness of Wordsworth's poetry. The growth and vicissitudes of Wordsworth's imagination constitute the subject of this new poetry.

CHAPTER THREE

Milton and William Blake
The Human Form Divine

Blake's *MILTON* IS A brief epic (1804–1810) in two books and two thousand lines, on the model of Milton's *Paradise Regained* (1671) and of their mutual ancestral work, the Book of Job (sixth century BCE). That sentence, accurate enough, belies the vigor and imaginative energy that William Blake—engraver, painter, prophetic poet, apocalyptic humanist, proletarian rebel, and visionary—poured into the fiery crucible of his composite art.

I have been teaching Blake and writing exegeses of his work for more than sixty years. In so long a span one undergoes many revisionary realizations, because knowing Blake entails everything in the way of knowledge and insight one can glean from turning and turning his illuminated texts and poems left in manuscript.

When I was very young, William Blake was for me a passion and a hope for human potential. Now that I am well on into my ninth decade, that passion and hope have receded. I reread and teach Blake as I do Milton or Wordsworth. What seemed prophecy has little place in our current nation and our suffering world. For me, Shakespeare has replaced God. Nietzsche seems right to me: "It is only as an aesthetic phenomenon that existence and the world are eternally justified."

Blake would have rejected Nietzsche's perspectivizing assertion. I have come to see that Blake's *Milton* is an aesthetic phenomenon, a remarkable poem but not a prelude to apocalypse. Shelley for me is an irreplaceable lyric poet; when I was young he seemed a spiritual force. Forlorn and perplexed when it comes to Tanakh, I want to trust in the Covenant but cannot. The Emersonian vision of Walt Whitman and of Hart Crane no longer prevails with me. *Song of Myself* and *The Bridge* are sublime poems, as is *The Auroras of Autumn*, yet I scarcely remember how once they seemed transfigurations.

I am confessing loss and am disheartened by it. Teaching remains a passion as does reading, but writing has entered the elegy season. Remarkable as my own students are, I am at least four times their age and cannot always know what it is that passes between us.

And yet I do not abandon hope that teaching others to apprehend more fully Shakespeare and the hidden channels that flow between major poets can still make some difference in the lives of my students. Transcendence is not to be hired. It will come if and when it will. There is a god within us and she speaks. Blake would repudiate that last sentence. He had a dread of what he unfortunately called "the Female Will," which misleads because he meant that dangerously it could prevail in men or in women. That must be why Blake had such a negative reaction to that marvelous vitalist the Wife of Bath:

> The characters of Women Chaucer has divided into two classes, the Lady Prioress and the Wife of Bath. Are not these leaders of the ages of men? The Lady Prioress in some ages predominates; and in some the Wife of Bath, in whose character Chaucer has been equally minute and exact; because she is also a scourge and a blight. I shall say no more of her, nor expose what Chaucer has left hidden; let the young reader study what he has said of her: it is useful as a scarecrow. There are of such characters born too many for the peace of the world.
> [Commentary on "Chaucers Canterbury Pilgrims" (1809)]

Once it would have been painful for me to consider Blake's limitations. Yet almost every great writer has blindnesses, prejudices, resentments, human fears, and anguishes not easily overcome. Shakespeare may be the exception, yet he is so hidden in his work that we never will know *him*, even if we have memorized every line he ever wrote. The young Robert Browning idolized Shelley as man and as poet, and was shocked when he later discovered Shelley's pragmatic performance as an apostle of free love, including his abandonment of his first wife and their children.

William Blake uniquely fused a visionary stance and the perspective of an intellectual satirist. He said that he must create his own system so as not to be enslaved by another man's. Here is the reaction of Thomas Stearns Eliot:

> We have the same respect for Blake's philosophy (and perhaps for that of Samuel Butler) that we have for an ingenious piece of home-made furniture: we admire the man who has put it together out of the odds and ends about the house. England has produced a fair number of these resourceful Robinson Crusoes; but we are not really so remote from the Continent, or from our own past, as to be deprived of the advantages of culture if we wish them.
>
> ["Blake" (1920)]

Originality doubtless must expect misunderstanding. Eliot still has his admirers, though mostly for the best of his poems, and not for his critical and polemical prose. I was gently amused when the courageous Anthony Julius, in his *T. S. Eliot, Anti-Semitism and Literary Form* (1995), observed that my lack of affection for Eliot has led me to underestimate him. Anyone who reads my *The Daemon Knows* (2015) will find my final analysis of Eliot's poetic achievement and my judicial dismissal of his misogyny, endless anti-Semitism, and lasting contempt for human nature. His character and personality puzzle me. Evidently always affable with his friends and courtly in his manner, he seemed incapable of escaping the prison of his self. He knew a great deal about his own sufferings, and not much about the vicissitudes of others. I can read St. John of the Cross, George Herbert, Christina Rossetti, and Gerard Manley Hopkins with wonder and gratitude, despite my deep ambivalence toward devotional poetry, but I am made uncomfortable when T. S. Eliot confuses himself with Dante.

William Blake did not confuse himself with John Milton. He wrote his brief epic *Milton* (1804) not to correct his heroic precursor but to invoke him as a savior for England and for Blake and all mankind.

I muse sometimes on Michael Drayton's vision of the poets' paradise in his *The Muses Elizium* (1630):

There in perpetuall Summers shade,
Apolloes Prophets sit
Among the flowres that never fade,
But flowrish like their wit;

To whom the Nimphes upon their Lyres,
Tune many a curious lay,
And with their most melodious Quires
Make short the longest day.

The thrice three Virgins heavenly Cleere,
Their trembling Timbrels sound,
Whilst the three comely Graces there
Dance many a dainty Round,

Decay nor Age there nothing knowes,
There is continuall Youth,
As Time on plant or creatures growes,
So still their strength renewth.

The Poets Paradice this is,
To which but few can come;
The Muses onely bower of blisse
Their Deare Elizium.

[ll. 85–104]

Drayton was a disciple of Edmund Spenser and a close friend of Shakespeare. Blake read Drayton and probably also William Warner's *Albion's England* (1596). Drayton's *Poly-Olbion* employs Spenserian alexandrines, but Warner uses the septenarius or fourteener that Blake chose as the metric for all his longer visionary poems.

I enjoy imagining John Milton in the poets' paradise confronting Blake's *Milton*, doubtless with considerable exasperation. On his title page Blake places "To Justify the Ways of God to Men." A highly polemical preface is followed by the now-famous and I would say badly misunderstood hymn sung everywhere in the English-speaking world under the title "Jerusalem":

And did those feet in ancient time
Walk upon Englands mountains green,
And was the holy Lamb of God,
On England's pleasant pastures seen?

And did the Countenance Divine
Shine forth upon our clouded hills?
And was Jerusalem builded here
Among these dark Satanic Mills?

Bring me my Bow of burning gold:
Bring me my arrows of desire:
Bring me my Spear: O clouds unfold!
Bring me my Chariot of fire!

I will not cease from Mental Fight,
Nor shall my sword sleep in my hand,
Till we have built Jerusalem,
In Englands green & pleasant Land.

Could we have heard Blake sing or recite this, I think his intona-
tions would have shown that the questions in the second quatrain are
not rhetorical but open. I also suggest that he would have emphasized:
"Bring me *my* Chariot of fire!" Blake had illustrated Thomas Gray's
Pindaric ode, *The Progress of Poesy* (1754), and would have remembered
its vision of Milton riding his own Chariot of Paternal Deity:

Nor second he, that rode sublime
Upon the seraph-wings of Ecstasy,
The secrets of th' Abyss to spy.
He pass'd the flaming bounds of Place and Time:
The living throne, the sapphire-blaze,
Where angels tremble, while they gaze,
He saw; but blasted with excess of light,
Clos'd his eyes in endless night.

[ll. 95–102]

"The living throne" ultimately derives from Isaiah's vision of
God:

In the year that king Uzziah died I saw also the Lord sitting upon a throne, high and lifted up, and his train filled the temple. Above it stood the seraphims: each one had six wings; with twain he covered his face, and with twain he covered his feet, and with twain he did fly. And one cried unto another, and said, Holy, holy, holy, is the Lord of hosts: the whole earth is full of his glory. And the posts of the door moved at the voice of him that cried, and the house was filled with smoke. Then said I, Woe is me! for I am undone; because I am a man of unclean lips, and I dwell in the midst of a people of unclean lips: for mine eyes have seen the King, the Lord of hosts. Then flew one of the seraphims unto me, having a live coal in his hand, which he had taken with the tongs from off the altar: And he laid it upon my mouth, and said, Lo, this hath touched thy lips; and thine iniquity is taken away, and thy sin purged. Also I heard the voice of the Lord, saying, Whom shall I send, and who will go for us? Then said I, Here am I; send me.

[Isaiah (KJV) 6:1–8]

Isaiah's vision engendered the shattering start of the prophecy of Ezekiel:

Now it came to pass in the thirtieth year, in the fourth month, in the fifth day of the month, as I was among the captives by the river of Chebar, that the heavens were opened, and I saw visions of God. In the fifth day of the month, which was the fifth year of king Jehoiachin's captivity, the word of the Lord came expressly unto Ezekiel the priest, the son of Buzi, in the land of the Chaldeans by the river Chebar; and the hand of the Lord was there upon him. And I looked, and, behold, a whirlwind came out of the north, a great cloud, and a fire infolding itself, and a brightness was about it, and out of the midst thereof as the colour of amber, out of the midst of the fire. Also out of the midst thereof came the likeness of four living creatures. And this was their appearance; they had the likeness of a man. And every one had four faces, and every one had four wings. And their feet were straight feet; and the sole of their feet was like the sole of a calf's foot: and they sparkled like the colour of burnished brass. And they had the hands of a man under their wings on their four sides; and they four had their faces and their wings. Their wings were joined one to another; they turned not when they went; they went every one straight forward. As for the likeness of their faces, they four had the face of a man, and the face of a lion, on the right side: and they four had the face of an ox on the left side; they four also had the face of an eagle. Thus were their faces: and their wings were stretched upward; two wings of every one were joined one to another, and two covered their bodies. And they went every one straight forward: whither the spirit was to go, they went; and they turned not when they went. As for the likeness of the living creatures, their appearance was like burning coals of fire, and like the appearance of lamps: it went up and down among the living creatures; and the fire was bright, and out of the fire went forth lightning. And the living creatures ran and returned as the appearance of a flash of lightning.

[Ezekiel (KJV) 1:1–13]

Inevitably Ezekiel's vision is travestied in Revelation:

And before the throne there was a sea of glass like unto crystal: and in the midst of the throne, and round about the throne, were four beasts full of eyes before and behind. And the first beast was like a lion, and the second beast like a calf, and the third beast had a face as a man, and the fourth beast was like a flying eagle. And the four beasts had each of them six wings about him; and they were full of eyes within: and they rest not day and night, saying, Holy, holy, holy, Lord God Almighty, which was, and is, and is to come.

[Revelation (KJV) 4:6–9]

To comprehend almost all of William Blake and much of Percy Bysshe Shelley, you need to begin with Ezekiel's vision of the divine chariot, which will pass on to Dante and to Petrarch, and from them to Milton and to his poetic descendants.

I cannot get away from Ezekiel, but he upsets me; he is more than half mad and chants in a spasmodic style. In Ezekiel everything breaks apart. God himself seems broken into shards. And yet the whirlwind and the frightening chariot overwhelm me. It is difficult to accept Ezekiel's Yahweh, who cares only that his name and his power be recognized and seems to have forgotten his covenant with the people of Judah. Literally Ezekiel's name means "God strengthens," though pragmatically God destroys.

The "wheels and their work," *merkabah* and throne, go back to Exodus 24 and 40, as well as to Isaiah 6 and Psalm 18. Why does this God keep roaring, "I am Yahweh!"? Triumphant in his chariot, horsed by the "living creatures" or cherubim, Yahweh glows with an aura called *hashmal*, which is untranslatable. The KJV "amber" is inadequate.

Dante evades this Yahweh in his Triumphal Chariot of the Church in *Purgatorio* 29:

Even as in heaven star followeth after star,
There came close after them four animals,
Incoronate each one with verdant leaf.

Plumed with six wings was every one of them,
The plumage full of eyes; the eyes of Argus
If they were living would be such as these.

Reader! to trace their forms no more I waste
My rhymes; for other spendings press me so,
That I in this cannot be prodigal.

But read Ezekiel, who depicteth them
As he beheld them from the region cold
Coming with cloud, with whirlwind, and with fire;

And such as thou shalt find them in his pages,
Such were they here; saving that in their plumage
John is with me, and differeth from him.

The interval between these four contained
A chariot triumphal on two wheels,
Which by a Griffin's neck came drawn along;

And upward he extended both his wings
Between the middle list and three and three,
So that he injured none by cleaving it

So high they rose that they were lost to sight;
His limbs were gold, so far as he was bird,
And white the others with vermilion mingled.

Not only Rome with no such splendid car
E'er gladdened Africanus, or Augustus,
But poor to it that of the Sun would be . . .

[ll. 91–117]

Petrarch imitated Dante thirty years after his death in his six
Triumphs (1351), of which the first was *The Triumph of Love:*

And there, amid the grasses, faint from weeping,
O'ercome with sleep, I saw a spacious light
Wherein were ample grief and little joy.

A leader, conquering and supreme, I saw,
Such as triumphal chariots used to bear
To glorious honour on the Capitol.

Never had I beheld a sight like this—
Thanks to the sorry age in which I live,
Bereft of valor, and o'erfilled with pride—

And I, desirous evermore to learn,
Lifted my weary eyes, and gazed upon
This scene, so wondrous and so beautiful

Four steeds I saw, whiter than whitest snow,
And on a fiery car a cruel youth
With bow in hand and arrows at his side.

No fear had he, nor armor wore, nor shield,
But on his shoulders he had two great wings
Of a thousand hues; his body was all bare.

And round about were mortals beyond count:
Some of them were but captives, some were slain,
And some were wounded by his pungent arrows.

Eager for tidings, I moved toward the throng,
So that I came near to becoming one
Of those who by his hand had lost their lives.

Then I moved closer still, to see if any
I recognized among the pressing host
Following the king ne'er satisfied with tears.

None did I seem to know; for if there were
Among them any I had known, their looks
Were changed by death or fierce captivity.
                              [ll. 10–39, translated by Peter Sadlon]

This was the direct impetus for Shelley's death poem *The Tri-umph of Life*. Blake could have read that, since it was published posthumously in 1824 and Blake died in 1827, but there is no evidence he ever read Shelley. Dante and Milton's Triumphal Chariot of the Church joins Ezekiel and Revelation as the spur to Blake's myth. In *Paradise Lost* the Son's Chariot of Paternal Deitie rushes forth "flashing thick flames, wheel within wheel, undrawn." Its four fierce cherubim

                    spread out their starry wings
With dreadful shade contiguous, and the orbs
Of his fierce chariot rolled, as with the sound
Of torrent floods, or of a numerous host.
He on his impious foes right onward drove,
Gloomiy as Night; under his burning wheels
The steadfast Empyrean shook throughout,
All but the throne itself of God. Full soon
Among them he arrived, in his right hand
Grasping ten thousand thunders, which he sent
Before him, such as in their souls infixed
Plagues. They, astonished, all resistance lost,
All courage; down thir idle weapons dropt;
O'er shields, and helms, and helmèd heads he rode
Of Thrones and mighty Seraphim prostrate,
That wished the mountains now might be again

Thrown on them, as a shelter from his ire.
Nor less on either side tempestuous fell
His arrows, from the fourfold-visaged Four,
Distinct with eyes, and from the living wheels,
Distinct alike with multitude of eyes;
One spirit in them ruled, and every eye
Glared lightning, and shot forth pernicious fire
Among the accursed, that withered all their strength . . .

[6.827–850]

The overthrown he raised, and, as a herd
Of goats or timorous flock together thronged,
Drove them before him thunderstruck, pursued
With terrors and with furies to the bounds
And crystal wall of Heaven; which, opening wide,
Rolled inward, and a spacious gap disclosed
Into the wasteful Deep. The monstrous sight
Strook them with horror backward; but far worse
Urged them behind: headlong themselves they threw
Down from the verge of Heaven: eternal wrath
Burnt after them to the bottomless pit.

[6.856–866]

I once compared this extraordinary Miltonic vision of Christ to a general leading an armored attack—Rommel, Patton, the Israeli Tal—but that was an overvaluation. Why did Milton do this? He had to overgo or transume Ezekiel and Dante, yet to transmute the Merkabah into a battle tank ironically prophesies the Israeli Defence Forces' naming of Merkava for its principal weapon. John Milton once practiced wielding a pike when it seemed that the Royalists might assault London.

Though it is the Chariot of Paternal Deity, its rider is the Son. Yahweh is a man of war, but is that identity appropriate for Jesus of Nazareth? Reread the Gospel of Mark. Could its protagonist mount a war chariot and lead the men of Galilee against the Roman oppressors? The hillmen of the tribes of Zebulon and Naphtali were the fierce Galilean warriors led by Deborah and Barak in Judges 5.

My concern here is William Blake, yet I realize again that I may never quite understand John Milton's stance *as a poet* in regard to Protestant Christianity. That does not mean that I fully grasp Blake's highly idiosyncratic spirituality. My first essay on Blake (1957) was on the dialectic of *The Marriage of Heaven and Hell.* More than sixty years later I continue to struggle with Blake. His difficulties are authentic and are justified by his rhetorical power and his cognitive acuity and originality. When I was young I loved Blake and thought he had found part of the truth of being human. In advanced old age, I am skeptical not of his aesthetic achievement but of whether any writer, except for Homer, the Yahwist, Chaucer, Montaigne, Cervantes, Shakespeare, and Tolstoy, can tell us the whole truth.

Blake identified himself with the poets of Sensibility and the Sublime, who were his immediate forerunners, including Thomas Gray, Thomas Chatterton, and above all William Cowper. In many respects he was a Bard of Sensibility more than he was a High Romantic poet like Wordsworth, Coleridge, Shelley, and Keats. Even more deeply he saw himself as a new Ezekiel, a prophet in exile seeking a return to a regenerated Jerusalem.

Compare the conclusion of Ezekiel with the final plate of Blake's *Jerusalem:*

It was round about eighteen thousand measures: and the name of the city from that day shall be, The LORD is there.

[Ezekiel (KJV) 48:35]

All Human Forms identified even Tree Metal Earth & Stone. all
Human Forms identified, living going forth & returning
    wearied
Into the Planetary lives of Years Months Days & Hours
    reposing
And then Awaking into his Bosom in the Life of Immortality.

And I heard the Name of their Emanations they are named
    Jerusalem

The End of The Song
of Jerusalem

[Plate 99]

Ezekiel for once is stark and almost simple; Blake is luminous and at peace with himself. Both prophets hope they have come home, though sorrowfully they are deluded. Poetic thinking can enlarge the contours of promise but cannot achieve a crossing into Canaan.

The final face-to-face conversation I enjoyed with the late Northrop Frye was in Toronto in 1981. He died a decade later at seventy-eight. I was giving a series of three lectures on successive late afternoons. To my surprise, he insisted upon introducing all three. They were thoroughly worked brief essays and all rather polemical. Frye's emphasis was on clearly delineating the critical differences that divided us. My lectures had no reference to him but came out of the theoretical and pragmatic disputes I had been having with Paul de Man and Jacques Derrida at Yale. They can now be found in my book *Agon* (1982).

On the final evening of my Toronto sojourn, I found myself alone with Frye at his club after dinner, sharing brandy and farewell. Our mutual friends Jay Macpherson and Eleanor Cook had departed and Frye wanted to talk about Blake. He remarked, as he had before, that I had a tendency to Hebraize Blake. I replied that Blake had preceded me in that process, having taught himself Hebrew and being highly aware of the analogies between his work and Kabbalah. As for Blake's complex relation to Neoplatonism and to ancient Gnosticism, I told Frye that it might never be fully disentangled. Frye, who was himself an ordained minister of the United Church of Canada, firmly insisted that Blake was, like Frye himself, a Protestant Christian.

I chose silence in that matter since I have little sympathy for historical Christianity. William Blake seems to me as much a sect of one as Milton, Emily Dickinson, Herman Melville, Walt Whitman, D. H. Lawrence, or the late Geoffrey Hill. Certainly Blake in temperament and social background emerged from the dissenting Protestant tradition. In Milton's own generation, Blake would have stood not with Cromwell and Milton but with the Levellers, the Diggers, the Ranters, and perhaps even the heroic Major General Thomas Harrison, martyred leader of the Fifth Monarchy Men.

Rereading some of my earlier works on Blake, I do not think I oversimplified him but at times I evaded his more sinuous wanderings. I still stand by my commentary in David V. Erdman's *The Com-*

plete Poetry and Prose of William Blake (1965), and by my introductory study *Blake's Apocalypse* (1963), but would revise them if current publishing mores allowed that, but they do not. This is certainly my last opportunity to be helpful to Blake's readers, and I hope I can accomplish that.

Ezekiel's Merkabah is the essential matrix for Blake's mythmaking since it gave him his four Zoas, the "living creatures" or Giant Forms whose strife, inner and outer, is the subject of his most ambitious poems. In Revelation 4, the four living creatures in Ezekiel's vision are translated by the Greek *zoa*. Blake uses this plural form as a singular in English. Together these four living creatures constitute Albion, the central man, unfallen and fallen, of Blake's myth.

Albion, an ancient name for the British Isles, in time tended to be used for Scotland. There are various etymologies, one perhaps based on the white cliffs of Dover. Legends tell that the original inhabitants were giants, who were subdued by Brutus, an exile from fallen Troy, whose name transmuted into Britain. Blake presumably found his Albion in the Elizabethan poets Drayton and Warner. Yet the Albion of Blake's epics is linked to many precursive gods/men, including Philo Judaeus of Alexandria's Moses, the Kabbalah's Adam Kadmon, the Hermetic Poimandres, and the Stranger God of the Gnostics. None of these, however, is as fundamental as Blake's Albion, since his unfallen form constituted all of reality and all of the human potential.

In discussions with my late friend David Erdman, we agreed once that Blake was more an apocalyptic humanist and social rebel than a spiritual reformer. And yet Blake rejected Dante for his pride and his hatreds. An apocalyptic humanist is as much an oxymoron as is a Christian humanist. Blake would have rejected my description since he insisted he was a Christian. He may have been one of the few Christians consonant with David Bentley Hart's translation of, and commentary upon, the New Testament. Doubtless there are such living Christians, and I may have met a few of them. It is difficult for me to believe that they are "multitudes, multitudes in the valley of decision" (Joel 3:14, KJV).

Blake knew that the best and oldest part of him was no part of the created world. He calls that part the Imagination, but I have begun to think that was a misnomer, and that he stated it best when he spoke of the Real Man the Imagination, at the close of his life. The ancient Gnostics called that part the *pneuma*, the breath or spark of divinity in each of us.

Though he has affinities to several more or less esoteric traditions, including Neoplatonism, Gnosticism, Kabbalah, the writings of Jacob Boehme and perhaps Paracelsus, Blake's true birthright is the greater Western poets, including Dante, Chaucer, Spenser, Shakespeare, and Milton. Setting aside Shakespeare, whose cognitive powers are beyond measure, Blake's difference from his poetic precursors is in his frightening capacity for representing schisms in consciousness.

Los is not William Blake the man, the poet, the painter, the engraver, but rather a trope for a creativity that is under no obligation to the created world. We do not know when *Jerusalem* was completed. There may have been revisions even after 1820. After a lifetime of study I still have a clearer sense of *The Four Zoas* and of *Milton* than I do of *Jerusalem*, though I regard it as Blake's masterwork. *Jerusalem* is a bitter and embattled poem that founds itself upon the structure of the Book of Ezekiel. I read *Jerusalem* with less anguish than I do Ezekiel, but there is more pain and suffering in both than I can bear.

Late yesterday afternoon I climbed up laboriously to my study and found a dust-covered paperback I had forgotten. It was the anthology *Romanticism and Consciousness: Essays in Criticism*, which I edited in 1970, a half century ago. I had not looked into it for some decades. At first it made me sad because all the scholars and critics in it had departed except for me. A number of them had been close friends: Geoffrey Hartman, Paul de Man, John Hollander, Martin Price; while others had been revered mentors: W. K. Wimsatt Jr., M. H. Abrams, Northrop Frye, Frederick A. Pottle. Then there were good acquaintances: Owen Barfield, Walter Jackson Bate, Josephine Miles, Alvin Kernan. Some I had never met: Samuel Monk, J. H. Van den Berg, Alfred Cobban, Humphry House.

I read through the volume, including my introductory essay, "The Internalization of Quest Romance," and the final essay, "The Unpastured Sea: An Introduction to Shelley," which I had written in 1965, at the middle of the journey. The book did not seem to me a period piece, but I suppose it now is for many. To my surprise it is still in print.

Reading it again, I was most impressed by John Hollander's essay, "Romantic Verse Form and the Metrical Contract"; Martin Price's "The Standard of Energy," which is on Blake; and Geoffrey Hartman's "The Romance of Nature and the Negative Way," which movingly traces Wordsworth's absolutely isolated position among the great English poets.

I see that Martin Price defined more clearly than I can the question of how best to describe William Blake: "Blake can hardly be identified as theist or humanist; the distinction becomes meaningless for him. God can only exist within man, but man must be raised to a perception of the infinite. Blake rejects both transcendental deity and natural man: 'God becomes as we are, that we may be as he is'" (*To the Palace of Wisdom* [1970]).

I do not think that there will ever be a clear way of formulating Blake's prophetic stance. He has flaws yet his largeness defies categorization. In my only conversation with Geoffrey Hill I was a little surprised at his strong preference for Blake's lyrics over *Jerusalem*, which he felt was "diffuse." Awed by Hill, who was a fierce presence, I did not respond, though *Jerusalem* is hardly diffuse. It is condensed, sometimes to a frightening degree.

The late Northrop Frye cautioned against searching for narrative continuity in Blake's epics but, while much indebted to Frye on Blake, I never agreed with him on that issue. Blake certainly experimented with disrupting narrative flow, particularly in *Milton* and *Jerusalem*, where dissolving backgrounds attempt to take the place of story. But all literary art has to tell a story, however strangely deferred or displaced it can be. Something in the mind remains a child who wants to hear wonders related in some sort of progression. Blake was fascinated by James Macpherson's Ossian forgeries, by Thomas Chatterton's Rowley impostures, by the Norse mythologies that he found in Mallet's *Northern Antiquities*. All these told stories.

No one would dispute that *The Four Zoas* tells a story, though at first it may seem estranged. Blake quotes Ephesians 6:12 as his epigraph: "For we wrestle not against flesh and blood, but against principalities, against powers, against the rulers of the darkness of this world, against spiritual wickedness in high places" (KJV). Those principalities and rulers of darkness are the Zoas: Tharmas, Luvah, Urizen, and Urthona. They are the four sons of Albion, who can no longer balance an instinct for wholeness or Organized Innocence with dark passion, self-curtailed intelligence, and the creating imagination.

That instinct for unity, or at least for harmony, is embodied by Tharmas, who before the Creation/Fall manifested a fused sense of touch and taste, which we encounter in sexual experience. I suspect that Blake may have derived the name from Thaumas, who in Hesiod was a sea god. Through the English Neoplatonist Thomas Taylor, author of *The Mystical Initiations, or Hymns of Orpheus*, Blake may have been aware that Plato interpreted Thaumas's name as "wonder."

Tharmas was a relative latecomer to Blake's mythology. I think one can surmise that Blake's difficulties in transforming his projected epic *Vala* into what became *The Four Zoas* were the stimuli that brought Tharmas into being:

Begin with Tharmas Parent power. darkning in the West

Lost! Lost! Lost! are my Emanations Enion O Enion
We are become a Victim to the Living We hide in secret
I have hidden Jerusalem in Silent Contrition O Pity Me
I will build thee a Labyrinth also O pity me O Enion
Why hast thou taken sweet Jerusalem from my inmost Soul
Let her Lay secret in the Soft recess of darkness & silence
It is not Love I bear to [Jerusalem] It is Pity
She hath taken refuge in my bosom & I cannot cast her out.
The Men have recieved their death wounds & their Emanations
    are fled
To me for refuge & I cannot turn them out for Pitys sake.
                                                    [1.18–28]

Neither Blake nor his reader finds it simple to achieve an image of Tharmas. He is the fallen sea of time and space, a rampaging chaos, John Milton's "universe of death." What happens to the human desire or instinct for wholeness when things fall apart? Even if you are William Blake, how can you represent an incoherence?

Most certainly, Blake was highly aware of his dilemma. He inherited and yet fought against the literary tradition of the Sublime. In a letter of reply to a clergyman who had urged the poet-painter to abandon the World of Spirits, Blake hit back hard:

> That which can be made Explicit to the Idiot is not worth my care.
>
> [Letter to Reverend John Trusler
> (August 23, 1799)]

The best insight I know regarding Tharmas is Northrop Frye's in his essay "The Keys to the Gates." Frye calls Tharmas "the power of renewing life" and therefore appropriately represented by the ocean, because it is the start and the finish of life. Since the Fall was also a deluge, we are ontologically underwater, as our true home ought to be Atlantis before it became the raging Atlantic. Frye rightly identifies Tharmas with the Sublime and Orc with the pathetic or the Picturesque.

The Four Zoas is divided into nine Nights, partly on the model of Edward Young's *Night-Thoughts* (1742–1745). As a graduate student in the early 1950s, I compelled myself to read through that entire, hopelessly dismal, quite inept chunk of verse. I cannot believe that Blake admired it. But the publisher Richard Edwards commissioned Blake to do the illustrations for a new edition of *Night-Thoughts*. Blake produced over five hundred watercolor illustrations, expecting to engrave some two hundred or so. Only the first volume was published (1797), but it did not sell and so the project was abandoned.

James Boswell was a remarkable personality and a great writer, but not exactly a literary critic. He refused patronage to Robert Burns and said this of Edward Young:

> "Night Thoughts" . . . I esteem as a mass of the grandest and richest poetry that human genius has ever produced.
>
> [*Life of Samuel Johnson* (1791)]

Dr. Johnson, as we might expect, expressed some reservations:

His verses are formed by no certain model; he is no more
like himself in his different productions than he is like others.
He seems never to have studied prosody, nor to have had any
direction but from his own ear. But with all his defects, he
was a man of genius and a poet.

["Life of Young" (1781)]

I cannot believe that Johnson was being other than gracious in
that last sentence. Here is the opening of *Night-Thoughts:*

Night First.
On Life, Death, and Immortality
Tired Nature's sweet restorer, balmy Sleep!
He, like the world, his ready visit pays
Where Fortune smiles; the wretched he forsakes;
Swift on his downy pinion flies from woe,
And lights on lids unsullied with a tear.

. . .

Be wise to-day; 'tis madness to defer;
Next day the fatal precedent will plead;
Thus on, till wisdom is push'd out of life.
Procrastination is the thief of time;
Year after year it steals, till all are fled,
And to the mercies of a moment leaves
The vast concerns of an eternal scene.

[Night First, ll. 1–5, 400–406]

If Young is remembered at all, aside from Blake's illustrations, it
is for that noble chestnut: "Procrastination is the thief of time." I
find it instructive to juxtapose with Young the opening of "Night
the First" of *The Four Zoas:*

The Song of the Aged Mother which shook the heavens
    with wrath
Hearing the march of long resounding strong heroic Verse
Marshalld in order for the day of Intellectual Battle

[1.1–3]

I cannot refrain from indulging in just one more juxtaposition, the opening of Young's apocalypse (to call it that) with the extraordinary whirlwind that commences Blake's "Night the Ninth":

The Consolation
As when a traveller, a long day past
In painful search of what he cannot find,
At night's approach, content with the next cot,
There ruminates, a while, his labour lost;
Then cheers his heart with what his fate affords,
And chants his sonnet to deceive the time,
Till the due season calls him to repose . . .

[Night Ninth, 1–7]

Night the Ninth
Being the Last Judgment
And Los & Enitharmon builded Jerusalem weeping
Over the Sepulcher & over the Crucified body
Which to their Phantom Eyes appear'd Still in the Sepulcher
But Jesus stood beside them in the Spirit Separating
Their Spirit from their body. Terrified at Non Existence
For such they deemd the death of the body. Los his vegetable
    hands
Outstretchd his right hand branching out in fibrous strength
Siezd the Sun. His left hand like dark roots coverd the
    Moon
And tore them down cracking the heavens across from im-
    mense to immense
Then fell the fires of Eternity with loud & shrill
Sound of Loud Trumpet thundering along from heaven to
    heaven
A mighty sound articulate Awake ye dead & come
To Judgment from the four winds Awake & Come away

Folding like scrolls of the Enormous volume of Heaven &
    Earth
With thunderous noise & dreadful shakings rocking to & fro
The heavens are shaken & the Earth removed from its place

The foundations of the Eternal hills discoverd
The thrones of Kings are shaken they have lost their robes &
    crowns
The poor smite their opressors they awake up to the harvest
The naked warriors rush together down to the sea shore
Trembling before the multitudes of slaves now set at liberty
They are become like wintry flocks like forests stripd of leaves
The opressed pursue like the wind there is no room for
    escape . . .

                                                      [9.1–23]

Cracking the heavens across from immense to immense might
have startled Young out of his ruminating slumbers. I slept very badly
last night because of pains in both knees and silently quoted to myself the subsequent passage of Night the Ninth:

The Spectre of Enitharmon let loose on the troubled deep
Waild shrill in the confusion & the Spectre of Urthona
Recievd her in the darkning South *their bodies lost they stood*
Trembling & weak a faint embrace a fierce desire as when
Two shadows mingle on a wall they wail & shadowy tears
Fell down & shadowy forms of joy mixd with despair & grief
Their bodies buried in the ruins of the Universe
Mingled with the confusion. Who shall call them from the
    Grave.

                              [9.24–31; emphasis added]

I would think that many of us, perhaps most, have suffered faint
embraces in which two shadows seemed to mingle on a wall. William Blake was the prophet of a fuller sexuality but prophecy, yielding to apocalyptic, diminishes every joy. When I stand back from
him and try to achieve perspective, I am likelier to apprehend the
terrible eloquence of loss more than any hope of fulfillment.

What drove Blake to his elaborate mythmakings? David Erdman told me it was the fear of being accused of sedition. It is true
that if Blake had been convicted in the trial resulting from his alter-
cation with the trooper John Scofield, the poet and his wife, Catherine, might well have been exiled to Australia. Fortunately he was

acquitted, but a pardonable touch of paranoia was the result. The wretched Scofield achieves immortality in *Jerusalem*, rather in the way that the roustabout Oliver St. John Gogarty is now remembered only as the outrageous Malachi "Buck" Mulligan of Joyce's *Ulysses*.

I vastly respected David Erdman as a historical and textual scholar, and a man of courage and conviction, yet I cannot read Blake's poetry as political allegory, though that strand indubitably is present. How shall we define allegory addressed to the intellectual powers? The best study of allegory remains Angus Fletcher's book of that title, but allegory is akin to irony: saying one thing and meaning another. I cannot find the exact term for Blake's project, and I no longer accept Northrop Frye's account of it as another great code of art. Neither the Bible nor Blake is such a code. Without the Isaiahs, Amos, Micah, Ezekiel, Jeremiah—there might have been no William Blake. What he made of them is another matter. He told his own story and not theirs. He misread them powerfully and productively.

Blake's agon with John Milton was even more an adventure in transumption. To emulate Milton was to make oneself another morning star and not to become, like William Cowper or Thomas Chatterton, another victim of belatedness. It was also to realize that there was a contemporary rival for the mantle of Milton: Wordsworth. In his annotations to Wordsworth's *Poems* (1815), Blake reacted to the poem addressed to little Hartley Coleridge with admiration and ambivalence:

> This is all in the highest degree Imaginative & equal to any Poet but not Superior   I cannot think that Real Poets have any competition   None are greatest in the Kingdom of Heaven it is so in Poetry

Annotating the Preface to *The Excursion* (1814), Blake exploded:

> You shall not bring me down to believe such fitting & fitted
> I know better & Please your Lordship

Wordsworth offended Blake by stating that the individual mind and the external world were exquisitely fitted to one another. That would destroy Blake. And yet Blake and Wordsworth were the children of Milton, more even than Shelley and Keats. Literary love tempered by ambivalence is very much like Freud's vision of what he called "family romances."

For many years I have urged that we read Freud as a major essayist in the tradition of Montaigne and Emerson, and not as a supposed scientist. He would not have been happy with that judgment, but nevertheless it is true. His authentic precursors were Schopenhauer and Nietzsche. He acknowledged Schopenhauer but was mute on Nietzsche. For many more years than I care to remember I labored on a large work that was to be called *Transference and Authority*, a study of all of Freud's writings. It defeated me and I abandoned the manuscript, fragments of which are scattered in my books from about 1980 onward, and some remain in my attic study, unpublished.

My Freud essentially was a theorist of the Sublime, not just in his essay "The Uncanny" (1919) but even more in *Beyond the Pleasure Principle* (1920) and *Inhibitions, Symptoms, Anxiety* (1926), which I consider his greatest single book. I would also add the invaluable *The Ego and the Mechanisms of Defense* (1936) by Anna Freud, without which I could not have written *A Map of Misreading*. If Freud gave us a science, it was a science of tropes, since his concepts are metaphoric and mythological. Wittgenstein complained that Freud reduced to "a powerful mythology," but I regard that as tribute. The Freud who goes on mattering is not the master of dream interpretation (where I doubt him) and certainly not the would-be therapist (talking cures) but the pessimistic seer of the human condition. He wrote once: "See for yourself that much has been gained if we succeed in turning your hysterical misery into ordinary unhappiness" (*Studies in Hysteria* [1895], co-written with Josef Breuer).

Freud wanted us to learn to live with what he called the Reality Principle or making friends with the necessity of dying. Though I regard him as fundamentally Judaic in most things, there we part. Jewish tradition exalts life. High literature, in my experience of it, is a saving lie against time, loss of individuality, premature death. Freud died at eighty-three after a virtually endless series of operations for cancer of the jaw, an illness brought on by his incessant cigar-smoking. At his request, morphine was employed to release him from endless pain.

Through the years I have speculated as to what Blake would have thought of Freud. I fear he would have assimilated that grand consciousness to his infernal trinity of Bacon, Locke, and Newton. Blake is not very persuasive when he attacks rival intellects. He had a touch of Jonathan Swift in him, but not enough to sustain mistaken assaults. The book that goes on upsetting me is *A Tale of a Tub* (1704), Swift's first and greatest work. I reread it twice a year to admonish myself. Blake, like Swift, feared the Mechanical Operation of the Spirit, through which our mind is violated by the excesses of our bodies. Satire corrodes and ultimately destroys. It is legitimate to associate Blake with Swift as an intellectual satirist, though that is only an aspect of Blake's visionary stance. Primarily he is what Swift would have dismissed as an Enthusiast, a kind of madman. Alas, Swift himself went mad, while Blake, in his triumphant final phase, was surrounded by a group of young disciples who called themselves "the Ancients" and regarded him as "the Interpreter." The three most important were Samuel Palmer, Edward Calvert, and George Richmond, remarkable painters of visionary landscapes and personages. Up in my study is George Richmond's pencil-and-chalk drawing of Blake on his deathbed, from the collection of William Inglis Morse, kindly given to me by Frederick W. Hilles, Morse's son-in-law. On the wall next to it is one of the few copies of the first plate of Blake's *The Gates of Paradise*, also originally owned by William Inglis Morse. Reproductions of Palmer and Calvert are strewn about the walls, reflecting my Blakean passions of more than sixty years ago. Old men digress, as I am doing here. I am taking a winding path back to Blake's Tharmas, but I am at last ready to expound him with what I hope will be a new clarity.

I do not enjoy a hidden channel to the mind and literary art of William Blake. All that I possess is a very long life of reading and rereading him. Close textual study in the tradition of David Erdman and his successors can be very useful indeed. I am aided by John Pierce's observation:

Even as Blake elaborates on the identity of Tharmas, he develops him beyond the immediate needs of the narrative. In the poem's narrative, he stands at the nodal point of the fall into the chaotic sea of time and space and acts as a source for the conditions of fallen existence. Enion's weaving of Tharmas into the Circle of Destiny and the form of the Spectre suggests that Tharmas' fall introduces fate and error. The weaving imagery also suggests Tharmas' incarnation into the limitations of the physical body, while the notion that he holds the Emanation Jerusalem within suggests the potential for redemption of the body when it contains the City of God. These associations suggest that Tharmas is analogous to the universal human form of the One Man, Jesus Christ. Such associations give Tharmas a symbolic equivalence with Albion.

> ["The Shifting Characterization of Tharmas
> and Enitharmon" (1988/1989)]

I am grateful to Pierce for this. One would expect that a parent power associated with the Atlantic Ocean has a tendency to be uncontrollable. Tharmas also had for Blake the fascination of largeness, of a comprehensiveness that could suggest a multiple series of biblical figures only apparently disparate. One of these is the Covering Cherub, identified by Ezekiel with the Prince of Tyre:

> Thou art the anointed cherub that covereth; and I have set thee so: thou wast upon the holy mountain of God; thou hast walked up and down in the midst of the stones of fire.
>
> Thou wast perfect in thy ways from the day that thou wast created, till iniquity was found in thee.
>
> By the multitude of thy merchandise they have filled the midst of thee with violence, and thou hast sinned: therefore I will cast thee as profane out of the mountain of God: and I will destroy thee, O covering cherub, from the midst of the stones of fire.
>
> [Ezekiel (KJV) 28:14–16]

This is a difficult text and scholars contend with one another as to the proper interpretation. But I think we can surmise how Blake construed it. In the Hebrew the Cherub is described as *mimshach* (widely extending). Ezekiel is haunted by his precursors: Isaiah, Amos, Micah, Jeremiah. I am still enough of a Blakean to see the Covering Cherub, in one aspect, to be these forerunners. Another aspect is the cherub with a flaming sword going every which way, guarding the gate back into Eden in Genesis and in Milton. The most vivid form is the most difficult: Is this a vision of the Fall of Lucifer? Is Ezekiel not alluding to Isaiah's account of the fall of the morning star?

> How art thou fallen from heaven, O Lucifer, son of the morning! how art thou cut down to the ground, which didst weaken the nations!
>
> For thou hast said in thine heart, I will ascend into heaven, I will exalt my throne above the stars of God: I will sit also upon the mount of the congregation, in the sides of the north:
>
> I will ascend above the heights of the clouds; I will be like the most High.
>
> Yet thou shalt be brought down to hell, to the sides of the pit.
>
> [Ezekiel (KJV) 14:12–15]

The Hebrew is *Helel ben Shahar*, rendered in Jerome's Vulgate as Lucifer. Presumably Isaiah prophesies the fall of the King of Babylon. But for Blake Babylon is where he and we still abide. We are in the world of fallen Tharmas, tumultuous ocean of space and time. All covering cherubim are blocking agents, keeping us from access to our lost Paradise. There is a dialectical complexity in Blake's Tharmas that ensues from his double aspect: unfallen he is a benign shepherd, as in the *Songs of Innocence;* fallen he is the god Atlas, king of the mythical Atlantis and prototype of Albion, drowned out with Atlantis by a primal flood. There is a lost giant fresco of Blake's of the Ancient Britons, described by him in his 1809 Descriptive Catalogue of the doomed exhibition, which sold nothing, and was nastily denounced by the *Examiner,* edited by the Hunt brothers.

Hesiod's Eione presumably becomes Blake's Earth Mother Enion, Emanation and bride of Tharmas. Their agonized relationship centers Night the First of *The Four Zoas.* Enion laments,

> I have lookd into the secret soul of him I lovd
> And in the Dark recesses found Sin & cannot return
> Trembling & pale sat Tharmas weeping in his clouds
> Why wilt thou Examine every little fibre of my soul

Spreading them out before the Sun like Stalks of flax to dry
The infant joy is beautiful but its anatomy
Horrible Ghast & Deadly nought shalt thou find in it
But Death Despair & Everlasting brooding Melancholy
Thou wilt go mad with horror if thou dost Examine thus
Every moment of my secret hours Yea I know
That I have sinnd & that my Emanations are become harlots
I am already distracted at their deeds & if I look
Upon them more Despair will bring self murder on my soul
O Enion thou art thyself a root growing in hell
Tho thus heavenly beautiful to draw me to destruction
Sometimes I think thou art a flower expanding
Sometimes I think thou art fruit breaking from its bud
In dreadful dolor & pain & I am like an atom
A Nothing left in darkness yet I am an identity
I wish & feel & weep & groan Ah terrible terrible

                                                          [1.36–55]

What does William Blake mean by "sin"? The New Testament
Greek word *harmatia* probably goes back to the notion of missing
the mark, possibly as in tossing a lance or spear. Curiously the Hebrew *hata* may have a common origin, since it means shooting an
arrow and missing the center of the target. But Blake does not seem
to mean just missing a mark. In his Laocoön engraving he scrawled
a bitter diatribe:

Money, which is The Great Satan or Reason the Root of Good
     & Evil
     In The Accusation of Sin

Where any view of Money exists Art cannot be carried on but
     War
     only (Read Matthew CX. 9 & 10 v) by pretenses to the
     Two Impossibilities
     Chastity & Abstinence Gods of the Heathen
Is not every Vice possible to Man described in the Bible openly

All is not Sin that Satan calls so all the Loves & Graces of
     Eternity

If Morality was Christianity Socrates was the Saviour
Art can never exist without Naked Beauty displayed
No Secresy in Art

[1826–1827]

For Blake, the state he terms Satan always goes back to the Satan of the Book of Job, God's authorized Accuser of Sin. Art and Sin are antithetical to one another: fulfilled desire that gratifies both partners is akin to Art; Chastity and Abstinence authentically constitute Sin. That would seem to turn normative Christianity upside down, but Blake is never that simplistic. My late mentor William K. Wimsatt, in one of the two graduate seminars I participated in under his fierce direction, erupted at my praise of one of Blake's Proverbs of Hell: "Sooner murder an infant in its cradle than nurse unacted desires." That was in 1952. Fourteen years later, Wimsatt published a book, *Hateful Contraries*, with this diatribe:

> The following collocation of materials has been arranged by me with the special design of provoking the Public. Of course they will cry "unfair." It must be unfair. But if any Promethean will make the effort to explain why it is unfair, much, very much may be explained.
>
> James Brown, 45 years old, of Devon, was sentenced to live in prison today for the strangling of a high school girl last October. . . . A confession read to the jury during the trial told how Brown became aroused as he watched the girl knitting during a committee meeting at the Devon County Grange last October 20. . . . Brown followed the girl in his car after the meeting. . . .
>
> —From a New England newspaper, during the spring of a
>   recent year (names and dates adapted)

He who desires but acts not, breeds pestilence.

Sooner murder an infant in its cradle than nurse unacted desires.

—William Blake again, *The Marriage of
Heaven and Hell*

There are two alternatives to *nursing* unacted desire. One is to suppress the desire; the other is to act it. I take it there can be no doubt as to which Blake thought he meant, if he had to mean either. The verbal achievement of this "Proverb of Hell" is that the starkness of a choice is covered in the ugly word *nurse*.

By 1966, Bill and I were argumentative friends and colleagues. He gave me this book and marked the appropriate passage. I evaded response. In January 1973, I published *The Anxiety of Influence* and dedicated it to him. He sent me a gracious note saying that while the book did not please him, nevertheless he granted that it made me a Plotinus to Emerson's American Plato. Bill stood seven feet tall and was broad with a wonderful craggy face. I had taught one of his sons, a charming and promising boy who died of cancer while still an undergraduate.

Wimsatt died at seventy-five after an accident. I felt and still experience deep grief. We never agreed, yet he was warm and compassionate. In retrospect I see how much I owed him for his teaching. We fought our way through every seminar, but I continued to learn despite our mutual contentiousness.

Bill was a gifted reader except when he became irate. He read Blake well enough when it was a song in quatrains but bridled when he sensed departures from normative Catholic morality or dogma. Wimsatt was a passionate Roman Catholic. Like his friend Cleanth Brooks, with whom I never had a civil exchange, Bill worshipped T. S. Eliot—as poet, critic, ideologue. By mutual consent we avoided discussing Eliot.

William Blake's provocation of normative stances testifies to his permanent strength. You cannot appropriate him and you need to be wary lest he appropriate you. All that I think he has in common either with Augustine or Freud is a certain tendentiousness. The three innovators were masters of dialectic and yet each felt he knew the truth.

Approaching ninety, I do not know the truth or any part of it. The writers who mean most to me—Montaigne, Cervantes, Shakespeare, Tolstoy, Proust—have brushed aside the partial truths I thought to have known. What would it mean to *believe* in the truth?

I believe in Montaigne and Shakespeare because they augment my freedom.

When I was very young, Blake seemed to expand my sense of human possibility and thus beckon me to freedom. I was never a Promethean Orc and do not find that I have aged into another Urizen. Struggling to apprehend Blake, I had the illusion of rendering the horizon ghostlier. A lifetime later, Plato shadows my rereadings of Blake. The deepest analogues to Blake are in Neoplatonism and in Gnosticism. But both of those transcendentalisms are strong misreadings of Plato. Plotinus and Valentinus necessarily are closer to Plato than Blake was.

Plato did not invent the soul's immortality. Ultimately that notion was shamanistic and may have come down through Thrace as an Orphism for which we lack documentation. The doctrine was Pythagorean and also stemmed from Empedocles. Yet Plato was so vivid a writer that he captured the myth of the soul: its exile from its true home in a kind of heavenly Athens. Socrates in *Republic* wistfully says that in heaven there is an ideal city, but only for those who strive for it. Through having a vision of it, the homesick soul for just an instant returns and partly gratifies its yearning.

Both Plotinus and his Gnostic opponents elaborated this Socratic dream. William Blake absorbed those refinements and vastly augmented them into his own mythological system. Yet as I ponder now I have to wonder to what extent Blake improved the post-Platonic vision of transcendence.

Blake attempted to destroy various cloven fictions, including the distinction between transcendence and immanence. What he termed Vision was a metonymic mode that discovered a divine immanence in all objects of perception. He had no use for the metaphor of a transcendent deity, unless it could be transumed into what he called the Human Form Divine.

Meister Eckhart (1260–1328) is generally called a mystic, but after years of reading him I think of him as a speculative psychologist. Famously he believed that only the selfhood burns in hell. William Blake primarily was a major poet, but he also was a considerable speculative psychologist. It does Blake violence to assimilate him to Jung, and while there are some genuine affinities to Freud, they become blind alleys soon enough. Blake speculates for himself and manages to turn both Platonic tradition and normative Christianity inside out.

I wonder now if my best essay on Blake was written half a century ago in 1970. I have just reread it and can hardly think that was me at forty. The curious reader can find it in my early book called *The Ringers in the Tower* (1971). Its title is "Blake's *Jerusalem:* The Bard of Sensibility and the Form of Prophecy." The essay's argument is that *Jerusalem* allies itself closely to the Book of Ezekiel.

Blake curiously foretells one aspect of Kierkegaard's *The Sickness unto Death* (1849), which is a treatise on religious despair. Blake's Los in *Jerusalem* confronts and has to master his own despair, named as the Spectre of Urthona:

> The Spectre builded stupendous Works, taking the Starry
>   Heavens
> Like to a curtain & folding them according to his will
> Repeating the Smaragdine Table of Hermes to draw Los
>   down
> Into the Indefinite, refusing to believe without demonstration[.]
> Los reads the Stars of Albion! the Spectre reads the Voids
> Between the Stars; among the arches of Albions Tomb
>   sublime
> Rolling the Sea in rocky paths: forming Leviathan
> And Behemoth: the War by Sea enormous & the War
> By Land astounding: erecting pillars in the deepest Hell,
> To reach the heavenly arches; Los beheld undaunted furious
> His heavd Hammer; he swung it round & at one blow,
> In unpitying ruin driving down the pyramids of pride
> Smiting the Spectre on his Anvil & the integuments of his Eye
> And Ear unbinding in dire pain, with many blows,
> Of strict severity self-subduing, & with many tears labouring.
> Then he sent forth the Spectre all his pyramids were grains
> Of sand & his pillars: dust on the flys wing: & his starry
> Heavens; a moth of gold & silver mocking his anxious grasp
> Thus Los alterd his Spectre & every Ratio of his Reason
> He alterd time after time, with dire pain & many tears
> Till he had completely divided him into a separate space.
>   [Plate 91]

This sublime sequence indeed smites like a series of hammer blows. Los cannot annihilate his selfhood, the Spectre of Urthona, but he can alter him until at last his personal despair or sickness unto death is confined to a separate region of the creative mind. I want now to revise and, I trust, improve the commentary on this that I composed in 1964, still available in David V. Erdman's *The Complete Poetry and Prose of William Blake* (1965, with several later textual revisions):

> In the final conflict with the Spectre of Urthona (91:32–57) Blake rejects all occultism, a point his myriads of esoteric interpreters have chosen not to understand. The Smaragdine Table of Hermes is a fundamental text in occult tradition, and is a brief statement of the correspondence of the suprasensual "above" and the sensual "below." Here it is an incantation of the Spectre to trap Los in the "below," and therefore only another "rational" mode of demonstration. William Butler Yeats, quite possibly the supreme poet of the Western World in the Twentieth Century, was a passionate occultist, having found his medium in his wife Georgie, whom he married in 1917, when he was fifty-two and she was twenty-five. The marriage worked, partly because Mrs. Yeats stoically accepted his frequent attachments to younger and younger women.
>
> In his youth, Yeats had produced a rather dreadful edition of Blake, in collaboration with one Ellis. I have to assume that Yeats chose to overlook Blake's repudiation of the Smaragdine Table of Hermes. There is no point chiding Yeats; his misreadings emanated in great poems and marmoreal prose reveries, in the mode of Walter Pater.

Who would want to quarrel with Yeats at his most passionate and persuasive? And yet some reservations crowd in. Yeats follows Nietzsche as well as Shelley, but has he earned this self-forgiveness? In some of the last poems, like "The Circus Animals' Desertion," "Man and the Echo," and most of all "Cuchalain Comforted," my question would be triumphantly answered. The Yeatsian self refuses annihilation since the Anglo-Irish Archpoet was totally Gnostic and identified his self with the "spark" or *pneuma* of the Valentinian adept.

Blake wanted to believe that he had been capable of overcoming his own Spectre of Urthona, but I think he knew better. Creative anxiety is self-renewing. In Blake's version of the Theater of Mind there is a dread that one's words never can become acts, and an allied sensation that consciousness cannot repair the trauma of a separately realized existence.

The awakening of Albion is properly elemental and provides some surprises:

> Her voice pierc'd Albions clay cold ear. he moved upon the
>   Rock
> The Breath Divine went forth upon the morning hills, Albion
>   mov'd
>
> Upon the Rock, he opend his eyelids in pain; in pain he mov'd
> His stony members, he saw England. Ah! shall the Dead live
>   again
>
> The Breath Divine went forth over the morning hills Albion
>   rose
> In anger: the wrath of God breaking bright flaming on all
>   sides around
> His awful limbs: into the Heavens he walked clothed in flames
> Loud thundring, with broad flashes of flaming lightning &
>   pillars
> Of fire, speaking the Words of Eternity in Human Forms, in
>   direful
> Revolutions of Action & Passion, thro the Four Elements on
>   all sides
> Surrounding his awful Members. Thou seest the Sun in heavy
>   clouds
> Struggling to rise above the Mountains. in his burning hand
> He takes his Bow, then chooses out his arrows of flaming
>   gold
> Murmuring the Bowstring breathes with ardor! clouds roll
>   around the

Horns of the wide Bow, loud sounding winds sport on the
    mountain brows
Compelling Urizen to his Furrow; & Tharmas to his
    Sheepfold;
And Luvah to his Loom: Urthona he beheld mighty
    labouring at
His Anvil, in the Great Spectre Los unwearied labouring &
    weeping
Therefore the Sons of Eden praise Urthonas Spectre in songs
Because he kept the Divine Vision in time of trouble.

                                     [*Jerusalem*, plate 95]

Blake/Los in the resurrection of Divine Man is the Great Spectre Los. I would not have expected Blake to redeem the Spectre of
Urthona as the poet/prophet/painter/engraver who "kept the Divine
Vision in time of trouble." Is that praise of a fear unwilling to be
fed? Does Blake exalt anxiety? Very subtly he suggests that trauma
can be redemptive. Most certainly my own experience teaches me
the reverse. But then, I am not William Blake. The mystery of his
highly original Christianity has to be involved in this. But Blake
hated mystery.

David Bentley Hart, an Eastern Orthodox theologian, seems to
me our best contemporary guide to early Christianity. He makes
clear that those who first followed Jesus would be totally unacceptable to almost everyone alive today who desire to call themselves
Christians. I have not discussed Blake with Hart, yet I suspect he
might find affinities between English Blake and the very radical Jewish
Christians or Ebionites, the "poor men" who accepted the leadership
of James the Just, who called himself the brother of Jesus. They rejected Saint Paul, regarded Jesus as the Messiah, not an incarnation
of God, and continued to observe the Law of Moses.

Blake certainly identified Jesus with the awakened Imagination. But did he believe in the Incarnation? The process through
which I began to disassociate myself from Northrop Frye's vision
of Blake began as early as 1950, though I did not achieve awareness
of this until a much later time. I had purchased Frye's *Fearful
Symmetry* (1947) in the autumn of 1947 in the Cornell University

bookstore. So many rereadings ensued that my first copy came apart, and I purchased a second one in New York City in June 1950. I have been looking at that now dilapidated volume this morning and am surprised by my marginalia, most of them admiring, but some severely dissenting. I had read three books on Blake before Frye's: Milton Percival's *Blake's Circle of Destiny* (1937), John Middleton Murry's *William Blake* (1933), and S. Foster Damon's *William Blake, His Philosophy and Symbols* (1924). Damon was the great pioneer of modern Blake studies, while Middleton Murry, then a disciple of D. H. Lawrence, read Blake through the lens of a Laurentian vitalist. Now, the day before we go into 2019, I find Percival the most useful of the three and more congenial to me than Frye because *Fearful Symmetry*, with all its brilliance, nevertheless is the work of a Protestant minister for whom the Incarnation is the basis of all human truth.

I am a little troubled by my own ingratitude because *Fearful Symmetry* was for me a holy book until I matured into a vision of literary influence inimical to Frye's rather generous sense of literary tradition. But my unhappiness with Frye came from an essay he published in 1957:

> The "Selfish father of men" who keeps Earth imprisoned is not God the Father, of course, but the false father that man visualizes as soon as he takes his mind off the Incarnation. To make God a Father is to make ourselves children: if we do this in the light of the Gospels, we see the world in the light of the state of innocence. But if we take the point of view of the child of ordinary experience, our God becomes a protection of ordinary childishness, a vision of undeveloped humanity. If we think of God as sulky, capricious, irritable, and mindlessly cruel, like Dante's primal love who made hell, or tied in knots of legal quibbles, like Milton's father-god, we may have a very awful divinity, but we have not got a very presentable human being. There is no excuse for keeping such a creature around when we have a clear revelation of God's human nature in the Gospels.
>
> ["Blake's Introduction to Experience"]

There is a fine line separating literary criticism from a United Church of Canada sermon, and I wondered if Frye had not crossed it. Not every reader of William Blake keeps her or his own mind on the Incarnation. I myself love the Tanakh or Hebrew Bible more than I possibly could care for Yahweh, since he has not kept his Covenant with us, whoever we are. Like William Blake I turn away from normative religion in favor of Hermetic tradition, Gnosticism, Neoplatonism, and Kabbalah, though not to occultism, again following Blake. Frye eloquently and humanely rejects Dante's so-called love that created hell and Milton's irascible God in *Paradise Lost*. But the final sentence of this paragraph grates me. Normally a master of tone, Frye sounds as though he is scolding, setting aside the question of the clarity of revelation in the Gospels. Which Gospel? Mark, which is marvelous, moves me to wonder. John, which is anti-Semitic, infuriates me. That the Spectre of Urthona is the man-in-the-poet as opposed to the poet-in-the-poet is a useful and accurate formulation. But why call him "the will," as Northrop Frye did? He is not a figure of desire but of anxiety, of anxious expectations. The Bhagavad Gita would see him as vacillating between passion and dark inertia, unable ever to achieve lucidity.

What directly precipitated my parting from Frye was one paragraph in *Fearful Symmetry:*

> The creative imagination perfects the form of its vision, and that vision may have a great influence on others, an influence which should be left to take care of itself. Once the artist thinks in terms of influence rather than of clarity of form, the effort of the imagination becomes an effort of will, and art is perverted into tyranny, the application of the principle of magic or mysterious compulsion to society. Here we come back to the opposition of visionary and hero, of the man who inspires with life as opposed to the man who inspires with death.

This is nobly phrased and is akin to T. S. Eliot's view of tradition and the individual talent. How can *any* poet avoid thinking in terms of influence? Even Shakespeare had to develop beyond his debts to Ovid, Chaucer, Marlowe, and the English Bible. He then became, in Blake's term, the Covering Cherub to John Milton, who assumed that role in regard to Blake. Frye's distinction between the will and the imagination is dubious, even in regard to Blake's own conceptualizations.

Allen Tate had a way of bothering me by saying that in Hart Crane the will tried to do the work of the imagination. We were on touchy enough terms, but once at dinner I asked Tate: "In your best poems—such as 'Ode to the Confederate Dead,' 'The Mediterranean,' 'Aeneas at Washington'—why is it that I hear your will to individuate wavering between the styles of T. S. Eliot and of Hart Crane?"

Tate frowned and was silent. Inwardly I regretted my remark, since he was thirty years my senior and I should have respected that. And yet the point is valid. It does not seem to me that the "will" is a Blakean notion. It certainly suits Shakespeare and, in an altogether different way, Schopenhauer, Nietzsche, William James, and Freud, but Blake *is* different. If you *see* as Blake did, then you need not will.

I return to Northrop Frye but just briefly. I cannot find William Blake's Jesus in the Gospels, not even in the enigmatic Mark. If Jesus is God and the only God, and so are you and I and Blake, then the Incarnation cannot be unique, a moment in and out of time. Aside from that, the Jesus of Mark is for Yahweh and Yahweh alone, though he is then forsaken by him. That also cannot be William Blake's Jesus.

It seems absurd for me to suggest that Frye absorbed Blake into a low church doctrine of the Incarnation. Frye was in Blake's own tradition of Protestant dissent, a lineage that included Milton, Bunyan, Vane, and the entire left wing of Cromwell's army. And yet Blake is so extraordinarily idiosyncratic that I would not even call him a sect of one, since his dialectic depends upon contraries in perpetual movement.

I turn finally to Blake's *Milton: A Poem in Two Books*, written between 1804 and 1810. Stand back and contemplate the outrageous audacity of Blake's project. Would John Milton have written *Spenser Agonistes?* Try to conceive of Wordsworth or Coleridge attempting an epic with Milton as the hero. Shelley was outrageous enough to try anything, but his urbanity and gentlemanly sense of decorum kept him from writing a *Wordsworth Bound*. But there was an imp in

Shelley, and in October 1819 he composed *Peter Bell the Third*, a dog-gerel devastating the turncoat Wordsworth (it could not be pub-lished until 1839, seventeen years after Shelley's drowning). Shelley used the pseudonym Miching Mallecho, Esq. His epigraphs are from Wordsworth and *Hamlet*:

Is it a party in a parlour,
Crammed just as they on earth were crammed,
Some sipping punch—some sipping tea;
But, as you by their faces see, or
All silent, and all—damned!
   Peter Bell, by w. wordsworth
Ophelia. — What means this, my lord?
Hamlet. — Marry, this is miching mallecho; it means
 mischief.
Here is the heart of Shelley's thrust:
He had a mind which was somehow
 At once circumference and centre
Of all he might or feel or know;
Nothing went ever out, although
 Something did ever enter.

He had as much imagination
 As a pint-pot; — he never could
Fancy another situation,
From which to dart his contemplation,
 Than that wherein he stood.

Yet his was individual mind,
 And new created all he saw
In a new manner, and refined
Those new creations, and combined
 Them, by a master-spirit's law.

Thus—though unimaginative—
 An apprehension clear, intense,
Of his mind's work, had made alive
The things it wrought on; I believe
 Wakening a sort of thought in sense.

But from the first 'twas Peter's drift
　　To be a kind of moral eunuch,
He touched the hem of Nature's shift,
Felt faint—and never dared uplift
　　The closest, all-concealing tunic.

She laughed the while, with an arch smile,
　　And kissed him with a sister's kiss,
And said—"My best Diogenes,
I love you well—but, if you please,
　　Tempt not again my deepest bliss.

"'Tis you are cold—for I, not coy,
　　Yield love for love, frank, warm, and true;
And Burns, a Scottish peasant boy—
His errors prove it—knew my joy
　　More, learnèd friend, than you."
　　　　　　　　　　　[Part Fourth (Sin), ll. 293–327]

The tribute to Robert Burns, splendidly lustful and active (he fathered twelve children and has a host of descendants) is apt and a good contrast to Wordsworth. Shelley did not know that Wordsworth, while in France during the Revolution, had a daughter with Annette Vallon and then fled back to England.

One can only conjecture other possibilities and improbabilities. I would like to think that in an archive somewhere is the text of a long poem on T. S. Eliot by Delmore Schwartz or a *Stevensiad* by the noble John Ashbery. But in the end only William Blake dared a visionary epic in which he is united with his great precursor.

"United" cannot be the precise word. Milton enters Blake, yet that is a self-purged Milton and a Blake who needs his forerunner to strengthen the later poet in an equally strenuous self-annihilation. The poem *Milton* could be judged overcondensed. It relies not only upon the reader's knowledge of John Milton's life and works but also on *The Four Zoas*, abandoned by Blake though certainly finished, and never engraved. *Milton*'s most troubling difficulty is that we need to know and understand Blake's sojourn, with his wife, Catherine, at Felpham, a village in Sussex, from 1800 to early 1804. Blake went there at the invitation of the poetaster William Hayley, who had been the friend and patron of the poet William Cowper. Hayley certainly meant well in regard to the Blakes. He settled them in a cottage near his home, and paid Blake generously to illustrate a *Life of Cowper* (published 1803–1804). But he sought to curb what he regarded as Blake's excesses in poetry and painting. Hayley rallied to Blake's sore need when John Scofield, a trooper, accused the great poet of violence and sedition. With Hayley's aid, Blake was acquitted. In those extreme circumstances, Blake seems to have indulged in a kind of paranoia. Something in him began to believe that Hayley regarded him as a problem in religious madness like that of William Cowper. The visionary poet and the insipid poetaster were so incompatible that the reader can benefit by contrasting the opening lines of Hayley's major poem *The Triumphs of Temper* (1781) with the opening of Blake's *Milton*:

The Mind's soft Guardian, who, tho' yet unsung,
Inspires with harmony the female tongue,
And gives, improving every tender grace,
The smile of angels to a mortal face;
Her powers I sing; and scenes of mental strife,
Which form the maiden for th' accomplish'd wife;
Where the sweet victor sees, with sparkling eyes,
Love her reward, and happiness her prize.
Daughters of Beauty, who the song inspire,
To your enchanting notes attune my lyre!
And O! if haply your soft hearts may gain
Or use, or pleasure from the motley strain,
Tho' formal critics, with a surly frown,
Deny your artless bard the laurel crown,
He still shall triumph, if ye deign to spread
Your sweeter myrtle round his honour'd head.

This is of a badness not to be believed. Even if you resist Blake's prophetic art, something in you must reverberate to the invocation that opens *Milton*:

Daughters of Beulah! Muses who inspire the Poet's Song,
Record the journey of immortal Milton thro' your Realms

Of terror & mild moony lustre, in soft sexual delusions
Of varied beauty, to delight the wanderer and repose
His burning thirst & freezing hunger! Come into my hand
By your mild power; descending down the Nerves of my
     right arm
From out the Portals of my Brain, where by your ministry
The Eternal Great Humanity Divine planted his Paradise,
And in it caus'd the Spectres of the Dead to take sweet form
In likeness of himself. Tell also of the False Tongue! vegetated
Beneath your land of shadows: of its sacrifices, and
Its offerings: even till Jesus, the image of the Invisible God,
Became its prey; a curse, an offering, and an atonement
For Death Eternal in the heavens of Albion, & before the Gates
Of Jerusalem his Emanation, in the heavens beneath Beulah.
                                                                [Plate 1]

What could William Hayley have done with that? What could
William Blake bear to think of *The Triumphs of Temper?* In fairness
to Hayley, the useful biography of him by Morchard Bishop, *Blake's
Hayley* (1951), makes clear how benignly he behaved throughout his
relationship with Blake. From Blake's perspective, a mutual ambivalence existed beneath the surface:

Thus Hayley on his toilette seeing the soap
Cries, "Homer is very much improved by Pope!"
          [Blake, *Apology for His Catalogue* (1809)]

Was I angry with Hayley who usd me so ill
Or can I be angry with Felphams old Mill
Or angry with Flaxman or Cromek or Stothard
Or poor Schiavonetti whom they to death botherd
Or angry with Macklin or Boydel or Bowyer
Because they did not say O what a Beau ye are
At a Friends Errors Anger shew
Mirth at the Errors of a Foe

Of H s birth this was the happy lot
His Mother on his Father him begot

When H——y finds out what you cannot do
That is the Very thing hell set you to
If you break not your Neck tis not his fault
But pecks of poison are not pecks of salt
And when he could not act upon my wife
Hired a Villain to bereave my Life

Thy Friendship oft has made my heart to ake
Do be my Enemy for Friendships sake

I write the Rascal Thanks till he & I
With Thanks & Compliments are quite drawn dry

Though vigorous, this is not exactly the Blake I love. Still, Blake was a poor man and had to live by his engraving abilities. Hayley rescued him but the patronage was too difficult to sustain. The Fates have been unkind to Hayley. Even his biographer titles the book *Blake's Hayley* ([1951], by Evelyn Morchard Bishop). Poor Hayley, who meant well, survives only in Blake.

The wretched Hayley also joined Blake's symbolic forms as Hyle, an invidious figure whose name plays upon a Greek word for "matter." One bids farewell to Hayley with a certain bittersweet regret, since he meant well but existed in a different cosmos from that inhabited by William Blake.

Epic irony undergoes metamorphoses as it moves from Homer to Virgil and on through Dante to Tasso, Spenser, Milton, Goethe, and the English Romantics. When you view irony as a diachronic trope, you discover that Homeric irony and Goethe's outrageous explosion of it in the second part of *Faust* are beyond reconciliation. In Virgil all is irony. An imperial epic that is Epicurean, the *Aeneid* owes almost as much to Lucretius as it does to Homer. Aeneas never escapes irony, from the loss of his first wife on through his abandonment of Dido to his slaughter of Turnus after that great warrior has been so stung by the Fury Allecto that he is hopelessly weakened.

But since Blake is an intellectual parodist, his epic ironies are incessant and virtually unlimited. It will always vex women readers of Blake to encounter his unfortunately named Female Will. Though he meant that malevolent will to be manifest in both men and women, he was inconsistent on this matter. I wish that he had called it the Natural Will, since sometimes that seems to be what he means. But something breaks loose in him. He fears female domination. There are speculations that he resented the competition of the remarkable Irish engraver Caroline Watson (1761–1814), who crowded him out from some vital commissions. Yet female power in Blake's epics courts sadomasochism and can be portrayed by him quite luridly.

In the poem *Milton* both Blake and Milton are literary characters, as are Dante the Pilgrim and Chaucer the Pilgrim in the *Commedia* and the *Tales of Canterbury*. Blake the Poet is overtly ironic in portraying Blake the man, and only a touch less ironic in portraying his precursor Milton. I accept that a feminist critic would have reservations about Blake as indeed about Milton, Dante, and Wordsworth. Catherine Blake in some ways owed everything to her husband: he taught her to read, write, draw, and color his engravings. The Blakes were childless, and there are dubious traditions that William once sought to bring another woman into the household. I see no evidence for this. How Blake could have had a better wife is beyond my imagination.

It is deliberately ironic that he seems to discount Ololon. As her name presumably indicates, a woman's ululation or crying-out to the divine can be either lamentation or rejoicing. Ololon progresses from a river of lamentation to a human virgin of twelve years who undergoes union with a renovated John Milton, who is partly fused with the historical figure William Blake, a man who suffered all our weaknesses, deprivations, forlorn expectations, yet ironically kept the Divine Vision in a time of troubles.

As Blake once wrote, he and Catherine ate little and drank less. On his deathbed, he made a sketch of her and called her his angel. At my age I am usually mourning some recently departed friend and so I have to fight against being sentimental.

I met the poet-critic John Crowe Ransom (1888–1974) only once, when I lectured at Kenyon College, from which he had retired some years before. The poems at their best remain wonderful, though the criticism I found alien to me. Ransom himself was charming and commended my book on Blake. In his doggerel "Survey of Literature," he strengthened my fear of sentimentality, though then I was quite young: "Then there was poor Willie Blake, / He foundered on sweet cake."

As John Ransom knew, Blake would have been very glad indeed to get hold of some sweet cake. All too often he wrote, painted, and engraved with no dinner. Sometimes I think my late friend David V. Erdman, who perfected our knowledge of Blake's text, understood Blake the man better than anyone else. David was a Nebraskan who stood on the extreme Left politically and socially, and was expelled by the union leadership from his position in the education department of the United Auto Workers. I recall conversations with David when I was working on my commentary to his Blake edition in which I ventured that perhaps the Anarchists rather than the Marxists were politically Blake's true heirs. Erdman, always whimsical, grinned his disagreement. I still think that, despite his idiosyncratic Christian stance, Blake possessed much in common with the Anarcho-Syndicalists of Catalonia who fought so gallantly against Franco and Spanish Fascism.

In a recent comment, David Bentley Hart gave the preference to the twentieth-century poet-painter David Jones (1895–1974) over Blake:

> As a poet, Jones was at least the equal of Blake (and certainly less prone to magnificent failures); as a visual artist, he was Blake's superior in every sense. Whereas Blake's best images are at most very arresting illustrations (often uncomfortably precursory of comic books), Jones's greatest paintings are endlessly absorbing products of an extravagantly rich and genuinely unique sensibility.
>
> ["The Lost Modernist" (2018)]

I am an admirer of David Bentley Hart, particularly for his translation of the New Testament. In 2014 I wrote a foreword to an edition of *In Parenthesis* by David Jones, expressing my fervent admiration for that extraordinary war poem and my warm memory of a visit to his home in London, at his invitation. Who am I to reprove Hart for hyperbole, as I am notoriously addicted to it? Still, Hart is rather too extravagant. It may be that Jones was the better visual artist, but William Blake is one of the six or seven major poets in the English language, and *The Four Zoas, Milton, Jerusalem* indeed are magnificent but distinctly not failures. David Jones was overpraised by W. H. Auden and others. I think *In Parenthesis, The Anathemata*, and *The Tribune's Visitation* are permanent poems and I vastly prefer them to Pound's *Cantos*, yet they are fragmentary and I would hesitate to surmise futurity's judgment of their eminence.

Despite the relatively high quality of critical scholarship that has been devoted to Blake's epics, they are unlikely ever to be read by the common reader. They are in the category of James Joyce's *Finnegans Wake*, a grand scripture doomed to an elitist audience. But then, the *Commedia, The Faerie Queene, Paradise Lost, Faust Part Two, The Prelude*, and other sublime works down to *Remembrance of Things Past* are now also fated to vanish beyond our horizons. We hold on to what we can.

In my old age I could wish that Blake had not elaborated so prodigiously. And yet he was isolated: "I am hid." Something in him had to fear he was speaking to himself only. John Milton had fit audience and actually more than a few even at the beginning. He spoke for the losing side even though it had won the Civil Wars. Even in disgrace, he remained a public figure. Blake was an autodidact. His tradition was lower-class Protestant dissent.

He still speaks for the wretched of the earth. I begin to think his deepest teaching is all but unbearable. Every morning at dawn I drink tea and try to read the *New York Times*. If I opened myself to all the suffering in those pages, I might cease to be. We survive by blocking the full range of our senses. Blake's prophecy stands against that desperate survival. To go on breathing we compromise ourselves. Blake indicts us:

> The ancient tradition that the world will be consumed in fire at the end of six thousand years is true, as I have heard from Hell.
>
> For the cherub with his flaming sword is hereby commanded to leave his guard at [the] tree of life, and when he does, the whole creation will be consumed and appear infinite and holy, whereas it now appears finite and corrupt.
>
> This will come to pass by an improvement of sensual enjoyment.

But first the notion that man has a body distinct from his soul is to be expunged; this I shall do by printing in the infernal method by corrosives, which in Hell are salutary and medicinal, melting apparent surfaces away, and displaying the infinite which was hid.

If the doors of perception were cleansed everything would appear to man as it is, infinite.

For man has closed himself up, till he sees all things through narrow chinks of his cavern.

[*The Marriage of Heaven and Hell*]

The late Aldous Huxley attempted to cleanse the doors of perception by absorbing psychedelic drugs. Alas, his novels have faded. In my youth I greatly enjoyed them but now they are period pieces. He was a remarkable essayist—his true gift—but *The Doors of Perception* (1954) and *Heaven and Hell* (1956) perplex and sadden me.

Aldous Huxley quested for what he called the perennial philosophy, which he quarried out of a grab bag that included Meister Eckhart, William Law, Shankara, St. John of the Cross, the Bhagavad Gita, Buddha, Christ, the Upanishads, and what you will. It is all very solemn, somber, sober, spiritual, where all things flow to all, like rivers to the sea. At least he did not recommend reading these sages while under the influence of sacred mushrooms and similar bits. I do not think that William Blake would have been much interested in the Huxleyan cleansing of perception.

Blake identified the enemy as reason, nature, and society. But by "reason" he meant Lockean reductionism and not cognition, in which Blake excelled. He did not mean the nature seen by him and by his painterly disciples Samuel Palmer and Edward Calvert, in which landscape is taken up into the imaginative mind. As to society, does that ever change? He set himself against autocratic and imperialist England, and he would reject the United States at its nadir in 2019.

I am hardly known to be a feminist literary critic, though I think I helped provoke several of them into their very useful labors. What troubles me now in my final return to William Blake is his stance toward sexual division and strife. His flaw is the Neoplatonist thrust in which the outering process becomes purely female. Neither Milton nor Blake, pragmatically speaking, is a misogynist. Unfortunately, both feminize the Creation/Fall. Hence Blake's obsession with the Female Will, which now seems to me a disfiguration, and is made manifest in his recoil from Chaucer's wonderful Wife of Bath. I wish he had further developed the Oothoon of *Visions of the Daughters of Albion*. Here his alternative tradition (Hermetic, Neoplatonic, Gnostic, Behmenite) served him ill. What could have saved him? Perhaps Shakespeare, but Milton challenged Blake more.

Fortunately Blake had a double vision of nature and could ascend into its celebration when appropriate:

> First eer the morning breaks joy opens in the flowery bosoms
> Joy even to tears, which the Sun rising dries; first the Wild
>   Thyme
> And Meadow-sweet downy & soft waving among the reeds.
> Light springing on the air lead the sweet Dance: they wake
> The Honeysuckle sleeping on the Oak: the flaunting beauty
> Revels along upon the wind; the White-thorn lovely May
> Opens her many lovely eyes: listening the Rose still sleeps
> None dare to wake her. soon she bursts her crimson curtaind bed
> And comes forth in the majesty of beauty; every Flower:
> The Pink, the Jessamine, the Wall-flower, the Carnation
> The Jonquil, the mild Lilly opes her heavens! every Tree,
> And Flower & Herb soon fill the air with an innumerable Dance
> Yet all in order sweet & lovely, Men are sick with Love!
> Such is a Vision of the lamentation of Beulah over Ololon.
>
> > [*Milton*, plate 31]

Beulah is the "married land" of Isaiah 62:4, which reads in the King James Version:

> It shall no more be said unto thee, Forsaken, neither shall it
> be said anymore to thy land, Desolate, but thou shalt be
> called Hephzibah, and thy land Beulah: for the Lord delight-
> eth in thee, and thy land shalt have an husband.

John Bunyan and Blake after him render Beulah as a kind of earthly paradise, a garden neither of Heaven nor of the unfallen

Eden. This is as close as Blake ever comes to a redemptive vision of the feminine aspect of the human. There is something harshly sublime about the descent of Blake's John Milton:

> And Milton collecting all his fibres into impregnable strength
> Descended down a Paved work of all kinds of precious stones
> Out from the eastern sky; descending down into my Cottage
> Garden: clothed in black, severe & silent he descended.
>
> The Spectre of Satan stood upon the roaring sea & beheld
> Milton within his sleeping Humanity! trembling & shuddring
> He stood upon the waves a Twenty-seven-fold mighty Demon
> Gorgeous & beautiful: loud roll his thunders against Milton
> Loud Satan thunderd, loud & dark upon mild Felpham shore
> Not daring to touch one fibre he howld round upon the Sea.
>
> I also stood in Satans bosom & beheld its desolations!
> A ruind Man: a ruind building of God not made with hands;
> Its plains of burning sand, its mountains of marble terrible:
> Its pits & declivities flowing with molten ore & fountains
> Of pitch & nitre: its ruind palaces & cities & mighty works;
> Its furnaces of affliction in which his Angels & Emanations
> Labour with blackend visages among its stupendous ruins
> Arches & pyramids & porches colonades & domes:
> In which dwells Mystery Babylon, here is her secret place
> From hence she comes forth on the Churches in delight
> Here is her Cup filld with its poisons, in these horrid vales
> And here her scarlet Veil woven in pestilence & war:
> Here is Jerusalem bound in chains, in the Dens of Babylon.
>
> [Milton, plate 38]

This makes me uncomfortable though it is superbly expressed. I think Blake, who rejected so much of orthodoxy, could well have avoided Revelation's Whore of Babylon. But I cannot cavil at Milton's grand affirmation:

> To bathe in the Waters of Life; to wash off the Not Human
> I come in Self-annihilation & the grandeur of Inspiration
> To cast off Rational Demonstration by Faith in the Saviour

To cast off the rotten rags of Memory by Inspiration
To cast off Bacon, Locke & Newton from Albions covering
To take off his filthy garments, & clothe him with Imagination
To cast aside from Poetry, all that is not Inspiration
That it no longer shall dare to mock with the aspersion of
    Madness
Cast on the Inspired, by the tame high finisher of paltry Blots,
Indefinite, or paltry Rhymes; or paltry Harmonies.
Who creeps into State Government like a catterpiller to destroy
To cast off the idiot Questioner who is always questioning,
But never capable of answering; who sits with a sly grin
Silent plotting when to question, like a thief in a cave;
Who publishes doubt & calls it knowledge; whose Science is
    Despair
Whose pretence to knowledge is Envy, whose whole Science is
To destroy the wisdom of ages to gratify ravenous Envy;
That rages round him like a Wolf day & night without rest
He smiles with condescension; he talks of Benevolence & Virtue
And those who act with Benevolence & Virtue, they murder
    time on time
These are the destroyers of Jerusalem, these are the murderers
Of Jesus, who deny the Faith & mock at Eternal Life:
Who pretend to Poetry that they may destroy Imagination;
By imitation of Natures Images drawn from Remembrance
These are the Sexual Garments, the Abomination of Desolation
Hiding the Human lineaments as with an Ark & Curtains
Which Jesus rent: & now shall wholly purge away with Fire
Till Generation is swallowd up in Regeneration.

                                   [*Milton*, plate 41]

If that should be my final quotation from Blake, I am content. I could wish he had taught not only the prevalence of the Idiot Questioner but how to cast it out. That is a necessary hazard of deep reading.

    The reader ideally is as free to read now as before. That is clearly an untruth. I get through the weekend *Times* in less than half an hour. There is nothing for me to absorb. Etymologically, "absorption" means inbreathing. One might hope that many among us read to breathe more deeply and to take the breath within as a benison.

CHAPTER FOUR

William Wordsworth and John Keats
Something Evermore About to Be

M ILTON'S BELIAL, LAMENTING IN Shakespearean accents the possible loss of thoughts that wander through
eternity, contributes vitally to Wordsworth and to
Keats:

> Visionary power
> Attends the motions of the viewless winds,
> Embodied in the mystery of words:
> There, darkness makes abode, and all the host
> Of shadowy things work endless changes,—there,
> As in a mansion like their proper home,
> Even forms and substances are circumfused
> By that transparent veil with light divine,
> And, through the turnings intricate of verse,
> Present themselves as objects recognised,
> In flashes, and with glory not their own.
>   [Wordsworth, *The Prelude* (1850), 5.595–605]

Away! away! for I will fly to thee,
    Not charioted by Bacchus and his pards,

But on the viewless wings of Poesy,
        Though the dull brain perplexes and retards:
Already with thee! tender is the night,
        And haply the Queen-Moon is on her throne,
                Cluster'd around by all her starry Fays;
                But here there is no light,
Save what from heaven is with the breezes blown
        Through verdurous glooms and winding mossy ways.
                                [Keats, "Ode to a Nightingale"]

Beth Lau, in her *Keats's "Paradise Lost"* (1998), studies his marginalia and notices only two negative comments: "Hell is finer than
this," and "Had not Shakespeare liv'd?" in response to 9.47, where
Milton credits his muse with inspiring, in Keats's words, "all that is
valuable in the poem." I am delighted to follow Keats's tracks in the
snow, as there was no better reader of William Shakespeare.

The radiant originality of John Keats is all the more remarkable
because he consciously worked in the hope of becoming a fourth
with Shakespeare, Milton, Wordsworth, and against Byron and Shelley, rather resenting their exaltation of the self. Whereas Shelley
was caught between two of the prime images of Western poetry—
the Fire for which all thirst and the Chariot (*Merkabah* in biblical
Hebrew, perhaps interpretable as "the Body of Spiritual Light")—
Keats at twenty-one seemed to see this image as a mark joining the
human and the poetic in continuity:

And can I ever bid these joys farewell?
Yes, I must pass them for a nobler life,
Where I may find the agonies, the strife
Of human hearts: for lo! I see afar,
O'er sailing the blue cragginess, a car
And steeds with streamy manes—the charioteer
Looks out upon the winds with glorious fear . . .
                ["Sleep and Poetry" (written 1816), ll. 122–128]

Wordsworth was an impatient auditor of Keats's "Hymn to Pan"
from *Endymion* (1818). His reaction was: "A very pretty piece of pa-
ganism, Mr. Keats." But then Wordsworth was always interested in

reciting reams of his own poetry even if his listeners suffered. Ralph Waldo Emerson, visiting Wordsworth, came away somewhat annoyed at being a captive audience. Keats's characterization of Wordsworth as the Egotistical Sublime remains highly useful.

One of my closest friendships, extending from 1955 to 2016, was with Geoffrey Hartman, a scholar-critic whose erudition, balance in judgment, and immense care in reading closely exceeded my own. Geoffrey, who came first to England and then to the United States, had been a child refugee from Nazi Germany. Genial and wise, he had a calm I envied but by temperament could not emulate.

Geoffrey taught me to read Wordsworth, his great love among the poets. Part of the teaching came through discussions across more than sixty years; the other from studying his major work, *Wordsworth's Poetry: 1787–1814* (1964). Hartman's devotion to Wordsworth was so great he argued against my conviction that everything truly permanent in the founder of modern poetry was the work of just one decade (1797–1807). So jealous was Geoffrey on his favorite poet's behalf that he deprecated the work of Coleridge and its importance to Wordsworth's development.

Wordsworth is so large a poet that it can be useful to approach him through a variety of perspectives. Hartman's angle of vision played consciousness against nature and therefore followed the tradition of A. C. Bradley rather than of Matthew Arnold. An admirer of Bradley since my youth, I have never taken to Arnold's criticism or to his poetry.

For me the central poem in Wordsworth is a passage he printed as a *Prospectus* to *The Excursion*. It is an extract from *Home at Grasmere* (written 1800–1806):

> —To these emotions, whencesoe'er they come,
> Whether from breath of outward circumstance,
> Or from the Soul—an impulse to herself,
> I would give utterance in numerous Verse.
> —Of Truth, of Grandeur, Beauty, Love, and Hope—
> And melancholy Fear subdued by Faith;
> Of blessed consolations in distress;
> Of moral strength, and intellectual power;
> Of joy in widest commonalty spread;

Of the individual Mind that keeps her own
Inviolate retirement, subject there
To Conscience only, and the law supreme
Of that Intelligence which governs all;
I sing:—"fit audience let me find though few!"
    So prayed, more gaining than he asked, the Bard,
Holiest of Men.—Urania, I shall need
Thy guidance, or a greater Muse, if such
Descend to earth or dwell in highest heaven!
For I must tread on shadowy ground, must sink
Deep—and, aloft ascending, breathe in worlds
To which the heaven of heavens is but a veil.
All strength—all terror, single or in bands,
That ever was put forth in personal form;
Jehovah—with his thunder, and the choir
Of shouting Angels, and the empyreal thrones,
I pass them, unalarmed. Not Chaos, not
The darkest pit of lowest Erebus,
Nor aught of blinder vacancy, scooped out
By help of dreams, can breed such fear and awe
As fall upon us often when we look
Into our Minds, into the Mind of Man,
My haunt, and the main region of my Song,
—Beauty—a living Presence of the earth,
Surpassing the most fair ideal Forms
Which craft of delicate Spirits hath composed
From earth's materials—waits upon my steps;
Pitches her tents before me as I move,
An hourly neighbour. Paradise, and groves
Elysian, Fortunate Fields—like those of old
Sought in the Atlantic Main, why should they be
A history only of departed things,
Or a mere fiction of what never was?
For the discerning intellect of Man,
When wedded to this goodly universe
In love and holy passion, shall find these
A simple produce of the common day.
—I, long before the blissful hour arrives,

Would chant, in lonely peace, the spousal verse
Of this great consummation:—and, by words
Which speak of nothing more than what we are,
Would I arouse the sensual from their sleep
Of Death, and win the vacant and the vain
To noble raptures; while my voice proclaims
How exquisitely the individual Mind
(And the progressive powers perhaps no less
Of the whole species) to the external World
Is fitted:—and how exquisitely, to
Theme this but little heard of among Men,
The external World is fitted to the Mind;
And the creation (by no lower name
Can it be called) which they with blended might
Accomplish:—this is our high argument.

[ll. 10–71]

Milton and Shakespeare are invoked here, as is the Bible, since Wordsworth wishes to emulate and to challenge all three. William Blake made some anxiously aggressive annotations on this *Prospectus:*

[Lines 31–35] All strength, all terror, single or in bands
That ever was put forth in personal Form
Jehovah—with his thunder & the choir
Of shouting Angels & the empyreal thrones—
I pass them unalarmed, . . .

Solomon when he married Pharohs daughter & became a Convert to the Heathen Mythology Talked exactly in this way of Jehovah as a Very inferior object of Mans Contemplations he also passed him by unalarmed & was permitted. Jehovah dropped a tear & followd him by his Spirit into the Abstract Void it is called the Divine Mercy Satan dwells in it but Mercy does not dwell in him he knows not to Forgive

[Lines 63–68] How exquisitely the individual Mind
(And the progressive powers perhaps no less
(Of the whole species) to the external World

Is fitted.—& how exquisitely too.
Theme this but little heard of among Men
The external World is fitted to the Mind.

You shall not bring me down to believe such fitting & fitted
I know now better & Please your Lordship

[Lines 71–82]   —Such grateful haunts forgoing. if I oft
                 Must turn elsewhere—to travel near the tribes
                 And fellowships of men, and see ill sights
                 Of madding passions mutually inflamd
                 Must hear *Humanity in fields and groves*
                 Pope solitary anguish; or must hang
                 Brooding above the fierce confederate storm
                 Of Sorrow barricaded evermore
                 Within the walls of cities; may these sounds
                 Have their authentic comment—that even these
                 Hearing I be not downcast nor forlorn

Does not this Fit & is it not Fitting most Exquisitely too but
to what not Mind but to the Vile Body only & to its Laws of
Good & Evil & its Enmities against Mind.

Wordsworth could have made nothing of this. Students of
Blake may find the first annotation somewhat ambiguous since the
poet of *The Book of Urizen* had no love for Jehovah. The remainder
is clear enough. Blake speaks both as an unreconstructed Cockney rebel against the established order and as a prophet who regards the external world as hindrance, not action, and therefore
no part of him.

Even in his darker, later years Wordsworth felt violated at the
thought nature would not recompense the heart that loved her. For
Geoffrey Hartman, Wordsworthian nature is a purgation for the
imagination. I agree with my departed friend that this seems a
variety of negative theology. You can describe God only by what
he is not. Wordsworth after 1807 seems to describe nature mostly
by what is not.

Was Wordsworth ever a "poet of nature"? His younger contemporary John Clare better merits that description, as here in "Badger":

When midnight comes a host of dogs and men
Go out and track the badger to his den,
And put a sack within the hole, and lie
Till the old grunting badger passes bye.
He comes and hears—they let the strongest loose.
The old fox hears the noise and drops the goose.
The poacher shoots and hurries from the cry,
And the old hare half wounded buzzes bye.
They get a forked stick to bear him down
And clap the dogs and take him to the town,
And bait him all the day with many dogs,
And laugh and shout and fright the scampering hogs.
He runs along and bites at all he meets:
They shout and hollo down the noisy streets.

He turns about to face the loud uproar
And drives the rebels to their very door.
The frequent stone is hurled where'er they go;
When badgers fight, then everyone's a foe.
The dogs are clapt and urged to join the fray;
The badger turns and drives them all away.
Though scarcely half as big, demure and small,
He fights with dogs for bones and beats them all.
The heavy mastiff, savage in the fray,
Lies down and licks his feet and turns away.
The bulldog knows his match and waxes cold,
The badger grins and never leaves his hold.
He drives the crowd and follows at their heels
And bites them through—the drunkard swears and reels.

The frighted women take the boys away,
The blackguard laughs and hurries on the fray.
He tries to reach the woods, and awkward race,
But sticks and cudgels quickly stop the chace.

He turns agen and drives the noisy crowd
And beats the many dogs in noises loud.
He drives away and beats them every one,
And then they loose them all and set them on.
He falls as dead and kicked by boys and men,
Then starts and grins and drives the crowd agen;
Till kicked and torn and beaten out he lies
And leaves his hold and cackles, groans, and dies.

Chanting this aloud is akin to watching a Roman candle rise up and burst. Your sympathy is with the fighting spirit of the badger and not with the dogs and men. Yet all is natural, too natural. Clare describes vividly, takes no side, and is one with his poem.

"Badger" is a wonderful poem by any standards. John Clare was a unique poet, a farm laborer, who attempted to support a wife and seven children through the sale of his poems. This proved not possible and patronage sustained him for a while. Mentally unstable, he underwent a number of confinements and finally yielded to the delusion that he was Shakespeare and Lord Byron as well as John Clare. He appreciated Wordsworth and Keats yet is very different from either. When I was young he seemed a kind of Wordsworth, but that mistaken notion abandoned me long ago. His poem that disturbs me most is the strangely Blakean "Song: Secret Love."

I hid my love when young till I
Couldn't bear the buzzing of a fly;
I hid my love to my despite
Till I could not bear to look at light:
I dare not gaze upon her face
But left her memory in each place;
Where eer I saw a wild flower lie
I kissed and bade my love good bye.

I met her in the greenest dells
Where dewdrops pearl the wood blue bells
The lost breeze kissed her bright blue eye,
The bee kissed and went singing by,
A sunbeam found a passage there,

A gold chain round her neck so fair;
As secret as the wild bee's song
She lay there all the summer long.

I hid my love in field and town
Till een the breeze would knock me down;
The bees seemed singing ballads oer,
The fly's bass turned a lion's roar;
And even silence found a tongue,
To haunt me all the summer long;
The riddle nature could not prove
Was nothing else but secret love.

One thinks of Blake's Sun-flower and of his sick Rose:

Ah Sun-flower! weary of time,
Who countest the steps of the Sun:
Seeking after that sweet golden clime
Where the travellers journey is done.

Where the Youth pined away with desire,
And the pale Virgin shrouded in snow:
Arise from their graves and aspire,
Where my Sun-flower wishes to go.

***

O Rose thou art sick.
The invisible worm,
That flies in the night
In the howling storm:

Has found out thy bed
Of crimson joy:
And his dark secret love
Does thy life destroy.

[*Songs of Innocence and Experience* (1789)]

What Shelley called "the ruin that is love's shadow" Blake names
as the Spectre. In Blake the Spectre is the shadow of the Self. The
Spectre was intended to guard inwardness but instead menaces by

keeping all otherness away. Geoffrey Hartman perhaps overpraises John Clare since Blake gives us a plethora of glories showing the Spectre:

> The single most beautiful depiction of that Spectre is, however, John Clare's poem beginning "I hid my love when young till I/ Couldn't bear the buzzing of a fly," in which the repressed or displaced love rises up in the forms of nature against the lover.
>
> [*Wordsworth's Poetry*]

I remember telling Geoffrey that I shared his admiration, but then I quoted:

> They are become like wintry flocks like forests stripd of leaves
> The opressed pursue like the wind there is no room for escape
> The Spectre of Enitharmon let loose on the troubled deep
> Waild shrill in the confusion & the Spectre of Urthona
> Recievd her in the darkning South their bodies lost they stood
> Trembling & weak a faint embrace a fierce desire as when
> Two shadows mingle on a wall they wail & shadowy tears
> Fell down & shadowy forms of joy mixd with despair & grief
> Their bodies buried in the ruins of the Universe
> Mingled with the confusion. Who shall call them from the
>   Grave.
>
> [*The Four Zoas*, 9.22–31]

That similitude: "as when / Two shadows mingle on a wall" is beyond John Clare's scope. Since Clare, even in his madness, remained a devout Anglican, the freedom of the prophet-poet was beyond him.

Wordsworth in his long freeze (1807–1850) was happy to be Anglican. Here is one of the results:

> Yet more,—round many a Convent's blazing fire
> Unhallowed threads of revelry are spun;
> There Venus sits disguisèd like a Nun,—
> While Bacchus, clothed in semblance of a Friar,

Pours out his choicest beverage high and higher
Sparkling, until it cannot choose but run
Over the bowl, whose silver lip hath won
An instant kiss of masterful desire—
To stay the precious waste. Through every brain
The domination of the sprightly juice
Spreads high conceits to madding Fancy dear,
Till the arched roof, with resolute abuse
Of its grave echoes, swells a choral strain,
Whose votive burthen is—"OUR KINGDOM'S HERE!"
    [*Ecclesiastical Sonnets*, 20, "Monastic Voluptuousness"]

Does one laugh or weep? This is Wordsworth 1821–1822. In 1839 he composed *Sonnets upon the Punishment of Death*, calling for more and swifter hangings of supposed malefactors in the desperate working class:

IS "Death," when evil against good has fought
With such fell mastery that a man may dare
By deeds the blackest purpose to lay bare?
Is Death, for one to that condition brought,
For him, or any one, the thing that ought
To be "most" dreaded? Lawgivers, beware,
Lest, capital pains remitting till ye spare
The murderer, ye, by sanction to that thought
Seemingly given, debase the general mind;
Tempt the vague will tried standards to disown,
Nor only palpable restraints unbind,
But upon Honour's head disturb the crown,
Whose absolute rule permits not to withstand
In the weak love of life his least command.
    [*Sonnets upon the Punishment of Death*, 4]

This is the poet who gave us *The Prelude*, "Intimations of Immortality," "Tintern Abbey," "Resolution and Independence," "Michael," "The Old Cumberland Beggar," and "The Tale of Margaret." We know *how* this debacle happened but not *why*. What can be surmised?

CHAPTER FIVE

Wordsworth
The Myth of Memory

THE GREAT DECADE, 1797–1807, involved what I go on calling a Myth of Memory. In his primordial power as a poet, Wordsworth was possessed by memory. Epiphanies termed "spots of time," moments of inherent excellence though darkly dreary to the young Wordsworth, returned with recuperative force after an interval. They became evidences of the power of the creative mind *over* what John Milton had called "a universe of death."

I suspect Wordsworth the poet could see and rejoice only in what he had estranged from himself. He had to alienate himself from nature and then derive rapture from the healing *ricorso* that recalled an earlier covenant with the external world.

Though I have been chided for this contention, I continue in my belief that Wordsworth hopes to save neither nature nor his own imagination, but to save himself from his awe, veneration, and ambivalent love for Milton. Still, for him the vital element in self was what he and Coleridge called imagination. Since his faith was that, in childhood, nature and imagination reconciled in him, I am aware that my distinction is disputable.

In his poetry Wordsworth tends to think by association, both temporal and spatial. His central poem for many readers remains "Tintern Abbey" (1798):

Five years have past; five summers, with the length
Of five long winters! and again I hear
These waters, rolling from their mountain-springs
With a soft inland murmur.—Once again
Do I behold these steep and lofty cliffs,
That on a wild secluded scene impress
Thoughts of more deep seclusion; and connect
The landscape with the quiet of the sky.
The day is come when I again repose
Here, under this dark sycamore, and view
These plots of cottage-ground, these orchard-tufts,
Which at this season, with their unripe fruits,
Are clad in one green hue, and lose themselves
'Mid groves and copses. Once again I see
These hedge-rows, hardly hedge-rows, little lines
Of sportive wood run wild: these pastoral farms,
Green to the very door; and wreaths of smoke
Sent up, in silence, from among the trees!
With some uncertain notice, as might seem
Of vagrant dwellers in the houseless woods,
Or of some Hermit's cave, where by his fire
The Hermit sits alone.

[ll. 1–22]

Four times in the opening verse paragraph of Wordsworth's return to the banks of the Wye, we hear "again" or "once again."

In a finer tone (I hope) than before, I want to meditate upon the surprise wreaths of smoke surmised by Wordsworth (in a second thought) to emanate from the fire in some Hermit's cave, a phantasmagoria in this landscape. Since the poet immediately after speaks of "a landscape to a blind man's eye," it is plausible that two allusions flow together:

And may at last my weary age
Find out the peaceful hermitage,
The hairy gown and mossy cell,
Where I may sit and rightly spell
Of every star that Heav'n doth shew,
And every herb that sips the dew;
Till old experience do attain
To something like prophetic strain.

[Milton, "Il Penseroso" (1645, written 1632), ll.
167–174]

Thus with the Year
Seasons return; but not to me returns
Day, or the sweet approach of even or morn,
Or sight of vernal bloom, or summer's rose,
Or flocks, or herds, or human face divine;
But cloud instead and ever-during dark
Surrounds me, from the cheerful wayes of men
Cut off, and, for the book of knowledge fair
Presented with a universal blank
Of Nature's works, to me expunged and rased,
And wisdom at one entrance quite shut out.

[*Paradise Lost*, 3.40–50]

The poetry of John Milton, deeply embedded in Wordsworth's consciousness, invades "these beauteous forms" of landscape unseen by the poet-prophet in both senses of seeing. Reading Wordsworth's biographers, I wonder how many "little, nameless, unremembered, acts / Of kindness and of love" were performed by the future laureate. There is an impressive departure from Milton in Wordsworth's quietistic or mystical Sublime in "Tintern Abbey":

we are laid asleep
In body, and become a living soul:
While with an eye made quiet by the power
Of harmony, and the deep power of joy,
We see into the life of things.

It cannot be accidental that the figure of the Hermit is followed by an intimation of allusion to the invocation of Book 3, *Paradise Lost:*

These beauteous forms,
Through a long absence, have not been to me
As is a landscape to a blind man's eye:
But oft, in lonely rooms, and 'mid the din
Of towns and cities, I have owed to them,
In hours of weariness, sensations sweet,
Felt in the blood, and felt along the heart;
And passing even into my purer mind
With tranquil restoration:—feelings too
Of unremembered pleasure: such, perhaps,
As have no slight or trivial influence
On that best portion of a good man's life,
His little, nameless, unremembered, acts
Of kindness and of love. Nor less, I trust,
To them I may have owed another gift,
Of aspect more sublime; that blessed mood,
In which the burthen of the mystery,
In which the heavy and the weary weight
Of all this unintelligible world,
Is lightened:—that serene and blessed mood,
In which the affections gently lead us on,—
Until, the breath of this corporeal frame
And even the motion of our human blood
Almost suspended, we are laid asleep
In body, and become a living soul:
While with an eye made quiet by the power
Of harmony, and the deep power of joy,
We see into the life of things.

[ll. 23–50]

After seventy years of reading and brooding upon this, it no longer seems esoteric to me. I think that most of us, particularly in youth, have known several such moments, or at least think we remember them. Were they illusions? It cannot be. There was a

time when what we saw seemed larger, fresher, more intensely
colored than what we see now. Wordsworth is anxious about his
own belief but turns to pragmatic consequences of remembered
glories:

> And now, with gleams of half-extinguished thought,
> With many recognitions dim and faint,
> And somewhat of a sad perplexity,
> The picture of the mind revives again:
> While here I stand, not only with the sense
> Of present pleasure, but with pleasing thoughts
> That in this moment there is life and food
> For future years. And so I dare to hope . . .
>
> . . .
>   For I have learned
> To look on nature, not as in the hour
> Of thoughtless youth; but hearing oftentimes
> The still sad music of humanity,
> Nor harsh nor grating, though of ample power
> To chasten and subdue.—And I have felt
> A presence that disturbs me with the joy
> Of elevated thoughts; a sense sublime
> Of something far more deeply interfused,
> Whose dwelling is the light of setting suns,
> And the round ocean and the living air,
> And the blue sky, and in the mind of man:
> A motion and a spirit, that impels
> All thinking things, all objects of all thought,
> And rolls through all things.
>
>   [ll. 60–67, 100–104]

The complete title is crucial: "Lines Composed a Few Miles
above Tintern Abbey, on *Revisiting* the Banks of the Wye during a
Tour. July 13, 1798." The italics are mine. The renewal of sound and
sight after five years seems to astonish the poet. Priority is given to
the "soft inland murmur" of the river Wye. The "Intimations" ode
(1807, written 1804) elaborates on this trope:

Hence in a season of calm weather
Though inland far we be,
Our Souls have sight of that immortal sea
Which brought us hither,
Can in a moment travel thither,
And see the Children sport upon the shore,
And hear the mighty waters rolling evermore.

A Platonic coloring, less evident in "Tintern Abbey," is an aspect that the Great Ode cannot fully work through. The Platonist Ralph Waldo Emerson, in his *Nature* (1836), employs Wordsworth as starting point for a leap into the more radical American Sublime:

Standing on the bare ground, my head bathed by the blithe air, and uplifted into infinite space,—all mean egotism vanishes. I become a transparent eye-ball; I am nothing; I see all; the currents of the Universal Being circulate through me; I am part or particle of God.

But Emerson turned away from Wordsworth because any myth of memory was abhorrent to him, as David Bromwich has emphasized. In the Wordsworthian vista, without memory we cannot be renovated.

For a while "Tintern Abbey" became a battleground. A medley of nouveau historicists, Marxists, would-be ecologists, and other fashionable lemmings battered the defenseless poem so vehemently that the splendidly sane Helen Vendler had to wonder what poem they were reading. Wordsworth indubitably was a coward in abandoning his mistress and their daughter during the French Revolution. He fled back to England and did not see his child or her mother, Annette Vallon, until 1802, when he met them in Calais and went for a walk along the beach with Caroline, who by then was nine years of age.

He had come to tell them of his forthcoming marriage to Mary Hutchinson. Belatedly but generously Wordsworth made a substantial financial agreement with Annette Vallon, so as to provide for her and Caroline.

I do not think I will ever comprehend Wordsworth's personality. Here is the poignant sonnet he wrote in August 1802 to commemorate his meeting with his daughter:

It is a beauteous Evening, calm and free,
The holy time is quiet as a Nun
Breathless with adoration; the broad sun
Is sinking down in its tranquility;
The gentleness of heaven is on the Sea;
Listen! the mighty Being is awake,
And doth with his eternal motion make
A sound like thunder—everlastingly.
Dear Child! dear Girl! that walkest with me here,
If thou appear'st untouch'd by solemn thought,
Thy nature is not therefore less divine:
Thou liest in Abraham's bosom all the year;
And worshipp'st at the Temple's inner shrine,
God being with thee when we know it not.

[Published 1807]

There is no more persuasive poem than this for establishing Wordsworth's natural piety, except for "Tintern Abbey," to which I return:

Therefore am I still
A lover of the meadows and the woods
And mountains; and of all that we behold
From this green earth; of all the mighty world
Of eye, and ear,—both what they half create,
And what perceive . . .

[ll. 104–109]

The enigmatic crux here is "half create." How can eye or ear only half create what does not reach them through perception or hearing? Wordsworth's implied answer is memory, supposed storehouse of images and sounds. The somewhat Shakespearean formula "remembering to forget" is what Sigmund Freud called *Verdrängung*, mistranslated as "repression" since that gives an inadequate impression of the violent drive involved. Wordsworthian memory is a romance of nature, a fantastic storytelling in which the collaborators are the poet and misremembered nature. The forms remembered are created half by Wordsworth and half by a distanced nature bordering upon a phantasmagoria.

That may seem a somewhat remote way of commenting upon a poem of passionate renovation and subdued distress at the loss of a heightened vision Wordsworth once enjoyed. My anxiety is that the diction of analysis might dim my own youthful memories of how strongly Wordsworth affected me in my twenties.

And yet, in my old age, I am overwhelmingly moved by a poem I have always loved and yet feared, "The Old Cumberland Beggar" (1800, written 1798), which concludes,

And, long as he can wander, let him breathe
The freshness of the vallies, let his blood
Struggle with frosty air and winter snows,
And let the charter'd wind that sweeps the heath
Beat his grey locks against his wither'd face.
Reverence the hope whose vital anxiousness
Gives the last human interest to his heart.
May never House, misnamed of industry,
Make him a captive; for that pent-up din,
Those life-consuming sounds that clog the air,
Be his the natural silence of old age.
Let him be free of mountain solitudes,
And have around him, whether heard or not,
The pleasant melody of woodland birds.
Few are his pleasures; if his eyes, which now
Have been so long familiar with the earth,
No more behold the horizontal sun
Rising or setting, let the light at least
Find a free entrance to their languid orbs.
And let him, *where* and *when* he will, sit down
Beneath the trees, or by the grassy bank
Of high-way side, and with the little birds
Share his chance-gather'd meal, and, finally,
As in the eye of Nature he has liv'd,
So in the eye of Nature let him die.

By normative moral standards this poem is an outrage, though somehow its critics overlook that. But that, I think, is to miss "The Old Cumberland Beggar" entirely.

Best to start far back with the question, What was it that provoked the Wordsworth of 1797 to dark images of human retrogres-
sion: beggary, idiocy, homeless wandering, deserted wives, lost
children? For that uncanny young poet, what you and I might call
images of estranged life could be images of the natural man or
woman somehow in harmony with the external world. Himself sep-
arated, by his own freedom, from consciousness of the past, the poet
of nature searches out the signature of all things in the outcast, the
lost child, the insane, the incredibly aged. His poetic reward, and
ours, is to intimate a gathering mortality to which he and we can be
reconciled.

"The Old Cumberland Beggar" has an ethos and ruggedness
with few parallels in Western literature. As I recite it I have to think
of Tolstoy, particularly in *The Cossacks*, *Hadji Murad*, and the episodes of *War and Peace* that describe the captivity of Pierre and of
Platon Karataev, wise and patient peasant who is executed by the
French. Wordsworth's ultra-senescent Cumberland beggar has nothing in common with Cossack and Avar warriors or with a saintly
Russian serf, but Tolstoy and Wordsworth have authentic affinities.

Since moving into my ninetieth year a few weeks ago, I find myself reading Wordsworth in a more primordial way than did my
mentors. What happens when you compare Wordsworth's "To a
Cuckoo," composed in 1802, to Shelley's "To a Skylark" (1820)?

O blithe New-comer! I have heard,
I hear thee and rejoice.
O Cuckoo! shall I call thee Bird,
Or but a wandering Voice?

While I am lying on the grass
Thy twofold shout I hear;
From hill to hill it seems to pass,
At once far off, and near.

Though babbling only to the Vale
Of sunshine and of flowers,
Thou bringest unto me a tale
Of visionary hours.

Thrice welcome, darling of the Spring!
Even yet thou art to me
No bird, but an invisible thing,
A voice, a mystery;

The same whom in my school-boy days
I listened to; that Cry
Which made me look a thousand ways
In bush, and tree, and sky.

To seek thee did I often rove
Through woods and on the green;
And thou wert still a hope, a love;
Still longed for, never seen.

And I can listen to thee yet;
Can lie upon the plain
And listen, till I do beget
That golden time again.

O blessèd Bird! the earth we pace
Again appears to be
An unsubstantial, faery place;
That is fit home for Thee!

At about this time Wordsworth wrote the opening four stanzas of the "Ode: Intimations of Immortality from Recollections of Early Childhood." It took five years to finish the ode, and Wordsworth could not resolve all the difficulties of the poem. The charm and wonder of "To a Cuckoo" is how freely the poet leaps over difficulties and experiences the joyous immediacy he had known before.

Can you sing face to face with a present joy? The question is slippery. Coleridge had doubts and qualms. Blake and Wordsworth found it difficult. John Clare, glad for anything he could find, in his madness identified himself with Lord Byron. Wallace Stevens wrote: "It was difficult to sing in the face of the object." I fall back on Shakespeare. The songs in his plays frequently sing gloriously, confronting the occasion and the person. Shakespeare is Shakespeare. This is hardly to be considered a limitation in all but the greatest of poets.

CHAPTER SIX

Percy Bysshe Shelley and
George Gordon, Lord Byron

Serpent and Eagle

BYRON AND SHELLEY BECAME one another's closest friends. It was a difficult relationship and more productive for Byron than for Shelley. In the long cavalcade of literary friendships between major writers, from Hellenistic Alexandria to the present day, the Byron/Shelley pairing is much the most significant. Many useful accounts of it are available and I will not sketch it here. Eventually it became a burden for Shelley, but the two men were too close to go apart. After Shelley drowned, Byron angrily defended him against a hypocritical society.

Shelley and Byron had many disagreements. Byron never got over his Calvinist upbringing and had Catholic yearnings. Shelley decidedly was not a Christian and something in him shocked Byron, though they were politically allied in most matters.

Shelley's professed atheism does not prevent him from being a religious poet, though no simple formulation of the salvific program of *Prometheus Unbound* (1820) will work. Revolutionary by temperament and conviction, Shelley in Italy wore a ring inscribed: "*Il buon tempo verra*" ("The good time will come").

The liveliest book on Shelley I have read and reread remains *Shelley: The Pursuit* by Richard Holmes (1974). My original copy of the book accompanied me on my Italian travels during the years I taught in Bologna and in Rome, and is now indeed in the condition Holmes happily prophesied: "battered and wine-stained from its voyages, its margins scrawled, its poetry underlined, its pages bent with maps and postcards, its cover bleached with sun and sea." I recently obtained the splendid reprint by New York Review Books (1994) since my first copy is falling apart.

I frequently disagree with Holmes as to his evaluation of particular poems by Shelley, but that scarcely matters. He gives us the astonishing man: swift, remorseless, capable of surprising cruelty, skeptical yet idealistic, erotically irresponsible, preternaturally gifted yet given to hallucinatory episodes and strange visitations by the night-world.

Cythna, the heroine of *The Revolt of Islam* (1818), charmingly addresses a group of piratical mariners and delivers Shelley's memorable casting-out of remorse as "the dark idolatry of self":

> "'Reproach not thine own soul, but know thyself,
> Nor hate another's crime, nor loathe thine own.
> It is the dark idolatry of self,
> Which, when our thoughts and actions once are gone,
> Demands that man should weep, and bleed, and groan;
> Oh, vacant expiation! be at rest!
> The past is Death's, the future is thine own;
> And love and joy can make the foulest breast
> A paradise of flowers, where peace might build her nest.'"
>
> [Canto 8, stanza 22]

Byron was outrageous beyond bounds. He was polymorphously perverse: sadomasochistic, bisexual, incestuous, and even attempted to purchase little girls for his interesting purposes. His letters and conversations show no remorse, but his poetry quite deliberately and frequently does, to its own enrichment. "The dark idolatry of self" accurately describes one of his principal poetic stances.

Byron and Shelley had a fierce disagreement about Hamlet:

BYRON: [Hamlet] is weak; so miserably weak as even to complain of his own weakness. He says,

> "The time is out of joint—O cruel spite,
> That ever I was born to set it right."

And yet he is always boasting and bragging of his own powers, and scorning every one else, and he swears he will sweep to his revenge, "with wings as swift as meditation or the thoughts of love." For revenge was his love. But in truth he loved it, Shelley, after your own heart, most platonically; for his heart is too faint to win it fairly, and he contents himself with laughing at himself, mocking his own conscious cowardice, and venting his spleen in names, instead of doing anything like a man. So irresolute is he, that he envies the players, he envies Fortinbras, Laertes, any one that can do any thing. Weak, irresolute, a talking sophist. Yet—O I am sick of this most lame and impotent hero!

SHELLEY: And yet we recognise in him something that we cannot but love and sympathise with, and a grandeur of tone which we instinctively reverence.

["Byron and Shelley on the Character of Hamlet" (1830)]

Like Hamlet, Shelley somehow has escaped a wounded name, though he certainly merits one. He was partly responsible for the suicides of his first wife, Harriet Westbrook, and his second wife Mary's half-sister, Fanny Imlay. Since he was a prophet of free love, his dizzying gyres from woman to woman required no defense from him. His greatest work, the unfinished and posthumously published *The Triumph of Life* (1824), can be taken, in conjunction with the speech of the last Fury in *Prometheus Unbound*, as his deepest understanding of the irreconcilable divide between good and the means of good, love and the means of love:

> In each human heart terror survives
> The ravin it has gorged: the loftiest fear
> All that they would disdain to think were true:
> Hypocrisy and custom make their minds
> The fanes of many a worship, now outworn.
> They dare not devise good for man's estate,
> And yet they know not that they do not dare.

The good want power, but to weep barren tears.
The powerful goodness want: worse need for them.
The wise want love; and those who love want wisdom;
And all best things are thus confused to ill.

[*Prometheus Unbound*, 1.618–628]

And much I grieved to think how power & will
In opposition rule our mortal day—

And why God made irreconcilable
Good & the means of good . . .

[*The Triumph of Life*, ll. 228–231]

Things fall apart; the centre cannot hold;
Mere anarchy is loosed upon the world,
The blood-dimmed tide is loosed, and everywhere
The ceremony of innocence is drowned;
The best lack all conviction, while the worst
Are full of passionate intensity.

The last passage is William Butler Yeats in "The Second Coming" ([1919], ll. 3–8), purloining Shelley's revolutionary insights of the permanent Left for the proto-Fascist annunciation of the German Freikorps sent against Trotsky's troops in a vain attempt to undo the Russian Revolution. It is hardly possible to stand left of Shelley: his *The Mask of Anarchy* (1819), an extraordinarily eloquent response to the Peterloo Massacre, was not published until 1832, a decade after the poet's death. Though much of Shelley's poetry and prose was successfully kept from the British public, radical printers pirated the early *Queen Mab* (1813), which contributed to the Chartist movement and to early Marxist agitation.

The final lines of *The Mask of Anarchy* remain alive in British radicalism:

"Rise like Lions after slumber
In unvanquishable number—
Shake your chains to earth like dew
Which in sleep had fallen on you—
Ye are many—they are few."

Labour Party leaders beginning with Michael Foot in the 1980s have quoted this repeatedly to enormous rallies. Shelley would have been happy to know that rebels, alas unsuccessful, in China and in Iran have also chanted these lines. Though he began as the disciple of his father-in-law, William Godwin, author of *Enquiry Concerning Political Justice* (1793), he swerved far to the left of Godwin and contributed to the dialectic of Karl Marx's *The Eighteenth Brumaire of Louis Bonaparte* (1852), as Marx recognized. In 1888, five years after Karl Marx's death, his daughter Eleanor Marx-Aveling and her husband, Edward Aveling, summed up his view of Shelley:

> [Shelley] was the child of the French Revolution. "The wild-eyed women" thronging round the path of Cythna as she went through the great city were from the streets of Paris, and he, more than any other of his time, knew the real strength and beauty of this wild mother of his and ours. With his singular poetical and historical insight he saw the real significance of the holy struggle. Another singer of that melodious time, Byron, was also a child of the same Revolution. But his intellectual fore-runners were Voltaire and his school, and the Rousseau of the *Nouvelle Héloise*, whilst those of Shelley were Baboeuf and the Rousseau of the *Contrat Social*. It is a wise child that knows his own father. As Marx, who understood the poets as well as he understood the philosophers and economists, was wont to say: "The real difference between Byron and Shelley is this: those who understand them and love them rejoice that Byron died at thirty-six, because if he had lived he would have become a reactionary bourgeois; they grieve that Shelley died at twenty-nine, because he was essentially a revolutionist, and he would always have been one of the advanced guard of Socialism."
>
> ["Shelley and Socialism"]

There is the difficulty that Shelley preached passive civil disobedience and so became an influence on figures as varied as Tolstoy, Thoreau, and Gandhi. I wonder though whether Shelley, who could be quite combative, would have preserved that stance. Lions rousing after slumber is hardly a trope for peaceful change. Leon Trotsky had a Promethean spirit that sustained him as a leader of revolutionary violence. I delight in telling students that Trotsky advised Communist writers to take Dante as their model—Shelleyan advice.

The silliest judgment ever rendered on Shelley was that of the egregious Matthew Arnold, who described the poet as a "beautiful and ineffectual angel, beating in the void his luminous wings in vain." Arnold had some later competitors. In his 1932 Charles Eliot Norton lectures at Harvard, T. S. Eliot dismissed Shelley as an adolescent:

> The ideas of Shelley seem to me always to be the ideas of adolescence—as there is every reason why they should be. And an enthusiasm for Shelley seems to me also to be an affair of adolescence: for most of us, Shelley has marked an intense period before maturity, but for how many does Shelley remain the companion of age?

As always, Eliot was autobiographical and quite mistaken. Shelley's *Alastor* gave Eliot an immortal wound. Eliot revised himself later, his usual practice, but his bad effect lingered on. I have a charming memory that goes back to the autumn of 1954, when I was a Fulbright Scholar at Pembroke College, Cambridge, and my adviser (who became a lifelong friend) Matthew Hodgart took me to tea with F. R. Leavis and his wife, Queenie. Soon after we were seated, Dr. Leavis asked me what the subject of my Yale doctoral dissertation-in-progress was. I answered: "Shelley." Dr. Leavis responded: "I have settled Shelley." At twenty-four I was rather brash and replied: "Shelley always buries his own undertakers." My host jumped up and left the room. His wife made a speechless gesture indicating that Hodgart and I were to depart, without taking tea. Matthew and I walked over to the Anchor pub and substituted Highland malt for tea and sausages for teacake.

Sometimes, in an attempt not to be unfair, I have tried to read Leavis on Shelley. I keep failing. Leavis accuses Shelley of having no firm grasp on the actual. The very sincere Cambridge don had no grasp at all on the actual Shelley or on the "Ode to the West Wind," which—incoherently—he finds incoherent. Leavis is all diluted T. S. Eliot and hardly even a period piece in 2019. My revered mentor Frederick Albert Pottle used to return my essays for him with the stern admonition: "Stop beating dead woodchucks." So I will cease.

And yet this matter was for me an intimate problem. I began teaching in the Yale English Department in September 1955 and was a kind of pariah. The department regarded T. S. Eliot as Christ's vicar upon earth. Professor Cleanth Brooks, with whom I never exchanged an amiable word, dismissed Shelley's major work with an Eliotic shrug: "What Shelley's world of *Prometheus Unbound* really has to fear is not resurrection of Jupiter but the resurrection of John Donne" (*Modern Poetry and the Tradition*, 1939).

It was Samuel Taylor Coleridge, not T. S. Eliot, who resurrected Donne, though he hardly needed revival, since he had never disappeared. There is a wonderful Coleridge quatrain on Donne:

> With Donne, whose muse on dromedary trots,
> Wreathe iron pokers into true-love knots;
> Rhyme's sturdy cripple, fancy's maze and clue,
> Wit's forge and fire-blast, meaning's press and screw.
> ["On Donne's Poetry" (1836, written ca. 1818)]

John Donne—whether he wrote erotic or devotional poems, plangent elegies or holy sonnets—was very much a unified being. We do not know the date of my favorite Donne poem, "A Nocturnal upon St. Lucy's Day," but I read it as lamenting the loss of his beloved wife, Anne More, who died giving birth to their stillborn twelfth child in 1617 at the age of thirty-three:

> Study me then, you who shall lovers be
> At the next world, that is, at the next spring;
>   For I am every dead thing,
>   In whom Love wrought new alchemy.
>   For his art did express
> A quintessence even from nothingness,
> From dull privations, and lean emptiness;
> He ruin'd me, and I am re-begot
> Of absence, darkness, death: things which are not.
> [ll. 10–18]

I have never seen any point in juxtaposing Donne and Shelley. I think that Shelley, who was always in the elegy season, would have been overwhelmed by this nocturnal, had he read it. The only link I can find is in a letter to Shelley and Mary by Leigh Hunt in 1819:

> Do you know Donne? I should like to have some more talk with you about him. He was one of those over-metaphysical headed men, who can find out connections between every thing and any thing, and allowed himself at last to become a clergyman after he had (to my conviction at least) been as free and deep a speculator in morals as yourself.

"A speculator in morals" is a charming description of both the young Donne and Shelley.

There are two major tropes in Shelley: Fire and the Chariot. *Adonais*, in its penultimate stanza 54, chants ecstatically a celebration of "the fire for which all thirst":

> That light whose smile kindles the Universe,
> That Beauty in which all things work and move,
> That Benediction which the eclipsing Curse
> Of birth can quench not, that sustaining Love
> Which, through the web of being blindly wove
> By man and beast and earth and air and sea,
> Burns bright or dim, as each are mirrors of
> The fire for which all thirst, now beams on me,
> Consuming the last clouds of cold mortality.
>
> [ll. 478–486]

Shelley, as T. S. Eliot finally testified, after earlier reluctance, is the most Dantesque poet in the English language. This fiery stanza alludes in a very subtle and complex way to the opening lines of the *Paradiso*, where we are told that God's glory moves everything, penetrates everywhere in the universe, and repeats its glow, more in one part than another. I myself, Dante tells us, have been in the sphere most favored by God's light.

Eliot does not mention Shelley's astonishing translation of Matelda gathering flowers in *Purgatorio*, Canto 28, lines 1–51:

My slow steps had already borne me o'er
Such space within the antique wood, that I
Perceived not where I entered any more,—

When, lo! a stream whose little waves went by,
Bending towards the left through grass that grew
Upon its bank, impeded suddenly

My going on. Water of purest hue
On earth, would appear turbid and impure
Compared with this, whose unconcealing dew,

Dark, dark, yet clear, moved under the obscure
Eternal shades, whose interwoven looms
The rays of moon or sunlight ne'er endure.

I moved not with my feet, but mid the glooms
Pierced with my charmed eye, contemplating
The mighty multitude of fresh May blooms

Which starred that night, when, even as a thing
That suddenly, for blank astonishment,
Charms every sense, and makes all thought take wing,—

A solitary woman! and she went
Singing and gathering flower after flower,
With which her way was painted and besprent.

Bright lady, who, if looks had ever power
To bear true witness of the heart within,
Dost bask under the beams of love, come lower

Towards this bank. I prithee let me win
This much of thee, to come, that I may hear
Thy song: like Proserpine, in Enna's glen,

Thou seemest to my fancy, singing here
And gathering flowers, as that fair maiden when
She lost the Spring, and Ceres her more dear.

[ca. 1820]

Shelley, always alert to influence and allusion, by his phrasing re-
prises the influence of Dante's earthly paradise upon Milton's Eden:

Thus was this place,
A happy rural seat of various view:
Groves whose rich trees wept odorous gums and balm;
Others whose fruit, burnish'd with golden rind,
Hung amiable—Hesperian fables true,
If true, here only—and of delicious taste.
Betwixt them lawns, or level downs, and flocks
Grazing the tender herb, were interposed,
Or palmy hillock; or the flowery lap
Of some irriguous valley spread her store,
Flowers of all hue, and without thorn the rose:
Another side, umbrageous grots and caves
Of cool recess, o'er which the mantling vine
Lays forth her purple grape, and gently creeps
Luxuriant; meanwhile murmuring waters fall
Down the slope hills, dispersed, or in a lake,
That to the fringed bank with myrtle crowned
Her crystal mirror holds, unite their streams.
The birds their quire apply; airs, vernal airs,
Breathing the smell of field and grove, attune
      The trembling leaves, while universal Pan,
Knit with the Graces and the Hours in dance,
Led on the eternal Spring. Not that fair field
Of Enna, where Proserpine gathering flowers,
Herself a fairer flower, by gloomy Dis
Was gather'd—which cost Ceres all that pain
To seek her through the world—nor that sweet grove
Of Daphne, by Orontes and the inspired
Castalian spring, might with this Paradise
Of Eden strive . . .

               [*Paradise Lost*, 4.246–275]

I return to the Shelleyan Condition of Fire, as W. B. Yeats learned to call it. Its major work is the visionary drama *Prometheus Unbound,* but its inception in Shelley is the destructive romance *Alastor,* composed in 1815, published a year later. Shelley's first attempt at a long poem in 1813 had been a rather mawkish exercise first titled *Queen Mab* after Mercutio's excursus upon her in *Romeo and*

Juliet, and later somewhat reworked as *The Daemon of the World* (1816). Since the poet was barely nineteen, its badness can be excused. What matters about it are the incendiary Notes, in which Shelley let loose his lucid rage against British society, religion, morals, economics, monarchy, and the exploitation of workers and the poor. Pirated, it achieved wide circulation in English radical circles and became a kind of scripture for the Chartist movement. Even a brief sample of a Shelleyan note shows why it had so large an impact:

> The state of society in which we exist is a mixture of feudal savageness and imperfect civilization. The narrow and unenlightened morality of the Christian religion is an aggravation of these evils. It is not even until lately that mankind have admitted that happiness is the sole end of the science of ethics, as of all other sciences; and that the fanatical idea of mortifying the flesh for the love of God has been discarded.

Before he became, from 1816 until his death in 1822, a great poet, Shelley was already a superb pamphleteer and agitator. Since he was in exile, and barely published in England, his revolutionary spirit had a delayed impact upon Marx and Engels, and on other burgeoning figures of revolution.

The chariot image appears in *Queen Mab* in a positive guise, since she rides it on her benignly mischievous missions. As a figuration the chariot rides remorselessly throughout Shelley's poetry until it culminates in *The Triumph of Life*, his death poem. In old age I have taken to running things backward in my mind, and so I will leap into the maelstrom of that darkening fragment and only afterward will I return to Shelley's more hopeful years.

When I think about *The Triumph of Life*, I cannot exclude my departed friend Paul de Man, whose brilliant disfiguration of the poem and the poet perpetually challenges everything I know in reading Shelley:

> *The Triumph of Life* warns us that nothing, whether deed, word, thought, or text, ever happens in relation, positive or negative, to anything that precedes, follows, or exists else-

where, but only as a random event whose power, like the power of death, is due to the randomness of its occurrence.

[*"Shelley Disfigured"* (1979)]

What would Shelley have thought of de Man's essay? I think this crucial sentence would have bothered him, but in 1822, just before dying, he might have endorsed it. His Humean skepticism had overcome the last vestiges of his Platonism. Herman Melville wrote a short, abrupt poem he called "Shelley's Vision":

Wandering late by morning seas
When my heart with pain was low—
Hate the censor pelted me—
Deject I saw my shadow go.

In elf-caprice of bitter tone
I too would pelt the pelted one:
At my shadow I cast a stone.

When lo, upon that sun-lit ground
I saw the quivering phantom take
The likeness of St. Stephen crowned:
Then did self-reverence awake.

[1891]

I think Shelley would have liked this as I do, except that he would have rejected any identity with the first Christian martyr. He might have enjoyed even more the two quatrains that Melville called "Fragments from a Lost Gnostic Poem of the Twelfth Century":

Found a family, build a state,
The pledged event is still the same:
Matter in end will never abate
His ancient brutal claim.

Indolence is heaven's ally here,
And energy the child of hell:
The Good Man pouring from his pitcher clear
But brims the poisoned well.

The Cathars, a Gnostic sect, flourished in southern France until a papal crusade exterminated them in a twenty-year campaign commencing in 1209. This butchery was sanctioned by a pious bishop who exhorted the crusaders: "Kill them all! God will know His own!" Melville, so far as I know, had never read William Blake, yet there is something Blakean about these quatrains. Melville took Shelley, together with Hawthorne and Shakespeare, for one of his heroes, and he echoes Shelley's complaint against the recalcitrance of matter, the unwilling dross that impedes the spirit's flight.

It would be accurate to say that Shelley, until *The Triumph of Life*, was a heretical religious poet, sounding the trumpet of a prophecy. I would not dispute Paul de Man's observation that religion has no relevance to Shelley's last and greatest poem. Though the posthumous revelations about Paul's early career in Belgium saddened me, my love for his memory has survived them. He goes on challenging the ways in which I read and reread.

My long experience as I approach ninety compels me to refuse the concept, attributed by de Man to *The Triumph of Life*, that no text ever happens in relation to anything that precedes; that a poem is to some extent a random event, and that every death is altogether random. Walking with Paul in 1978, after I had read his stringent essay, I remarked that I could not think of a poem as a death since even *The Triumph of Life* augmented my desire to go on living. He replied that he was eleven years my senior and that my statement was meaningless. Paul died at sixty-four in 1983 of pancreatic cancer. My wife and I visited him every other day during his final two weeks. When I bent over to say that I would see him the day after tomorrow, he replied that I would not because he expected to die very soon. I tried to remonstrate, but he said farewell with his usual irony: "You know, Harold, you are the only person who could have made New Haven interesting to me." It was rather like his constant attendance at my weekly lectures when I held the DeVane Professorship: I remember asking him, "Paul, why do you go to my lectures even when they are on authors that do not interest you?" He replied cheerfully that it was wonderful to hear so many new errors in constant creation. Paul loved rigor and believed he found it in Shelley. Perhaps he was right.

In 1979 I joined four friends in bringing out a volume called *Deconstruction and Criticism*. I gave it that title, meaning that my four associates were deconstructors and I was not. Two of them—J. Hillis Miller and Paul de Man—chose to write about *The Triumph of Life*. Geoffrey Hartman chose Wordsworth, and Jacques Derrida, more or less, Blanchot. I had already written so many commentaries on *The Triumph of Life* that I chose instead John Ashbery's "Self-Portrait in a Convex Mirror" (1974) as my proof text. Before commenting on that wonderful poem, I wrote a brief essay on "The Breaking of Form." The book is out of print, so I feel justified in quoting what for me was my central contention:

> No strong poem merely alludes to another, and what look like overt allusions and even echoes in strong poems are disguises for darker relationships. A strong authentic allusion to another strong poem can be only by and in what the later poem *does not say*, by what it represses. This is another aspect of a limitation of poetry that defines poetry: a poem can be *about* experience or emotion or whatever only by initially encountering another poem, which is to say a poem must handle experience and emotion as if they already were rival poems. Poetic knowledge is necessarily a knowledge by tropes, an experience of emotion as trope, and an expression of knowledge and emotion by a revisionary further troping. Since a poem is necessarily still further troped in any strong reading, there is a bewildering triple intertropicality at work that makes a mockery of most attempts at reading. I do not agree wholly with de Man that reading is impossible, but I acknowledge how very difficult it is to read a poem properly, which is what I have meant by my much-attacked critical trope of "misreading" or "misprision." With three layers of troping perpetually confronting us, the task of restituting meaning or of healing a wounded rhetoricity is a daunting one. Yet it can and must be attempted. The only alternative I can see is the triumph of Romantic irony in purified form by way of the allegory of reading formulated by Paul de Man. But this most advanced version of Deconstruction cheerfully

accepts the risk warned against by de Man's truest precursor, Friedrich Schlegel: "The irony of irony is the fact that one becomes weary of it if one is offered it everywhere and all the time."

The alternative to endless irony is what the ancients called transumption, by which belatedness is transformed into earliness, and the dead return in our colors and at our will. Milton, as I keep noting, remains the greatest master of transumption in the language. Shakespeare was an all but absolute original, despite his debts to Ovid, Chaucer, Marlowe, and the English Bible. He cannot be transumed and had no need to practice it. By the time he wrote *Henry IV, Part 1* (1597), his agon with competitors was not concluded, but victory was assured.

The one time I angered Paul de Man was when, in a lecture that he attended, I dismissed the deconstructive gospel, "There is no outside-text," by remarking that this was just a version of Bishop George Berkeley's Idealism:

> But say you, though the ideas themselves do not exist without the mind, yet there may be things like them whereof they are copies or resemblances, which things exist without the mind, in an unthinking substance. I answer, an idea can be like nothing but an idea; a colour or figure can be like nothing but another colour or figure.
>
> [*Of the Principles of Human Knowledge* (1710)]

My offending statement was that just as an idea can be like nothing but an idea, the overstuffed old armchair in my study could be like nothing but another overstuffed armchair. Nothing can be like a trope except another trope, except that all tropes can vary, and need not be ironies. I was very fond of that overstuffed ancient armchair, which perpetually was falling apart.

There is no single way of reading Shelley when, as in the "Ode to the West Wind," *The Witch of Atlas, Adonais, The Triumph of Life,* he surpasses himself. Yet he does this by taking on the magnificent forerunners: Isaiah, Ezekiel, Plato, Aeschylus, Lucretius, Ovid, Dante, Petrarch, Spenser, Shakespeare, Milton, Rousseau, Wordsworth. In spite of Paul de Man, I do not know how to exclude these giant forms from my consciousness each time I return to *The Triumph of Life*. Nor can I banish Shelley's followers: Robert Browning, Swinburne, Thomas Hardy, George Bernard Shaw, D. H. Lawrence, Virginia Woolf, on to Wallace Stevens and Hart Crane.

Essentially I read Shelley as Wallace Stevens did when he wrote, "Mesdames, one might believe that Shelley lies / Less in the stars than in their earthy wake."

Shelley's presence in Stevens is constant. The one time I had the privilege of meeting Stevens, we talked about Shelley. To my delight he quoted the last six lines of stanza 27 of *The Witch of Atlas* (1824, written 1820)—Shelley at his most visionary:

Men scarcely know how beautiful fire is—
    Each flame of it is as a precious stone
Dissolved in ever-moving light, and this
    Belongs to each and all who gaze upon.
The Witch beheld it not, for in her hand
She held a woof that dimmed the burning brand.

Shelley in his final year, 1822, wrote many love poems to Jane Williams, one entitled "With a Guitar. To Jane," and another celebrating her song as she played the guitar to her lover, and revealed "some world far from ours, / Where music and moonlight and feeling / Are one." Both poems, with their star and moon imagery, are echoed in *Mr. Burnshaw and the Statue*, where Stevens invokes a "mortal lullaby" that will "suddenly with lights, / Astral and Shelleyan, diffuse new day."

I have never understood how anyone could take this as an attack on Shelley, which Stevens, in a letter, clearly disowns, in a strong tribute to the harmonious skeptic among his Romantic precursors: "The astral and Shelleyan lights are not going to alter the structure of nature. Apples will always be apples, and whoever is a ploughman hereafter will be what the ploughman has always been. For all that, the astral and the Shelleyan will have transformed the world" (Letter to Hi Simons [August 27, 1940]).

Stevens owned a copy of Shelley's *A Defence of Poetry*, which he seems to have read repeatedly. The book is in the Huntington

Library, San Marino, California, where there are many check marks in the margins. Many people can recognize the famous closing sentence, which infuriated W. H. Auden, who repeated to me a version of his curious judgment, "How glad I am that the silliest remark ever made about poets, 'the unacknowledged legislators of the world,' was made by a poet whose work I detest" ("Squares and Oblongs" [1947]). Auden believed that this meant poets were in league with the secret police. Let Shelley speak eloquently for himself:

> It is impossible to read the compositions of the most cele-
> brated writers of the present day without being startled with
> the electric life which burns within their words. They mea-
> sure the circumference and sound the depths of human na-
> ture with a comprehensive and all-penetrating spirit, and
> they are themselves perhaps the most sincerely astonished at
> its manifestations; for it is less their spirit than the spirit of
> the age. Poets are the hierophants of an unapprehended in-
> spiration; the mirrors of the gigantic shadows which futu-
> rity casts upon the present; the words which express what
> they understand not; the trumpets which sing to battle, and
> feel not what they inspire; the influence which is moved not,
> but moves. Poets are the unacknowledged legislators of the
> world.

Like Stevens and Yeats, I regard Shelley's *Defence* as a profound essay on the nature and use of poetry. We would be much poorer without it.

The poet Wystan Hugh Auden was humane and charming, if somewhat disconcerting. Once, at his request, he stayed overnight with my wife and me at our New Haven house. I remember that was in the mid-1960s and that he had come to read his poems at Ezra Stiles College. He had a battered attaché case, which he opened to reveal a bottle of gin, a smaller one of vermouth, a plastic drinking cup, and a sheaf of poems.

The next morning, after a somewhat contentious breakfast, in which Auden denounced Lucretius, Walt Whitman, Shelley, and Stevens, saying that none of them had an ear for language, the poet and I walked to campus, where I was to teach a class on Shelley.

Though I urged him to feel free to take the train back to New York City, he insisted upon accompanying me to class. His presence inspired me to teach Shelley with incredible ferocity. Auden sat silently, without expression, and then courteously walked out with me. We shook hands and he encouraged me to visit him in New York City, but I cannot remember ever doing so.

When I was young I read early Auden with considerable pleasure. In old age I sometimes reread one or another of his quirky essays, but his poems frequently seem to me period pieces. His dislike of Shelley is much less interesting than T. S. Eliot's ambivalent statements of aversion. Eliot is a classic instance of defense against true precursors: Shakespeare, Shelley, Walt Whitman, Tennyson, Dante Gabriel Rossetti, and Swinburne, by substituting idealized forerunners: Dante Alighieri, Jacobean dramatists, metaphysical poets, and such minor French figures as Tristan Corbière and Jules Laforgue. Eliot could not have missed the irony that the free verse of Laforgue is an imitation of Whitman, whom Laforgue translated.

Walt Whitman is so powerful a poet and human presence that his imaginative descendants always have to defend against him, to one degree or another. If you read *The Waste Land* and "When Lilacs Last in the Dooryard Bloom'd" side by side, and read deeply and closely enough, they begin to merge. Walt is one of Eliot's daemons; Shelley is another. Shakespeare is a flood threatening to drown Eliot. Someday there will be a definitive biography of Eliot, after all the letters and other documents by the poet, family, and friends are finally available. He was the last of seven children, six of whom lived. Both his parents were forty-four when he was born. He grew up with four older sisters, eleven to nineteen years older, and one brother eight years his senior. Physically rather weak, with hernia problems, he sheltered himself in books, and wrote poetry at a very early age. Both his parents were strong-willed, and there is something problematic about his relation to his mother.

His extraordinary resistance to *Hamlet* caused him to describe that poem unlimited as "certainly an aesthetic failure," and led to his preference for *Coriolanus*. One wonders if his praise of *Coriolanus* was primarily political, and yet he may have seen Volumnia as Charlotte Champe Stearns, his mother, an aesthetic sensibility who failed as a poet.

Shelley, even as a preadolescent, had a tormented relationship with both his parents. Biographers offer ample material for his endless battle with his father, Sir Timothy Shelley, but rather little in regard to his mother, Lady Elizabeth Shelley. The image of a father throughout Shelley's poetry has much in common with Blake's Nobodaddy. Shelley was ambivalent on the question of incest. *The Cenci* (1819), his now neglected, rather too-Shakespearean tragedy, turns on the repeated rapes and sadistic treatment of the heroine, Beatrice, by her father, Count Cenci, who resembles the monstrous Jupiter of Shelley's masterwork *Prometheus Unbound*.

I observe that fire in Shelley battles Jupiter and the varied chariots of destruction in which divinity drives. The Veiled Maid of *Alastor* is a kind of sister to the doomed Poet, who represents fire and who wastes away, consumed by his longing to renew that incestuous coupling:

> But thou art fled
> Like some frail exhalation; which the dawn
> Robes in its golden beams,—ah! thou hast fled!
> The brave, the gentle, and the beautiful,
> The child of grace and genius. Heartless things
> Are done and said i' the world, and many worms
> And beasts and men live on, and mighty Earth
> From sea and mountain, city and wilderness,
> In vesper low or joyous orison,
> Lifts still its solemn voice:—but thou art fled—
> Thou canst no longer know or love the shapes
> Of this phantasmal scene, who have to thee
> Been purest ministers, who are, alas!
> Now thou art not. Upon those pallid lips
> So sweet even in their silence, on those eyes
> That image sleep in death, upon that form
> Yet safe from the worm's outrage, let no tear
> Be shed—not even in thought. Nor, when those hues
> Are gone, and those divinest lineaments,
> Worn by the senseless wind, shall live alone
> In the frail pauses of this simple strain,
> Let not high verse, mourning the memory

Of that which is no more, or painting's woe
Or sculpture, speak in feeble imagery
Their own cold powers. Art and eloquence,
And all the shows o' the world are frail and vain
To weep a loss that turns their lights to shade.
It is a woe too "deep for tears," when all
Is reft at once, when some surpassing Spirit,
Whose light adorned the world around it, leaves
Those who remain behind, not sobs or groans,
The passionate tumult of a clinging hope;
But pale despair and cold tranquillity,
Nature's vast frame, the web of human things,
Birth and the grave, that are not as they were.

[ll. 686–720]

The most suggestive and perspicuous reading of *Alastor* I know is by the late Jay Macpherson, Canadian poet-scholar, in her *The Spirit of Solitude: Conventions and Continuities in Late Romance* (1982):

Shelley believed when he wrote *Alastor* that "Mind . . . cannot create, it can only perceive" ("On Life," [1815], *Works* VI, 197). In the poem, the Poet's mind is a mirror surface waiting for meaning to be "flashed" onto it. Nature, not man, is the creator, seizing on a passive sensibility and making it if anything still more passive. As Goethe indicated in *Werther* and Shelley in *Alastor* seems to suspect, such determined passivity is the way to possession and madness: "We receive but what we give, / And in our life along does Nature live." So far as the name "Alastor" relates to the Poet himself, the Muse of him who is unable to forget will be one of "Dame Memory's Siren daughters" . . . beckoning to reflection on the past as well as on the secrets of nature; this interest the Poet clearly shares with his author. Hence his inability to recognize in the visionary maiden his own creation. In so far as she is a "siren," she is, as the preface says, assembled out of scraps of experience in his memory. To that extent she is "demonic," since I take it that the true demonic is precisely something of oneself that splits off and becomes recognized as "the other"; recognition of the "other" assumes a relation to oneself, so that one sees it as "obsessing," "haunting," or "possessing."

Shelley refuses the suicide of Werther and the madness of Tasso. William Hazlitt disliked Shelley the man and weakly misread Shelley's greatest poetry. I never know what to make of this. The great English critics of the nineteenth century include Coleridge, Ruskin, Pater, and Hazlitt, who at his best raised journalism into authentic wisdom. Somehow Shelley blinded him. In 1824 he reviewed *Posthumous Poems* in a manner I find confused:

> He mistook the nature of the poet's calling, which should be guided by involuntary, not by voluntary impulses. He shook off, as an heroic and praiseworthy act, the trammels of sense, custom, and sympathy, and became the creature of his own will. He was "all air," disdaining the bars and ties of mortal mould. He ransacked his brain for incongruities, and believed in whatever was incredible. Almost all is effort, almost all is extravagant, almost all is quaint, incomprehensible, and abortive, from aiming to be more than it is. Epithets are applied, because they do not fit: subjects are chosen, because they are repulsive: the colours of his style, for their gaudy, changeful, startling effect, resemble the display of fire-works in the dark, and, like them, have neither durability, nor keeping, nor discriminate form. Yet Mr. Shelley, with all his faults, was a man of genius; and we lament that uncontrollable violence of temperament which gave it a forced and false direction. He has single thoughts of great depth and force, single images of rare beauty, detached passages of extreme tenderness; and, in his smaller pieces, where he has attempted little, he has done most. . . .
>
> Mr. Shelley was a remarkable man. His person was a type and shadow of his genius. His complexion, fair, golden, freckled, seemed transparent with an inward light, and his spirit within him
>
> —so divinely wrought,
> That you might almost say his body thought.

He reminded those who saw him of some of Ovid's fables. His form, graceful and slender, drooped like a flower in the breeze. But he was crushed beneath the weight of thought which he aspired to bear, and was withered in the lightning-glare of a ruthless philosophy! He mistook the nature of his own faculties and feelings—the lowly children of the valley, by which the skylark makes its bed, and the bee murmurs, for the proud the mountain-pine, in which the eagle builds its eyry, "and dallies with the wind, and scorns the sun."—He wished to make of idle verse and idler prose the frame-work of the universe, and to bind all possible existence in the visionary chain of intellectual beauty.

Hazlitt seemed baffled by *The Witch of Atlas* and rather irritated by *The Triumph of Life*. Shelley offended Hazlitt's empiricism and perhaps also the naturalistic humanism the critic shared with John Keats. A fierce Shelleyan from my childhood to my now advanced old age, I have learned to dismiss most negative criticisms of the Promethean poet, including those of Matthew Arnold, F. R. Leavis, T. S. Eliot, W. H. Auden, Allen Tate, Cleanth Brooks, and their minor followers. Hazlitt is a different matter. He is outweighed by Shelley's progeny: Thomas Lovell Beddoes, Robert Browning, Arthur Henry Hallam, Alfred Tennyson, Algernon Charles Swinburne, Dante Gabriel Rossetti, William Morris, Oscar Wilde, William Butler Yeats, Thomas Hardy, Francis Thompson, Lionel Johnson, Virginia Woolf, and James Joyce; and in America: Elinor Wylie, Wallace Stevens, Conrad Aiken, and Hart Crane.

T. S. Eliot finally seems to have resolved his conflicts with regard both to Walt Whitman and to Shelley. He became obsessed with the image of Rousseau in *The Triumph of Life*, rather strangely echoing it in "Sweeney Erect" (1919), but more acutely in "Little Gidding" (1942).

The Victorian James Thomson, who called himself "Bysshe Vanolis" in honor of Shelley and Novalis, should be remembered for his grim *The City of Dreadful Night* (1874), a long poem fusing Shelley and Browning in the wake of "Childe Roland to the Dark Tower Came" (1855, written 1852):

As I came through the desert thus it was,
As I came through the desert: From the right
A shape came slowly with a ruddy light;
A woman with a red lamp in her hand,
Bareheaded and barefooted on that strand;
O desolation moving with such grace!
O anguish with such beauty in thy face.
    I fell as on my bier,
    Hope travailed with such fear.

[4.61–69]

That is not particularly Eliotic, but there are several passages in Thomson that make their way into Eliot's poetry. The Scottish poet-critic Robert Crawford convincingly demonstrates a number of verbal echoings and suggests, with some justice, that Thomson be added to that rather crowded "familiar compound ghost."

Shelley's major poem *Prometheus Unbound*, a lyrical drama in four acts, takes as its models the *Prometheus Bound* attributed to Aeschylus and, more subversively, *Paradise Lost.* I reread it a few evenings ago, for the first time in some years, and found it stronger even than I remembered. I wrote extensive commentaries on it when I was very young, and would not want to look at them now. Probably they idealized what now seems to me superb in its severe vision of human renovation.

In the ancient tragedy, possibly by Aeschylus, the Titan Prometheus is punished by Zeus for bringing fire to humankind and thus frustrating Zeus's design of obliterating them. Bound to a vast rock, he endures endless torment, and refuses to tell Zeus the secret of the forthcoming birth of Hercules, and of prophecies foretelling the downfall of Zeus. At the play's conclusion, a thunderbolt sends Prometheus into the abyss.

Shelley modifies this with subtle originality. Despite his suffering, the major impulse of this High Romantic Prometheus is to revoke his curse against Zeus. Since he has forgotten the wording, he appeals to Mother Earth:

Prometheus
Venerable mother!

All else who live and suffer take from thee
Some comfort; flowers, and fruits, and happy sounds,
And love, though fleeting; these may not be mine.
But mine own words, I pray, deny me not.

The Earth

They shall be told. Ere Babylon was dust,
The Magus Zoroaster, my dead child,
Met his own image walking in the garden.
That apparition, sole of men, he saw.
For know there are two worlds of life and death:
One that which thou beholdest; but the other
Is underneath the grave, where do inhabit
The shadows of all forms that think and live,
Till death unite them and they part no more;
Dreams and the light imaginings of men,
And all that faith creates or love desires,
Terrible, strange, sublime and beauteous shapes.
There thou art, and dost hang, a writhing shade,
'Mid whirlwind-peopled mountains; all the gods
Are there, and all the powers of nameless worlds,
Vast, sceptred phantoms; heroes, men, and beasts;
And Demogorgon, a tremendous gloom;
And he, the supreme Tyrant, on his throne
Of burning gold. Son, one of these shall utter
The curse which all remember. Call at will
Thine own ghost, or the ghost of Jupiter,
Hades or Typhon, or what mightier Gods
From all-prolific Evil, since thy ruin,
Have sprung, and trampled on my prostrate sons.
Ask, and they must reply: so the revenge
Of the Supreme may sweep through vacant shades,
As rainy wind through the abandoned gate
Of a fallen palace . . .

[1.186–218]

Shelley possessed (or was afflicted by) a Macbeth-like capacity for hallucination: on one occasion, out walking, he met his double, who asked him, "How long do you mean to be content?" The poet fainted and the apparition vanished. The Magus Zoroaster (Zarathustra) cannot be firmly dated, but the dualistic religion he founded became the governing faith of Iran. Shelley's friend Thomas Love Peacock, poet and satirical novelist, probably introduced the Promethean poet to legends of Zoroaster.

The curious vision of two parallel universes has mythographic origins, yet Shelley's version is essentially his own:

For know there are two worlds of life and death:
One that which thou beholdest; but the other
Is underneath the grave, where do inhabit
The shadows of all forms that think and live,
Till death unite them and they part no more . . .

There seems no end to the presence of Shelley in T. S. Eliot. "The Love Song of J. Alfred Prufrock" (1915) can be shown to be a weird parody of *Alastor*. I am not an admirer of Eliot's plays, with the exception of *Sweeney Agonistes* (1932). *The Cocktail Party* (1948) seems to me wantonly cruel and finally quite silly. Eliot models himself on the *Alcestis* of Euripides, and his egregious version of Heracles is Sir Henry Harcourt-Reilly, a very odd and intrusive psychiatrist who thinks that being crucified near an anthill and then cannibalized is a proper spiritual destiny for the unfortunate Celia Coplestone. Harcourt-Reilly quotes verbatim the Magus Zoroaster passage from *Prometheus Unbound* and then—shall we say smugly?—expresses approval in his own spiritual insights: "And if that is not a happy death, what death is happy?" (Act 1, Scene 1).

That is hardly a Shelleyan sentiment. Perhaps Flannery O'Connor might have agreed with this, and certainly Eliot relished it. What are the rest of us to think?

Northrop Frye, when we first met in London in 1958, seemed amused when I urged him to be more explicit about his distaste for Eliot. I was young and foolish. Frye had his own way of eviscerating Eliot, splendidly exemplified in the first chapter, "Antique Drum," of his little book on Eliot (1981). It leaves not much.

In his brief book *A Study of English Romanticism* (1968), Frye centered on three poems: *Death's Jest-Book* (1850), the macabre drama by Thomas Lovell Beddoes, Shelley's disciple; *Prometheus Unbound*; Keats's *Endymion*. There are keen insights throughout, particularly on Shelley. Frye emphasizes that Prometheus is not a poet or a creator of any kind and so hardly a surrogate for Shelley. This Prometheus is a *hearer:* he is listening for a primordial voice that will release him. The only action in *Prometheus Unbound* is the Titan's recantation of his curse upon Jupiter. He has forgotten it, hears it repeated, rejects it, is released. Jupiter falls as soon as Prometheus gives up hatred and his desire for revenge.

Shelley always acknowledges his divided allegiance: he is a Lucretian skeptic intellectually, yet emotionally unable to forsake Platonic eros. Frederick Pottle catches this in his meditation on Asia's role in the lyrical drama:

Asia must go down to the Cave of Demogorgon, the affections must sink back on themselves down into the unconscious depths of being and be made over. Specifically, the affections must exorcize the demons of infancy, whether personal or of the race, and must rebuild themselves in accord with a mature theology. But is not this to turn matters precisely upside down? Surely it is the function of the heart to forgive and of the head to construct theologies? No, would certainly be Shelley's firm rejoinder. The head must sincerely forgive, must willingly eschew hatred on purely experimental grounds. "Revenge, retaliation, atonement, are pernicious *mistakes*"; intellect must "discover the *wisdom* of universal love." And since the evidence on which all religions are founded is revealed to the heart and does not have the character of experimental verifiability which the intellect demands for its operations, intellect, to be true to itself, must remain scrupulously agnostic. If it does apply the operations of logic to the content of revelation, it produces precisely Jupiter. Theology, in the form of concrete poetic speculation, is the domain and the duty of the imagination.

["The Role of Asia in the Dramatic Action of Shelley's
Prometheus Unbound" (1965)]

In Shelley's gnosis, Jupiter believes he has engendered a son stronger than himself who will join him in the imposition of tyranny. Ironically—a critique of God and Christ in *Paradise Lost*—Jupiter has begotten nothing, and Demogorgon, invented by Boccaccio as "the father of the Gentile gods," rises up from his cave to drag the sky-god down into the abyss. Shelley's greatest poetic disciple of the twentieth century, William Butler Yeats, when in the middle of the journey (1900), found Blake and Shelley alike to have been founders of an *antithetical* religion replacing Christianity:

It was therefore natural that Blake who was always praising energy, and all exalted overflowing of oneself, and who though art an impassioned labour to keep men from doubt and despondency, and woman's love an evil, when it would trammel man's will, should see the poetic genius not in a woman star but in the Sun, and should rejoice throughout his poetry in "the Sun in his strength." Shelley, however, except when he uses it to describe the peculiar beauty of Emilia Viviani, who was like "an incarnation of the Sun when light is changed to love," saw it with less friendly eyes. He seems to have seen it with perfect happiness only when veiled in mist, or glimmering upon water, or when faint enough to do no more than veil the brightness of his own Star; and in *The Triumph of Life*, the one poem in which it is part of the avowed symbolism, its power is the being and the source of all tyrannies. When the woman personifying the Morning Star has faded from before his eyes, Rousseau sees a "new vision" in "a cold bright car" with a rainbow hovering over her, and as she comes the shadow passes from "leaf and stone" and souls she has enslaved seem "in that light, like atomies to dance within a sunbeam," or they dance among the flowers that grow up newly in "the grassy vesture of the desert," unmindful of the misery that is to come upon them. These are "the great, the unforgotten," all who have worn "mitres and helms and crowns, or wreaths of light," and yet have not known themselves. Even "great Plato" is there, because he knew joy and sorrow, because life that could not subdue him by gold or pain, by "age, or sloth, or slavery,"

subdued him by love. All who have ever lived are there except Christ and Socrates and the "sacred few" who put away
all life could give, being doubtless followers throughout their
lives of the forms borne by the flying ideal, or who, "as soon
as they had touched the world with living flame, fled back
like eagles to their native noon."

[*"The Philosophy of Shelley's Poetry"*]

Yeats later rather defensively changed his mind:

Demogorgon made his plot incoherent, its interpretation impossible, it was thrust there by that something which again
and again forced him to balance the object of desire conceived as miraculous and superhuman, with nightmare.
Shelley told his friends of attempts upon his life or his liberty, elaborating details between delusion and deceit, believing himself infected with elephantiasis because he had sat
opposite a fat woman in an omnibus, encountered terrify-
ing apparitions, one woman with eyes in her breasts.

[*"Prometheus Unbound" (1932)*]

After years of intermittent pondering, I still cannot apprehend
this. Demogorgon is not a nightmare: he is a skeptical myth of release. C. E. Pulos, in *The Deep Truth: A Study of Shelley's Skepticism*
(1954), describes Demogorgon as "the inconceivable ultimate reality of skepticism," by which Pulos intends the Necessity of David
Hume, marked by wariness and a certain irony. One might call this
Necessity "the unknown God."

It seems odd to me that *Prometheus Unbound* is more baroque
than *Paradise Lost*. The longer I know Shelley's poetry, the less I know
it. Surprise, speed, abandon, breathlessness, and vaultings upward
and downward are its stigmata. In a sense there can be no epiphanies
in Shelley since everything flashes by against darkening backgrounds.
And yet there were for him times of inherent excellence when hope
seemed rationally possible, when desire and the means of desire could
be reconciled. Unrolling ecstasies did not always yield to roilings.

Half a century ago I published a large study of William Butler
Yeats. Since it is out of print, I venture a relevant quotation:

In the apocalyptic afterthought of *Prometheus Unbound*, Act IV, a chorus of rejoicing spirits comes from "Thought's crowned powers" to watch the dance of redeemed time. These skiey towers of joy are invoked ironically by Yeats, in further mockery of the emblematic tower he sets up as mockery of our "time / Half dead at the top." . . . His tower and his winding stair represent what Romantic tradition has found so many emblems for, the power of the mind, of the most terrible force in the world, over Milton's universe of death: "Everything that is not God consumed with intellectual fire." The problem with this luminous line is that, as I think Frye remarks somewhere, God occupies the place of death in the Yeatsian vision, and indeed we are being told that the mind's fire consumes all that is alive here. Intellectual power, in the poem, is knowledge but hardly wisdom.

[1970]

"For wisdom is the property of the dead, / A something incompatible with life . . ." Those lines are from "Blood and the Moon" (written 1928, ll. 49–54) and sound curiously Eliotic, probably because they echo the style of such Jacobean tragedians as John Webster and Cyril Tourneur. Shelley, more than Blake, so contaminated Yeats that he could never fight free of the revolutionary Romantic since that would have meant abandoning his own inmost self.

Shelley is so strange a person and poet that he seems all inmost self. Between the composition of Acts 3 and 4 of *Prometheus Unbound*, he composed his most important shorter poem, the "Ode to the West Wind." This sequence of five *terza rima* sonnets is inexhaustible; you can go on reading it all your life and it will keep changing. Though I have always believed that it is Shelley's version of Job, it also seems to meditate upon his own stance in regard to *Prometheus Unbound*. It is as though Plato and Dante, Leon Trotsky and Gandhi, David Hume and William Blake cohabited beyond sexuality. Few poems in the language open so explosively as the "Ode":

O wild West Wind, thou breath of Autumn's being,
Thou, from whose unseen presence the leaves dead
Are driven, like ghosts from an enchanter fleeing,

Yellow, and black, and pale, and hectic red,
Pestilence-stricken multitudes: O thou,
Who chariotest to their dark wintry bed

The winged seeds, where they lie cold and low,
Each like a corpse within its grave, until
Thine azure sister of the Spring shall blow

Her clarion o'er the dreaming earth, and fill
(Driving sweet buds like flocks to feed in air)
With living hues and odours plain and hill:

Wild Spirit, which art moving everywhere;
Destroyer and preserver; hear, oh hear!

Shelley relies upon the fiction of the leaves in Homer, Virgil, Dante, Milton, and others, but alters the balance in favor of preservation over destruction. The winged seeds will be resurrected by the Spring West Wind, whose gender Shelley changes to feminine. Since Shelley is a revolutionary agitator, he anticipates a fresh wave of rebellions. The "black rain" of the next *terza rima* sonnet may well suggest a burning city.

"Some fierce Maenad" implies the Orphic rending apart the poet risks. A poignance of cultural loss pervades the third sonnet. It is with the fourth that Shelley himself enters:

If I were a dead leaf thou mightest bear;
If I were a swift cloud to fly with thee;
A wave to pant beneath thy power, and share

The impulse of thy strength, only less free
Than thou, O uncontrollable! If even
I were as in my boyhood, and could be

The comrade of thy wanderings over Heaven,
As then, when to outstrip thy skiey speed
Scarce seem'd a vision; I would ne'er have striven

As thus with thee in prayer in my sore need.
Oh, lift me as a wave, a leaf, a cloud!
I fall upon the thorns of life! I bleed!

A heavy weight of hours has chain'd and bow'd
One too like thee: tameless, and swift, and proud.

"Too like" means both "also" and "too much like." Job and not
Jesus is the clear analogue. Apostrophe has become prayer, but for
what? The magnificent final sonnet is the answer:

Make me thy lyre, even as the forest is:
What if my leaves are falling like its own!
The tumult of thy mighty harmonies

Will take from both a deep, autumnal tone,
Sweet though in sadness. Be thou, Spirit fierce,
My spirit! Be thou me, impetuous one!

Drive my dead thoughts over the universe
Like wither'd leaves to quicken a new birth!
And, by the incantation of this verse,

Scatter, as from an unextinguish'd hearth
Ashes and sparks, my words among mankind!
Be through my lips to unawaken'd earth

The trumpet of a prophecy! O Wind,
If Winter comes, can Spring be far behind?

There are multiple responses possible to this great chant. The
most remarkable is by Wallace Stevens. "Bethou me as you blow,"
Stevens writes in *Notes toward a Supreme Fiction* (1942) ("It Must
Change," section 6), "It is / A sound like any other. It will end." Stevens greatly admired Shelley, and the ironies here are turned
against the later poet. The trumpet of a prophecy is not available to
Stevens, and for him the hearth is all but extinguished. The "Ode
to the West Wind" haunts Stevens.

What precisely is Shelley's prayer in the final sonnet of the
"Ode"? Ostensibly he desires to be an Aeolian harp, but he asks for
an amazing identification with the wind: "Be thou, Spirit fierce, / My
spirit! Be thou me, impetuous one!" "Impetuous" takes the double
nuance of "rash" and "relentless," Shelley's accurate self-recognition.

One feels that Shelley was always writing a nonstop *Revolution-ist's Handbook*, like John Tanner's in Shaw's *Man and Superman* (1903). When he urges the wind, "Drive my dead thoughts over the uni-verse / Like wither'd leaves to quicken a new birth!" the sublime agi-tator knows his thoughts are undying. The word "incantation" has magic in it: if the "enchanter" of the first sonnet was an exorcist, Shelley, declaiming his poem, resurrects the dead:

> In a moment, in the twinkling of an eye, at the last trump:
> for the trumpet shall sound, and the dead shall be raised in-
> corruptible, and we shall be changed.
>
>   [1 Corinthians (KJV) 15:52]

Can there be an altogether secular prophecy? Only if you strip away from "prophecy" all that belonged to Amos, Micah, first Isa-iah, and here St. Paul. Shelley is the trumpet of a prophecy. He does not want the great winter of the world to be perpetual. I repeat the speech of the last Fury in *Prometheus Unbound:*

> In each human heart terror survives
> The ravin it has gorged: the loftiest fear
> All that they would disdain to think were true:
> Hypocrisy and custom make their minds
> The fanes of many a worship, now outworn.
> They dare not devise good for man's estate,
> And yet they know not that they do not dare.
> The good want power, but to weep barren tears.
> The powerful goodness want: worse need for them.
> The wise want love; and those who love want wisdom;
> And all best things are thus confused to ill.
> Many are strong and rich, and would be just,
> But live among their suffering fellow-men
> As if none felt: they know not what they do.
>
>   [1.618–631]

Does nothing change? It is exactly two centuries since Shelley composed these lines. Are they less true? I once told Paul de Man that *The Triumph of Life*, most despairing of great poems, still did not reduce either itself or earlier Shelleyan works to nought. It comes down to the question of metaphor and of metaphoric thinking. Does the epistemology of metaphor outweigh suggestiveness and persuasiveness? Can it be that this is simply another version of the ancient quarrel between Socrates and the Sophists?

The best analysis I have read of Protagoras, Gorgias, and their successors remains Mario Untersteiner's *The Sophists*, translated by Kathleen Freeman (1954). Gorgias, following Pindar and Athenian tragedians, worked out a tragic epistemology. Nothing exists. If anything does exist, it cannot be known. Even if known, it cannot be conveyed to others.

This profound commitment to irrationalism voids mere skepticism. There may be virtues but they are incommunicable. Art, however, can give the pleasure of aesthetic recognition. Perhaps most important, to quote Untersteiner: "It cannot be claimed that the epistemological essence of rhetoric is opposed to that of the universe." In the universe, everything is tragic.

Against Gorgias, Plato gives us the Socratic irony that rhetoric teaches everything and knows nothing. There is of course Plato's rhetoric that elevates the spirit and seems to know everything. I have learned slowly to go with Gorgias since everything I have come to know is tragic at its most dignified. Most of it is merely loss.

The greatest poetry—Homer, Sophocles, Pindar, Virgil, Dante, Chaucer, above all Shakespeare—transfigures rhetoric into forms of life and so of loss. Magnificent but more limited poets—Spenser, Milton, Goethe, Wordsworth, Shelley, Leopardi, Victor Hugo, Baudelaire—struggle to achieve that transfiguration and manage it only intermittently.

Prometheus Unbound, baroque splendor though it be, is uneven when it confronts Shelley's greatest challenges at sublime representation. Acts 3 and 4 really do attempt the impossible in seeking to show us a renovated universe and restored human beings. Shelley was barely twenty-eight, possessed enormous learning, a zest for revolutionizing society, a mission for freeing love, and a strange capacity for apprehending unknown modes of being. He also knew a great deal more about himself than many critics would concede. It may not be true that Shelley's Condition of Fire is thirsted for by all of us, but he believed it was. To him it was the inevitable image for longing.

Act 2 of *Prometheus Unbound* concludes with two memorable chants:

Voice in the Air, Singing:
Life of Life! thy lips enkindle
  With their love the breath between them;
And thy smiles before they dwindle
  Make the cold air fire; then screen them
In those looks, where whoso gazes
Faints, entangled in their mazes.
Child of Light! thy limbs are burning
  Through the vest which seems to hide them;
As the radiant lines of morning
  Through the clouds ere they divide them;
And this atmosphere divinest
Shrouds thee wheresoe'er thou shinest.

Fair are others; none beholds thee,
  But thy voice sounds low and tender
Like the fairest, for it folds thee
  From the sight, that liquid splendour,
And all feel, yet see thee never,
As I feel now, lost for ever!

Lamp of Earth! where'er thou movest
  Its dim shapes are clad with brightness,
And the souls of whom thou lovest
  Walk upon the winds with lightness,
Till they fail, as I am failing,
Dizzy, lost, yet unbewailing!

                                              [2.5.48–71]

Exegesis of a rapture this evasive is close to impossible. Asia in her glory appears to be a manifestation of the Neoplatonic astral body. Walter Benjamin, possibly stimulated by his close friend Gershom Scholem, secularized this as the aura, his version of the zelem, the image of Yahweh reflected in Adam, the principle of individuation in each of us.

In 1994 I reviewed an edition of Benjamin's correspondence in *Artforum* magazine. I had forgotten the review and discovered it by accident. I find it felicitous to use here:

> Brilliantly carrying Freud and Valéry back to Baudelaire, Benjamin found the trope of shock and catastrophe in the aura: "To perceive the aura of an object we look at means to invest it with the ability to look at us in return." That wonderful formula hovers in our consciousness and perhaps will become even more prevalent as the millennium comes closer.

The most famous image shared by Scholem and Benjamin, Paul Klee's painting Angelus Novus, became the final emblem of the aura. Benjamin wrote to Scholem that "the angels—new ones each moment in innumerable bands—are created so that after they have sung their hymn before God, they cease and dissolve into the naught." Scholem related this idea to the cabalistic tradition of the personal angel who is one's secret self yet whose very name remains unknown to one, an angel indeed less one's guardian (as in current American moonshine) than essentially opposed to the self, even working against the interests of the self, and so the veritable aura, the double able to gaze back upon us precisely because we unseeingly gaze at it.

In Genesis 1:26 we are told that we are made in God's *zelem* or image, an idea that rabbinical orthodoxy necessarily scanted, but that has delighted Jewish gnostics from ancient Alexandria down to Scholem. In cabala, as Scholem powerfully expounded it, the *zelem* is at once the mark of human individuality and also the subtle or astral body that defends our material body from the fires of our own soul. As in ancient gnosticism, where the pneuma (self or spark) was preferred to the psyche, so Benjamin chose the *zelem* or aura, his antithetical self, over the Freudian psyche. The aura is authentic individuality, both of the work of art and of the self, and its descent from the *zelem* or astral body suggests Benjamin's strange visionary materialism, the luminous envelope of appearances that defends the critic, however politically or historically oriented, from the chaos of the city in the 19th and 20th centuries.

The "Life of Life" lyric brilliantly captures Asia's aura or astral body. Her chant in response is a Shelleyan triumph, dexterously fusing the Neoplatonic with the Wordsworthian:

Asia:
    My soul is an enchanted boat,
    Which, like a sleeping swan, doth float
Upon the silver waves of thy sweet singing;
    And thine doth like an angel sit
    Beside a helm conducting it,
Whilst all the winds with melody are ringing.
    It seems to float ever, for ever,
    Upon that many-winding river,
    Between mountains, woods, abysses,
    A paradise of wildernesses!
Till, like one in slumber bound,
Borne to the ocean, I float down, around,
    Into a sea profound, of ever-spreading sound.

                                              [2.5.72–84]

The ocean is that of Wordsworth's Immortality Ode:

      Hence, in a season of calm weather
        Though inland far we be,
    Our Souls have sight of that immortal sea
        Which brought us hither,
        Can in a moment travel thither,
    And see the Children sport upon the shore,
    And hear the mighty waters rolling evermore.

Asia's voyage takes us by stages back to origins. Time in Shelley is not the mercy of eternity, as it is in Blake:

    Meanwhile thy spirit lifts its pinions
    In music's most serene dominions;

Catching the winds that fan that happy heaven.
   And we sail on, away, afar,
   Without a course, without a star,
But, by the instinct of sweet music driven;
   Till through Elysian garden islets
   By thee most beautiful of pilots,
   Where never mortal pinnace glided,
   The boat of my desire is guided:
Realms where the air we breathe is love,
Which in the winds on the waves doth move,
Harmonizing this earth with what we feel above.

                        [2.5.85–97]

It is as though Shelley seeks to redeem the doomed quest of the Poet in *Alastor*. We are offered a transmutation of narcissism into the atmosphere of a purified Eros:

   We have passed Age's icy caves,
   And Manhood's dark and tossing waves,
And Youth's smooth ocean, smiling to betray:
   Beyond the glassy gulfs we flee
   Of shadow-peopled Infancy,
Through Death and Birth, to a diviner day;
   A paradise of vaulted bowers,
   Lit by downward-gazing flowers,
   And watery paths that wind between
   Wildernesses calm and green,
Peopled by shapes too bright to see,
And rest, having beheld; somewhat like thee;
Which walk upon the sea, and chant melodiously!

                       [2.5.98–110]

Those "shapes too bright to see" are forms more real than living men and women. Dante and Spenser inform aspects of this vision, which has analogues in Bunyan and in Blake. Shelley allows the final line an inevitable association with the image of Jesus walking upon the water.

There is something unbounded in Shelley's aspirations that is unfulfillable. Acts 3 and 4 of the lyrical drama attempt the impossible: depiction of a renovated humankind and of a redeemed cosmos. The project is comparable to Blake's, but the style and spirit are totally remote from Blake's apocalyptic fireworks.

Act 3 commences with the fall of Jupiter, pulled down into the abyss by Demogorgon. It is as though Milton's supposed God suffered what he inflicted upon the rebel angels. Though I find this emotionally satisfying, it is really too outward for Shelley's transcendental art. From Scene 2 on, Shelley finds himself. At the mouth of a great river in the island of Atlantis, Ocean and Apollo stand side by side near the shore. They discuss with relish the tyrant's fall and welcome an end to all bloodshed. I take particular pleasure in the tone of Ocean as a pastoral shepherd:

Ocean
>   Thou must away;
> Thy steeds will pause at even, till when farewell.
> The loud deep calls me home even now to feed it
> With azure calm out of the emerald urns
> Which stand forever full beside my throne.
> Behold the Nereids under the green sea,
> Their wavering limbs borne on the wind-like stream,
> Their white arms lifted o'er their streaming hair
> With garlands pied and starry sea-flower crowns,
> Hastening to grace their mighty sister's joy.
>   [*A sound of waves is heard.*]

> It is the unpastured Sea hung'ring for Calm.
> Peace, Monster; I come now. Farewell.

Apollo
>   Farewell.
>   [3.2.39–50]

Shelley's urbanity was first noted by the late Donald Davie. I elaborated on Davie's view by demonstrating its uniqueness in representing the sublime. The wonderful *Letter to Maria Gisborne* (1820) is Shelley at play, rendering all finalities light and clear:

> Though we eat little flesh and drink no wine,
> Yet let's be merry! we'll have tea and toast;
> Custards for supper, and an endless host
> Of syllabubs and jellies and mince-pies,
> And other such lady-like luxuries—
> Feasting on which we will philosophize!
> And we'll have fires out of the Grand Duke's wood,
> To thaw the six weeks' winter in our blood.
> And then we'll talk—what shall we talk about?
> Oh, there are themes enough for many a bout
> Of thought-entangled descant;—as to nerves
> With cones and parallelograms and curves
> I've sworn to strangle them if once they dare
> To bother me—when you are with me there,
> And they shall never more sip laudanum,
> From Helicon or Himeros;—well, come,
> And in despite of God and of the devil
> We'll make our friendly philosophic revel
> Outlast the leafless time—till buds and flowers
> Warn the obscure inevitable hours
> Sweet meeting by sad parting to renew—
> "To-morrow to fresh woods and pastures new."
>
> [ll. 302–323]

By concluding with the final line of Milton's pastoral elegy *Lycidas*, Shelley civilizes poetic ambition, almost as though you could domesticate the sublime. His pastoral Ocean dispenses quiescence to the waves. There is an astonishing luster to the grand line: "It is the unpastured Sea hung'ring for Calm." What follows is beautifully paced: the rough affection of "Peace, Monster; I come now," and then the two modulated "Farewells." The uncanniness of this haunts me. It vindicates Wordsworth's remark: "Shelley is one of the best artists of us all: I mean in workmanship of style."

From first to last, Shelley made friends with the necessity of dying. And yet he believed passionately that there is something in us that prevails, beyond the natural and its limitations. Whatever that something was, it had to be discovered in Plato and Sophocles, Dante and Shakespeare, Milton and Goethe, and not in the New Testament. There is a delightful note in *Queen Mab* that retains pungency:

> But even supposing that a man should raise a dead body to life before
> our eyes, and on this fact rest his claim to being considered the son of
> God;—the Humane Society restores drowned persons, and because it makes
> no mystery of the method it employs, its members are not mistaken for
> the sons of God. All that we have a right to infer from our ignorance of
> the cause of any event is that we do not know it . . .

Though Shelley learned to endure his lack of a contemporary audience, he actually became widely known and admired by working-class radicals and their followers. Pirated texts of *Queen Mab* from 1821 all through the 1830s were profuse, and became the Bible for the Chartist movement. Friedrich Engels, friend and collaborator of Karl Marx, accurately remarked that the English working classes were passionately imbued with Shelley. I myself suspect that had Shelley lived, he would have been more at home with the anarchism of Proudhon and Kropotkin than with the communism of Marxism. And yet the instincts of the suffering workers of England were precisely accurate: Shelley was their poet and their prophet. He still is.

Old age has taught me that everything in Shelley is dialectical. Immortality, resurrection, and redemption are wavering entities in his speculation. What we might call the Shelleyan speculation could be applied as a critique to such figures as Nietzsche, Kierkegaard, Freud, and poets like Yeats, Brecht, Trakl, and Stevens. Consider the exchange between Earth and Asia:

The Earth

> And men and beasts in happy dreams shall gather
> Strength for the coming day, and all its joy;
> And death shall be the last embrace of her
> Who takes the life she gave, even as a mother,
> Folding her child, says, "Leave me not again."

Asia

> Oh, mother! wherefore speak the name of death?
> Cease they to love, and move, and breathe, and speak,
> Who die?

The Earth

> It would avail not to reply;
> Thou art immortal and this tongue is known
> But to the uncommunicating dead.
> Death is the veil which those who live call life;
> They sleep, and it is lifted . . .

> [3.3.103–114]

Shelley's first major poet-disciple was Thomas Lovell Beddoes, who committed suicide by poison at the age of forty-five in 1849. His outrageous masterpiece, *Death's Jest-Book*, was abandoned unfinished. It is a kind of Jacobean revenge tragedy in five sublimely mad acts, in which the line between human and ghostly existence becomes very indistinct. Beddoes was a remarkable medical anatomist and sought in his studies whatever evidence could be found for the survival of the spirit. He found none, and all of his work is a parody of resurrection.

Beddoes was homosexual and politically radical. He was expelled from various cities in Germany and Switzerland in response to his revolutionary agitation. Increasingly unbalanced, he attempted death by self-dissection and failed. Had Shelley lived, I think he could have saved Beddoes, but he drowned when his young Oxford disciple was just nineteen.

How are we to interpret Earth's cryptic pronouncement:

> Death is the veil which those who live call life;
> They sleep, and it is lifted . . .

In a sonnet of uncertain date (perhaps 1820), Shelley wrote variations on the same trope:

Lift not the painted veil which those who live
Call Life: though unreal shapes be pictured there,
And it but mimic all we would believe
With colours idly spread,—behind, lurk Fear
And Hope, twin Destinies; who ever weave
Their shadows, o'er the chasm, sightless and drear.
I knew one who had lifted it—he sought,
For his lost heart was tender, things to love,
But found them not, alas! nor was there aught
The world contains, the which he could approve.
Through the unheeding many he did move,
A splendour among shadows, a bright blot
Upon this gloomy scene, a Spirit that strove
For truth, and like the Preacher found it not.

Shelley is "a splendour among shadows" yet still only a shadow. He identifies himself with Koheleth, Hebrew for "the assembler," speaker of the strange book known as Ecclesiastes, by tradition associated with King Solomon the Wise. Truth cannot be found because everything is *hevel*, "vapor," just so much emptiness. Shelley's Demogorgon tells Asia: "The deep truth is imageless" (2.4.116).

Well, my path lately lay through a great city
Into the woody hills surrounding it:
A sentinel was sleeping at the gate:
When there was heard a sound, so loud, it shook
The towers amid the moonlight, yet more sweet
Than any voice but thine, sweetest of all . . .

[3.3.51–56]

In Act 3, Scene 4, the Spirit of the Earth embodies *kairos*, the opportune and appropriate moment in which an act can be truly significant. He tells Prometheus that he entered a city where suddenly the music of apocalypse was heard:

A long, long sound, as it would never end:
And all the inhabitants leaped suddenly
Out of their rest, and gathered in the streets,
Looking in wonder up to Heaven, while yet
The music pealed along. I hid myself
Within a fountain in the public square,
Where I lay like the reflex of the moon
Seen in a wave under green leaves; and soon
Those ugly human shapes and visages
Of which I spoke as having wrought me pain,
Passed floating through the air, and fading still
Into the winds that scattered them; and those
From whom they passed seemed mild and lovely forms
After some foul disguise had fallen, and all
Were somewhat changed, and after brief surprise
And greetings of delighted wonder, all
Went to their sleep again . . .

[3.4.57–73]

I recall commenting on this passage some sixty years ago in a book called *The Visionary Company* (1961). Now it seems even more magically urbane and graciously understated. "Somewhat changed" is delicately etched, and everyone sensibly goes back to sleep. I wonder what William Blake would have made of this quietude?

The Shelleyan chariot is permitted a singular apotheosis in a double vision of our possible redemption:

Ione

I see a chariot like that thinnest boat,
In which the Mother of the Months is borne
By ebbing light into her western cave,
When she upsprings from interlunar dreams;
O'er which is curved an orblike canopy
Of gentle darkness, and the hills and woods,
Distinctly seen through that dusk aery veil,
Regard like shapes in an enchanter's glass;
Its wheels are solid clouds, azure and gold,
Such as the genii of the thunderstorm

Pile on the floor of the illumined sea
When the sun rushes under it; they roll
And move and grow as with an inward wind;
Within it sits a wingèd infant, white
Its countenance, like the whiteness of bright snow,
Its plumes are as feathers of sunny frost,
Its limbs gleam white, through the wind-flowing folds
Of its white robe, woof of ethereal pearl.
Its hair is white, the brightness of white light
Scattered in strings; yet its two eyes are heavens
Of liquid darkness, which the Deity
Within seems pouring, as a storm is poured
From jaggèd clouds, out of their arrowy lashes,
Tempering the cold and radiant air around,
With fire that is not brightness; in its hand
It sways a quivering moonbeam, from whose point
A guiding power directs the chariot's prow
Over its wheelèd clouds, which as they roll
Over the grass, and flowers, and waves, wake sounds,
Sweet as a singing rain of silver dew.

[4.206–235]

The "fire that is not brightness," dark flame rising like the *duende* of the poet's breath-soul from the abyss now yielding a secret, tempers not only the air but the onrushing sound of the chariot that is no longer a vehicular form of divinity but of the human. Subsequently Shelley gifts us a humanized revision of the chariot that went from Ezekiel and Revelation through Dante and Milton onto the mischief-making advent of Queen Mab:

Panthea
With mighty whirl the multitudinous orb
Grinds the bright brook into an azure mist
Of elemental subtlety, like light;
And the wild odour of the forest flowers,
The music of the living grass and air,
The emerald light of leaf-entangled beams
Round its intense yet self-conflicting speed,

Seem kneaded into one aëreal mass
Which drowns the sense. Within the orb itself,
Pillowed upon its alabaster arms,
Like to a child o'erwearied with sweet toil,
On its own folded wings, and wavy hair,
The Spirit of the Earth is laid asleep,
And you can see its little lips are moving,
Amid the changing light of their own smiles,
Like one who talks of what he loves in dream.

Ione
'Tis only mocking the orb's harmony.

[4.253–269]

Ione's response is a candidate for one of my favorite lines in Shelley. The infant spirit of the earth mocks the harmony of the orb and of all that whirling kaleidoscope of spheres and axles. Shelley is wickedly funny when *kairos* calls for it.

This morning (January 20, 2019) I looked at the Sunday *Times* Style section and was bemused by the account of a young Japanese fellow in a white tuxedo who was formally marrying his sex robot. One of my favorite short stories is "Gogol's Wife" (1963) by Tommaso Landolfi (1908–1979), with whom I conversed occasionally when I was teaching in Rome. I told Landolfi how much I loved the story and he replied, rather impassively, that he was a scholar of Russian literature and could vouch for the truth of Gogol's married life.

I would not have wanted to play poker with Landolfi because he controlled his expression like a great mime. The narrator of "Gogol's Wife" presents himself as a faithful biographer, and tells us that the writer married a balloon, created according to his specifications. She had all the female charms, could speak, and was named Caracas by her insane and loving husband. However, she spoke infrequently and Gogol became furious at her silence. Employing a pump, Gogol inflated poor Caracas until she exploded. Her remains, including a baby boy balloon, were thrown into the fire, a familiar pattern for Gogol, who burned some magnificent manuscripts that are lost forever.

A literary critic is not qualified to prophesy whether the Japanese sex-robot bride will come to as sorrowful an end. All this is relevant to Shelley because after a few more observations on *Prometheus Unbound*, I will pass on to *The Witch of Atlas*, probably my favorite among all his longer poems.

The Earth chants what could be called Shelley's Hymn of Man:

> Man, one harmonious soul of many a soul,
>   Whose nature is its own divine control,
> Where all things flow to all, as rivers to the sea;
>   Familiar acts are beautiful through love;
>   Labour, and pain, and grief, in life's green grove
> Sport like tame beasts, none knew how gentle they could be!
>
> His will, with all mean passions, bad delights,
>   And selfish cares, its trembling satellites,
> A spirit ill to guide, but mighty to obey,
>   Is as a tempest-wingèd ship, whose helm
>   Love rules, through waves which dare not overwhelm,
> Forcing life's wildest shores to own its sovereign sway.
>
> All things confess his strength. Through the cold mass
>   Of marble and of colour his dreams pass;
> Bright threads whence mothers weave the robes their children
>   wear;
>   Language is a perpetual Orphic song,
>   Which rules with Dædal harmony a throng
> Of thoughts and forms, which else senseless and shapeless
>   were.
>
> The lightning is his slave; heaven's utmost deep
>   Gives up her stars, and like a flock of sheep
> They pass before his eye, are numbered, and roll on!
>   The tempest is his steed, he strides the air;
>   And the abyss shouts from her depth laid bare,
> Heaven, hast thou secrets? Man unveils me; I have none.

> [4.400–423]

How shall we interpret "Language is a perpetual Orphic song"?
For Shelley it may be that all of language is constituted by the ruins of
an abandoned cyclic poem. That may sound Borgesian, yet the Argen-
tine magus agreed with Shelley and Emerson (who did not like Shelley)
that the literary cosmos could seem the work of a single author.

Prometheus Unbound concludes with the baroque eloquence of
Demogorgon:

> This is the day, which down the void abysm
> At the Earth-born's spell yawns for Heaven's despotism,
>   And Conquest is dragged captive through the deep:
> Love, from its awful throne of patient power
> In the wise heart, from the last giddy hour
>   Of dread endurance, from the slippery, steep,
> And narrow verge of crag-like agony, springs
> And folds over the world its healing wings.
>
> Gentleness, Virtue, Wisdom, and Endurance,
> These are the seals of that most firm assurance
>   Which bars the pit over Destruction's strength;
> And if, with infirm hand, Eternity,
> Mother of many acts and hours, should free
>   The serpent that would clasp her with his length;
> These are the spells by which to reassume
> An empire o'er the disentangled doom.
>
> To suffer woes which Hope thinks infinite;
> To forgive wrongs darker than death or night;
>   To defy Power, which seems omnipotent;
> To love, and bear; to hope till Hope creates
> From its own wreck the thing it contemplates;
>   Neither to change, nor falter, nor repent;
> This, like thy glory, Titan, is to be
> Good, great and joyous, beautiful and free;
> This is alone Life, Joy, Empire, and Victory.

[4.554–578]

There are readers for whom this trumpet blast seems vainglori-
ous. I am not among them. Read closely, this is qualified and dialec-

tical. Time's serpent is poised to clasp an unwary Eternity that relaxes its hold. One can wonder at the process by which Hope creates what it desires from its own wreckage. All of us live, to one degree or another, with unfulfilled desires. We worry that we have failed to become ourselves. But who is Demogorgon to teach us this?

The joke is that Demogorgon began as a spelling error when a monk at work copying added an additional letter to Plato's Demiurge of the *Timaeus*. Boccaccio, churning out his *Genealogy of the Gentile Gods* (1360–1374), decided that Demogorgon was the dreadful father of all those false divinities. Shelley was too subtle to accept such an identification. His Demogorgon is rather like William Blake's Circle of Destiny. William Butler Yeats was unhappy with Shelley's Demogorgon, whom he thought incoherent. But Demogorgon is always at the turning: he rises up from his deep cave to overturn custom, ceremony, status, and the way things are. He is Shelley's conviction that the Unexpected will keep breaking into our days and nights. Chaucer's Knight tells us to bear ourselves always with equanimity, for constantly we are keeping appointments that we never made.

With considerable joy I turn to *The Witch of Atlas* (1824, written 1820). T. S. Eliot dismissed it as "a trifle," not one of his more auspicious pronouncements. Mary Shelley was enough of a Godwinian to see it as a waste of her husband's genius. Shelley himself knew better. G. Wilson Knight—whom I first met in the autumn of 1957 in Leeds, where he taught—in his book *The Starlit Dome* (1941), accurately compared *The Witch of Atlas* to the Byzantium poems of W. B. Yeats. I elaborated upon Wilson Knight in my books on Shelley (1959) and on Yeats (1970), following his tracks in the snow. He and I met a number of times through the years and corresponded. Several times we discussed *The Witch of Atlas*, a poem of seventy-eight *ottava rima* stanzas with a tonality markedly different from Byron's ventures in the same form. How shall we characterize Shelley's tone in the opening stanzas:

I.
Before those cruel Twins, whom at one birth
　Incestuous Change bore to her father Time,
Error and Truth, had hunted from the Earth

All those bright natures which adorned its prime,
And left us nothing to believe in, worth
    The pains of putting into learnèd rhyme,
A lady-witch there lived on Atlas' mountain
Within a cavern, by a secret fountain.

II.

Her mother was one of the Atlantides:
    The all-beholding Sun had ne'er beholden
In his wide voyage o'er continents and seas
    So fair a creature, as she lay enfolden
In the warm shadow of her loveliness;—
    He kissed her with his beams, and made all golden
The chamber of gray rock in which she lay—
She, in that dream of joy, dissolved away.

III.

'Tis said, she first was changed into a vapour,
    And then into a cloud, such clouds as flit,
Like splendour-wingèd moths about a taper,
    Round the red west when the sun dies in it:
And then into a meteor, such as caper
    On hill-tops when the moon is in a fit:
Then, into one of those mysterious stars
Which hide themselves between the Earth
        and Mars.

IV.

Ten times the Mother of the Months had bent
    Her bow beside the folding-star, and bidden
With that bright sign the billows to indent
    The sea-deserted sand—like children chidden,
At her command they ever came and went—
    Since in that cave a dewy splendour hidden
Took shape and motion: with the living form
Of this embodied Power, the cave grew warm.

[ll. 49–80]

Shelley's "Mont Blanc" (1816) introduced us to "the still cave of the witch Poesy." The tone of "Mont Blanc" is high sublime, quite unlike the gently darting inflection of *The Witch of Atlas*. Shelley probably was indebted to his own translation of the *Homeric Hymn to Mercury* (1818):

I.

Sing, Muse, the son of Maia and of Jove,
The Herald-child, king of Arcadia
And all its pastoral hills, whom in sweet love
Having been interwoven, modest May
Bore Heaven's dread Supreme. An antique grove
Shadowed the cavern where the lovers lay
In the deep night, unseen by Gods or Men,
And white-armed Juno slumbered sweetly then.

II.

Now, when the joy of Jove had its fulfilling,
And Heaven's tenth moon chronicled her relief,
She gave to light a babe all babes excelling,
A schemer subtle beyond all belief;
A shepherd of thin dreams, a cow-stealing,
A night-watching, and door-waylaying thief,
Who 'mongst the Gods was soon about to
    thieve,
And other glorious actions to achieve.

III.

The babe was born at the first peep of day;
He began playing on the lyre at noon,
And the same evening did he steal away
Apollo's herds;—the fourth day of the moon
On which him bore the venerable May,
From her immortal limbs he leaped full soon,
Nor long could in the sacred cradle keep,
But out to seek Apollo's herds would creep.

[ll. 1–24]

This imp is considerably less dignified than the beautiful Witch of Atlas yet he presages her mischievous spirit. Entirely her own is a universal magnetic appeal:

V.
A lovely lady garmented in light
    From her own beauty—deep her eyes, as are
Two openings of unfathomable night
    Seen through a Temple's cloven roof—her hair
Dark—the dim brain whirls dizzy with delight,
    Picturing her form—her soft smiles shone afar,
And her low voice was heard like love, and drew
All living things towards this wonder new.

[ll. 81–88]

I interrupt myself here for a personal digression that may enrich my exegesis of Shelley's visionary rhyme. During the academic year 1954–1955, I lived in Pembroke College, Cambridge. I was a Fulbright Fellow at work on my Yale dissertation that in time became my first book, *Shelley's Mythmaking* (1959). Pembroke was very convivial and I spent much of my time with a group of mostly Celtic undergraduates devoted to poetry and fairly heavy imbibings of sherry and many other liquors. I became particularly fond of the charming Dean of Pembroke, the Reverend Meredith Dewey, splendidly eccentric and indomitable. We surmounted our religious difference, dined together frequently, and discussed the complexities of human nature. Meredith was devout and evidently ascetic, yet with a wild sense of humor.

Nearing the close of the second of the year's three terms, the Dean asked me what I intended to do with the six-week break. I replied cheerfully that I intended to go back to Scotland and Ireland with my cronies and travel from pub to pub. "No!" said Dewey. "You are going to Saint Deiniol's Rectory in Hawarden, Wales, across the border from Chester. It is William Ewart Gladstone's estate and library which he left to the Church. For company you will have only young Anglican priests studying or on retreat, and with the help of Gladstone's library you will write your Shelley dissertation for Yale."

"Nothing," I replied, "could be as dismal as that ghastly prospect!" At this the Dean pulled a letter from his pocket and handed it to me. I shuddered as I recognized the handwriting of Professor Frederick Albert Pottle, my mentor and dissertation adviser, whom I held in the utmost awe. The gist of the note was that I had departed for Pembroke after writing only one chapter and he had not heard from me since. Against fierce opposition he had demanded a faculty instructorship for me at Yale, but it depended on my returning in September with a finished dissertation.

I wrote some six hundred pages at Saint Deiniol's, talking to almost no one, and absorbing much too much sherry and claret. My only recreation was a daily afternoon croquet match with the Warden of Saint Deiniol's and the Bishop of Chester, for a shilling a game. Since I was absorbed by Shelley and not very adept anyway, I tended to lose. One day, however, as I was looking up at the clouds and thinking about *The Witch of Atlas*, upon which I was writing a commentary, I glanced down to see that the Bishop of Chester slyly was nudging the ball over. He then slammed it home with a chuckle. When I remonstrated, the cheerful Warden sang out: "That will teach you, Bloom, to keep sharp lookout when you contend with gentlemen of the cloth!"

I have held on to that sensible advice ever since. Sometimes I think that the Witch of Atlas herself might have appreciated this mercurial wickedness, particularly because she shared in Shelley's anti-clericalism:

LXXIII.
The priests would write an explanation full,
   Translating hieroglyphics into Greek,
How the God Apis really was a bull,
   And nothing more; and bid the herald stick
The same against the temple doors, and pull
   The old cant down; they licensed all to speak
What'er they thought of hawks, and cats, and geese,
By pastoral letters to each diocese.

[ll. 625–632]

I still associate Shelley's dazzling epyllion with my somber sojourn at Gladstone's library. Last night I dreamed about the Witch of Atlas. I was floating downriver in a curious craft, alone with that beautiful apparition, and tried to speak to her, but she maintained silence. I woke up at dawn unsure as to whether the dream was over. Some stanzas flashed into my mind:

XXII.

The Ocean-nymphs and Hamadryades,
　Oreads and Naiads, with long weedy locks,
Offered to do her bidding through the seas,
　Under the earth, and in the hollow rocks,
And far beneath the matted roots of trees,
　And in the gnarlèd heart of stubborn oaks,
So they might live for ever in the light
Of her sweet presence—each a satellite.

XXIII.

"This may not be," the wizard maid replied;
　"The fountains where the Naiades bedew
Their shining hair, at length are drained and dried;
　The solid oaks forget their strength, and strew
Their latest leaf upon the mountains wide;
　The boundless ocean like a drop of dew
Will be consumed—the stubborn centre must
Be scattered, like a cloud of summer dust.

XXIV.

"And ye with them will perish, one by one;—
　If I must sigh to think that this shall be,
If I must weep when the surviving Sun
　Shall smile on your decay—oh, ask not me
To love you till your little race is run;
　I cannot die as ye must—over me
Your leaves shall glance—the streams in which ye dwell
Shall be my paths henceforth, and so—farewell!"—

XXV.

She spoke and wept:—the dark and azure well
　Sparkled beneath the shower of her bright tears,
And every little circlet where they fell

Flung to the cavern-roof inconstant spheres
And intertangled lines of light:—a knell
   Of sobbing voices came upon her ears
From those departing Forms, o'er the serene
Of the white streams and of the forest green.

[ll. 217–248]

Shelley defended *The Witch of Atlas* against his wife, Mary, who lamented its lack of human interest. The seer of *Frankenstein* took too narrow a view. Ambivalence, ambiguity, forebodings of sorrow, anguish of separation—all these throng the poem. The Witch's immortality cuts her off even from the Naiades, who live far longer than humans yet eventually must die. A presage of William Butler Yeats, who was deeply imbued with *The Witch of Atlas*, can be felt in:

the stubborn centre must
Be scattered, like a cloud of summer dust.

But for Shelley the visionary center *can* hold since the Witch is the ministry of how meaning gets started and then is augmented:

XXVI.
All day the wizard lady sate aloof,
   Spelling out scrolls of dread antiquity,
Under the cavern's fountain-lighted roof;
   Or broidering the pictured poesy
Of some high tale upon her growing woof,
   Which the sweet splendour of her smiles could dye
In hues outshining heaven—and ever she
Added some grace to the wrought poesy.

XXVII.
While on her hearth lay blazing many a piece
   Of sandal wood, rare gums, and cinnamon;
Men scarcely know how beautiful fire is—
   Each flame of it is as a precious stone
Dissolved in ever-moving light, and this
   Belongs to each and all who gaze upon.

The Witch beheld it not, for in her hand
She held a woof that dimmed the burning brand.

XXVIII.
This lady never slept, but lay in trance
    All night within the fountain—as in sleep.
Its emerald crags glowed in her beauty's glance;
    Through the green splendour of the water deep
She saw the constellations reel and dance
    Like fire-flies—and withal did ever keep
The tenour of her contemplations calm,
With open eyes, closed feet, and folded palm.

XXIX.
And when the whirlwinds and the clouds descended
    From the white pinnacles of that cold hill,
She passed at dewfall to a space extended,
    Where in a lawn of flowering asphodel
Amid a wood of pines and cedars blended,
    There yawned an inextinguishable well
Of crimson fire—full even to the brim,
And overflowing all the margin trim.

XXX.
Within the which she lay when the fierce war
    Of wintry winds shook that innocuous liquor
In many a mimic moon and bearded star
    O'er woods and lawns;—the serpent heard it
        flicker
In sleep, and dreaming still, he crept afar—
    And when the windless snow descended thicker
Than autumn leaves, she watched it as it came
Melt on the surface of the level flame.

[ll. 249–288]

This Shelleyan fire of fires ignited both Yeats and Wallace Stevens
in rather different ways. In Stevens's pre-elegy for the philosopher

George Santayana, "To an Old Philosopher in Rome" (1952), the Shelleyan flame burns on as "a light on the candle tearing against the wick / To join a hovering excellence."

Santayana had taught Stevens at Harvard; the two even engaged in a sonnet-writing competition. As the atheist philosopher approached death in Rome, he was cared for by nuns; appropriate because his deep respect for Roman Catholic culture survived his unbelief.

The Witch rests in trance, her bed being a well of crimson fire. A true Shelleyan, she requires a boat for perpetual voyaging:

XXXIV.
This boat she moored upon her fount, and lit
  A living spirit within all its frame,
Breathing the soul of swiftness into it.
  Couched on the fountain like a panther tame,
One of the twain at Evan's feet that sit—
  Or as on Vesta's sceptre a swift flame—
Or on blind Homer's heart a wingèd thought,—
In joyous expectation lay the boat.

XXXV.
Then by strange art she kneaded fire and snow
  Together, tempering the repugnant mass
With liquid love—all things together grow
  Through which the harmony of love can pass;
And a fair Shape out of her hands did flow—
  A living Image, which did far surpass
In beauty that bright shape of vital stone
Which drew the heart out of Pygmalion.

XXXVI.
A sexless thing it was, and in its growth
  It seemed to have developed no defect
Of either sex, yet all the grace of both,—
  In gentleness and strength its limbs were decked;
The bosom swelled lightly with its full youth,

The countenance was such as might select
Some artist that his skill should never die,
Imaging forth such perfect purity.

XXXVII.
From its smooth shoulders hung two rapid wings,
    Fit to have borne it to the seventh sphere,
Tipped with the speed of liquid lightenings,
    Dyed in the ardours of the atmosphere:
She led her creature to the boiling springs
    Where the light boat was moored, and said: "Sit here!"
And pointed to the prow, and took her seat
Beside the rudder, with opposing feet.

[ll. 313–344]

Subtly Shelley foreshadows the limitation of his visionary cosmocrator: the Hermaphrodite, with all its incapacities, is the best she can do, one more False Florimell. The classical Hermaphroditus was the son of Hermes and Aphrodite. Shelley's Hermaphrodite is more a robot than a transgendered human. It provides the Witch with a mode of fantastic voyaging:

LVII.
But her choice sport was, in the hours of sleep,
    To glide adown old Nilus, where he threads
Egypt and AEthiopia, from the steep
    Of utmost Axumè, until he spreads,
Like a calm flock of silver-fleecèd sheep,
    His waters on the plain: and crested heads
Of cities and proud temples gleam amid,
And many a vapour-belted pyramid.

LVIII.
By Moeris and the Mareotid lakes,
    Strewn with faint blooms like bridal chamber floors,
Where naked boys bridling tame water-snakes,
    Or charioteering ghastly alligators,

Had left on the sweet waters mighty wakes
  Of those huge forms—within the brazen doors
Of the great Labyrinth slept both boy and beast,
Tired with the pomp of their Osirian feast.

LIX.
And where within the surface of the river
  The shadows of the massy temples lie,
And never are erased—but tremble ever
  Like things which every cloud can doom to die,
Through lotus-paven canals, and wheresoever
  The works of man pierced that serenest sky
With tombs, and towers, and fanes, 'twas her delight
To wander in the shadow of the night.

[ll. 497–520]

William Butler Yeats wrote two sublime death poems, "Cuchulain Comforted" (1939) and "Man and the Echo" (1938). His official
death poem, "Under Ben Bulben" (1938), is not very good, but two
among the opening quatrains come alive by drawing upon Shelley's
Witch:

I
Swear by what the Sages spoke
Round the Mareotic Lake
That the Witch of Atlas knew,
Spoke and set the cocks a-crow . . .

II

. . .
Though grave-diggers' toil is long,
Sharp their spades, their muscle strong,
They but thrust their buried men
Back in the human mind again.

[ll. 1–4, 21–24]

That second quatrain echoes the Witch at her most exuberant:

LXII.

But other troubled forms of sleep she saw,
   Not to be mirrored in a holy song—
Distortions foul of supernatural awe,
   And pale imaginings of visioned wrong;
And all the code of Custom's lawless law
   Written upon the brows of old and young:
"This," said the wizard maiden, "is the strife
Which stirs the liquid surface of man's life."

LXIII.

And little did the sight disturb her soul.—
   We, the weak mariners of that wide lake
Where'er its shores extend or billows roll,
   Our course unpiloted and starless make
O'er its wild surface to an unknown goal:—
   But she in the calm depths her way could take,
Where in bright bowers immortal forms abide
Beneath the weltering of the restless tide. . . .
. . .

LXX.

For on the night when they were buried, she
   Restored the embalmers' ruining, and shook
The light out of the funeral lamps, to be
   A mimic day within that deathly nook;
And she unwound the woven imagery
   Of second childhood's swaddling bands, and
      took
The coffin, its last cradle, from its niche,
And threw it with contempt into a ditch. . . .

                    [ll. 537–552, 601–608]

Yeats consciously never got over the influence of Shelley's Witch. She became for him the patroness of his great "Byzantium" poem (1930) and also a guiding spirit for his occult system *A Vision* (1925, 1937). Anticipating Yeats, Shelley writes,

LXXIV.

The king would dress an ape up in his crown
  And robes, and seat him on his glorious seat,
And on the right hand of the sunlike throne
  Would place a gaudy mock-bird to repeat
The chatterings of the monkey.—Every one
  Of the prone courtiers crawled to kiss the feet
Of their great Emperor, when the morning came,
And kissed—alas, how many kiss the same!

LXXV.

The soldiers dreamed that they were blacksmiths, and
  Walked out of quarters in somnambulism;
Round the red anvils you might see them stand
  Like Cyclopses in Vulcan's sooty abysm,
Beating their swords to ploughshares;—in a band
  The jailors sent those of the liberal schism
Free through the streets of Memphis, much, I wis,
To the annoyance of king Amasis. . . .

                                        [ll. 633–648]

This is a jocular version of what Yeats will call Byzantium, not so much a city as the condition of being a poem and also a stage in the soul's wandering after death and before rebirth. Shelley finds the perfect pitch for concluding his fantastic vision:

LXXVIII.

These were the pranks she played among the cities
  Of mortal men, and what she did to Sprites
And Gods, entangling them in her sweet ditties
  To do her will, and show their subtle sleights,
I will declare another time; for it is
  A tale more fit for the weird winter nights
Than for these garish summer days, when we
Scarcely believe much more than we can see.

That promise was not fulfilled. Shelley abandoned this playful splendor so as to go on to what Keats called the shores of darkness:

Standing aloof in giant ignorance,
   Of thee I hear and of the Cyclades,
As one who sits ashore and longs perchance
   To visit dolphin-coral in deep seas.
So thou wast blind;—but then the veil was rent,
   For Jove uncurtain'd Heaven to let thee live,
And Neptune made for thee a spumy tent,
   And Pan made sing for thee his forest-hive;
Aye on the shores of darkness there is light,
   And precipices show untrodden green,
There is a budding morrow in midnight,
   There is a triple sight in blindness keen;
Such seeing hadst thou, as it once befel
To Dian, Queen of Earth, and Heaven, and Hell.

                [Keats, "To Homer" (1818)]

The formidable scholar-critic Jerome McGann once suggested that Shelley, in his final years, was moving toward a stance closer to Keats's. I admire McGann for many reasons, though we agree on very little. His critique of my own work emphasizes the notion of "care." I would think he urges a sense of otherness upon me, a reminder that the social world always exists. But that seems to me a kind of double-entry bookkeeping: historical society frames every poem. Remove the frame and the essential poem remains. It struggles with prior poems and with the pastness of language history. In any case, McGann is McGann and Bloom is Bloom. The issue is the liveliness of interpretation. He works his work, I mine.

Transumption is a diachronic trope and so is involved in history. That chronicle is more linguistic, rhetorical, cognitive, psychological, and cosmological than it is social, political, and economic. Shelley was supremely intelligent and, as a revolutionary agitator, immensely concerned with the wickedness of state, church, the upper classes, and what Blake called "mind-forged manacles." Primarily, though, he was a major lyric poet, concerned to work out his relationship to Plato and Aeschylus, Lucretius and Ovid, Dante and Milton, Goethe and Wordsworth, Byron and Keats, among others, including Rousseau. He is highly aware of the dialectical nature of literary influence: what it gives with one hand, it takes away with the other.

Before following him through the major sequence of *Epipsychid-ion* (1821), *Adonais*, *Hellas* (1821), the final lyrics to Jane Williams, and *The Triumph of Life*, I turn to the remarkable hymns he wrote for his wife Mary's mythological drama *Midas* (1820).

> Liquid Peneus was flowing,
>   And all dark Tempe lay
> In Pelion's shadow, outgrowing
>   The light of the dying day,
>   Speeded by my sweet pipings.
> The Sileni, and Sylvans, and Fauns,
>   And the Nymphs of the woods and the
>   waves,
> To the edge of the moist river-lawns,
>   And the brink of the dewy caves,
> And all that did then attend and follow,
> Were silent with love, as you now, Apollo,
>   With envy of my sweet pipings.
> I sang of the dancing stars,
>   I sang of the daedal Earth,
> And of Heaven, and the giant wars,
>   And Love, and Death, and Birth—
>   And then I chang'd my pipings,
> Singing how down the vale of Maenalus
>   I pursu'd a maiden and clasp'd a reed.
> Gods and men, we are all deluded thus!
>   It breaks in our bosom and then we bleed.
> All wept, as I think both ye now would,
> If envy or age had not frozen your blood,
>   At the sorrow of my sweet pipings.

The rush and delight of this tumultuous rhapsody initially con-ceal its sting:

> I pursu'd a maiden and clasp'd a reed.
> Gods and men, we are all deluded thus!
>   It breaks in our bosom and then we bleed.
>   ["Hymn of Pan" (written 1820)]

An erotomaniac, Pan pursues the nymph Syrinx, who metamor-
phosizes into a reed. Still inflamed, the goatish god binds seven reeds
together and thus creates panpipes, the musical instrument he
wistfully names Syrinx. I think we can hear in this song ironic
self-recognition. Shelley could not stop falling in love. As if to recompense for this ruefulness, something like the Andalusian *duende*,
or "black sounds," rises up from the foundations of Shelley's being
to chant the glory of Apollo, archetypal poet:

> The sleepless Hours who watch me as I lie,
>   Curtained with star-inwoven tapestries,
> From the broad moonlight of the sky;
>   Fanning the busy dreams from my dim eyes,
> Waken me when their Mother, the gray Dawn,
> Tells them that Dreams and that the moon is gone.
>
> Then I arise, and climbing Heaven's blue dome,
>   I walk over the mountains and the waves,
> Leaving my robe upon the Ocean foam;
>   My footsteps pave the clouds with fire; the caves
> Are filled with my bright presence, and the air
> Leaves the green Earth to my embraces bare.
>
> The sunbeams are my shafts, with which I kill
>   Deceit, that loves the night and fears the day.
> All men who do, or even imagine ill
>   Fly me, and from the glory of my ray
> Good minds and open actions take new might,
> Until diminished, by the reign of night.
>
> I feed the clouds, the rainbows and the flowers,
>   With their ethereal colors; the moon's globe
> And the pure stars in their eternal bowers
>   Are cinctured with my power as with a robe;
> Whatever lamps on Earth or Heaven may shine,
> Are portions of one power; which is mine.
>
> I stand at noon upon the peak of Heaven;
>   Then with unwilling steps, I linger down
> Into the clouds of the Atlantic even.

For grief that I depart they weep and frown—
What look is more delightful than the smile
With which I soothe them from the western isle?

I am the eye with which the Universe
    Beholds itself, and knows it is divine;
All harmony of instrument or verse,
    All prophecy, all medicine, is mine,
All light of art or nature;—to my song
Victory and praise in its own right belong.
                    ["Hymn of Apollo" (written 1820)]

What I would call Shelley's gnosis is concentrated in one astonishing metaphor:

I am the eye with which the Universe
    Beholds itself, and knows it is divine . . .

Wallace Stevens, Shelley depoliticized, renders the trope more
aggressively when he pictures at the end of his *Notes toward a Supreme Fiction* "a war between the mind / And sky, between thought
and day and night." Stevens adds, "It is / For that the poet is always
in the sun" ("It Must Give Pleasure").

In the war between sky and mind, the poet cannot win. Stevens
knows that but fights on. Shelley's Orphism will not yield. His is the
ocular revelation through which the cosmos knows and beholds its
own divinity. Even a momentary fusion with Apollo destroys the vital reserves upon which further poetic making relies. After this,
Shelley takes the path downward and outward in which the Condition of Fire begins to consume more than it awards. As I read it, that
is the story of *Epipsychidion*.

In a letter of June 18, 1822, to John Gisborne, Shelley described
the work:

The "Epipsychidion" I cannot look at; the person whom it
celebrates was a cloud instead of a Juno; and poor Ixion starts
from the Centaur that was the offspring of his own embrace.
If you are curious, however, to hear what I am and have been,
it will tell you something thereof. It is an idealized history of

my life and feelings. I think one is always in love with something or other; the error, and I confess it is not easy for spirits cased in flesh and blood to avoid it, consists in seeking in a mortal image the likeness of what is, perhaps, eternal.

I am uncertain as to how this disavowal should affect our reading of *Epipsychidion*. Much of Shelley's prose is remarkable, but he is not one of the great letter writers like John Keats. It is doubtful that the twenty-eight-year-old Shelley and the nineteen-year-old Teresa Viviani actually had a sexual relationship, as circumstances made it all but impossible. Shelleyan eros usually was palpable enough: he and Claire Clairmont maintained a discontinuous but enduring liaison until his death. Like Byron, he may have fathered a daughter upon her who, like Claire's daughter Allegra by Byron, died young.

Following Chaucer's Knight's Tale and its source in Boccaccio, Shelley, Mary, and Claire called Teresa by the name Emilia. Since Shelley had addressed *Epipsychidion* to Teresa Viviani, under the name of Emily, Emily Dickinson felt authorized to answer a poet who, like herself, favored the image of volcanoes. Only ten days or so before her lover Judge Lord died, she composed a remarkable quatrain in his honor (and her own):

> Circumference thou Bride of Awe
> Possessing thou shalt be
> Possessed by every hallowed Knight
> That dares—to covet thee.

[Poem 1620]

Dickinson's biographer Richard Sewall noted the interplay with some lines in *Epipsychidion*:

> Possessing and possest by all that is
> Within that calm circumference of bliss,
> And by each other, till to love and live
> Be one:—

[ll. 549–552]

Dickinson's trope of "circumference" has a number of sources, including Emerson, but this Shelleyan context clearly is one of them. I have always wondered how Dickinson reacted to Shelley's doctrine of free love in *Epipsychidion:*

> Thy wisdom speaks in me, and bids me dare
> Beacon the rocks on which high hearts are wrecked.
> I never was attached to that great sect,
> Whose doctrine is, that each one should select
> Out of the crowd a mistress or a friend,
> And all the rest, though fair and wise, commend
> To cold oblivion, though it is in the code
> Of modern morals, and the beaten road
> Which those poor slaves with weary footsteps tread,
> Who travel to their home among the dead
> By the broad highway of the world, and so
> With one chained friend, perhaps a jealous foe,
> The dreariest and the longest journey go.
>
> True Love in this differs from gold and clay,
> That to divide is not to take away.
> Love is like understanding, that grows bright,
> Gazing on many truths; 'tis like thy light,
> Imagination! which from earth and sky,
> And from the depths of human phantasy,
> As from a thousand prisms and mirrors, fills
> The Universe with glorious beams, and kills
> Error, the worm, with many a sun-like arrow
> Of its reverberated lightning. Narrow
> The heart that loves, the brain that contemplates,
> The life that wears, the spirit that creates
> One object, and one form, and builds thereby
> A sepulchre for its eternity.

[ll. 147–173]

Shelley had a rare gift for arguing cogently in verse, and here he surpasses himself. I would think Emily Dickinson accepted these

strong notions. Mary Shelley, reading this, must have been made unhappy. One feels that Shelley would have been best off with Mary
Wollstonecraft, who died giving birth to Mary Godwin, who became the second Mrs. Shelley.

When I was younger, I greatly admired *Epipsychidion*. In late old
age I like it only in certain passages. It is a fireworks display of extraordinary imagery, bursting like a Roman candle and returning
soon enough to an experiential darkness:

> We shall become the same, we shall be one
> Spirit within two frames, oh! wherefore two?
> One passion in twin-hearts, which grows and grew,
> Till like two meteors of expanding flame,
> Those spheres instinct with it become the same,
> Touch, mingle, are transfigured; ever still
> Burning, yet ever inconsumable:
> In one another's substance finding food,
> Like flames too pure and light and unimbued
> To nourish their bright lives with baser prey,
> Which point to Heaven and cannot pass away:
> One hope within two wills, one will beneath
> Two overshadowing minds, one life, one death,
> One Heaven, one Hell, one immortality.

[ll. 573–586]

Shelley is his own tradition even if Plato and Dante are shadowy presences. The rhapsodies of *Prometheus Unbound* are validated
by a context carefully constructed to accommodate their coherence.
Epipsychidion is another story. Depending upon the perspective you
bring to it, the poem is either a spectacular failure or a success we
do not know how to apprehend. There is something ruthlessly experimental about Shelley's poetics. Every other genre is converted
into lyric. I think of a reflection by Henry James in *The Bostonians*
(1886), commenting upon Olive Chancellor: "She was a spinster as
Shelley was a lyric poet."

I cannot abandon *Epipsychidion* without a brief meditation on
Shelley's vision of love between the sexes. Ultimately Shelley came to
believe that good and the means of good were irreconcilable. This

held also for love. The most terrible aspect of *The Triumph of Life* is its bitter demonstration that love and the means of love are antithetical:

They, tortured by their agonizing pleasure,
Convulsed and on the rapid whirlwinds spun
Of that fierce spirit, whose unholy leisure

Was soothed by mischief since the world begun,
Throw back their heads and loose their streaming hair,
And in their dance round her who dims the sun,

Maidens and youths fling their wild arms in air
As their feet twinkle; they recede, and now
Bending within each other's atmosphere

Kindle invisibly—and as they glow,
Like moths by light attracted and repelled,
Oft to new bright destruction come and go,

Till like two clouds into one vale impelled
That shake the mountains when their lightnings mingle
And die in rain—the fiery band which held

Their natures, snaps—the shock still may tingle;
One falls and then another in the path
Senseless,—nor is the desolation single,

Yet ere I can say *where*—the chariot hath
Past over them—nor other trace I find
But as of foam after the ocean's wrath

Is spent upon the desert shore.—Behind,
Old men, and women foully disarrayed
Shake their grey hairs in the insulting wind,

To seek, to [ ], to strain with limbs decayed
Limping to reach the light which leaves them still
Farther behind and deeper in the shade.

But not the less with impotence of will
They wheel, though ghastly shadows interpose
Round them and round each other, and fulfill

Their work, and in the dust whence they rose
Sink, and corruption veils them as they lie . . .

[ll. 143–174]

Nathaniel Hawthorne, as his notebooks show, read Shelley with considerable interest and discernment. I do not know whether he read *The Triumph of Life*, but it was available to him. Whenever I recite those disheartening lines in which old men and women foully disarrayed limp and strain to join the erotic dance of death, I remember Hawthorne's mordant tale in which three aged lechers and a withered hoyden momentarily return to youth after quaffing a magic elixir:

> They all gathered round her. One caught both her hands in his passionate grasp,—another threw his arm about her waist,—the third buried his hand among the glossy curls that clustered beneath the widow's cap. Blushing, panting, struggling, chiding, laughing, her warm breath fanning each of their faces by turns, she strove to disengage herself, yet still remained in their triple embrace. Never was there a livelier picture of youthful rivalship, with bewitching beauty for the prize. Yet, by a strange deception, owing to the duskiness of the chamber, and the antique dresses which they still wore, the tall mirror is said to have reflected the figures of the three old, gray, withered grandsires, ridiculously contending for the skinny ugliness of a shrivelled grandam··
>
> ["Dr. Heidegger's Experiment" (1837)]

Hawthorne, whose marriage to Sophia Peabody was the happiest in literary history, can be more detached than Shelley in confronting a rancid eros. For Shelley it mocked his hope for human love. The death of John Keats, aged just twenty-five and four months, on February 23, 1821, prompted Shelley to compose the major pastoral elegy in English since *Lycidas*, the rhapsodic *Adonais*, in fifty-five Spenserian stanzas. It is in the final seventeen stanzas that the poem soars:

XXXVIII.

Nor let us weep that our delight is fled
Far from these carrion kites that scream below;
He wakes or sleeps with the enduring dead;
Thou canst not soar where he is sitting now.—
Dust to the dust! but the pure spirit shall flow
Back to the burning fountain whence it came,
A portion of the Eternal, which must glow
Through time and change, unquenchably the same,
Whilst thy cold embers choke the sordid hearth of shame.

[ll. 334–342]

That burning fountain goes back to Plotinus, yet Shelley appropriates it so deftly that it has become his own. In him it merges with the Promethean fire or human protest against mortality.

XXXIX.

Peace, peace! he is not dead, he doth not sleep—
He hath awakened from the dream of life—
'Tis we, who lost in stormy visions, keep
With phantoms an unprofitable strife,
And in mad trance, strike with our spirit's knife
Invulnerable nothings.—*We* decay
Like corpses in a charnel; fear and grief
Convulse us and consume us day by day,
And cold hopes swarm like worms within our living clay.

[ll. 343–351]

Brilliantly Shelley evokes Macbeth:

Is this a dagger which I see before me,
The handle toward my hand? Come, let me clutch thee.
I have thee not, and yet I see thee still.
Art thou not, fatal vision, sensible
To feeling as to sight? or art thou but
A dagger of the mind, a false creation,
Proceeding from the heat-oppressèd brain?

I see thee yet, in form as palpable
As this which now I draw.

[2.1.33–41]

A false creation suggests Gnosticism rather than Plotinus. Hallucination substitutes for vision. But Shelley presses on and recalls the
Dantesque image of the earth's shadow ceasing at the sphere of Venus:

XL.

He has outsoared the shadow of our night;
Envy and calumny and hate and pain,
And that unrest which men miscall delight,
Can touch him not and torture not again;
From the contagion of the world's slow stain
He is secure, and now can never mourn
A heart grown cold, a head grown grey in vain;
Nor, when the spirit's self has ceased to burn,
With sparkless ashes load an unlamented urn.

[ll. 352–360]

One might wish that the reference of those closing lines could
be restricted to the wretched Robert Southey, but the allusion certainly includes Wordsworth and Coleridge.

XLII.

He is made one with Nature: there is heard
His voice in all her music, from the moan
Of thunder, to the song of night's sweet bird;
He is a presence to be felt and known
In darkness and in light, from herb and stone,
Spreading itself where'er that Power may move
Which has withdrawn his being to its own;
Which wields the world with never-wearied love,
Sustains it from beneath, and kindles it above.

[ll. 370–378]

The tribute to Keats is gloriously deserved, since he has captured
the song of the nightingale once and for all time. How can we de-

fine that Power of cosmic love whose being has absorbed Keats and at once sustains us from the depths and changes us to sparks moving upward?

XLIII.

> He is a portion of the loveliness
> Which once he made more lovely: he doth bear
> His part, while the one Spirit's plastic stress
> Sweeps through the dull dense world, compelling there,
> All new successions to the forms they wear;
> Torturing th'unwilling dross that checks its flight
> To its own likeness, as each mass may bear;
> And bursting in its beauty and its might
> From trees and beasts and men into the Heavens' light.
>
> [ll. 379–387]

Whatever that one Spirit may be, it seems too purgative to be Neoplatonic. Bursting upward is not so much an apocalyptic movement as it is redemptive. Yet we sense that *Prometheus Unbound*, with its curiously baroque urbanity, is very different from what Shelley aspires to describe.

XLIV.

> The splendours of the firmament of time
> May be eclipsed, but are extinguished not;
> Like stars to their appointed height they climb
> And death is a low mist which cannot blot
> The brightness it may veil. When lofty thought
> Lifts a young heart above its mortal lair,
> And love and life contend in it, for what
> Shall be its earthly doom, the dead live there
> And move like winds of light on dark and stormy air.
>
> [ll. 388–396]

It is difficult not to apprehend this as a mode of resurrection. How can that be Shelleyan? Has he changed, or is this just a question of perspectivism?

XLV.

The inheritors of unfulfilled renown
Rose from their thrones, built beyond mortal thought,
Far in the Unapparent. Chatterton
Rose pale, his solemn agony had not
Yet faded from him; Sidney, as he fought
And as he fell and as he lived and loved
Sublimely mild, a Spirit without spot,
Arose; and Lucan, by his death approved:
Oblivion as they rose shrank like a thing reproved.

[ll. 397–405]

Shelley had more of an audience than he realized but that was to be found in revolutionary agitators and the English working class. He also wanted learned readers steeped in Milton and in Wordsworth but had few of them indeed until after his death. He may have feared a fate of unfulfilled renown but was mistaken. Thomas Chatterton poisoned himself at seventeen. Sir Philip Sidney was only thirty-one when he died of a battle wound. Lucan at twenty-five had to bleed himself to death after he joined in an unsuccessful plot against the emperor Nero. Keats was considerably beyond all of these in aesthetic eminence, yet none has experienced the iniquity of oblivion.

XLVI.

And many more, whose names on Earth are dark,
But whose transmitted effluence cannot die
So long as fire outlives the parent spark,
Rose, robed in dazzling immortality.
"Thou art become as one of us," they cry,
"It was for thee yon kingless sphere has long
Swung blind in unascended majesty,
Silent alone amid an Heaven of song.
Assume thy winged throne, thou Vesper of our throng!"

[ll. 406–414]

It is a superb salute to Keats that acclaims him the morning and evening star of canonical poetry. I am haunted by Trelawney's vivid description of the drowned Shelley's jacket, "with the volume of

Sophocles in one pocket, and Keats's poems in the other, doubled back, as if the reader, in the act of reading, had hastily thrust it away" [*Recollections of the Last Days of Shelley and Byron* (1858)].

XLVIII.

 Or go to Rome, which is the sepulchre,
 O, not of him, but of our joy: 'tis nought
 That ages, empires, and religions, there
 Lie buried in the ravage they have wrought;
 For such as he can lend—they borrow not
 Glory from those who made the world their prey;
 And he is gathered to the kings of thought
 Who waged contention with their time's decay,
And of the past are all that cannot pass away.

[ll. 424–432]

There is a weight and dignity to those last three lines worthy of John Milton. Shelley undergoes a metamorphosis as he composes *Adonais;* something of Keats's spirit enters the revolutionary poet and slows him down. But Shelley is Shelley and is carried up by his aspiring spirit into the high splendor of annunciation, not of the Christ but of an angelic form that knows its own resurrection *before* dying:

LII.

 The One remains, the many change and pass;
 Heaven's light forever shines, earth's shadows fly;
 Life, like a dome of many-coloured glass,
 Stains the white radiance of Eternity,
 Until Death tramples it to fragments.—Die,
 If thou wouldst be with that which thou dost seek!
 Follow where all is fled!—Rome's azure sky,
 Flowers, ruins, statues, music, words, are weak
The glory they transfuse with fitting truth to speak.

LIII.

 Why linger, why turn back, why shrink, my Heart?
 Thy hopes are gone before: from all things here

They have departed; thou shouldst now depart!
A light is past from the revolving year,
And man, and woman; and what still is dear
Attracts to crush, repels to make thee wither.
The soft sky smiles,—the low wind whispers near:
'Tis Adonais calls! oh hasten thither!
No more let Life divide what Death can join together.

LIV.

That Light whose smile kindles the Universe,
That Beauty in which all things work and move,
That Benediction which the eclipsing Curse
Of birth can quench not, that sustaining Love
Which through the web of being blindly wove
By man and beast and earth and air and sea,
Burns bright or dim, as each are mirrors of
The fire for which all thirst, now beams on me,
Consuming the last clouds of cold mortality.

[ll. 460–486]

John Keats has transmogrified into Adonais, at once the reviving god Adonis and the Hebrew *Adonai* ("my Lord"), the substitute for the forbidden name Yahweh. Shelley's transmemberment is even more mysterious. Orphic, Neoplatonic, Hermetic, and Gnostic strains amalgamate in something less than a synthesis.

Shelley has done something very radical to the idea of elegy. It does not accomplish what Sigmund Freud called "the work of mourning." The death drive beyond the pleasure principle very nearly appropriates the Platonic Eros. Pragmatically the poet offers himself only suicidal resolution. Yet that is the poet as man, not the poet *in* the poet. That inward maker quests for canonization, thus joining himself to Dante, Milton, Wordsworth, Byron, and John Keats.

LV.

The breath whose might I have invoked in song
Descends on me; my spirit's bark is driven,
Far from the shore, far from the trembling throng
Whose sails were never to the tempest given;

The massy earth and spherèd skies are riven!
I am borne darkly, fearfully, afar:
Whilst, burning through the inmost veil of Heaven,
The soul of Adonais, like a star,
Beacons from the abode where the Eternal are.

[ll. 487–495]

Daringly Shelley invokes his own "Ode to the West Wind," a gesture that takes the risk of reducing his conclusion to the status of a self-aware fiction. Shelley could never have said, with Wallace Stevens, that the final belief is to believe in a fiction, with the nicer knowledge of belief, that what one believes in is not true.

I have always assumed that Shelley somehow was aware that his speculations on the veil repeated, in his own tonality, Vedanta's idea of Maya, very roughly that the phenomenal world is an illusion, as is the individual ego. Blake invented Vala, the emanation of Luvah, as the presiding deity of fallen nature. An ultimate source has to be Matthew 27:51:

And, behold, the veil of the temple was rent in twain from the top to the bottom; and the earth did quake, and the rocks rent. (KJV)

It may be that Shelley is far more audacious here than ever before. If the soul of John Keats, at once Adonai and Adonis, burns *through* the inmost veil of heaven, then Keats has achieved more than poetic immortality. He is a beacon among the Eternals who are gods of resurrection. The Gnostics would have called him an Aeon rather than an Archon. He has become an intrinsic element in a heretical cosmic structure of redemption.

Shelley says that his personal hopes have gone before him. The death of his children, loves ending in estrangements, mistakes that could not be negated, the dearth of a responsive readership: all presage a drive beyond life. He seems to have courted death by water and found it.

The eloquent urgency of the final stanzas of *Adonais* sometimes leaves me breathless. Is there any consolation to be found? The Shelleyan Yeats asked that question and replied: "Man is in love and loves what vanishes / What more is there to say?" *Adonais* implies a considerable rejoinder, yet how can it be formulated?

When *Adonais* comes to its end, I seem to *know* something withheld from me before. It is that kind of knowing in which somehow the knower becomes the known. That seems absurdly cryptic but I wonder: Is it so? Perhaps on some level of consciousness Shelley has joined Keats in finding that what is best and oldest in him was never created and so never fell. Birth may be an eclipsing curse, but it will not dim the spark or breath in one that mirrors the fire for which many among us continue to thirst.

For Shelley the burning fountain is more than a trope. He cannot *be* the Witch of Atlas or a restored Prometheus. The function of his most visionary poems is to intimate a state of being that is far away in the Unapparent.

Hellas, a lyrical drama composed in 1821 and published a year later, before Shelley's death, is a work that always leaves me disappointed yet still grateful for its remarkable passages and songs. Its purpose was political: to support the Greeks in their uprising against their Turkish overlords. In 1824 Byron died in Greece, where he had gone to help organize, finance, and lead a rather dubious rabblement of ruffians, mercenaries, idealists, and volunteers into a force capable of achieving independence.

Something in Shelley starts to break apart in *Hellas*. Rumination goes one way, lyricism the other. His genius for improvisation becomes a stumbling block. He shows some awareness that he is being rather too hasty and facile, but Hobgoblin runs away with the garland of Apollo, to borrow yet once more Gabriel Harvey's curious remark about Spenser's *The Faerie Queene*.

When very young, Shelley wrote quite a bad poem called *The Wandering Jew*, unpublished for half a century after his death. Ahasuerus is a traditional name for the Jew who supposedly mocked Jesus and is condemned to be an immortal vagrant throughout history. One of the impressive passages in *Hellas* is the description of Ahasuerus by Hassan, the henchman of the Sultan Mahmud:

> The Jew of whom I spake is old,—so old
> He seems to have outlived a world's decay;
> The hoary mountains and the wrinkled ocean

Seem younger still than he—his hair and beard
Are whiter than the tempest-sifted snow.
His cold pale limbs and pulseless arteries
Are like the fibres of a cloud instinct
With light, and to the soul that quickens them
Are as the atoms of the mountain-drift
To the winter wind—but from his eye looks forth
A life of unconsumed thought which pierces
The present, and the past, and the to-come.
Some say that this is he whom the great prophet
Jesus, the son of Joseph, for his mockery
Mocked with the curse of immortality.—
Some feign that he is Enoch—others dream
He was preadamite and has survived
Cycles of generation and of ruin.
The sage, in truth, by dreadful abstinence
And conquering penance of the mutinous flesh,
Deep contemplation and unwearied study
In years outstretched beyond the date of man,
May have attained to sovereignty and science
Over those strong and secret things and thoughts
Which others fear and know not.

[ll. 137–161]

We are given several rather antithetical possibilities for Ahasuerus: he is either the mocker of Jesus, or Enoch who walked
with God and then God took him, or a kind of God-Man who
lived before the creation of Adam. Why does Shelley want him in
Hellas?

Ahasuerus delivers a weighty discourse yet it is meretricious.
The reader scarcely needs or wants it. Whether the reeling Sultan
Mahmud derives enlightenment from it is uncertain. Shelley attempts to imitate the structure of *The Persians* of Aeschylus and of
Shakespeare's *Antony and Cleopatra*, in which messengers arrive con-
tinuously to convey bad news. Fierce Shelleyan as I am, I become
irritated as one war whoop succeeds another.

Hellas survives in the best of its lyrics, particularly the concluding chant:

The world's great age begins anew,
    The golden years return,
The earth doth like a snake renew
    Her winter weeds outworn;
Heaven smiles, and faiths and empires gleam
Like wrecks of a dissolving dream.

A brighter Hellas rears its mountains
    From waves serener far,
A new Peneus rolls his fountains
    Against the morning-star,
Where fairer Tempes bloom, there sleep
Young Cyclads on a sunnier deep.

A loftier Argo cleaves the main,
    Fraught with a later prize;
Another Orpheus sings again,
    And loves, and weeps, and dies;
A new Ulysses leaves once more
Calypso for his native shore.

Oh, write no more the tale of Troy,
    If earth Death's scroll must be!
Nor mix with Laian rage the joy
    Which dawns upon the free;
Although a subtler Sphinx renew
Riddles of death Thebes never knew.

Another Athens shall arise,
    And to remoter time
Bequeath, like sunset to the skies,
    The splendour of its prime,
And leave, if nought so bright may live,
All earth can take or Heaven can give.

Saturn and Love their long repose
    Shall burst, more bright and good
Than all who fell, than One who rose,
    Than many unsubdued;
Not gold, not blood, their altar dowers
But votive tears and symbol flowers.

Oh, cease! must hate and death return?
    Cease! must men kill and die?
Cease! drain not to its dregs the urn
    Of bitter prophecy.
The world is weary of the past,
Oh, might it die or rest at last!

[ll. 1060–1101]

This is not a paean of revolutionary triumph; it seems more cyclic than not. William Butler Yeats, soaked with Shelley, emulates it
brilliantly in the "Two Songs from a Play," the play being *The Resurrection* (1927):

I

I saw a staring virgin stand
Where holy Dionysus died,
And tear the heart out of his side,
And lay the heart upon her hand
And bear that beating heart away;
And then did all the Muses sing
Of Magnus Annus at the spring,
As though God's death were but a play.

Another Troy must rise and set,
Another lineage feed the crow,
Another Argo's painted prow
Drive to a flashier bauble yet.
The Roman Empire stood appalled:
It dropped the reins of peace and war
When that fierce virgin and her Star
Out of the fabulous darkness called.

II

In pity for man's darkening thought
He walked that room and issued thence
In Galilean turbulence;
The Babylonian starlight brought
A fabulous, formless darkness in;

Odour of blood when Christ was slain
Made all Platonic tolerance vain
And vain all Doric discipline.

Everything that man esteems
Endures a moment or a day.
Love's pleasure drives his love away,
The painter's brush consumes his dreams;
The herald's cry, the soldier's tread
Exhaust his glory and his might:
Whatever flames upon the night
Man's own resinous heart has fed.

It is a close contest between Shelley and Yeats for the laurel of visionary cynicism. Behind both chants is Virgil's *Fourth Eclogue:*

Now the last age by Cumae's Sibyl sung
Has come and gone, and the majestic roll
Of circling centuries begins anew:
Justice returns, returns old Saturn's reign,
With a new breed of men sent down from heaven.
Only do thou, at the boy's birth in whom
The iron shall cease, the golden race arise,
Befriend him, chaste Lucina; 'tis thine own
Apollo reigns.
. . .
    Yet shall there lurk within of ancient wrong
Some traces, bidding tempt the deep with ships,
Gird towns with walls, with furrows cleave the earth.
Therewith a second Tiphys shall there be,
Her hero-freight a second Argo bear;
New wars too shall arise, and once again
Some great Achilles to some Troy be sent.
              [translated by J. B. Greenough]

For the Latin Middle Ages, culminating in Dante, this was a pagan prophecy of the coming of Christ. You might call that a canonical misreading. Virgil was the actual prophet of Roman dominion and so of the destruction of Jerusalem and the scattering of its people. Yet Virgil was the Epicurean disciple of Lucretius and so a metaphysical materialist far removed from the Platonism of Dante, Shelley, and Yeats.

It is with some relief that I turn away from *Hellas* to Shelley's final lyrics, most of them addressed to his last muse, Jane Williams. Since both Shelley and Jane believed in free love, we can assume that their relationship was consummated. Jane Williams possessed remarkable serenity. After the drowning of Shelley and Edward Williams, she eventually became the common-law wife of Thomas Jefferson Hogg, Shelley's lifelong friend, with whom she had two children.

Shelley's lyrics to Jane Williams at their best have a Shakespearean resonance. They are subtler and more nuanced than Shelley's earlier works and indeed introduce tonalities and implications previously unknown in the poetry of the English language. Something uncanny entered Shelley's consciousness as he faced toward what he sensed would be his final days that included the composition of *The Triumph of Life*.

Here is one of my favorites, "With a Guitar. To Jane" (1822):

Ariel to Miranda:—Take
This slave of music for the sake
Of him who is the slave of thee,
And teach it all the harmony,
In which thou canst, and only thou,
Make the delighted spirit glow,
Till joy denies itself again
And, too intense, is turned to pain;
For by permission and command
Of thine own Prince Ferdinand,
Poor Ariel sends this silent token
Of more than ever can be spoken;
Your guardian spirit, Ariel, who
From life to life must still pursue
Your happiness;—for thus alone
Can Ariel ever find his own.
From Prospero's enchanted cell,

As the mighty verses tell,
To the throne of Naples, he
Lit you o'er the trackless sea,
Flitting on, your prow before,
Like a living meteor.
When you die, the silent Moon,
In her interlunar swoon,
Is not sadder in her cell
Than deserted Ariel.
When you live again on earth,
Like an unseen star of birth,
Ariel guides you o'er the sea
Of life from your nativity.
Many changes have been run
Since Ferdinand and you begun
Your course of love, and Ariel still
Has tracked your steps, and served your will;
Now, in humbler, happier lot,
This is all remembered not;
And now, alas! the poor sprite is
Imprisoned, for some fault of his,
In a body like a grave;—
From you he only dares to crave,
For his service and his sorrow,
A smile today, a song to-morrow.

The poem is a kind of dyptich; what holds its hinges together can be difficult to discern. Ariel vanishes from the second part, but this is more Shelley's sprite than Shakespeare's. Caliban's mother, the wicked witch Sycorax, imprisoned Ariel in a tree, from which Prospero rescued him. But Shelley-as-Ariel is imprisoned in his own body as if it were his grave.

The artist who this idol wrought,
To echo all harmonious thought,
Felled a tree, while on the steep
The woods were in their winter sleep,
Rocked in that repose divine

On the wind-swept Apennine;
And dreaming, some of autumn past
And some of Spring approaching fast,
And some of April buds and showers,
And some of songs in July bowers,
And all of love; and so this tree,—
O that such our death may be!—
Died in sleep, and felt no pain,
To live in happier form again:
From which, beneath Heaven's fairest star,
The artist wrought this loved Guitar,
And taught it justly to reply,
To all who question skilfully,
In language gentle as thine own;
Whispering in enamoured tone
Sweet oracles of woods and dells,
And summer winds in sylvan cells;
For it had learnt all harmonies
Of the plains and of the skies,
Of the forests and the mountains,
And the many-voicèd fountains,
The clearest echoes of the hills,
The softest notes of falling rills,
The melodies of birds and bees,
The murmuring of summer seas,
The pattering rain, and breathing dew,
And airs of evening; and it knew
That seldom-heard mysterious sound,
Which, driven on its diurnal round
As it floats through boundless day,
Our world enkindles on its way.—
All this it knows, but will not tell
To those who cannot question well
The spirit that inhabits it;
It talks according to the wit
Of its companions; and no more
Is heard than has been felt before,
By those who tempt it to betray

These secrets of an elder day:
But, sweetly as its answers will
Flatter hands of perfect skill,
It keeps its highest, holiest tone
For our belovèd Jane alone.

Famously Shelley identified with Ariel. Jane becomes Miranda, and Edward Williams is Ferdinand. Yet this poem concerns the "secrets of an elder day." Rimbaud, a poet who is the middle term between Shelley and Hart Crane, insisted that the "I" is another. If the brass wakes the trumpet, that is not its fault. Even so, Shelley tells us that if the wood wakes the guitar, that is its holiness. Hart Crane more pungently asserts that the Brooklyn Bridge is his Shelleyan lyre or giant Aeolian Harp.

"That seldom-heard mysterious sound" is the music of the Spheres. The two versions of that figuration received a classical exposition by the late John Hollander:

> In the Republic, Book X, Socrates' relation of the myth of Er includes mention of this Pythagorean myth; it describes the heavenly spheres bearing "on the upper surface of each" a siren, "who goes round with them, hymning a single tone or note. The eight together form one harmony. . . ." It is not, of course, that we are to think of *a chord of eight tones* here; rather, the "harmony" is an ordered intervallic relationship among all of these tones, more in the manner of the intervals obtainable by step or skip in a scale. The singing siren that produces the tone on each sphere, of course, becomes beautifully adaptable, eventually, to membership in a Christian angelic choir. But the more common version of the myth, such as is put down elaborately by Aristotle in *De Caelo*, maintained that it was the rubbing against each other of the supposedly hard, glassy celestial spheres that produced the sound. In answer to the objection that no mortal had ever heard that music, it was often retorted that the constant droning of that noise deadened the ears of earthly inhabitants by custom alone, and that because it was so constant, it was inaudible.
>
> [*The Untuning of the Sky* (1961)]

"These secrets of an elder day": Do they comprise more than the music of the Spheres? Shelley had no belief that the past once was a Golden Age. And yet he was desperately optimistic. A religious poet by temperament and vocation who is also an atheist and an advocate of working-class insurrection, he embodies a siege of contraries that was bound to tear him apart. His poems to Jane Williams, necessarily shaded by troubles, nevertheless represent the only peace he ever achieved.

In my judgment the summit of these lyrics and perhaps of Shelley's poetry is attained in the last poem he wrote except for *The Triumph of Life:*

> She left me at the silent time
> When the moon had ceased to climb
> The azure path of Heaven's steep,
> And like an albatross asleep,
> Balanced on her wings of light,
> Hovered in the purple night,
> Ere she sought her ocean nest
> In the chambers of the West.
> She left me, and I stayed alone
> Thinking over every tone,
> Which, though now silent to the ear
> The enchanted heart could hear,
> Like notes which die when born, but still
> Haunt the echoes of the hill;
> And feeling ever—oh, too much!—
> The soft vibration of her touch,
> As if her gentle hand, even now,
> Lightly trembled on my brow;
> And thus, although she absent were,
> Memory gave me all of her
> That even Fancy dares to claim:—
> Her presence had made weak and tame
> All passions, and I lived alone
> In the time which is our own;
> The past and future were forgot,
> As they had been, and would be, not.—

But soon, the guardian angel gone,
The daemon reassumed his throne
In my faint heart. I dare not speak
My thoughts, but thus disturbed and weak
I sat and saw the vessels glide
Along the ocean bright and wide,
Like spirit-wingèd chariots sent
O'er some serenest element
For ministrations strange and far;
As if to some Elysian star
They sailed for drink to medicine
Such sweet and bitter pain as mine.
And the wind that winged their flight
From the land came fresh and light,
And the scent of wingèd flowers
And the coolness of the hours
Of dew, and sweet warmth of day
Was scattered o'er the twinkling bay,
And the fisher with his lamp
And spear about the low rocks damp
Crept, and struck the fish who came
To worship the delusive flame.
Too happy they, whose pleasure sought
Extinguishes all sense and thought
Of the regret that pleasure [   ]
Destroying life alone, not peace!

Shelley gave this no title, but it is now known as "Lines Written in the Bay of Lerici." He left a blank as the last word of the penultimate line. Probably it was written only two weeks before his death. There is a sense of gracious renunciation throughout. And yet most vividly we are given the representation of a condition of immediacy so intense that Shelley, for just a moment, wonders at the hope of coming alive again in present time. The daemon or genius again usurps the poet's heart, and Shelley compels himself to recall the perpetual hopelessness of his lifelong quest for the Absolute. In a lovely gesture he gazes at the sea and has intimations of an Elysium. Reality returns with the fisher's spear. As Yeats, following Shelley, would phrase it: love's pleasure drives his love away. Life, mere life, triumphs over all imaginings that might redeem it, and the poem ends mixing devastation and a lingering peace.

I return finally to *The Triumph of Life*. Though scholars regard it as unfinished, I suspect Shelley would not have agreed with them. He had nothing more to add. Paul Valéry cunningly said no poem is ever finished. It is merely abandoned.

As always I must deal with my late friend Paul de Man, who so powerfully saw the poem as being disjunctive in regard to any other poem by Shelley or by anyone else. It comes down to a choice of tropes: the irony of irony as against the work of transumption, which is the transference of later figures to the place of earlier ones. John Hollander called this "the figure of interpretive allusion." I continue to search for a simpler way of presenting how a great poet's command of allusion becomes primal in her or his revision of literary history. A Dante or a Milton, a Goethe or a Wordsworth, a Victor Hugo or a Pushkin obeys the drive to evade belatedness and establish himself as an ever-early "candor," a word whose etymology suggests whiteness or brilliance.

I have been rereading Paul's essay "Shelley Disfigured: *The Triumph of Life*" for some forty years now. It charms and exasperates me:

The appearance and the waning of the light-shape . . . is . . . a single, and therefore violent, act of power achieved by the positional power of language considered by and in itself: the sun masters the stars because it *posits* forms, just as "life" subsequently masters the sun because it posits, by inscription, the "track" of historical events.

. . .

The Triumph of Life differs entirely from such Promethean or titanic myths as Keats's *Hyperion* or even *Paradise Lost* which thrive on the agonistic pathos of dialectical battle. It is unimaginable that Shelley's non-epic, non-religious poem would begin by elegiacally or rebelliously evoking the tragic defeat of the former gods, the stars, at the hands of the sun.

The text has no room for the tragedy of defeat or the victory among next-of-kin, or among gods and men.

An inveterate poker player in youth and middle age, my initial response is that Paul has stacked the deck. His invariable demiurge "language" usurps Shelley's "shape all light," the triumphal conqueror Life. The pivot is de Man's "posit," an initiative he assigns to language alone. It is unclear to me how he thinks to exclude "the agonistic pathos of dialectical battle." Nor can I comprehend Paul's ascetic confidence as he detaches *The Triumph of Life* from the *Commedia* and from *Paradise Lost:*

> It is unimaginable that Shelley's non-epic, non-religious poem would begin by elegiacally or rebelliously evoking the tragic defeat of the former gods, the stars, at the hands of the sun. The text has no room for the tragedy of defeat or the victory among next-of-kin, or among gods and men.

"The tragedy of defeat" of the poet's spirit by death-in-life *is* the story of Rousseau and—by implication—Wordsworth in *The Triumph of Life.* Whether or not Shelley's spirit sustains a similar defeat is open to question. I think it does not.

Subtlest of sophists, de Man sneaks his strategy into the "now" of this passage's first sentence:

> We now understand the shape to be the figure for the figurality of all signification.

To give Paul that would be to lose the game from the beginning. You can reduce any figuration to a generic figurality at will. I can conceive of many interpretive possibilities for Shelley's "shape all light" but none by which all meaning is sent into exile. Paul de Man's Shelley is a continental Romantic ironist, addicted to a permanent parabasis of meaning. There are indeed many Shelleys in Shelley but not Paul's. *Death's Jest-Book*, by Thomas Lovell Beddoes, would have served de Man better.

The dialectical agon in *The Triumph of Life* is waged between a fire smoldering as an ember and the fearsome rush of the chariot of so many dubious divinities. Aside from the tradition that goes from Ezekiel through Revelation on to Dante and Petrarch, there is Spenser's Lucifera:

> So forth she comes, and to her coche does clyme,
>   Adorned all with gold, and girlonds gay,
>   That seem'd as fresh as *Flora* in her Prime;
>   And stroue to match, in royall rich array,
>   Great *Iunoes* golden chaire, the which they say
>   The Gods stand gazing on, when she does ride
>   To *Iues* high house through heauens bras-paued way
>   Drawne of faire Pecocks, that excel in pride,
> And full of *Argus* eyes their tailes dispredden wide.
>   [*The Faerie Queene* (1590), 1.4.17]

I return to the opening of *The Triumph of Life:*

> Swift as a spirit hastening to his task
> Of glory and of good, the Sun sprang forth
> Rejoicing in his splendour, and the mask
>
> Of darkness fell from the awakened Earth—
> The smokeless altars of the mountain snows
> Flamed above crimson clouds, and at the birth
>
> Of light, the Ocean's orison arose
> To which the birds tempered their matin lay.
> All flowers in field or forest which unclose
>
> Their trembling eyelids to the kiss of day,
> Swinging their censers in the element,
> With orient incense lit by the new ray
>
> Burned slow and inconsumably, and sent
>   Their odorous sighs up to the smiling air;
> And, in succession due, did continent,
>
> Isle, ocean, and all things that in them wear
> The form and character of mortal mould
> Rise as the Sun their father rose, to bear

Their portion of the toil, which he of old
Took as his own, and then imposed on them . . .

[ll. 1–20]

Though W. B. Yeats thought otherwise, I no longer discover any negativity in this strong opening. Shelley the Pilgrim provides it with his entrance:

But I, whom thoughts which must remain untold

Had kept as wakeful as the stars that gem
The cone of night, now they were laid asleep
Stretched my faint limbs beneath the hoary stem

Which an old chestnut flung athwart the steep
Of a green Apennine: before me fled
The night; behind me rose the day; the deep

Was at my feet, and Heaven above my head,—
When a strange trance over my fancy grew
Which was not slumber, for the shade it spread

Was so transparent, that the scene came through
As clear as when a veil of light is drawn
O'er evening hills, they glimmer; and I knew

That I had felt the freshness of that dawn
Bathed in the same cold dew my brow and hair,
And sate as thus upon that slope of lawn

Under the self same bough, and heard as there
The birds, the fountains and the ocean hold
Sweet talk in music through the enamoured air,

And then a vision on my brain was rolled.

[ll. 21–40]

This is a repetition of that scene in which the Poetical Character undergoes cyclic juvescence. We and Shelley have been here before.

As in that trance of wondrous thought I lay
This was the tenour of my waking dream:—
Methought I sate beside a public way

Thick strewn with summer dust, and a great stream
Of people there was hurrying to and fro,
Numerous as gnats upon the evening gleam,

All hastening onward, yet none seemed to know
Whither he went, or whence he came, or why
He made one of the multitude, and so

Was borne amid the crowd, as through the sky
One of the million leaves of summer's bier;
Old age and youth, manhood and infancy,

Mixed in one mighty torrent did appear,
Some flying from the thing they feared, and some
Seeking the object of another's fear;

And others, as with steps towards the tomb,
Pored on the trodden worms that crawled beneath,
And others mournfully within the gloom

Of their own shadow walked, and called it death;
And some fled from it as it were a ghost,
Half fainting in the affliction of vain breath:

But more, with motions which each other crossed,
Pursued or shunned the shadows the clouds threw,
Or birds within the noonday aether lost,

Upon that path where flowers never grew,—
And weary with vain toil and faint for thirst
Heard not the fountains, whose melodious dew

Out of their mossy cells forever burst;
Nor felt the breeze which from the forest told
Of grassy paths and wood-lawns interspersed

With overarching elms and caverns cold,
And violet banks where sweet dreams brood,
     but they
Pursued their serious folly as of old.

[ll. 41–73]

As an indictment of our *busyness* this stings and stings again. "Serious folly" is not even oxymoronic here. It is an intensification. I can only surmise that seven years of questing, commencing with *Alastor*, had worn down even Shelley's optimistic spirit. The marriage to Mary was strained, though she was exemplary in her steadfastness. Byron, once a resource and a friend, had become a vexation. The perpetual romance with Claire continued but was intermittent. The children Clara and William had died. English law denied him any access to his two children by Harriet. The suicides of Harriet and of Fannie Imlay must have haunted him. He did not know that he had biblical status with British radicals and the working class they tried to lead. Unlike Byron, he seemed to have no audience. He knew that his love for Jane Williams was likely to end in catastrophe for his entire circle. And yet I am uncertain precisely how he represents himself in *The Triumph of Life:*

> And as I gazed, methought that in the way
> The throng grew wilder, as the woods of June
> When the South wind shakes the extinguished day,
>
> And a cold glare, intenser than the noon,
> But icy cold, obscured with [   ] light
> The sun, as he the stars. Like the young moon—
>
> When on the sunlit limits of the night
> Her white shell trembles amid crimson air,
> And whilst the sleeping tempest gathers might—
>
> Doth, as the herald of its coming, bear
> The ghost of its dead mother, whose dim form
> Bends in dark aether from her infant's chair,—
>
> So came a chariot on the silent storm
> Of its own rushing splendour, and a Shape
> So sate within, as one whom years deform,
>
> Beneath a dusky hood and double cape,
> Crouching within the shadow of a tomb;
> And o'er what seemed the head a cloud-like crape

Was bent, a dun and faint aethereal gloom
Tempering the light. Upon the chariot-beam
A Janus-visaged Shadow did assume

The guidance of that wonder-wingèd team.
The shapes which drew it in thick lightenings
Were lost:—I heard alone on the air's soft stream

The music of their ever-moving wings.
All the four faces of that Charioteer
Had their eyes banded; little profit brings

Speed in the van and blindness in the rear,
Nor then avail the beams that quench the sun,—
Or that with banded eyes could pierce the sphere

Of all that is, has been or will be done;
So ill was the car guided, but it passed
With solemn speed majestically on.

[ll. 74–106]

Of all the images of the Merkabah, Shelley's is the most destructive distortion of Ezekiel's vision that literary tradition affords
us, except for the rather desperate attempt by Moses Maimonides
to reduce the Work of the Chariot to a dubious physics. How much
Shelley knew about the complex origins of the Merkabah tradition
is unclear to me. Scholars now trace its beginnings to Mithraism. Before the advent of Zoroaster, Mithra was the Iranian sun
god, and also the god of war. In the Roman Empire of the second
century CE, soldiers in particular and many citizens honored Mithra
as the guardian of their loyalty to the emperor. When Constan-
tine early in the fourth century made Christianity the Empire's
religion, Mithraism vanished quickly. But its chariot visions per-
meated the Middle East and possibly by way of Egypt entered
Jewish circles from Philo on to the Talmudists and then the esoteric tradition.

What Shelley did know was the poetic sequence of Dante, Petrarch, Spenser, and Milton, and also the biblical texts of Isaiah, Ezekiel, and Revelation. As I have remarked, despite his professed
atheism, Shelley is a new kind of religious poet. In a letter to Maria

Gisborne (October 14, 1819), he wrote: "Let us believe in a kind of optimism in which we are our own gods."

The Shelley of *The Triumph of Life* would seem to have abandoned that kind of optimism. And yet the role he assigns to himself in the poem is either quietistic or despairing. If he subsided in quietism, he would still have believed that the good time would come.

For me the particular enigma of *The Triumph of Life* is Rousseau, intended to be the Virgil of Shelley-as-Dante. And here I return to Paul de Man, in his notebooks for 1978, where he is at his most forceful:

> Lucifer, *photon-phorein*, lampadephore or Prometheus, the carrier (*porteur*) of fire who trans*ports* the light of the senses and of sense (*des sens et du sens*) from events and entities to their meaning (*signification*), it is the metaphor that is undone and dispossessed under our eyes in the very act of figural comprehension. Disfiguration brought about by (*sous l'empire de*) the performative power of language is irrevocable. It parades in front of us in the *Trionfo* where the figure first appears as water music, then as rainbow, then as measure to finally sink "below the watery floor," trampled by its own power. Unlike *Lycidas* or *Adonais*, in the elegies of Milton and Shelley that bear these names, it is not reborn in the form of a star, but is repeated at a lower and more violent level of literality. The process is endless, since the knowledge of language's performative power is itself a figure and thus bound to repeat the disfiguration of metaphor, just as Shelley's poem is condemned to repeat the ambient violence of *Julie* in the more violent mode that also implies its forgetting and erasure.
>
> That Shelley chose to give the name of Rousseau to the process of disfiguration indicates that his understanding of Rousseau is something we are only just beginning to perceive ourselves. But this also serves as a warning that such an understanding risks not being able to provide (*apporter*) us with any kind of reassurance.

I am very moved by this because I understand that Paul struggled inwardly with those dark years in occupied Belgium when he wrote so many collaborationist articles, including at least one that is anti-Semitic. Only in retrospect can I now apprehend that on more than one occasion he attempted to talk to me about this. Since I had no idea what he could have meant except perhaps Flemish nationalism, I never encouraged him to say more. Once, discussing *The Triumph of Life*, Paul persuaded me to reread *Julie, or The New Héloïse* (1761), Rousseau's epistolary novel deeply influenced by my favorite narrative, Samuel Richardson's *Clarissa* (1748).

The protagonist Saint-Preux has to renounce the intense passion he shares with Julie, because she virtuously returns to her existence as a mother and a wife. Julie has an aura of a curious destructiveness, undoubtedly a suggestion to Shelley for his "shape all light."

I can hear Paul's voice in the sentence I find fascinating but unacceptable: "Disfiguration brought about by (*sous l'empire de*) the performative power of language is irrevocable." To speak of language's performative power is itself a figuration, as Paul says, but figuration is not in itself a trackless forest or a meandering river. Parabasis, originally the concluding chorus in ancient Greek comedy, is also a digression in narrative or any other discourse. To equate it with the trope of irony is an arbitrary and tendentious gesture.

In a great poem's dance of tropes, irony is just an opening move. Nor is irony immune from historical change: one era's irony is quite likely to become a noble synecdoche in another time. It can be maddening to speak of the metalepsis of a metalepsis, which is transumption, but the closing figure of most strong poems in the Western tradition tends to be a scheme of transumption. The effect of that scheme is to accomplish an ellipsis of further figuration. For Paul de Man, such an ellipsis was elusory: figuration never ends. My late friend John Hollander liked to jest: "All is trope except in games." Ludic dances and frolics are the joy of poems that reverse tradition and make themselves earlier than their forerunners.

And yet Paul de Man continues to challenge my transumptive stance. I remember that when I handed him a copy of my book *A Map of Misreading*, playfully yet affectionately dedicated to him in response to his zealous review of *The Anxiety of Influence*, I remarked gently: "I am trying to put pathos back into the tropes." Paul's response was: "But Harold, pathos is itself a trope." That stopped me but only for a time.

Pathos is more than a trope. Are all our sorrowings only metaphors? If ethos is character, and logos is cognition, then pathos is personality. When I think back fondly to the complexities of Paul de Man's personality, am I recalling only tropes? His favorite rejoinder as we walked along together was: "The trouble with you, Harold, is that you do not believe in the truth." Perhaps Shelley attracted him because they both hoped to arrive at some truth.

Where in *The Triumph of Life* are we to locate Shelley's truth? The poem affords only a few options. You can join the dance, as Rousseau did, or, like the sacred few of Athens and Jerusalem, you can fly back to some celestial fire. Or, like the peregrine in Shelley, you can stand aside and forbear. But you end crying out: "Then what is Life?" And the answer would have to be: life is death-in-life that triumphs over almost every individual's integrity.

Shelley, like Dante and Milton, never compromised. All of them maintained their integrity. The costs were steep. Shelley and Dante lived in exile. Blind Milton accepted internal exile, as did the uncompromising William Blake in a later time.

Something in Paul de Man chose both modes of exile. Like Shelley he regarded remorse as another dark self-idolatry. For him literature was a dialectic of truth and error. Even if you sharpened the terms as he did, I find this off-center in regard to the pragmatics of reading. I teach *Hamlet* every year, ransacking it afresh because it changes incessantly. Hamlet frequently does not mean what he says or say what he means. His mind is too quick for me. I cannot keep up. Shakespeare has created a consciousness so capacious that I cannot find its limits.

I apprehend that for Hamlet the truth is death. Yet our life is both error and eros. Agata Bielik-Robson employs that wordplay in the Freudian context of the defense against dying. Though I have been preoccupied with Shelley for sixty-five years, it may be that a darkness in Paul de Man's spirit gave him insights into the Promethean revolutionary more intense than my own.

Still, there is both light and dark in Shelley's spirit, however equivocal light becomes in *The Triumph of Life*. But all is equivocal in that infernal vision:

Struck to the heart by this sad pageantry,
Half to myself I said—"And what is this?
Whose shape is that within the car? and why—"

I would have added—"is all here amiss?—"
But a voice answered—"Life!"—I turned, and knew
(O Heaven, have mercy on such wretchedness!)

That what I thought was an old root which grew
To strange distortion out of the hill side,
Was indeed one of those deluded crew,

And that the grass, which methought hung so wide
And white, was but his thin discoloured hair,
And that the holes he vainly sought to hide,

Were or had been eyes:—"If thou canst forbear
To join the dance, which I had well forborne!"
Said the grim Feature (of my thought aware),

"I will unfold that which to this deep scorn
Led me and my companions, and relate
The progress of the pageant since the morn;

If thirst of knowledge shall not then abate,
Follow it even to the night, but I
Am weary."—Then like one who with the weight

Of his own words is staggered, wearily
He paused, and ere he could resume, I cried,
"First, who art thou?"—"Before thy memory

"I feared, loved, hated, suffered, did and died,
And if the spark with which Heaven lit my spirit
Earth had with purer nutriment supplied,

"Corruption would not now thus much inherit
Of what was once Rousseau,—nor this disguise
Stain that within which still disdains to wear it . . ."

[ll. 176–205]

I have always been uncertain why Shelley compares Rousseau's pride to that of Farinata in Canto 10 of the *Inferno:*

Ed el mi disse: «Volgiti! Che fai?
Vedi là Farinata che s'è dritto:
da la cintola in sù tutto 'l vedrai».

Io avea già il mio viso nel suo fitto;
ed el s'ergea col petto e con la fronte
com' avesse l'inferno a gran dispitto.

———

And unto me he said: "Turn thee; what dost thou?
  Behold there Farinata who has risen;
  From the waist upwards wholly shalt thou see him."

I had already fixed mine eyes on his,
  And he uprose erect with breast and front
  E'en as if Hell he had in great despite.
        [10.31–36, translated by H. W. Longfellow]

I think Shelley would have rendered "com' avesse l'inferno a gran dispitto," "as if of Hell he had a great disdain." Hence: "nor this disguise / Stain that which ought to have disdained to wear it." Farinata was an Epicurean and so a heretic. Rousseau had an individual channel to God but championed civil religion and regarded Christianity as a menace to the social contract. It is probably true that in this sphere Shelley was far more influenced by Rousseau than by William Godwin or anyone else.

"If I have been extinguished, yet there rise
A thousand beacons from the spark I bore"—
"And who are those chained to the car?"—"The wise,

"The great, the unforgotten,—they who wore
Mitres and helms and crowns, or wreaths of light,
Signs of thought's empire over thought—their lore

"Taught them not this, to know themselves; their might
Could not repress the mutiny within,
And for the morn of truth they feigned, deep night

"Caught them ere evening."
                    [The Triumph of Life, ll. 206–215]

Shelley was one of those beacons. The great phrase here is "the mutiny within." The word "mutiny" goes back to the Latin *movere*, meaning "to move." Wisdom is insufficient in self-knowledge and therefore unaware of inward movements of rebellion. Shelley's Rousseau at this point could be Montaigne or Sigmund Freud.

> And much I grieved to think how power and will
> In opposition rule our mortal day,
>
> And why God made irreconcilable
> Good and the means of good; and for despair
> I half disdained mine eyes' desire to fill
>
> With the spent vision of the times that were
> And scarce have ceased to be . . . "Dost thou behold,"
> Said my guide, "those spoilers spoiled, Voltaire,
>
> "Frederic, and Kant, Catherine, and Leopold,
> And hoary anarchs, demagogues, and sage—
> [   ] names which the world thinks always old—
>
> "For in the battle Life and they did wage,
> She remained conqueror. I was overcome
> By my own heart alone, which neither age,
>
> "Nor tears, nor infamy, nor now the tomb
> Could temper to its object."
>   [ll. 228–243]

Setting aside the rather startling denigration of Immanuel Kant, one expects that the poet of *Prometheus Unbound* might confront the puzzle of why God made irreconcilable good and the means of good, love and the means of love, poetry and the limits of figuration. Rousseau could as well be Shelley when he insists that life did not conquer him but that his own heart could not be fitted to any single and particular object. I think that Shelley at least, here near the end of

The Triumph of Life, understands that he was the subject and object
of his own quest.

"And still her feet, no less than the sweet tune
To which they moved, seemed as they moved to blot
The thoughts of him who gazed on them; and soon

"All that was seemed as if it had been not;
As if the gazer's mind was strewn beneath
Her feet like embers; and she, thought by thought,

"Trampled its sparks [fires] into the dust of death;
As day upon the threshold of the east
Treads out the lamps of night, until the breath

"Of darkness reillumines even the least
Of heaven's living eyes—like day she came,
Making the night a dream; and ere she ceased

"To move, as one between desire and shame
Suspended, I said—If, as it doth seem,
Thou comest from the realm without a name,

"Into this valley of perpetual dream,
Shew whence I came, and where I am, and why—
Pass not away upon the passing stream.

"Arise and quench thy thirst," was her reply.
And as a shut lily, stricken by the wand
Of dewy morning's vital alchemy,

"I rose; and, bending at her sweet command,
Touched with faint lips the cup she raised,
And suddenly my brain became as sand

"Where the first wave had more than half erased
The track of deer on desert Labrador;
Whilst the fierce wolf from which they fled amazed,

"Leaves his stamp visibly upon the shore,
Until the second bursts;—so on my sight
Burst a new vision, never seen before,

"And the fair shape waned in the coming light,
As veil by veil the silent splendour drops
From Lucifer, amid the chrysolite

"Of sunrise, ere it tinge [strike] the mountain tops . . ."

[ll. 382–415]

Wordsworth's embers lived even though the celestial light had departed forever. Shelley's fire always remained an unextinguished hearth. I cannot pretend sufficient insight into Rousseau to judge what survived his many vicissitudes. Here he drinks the shape's nepenthe and his brain is reduced to sand. Shelley plays with fearsome irony on the nepenthe of Homer's *Odyssey*, the taste of which takes away our grief.

Though Dante gives Shelley the essential form of his poem, it seems another irony to remark that the *Commedia* tells us "The words of hate and awe." The *Inferno* is awash with hatred and our awe is tinged by fear, Shelley stresses in *The Triumph of Life*:

"Before the chariot had begun to climb
The opposing steep of that mysterious dell,
Behold a wonder worthy of the rhyme

"Of him who from the lowest depths of hell,
Through every paradise and through all glory,
Love led serene, and who returned to tell

"The words of hate and awe; the wondrous story
How all things are transfigured except Love;
For deaf as is a sea, which wrath makes hoary,

"The world can hear not the sweet notes that move
The sphere whose light is melody to lovers—
A wonder worthy of his rhyme.—"

[ll. 469–480]

The wonder reminds me of Hamlet's "woe or wonder":

each one
Of that great crowd sent forth incessantly
These shadows, numerous as the dead leaves blown

"In autumn evening from a poplar tree.
Each like himself and like each other were,
At first; but soon distorted seemed to be

"Obscure clouds, moulded by the casual air;
And of this stuff the car's creative ray
Wrought all the busy phantoms that were there,

"As the sun shapes the clouds; thus on the way
Mask after mask fell from the countenance
And form of all; and long before the day

"Was old, the joy which waked like heaven's glance
The sleepers in the oblivious valley, died,
And some grew weary of the ghastly dance

"And fell, as I have fallen, by the wayside;—
Those soonest from whose forms most shadows passed,
And least of strength and beauty did abide."

Then, what is Life? I cried . . .

[ll. 526–544]

"The car's creative ray" must be the harshest use of "creative" in any major poet. Shelley's final question—"Then, what is Life?"— is purely rhetorical. He has shown us, through Rousseau, what it is and is not. What then remains of Shelley's tough optimism? In a letter to Leigh Hunt (December 1819) he had observed:

I am one of those whom nothing will fully satisfy, but who am ready to be partially satisfied by all that is practicable.

And yet *The Triumph of Life* is hardly a pragmatist's poem. Its stance, like that of *Adonais*, is suicidal. Shelley's life and his achievement resemble Hamlet's. Both look before and after and conclude that the rest is silence.

Whether Shelley in his final hours might have agreed with that, we cannot know. Shelley's skepticism has always been recognized as founding itself at least in part on David Hume. The Scottish philosopher and historian had little use for Shakespeare and probably would have found Shelley unreadable. Yet Hume, more than William Godwin, converted Shelley to empiricism. The major Humean poem by Shelley is the fierce meditation "Mont Blanc," written in Switzerland in 1816:

I

The everlasting universe of things
Flows through the mind, and rolls its rapid waves,
Now dark—now glittering—now reflecting gloom—
Now lending splendour, where from secret springs
The source of human thought its tribute brings
Of waters,—with a sound but half its own,
Such as a feeble brook will oft assume,
In the wild woods, among the mountains lone,
Where waterfalls around it leap for ever,
Where woods and winds contend, and a vast river
Over its rocks ceaselessly bursts and raves.

[ll. 1–11]

I have written several commentaries on "Mont Blanc," but I now agree with them only in part. Like its companion "Hymn to Intellectual Beauty" (1816), which revises Wordsworth's "Intimations" ode, Shelley's meditation on the tallest mountain in the Alps struggles with Coleridge, and reworks any Christian understanding of nature. "Kubla Khan" (1797, published 1816) courses along throughout the initial section of "Mont Blanc." It is "Alph, the sacred river," that runs through both poems, and the Coleridgean fountain will in time become the fire for which all thirst:

II

. . .
Thou art pervaded with that ceaseless motion,
Thou art the path of that unresting sound—
Dizzy Ravine! and when I gaze on thee
I seem as in a trance sublime and strange
To muse on my own separate fantasy,
My own, my human mind, which passively
Now renders and receives fast influencings,

Holding an unremitting interchange
With the clear universe of things around;
One legion of wild thoughts, whose wandering wings
Now float above thy darkness, and now rest
Where that or thou art no unbidden guest,
In the still cave of the witch Poesy,
Seeking among the shadows that pass by
Ghosts of all things that are, some shade of thee,
Some phantom, some faint image; till the breast
From which they fled recalls them; thou art there!

[ll. 32–48]

"The witch Poesy" will mature into the Witch of Atlas. Wordsworth, more than Coleridge, is the undersong of the passage so antithetical that I become breathless keeping up. How do you *passively*
both render and receive influencings? If there is an unremitting interchange, how can you know when your mind and the universe of
things are demarcated?

Shelley launches himself into his visionary sublime in subtle opposition to Wordsworthian interchanges between poet and external
world. Whatever the prompting, he ascends into empyrean speculations on the veil tenuously separating life and death:

III

Some say that gleams of a remoter world
Visit the soul in sleep,—that death is slumber,
And that its shapes the busy thoughts outnumber
Of those who wake and live.—I look on high;
Has some unknown omnipotence unfurled
The veil of life and death? or do I lie
In dream, and does the mightier world of sleep
Spread far around and inaccessibly
Its circles? For the very spirit fails,
Driven like a homeless cloud from steep to steep
That vanishes among the viewless gales!
Far, far above, piercing the infinite sky,
Mont Blanc appears,—still, snowy, and serene—
. . .

Is this the scene
Where the old Earthquake-daemon taught her young
Ruin? Were these their toys? or did a sea
Of fire envelop once this silent snow?
None can reply—all seems eternal now.
The wilderness has a mysterious tongue
Which teaches awful doubt, or faith so mild,
So solemn, so serene, that man may be,
But for such faith, with Nature reconciled;
Thou hast a voice, great Mountain, to repeal
Large codes of fraud and woe; not understood
By all, but which the wise, and great, and good
Interpret, or make felt, or deeply feel.

[ll. 49–61, 71–83]

Shelley rejected "in such a faith" and instead chose "But for such faith." How much difference is there in this daemonic context? "Faith so mild, / So solemn, so serene" is a critique of Wordsworth. The polemic goes on, rather more mildly, in the voice of Mont Blanc, which is properly "interpret[ed]" by the "wise" William Godwin, "felt" by the "great" William Wordsworth, and "deeply" felt by the "good" Samuel Taylor Coleridge. The revelation of Mont Blanc can free us from the revelation of Mount Sinai, with its Mosaic codes now rejected as fraudulent and woeful. Though his poetic power has augmented, this is still the Shelley of the early and subversive *Queen Mab:*

IV

. . .

Power dwells apart in its tranquillity,
Remote, serene, and inaccessible:
And *this*, the naked countenance of earth,
On which I gaze, even these primaeval mountains
Teach the adverting mind. The glaciers creep
Like snakes that watch their prey, from their far fountains,
Slow rolling on; there, many a precipice,
Frost and the Sun in scorn of mortal power
Have piled: dome, pyramid, and pinnacle,
A city of death, distinct with many a tower

And wall impregnable of beaming ice.
Yet not a city, but a flood of ruin
Is there, that from the boundaries of the sky
Rolls its perpetual stream; vast pines are strewing
Its destin'd path, or in the mangled soil
Branchless and shattered stand; the rocks, drawn down
From yon remotest waste, have overthrown
The limits of the dead and living world,
Never to be reclaimed. The dwelling-place
Of insects, beasts, and birds, becomes its spoil;
Their food and their retreat for ever gone,
So much of life and joy is lost. The race
Of man flies far in dread; his work and dwelling
Vanish, like smoke before the tempest's stream,
And their place is not known. Below, vast caves
Shine in the rushing torrents' restless gleam,
Which from those secret chasms in tumult welling
Meet in the vale, and one majestic River,
The breath and blood of distant lands, for ever
Rolls its loud waters to the ocean-waves,
Breathes its swift vapours to the circling air.

[ll. 96–126]

It is rather wicked of Shelley to follow so much desolation with a direct tribute to "Kubla Khan." His preferred audience for "Mont Blanc" would have been Coleridge and Wordsworth.

V
Mont Blanc yet gleams on high:—the power is there,
The still and solemn power of many sights,
And many sounds, and much of life and death.
In the calm darkness of the moonless nights,
In the lone glare of day, the snows descend
Upon that Mountain; none beholds them there,
Nor when the flakes burn in the sinking sun,
Or the star-beams dart through them:—Winds contend
Silently there, and heap the snow with breath
Rapid and strong, but silently! Its home

The voiceless lightning in these solitudes
Keeps innocently, and like vapour broods
Over the snow. The secret Strength of things
Which governs thought, and to the infinite dome
Of Heaven is as a law, inhabits thee!
And what were thou, and earth, and stars, and sea,
If to the human mind's imaginings
Silence and solitude were vacancy?

[ll. 127–144]

Demogorgon was called the father of the Gentile gods by Boccaccio, who did not know that this fanciful being started as a spelling
error. Two years after composing "Mont Blanc," Shelley was at work
on his lyrical drama *Prometheus Unbound*, where "The secret Strength
of things" will be named as Demogorgon, deplored by William Butler Yeats as an incoherence, yet the remarkable agent of Jupiter's fall,
and certainly one of Shelley's most extravagant inventions.

The concluding question of "Mont Blanc" is not rhetorical. Shelley's skepticism cuts all ways. Something in him, a kind of nihilism
that will develop into *The Triumph of Life*, wonders whether the mountain, earth, stars, and sea are indeed vacancy. An uncanny personality,
in life as in poetry, Shelley lets his poem take him where it will. The
companion piece of 1816, "Hymn to Intellectual Beauty," is even freer:

I

The awful shadow of some unseen Power
    Floats though unseen among us,—visiting
    This various world with as inconstant wing
As summer winds that creep from flower to flower,—
Like moonbeams that behind some piny mountain shower,
    It visits with inconstant glance
    Each human heart and countenance;
Like hues and harmonies of evening,
    Like clouds in starlight widely spread,
    Like memory of music fled,—
    Like aught that for its grace may be
Dear, and yet dearer for its mystery.
. . .

VI

I vow'd that I would dedicate my powers
  To thee and thine—have I not kept the vow?
  With beating heart and streaming eyes, even now
I call the phantoms of a thousand hours
Each from his voiceless grave: they have in visioned bowers
    Of studious zeal or love's delight
    Outwatched with me the envious night—
  They know that never joy illumed my brow
    Unlinked with hope that thou wouldst free
    This world from its dark slavery,
    That thou—O awful LOVELINESS,
Wouldst give whate'er these words cannot express.

VII

The day becomes more solemn and serene
  When noon is past—there is a harmony
  In autumn, and a lustre in its sky,
Which through the summer is not heard or seen,
As if it could not be, as if it had not been!
    Thus let thy power, which like the truth
    Of nature on my passive youth
Descended, to my onward life supply
    Its calm—to one who worships thee,
    And every form containing thee,
    Whom, SPIRIT fair, thy spells did bind
To fear himself, and love all human kind.

[ll. 1–12, 61–71, 73–84]

I would no longer say that Wordsworth legislated for Shelley, but the ode "Intimations of Immortality" seems to have given the disciple of Plato and Dante an enduring wound. Palpably Shelley's *Hymn* would not exist had Wordsworth not composed "Tintern Abbey" and the "Intimations" ode. Nietzsche, in *Twilight of the Idols* (1889), said cause and effect were fictions: tracing something unknown back to something known yields a sense of power. My first sentence in this paragraph is certainly open to Nietzsche's critique. Paul de Man relied on it in his highly ironic review of my book *The Anxiety of Influence.* My reply in *A Map of Misreading* was to observe, not without irony, that anything you said about a fiction could only be another fiction. I would refine this now. To cite Hollander again, "All is trope save in games."

Angus Fletcher, a theorist of thresholds, saw them as standing between labyrinth and temple. Irony is labyrinthine. Temples, whether sacred or secular-poetic, are synecdochal. They increase meaning by representing it. Labyrinthic irony limits and at last withdraws meaning. Kenneth Burke and I gave several joint lectures exploring his four master tropes and my desire to add hyperbole and transumption to them. Genial and generous, Kenneth bestowed more clarity on my endeavor than I could manage at that moment.

Exchanges through the years with John Hollander and Angus Fletcher enlarged my notion of transumption, a trope leaping over simple allusions to reverse the meanings and temporal priority of an earlier trope. Transumption therefore is diachronic. Many of the implications of a truly diachronic rhetoric are worked through in Peter de Bolla's *Harold Bloom: Towards Historical Rhetorics* (1988; reissued 2014). De Bolla accurately cites my chagrin at never quite achieving a fully diachronic rhetoric.

Lest this appear abstract, I return us to Shelley's "Hymn to Intellectual Beauty." The intellectual beauty may have traces in it of Edmund Spenser's *Fowre Hymnes* (1596), but the Puritanism is absent. Shelley has caught a noble fever of intermittent transcendence from Wordsworth, whose rhetorical accents are omnipresent here:

VII
The day becomes more solemn and serene
    When noon is past—there is a harmony
    In autumn, and a lustre in its sky,
Which through the summer is not heard or seen,
As if it could not be, as if it had not been!

               [ll. 73-77]

The emphasis is Shelleyan on not hearing and not seeing yet apprehending what cannot be there and yet is.

In his *The Vision of Judgment* (1822), George Gordon, Lord Byron, replied to Robert Southey's *Vision of Judgement* (1820), in which the wretched King George III entered into Heaven. Possibly to Byron's chagrin, his very public association with Shelley had made him a target for the Tory regime and its supporters, including the egregious Southey, turncoat and enemy of the free imagination. The unfortunate Southey also attacked what he called "the Satanic School" of Byron, Shelley, Leigh Hunt, and their friends. Southey, poet laureate, suggested that Parliament should take action against these Satanists. What little immortality Southey now possesses is Byron's gift. But I restrict Byron here to the majestic meeting of Michael and Satan:

XXIV

But bringing up the rear of this bright host
    A Spirit of a different aspect waved
His wings, like thunder-clouds above some coast
    Whose barren beach with frequent wrecks is paved;
His brow was like the deep when tempest-tossed;
    Fierce and unfathomable thoughts engraved
Eternal wrath on his immortal face,
And where he gazed a gloom pervaded space.
  . . .

XXXII

He and the sombre, silent Spirit met—
    They knew each other both for good and ill;
Such was their power, that neither could forget
    His former friend and future foe; but still
There was a high, immortal, proud regret
    In either's eye, as if 'twere less their will
Than destiny to make the eternal years
Their date of war, and their "Champ Clos" the spheres.

XXXIII

But here they were in neutral space: we know
    From Job, that Satan hath the power to pay
A heavenly visit thrice a-year or so;
    And that the "Sons of God," like those of clay,

Must keep him company; and we might show
　　From the same book, in how polite a way
The dialogue is held between the Powers
Of Good and Evil—but 'twould take up hours.
. . .

XXXVI

The Archangel bowed, not like a modern beau,
　　But with a graceful oriental bend,
Pressing one radiant arm just where below
　　The heart in good men is supposed to tend;
He turned as to an equal, not too low,
　　But kindly; Satan met his ancient friend
With more hauteur, as might an old Castilian
Poor Noble meet a mushroom rich civilian.
. . .

XL

"Look to our earth, or rather mine; it was,
　　Once, more thy master's: but I triumph not
In this poor planet's conquest; nor, alas!
　　Need he thou servest envy me my lot:
With all the myriads of bright worlds which pass
　　In worship round him, he may have forgot
Yon weak creation of such paltry things:
I think few worth damnation save their kings,

XLI

"And these but as a kind of quit-rent, to
　　Assert my right as Lord: and even had
I such an inclination, 'twere (as you
　　Well know) superfluous; they are grown so bad,
That Hell has nothing better left to do
　　Than leave them to themselves: so much more mad
And evil by their own internal curse,
Heaven cannot make them better, nor I worse."

　　　　　　[ll. 185–192, 249–264, 281–288, 313–328]

I delight to imagine John Milton listening to these stanzas read aloud to him. Probably once would have been enough. When it comes to Byron's *Cain, a Mystery* (1821), Milton's reaction would be unimaginable:

Cain.
Haughty spirit!
Thou speak'st it proudly; but thyself, though proud,
Hast a superior.

Lucifer.
No! By heaven, which He
Holds, and the abyss, and the immensity
Of worlds, and life, which I hold with him, No!
I have a victor true; but no superior.
Homage he has from all but none from me;
I battle it against him, as I battled
In highest heaven. Through all eternity,
And the unfathomable gulphs of Hades,
And the interminable realms of space,
And the infinity of endless ages,
All, all, will I dispute! And world by world,
And star by star and universe by universe
Shall tremble in the balance, till the great
Conflict shall cease, if ever it shall cease,
Which it ne'er shall, till he or I be quench'd!
And what can quench our immortality,
Or mutual and irrevocable hate?
He as a conqueror will call the conquer'd
Evil; but what will be the good he gives I
Were I the victor, his works would be deem'd
The only evil ones. And you, ye new
And scarce-born mortals, what have been his gifts
To you already in your little world?

Cain.
But few; and some of those but bitter.

Lucifer.
Back
With me, then, to thine Earth, and try the rest . . .

[Act 2, Scene 2, ll. 424–450]

I juxtapose a recent admirable poem by Rowan Ricardo Phillips, "An Excuse for Mayhem":

The Kingdom of Heaven, the Kingdom of
God, Kingdom of the Father, the Kingdom
Of Christ, House of the Father, the City
Of God, the Heavenly Jerusalem,
The Holy Place, Paradise of Life, Life
Everlasting, the Joy of the Lord, Crown
Of Life, Crown of Justice, Crown of Glory,
Incorruptible Crown, the Great Reward,
The Inheritance of Christ, Eternal
Inheritance, the Immutable Change,
The Belt of Venus, the sublime blue hour
Of the voice, the mute light, mute church, mute choice.

[2015]

That leaves not much, but how much is there left to leave? William Blake attempted an answer in his last engraved work, *The Ghost of Abel* (1822), addressed to "Lord Byron in the Wilderness." Always exuberantly, I return to the hero-villain of *Paradise Lost*, and to Shelley's posthumously published essay, "On the Devil and Devils":

Thus much is certain, that Milton gives the Devil all imaginable advantage; and the arguments with which he exposes the injustice and impotent weakness of his adversary, are such as, had they been printed, distinct from the shelter of any dramatic order, would have been answered by the most conclusive of syllogisms—persecution. As it is, Paradise Lost has conferred on the modern mythology a systematic form; and when the immeasurable and unceasing mutability of time shall have added one more superstition to those which have already arisen and decayed upon the earth, commentators and critics will be learnedly employed in elucidating the religion of ancestral Europe, only not utterly forgotten because it will have participated in the eternity of genius. The Devil owes everything to Milton. Dante and Tasso present us with a very gross idea of him. Milton divested him of a sting, hoof, and horns, and clothed him with the sublime grandeur of a graceful but tremendous spirit.

Byron was much given to calling Shelley "the Snake," whether in the second person or the third. This private joke became a poetic mythology for both, snake and eagle contending.

Shelley wrote a sonnet "To Byron," unpublished until 1832, a decade after Shelley's death by water. It is difficult to believe that he showed it to Byron. It makes me very unhappy:

[I am afraid these verses will not please you, but]

If I esteemed you less, Envy would kill
Pleasure, and leave to Wonder and Despair
The ministration of the thoughts that fill
The mind which, like a worm whose life may share
A portion of the unapproachable,
Marks your creations rise as fast and fair
As perfect worlds at the Creator's will.

But such is my regard that nor your power
To soar above the heights where others [climb],
Nor fame, that shadow of the unborn hour
Cast from the envious future on the time,
Move one regret for his unhonoured name
Who dares these words:—the worm beneath the sod
May lift itself in homage of the God.

Shelley did not lack self-esteem, as person and as poet. Not even the most extreme idolators among Byron's scholars have a more exalted estimate of the noble lord's poetry than Shelley did. He went so far as to judge *Don Juan* (1819) the great poem of the age, surpassing Goethe and Wordsworth. After six years of almost constant

communication, in conversation and in correspondence, Byron became a stifling weight for Shelley. Aside from differences in temperament, and the perplexities caused by Claire Clairmont's pursuit of,
brief affair with, and subsequent angry rejection by Byron, Shelley
was a poet banned and largely unread in England, except by the
working classes, who enthused and were roused by pirated editions
of the revolutionary *Queen Mab*. Byron had an enormous readership,
immense personal wealth, and was both famous and infamous. Shelley was notorious mostly for the wrong reasons.

Byron's *Manfred* (1817) was deeply influenced by Shelley's *Alastor*
but in a rather defiant way. *Julian and Maddalo* (1824, written 1818–
1819) was Shelley's most remarkable portrait of Byron, but the celeb-
rity poet also appears in *Lines Written in the Euganean Hills* (1819,
written 1818) and in *Adonais*. Byron is significantly absent from *The
Triumph of Life*, and perhaps Shelley at the very end had exorcised him.

There were only glancing allusions to Shelley, never by name,
in Byron's poetry until the close, where the aura of the revolutionary poet finds its way into *The Island* (1823), a strange performance
that rehearses the mutiny on the *Bounty*, the saga of Captain Bligh
and the rebel first mate Fletcher Christian. Byron's Fletcher Christian is most certainly not a portrait of Shelley, yet there are fleeting
overtones of the most revolutionary of all major English poets (except perhaps for William Blake).

The friendship of Byron and Shelley was too intricate for historical and scholarly understanding. It abounded in contradictions.
When they were together they frequently stayed up until dawn in
animated conversation. We do not have records of what they said to
one another. Byron, as I read him, is at once the most amiable and
most bitter of nihilists. Shelley, again as I read him, arrives at his
own nihilism in *Adonais* and even more in *The Triumph of Life*. But
there are nihilists and nihilists, and the ethos of Byron's *Cain* is very
different from Shelley's descent into the abyss in *The Cenci*.

Shelley's influence and encouragement ultimately were benefi-
cial for Byron. He read most of Byron's work in progress and seems
to have made specific suggestions. It is always worth repeating that
Shelley was a great reader. Sadly Byron, identified by both poets with
the eagle, finally had a negative effect on the serpentine Shelley. If
the eagle represents the immensity of space, the snake stands for

time. William Blake called time "the Mercy of Eternity," but most poets regard it as destructive.

Shelley died at twenty-nine in what appears to have been a boating accident. Byron died in Greece, financing a mercenary army of brigands in an uprising against the Turks. The Greek adventure was not what the noble lord expected. Ostensibly in command, Byron was tormented by the anarchistic behavior of the ruffians he had hired. He also conceived his last mad passion for his teenaged Greek page Lukas Chalandritsanos, who raked in the infatuated poet's considerable wealth while declining to yield up his body to Byronic bumbuggery.

Byron wanted to die in battle, gallantly leading his reprobates to victory, but ill fortune prevented it. He died rather miserably in camp of sepsis. Almost from the moment of his death he became universally known and revered, on a scale starting with Goethe upon the heights, and concluding with the schoolgirls of Britain and the world, who conducted imaginary romances with him.

What moves us most if we contemplate the lives and deaths of Byron (thirty-six years) and Shelley (twenty-nine years)? Hart Crane, in the final lines of *The Bridge* (1930), is counterpointing intricately, but part of his burden is an apt requiem for Shelley and Byron, reconciled by the rainbows of pity, allied to Walt Whitman's prophecy of the grass; the American bard whispering antiphons in the blue of the imagination:

> Now pity steeps the grass and rainbows ring
> The serpent with the eagle in the leaves . . . ?
> Whispers antiphonal in azure swing.

CHAPTER SEVEN

Keats

They Seek No Wonder but the Human Face

KEATS HAS BECOME SO universally accepted as a major poet that I wonder what ailed most of his contemporary readers. The noble exceptions were William Hazlitt, Leigh Hunt, and Shelley.

My late friend Paul de Man called Keats's poetic stance prospective, yearning for realities and accepting no compromises between aspiration and fulfillment. That certainly is a part of *Endymion*'s agon with English poetic tradition. Yet I think this changed radically when Keats's mature odes and sonnets and the two *Hyperion* fragments broke a new path into meaning and rhetorical structures.

Keats matured into a vital struggle with Shakespeare, Milton, and Wordsworth. The consciousness of Shakespeare and his Prince Hamlet led the young poet to the shores of darkness rediscovered in English tragedy. Keats attempted to overgo Milton in the war of Titans, and with utmost seriousness to outdo Wordsworth in words of what we speak when we are most ourselves.

All through the poetry of Wallace Stevens there are references to porcelain and to the necessary evil and suffering of being completely physical in a physical world. In "Extracts from Addresses to the Academy of Fine Ideas" (1940) Keats is hailed as the Secretary of Porcelain, clearly alluding to "Ode on a Grecian Urn." In a central meditation, "The Poems of Our Climate" (1942), we can overhear an authentic American revision of "Ode on a Grecian Urn."

Stevens was interested in the art of Japanese flower arrangement. When he had walked home after a day's work as an insurance lawyer, he would prepare a drink and then turn to his daily order from the florist. Japanese flower arrangement depends upon turning some simple elements into a subtly suggestive pattern insinuating order. Here the brilliant bowl, clear water, and pink and white carnations are so transmuted as to produce a light in the room more like a newly fallen snow, at that moment in Connecticut winter when afternoons return. The achieved effect is a wintery air but at the end of winter.

The taste of bitterness at erotic loss is conveyed by a negative dialectic as one realizes that the speaker says "more" when he means "less": "Pink and white carnations—one desires / So much more than that."

The aesthetic of Wallace Stevens, like that of Walter Pater and of W. B. Yeats, relies upon simplification through intensity. I do not think that is the aesthetic of John Keats. He emphasizes so *stationing* perplexities that apprehension itself becomes a central act of imagination. Keats's Grecian Urn with its Cold Pastoral becomes Stevens's Cold Porcelain. And the arrangement had been too successful. The day itself outside has become a bowl of white echoing Fitzgerald's *Rubaiyat of Omar Khayyam* (1859):

> And that inverted Bowl they call the Sky,
> Whereunder crawling cooped we live and die,
>   Lift not your hands to It for help—for It
> As impotently moves as you or I.

Stevens gives two very different stances for concluding his poem:

II
Say even that this complete simplicity
Stripped one of all one's torments, concealed
The evilly compounded, vital I
And made it fresh in a world of white,
A world of clear water, brilliant-edged,

Still one would want more, one would need more,
More than a world of white and snowy scents.

Like Emily Dickinson, Stevens learned from Keats the uses of
oxymoronic imagery. He himself invents adverbial antitheses, as in
the complete simplicity of stripping and concealing. Then there is
the vital I so curiously compounded by the Keatsian evil of being a
natural man or woman in a natural world. The entire enterprise of
the poem comes to rest and is defeated in the line "A world of clear
water, brilliant-edged." Neither art nor nature has been enhanced,
but the demarcation between the two has been made more brilliant.
One of the more-is-less formulae now takes us to the need for "More
than a world of white and snowy scents."

The poet's mind, not restless, but never-resting, exercises its
power so that one would want to escape and return to what Nietzsche
called the primordial poem of mankind, so long ago composed.
There remains Stevens's shrewd interpellation of one of his prose
Adagia, "The Imperfect Paradise." This would seem to imply that
our Eden is unfinished. Finally, in this bitterness or brokenness, we
can find delight, the imperfect being so lustful in it, but what we will
find is that delight lies in, tells us untruths in flawed words and stubborn sounds.

The odes of John Keats have had so large an influence on poetry in the language that it hardly seems possible or desirable to read
Keats except in the full context of his precursors—Spenser, Shakespeare, Milton, Wordsworth—and of his successors—Tennyson,
Dante Gabriel Rossetti, Gerard Manley Hopkins, and Wilfred
Owen. In the United States they would include the very different
figures of Stevens and W. C. Williams.

I find Hopkins an astonishing cross between Keats and Walt
Whitman. Hart Crane excitedly discovered Hopkins late, and made
some remarkable amalgamations of the Jesuit poet with Keats and
with Whitman. Before joining the Society of Jesus, Hopkins had
shared a brief but intense affection with the young poet Digby Dolben, who drowned at seventeen. Dolben did not answer the passionate letters of Hopkins. Doubtless it was better that he did not. Both
young men were excitable idealists and potentially authentic poets.
Hopkins had a difficult life, dying a month short of forty-five while

suffering through an excruciating teaching situation with too many students and barely sustained by a rigorous Jesuit privation.

Considering the difficulties Hopkins imposed upon himself, it is heroic that he broke through into a new variation of the naturalistic humanism of John Keats. There was nothing religious in Keats's temperament: he sought no wonder but the human face. His epiphanies are all secular and anticipate the speculative aestheticism of Walter Pater. In a most curious relation of literary history, Walter Pater was the undergraduate tutor for Hopkins, and set and graded his weekly essays. Hopkins made every attempt to return the epiphanies of Walter Pater to their alternate origins in Christian belief. That is hardly a simple project. In most of his major poems, Hopkins manifests a struggle with a composite angel of Keats, Pater, and, most alarmingly for him, Walt Whitman.

Truthful in all other regards, Hopkins had trouble recalling just how much Whitman he had read. William Michael Rossetti's *Selected Poems of Walt Whitman* was easily available from 1868 on. Fearful of censorship, Rossetti de-eroticized Whitman as best he could, but of course it cannot be done. Walt *is* an erotic poet. It is possible that Hopkins never looked into Rossetti's volume but I find that difficult to believe.

Here is one of the final poems composed shortly before Hopkins died, "That Nature Is a Heraclitean Fire and of the Comfort of the Resurrection" (1889):

> Cloud-puffball, torn tufts, tossed pillows | flaunt forth, then
>   chevy on an air-
> Built thoroughfare: heaven-roysterers, in gay-gangs | they
>   throng; they glitter in marches.
> Down roughcast, down dazzling whitewash, | wherever an elm
>   arches,
> Shivelights and shadowtackle ín long | lashes lace, lance, and
>   pair.
> Delightfully the bright wind boisterous | ropes, wrestles, beats
>   earth bare
> Of yestertempest's creases; | in pool and rut peel parches
> Squandering ooze to squeezed | dough, crust, dust; stanches,
>   starches

Squadroned masks and manmarks | treadmire toil there
Footfretted in it. Million-fuelèd, | nature's bonfire burns on.
But quench her bonniest, dearest | to her, her clearest-selvèd
  spark
Man, how fast his firedint, | his mark on mind, is gone!
Both are in an unfathomable, all is in an enormous dark
Drowned. O pity and indig | nation! Manshape, that shone
Sheer off, disseveral, a star, | death blots black out; nor mark
              Is any of him at all so stark
But vastness blurs and time | beats level. Enough! the Resur-
  rection,
A heart's-clarion! Away grief's gasping, | joyless days, dejection.
              Across my foundering deck shone
A beacon, an eternal beam. | Flesh fade, and mortal trash
Fall to the residuary worm; | world's wildfire, leave but ash:
              In a flash, at a trumpet crash,
I am all at once what Christ is, | since he was what I am, and
This Jack, joke, poor potsherd, | patch, matchwood, immortal
  diamond,
              Is immortal diamond.

Nowhere in his letters to Robert Bridges does Hopkins mention
Whitman's great poem "The Sleepers." "Cloud-puffball, torn tufts,
tossed pillows | flaunt forth, then chevy on an air- / Built thorough-
fare: heaven-roysterers, in gay-gangs | they throng; they glitter in
marches." This clearly echoes:

Well do they do their jobs those journeymen divine,
Only from me can they hide nothing, and would not if they
  could,
I reckon I am their boss and they make me a pet besides,
And surround me and lead me and run ahead when I walk,
To lift their cunning covers to signify me with stretch'd arms,
  and resume the way;
Onward we move, a gay gang of blackguards! with mirth-
  shouting music and wild-flapping pennants of joy!
              ["The Sleepers," *Leaves of Grass*
              (1881–1882 edition), ll. 36–41]

I always knew in my heart Walt Whitman's mind to be more like my own than any other man's living. As he is a very great scoundrel this is not a pleasant confession.
[Hopkins, letter to Robert Bridges (October 1882)]

The confession is precise and accurate. The minds of Whitman and of Hopkins are in certain regards similar. It is a little sad that the Oxford-educated Jesuit could have thought that the heroic wound-dresser and ministering angel of the Washington, D.C., Civil War's so-called hospitals was a very great scoundrel. As much as Abraham Lincoln, Walt Whitman is now an American saint and healer.

Gerard Manley Hopkins necessarily is a smaller figure on the scale of Whitman or of Keats. His aesthetic eminence is beyond question, but it does him violence to overpraise him. Variety is hardly one of his characteristics. The spiritual anguish of his poems is sustained at the rather high cost of a dark sameness of affect. His extraordinary sonnet directed to Robert Bridges puts the lie to my observation:

The fine delight that fathers thought; the strong
Spur, live and lancing like the blowpipe flame,
Breathes once and, quenchèd faster than it came,
Leaves yet the mind a mother of immortal song.
Nine months she then, nay years, nine years she long
Within her wears, bears, cares and moulds the same:
The widow of an insight lost she lives, with aim
Now known and hand at work now never wrong.
    Sweet fire the sire of muse, my soul needs this;
I want the one rapture of an inspiration.
O then if in my lagging lines you miss
The roll, the rise, the carol, the creation,
My winter world, that scarcely breathes that bliss
Now, yields you, with some sighs, our explanation.
["To R.B." (1889)]

It is marvelous that the tribute to the Keatsian delight in imagination fathers this sonnet's thought, in which the mothering image is crucial. I think Keats would have appreciated "The widow of an insight lost." Though Hopkins laments lack of inspiration, his poem banishes all that is not celebration: "The roll, the rise, the carol, the creation." The two final lines graciously expend themselves in catching up all the cognitive threads of the poem.

Because Hopkins achieved his reputation only in the twentieth century, it remains tempting to distort the nature of his highly individual achievement. Reading him side by side with the principal pre-Raphaelite poets—Dante Gabriel Rossetti, George Meredith, Algernon Charles Swinburne, and William Morris—does not greatly illuminate him or them. I think now that his true contemporary was Christina Rossetti, a devotional poet of comparable achievement. My particular favorite by her is the chant founded on the biblical Song of Songs:

> Passing away, saith the World, passing away:
> Chances, beauty and youth, sapped day by day:
> Thy life never continueth in one stay.
> Is the eye waxen dim, is the dark hair changing to grey
> That hath won neither laurel nor bay?
> I shall clothe myself in Spring and bud in May:
> Thou, root-stricken, shalt not rebuild thy decay
> On my bosom for aye.
> Then I answered: Yea.
>
> Passing away, saith my Soul, passing away:
> With its burden of fear and hope, of labour and play,
> Hearken what the past doth witness and say:
> Rust in thy gold, a moth is in thine array,
> A canker is in thy bud, thy leaf must decay.
> At midnight, at cockcrow, at morning, one certain day
> Lo, the Bridegroom shall come and shall not delay:
> Watch thou and pray.
> Then I answered: Yea.
>
> Passing away, saith my God, passing away:
> Winter passeth after the long delay:
> New grapes on the vine, new figs on the tender spray,
> Turtle calleth turtle in Heaven's May.
> Though I tarry, wait for Me, trust Me, watch and pray.
> Arise, come away, night is past and lo it is day,

My love, My sister, My spouse, thou shalt hear Me say.
Then I answered: Yea.

[1862]

This ecstatic yet troubled lyric sustains itself upon a single rhyming sound. Approaching meridian, the poet confronts loss: bodily beauty, unrecognized achievement, unfulfilled spirituality. And yet she keeps replying: Yea. Still, this is not affirmation. She invokes the Song of Solomon but more in plangency than in celebration. Yet who could judge her except herself?

Unlike her brothers and their friends, Christina Rossetti was an original Anglican speculator upon theology. Here is her mysterious lyric "Up-Hill":

Does the road wind up-hill all the way?
    Yes, to the very end.
Will the day's journey take the whole long day?
    From morn to night, my friend.

But is there for the night a resting-place?
    A roof for when the slow dark hours begin.
May not the darkness hide it from my face?
    You cannot miss that inn.

Shall I meet other wayfarers at night?
    Those who have gone before.
Then must I knock, or call when just in sight?
    They will not keep you standing at that door.

Shall I find comfort, travel-sore and weak?
    Of labour you shall find the sum.
Will there be beds for me and all who seek?
    Yea, beds for all who come.

[1862]

Christina Rossetti believed in what she called soul sleep, a kind of Christian mortalism in which the dead enter an intermediate condition until at last their souls and bodies will reunite in a final resurrection. Alas, that seems to me a mere evasion, but I cannot dispute what splendid *materia poetica* it provided for her.

George Meredith in my youth was more widely and deeply read as a novelist than he is now. *The Egoist* (1879) is his comic masterpiece but no longer makes a universal interest among the younger readers I know. As a poet Meredith is greatly undervalued. His bitter yet lucid sequence of fifty sixteen-line sonnets, *Modern Love* (1862), achieves highly individual power in the three poems closing it out:

XLVIII

Their sense is with their senses all mixed in,
Destroyed by subtleties these women are!
More brain, O Lord, more brain! or we shall mar
Utterly this fair garden we might win.
Behold! I looked for peace, and thought it near.
Our inmost hearts had opened, each to each.
We drank the pure daylight of honest speech.
Alas! that was the fatal draught, I fear.
For when of my lost Lady came the word,
This woman, O this agony of flesh!
Jealous devotion bade her break the mesh,
That I might seek that other like a bird.
I do adore the nobleness! despise
The act! She has gone forth, I know not where.
Will the hard world my sentence of her share?
I feel the truth; so let the world surmise.

XLIX

He found her by the ocean's moaning verge,
Nor any wicked change in her discerned;
And she believed his old love had returned,
Which was her exultation, and her scourge.
She took his hand, and walked with him, and seemed
The wife he sought, though shadow-like and dry.
She had one terror, lest her heart should sigh,
And tell her loudly she no longer dreamed.
She dare not say, "This is my breast: look in."
But there's a strength to help the desperate weak.
That night he learned how silence best can speak
The awful things when Pity pleads for Sin.

About the middle of the night her call
Was heard, and he came wondering to the bed.
"Now kiss me, dear! it may be, now!" she said.
Lethe had passed those lips, and he knew all.

L
Thus piteously Love closed what he begat:
The union of this ever-diverse pair!
These two were rapid falcons in a snare,
Condemned to do the flitting of the bat.
Lovers beneath the singing sky of May,
They wandered once; clear as the dew on flowers:
But they fed not on the advancing hours:
Their hearts held cravings for the buried day.
Then each applied to each that fatal knife,
Deep questioning, which probes to endless dole.
Ah, what a dusty answer gets the soul
When hot for certainties in this our life!—
In tragic hints here see what evermore
Moves dark as yonder midnight ocean's force,
Thundering like ramping hosts of warrior horse,
To throw that faint thin line upon the shore!

Meredith was twenty-one when he married a beautiful widow,
who was seven years his senior. She was the daughter of Thomas
Love Peacock, satirical poet and novelist and friend of Shelley. Famously Meredith was the model for the painting *The Death of Chatterton* (1856) by Henry Wallis. The ebullient Mrs. Meredith ran off
with Wallis and bore him a child. Though Meredith eventually married again and was reasonably happy, the sequence *Modern Love*
should be called *The Death of Love*. Something abandoned Meredith
after the debacle of his first marriage:

Ah, what a dusty answer gets the soul
When hot for certainties in this our life!—

Call this a sense of past meridian, of being a man upon whom
the sun has gone down. My dark favorite among Meredith's poems
is "A Ballad of Past Meridian" (1876):

I

Last night returning from my twilight walk
I met the grey mist Death, whose eyeless brow
Was bent on me, and from his hand of chalk
He reached me flowers as from a withered bough:
O Death, what bitter nosegays givest thou!

II

Death said, I gather, and pursued his way.
Another stood by me, a shape in stone,
Sword-hacked and iron-stained, with breasts of clay,
And metal veins that sometimes fiery shone:
O Life, how naked and how hard when known!

III

Life said, As thou hast carved me, such am I.
Then memory, like the nightjar on the pine,
And sightless hope, a woodlark in night sky,
Joined notes of Death and Life till night's decline
Of Death, of Life, those inwound notes are mine.

You might call this a ballad of imbalance. Death is aesthetically stronger and therefore more memorable. Meredith had too acute a comic sense to find his depiction of Life successful. The final stanza just barely works. Neither we nor Meredith is persuaded that Life is as he carved it, whereas a Death that gathers is all too adequate. Like most of Meredith's better poems, this is flawed. As an instance of superb execution, I give his sonnet "Lucifer in Starlight" (1883):

On a starred night Prince Lucifer uprose.
Tired of his dark dominion swung the fiend
Above the rolling ball in cloud part screened,
Where sinners hugged their spectre of repose.
Poor prey to his hot fit of pride were those.
And now upon his western wing he leaned,
Now his huge bulk o'er Afric's sands careened,
Now the black planet shadowed Arctic snows.
Soaring through wider zones that pricked his scars

With memory of the old revolt from Awe,
He reached a middle height, and at the stars,
Which are the brain of heaven, he looked, and sank.
Around the ancient track marched, rank on rank,
The army of unalterable law.

This is and is not Milton's Satan or the Prince Lucifer he never shows us. Meredith's Lucifer suffers weariness of his own limited success and tries to raise himself to a higher vision. But what he beholds is his own aesthetic defeat:

Around the ancient track marched, rank on rank,
The army of unalterable law.

Meredith, like Dante Gabriel Rossetti, tracks Keats even when he is unaware whose steps he follows. Though Rossetti is a poet who thinks things through for himself, he knows that Keats is always with him. Since boyhood I have been moved to wonder by Rossetti's translation of Dante's stony sestina:

To the dim light and the large circle of shade
I have clomb, and to the whitening of the hills,
There where we see no colour in the grass.
Natheless my longing loses not its green,
It has so taken root in the hard stone
Which talks and hears as though it were a lady.

Utterly frozen is this youthful lady,
Even as the snow that lies within the shade;
For she is no more moved than is the stone
By the sweet season which makes warm the hills
And alters them afresh from white to green,
Covering their sides again with flowers and grass.

When on her hair she sets a crown of grass
The thought has no more room for other lady,
Because she weaves the yellow with the green
So well that Love sits down there in the shade,—
Love who has shut me in among low hills
Faster than between walls of granite-stone.

She is more bright than is a precious stone;
The wound she gives may not be healed with grass:
I therefore have fled far o'er plains and hills
For refuge from so dangerous a lady;
But from her sunshine nothing can give shade,—
Not any hill, nor wall, nor summer-green.

A while ago, I saw her dressed in green,—
So fair, she might have wakened in a stone
This love which I do feel even for her shade;
And therefore, as one woos a graceful lady,
I wooed her in a field that was all grass
Girdled about with very lofty hills.

Yet shall the streams turn back and climb the hills
Before Love's flame in this damp wood and green
Burn, as it burns within a youthful lady,
For my sake, who would sleep away in stone
My life, or feed like beasts upon the grass,
Only to see her garments cast a shade.

How dark soe'er the hills throw out their shade,
Under her summer green the beautiful lady
Covers it, like a stone covered in grass.

[1861]

This is Dante at his most intense as a lyric poet. Petrarch never transcended this poem though his endeavors caught something of Dante's negative exuberance. Rossetti, awed but liberated by Dante and Petrarch, surpassed himself in stylistic stance and metric perhaps more here than anywhere else. And yet I chant the poem through so many decades and hear more and more the images of voice, stationing, and incipient tragedy of John Keats.

Partly this is Rossetti absorbing the Keatsian advice to load every rift with ore. A darker share evokes the Belle Dame sans Merci whose seductions, however unintended, condemn the quester to starvation and to the thralldom that must end in a perpetual dying always short of actual death.

For Keats there was neither a Beatrice nor a Laura, but he was too sane to fall a victim to another Lady Pietra degli Scrovigni, in the unlikely event of stumbling upon her in London. After touching upon so many disciples of Keats, I remember Robert Browning's acerbic "Popularity" (1855):

I
Stand still, true poet that you are!
    I know you; let me try and draw you.
Some night you'll fail us: when afar
    You rise, remember one man saw you,
Knew you, and named a star!
. . .

V
Meantime, I'll draw you as you stand,
    With few or none to watch and wonder:
I'll say—a fisher, on the sand
    By Tyre the old, with ocean-plunder,
A netful, brought to land.

VI
Who has not heard how Tyrian shells
    Enclosed the blue, that dye of dyes
Whereof one drop worked miracles,
    And coloured like Astarte's eyes
Raw silk the merchant sells?
. . .

IX
Enough to furnish Solomon
    Such hangings for his cedar-house,
That, when gold-robed he took the throne
    In that abyss of blue, the Spouse
Might swear his presence shone
. . .

XII
And there's the extract, flasked and fine,
    And priced and saleable at last!

And Hobbs, Nobbs, Stokes and Nokes combine
 To paint the future from the past,
Put blue into their line.

XIII

Hobbs hints blue,—Straight he turtle eats:
 Nobbs prints blue,—claret crowns his cup:
Nokes outdares Stokes in azure feats,—
 Both gorge. Who fished the murex up?
What porridge had John Keats?

The true subject is Robert Browning, who by 1855 had achieved
no popularity as a poet. Hobbs, Nobbs, Stokes, and Nokes might be
named as Dante Gabriel Rossetti, George Meredith, William Morris, and whatever Spasmodic you would want to toss in. It is unlikely
that Keatsian poems provided much income for pre-Raphaelite banquets, and while John Keats had financial problems, he did not subsist on porridge. Still, Browning argues strenuously for his point
against imitators and in favor of originals.

 When Keats was working to complete *Endymion*, he dashed off an
odd variant on John Dryden's song "Farewell, ungrateful traitor" (1680):

In drear nighted December,
 Too happy, happy tree,
Thy branches ne'er remember
 Their green felicity:
The north cannot undo them,
With a sleety whistle through them;
Nor frozen thawings glue them
 From budding at the prime.

In drear-nighted December,
 Too happy, happy brook,
Thy bubblings ne'er remember
 Apollo's summer look;
But with a sweet forgetting,
They stay their crystal fretting,
Never, never petting
 About the frozen time.

Ah! would 'twere so with many
    A gentle girl and boy!
But were there ever any
    Writhed not at passed joy?
The feel of not to feel it,
When there is none to heal it,
Nor numbed sense to steel it,
    Was never said in rhyme.

[1817]

Those last four lines stay in the memory, but can Keats be right? Perhaps not in rhyme but certainly in Shakespeare's blank verse we are taught, as Keats was, the feel of not to feel it, as Macbeth recedes further and further from any affect except a sense of outrage. Keats is pressing against a hard limitation that poems have to learn to accept.

Walt Whitman stressed that poems emanated from the powerful press of himself. He was opposing Keats's notion of Negative Capability, as expressed in a letter to his brothers, George and Thomas:

which Shakespeare possessed so enormously—I mean Negative Capability, that is, when a man is capable of being in uncertainties, mysteries, doubts, without any irritable reaching after fact and reason—

[December 21–27, 1817]

This has been so much discussed as to produce a certain distortion. The single subject is Shakespeare, and Keats's observation is totally justified: the major Shakespearean protagonists abide in mysteries, and we are not encouraged to obliterate these by supposed fact or inadequate ideas of reason. We cannot pluck out the heart of Hamlet's mystery.

"Lord Byron cuts a figure but he is not figurative—Shakespeare led a life of Allegory: his works are the comments on it." That remark of Keats fascinates because we know almost nothing of Shakespeare's inward life. With Keats we know a great deal and can surmise the labyrinthine ways in which the Great Odes and the *Hyperion* fragments comment upon his allegorical reading of his own life.

Every student I encounter is challenged by the "Ode to a Nightingale" to confront herself or himself in a meditation upon the passing of youth and the ultimate necessity of dying:

I

My heart aches, and a drowsy numbness pains
    My sense, as though of hemlock I had drunk,
Or emptied some dull opiate to the drains
    One minute past, and Lethe-wards had sunk:
'Tis not through envy of thy happy lot,
    But being too happy in thine happiness,—
        That thou, light-winged Dryad of the trees,
          In some melodious plot
        Of beechen green, and shadows numberless,
          Singest of summer in full-throated ease.

II

O, for a draught of vintage! that hath been
    Cool'd a long age in the deep-delved earth,
Tasting of Flora and the country green,
    Dance, and Provençal song, and sunburnt mirth!
O for a beaker full of the warm South,
    Full of the true, the blushful Hippocrene,
        With beaded bubbles winking at the brim,
          And purple-stained mouth;
        That I might drink, and leave the world unseen,
          And with thee fade away into the forest dim:

III

Fade far away, dissolve, and quite forget
    What thou among the leaves hast never known,
The weariness, the fever, and the fret
    Here, where men sit and hear each other groan;
Where palsy shakes a few, sad, last gray hairs,
    Where youth grows pale, and spectre-thin, and dies;
        Where but to think is to be full of sorrow
          And leaden-eyed despairs,
        Where Beauty cannot keep her lustrous eyes,
          Or new Love pine at them beyond tomorrow.

IV

Away! away! for I will fly to thee,
    Not charioted by Bacchus and his pards,
But on the viewless wings of Poesy,
    Though the dull brain perplexes and retards:
Already with thee! tender is the night,
      And haply the Queen-Moon is on her throne,
        Cluster'd around by all her starry Fays;
          But here there is no light,
        Save what from heaven is with the breezes blown
          Through verdurous glooms and winding mossy ways.

V

I cannot see what flowers are at my feet,
    Nor what soft incense hangs upon the boughs,
But, in embalmed darkness, guess each sweet
    Wherewith the seasonable month endows
The grass, the thicket, and the fruit-tree wild;
    White hawthorn, and the pastoral eglantine;
      Fast fading violets cover'd up in leaves;
        And mid-May's eldest child,
    The coming musk-rose, full of dewy wine,
      The murmurous haunt of flies on summer eves.

VI

Darkling I listen; and, for many a time
    I have been half in love with easeful Death,
Call'd him soft names in many a mused rhyme,
    To take into the air my quiet breath;
Now more than ever seems it rich to die,
    To cease upon the midnight with no pain,
      While thou art pouring forth thy soul abroad
        In such an ecstasy!
      Still wouldst thou sing, and I have ears in vain—
        To thy high requiem become a sod.

VII

Thou wast not born for death, immortal Bird!
    No hungry generations tread thee down;

The voice I hear this passing night was heard
   In ancient days by emperor and clown:
Perhaps the self-same song that found a path
    Through the sad heart of Ruth, when, sick for home,
      She stood in tears amid the alien corn;
        The same that oft-times hath
     Charm'd magic casements, opening on the foam
       Of perilous seas, in faery lands forlorn.

VIII

Forlorn! the very word is like a bell
   To toll me back from thee to my sole self!
Adieu! the fancy cannot cheat so well
   As she is fam'd to do, deceiving elf.
Adieu! adieu! thy plaintive anthem fades
    Past the near meadows, over the still stream,
      Up the hill-side; and now 'tis buried deep
        In the next valley-glades:
     Was it a vision, or a waking dream?
       Fled is that music:—Do I wake or sleep?

Doubtless there can be no such thing as a perfect poem. Between poet and performance, shadows must fall. You could pick away at a phrase or two here in search of some flaw, but then you would lack all grace and all gratitude.

Tom, the poet's younger brother, died of tuberculosis at nineteen. Denise Gigante, an admirable scholar of Romantic poetry, has emphasized with total clarity the extent to which the nightingale ode is an elegy for Tom; a lament for the other brother, George, struggling with the economics of existence in Kentucky; and inevitably a threnody for the poet himself, who died in Rome less than two years later.

At my age I sometimes find it helpful to think of poems in clusters. Shelley's "Ode to the West Wind" and Stevens's "The Course of a Particular" (1951) frame "Ode to a Nightingale." Shelley is the force of the Spirit descending. Keats struggles with love and death while enveloped in the song that edges the first toward the second. Stevens, aware of both, shows the American difference, with his "cry of leaves that do not transcend themselves, / In the absence of fantasia . . ."

Shelleyan as always, this knowingly belies itself. The leaves cry. The poet will not let himself hear this as an image of transcendence. But since the leaves continue to cry, they do transcend themselves. Shelley's wind blows through New England winter.

Keats is so firmly rooted in his vision that transcendence becomes irrelevant. We are moved by his hyperbole that the nightingale is immortal though immortality, were it to exist, would destroy this great ode.

A major confusion in many of us involves the three very different speculations we call immortality, resurrection, and redemption. Immortality is an ancient Greek surmise we associate most firmly with Plato. Resurrection, Indo-Iranian in origins, became a Pharasaic doctrine and then was absorbed by early Christianity. Redemption in very different ways informs Judaism, Christianity, and Islam.

Setting aside Shakespeare, Keats is the first major English poet free of religion. This is palpable yet hard to keep in mind. He rightly believed that he would be among the English poets after his death. Since he thought that the imagination had to work out its own salvation in any poet, he had to intimidate those who came after him. His principal disciple was Tennyson, who seemed to have no realization that Keats was not a Christian. In his inmost core, which was daemonic, Tennyson also was scarcely a Christian, despite the colorings of *Idylls of the King* (1859–1885) and *In Memoriam* (1850, written 1849).

I write this on March 16, 2019, grieving for the death of my old friend, the poet William Merwin, news of which arrived this morning. That sharpens my sense that the question concluding "Ode to a Nightingale" has to be confronted as we interpret the poem: "Do I wake or sleep?" It is capable of various turnings. Am I awake or still asleep? Shall I now seek to be more wakeful or go to sleep? How much longer will it be until my final sleep?

VI

Darkling I listen; and, for many a time
    I have been half in love with easeful Death,
Call'd him soft names in many a mused rhyme,
    To take into the air my quiet breath;

Now more than ever seems it rich to die,
    To cease upon the midnight with no pain,
      While thou art pouring forth thy soul abroad
        In such an ecstasy!
    Still wouldst thou sing, and I have ears in vain—
      To thy high requiem become a sod.

I repeat this glorious stanza because I can never come to the end of its tropological refinements. Milton is invoked with high deliberation in that rich "Darkling." What does it mean to be "half in love"? "Rich to die" would fit well in Shakespeare's *Antony and Cleopatra*. "Cease" is another wealthy word. "Ecstasy" is and is not madness. I overhear Hamlet as well as Cleopatra.

Nothing else in Keats is pitched so high as "Ode to a Nightingale." Keats has no illusion that he can storm heaven, whatever that heaven can be. The strength of his elevated image of voice can be surmised by the influence it exercises upon Shelley's *Adonais*:

LIV

    That Light whose smile kindles the Universe,
    That Beauty in which all things work and move,
    That Benediction which the eclipsing Curse
    Of birth can quench not, that sustaining Love
    Which through the web of being blindly wove
    By man and beast and earth and air and sea,
    Burns bright or dim, as each are mirrors of
    The fire for which all thirst; now beams on me,
Consuming the last clouds of cold mortality.

                        [ll. 478–486]

There are no Keatsian echoes here. Emulation enters as it might with two flamenco dancer-singers, each transcending the other in "black sounds." Lorca, expounding the *duende*, said that it had to come up from the soles of a man's feet. It is the daemon of Socrates.

Shelley recognizes that Keats broke limits in his ode to his spirit sister, the *lorn* nightingale alluding to "forlorn," transition between Keats's two final stanzas:

XVII

Thy spirit's sister, the lorn nightingale
Mourns not her mate with such melodious pain;
Not so the eagle, who like thee could scale
Heaven, and could nourish in the sun's domain
Her mighty youth with morning, doth complain,
Soaring and screaming round her empty nest,
As Albion wails for thee . . .

[ll. 145–151]

Keats soars upward into the realm of the sun, his *Hyperion*. Shelley is moved to his own fiercest flight and so to the fountain for which all thirst. In that sense *Adonais* is both challenge and response.

It now seems inevitable to associate Shelley and Keats. But that is a quirk of literary history. Shelley is the most convinced revolutionary among all the poets. His ideas shocked Byron and have not lost their capacity to infuriate. Courageous students worldwide continue to chant the conclusion to his *The Mask of Anarchy*.

Shelley is a great unrest inducer. He wanted to turn over everything and keep it from merely repeating itself. Keats possibly would have been aesthetically disdainful of this as revolutionary rant. His own dismissal of Christianity is rather elegant:

The church bells toll a melancholy round,
 Calling the people to some other prayers,
 Some other gloominess, more dreadful cares,
More harkening to the sermon's horrid sound.
Surely the mind of man is closely bound
 In some black spell; seeing that each one tears
 Himself from fireside joys, and Lydian airs,
And converse high of those with glory crown'd
Still, still they too, and I should feel a damp,
 A chill as from a tomb, did I not know
That they are dying like an outburnt lamp;
 That 'tis their sighing, wailing ere they go
 Into oblivion—that fresh flowers will grow,
And many glories of immortal stamp.

["Written in Disgust of Vulgar Superstition" (1816)]

The vulgar superstition is English Christianity. It is a lasting puzzle that a dominant school of scholarly critics, historicizers old and new, have made too much of Keats's Cockney identity, as though such rigorously *thought* poems might as well have been written by Leigh Hunt.

Keats omitted the original first stanza of the "Ode on Melancholy," probably because it was so grisly.

Though you should build a bark of dead men's bones,
And rear a phantom gibbet for a mast,
Stitch creeds [shrouds interlined above] together for a sail,
                                                    with groans
    To fill it out, blood-stained and aghast;
Although your rudder be a Dragon's tail,
                Long sever'd, yet still hard with agony,
    Your cordage large uprootings from the skull
Of bald Medusa, certes you would fail
        To find the Melancholy—whether she
        Dreameth in any isle of Lethe dull.

Keats's final version of the "Ode on Melancholy" reads:

I
No, no, go not to Lethe, neither twist
    Wolf's-bane, tight-rooted, for its poisonous wine;
Nor suffer thy pale forehead to be kiss'd
    By nightshade, ruby grape of Proserpine;
        Make not your rosary of yew-berries,
    Nor let the beetle, nor the death-moth be
        Your mournful Psyche, nor the downy owl
A partner in your sorrow's mysteries;
    For shade to shade will come too drowsily,
        And drown the wakeful anguish of the soul.

II
But when the melancholy fit shall fall
    Sudden from heaven like a weeping cloud,
That fosters the droop-headed flowers all,

And hides the green hill in an April shroud;
Then glut thy sorrow on a morning rose,
   Or on the rainbow of the salt sand-wave,
     Or on the wealth of globed peonies;
Or if thy mistress some rich anger shows,
    Emprison her soft hand, and let her rave,
     And feed deep, deep upon her peerless eyes.

III

She dwells with Beauty—Beauty that must die;
   And Joy, whose hand is ever at his lips
Bidding adieu; and aching Pleasure nigh,
    Turning to poison while the bee-mouth sips:
Ay, in the very temple of Delight
   Veil'd Melancholy has her sovran shrine,
     Though seen of none save him whose strenuous tongue
    Can burst Joy's grape against his palate fine;
His soul shalt taste the sadness of her might,
    And be among her cloudy trophies hung.

I have very complex memories of Walter Jackson Bate, who lives on in his critical biographies of Samuel Johnson and of John Keats. Jack was twelve years my senior and we had very different personalities. But we found common ground whenever we met, particularly during my Charles Eliot Norton Professorship at Harvard, 1987–1988. I found it poignant that Jack, who had just retired, strongly urged me to stay on at Harvard rather than return to Yale.

When I made a later lecture visit to Harvard, Jack sent word he was unwell so we did not meet for a final time. But his friends and former students startled me by saying that he wished me to know of his discovery that he was of Jewish ancestry. In a subsequent phone call Jack said that he was studying Hebrew and hoping to absorb some Talmud.

In 1999, aged eighty-one, Jack died at a Jewish medical center and told friends he was dying as a Jew. I had always believed that Jack's great strength as a critical biographer came from his own deeply ingrained melancholy. His remarks on Keats's "Ode on Melancholy" are worthy of the poem:

The knowledge of both of our own brevity and of the brevity of what we seek to hold awakens the drowsy, easily distracted attention, and fosters a heightened awareness that will match the transient process it salutes—an awareness that itself inevitably leads to the "Sovran shrine" of melancholy. For it is not simply the knowledge of transience that brings sorrow or pain. In a response sufficiently intense—a response duplicating and identifying itself with the active process it acknowledges and shares—the full emotional resources of our nature are called into play. Pain and "aching pleasure" pass organically into each other as the nectar sipped by the bee passes into the poison sting within its body. Images of pleasure and pain are now coalesced in the final stanza. For the contrast now is not of one with the other but rather of both, in organic combination, with the dimly allegorical background (the "temple," "Veiled Melancholy" and her "Sovran shrine," the "cloudy trophies")—allegorical images that Keats had once so warmly incorporated in narrative but that now (as later in the *Fall of Hyperion*) loom abstract and shadowlike, suggesting the permanence of the nonhuman.

[*John Keats* (1964)]

It is a fine insight to speak of Keats as a seer of "the permanence of the nonhuman." He had been reading Burton's *Anatomy of Melancholy*, which in one respect is a phantasmagoria suggesting that we are walled in or framed by the nonhuman. The condition of melancholy has to be accepted as a basis of our being. I think Keats may have brooded on the speech of the Player King in *Hamlet*:

I do believe you think what now you speak;
But what we do determine oft we break.
Purpose is but the slave to memory,
Of violent birth, but poor validity;
Which now, like fruit unripe, sticks on the tree;
But fall, unshaken, when they mellow be.
Most necessary 'tis that we forget
To pay ourselves what to ourselves is debt:
What to ourselves in passion we propose,

The passion ending, doth the purpose lose.
The violence of either grief or joy
Their own enactures with themselves destroy:
Where joy most revels, grief doth most lament;
Grief joys, joy grieves, on slender accident.
This world is not for aye, nor 'tis not strange
That even our loves should with our fortunes change;
For 'tis a question left us yet to prove,
Whether love lead fortune, or else fortune love.
The great man down, you mark his favourite flies;
The poor advanced makes friends of enemies.
And hitherto doth love on fortune tend;
For who not needs shall never lack a friend,
And who in want a hollow friend doth try,
Directly seasons him his enemy.
But, orderly to end where I begun,
Our wills and fates do so contrary run
That our devices still are overthrown;
Our thoughts are ours, their ends none of our own.

[3.2.190–217]

We are listening to Prince Hamlet as author here, as these are the lines he wrote to help transform *The Murder of Gonzago* into *The Mousetrap*. David Bromwich a long time ago dismissed two delusions about Keats. Far from irenic, he was pugnacious, as was his moral guide William Hazlitt. And like Hazlitt, he had metaphysical interests, but was delaying them until he was further along in his self-education. Had he lived, he would have gone to Hazlitt to ask for instruction as to which metaphysicians required deep reading.

If you seek no wonder but the human face, the music of a happy noted voice, what does it mean to be haunted by the permanence of the nonhuman? In Shelley there is a recalcitrance, a dross in human being that hinders the spirit's flight. Shelley wanted to name that negation as the principle of self or Mammon. But Keats, like Blake, had come up from below, working-class London. He distrusted Shelley's aristocratic idealism and kept the Promethean poet at a distance.

What would Shelley have made of the quality expounded famously by Keats in a letter to his brothers (December 22, 1817)?

I had not a dispute, but a disquisition, with Dilke upon various subjects; several things dove-tailed in my mind, and at once it struck me what quality went to form a Man of Achievement, especially in Literature, and which Shakspeare possessed so enormously—I mean *Negative Capability*, that is, when a man is capable of being in uncertainties, mysteries, doubts, without any irritable reaching after fact and reason. Coleridge, for instance, would let go by a fine isolated verisimilitude caught from the Penetralium of mystery, from being incapable of remaining content with half-knowledge. This pursued through volumes would perhaps take us no further than this, that with a great poet the sense of Beauty overcomes every other consideration, or rather obliterates all consideration.

By now *Negative Capability* is pretty much what you can make of it. No single reader, not even Hazlitt or Jack Bate, can absorb and give back whatever is most vital in Keats. Each one of us confronts Moneta as best she can:

As near as an immortal's sphered words
Could to a mother's soften, were these last:
And yet I had a terror of her robes,
And chiefly of the veils, that from her brow
Hung pale, and curtain'd her in mysteries
That made my heart too small to hold its blood.
This saw that Goddess, and with sacred hand
Parted the veils. Then saw I a wan face,
Not pined by human sorrows, but bright-blanch'd
By an immortal sickness which kills not;
It works a constant change, which happy death
Can put no end to; deathwards progressing
To no death was that visage; it had pass'd
The lily and the snow; and beyond these
I must not think now, though I saw that face.
But for her eyes I should have fled away.
They held me back, with a benignant light,
Soft mitigated by divinest lids

Half closed, and visionless entire they seem'd
Of all external things—they saw me not,
But, in blank splendor, beam'd like the mild moon,
Who comforts those she sees not, who knows not
What eyes are upward cast. As I had found
A grain of gold upon a mountain's side,
And twing'd with avarice, strain'd out my eyes
To search its sullen entrails rich with ore,
So, at the view of sad Moneta's brow,
I ached to see what things the hollow brain
Behind enwombed: what high tragedy
In the dark secret Chambers of her skull
Was acting, that could give so dread a stress
To her cold lips, and fill with such a light
Her planetary eyes . . .
                    [Keats, *The Fall of Hyperion*, 1.249–281]

Farewell to an idea . . . The mother's face,
The purpose of the poem, fills the room.
                    [Stevens, *The Auroras of Autumn* (1950), Section 3]

Keats's father died in an accident when the boy was just eight. Two months later his mother ran off. The poet had vivid memories of both but said little overtly about his mother. Wallace Stevens is both Freudian and Keatsian in finding the purpose of the poem to be the mother's face.

Moneta is hardly a mother. She is harsh and admonitory. Keats has won her over by a shocking outburst against his poetic contemporaries:

                                    Then shouted I
Spite of myself, and with a Pythia's spleen,
"Apollo! faded! O far-flown Apollo!
Where is thy misty pestilence to creep
Into the dwellings, through the door crannies
Of all mock lyrists, large self-worshippers
And careless Hectorers in proud bad verse?

Though I breathe death with them it will be life
To see them sprawl before me into graves."

[1.202–210]

It is not unreasonable to surmise that Shelley is one of the mock lyrists, Wordsworth the most eminent of large self-worshippers, and Lord Byron chief of the careless Hectorers in proud bad verse. The closing sentiment can be excused since the young poet knows he will live only briefly, will not consummate his love for Fanny Brawne, will enjoy poetic fame only posthumously.

I continue to believe that *The Triumph of Life* was a palinode to *Prometheus Unbound*. Difficult as it is to characterize *The Fall of Hyperion*, the poem is not a critique of earlier Keats, including *Lamia* or *Hyperion*. For my friend the late Geoffrey Hartman it was only in the ode "To Autumn" that Keats achieved "true impersonality."

All sensitive readers find in "To Autumn" (1819) the virtually perfect poem. Does its implied speaker seem selfless?

I

Season of mists and mellow fruitfulness,
    Close bosom-friend of the maturing sun;
Conspiring with him how to load and bless
    With fruit the vines that round the thatch-eves run;
To bend with apples the moss'd cottage-trees,
    And fill all fruit with ripeness to the core;
        To swell the gourd, and plump the hazel shells
    With a sweet kernel; to set budding more,
And still more, later flowers for the bees,
Until they think warm days will never cease,
        For summer has o'er-brimm'd their clammy cells.

II

Who hath not seen thee oft amid thy store?
    Sometimes whoever seeks abroad may find
Thee sitting careless on a granary floor,
    Thy hair soft-lifted by the winnowing wind;
Or on a half-reap'd furrow sound asleep,

Drows'd with the fume of poppies, while thy hook
Spares the next swath and all its twined flowers:
And sometimes like a gleaner thou dost keep
Steady thy laden head across a brook;
Or by a cyder-press, with patient look,
Thou watchest the last oozings hours by hours.

III

Where are the songs of Spring? Ay, where are they?
Think not of them, thou hast thy music too,—
While barred clouds bloom the soft-dying day,
And touch the stubble-plains with rosy hue;
Then in a wailful choir the small gnats mourn
Among the river sallows, borne aloft
Or sinking as the light wind lives or dies;
And full-grown lambs loud bleat from hilly bourn;
Hedge-crickets sing; and now with treble soft
The red-breast whistles from a garden-croft;
And gathering swallows twitter in the skies.

[ll. 1–33]

"And fill all fruit with ripeness to the core" recalls Edgar in *King Lear*:

Men must endure
Their going hence even as their coming hither.
Ripeness is all.

[5.2.9–11]

As I have learned to read *King Lear*, Edgar begins as a gullible young nobleman who seems lacking in self. Through a terrible act of self-abnegation, he chooses the bottom of the social scale for his disguise as poor Tom O'Bedlam, wandering maniac and beggar. He shows astonishing command of rhetoric in this dissimulation. In defense of his blinded father, Gloucester, he changes disguises and becomes a country peasant with authentic accent and clubs to death the monstrous Oswald, who is about to cut down the helpless old man. Finding in Oswald's possession the fatal note from Goneril to

Edmund that threatens Albany and reveals their adultery, he sensibly transmits this to Albany. At the third sound of the trumpet that precedes a possible duel between Albany and Edmund, he appears in arms and armor as a nameless knight seeking revenge. Quite properly he gives his half brother a death wound and precipitates the final actions of the drama.

I do not think that "ripeness is all" is to be taken as some final wisdom that the recalcitrant Edgar has learned. Keats seems to have intended some complex allusion in linking "ripeness is all" with "ripeness to the core."

Edgar painfully earns a new personality. Keats ripened astonishingly in the last two years of his life. But he achieved neither selflessness nor a new self. And though he played with an idea of impersonality, I wonder whether he achieved it.

Like his mentor William Hazlitt, Keats appreciates the paradox that Shakespeare in regard to his work is the sublime of impersonality, yet the plays are miracles thronged with strong personalities. Like all the Romantics, Keats wanted to compose stage dramas. His surviving efforts at theater are unpromising. I have seen productions of Byron's *Cain* and his *Manfred*. They fell short. Shelley surprisingly wrote *The Cenci*, which I have seen twice and found intermittently effective, but am unhappy reading it. That leaves Wordsworth's *The Borderers* (1795–1797), which I have never seen but sustains rereading. There is *Death's Jest-Book*, by Thomas Lovell Beddoes. I read it constantly for shock and pleasure but do not see how it could be staged.

Hazlitt's power as a critic of Shakespeare emanates from his gusto in describing and extolling the creation of character and of personality. Like Samuel Johnson before him and A. C. Bradley at a later time, he does not hesitate to bring together literature and the common life.

David Bromwich, always acute on the relation between Keats and Hazlitt, catches the threshold stance of Keats poised on the precarious verge of risking the self:

He hoped to attain a point of view from which sublime emotions could be his as a more than temporary privilege. At the same time he needed to be invulnerable to the charge of egotism that he had brought against Wordsworth. He was reconciled to seeing the self dominate his poetry as much as it had Wordsworth's; but unlike Wordsworth he would leave the way open to feel as someone or something else. The change has to do with dramatic situation. The narrator of a Keats ode is always on the verge of becoming not quite himself, and he makes us believe that to remain so is to widen experience.

[*Hazlitt* (1983)]

As a critical formulation this is suggestive and itself rather precarious. There are so many ways of becoming not quite oneself. Shakespeare's personalities change through self-overhearing and self-otherseeing. Much the same is true of Keats as lyric narrator. Since he strives not to resemble himself, whatever self that be, he takes care not to speak with the resonances of Hamlet and all the other Shakespearean protagonists.

> Where are the songs of Spring? Ay, where are they?
>   Think not of them, thou hast thy music too . . .

The Keats who wished to be always prospective asks the first question. The next question is spoken by the tragic Keats, and is purely rhetorical. There is something of Antony saying to his freedman: Unarm Eros, the long day's work is done and we are for the night.

You could argue the Keatsian difference from Wordsworth as lyric narrator of the great "Ode: Intimations of Immortality from Recollections of Early Childhood" is that the Wordsworthian singer sees nothing in the departed glory he did not estrange from himself. There is always a dialectical tension in Wordsworth between the sublime sense of self and the outward scene, whether glorious or fallen away. But Keats is almost always at home with his own landscapes.

In my youth I was greatly influenced by a highly original study, J. H. Van den Berg's *The Changing Nature of Man* (1961). The book chronicles the growing inner self, the consequent estrangement of landscape, and the ironic emergence into visibility of what had been there, but with scarce prior notice. I have begun to doubt Van den

Berg's humane observations. The poets were always there before all discursiveness. That is one of the great teachings of Giambattista Vico. In his bravura W. B. Yeats said the world knew nothing because it had made nothing. The poets knew everything because they made everything. Yeats, as he so frequently does, carries Vico to an irreality that stuns us rhetorically but leaves us with empty hands.

Of all poets, Yeats was most wrong about John Keats. He compared Keats's supposed desire for ideal forms to a poor child gazing through a bakery window and longing for the sweets within. Negative capability decidedly was not a Yeatsian mode. Keats hoped to emulate Shakespeare by developing so comprehensive a consciousness that the poet's self pragmatically might vanish. All readers of Keats have personal favorites; mine is "Ode to Psyche," which set some of the patterns of the subsequent odes of 1819:

O Goddess! hear these tuneless numbers, wrung
    By sweet enforcement and remembrance dear,
And pardon that thy secrets should be sung
    Even into thine own soft-conched ear:
Surely I dreamt to-day, or did I see
    The winged Psyche with awaken'd eyes?
I wander'd in a forest thoughtlessly,
    And, on the sudden, fainting with surprise,
Saw two fair creatures, couched side by side
    In deepest grass, beneath the whisp'ring roof
    Of leaves and trembled blossoms, where there ran
        A brooklet, scarce espied:
'Mid hush'd, cool-rooted flowers, fragrant-eyed,
    Blue, silver-white, and budded Tyrian,
They lay calm-breathing, on the bedded grass;
    Their arms embraced, and their pinions too;
    Their lips touch'd not, but had not bade adieu,
As if disjoined by soft-handed slumber,
And ready still past kisses to outnumber
    At tender eye-dawn of aurorean love:
        The winged boy I knew;
    But who wast thou, O happy, happy dove?
        His Psyche true!

O latest born and loveliest vision far
   Of all Olympus' faded hierarchy!
Fairer than Phoebe's sapphire-region'd star,
   Or Vesper, amorous glow-worm of the sky;
Fairer than these, though temple thou hast none,
      Nor altar heap'd with flowers;
Nor virgin-choir to make delicious moan
      Upon the midnight hours;
No voice, no lute, no pipe, no incense sweet
   From chain-swung censer teeming;
No shrine, no grove, no oracle, no heat
   Of pale-mouth'd prophet dreaming.

O brightest! though too late for antique vows,
   Too, too late for the fond believing lyre,
When holy were the haunted forest boughs,
   Holy the air, the water, and the fire;
Yet even in these days so far retir'd
   From happy pieties, thy lucent fans,
   Fluttering among the faint Olympians,
I see, and sing, by my own eyes inspir'd.
So let me be thy choir, and make a moan
      Upon the midnight hours;
Thy voice, thy lute, thy pipe, thy incense sweet
   From swinged censer teeming;
Thy shrine, thy grove, thy oracle, thy heat
   Of pale-mouth'd prophet dreaming.

Yes, I will be thy priest, and build a fane
   In some untrodden region of my mind,
Where branched thoughts, new grown with pleasant pain,
   Instead of pines shall murmur in the wind:
Far, far around shall those dark-cluster'd trees
   Fledge the wild-ridged mountains steep by steep;
And there by zephyrs, streams, and birds, and bees,
   The moss-lain Dryads shall be lull'd to sleep;
And in the midst of this wide quietness
A rosy sanctuary will I dress
With the wreath'd trellis of a working brain,

With buds, and bells, and stars without a name,
With all the gardener Fancy e'er could feign,
　Who breeding flowers, will never breed the same:
And there shall be for thee all soft delight
　　That shadowy thought can win,
A bright torch, and a casement ope at night,
　　To let the warm Love in!

I have written and published so many commentaries on this inaugural ode that I think it best to begin anew, and not consult any of my timeworn remarks. There is a disproportion between Keats's benignity and the ironic history, down to his own day, of the literary myth of Cupid and Psyche that more or less begins with *The Golden Ass* of Apuleius, as Augustine called the book, whose actual title is *The Metamorphoses* (second century CE).

Copious accounts of Venus, from the most ancient on to the Age of Keats, combine to make her a vain, malicious, revengeful goddess, second perhaps only to Juno. Apuleius makes her frightening yet ridiculous, when she sends her son Cupid to seduce and defame Psyche. Instead the imp falls in love but will visit Psyche only in the darkness. Already, though, I disfigure the "Ode to Psyche," a poem so affirmative in its celebration of fulfilled sexual love as to have few competitors.

And there shall be for thee all soft delight
　　That shadowy thought can win,
A bright torch, and a casement ope at night,
　　To let the warm Love in!

I repeat these final lines because of their beauty, their complexities, and their fruitful ambiguities. Keats slyly recalls a delicious exchange in *As You Like It:*

AUDREY: I do not know what "poetical" is. Is it honest in deed and word? is it a true thing?
TOUCHSTONE: No, truly; for the truest poetry is the most feigning; and lovers are given to poetry, and what they swear in poetry may be said as lovers they do feign.

[3.3.14–18]

Keats is exalted yet wary. He knows that what he offers Psyche is transitory. Yet, though there are limits to what *shadowy* thought can win, apotheosis triumphs over caution. What matters are the poet's gestures of generosity. He will illuminate Cupid and throw open the nocturnal casement to abet the warmth of consummation.

There are no final observations I am moved to make about Keats. Had he lived, he might well have surpassed Wordsworth, Byron, and Shelley as the poet of the age. He was moving toward the composition of Shakespearean tragedy, but all we have is one remarkable fragment:

> This living hand, now warm and capable
> Of earnest grasping, would, if it were cold
> And in the icy silence of the tomb,
> So haunt thy days and chill thy dreaming nights
> That thou would[st] wish thine own heart dry of blood
> So in my veins red life might stream again,
> And thou be conscience-calm'd—see here it is—
> I hold it towards you.
>
> [1819]

CHAPTER EIGHT

Robert Browning

What in the Midst Lay but the Tower Itself?

A T THIS TIME ROBERT BROWNING seems to be among the least read of the major poets of the English language. I wish that sentence were inaccurate, but I fear it is valid. I teach Browning annually and always find time to devote at least two seminars to his strongest dramatic lyrics and monologues. My students take to him very quickly and become profoundly engrossed in such poems as "Andrea del Sarto" (ca. 1853), "Childe Roland to the Dark Tower Came" (1855), "Caliban upon Setebos" (1864), "Fra Lippo Lippi" (1853), and a group of the music poems.

Browning met considerable early resistance to his poetry. Some of it endured. Gerard Manley Hopkins called him "bouncing Browning," and remarked that this bouncer had "a way of talking (and making his people talk) with the air and spirit of a man bouncing up from table with mouth full of bread and cheese and saying that he meant to stand no blasted nonsense" (letter to R. W. Dixon, October 12, 1881).

That is hardly the Robert Browning I reread and revere. He is not Chaucer or Shakespeare, but who is? He cannot really persuade you that his representations could be living men or women. The Wife of Bath and Sir John Falstaff, Sancho Panza and Don Quixote, Pierre Bezukhov and Hadji Murad: these rise from the earth and in them it cries out. Shakespeare's Caliban is with them; Browning's is not. Each of Browning's major figures is a polyphony of voices, and all are constituent aspects of his own buried personalities. On the surface we see the Robert Browning who became an absurd lion of London society. Beneath are a cauldron of failed questers, confidence men, charlatans, compromised artists, deranged aristocrats, and some authentic visionaries nearing the border of their own madness.

I once discussed Browning with the Anglo-Irish poet Louis MacNeice, whose work I continue to admire. I think it was London in the late 1950s. MacNeice was a heavy drinker and that may have contributed to his early death in 1963 at the age of fifty-five. We were in a pub drinking Highland malt whiskey and I told him Browning would have liked my own favorite among MacNeice's poems, "Bagpipe Music." Its boisterousness seemed to play off Browning's music poems. MacNeice was amenable, particularly when I quoted the wonderful conclusion of his poem:

> The glass is falling hour by hour, the glass will fall for ever,
> But if you break the bloody glass you won't hold up the weather.
>
> [1938]

Here are the two final stanzas of Browning's *A Toccata of Galuppi's*:

XIV

"As for Venice and her people, merely born to bloom and drop,
Here on earth they bore their fruitage, mirth and folly were
    the crop:
What of soul was left, I wonder, when the kissing had to stop?

XV

"Dust and ashes!" So you creak it, and I want the heart to scold.
Dear dead women, with such hair, too—what's become of all
    the gold
Used to hang and brush their bosoms? I feel chilly and grown old.

Browning is darker though MacNeice is dark enough. I studied Browning in 1953–1954 with William Clyde DeVane, Dean of Yale

College, who kindly gave me a number of rare items from his Browning collection. In 1955–1956, though it was only my first year as a faculty instructor at Yale, DeVane insisted that I conduct his graduate course in the Victorian poets, so that I spent the better part of a semester teaching Browning. My students were older than I was but they kindly accepted me. Though it is nearly two-thirds of a century ago, I still remember a remarkable session on "The Pope" section of *The Ring and the Book* (1868–1869).

He would not have liked my saying this, but Browning essentially is a poet of the Grotesque. I am in the wake of the boisterous Gilbert Keith Chesterton (1874–1936), in his admirable study of Browning (1903):

> This queer trait in Browning, his inability to keep a kind of demented ingenuity even out of poems in which it was quite inappropriate, is a thing which must be recognised, and recognised all the more because as a whole he was a very perfect artist, and a particularly perfect artist in the use of the grotesque. But everywhere when we go a little below the surface in Browning we find that there was something in him perverse and unusual despite all his working normality and simplicity. His mind was perfectly wholesome, but it was not made exactly like the ordinary mind. It was like a piece of strong wood with a knot in it.

There is indeed a kind of quirk or knot in Browning's consciousness. Who else could have written "The Heretic's Tragedy" in *Dramatic Romances and Lyrics* (1845)?

A Middle-Age Interlude

ROSA MUNDI; SEU, FULCITE ME FLORIBUS.
A CONCEIT OF MASTER GYSBRECHT,
CANON-REGULAR OF SAINT JODOCUS-BY-
THE-BAR, YPRES CITY. CANTUQUE,
Virgilius. AND HATH OFTEN BEEN SUNG
AT HOCK-TIDE AND FESTIVALS. GAVISUS
ERAM, Jessides.

(It would seem to be a glimpse from the burning
of Jacques du Bourg-Molay, at Paris, A.D. 1314,
as distorted by the refraction from Flemish brain to
brain, during the course of a couple of centuries.)

[Molay was Grand Master of the Templars
when that order was suppressed in 1312.]
. . .

II

[ONE SINGETH]
John, Master of the Temple of God,
  Falling to sin the Unknown Sin,
What he bought of Emperor Aldabrod,
  He sold it to Sultan Saladin:
Till, caught by Pope Clement, a-buzzing there,
  Hornet-prince of the mad wasps' hive,
And clipt of his wings in Paris square,
  They bring him now to be burned alive.
    [And wanteth there grace of lute or
     clavicithern, ye shall say to
     confirm him who singeth—
We bring John now to be burned alive.

III

In the midst is a goodly gallows built;
  'Twixt fork and fork, a stake is stuck;
But first they set divers tumbrils a-tilt,
  Make a trench all round with the city muck;
Inside they pile log upon log, good store;
  Faggots no few, blocks great and small,
Reach a man's mid-thigh, no less, no more,—
  For they mean he should roast in the sight
  of all.
CHORUS.
  We mean he should roast in the sight of all.

IV

Good sappy bavins that kindle forthwith;
    Billets that blaze substantial and slow;
Pine-stump split deftly, dry as pith;
    Larch-heart that chars to a chalk-white glow:
They up they hoist me John in a chafe,
    Sling him fast like a hog to scorch,
Spit in his face, then leap back safe,
Sing "Laudes" and bid clap-to the torch.

CHORUS.
    Laus deo—who bids clap-to the torch.

V

John of the Temple, whose fame so bragged,
    Is burning alive in Paris square!
How can he curse, if his mouth is gagged?
    Or wriggle his neck, with a collar there?
Or heave his chest, which a band goes round?
    Or threat with his fist, since his arms are
        spliced?
Or kick with his feet, now his legs are bound?
    —Thinks John, I will call upon Jesus Christ.
        [Here one crosseth himself.]

VI

Jesus Christ—John had bought and sold,
    Jesus Christ—John had eaten and drunk;
To him, the Flesh meant silver and gold.
    (Salva reverentia.)
Now it was, "Saviour, bountiful lamb,
    "I have roasted thee Turks, though men roast me!
"See thy servant, the plight wherein I am!
    "Art thou a saviour? Save thou me!"

CHORUS.
    'Tis John the mocker cries, "Save thou me!"

. . .

IX

Ha ha, John plucketh now at his rose
    To rid himself of a sorrow at heart!
Lo,—petal on petal, fierce rays unclose;
    Anther on anther, sharp spikes outstart;
And with blood for dew, the bosom boils;
    And a gust of sulphur is all its smell;
And lo, he is horribly in the toils
    Of a coal-black giant flower of hell!

CHORUS.
    What maketh heaven, That maketh hell.

X

So, as John called now, through the fire amain,
    On the Name, he had cursed with, all his life—
To the Person, he bought and sold again—
    For the Face, with his daily buffets rife—
Feature by feature It took its place:
    And his voice, like a mad dog's choking bark,
At the steady whole of the Judge's face—
    Died. Forth John's soul flared into the dark.

SUBJOINETH THE ABBOT DEODAET.
    God help all poor souls lost in the dark!

I cannot say that reading this gives me pleasure, and yet it is a remarkably accomplished poem. Robert Browning was not a sado-masochist but he must have relished—as we do, with a shudder—this delicious line:

For they mean he should roast in the sight of all.

You need to chant "The Heretic's Tragedy" out loud to yourself and thus enjoy—however equivocally—Browning's gusto as he mouths delicious syllables mingling grotesque horrors and splendors:

Good sappy bavins that kindle forthwith;
    Billets that blaze substantial and slow;

Pine-stump split deftly, dry as pith;
    Larch-heart that chars to a chalk-white glow:
They up they hoist me John in a chafe,
    Sling him fast like a hog to scorch,
Spit in his face, then leap back safe,
    Sing "Laudes" and bid clap-to the torch.

"Sling him fast like a hog to scorch" is the purest Browning. What is the aesthetic gratification that this poem affords us?

Partly it is Browning's diction; partly his inventiveness at fresh metrics; mostly heroic verve. We sense his pleasure as he mouths the madness of a public burning and its flowering climax:

And with blood for dew, the bosom boils;
    And a gust of sulphur is all its smell;
And lo, he is horribly in the toils
    Of a coal-black giant flower of hell!

CHORUS.
    What maketh heaven, That maketh hell.

I wonder if Gerard Manley Hopkins had read this poem. Both form and matter would have distressed him. What was Browning trying to do for himself, as poet and as person, by composing this delicious ghastliness?

You achieve a nice juxtaposition when you contrast "The Heretic's Tragedy" to Browning's "Holy-Cross Day" (1855):

On Which the Jews Were Forced to Attend an Annual Christian Sermon in Rome

[The passage from a mock-historic Diary which follows is by Browning himself.]

"Now was come about Holy-Cross Day, and now must my lord preach his first sermon to the Jews: as it was of old cared for in the merciful bowels of the Church, that, so to speak, a crumb at least from her conspicuous table here in Rome should be, though but once yearly, cast to the famishing dogs, under-trampled and bespitten-upon beneath the feet of the guests. And a moving sight in truth, this, of so

many of the besotted blind restif and ready-to-perish Hebrews! now maternally brought—nay, (for He saith, 'Compel them to come in') haled, as it were, by the head and hair,
and against their obstinate hearts, to partake of the heavenly
grace. What awakening, what striving with tears, what working of a yeasty conscience! Nor was my lord wanting to
himself on so apt an occasion; witness the abundance of con-
versions which did incontinently reward him: though not to
my lord be altogether the glory."—Diary by the Bishop's
Secretary, 1600.

    What the Jews really said, on thus being driven to
church, was rather to this effect:—

Fee, faw, fum! bubble and squeak!
Blessedest Thursday's the fat of the week.
Rumble and tumble, sleek and rough,
Stinking and savory, smug and gruff,
Take the church-road, for the bell's due chime
Gives us the summons—'t is sermon-time!
Boh, here's Barnabas! Job, that's you?
Up stumps Solomon—bustling too?
Shame, man! greedy beyond your years
To handsel the bishop's shaving-shears?
Fair play's a jewel! Leave friends in the lurch?
Stand on a line ere you start for the church!
Higgledy piggledy, packed we lie,
Rats in a hamper, swine in a sty,
Wasps in a bottle, frogs in a sieve,
Worms in a carcass, fleas in a sleeve.
Hist! square shoulders, settle your thumbs
And buzz for the bishop—here he comes.
Bow, wow, wow—a bone for the dog!
I liken his Grace to an acorned hog.

. . .

See to our converts—you doomed black dozen—
No stealing away—nor cog nor cozen!
You five, that were thieves, deserve it fairly;
You seven, that were beggars, will live less sparely;

You took your turn and dipped in the hat,
Got fortune—and fortune gets you; mind that!
Give your first groan—compunction's at work;
And soft! from a Jew you mount to a Turk.
Lo, Micah,—the selfsame beard on chin
He was four times already converted in!
Here's a knife, clip quick—it's a sign of grace—
Or he ruins us all with his hanging-face.
Whom now is the bishop a-leering at?
I know a point where his text falls pat.
I'll tell him to-morrow, a word just now
Went to my heart and made me vow
I meddle no more with the worst of trades—
Let somebody else pay his serenades.
Groan all together now, whee—hee—hee!
It's a-work, it's a-work, ah, woe is me!
It began, when a herd of us, picked and placed,
Were spurred through the Corso, stripped to the waist;
Jew brutes, with sweat and blood well spent
To usher in worthily Christian Lent.
It grew, when the hangman entered our bounds,
Yelled, pricked us out to his church like hounds:
It got to a pitch, when the hand indeed
Which gutted my purse would throttle my creed:
And it overflows, when, to even the odd,
Men I helped to their sins help me to their God.
But now, while the scapegoats leave our flock,
And the rest sit silent and count the clock,
Since forced to muse the appointed time
On these precious facts and truths sublime,—
Let us fitly employ it, under our breath,
In saying Ben Ezra's Song of Death.
. . .
"Thou art the Judge. We are bruisèd thus.
But, the Judgment over, join sides with us!
Thine too is the cause! and not more thine
Than ours, is the work of these dogs and swine,
Whose life laughs through and spits at their creed,

Who maintain thee in word, and defy thee in deed!
"We withstood Christ then? Be mindful how
At least we withstand Barabbas now!
Was our outrage sore? But the worst we spared,
To have called these—Christians, had we dared!
Let defiance to them pay mistrust of thee,
And Rome make amends for Calvary!
"By the torture, prolonged from age to age.
By the infamy, Israel's heritage,
By the Ghetto's plague, by the garb's disgrace,
By the badge of shame, by the felon's place,
By the branding-tool, the bloody whip,
And the summons to Christian fellowship,—
"We boast our proof that at least the Jew
Would wrest Christ's name from the Devil's crew.
Thy face took never so deep a shade
But we fought them in it, God our aid!
A trophy to bear, as we march, thy band,
South, East, and on to the Pleasant Land!"

This is so audacious, even for Robert Browning, that I am dazzled into breathlessness. Browning was so philo-Semitic that some
early readers wondered if he had Jewish ancestry, which certainly he
did not. But he picked up a great deal of rabbinic learning, and by a
curious swerve of imaginative appropriation, he thought himself into
the condition of the Diaspora. He particularly identified himself with
the poet-scholar Abraham ibn Ezra (1092–1167), one of the major figures of Judaic culture in twelfth-century Spain.

Aside from the rollicking play of dancing syllables, puns, weird
rhymes, "Holy-Cross Day" surprisingly turns the relationship between Judaism and Christianity inside out and all but lunatic. The exuberant rhapsodists on their way to suffer a conversionary sermon assert
their intention of reclaiming Christ from the apparent Christians.

"Holy-Cross Day" is not one of Browning's masterworks: it is
fierce fun, mischief-making, polemic by the endlessly strange
poet who somehow achieved a balance between his mother's
evangelical Protestantism and Shelley's relentless questings in

pursuit of the Sublime. "Rabbi Ben Ezra" (1864) no longer enjoys much critical esteem, but I think it tends now to be misunderstood:

I
    Grow old along with me!
The best is yet to be,
The last of life, for which the first was made:
    Our times are in His hand
    Who saith "A whole I planned,
Youth shows but half; trust God: see all, nor be afraid!"
. . .

XXVI
    Ay, note that Potter's wheel,
That metaphor! and feel
Why time spins fast, why passive lies our clay,—
    Thou, to whom fools propound,
    When the wine makes its round,
"Since life fleets, all is change; the Past gone, seize to-day!"

XXVII
    Fool! All that is, at all,
Lasts ever, past recall;
Earth changes, but thy soul and God stand sure:
    What entered into thee,
    That was, is, and shall be:
Time's wheel runs back or stops; Potter and clay endure.
. . .

XXXII
    So, take and use Thy work,
Amend what flaws may lurk,
What strain o' the stuff, what warpings past the aim!
    My times be in Thy hand!
    Perfect the cup as planned!
Let age approve of youth, and death complete the same!

From my perspective, that is the pith of "Rabbi Ben Ezra." Too quickly you might judge that the great Hebrew poet and sage was being reduced to only another mouthpiece for bouncing Browning. And indeed the metric here is at times annoying since it is upbeat without variation. But the argument is subtle and rather dark. Addressing the biblical godhead, it accepts his handiwork and asks only to be perfected by him. I find that a harsh stance. It would hurt me to accept it. Browning shrewdly goes past Rabbi Ben Ezra to the prophets Isaiah and Jeremiah and their great figuration of the potter and his vessels.

> But now, O LORD, thou art our father; we are the clay, and thou our potter; and we all are the work of thy hand.
>   [Isaiah (KJV) 64:8]

> Arise, and go down to the potter's house, and there I will cause thee to hear my words. Then I went down to the potter's house, and, behold, he wrought a work on the wheels. And the vessel that he made of clay was marred in the hand of the potter: so he made it again another vessel, as seemed good to the potter to make it. Then the word of the LORD came to me, saying, O house of Israel, cannot I do with you as this potter? saith the LORD. Behold, as the clay is in the potter's hand, so are ye in mine hand, O house of Israel.
>   [Jeremiah (KJV) 18:2–6]

The trope of being in the hands of the living God is so strong as to endure any ironies. I fear the same cannot be said for the ecstatic "Saul," where the young harpist and singer David attempts to put some life back into the dour and unfortunate first King of Israel. There is a dreadful dull repetitive sameness in "Saul." It is as though Browning loses touch not only with his audience but with himself. Better to go to him at his strongest. Throughout my life I have found his crucial poem to be "Childe Roland to the Dark Tower Came." Before this chapter concludes, I will return to that disturbing parable for my final time in this life. Yet I begin to accept the notion of my former student Kenneth Gross that Browning's agon with William Shakespeare in "Caliban upon Setebos" may seem more illuminating of a transumptive stance against tradition than even the ordeal by landscape that is "Childe Roland."

> ['Will sprawl, now that the heat of day is best,
> Flat on his belly in the pit's much mire,
> With elbows wide, fists clenched to prop his chin;
> And, while he kicks both feet in the cool slush,
> And feels about his spine small eft-things course,
> Run in and out each arm, and make him laugh;
> And while above his head a pompion-plant,
> Coating the cave-top as a brow its eye,
> Creeps down to touch and tickle hair and beard,
> And now a flower drops with a bee inside,
> And now a fruit to snap at, catch and crunch:
> He looks out o'er yon sea which sunbeams cross
> And recross till they weave a spider-web,
> (Meshes of fire, some great fish breaks at times)
> And talks to his own self, howe'er he please,
> Touching that other, whom his dam called God . . .]
>   [ll. 1–16]

Browning confronted two enormous quandaries in seeking to compose a major poem on *The Tempest*'s Caliban. One perhaps had to be insurmountable: How can you capture a Shakespearean character and make him your own? The other was to invent fit speech for your new Caliban so as to make him persuasive.

The marvelous achievement of "Caliban upon Setebos" is the diction, metric, low-pitched style manifested by this new hybrid half human, half sea beast. Clearly Browning follows, as best he can, some aspects of Shakespeare's language. But he did not want Shakespeare's Caliban. Various historicisms and social resentments have made it very difficult to discuss and act the part of Caliban in the last generation or so. However, I seem no longer to be the only reader weary of postcolonialist discourse. Shakespeare's Caliban is hardly a heroic freedom fighter. He is cowardly, perpetually terrorized by Prospero's punishments and by the uncharacteristic fury of Miranda, whom he attempted to rape. Shakespeare is giving us a vision of a failed adoption with all the bitterness and torment of a family romance gone bad. When Prospero finally confronts his responsibility and says, "This thing of darkness / I acknowledge mine," he takes on the task of bringing Caliban back to Milan with him, in order to try a second time.

But that is not at all the Caliban of Robert Browning. I have difficulty imagining precisely why the brilliant dramatic monologist and failed playwright decided to rework what he took to be Shakespeare's farewell drama. I speculate that it had much to do with Browning's early idol Shelley, who had made the young evangelical into a poet. Shelley identified with Ariel. He was moved by the image of his final love, Jane Williams, as a new Miranda.

Browning never quite got over Shelley; it was a love that endured, even though the revelations of Shelley's sexual freedom became quite distasteful for the later poet. There is nothing of Shelley's visionary intensity in Browning's representation of Caliban, but Setebos, the god of Caliban's mother, the witch Sycorax, is a copy of the sky tyrant Jupiter in *Prometheus Unbound*.

Browning begins his poem by using Psalm 50:21 KJV as the epigraph:

> These things hast thou done, and I kept silence; thou thoughtest that I was altogether such an one as thyself: but I will reprove thee, and set them in order before thine eyes.

This is Yahweh telling the Psalmist: you thought I was as bad you were. Browning's Caliban, a desperate child, imputes all his own worst qualities to Setebos and even more besides. I do not think Browning merely mocks anthropomorphism. His quarry is larger:

> But wherefore rough, why cold and ill at ease?
> Aha, that is a question! Ask, for that,
> What knows,—the something over Setebos
> That made Him, or He, may be, found and fought,
> Worsted, drove off and did to nothing, perchance.
> There may be something quiet o'er His head,
> Out of His reach, that feels nor joy nor grief,
> Since both derive from weakness in some way.
>
> [ll. 127–134]

The Quiet is beyond Setebos, beyond Caliban, beyond poetry. Silence is unfallen. Poor Caliban, playing his dark games in a hopeless attempt to reverse his expulsion from grace and favor by Prospero, persuades us that Setebos depends upon the son of Sycorax as his model.

Can this new Caliban conceive an end to sorrow?

If He surprise not even the Quiet's self
Some strange day,—or, suppose, grow into it
As grubs grow butterflies: else, here are we,
And there is He, and nowhere help at all.

"Believeth with the life, the pain shall stop.
His dam held different, that after death
He both plagued enemies and feasted friends:
Idly! He doth His worst in this our life,
Giving just respite lest we die through pain,
Saving last pain for worst—with which, an end.
Meanwhile, the best way to escape His ire
Is, not to seem too happy . . ."

[ll. 246–257]

Browning once remarked that Shelley, had he lived long enough, would have ranged himself among the Christians. That may be the silliest suggestion ever made about the revolutionary prophet who quested for a god unknown within his own spirit. It is not unfair to say that something recalcitrant in Browning is the indwelling presence of his evangelical mother. Generally, I read Herbert Tucker on Browning with unmixed admiration, but I touch a limit in a careless transcendence (Browning's, not Tucker's) that is ultimately incoherent. I do not want Browning to tell me that God is the perfect poet or to boom out: "God is it that transcends." Tucker is justified when he says that Browning is "a great artist." To engage the obstacles to art as strenuously as Browning did is very rare among the major poets.

Rereading and teaching "Caliban upon Setebos," I become both exhilarated and annoyed. You cannot say that Browning—like Milton, Blake, and Emily Dickinson—was a Protestant sect of one because there is no "one" self in Browning. He is a whirligig of selves, gyring around and around, and no one of these selves is capable of hearing all the others. His Protestantism is half gusto, half Incarnationism. Luther, Calvin, and their ilk vanish away and all that remains is that God once became man.

Browning's largest contrast with Shelley is in the nature of their optimism. To believe, with Shelley, that we can become our own gods is a cosmos apart from a temperamental tub-thumping that our reach should exceed our grasp. I am grateful to Browning for his wild array of self-deceivers: they expose my own imaginative flaws. Shakespeare's protagonists are larger than I can apprehend, though I strive mightily to keep up with them. Walter Savage Landor thought that the genius of Geoffrey Chaucer came to life again in Robert Browning. That over-praise is dangerous. The Wife of Bath, the Pardoner, and even the Knight take us to a scale that Browning cannot approach. He does not represent human beings in their full depth or on their final heights. His own consciousness is far more divided than he allows himself to realize. My own nightmares are informed, all too often, by "Childe Roland to the Dark Tower Came." Yet no one in Browning, including the poet himself, can teach me the lesson of Chaucer's Knight: a man should learn to bear himself always with equanimity, for we are constantly keeping appointments that we never made. I am back in the hospital unexpectedly as I dictate this. For the very old with heart failure, the sudden appearance of water in the lungs condemns one to a week's impatience with yet once more being a patient.

I write as always in praise and appreciation of the poetry of Robert Browning. It seems apt that at this difficult moment I return, surely for the last time, to Roland and his trial by landscape. In teaching the poem it seems useful to tell my students that if they rode by Roland's side, they would not see the deformed and broken vistas that he encounters.

A quester who hopes only to be fit to fail imposes a will that romance cannot accommodate. That perfect a knowledge is daemonic. The nameless candidate for knighthood desires to join a beloved band of traitors who ended badly at the Dark Tower. Traitors to what? The poem is not Christian. Is it even the Browning version of Protestantism? For me the grandest moment in the poem is its extraordinary negative epiphany:

XXX

Burningly it came on me all at once,
   This was the place! those two hills on the right
   Crouched like two bulls locked horn in horn in fight;
While to the left, a tall scalped mountain . . . Dunce,
Dotard, a-dozing at the very nonce,
   After a life spent training for the sight!

In matters both military and erotic, nothing is more fatal than overpreparing the event. Excessive expectation can blind one to the site so long anticipated. The next line is an outcry of startlement and of revelation:

XXXI

What in the midst lay but the Tower itself?
   The round squat turret, blind as the fool's heart,
   Built of brown stone, without a counterpart
In the whole world. The tempest's mocking elf
Points to the shipman thus the unseen shelf
   He strikes on, only when the timbers start.

The turret, being windowless, is blind. It is utterly commonplace and yet unique. Toquarto Tasso, supposedly mad through erotic frustration, was imprisoned in the tower described in Shelley's *Julian and Maddalo*, where Shelley as Julian and Lord Byron as Count Maddalo clash in their visions of human character and destiny.

XXXII

Not see? because of night perhaps?—why, day
   Came back again for that! before it left,
   The dying sunset kindled through a cleft:
The hills, like giants at a hunting, lay,
Chin upon hand, to see the game at bay,—
   "Now stab and end the creature—to the heft!"

XXXIII

Not hear? when noise was everywhere! it tolled
   Increasing like a bell. Names in my ears

Of all the lost adventurers my peers,—
How such a one was strong, and such was bold,
And such was fortunate, yet each of old
    Lost, lost! one moment knelled the woe of years.

"The lost adventurers my peers" include Tasso, Thomas Chatterton, Christopher Smart, and above all Shelley. The tolling catalogues the names of those ringers in the tower who have become its sexton slaves (so to speak). Their tongues appoint for the hymen of the soul a passing bell.

XXXIV

There they stood, ranged along the hill-sides, met
    To view the last of me, a living frame
    For one more picture! in a sheet of flame
I saw them and I knew them all. And yet
Dauntless the slug-horn to my lips I set,
    And blew. *"Childe Roland to the Dark Tower came."*

[ll. 174–204]

That sheet of flame is Shelley's fire for which all thirst. It will become Yeats's Condition of Fire in Byzantium. The nameless candidate for knighthood suddenly recovers from his long day's dying and transmutes into Robert Browning at his most buoyant. He takes Thomas Chatterton's slug-horn (slogan) and transumes Shelley's trumpet of a prophecy. What is Browning's prophecy? We are not told but something is intimated. Edgar's mad song from *King Lear* returns as a final line, unaltered from the poem's title. What is absent is any ogre to smell the blood of an Englishman. All that you can find at the Dark Tower is yourself and the poets who failed sublimely there before you.

What is it to say that you knew them all? Recognition is the resolution of tragedy. It is an ungainly visitor in romance. Perhaps Browning approximates Keats. Intelligences are atoms of perception. They see and they know and therefore they are gods.

It comes down, as so often it does, to Shelley and Browning. I reflect that Shelley's progeny are profusely varied: Beddoes, Browning, Swinburne, Bernard Shaw, Thomas Hardy, Yeats, Lionel Johnson, D. H. Lawrence, Elinor Wylie, Conrad Aiken, Wallace Stevens, Hart Crane. And then there is the hidden legatee T. S. Eliot. They found in Shelley what they needed: an image of the absolute that dismisses all compromise.

The unnamed quester at the Dark Tower is most certainly not Browning. And yet he is not the prophetic and religion-making Shelley. It may be that he is the poet yet to come among us, destroyer and preserver, an Ishmael spared from our wreckage.

At his best Browning knows when to curtail himself. His largest fault is just to keep on going page after page, so that all too frequently his dramatic lyrics and monologues do not know when and where to stop. The Roland monologue is perfect in its length of thirty-four six-line stanzas. Every poem is a fiction of duration. The chanting of Roland's poem, properly paced, is very close to the lapsed time of his ordeal.

There are poems by Browning I could enjoy if only he had curbed his sometimes-negative gusto. One of them is "Mr. Sludge: 'The Medium,'" which continues for 1,525 lines. Browning's wife, the poet Elizabeth Barrett Browning, was a convinced spiritualist. He was not.

The Sludge poem has had distinguished advocates from G. K. Chesterton to Isobel Armstrong. Chesterton shrewdly notes that the self-confessed charlatan nevertheless *believes* in spiritualism. Like Browning, Chesterton is not to be argued with when it comes to theism and the Incarnation.

It is unclear to me whether Browning's intense Incarnationism mars the conclusion of the troublesome dramatic monologue "Cleon" (1855). The imaginary Cleon is a Hellenistic poetaster possibly modeled on Matthew Arnold, greatest of school inspectors. Cleon's monologue is an epistle directed to his tyrant-patron:

> Thy letter's first requirement meets me here.
> It is as thou hast heard: in one short life
> I, Cleon, have effected all those things
> Thou wonderingly dost enumerate.
> That epos on thy hundred plates of gold
> Is mine, and also mine the little chant,
> So sure to rise from every fishing-bark
> When, lights at prow, the seamen haul their net.

The image of the sun-god on the phare,
Men turn from the sun's self to see, is mine;
The Pœcile o'er-storied its whole length,
As thou didst hear, with painting, is mine too.
I know the true proportions of a man
And woman also, not observed before;
And I have written three books on the soul,
Proving absurd all written hitherto,
And putting us to ignorance again.
For music,—why, I have combined the moods,
Inventing one. In brief, all arts are mine;
Thus much the people know and recognize,
Throughout our seventeen islands. Marvel not.
We of these latter days, with greater mind
Than our forerunners, since more composite,
Look not so great, beside their simple way,
To a judge who only sees one way at once,
One mind-point and no other at a time,—
Compares the small part of a man of us
With some whole man of the heroic age,
Great in his way—not ours, nor meant for ours.
And ours is greater, had we skill to know:
For, what we call this life of men on earth,
This sequence of the soul's achievements here
Being, as I find much reason to conceive,
Intended to be viewed eventually
As a great whole, not analyzed to parts,
But each part having reference to all,—
How shall a certain part, pronounced complete,
Endure effacement by another part?
Was the thing done?—then, what's to do again?

[ll. 43–81]

We can assume Cleon to be as mediocre a composer and painter as he is a poet. He evidences considerable anguish of contamination in regard to heroic forerunners. I hear a trace of Matthew Arnold's "the best that has been thought and said" in Cleon's defensiveness:

I have not chanted verse like Homer, no—
Nor swept string like Terpander, no—nor carved
And painted men like Phidias and his friend:
I am not great as they are, point by point.
But I have entered into sympathy
With these four, running these into one soul,
Who, separate, ignored each other's art.
Say, is it nothing that I know them all?
The wild flower was the larger; I have dashed
Rose-blood upon its petals, pricked its cup's
Honey with wine, and driven its seed to fruit,
And show a better flower if not so large . . .

[ll. 139–150]

There is no single answer to the feeble question: "Say, is it nothing that I know them all?" I wish Browning had ended the poem there, but he bounces into belief:

Live long and happy, and in that thought die:
Glad for what was! Farewell. And for the rest,
I cannot tell thy messenger aright
Where to deliver what he bears of thine
To one called Paulus; we have heard his fame
Indeed, if Christus be not one with him—
I know not, nor am troubled much to know.
Thou canst not think a mere barbarian Jew,
As Paulus proves to be, one circumcised,
Hath access to a secret shut from us?
Thou wrongest our philosophy, O king,
In stooping to inquire of such an one,
As if his answer could impose at all!
He writeth, doth he? well, and he may write.
Oh, the Jew findeth scholars! certain slaves
Who touched on this same isle, preached him and Christ;
And (as I gathered from a bystander)
Their doctrine could be held by no sane man.

[ll. 336–353]

Something in Browning may have sympathized with that final
line. He is a labyrinth within a labyrinth and offers us no exit that
will work. I am enough of a gleaner and preserver of better words
than I can summon on my own so that "Cleon" wounds me enough to
be memorable.

I find it difficult to conclude any meditation on Browning. He
evades me. His painters and musicians find me. The love poems,
even "By the Fire-Side" (1855), do not work with me, but that is my
flaw. It may be my inability to appreciate his wife's poetry. *Aurora
Leigh* (1856) constitutes eleven thousand lines of very blank verse. I
got through it just once and will not return.

Robert Browning ended strongly with *Asolando: Fancies and Facts*
(1889). My favorite is the third of a series of four "Bad Dreams":

> This was my dream: I saw a Forest
>   Old as the earth, no track nor trace
> Of unmade man. Thou, Soul, explorest—
>   Though in a trembling rapture—space
> Immeasurable! Shrubs, turned trees,
> Trees that touch heaven, support its frieze
> Studded with sun and moon and star:
> While—oh, the enormous growths that bar
> Mine eye from penetrating past
>   Their tangled twine where lurks—nay, lives
> Royally lone, some brute-type cast
>   I' the rough, time cancels, man forgives.
>
> On, Soul! I saw a lucid City
>   Of architectural device
> Every way perfect. Pause for pity,
>   Lightning! nor leave a cicatrice
> On those bright marbles, dome and spire,
> Structures palatial,—streets which mire
> Dares not defile, paved all too fine
> For human footstep's smirch, not thine—
> Proud solitary traverser,
>   My Soul, of silent lengths of way—
> With what ecstatic dread, aver,
>   Lest life start sanctioned by thy stay!

Ah, but the last sight was the hideous!
    A City, yes,—a Forest, true,—
But each devouring each. Perfidious
    Snake-plants had strangled what I knew
Was a pavilion once: each oak
Held on his horns some spoil he broke
By surreptitiously beneath
Upthrusting: pavements, as with teeth,
Griped huge weed widening crack and split
    In squares and circles stone-work erst.
Oh, Nature—good! Oh, Art—no whit
    Less worthy! Both in one—accurst!

Yeats confessed that Browning was a bad influence on him. The second stanza here worked its way into the "Byzantium" poems. In the final stanza, Browning would have disturbed Yeats's project to flee from nature to Byzantium. This interfusion of Nature and Art curses both. One of Shakespeare's larger conceptions is that the art itself is nature. The older formulation is still true. Shakespeare's art has usurped human nature and much of the nature in which we have to abide.

CHAPTER NINE

Alfred, Lord Tennyson

Lest One Good Custom Should Corrupt the World

MY FAVORITE DRAMATIC MONOLOGUE is Tennyson's "Tithonus" (1860). Many of my students greatly prefer "Ulysses" (1842, written 1833):

> It little profits that an idle king,
> By this still hearth, among these barren crags,
> Match'd with an aged wife, I mete and dole
> Unequal laws unto a savage race,
> That hoard, and sleep, and feed, and know not me.

Homeric homecoming has staled. Penelope has aged rather more quickly. The Ithacans are guilty of the unpardonable sin: they know not me. And the I beats on:

> I cannot rest from travel: I will drink
> Life to the lees: All times I have enjoy'd
> Greatly, have suffer'd greatly, both with those
> That loved me, and alone, on shore, and when
> Thro' scudding drifts the rainy Hyades
> Vext the dim sea: I am become a name;

For always roaming with a hungry heart
Much have I seen and known; cities of men
And manners, climates, councils, governments,
Myself not least, but honour'd of them all;
And drunk delight of battle with my peers,
Far on the ringing plains of windy Troy.

The hungry heart cannot be appeased:

I am a part of all that I have met;
Yet all experience is an arch wherethro'
Gleams that untravell'd world whose margin fades
For ever and forever when I move.
How dull it is to pause, to make an end,
To rust unburnish'd, not to shine in use!
As tho' to breathe were life! Life piled on life
Were all too little, and of one to me
Little remains: but every hour is saved
From that eternal silence, something more,
A bringer of new things; and vile it were
For some three suns to store and hoard myself,
And this gray spirit yearning in desire
To follow knowledge like a sinking star,
Beyond the utmost bound of human thought.

Increasingly we hear the Ulysses of Dante: the desire uttered out
of the double flame shared with Diomedes is to break all bounds and
achieve knowledge of the unknown worlds.

This is my son, mine own Telemachus,
To whom I leave the sceptre and the isle,—
Well-loved of me, discerning to fulfil
This labour, by slow prudence to make mild
A rugged people, and thro' soft degrees
Subdue them to the useful and the good.
Most blameless is he, centred in the sphere
Of common duties, decent not to fail
In offices of tenderness, and pay

Meet adoration to my household gods,
When I am gone. He works his work, I mine.

The blameless son Telemachus is shrugged aside. What remains
is the final enterprise:

There lies the port; the vessel puffs her sail:
There gloom the dark, broad seas. My mariners,
Souls that have toil'd, and wrought, and thought with me—
That ever with a frolic welcome took
The thunder and the sunshine, and opposed
Free hearts, free foreheads—you and I are old;
Old age hath yet his honour and his toil;
Death closes all: but something ere the end,
Some work of noble note, may yet be done,
Not unbecoming men that strove with Gods.
The lights begin to twinkle from the rocks:
The long day wanes: the slow moon climbs: the deep
Moans round with many voices. Come, my friends,
'T is not too late to seek a newer world.
Push off, and sitting well in order smite
The sounding furrows; for my purpose holds
To sail beyond the sunset, and the baths
Of all the western stars, until I die.
It may be that the gulfs will wash us down:
It may be we shall touch the Happy Isles,
And see the great Achilles, whom we knew.
Tho' much is taken, much abides; and tho'
We are not now that strength which in old days
Moved earth and heaven, that which we are, we are;
One equal temper of heroic hearts,
Made weak by time and fate, but strong in will
To strive, to seek, to find, and not to yield.

Who are those friends and fellow mariners invited to this final
voyaging? Are they phantoms? Ulysses was the sole survivor of all
his crew. So exquisitely and precisely measured are these cadences
that we hardly can dismiss them as phantasmagoria.

We have passed from Dante to Milton. It was the sublime Satan who chanted:

> And courage never to submit or yield
> And what is else not to be overcome?
>
> [*Paradise Lost*, 1.108–109]

Tennyson's intentions frequently are irrelevant to the drive and fury of his personae. He thought his Ulysses represented his own desire to keep going after the sudden death of Arthur Henry Hallam, his closest friend and critical guide. Clearly he was providentially mistaken.

"Tithonus" began as a monological fragment and expanded into the most beautiful Virgilian poem in the English language. We possess an almost complete poem by Sappho in which she meditates upon aging and tells her young women that their music will prevail even as their beauty fades. She compares herself to the mythical Tithonus, a prince of Troy beloved by Eos the dawn goddess. Unfortunately, Eos, petitioning Zeus to give Tithonus eternal life, forgot to ask for perpetual youth. Tennyson's monologist has become a Swiftian struldbrug or a Borgesian Immortal. Though this Tithonus wishes only to die, he incants with the grand dying music of Virgil:

> The woods decay, the woods decay and fall,
> The vapours weep their burthen to the ground,
> Man comes and tills the field and lies beneath,
> And after many a summer dies the swan.
> Me only cruel immortality
> Consumes: I wither slowly in thine arms,
> Here at the quiet limit of the world,
> A white-hair'd shadow roaming like a dream
> The ever-silent spaces of the East,
> Far-folded mists, and gleaming halls of morn.

One is grateful for the cadence and the diction, but though the speaker's situation is extreme, he verges on solipsism and manifests no affection for Eos, in whose arms he is lying.

Alas! for this gray shadow, once a man—
So glorious in his beauty and thy choice,
Who madest him thy chosen, that he seem'd
To his great heart none other than a God!
I ask'd thee, "Give me immortality."
Then didst thou grant mine asking with a smile,
Like wealthy men, who care not how they give.
But thy strong Hours indignant work'd their wills,
And beat me down and marr'd and wasted me,
And tho' they could not end me, left me maim'd
To dwell in presence of immortal youth,
Immortal age beside immortal youth,
And all I was, in ashes. Can thy love,
Thy beauty, make amends, tho' even now,
Close over us, the silver star, thy guide,
Shines in those tremulous eyes that fill with tears
To hear me? Let me go: take back thy gift:
Why should a man desire in any way
To vary from the kindly race of men
Or pass beyond the goal of ordinance
Where all should pause, as is most meet for all?

Is Tennyson allowing his Tithonus to sound more Hebraic than
Virgilian? There is hardly enough inwardness in this monologist to
justify the question.

A soft air fans the cloud apart; there comes
A glimpse of that dark world where I was born.
Once more the old mysterious glimmer steals
From thy pure brows, and from thy shoulders pure,
And bosom beating with a heart renew'd.
Thy cheek begins to redden thro' the gloom,
Thy sweet eyes brighten slowly close to mine,
Ere yet they blind the stars, and the wild team
Which love thee, yearning for thy yoke, arise,
And shake the darkness from their loosen'd
      manes,
And beat the twilight into flakes of fire.

Tennyson's unrivaled power of assonance and of writing English verse as though it could be quantified like Latin achieves magnificence in those last five lines.

> Lo! ever thus thou growest beautiful
> In silence, then before thine answer given
> Departest, and thy tears are on my cheek.
>
> Why wilt thou ever scare me with thy tears,
> And make me tremble lest a saying learnt,
> In days far-off, on that dark earth, be true?—
> "The Gods themselves cannot recall their gifts."
>
> Ay me! ay me! with what another heart
> In days far-off, and with what other eyes
> I used to watch—if I be he that watch'd—
> The lucid outline forming round thee; saw
> The dim curls kindle into sunny rings;
> Changed with thy mystic change, and felt my blood
> Glow with the glow that slowly crimson'd all
> Thy presence and thy portals, while I lay,
> Mouth, forehead, eyelids, growing dewy-warm
> With kisses balmier than half-opening buds
> Of April, and could hear the lips that kiss'd
> Whispering I knew not what of wild and sweet,
> Like that strange song I heard Apollo sing,
> While Ilion like a mist rose into towers.

The winning eroticism of this culminates in those two final lines with their mysterious aura. Apollo sang Troy into existence by music eternally strange to us.

> Yet hold me not for ever in thine East:
> How can my nature longer mix with thine?
> Coldly thy rosy shadows bathe me, cold
> Are all thy lights, and cold my wrinkled feet
> Upon thy glimmering thresholds, when the steam
> Floats up from those dim fields about the homes
> Of happy men that have the power to die,

And grassy barrows of the happier dead.
Release me, and restore me to the ground;
Thou seëst all things, thou wilt see my grave:
Thou wilt renew thy beauty morn by morn;
I earth in earth forget these empty courts,
And thee returning on thy silver wheels.

The cruelty of this is enhanced by the assurance that she will
see the grave of her beloved. Like the laureate's Ulysses, that pinnacle of self-love, Tithonus leaves us with a bitter residue. Self-pity
seems little different from self-vaunting. In teaching Tennyson I begin with "Ulysses" and "Tithonus" and then go on to the harshness
and controlled hysteria of "Lucretius" (1868):

Lucilia, wedded to Lucretius, found
Her master cold; for when the morning flush
Of passion and the first embrace had died
Between them, tho' he lov'd her none the less,
Yet often when the woman heard his foot
Return from pacings in the field, and ran
To greet him with a kiss, the master took
Small notice, or austerely, for—his mind
Half buried in some weightier argument,
Or fancy-borne perhaps upon the rise
And long roll of the Hexameter—he past
To turn and ponder those three hundred scrolls
Left by the Teacher, whom he held divine.
She brook'd it not; but wrathful, petulant,
Dreaming some rival, sought and found a witch
Who brew'd the philtre which had power, they said,
To lead an errant passion home again.
And this, at times, she mingled with his drink,
And this destroy'd him; for the wicked broth
Confused the chemic labour of the blood.
And tickling the brute brain within the man's
Made havock among those tender cells, and check'd
His power to shape: he loathed himself; and once

After a tempest woke upon a morn
That mock'd him with returning calm, and cried:

"Storm in the night! for thrice I heard the rain
Rushing; and once the flash of a thunderbolt—
Methought I never saw so fierce a fork—
Struck out the streaming mountain-side, and show'd
A riotous confluence of watercourses
Blanching and billowing in a hollow of it,
Where all but yester-eve was dusty-dry.

"Storm, and what dreams, ye holy Gods, what dreams!
For thrice I waken'd after dreams. Perchance
We do but recollect the dreams that come
Just ere the waking: terrible! for it seem'd
A void was made in Nature; all her bonds
Crack'd; and I saw the flaring atom-streams
And torrents of her myriad universe,
Ruining along the illimitable inane,
Fly on to clash together again, and make
Another and another frame of things
For ever: that was mine, my dream, I knew it—
Of and belonging to me, as the dog
With inward yelp and restless forefoot plies
His function of the woodland: but the next!
I thought that all the blood by Sylla shed
Came driving rainlike down again on earth,
And where it dash'd the reddening meadow, sprang
No dragon warriors from Cadmean teeth,
For these I thought my dream would show to me,
But girls, Hetairai, curious in their art,
Hired animalisms, vile as those that made
The mulberry-faced Dictator's orgies worse
Than aught they fable of the quiet Gods.
And hands they mixt, and yell'd and round me drove
In narrowing circles till I yell'd again
Half-suffocated, and sprang up, and saw—
Was it the first beam of my latest day?

"Then, then, from utter gloom stood out the breasts,
The breasts of Helen, and hoveringly a sword
Now over and now under, now direct,
Pointed itself to pierce, but sank down shamed
At all that beauty; and as I stared, a fire,
The fire that left a roofless Ilion,
Shot out of them, and scorch'd me that I woke.

. . .

"The mountain quickens into Nymph and Faun;
And here an Oread—how the sun delights
To glance and shift about her slippery sides,
And rosy knees and supple roundedness,
And budded bosom-peaks—who this way runs
Before the rest—A satyr, a satyr, see,
Follows; but him I proved impossible;
Twy-natured is no nature: yet he draws
Nearer and nearer, and I scan him now
Beastlier than any phantom of his kind
That ever butted his rough brother-brute
For lust or lusty blood or provender:
I hate, abhor, spit, sicken at him; and she
Loathes him as well; such a precipitate heel,
Fledged as it were with Mercury's ankle-wing,
Whirls her to me: but will she fling herself,
Shameless upon me? Catch her, goat-foot: nay,
Hide, hide them, million-myrtled wilderness,
And cavern-shadowing laurels, hide! do I wish—
What?—that the bush were leafless? or to whelm
All of them in one massacre? O ye Gods,
I know you careless, yet, behold, to you
From childly wont and ancient use I call—
I thought I lived securely as yourselves—
No lewdness, narrowing envy, monkey-spite,
No madness of ambition, avarice, none:
No larger feast than under plane or pine
With neighbours laid along the grass, to take
Only such cups as left us friendly-warm,

Affirming each his own philosophy—
Nothing to mar the sober majesties
Of settled, sweet, Epicurean life.
But now it seems some unseen monster lays
His vast and filthy hands upon my will,
Wrenching it back ward into his; and spoils
My bliss in being; and it was not great;
For save when shutting reasons up in rhythm,
Or Heliconian honey in living words,
To make a truth less harsh, I often grew
Tired of so much within our little life,
Or of so little in our little life—
Poor little life that toddles half an hour
Crown'd with a flower or two, and there an end—
And since the nobler pleasure seems to fade,
Why should I, beastlike as I find myself,
Not manlike end myself?—our privilege—
What beast has heart to do it? And what man,
What Roman would be dragg'd in triumph thus?
Not I; not he, who bears one name with her
Whose death-blow struck the dateless doom of kings,
When, brooking not the Tarquin in her veins,
She made her blood in sight of Collatine
And all his peers, flushing the guiltless air,
Spout from the maiden fountain in her heart.
And from it sprang the Commonwealth, which breaks
As I am breaking now!

         "And therefore now
Let her, that is the womb and tomb of all,
Great Nature, take, and forcing far apart
Those blind beginnings that have made me man,
Dash them anew together at her will
Thro' all her cycles—into man once more,
Or beast or bird or fish, or opulent flower:
But till this cosmic order everywhere
Shatter'd into one earthquake in one day
Cracks all to pieces,—and that hour perhaps

Is not so far when momentary man
Shall seem no more a something to himself,
But he, his hopes and hates, his homes and fanes,
And even his bones long laid within the grave,
The very sides of the grave itself shall pass,
Vanishing, atom and void, atom and void,
Into the unseen for ever,—till that hour,
My golden work in which I told a truth
That stays the rolling Ixionian wheel,
That numbs the Fury's ringlet-snake, and plucks
The mortal soul from out immortal hell,
Shall stand: ay, surely: then it fails at last
And perishes as I must; for O Thou,
Passionless bride, divine Tranquillity,
Yearn'd after by the wisest of the wise,
Who fail to find thee, being as thou art
Without one pleasure and without one pain,
Howbeit I know thou surely must be mine
Or soon or late, yet out of season, thus
I woo thee roughly, for thou carest not
How roughly men may woo thee so they win—
Thus—thus: the soul flies out and dies in the air."

With that he drove the knife into his side:
She heard him raging, heard him fall; ran in,
Beat breast, tore hair, cried out upon herself
As having fail'd in duty to him, shriek'd
That she but meant to win him back, fell on him,
Clasp'd, kiss'd him, wail'd: he answer'd, "Care not thou!
Thy duty? What is duty? Fare thee well!"

[ll. 1–66, 187–281]

As a pious Epicurean I am outraged by this magnificent slander
of the great Lucretius. It may well be that Tennyson in 1868 was answering the challenge of Swinburne's *Poems and Ballads* (1866).
More crucially he was wrestling with his own daemon and lost.

The classicist Charles Segal, who died at the age of sixty-five in
2002, made a memorable remark about the relation of Lucretius to

Epicureanism. He compared it to Homer's reliance on the poetry of the past. That seems to me the Lucretius I go on reading. He is the greatest of Latin poets, surpassing even his extraordinary disciple, Virgil.

Saint Jerome gathered together various Christian calumnies of Lucretius, including the absurd myth that he died of a love potion administered by his neglected wife. One can doubt that Tennyson believed this absurdity, but it gave him a dubious yet fecund starting point for the dramatic monologue "Lucretius," in which he seems to take up a rather aggressive stance against Swinburne, Robert Browning, and Edward Fitzgerald, who composed the *Rubaiyat of Omar Khayyam.*

Though I teach Tennyson's "Lucretius" annually, the poem makes me nervous. It is not just that it travesties Lucretius, but Tennyson indulges in a kind of acid bath of sensuality:

And here an Oread—how the sun delights
To glance and shift about her slippery sides,
And rosy knees and supple roundedness,
And budded bosom-peaks—who this way runs
Before the rest . . .

That naughty sun might be silly except that Tennyson's talent for erotic excitation compels many of us to share in its delight. I have no final word to speak about Tennyson's "Lucretius"; I find it to be a guilty pleasure.

To me the perfect poem by Tennyson is his lyrical monologue "Mariana" (1830). Perhaps I should say the consummate poem by his daemon, without the censorious superego impeding the dark flowering of Tennyson's isolate consciousness. Sometimes I feel like Dr. Johnson defending Alexander Pope: If "Mariana" is not a totally accomplished poem, can there be one?

"Mariana in the Moated Grange"—*Measure for Measure*

With blackest moss the flower-plots
    Were thickly crusted, one and all:
The rusted nails fell from the knots

That held the pear to the gable-wall.
The broken sheds look'd sad and strange:
    Unlifted was the clinking latch;
    Weeded and worn the ancient thatch
Upon the lonely moated grange.
    She only said, "My life is dreary,
        He cometh not," she said;
    She said, "I am aweary, aweary,
        I would that I were dead!"

Her tears fell with the dews at even . . .

    . . .

About a stone-cast from the wall
    A sluice with blacken'd waters slept,
And o'er it many, round and small,
    The cluster'd marish-mosses crept.
Hard by a poplar shook alway,
    All silver-green with gnarled bark:
    For leagues no other tree did mark
The level waste, the rounding gray.
    She only said, "My life is dreary,
        He cometh not," she said;
    She said "I am aweary, aweary
        I would that I were dead!"

And ever when the moon was low,
    And the shrill winds were up and away,
In the white curtain, to and fro,
    She saw the gusty shadow sway.
But when the moon was very low
    And wild winds bound within their cell,
    The shadow of the poplar fell
Upon her bed, across her brow.
    She only said, "The night is dreary,
        He cometh not," she said;
    She said "I am aweary, aweary,
        I would that I were dead!"

All day within the dreamy house,
   The doors upon their hinges creak'd;
The blue fly sung in the pane; the mouse
   Behind the mouldering wainscot shriek'd,
Or from the crevice peer'd about.
   Old faces glimmer'd thro' the doors
   Old footsteps trod the upper floors,
Old voices called her from without.
   She only said, "My life is dreary,
     He cometh not," she said;
   She said, "I am aweary, aweary,
     I would that I were dead!"

The sparrow's chirrup on the roof,
   The slow clock ticking, and the sound
Which to the wooing wind aloof
   The poplar made, did all confound
Her sense; but most she loathed the hour
   When the thick-moted sunbeam lay
   Athwart the chambers, and the day
Was sloping toward his western bower.
   Then said she, "I am very dreary,
     He will not come," she said;
   She wept, "I am aweary, aweary,
     Oh God, that I were dead!"

           [ll. 1–13, 37–84]

I have never met James R. Kincaid, liveliest of Victorian scholars, but I wish I had, as he writes with a charming boisterousness and also seems to understand me better than I can manage in my closing years. Here is Kincaid on Tennyson, Keats, and a much younger Bloom:

The interpretation of "Mariana" is perhaps most impressive. Bloom begins with what appears to be one more mildly alarming example of his distance from our usual restraints: "'Mariana,'" he says, "is as genuinely alarming in its deepest

implications as are even the darkest speculations of Freud."
By the time he is through, however, he convinces me absolutely. The poem is, at base, an expression of resistance to
Keats's influence. The grotesque images are a reversal of
Keats's "heroic and proleptic naturalism." Keats's tactile
natural images are there but subtly transformed out of nature
into "phantasmagoria, imagery of absence despite the apparent imagery of presence." And the person being absented
by this inversion is John Keats. Mariana's sexual anguish is
"a mask of poetic anxiety," an expression of her desire for
"priority in poetic invention." But she becomes just as obsessed with the equal "quasi-sexual pleasure" she finds in her
intense self-absorption. The poem is more deliciously un-
healthy than any of its decadent sons, Bloom says: it is the
"finest example in the language of an embowered consciousness representing itself as being too happy in its unhappiness
to want anything more." To put it more clearly, Bloom says
that Mariana is finally repressing the fact "that she doesn't
want or need the other who cometh not. What would she do
with him, what mental space has she left for him?"

[*Annoying the Victorians* (1995)]

Old Bloom at ninety is much more passionate about Mariana. She
centers a poem that edges on erotomania and self-gratification. I wonder whether Wallace Stevens found in her an image for what he called
the "interior paramour" that courses through his work from "Sunday
Morning" (1915) to the "Final Soliloquy of the Interior Paramour."
Tennyson was named by the admiring Walt Whitman as "the boss of
us all" in anticipation of Bruce Springsteen. The laureate returned the
compliment by unsuccessfully inviting Whitman to England.

Gerard Manley Hopkins, who now seems to me a startling fusion of John Keats and Walt Whitman, began by admiring Tennyson
but increasingly expressed doubts. I wish we had some comments on
"Mariana" by Hopkins. The poem's well-seasoned unhealthiness might
have induced a strong reaction in the suffering Jesuit. I go back to
it now in the hope of rendering it authentic literary appreciation.

John Keats, in a letter, urged Percy Shelley to "load every rift of
your subject with ore" (August 16, 1820). Tennyson and his muse

Mariana seek to overgo Keats. Every phrase, indeed nearly every word, of the poem is hefted so deeply that the effect stops just short of being overripe:

> With blackest moss the flower-plots
>   Were thickly crusted, one and all:
> The rusted nails fell from the knots
>   That held the pear to the gable-wall.
> The broken sheds look'd sad and strange:
>   Unlifted was the clinking latch;
>   Weeded and worn the ancient thatch
> Upon the lonely moated grange.

An English country house with moat seems rather singular. Doubtless they exist, though I have never seen one. Mariana's grange and moat are Shakespeare's in *Measure for Measure*, but only the line used as epigraph seems relevant. Like granges I have seen, Mariana's is surrounded by farm buildings but everything is in neglect. Her flower pots go unattended; the pear tree sags; sheds are broken; the latch never lifts; the roof cover is worn to weeds. "Lonely" is the precise word for this dismal dwelling. We properly expect a dark refrain:

> She only said, "My life is dreary,
>   He cometh not," she said;
> She said, "I am aweary, aweary,
>   I would that I were dead!"

It is splendidly appropriate that the surrounding landscape is a waste land. The opening eight lines of stanza 4 reverberate:

> About a stone-cast from the wall
>   A sluice with blacken'd waters slept,
> And o'er it many, round and small,
>   The cluster'd marish-mosses crept.
> Hard by a poplar shook alway,
>   All silver-green with gnarled bark:
>   For leagues no other tree did mark
> The level waste, the rounding gray.

That wretched poplar is unhappy enough without being desig-
nated as a phallus, a fairly widespread interpretation. More plausi-
bly it marks the border between Mariana's phantasmagoria and her
bleak reality:

> But when the moon was very low
>   And wild winds bound within their cell,
>   The shadow of the poplar fell
> Upon her bed, across her brow.

Whenever I recite or teach "Mariana," I become dazzled by Tennyson's daemonic craft at just this point:

> All day within the dreamy house,
>   The doors upon their hinges creak'd;
> The blue fly sung in the pane; the mouse
>   Behind the mouldering wainscot shriek'd,
> Or from the crevice peer'd about.
>   Old faces glimmer'd thro' the doors
>   Old footsteps trod the upper floors,
> Old voices called her from without.

How can one overpraise this? Dimly I recall that T. S. Eliot was
much taken with it. *Wuthering Heights* (1847) and *Jane Eyre* (1847) are
oaks to its acorn. Phantasmagoria works as an arch through which
gleams that undiscovered country from whose bourn no traveler returns. Challenged for adequate completion, Tennyson's daemon offers a temporal dimension that exposes Mariana's self-gratified stasis,
which no lover could move:

> The sparrow's chirrup on the roof,
>   The slow clock ticking, and the sound
> Which to the wooing wind aloof
>   The poplar made, did all confound
> Her sense; but most she loathed the hour
>   When the thick-moted sunbeam lay
>   Athwart the chambers, and the day
> Was sloping toward his western bower.

Then said she, "I am very dreary,
    He will not come," she said;
    She wept, "I am aweary, aweary,
    Oh God, that I were dead!"

In Tennyson love is almost as doubtful as Christianity. When he died the laureate declared himself agnostic and pan-deist and at one with the great heretics Giordano Bruno (who was a Hermetist and burned alive by the Church) and Baruch Spinoza (who was excommunicated by the Jews).

Tennyson had known Emily Sellwood since their mutual childhood but delayed marrying her until 1850 when he was already forty. There were two sons, the first named after Arthur Henry Hallam, not only Tennyson's closest friend but probably the major emotional relationship of his entire life. Hallam died in 1833 of a stroke, aged twenty-two. It is accurate to say that most of what is still alive in Tennyson's poetry elegizes Hallam.

The great instance is *In Memoriam A.H.H.* (1850), a discontinuous series of lyrics of varied merit. To me the two greatest are sections XCV and CII:

By night we linger'd on the lawn,
    For underfoot the herb was dry;
    And genial warmth; and o'er the sky
The silvery haze of summer drawn;

And calm that let the tapers burn
    Unwavering: not a cricket chirr'd:
    The brook alone far-off was heard,
And on the board the fluttering urn:

And bats went round in fragrant skies,
    And wheel'd or lit the filmy shapes
    That haunt the dusk, with ermine capes
And woolly breasts and beaded eyes;

While now we sang old songs that peal'd
    From knoll to knoll, where, couch'd at ease,
    The white kine glimmer'd, and the trees
Laid their dark arms about the field.

But when those others, one by one,
    Withdrew themselves from me and night,
    And in the house light after light
Went out, and I was all alone,

A hunger seized my heart; I read
    Of that glad year which once had been,
    In those fall'n leaves which kept their green,
The noble letters of the dead:

And strangely on the silence broke
    The silent-speaking words, and strange
    Was love's dumb cry defying change
To test his worth; and strangely spoke

The faith, the vigour, bold to dwell
    On doubts that drive the coward back,
    And keen thro' wordy snares to track
Suggestion to her inmost cell.

So word by word, and line by line,
    The dead man touch'd me from the past,
    And all at once it seem'd at last
The living soul was flash'd on mine,

And mine in his was wound, and whirl'd
    About empyreal heights of thought,
    And came on that which is, and caught
The deep pulsations of the world,

Æonian music measuring out
    The steps of time—the shocks of Chance—
    The blows of Death. At length my trance
Was cancell'd, stricken thro' with doubt.

Vague words! but ah, how hard to frame
    In matter-moulded forms of speech,
    Or ev'n for intellect to reach
Thro' memory that which I became:

Till now the doubtful dusk reveal'd
    The knolls once more where, couch'd at ease,

The white kine glimmer'd, and the trees
Laid their dark arms about the field:

And suck'd from out the distant gloom
   A breeze began to tremble o'er
   The large leaves of the sycamore,
And fluctuate all the still perfume,

And gathering freshlier overhead,
   Rock'd the full-foliaged elms, and swung
   The heavy-folded rose, and flung
The lilies to and fro, and said,

"The dawn, the dawn," and die away;
   And East and West, without a breath,
   Mixt their dim lights, like life and death,
To broaden into boundless day.

I think my admiration for this lyric all through the years may have been rather abstract. It is a kind of Tennysonian variant on Wordsworth's "Intimations" ode. It is May 19, 2019, and I approach my eighty-ninth birthday. Rereading my departed friends, I strain to hear their voices, the particular inflections of their eloquence. I grow superstitious. I find myself resting my hand on a favorite book by one of them and imagining a hand's response. Tennyson wanted to believe that the dead were not dead but alive. He knew better. I am uncertain what I know. Surviving one's own generation makes me care more than ever about younger friends and students. I believe in ghosts and yet do not value my own belief. Here is Tennyson recovering Hallam in a phantasmagoria edging on replacing reality:

CII.

On that last night before we went
   From out the doors where I was bred,
   I dream'd a vision of the dead,
Which left my after-morn content.

Methought I dwelt within a hall,
   And maidens with me: distant hills

From hidden summits fed with rills
A river sliding by the wall.

The hall with harp and carol rang.
    They sang of what is wise and good
    And graceful. In the centre stood
A statue veil'd, to which they sang;

And which, tho' veil'd, was known to me,
    The shape of him I loved, and love
    For ever: then flew in a dove
And brought a summons from the sea:

And when they learnt that I must go
    They wept and wail'd, but led the way
    To where a little shallop lay
At anchor in the flood below;

And on by many a level mead,
    And shadowing bluff that made the banks,
    We glided winding under ranks
Of iris, and the golden reed;

And still as vaster grew the shore
    And roll'd the floods in grander space,
    The maidens gather'd strength and grace
And presence, lordlier than before;

And I myself, who sat apart
    And watch'd them, wax'd in every limb;
    I felt the thews of Anakim,
The pulses of a Titan's heart;

As one would sing
    And one would chant the history
    Of that great race, which is to be,
And one the shaping of a star;

Until the forward-creeping tides
    Began to foam, and we to draw
    From deep to deep, to where we saw
A great ship lift her shining sides.

The man we loved was there on deck,
    But thrice as large as man he bent
    To greet us. Up the side I went,
And fell in silence on his neck;

Whereat those maidens with one mind
    Bewail'd their lot; I did them wrong:
    "We served thee here," they said, "so long,
And wilt thou leave us now behind?"

So rapt I was, they could not win
    An answer from my lips, but he
    Replying, "Enter likewise ye
And go with us:" they enter'd in.

And while the wind began to sweep
    A music out of sheet and shroud,
    We steer'd her toward a crimson cloud
That landlike slept along the deep.

Tennyson or his daemon transmembers into one of the Anakim, Canaanite giants driven out by Joshua, some of them joining the Philistines and thus engendering Goliath. They are identified here with the Titans, who were usurped by the Olympians and resurrected in the *Hyperion* fragments of John Keats. The very Tennysonian maidens, his muses, themselves are enhanced.

That shining great ship is apocalyptic. Hallam, three times enlarged, graciously accepts the muses as he and Tennyson steer toward a crimson cloud more landlike than oceanic, though it rests on the sea.

My inner ear catches strains of *Alastor*, *Epipsychidion*, and *Adonais*. There are traces of *The Winter's Tale* and of *Endymion*. The Tennysonian difference is the homoerotic element in the fantasy. It is more than unlikely that either Hallam or Tennyson ever consciously realized that their comprehensive love had a sexual component. The poetry is better for that.

Walt Whitman was partly responsible for Tennyson's interest in Bruno, having sent him essays on the martyred Hermetist. The American Bard took with gusto to the novels of George Sand, particularly *Consuelo* (1842–1843) and *La Comtesse de Rudolstadt* (1843).

George Sand was enough of a hermetic adept to give Walt useful clues about the Hermetic Corpus, which was a bible for Bruno.

Many years ago, both in London and in Ithaca, New York, I benefited from conversations with Frances Yates on the Hermetic tradition and English poetry. Frances, who was a good friend, was a little wild on hermeticizing Shakespeare but very useful on Henry Vaughan, George Herbert, Andrew Marvell, John Donne, and others. I wish now I could get Frances back so as to discuss Tennyson with her.

Like Bruno, Tennyson believed in alternative universes, planets populated like our own, so the Incarnation waned in his imaginings. It is decidedly odd that anyone should still think of Tennyson as a Christian poet. I suppose it is partly Tennyson's fault; as laureate he had to *sound* pious. There is some rich confusion also. Read again his official death poem "Crossing the Bar" (1889):

> Sunset and evening star,
>   And one clear call for me!
> And may there be no moaning of the bar,
>   When I put out to sea,
>
>   But such a tide as moving seems asleep,
>   Too full for sound and foam,
> When that which drew from out the boundless deep
>   Turns again home.
>
>   Twilight and evening bell,
>   And after that the dark!
> And may there be no sadness of farewell,
>   When I embark;
>
>   For tho' from out our bourne of Time and Place
>   The flood may bear me far,
> I hope to see my Pilot face to face
>   When I have crost the bar.

It is noble, eloquent, and highly ambiguous. Who is the Pilot? The reader is free to choose, yet that freedom blurs the poem. "Boundless deep" and "bourne of Time and Place" could be normative Christian or just as likely Hermetist.

CHAPTER TEN

Walt Whitman

I Stop Somewhere Waiting for You

I concentrate toward them that are nigh . . . . I wait on the
    door-slab.

Who has done his day's work and will soonest be through with
    his supper?
Who wishes to walk with me?

Will you speak before I am gone? will you prove already too
    late?

The spotted hawk swoops by and accuses me . . . . he complains
    of my gab and my loitering.

I too am not a bit tamed . . . . I too am untranslatable,
I sound my barbaric yawp over the roofs of the world.

The last scud of day holds back for me,
It flings my likeness after the rest and true as any on the
    shadowed wilds,
It coaxes me to the vapor and the dusk.

I depart as air . . . . I shake my white locks at the runaway sun,
I effuse my flesh in eddies and drift it in lacy jags.

I bequeath myself to the dirt to grow from the grass I love,
If you want me again look for me under your boot-soles.

You will hardly know who I am or what I mean,
But I shall be good health to you nevertheless,
And filter and fibre your blood.

Failing to fetch me at first keep encouraged,
Missing me one place search another,
I stop some where waiting for you

This is the end of the untitled long poem of 1855 that Whitman
was to call *Song of Myself*. Ralph Waldo Emerson responded by saluting the unknown poet for his wit and his wisdom. In time Emerson developed some reservations, and Whitman told conflicting
stories as to whether he had read Emerson before composing the
1855 volume. That does not matter. Emerson had the critical discernment to absorb and appreciate the strangeness and difficulty of
Whitman's originality.

Whitman is where he always wants to be: close enough to be
touching us. In the 1856 *Leaves of Grass* second edition, he declares:
"Whoever you are, now I place my hand upon you, that you be my
poem." That immediacy in reaching for the reader in an erotic embrace has some biblical precedents, but little in Western secular tradition provides the clew Whitman seeks.

Walt waits at the door. If we wish to walk with him, we must be
ready. Belatedness awaits us if we do not instantly respond.

This American Christ willfully dissolves himself. To find him
we must look under our boot-soles.

Are we would-be disciples journeying to Emmaus?

And, behold, two of them went that same day to a village
called Emmaus, which was from Jerusalem about threescore
furlongs. And they talked together of all these things which
had happened. And it came to pass, that, while they com-
muned together and reasoned, Jesus himself drew near, and
went with them. But their eyes were holden that they should
not know him. And he said unto them, What manner of
communications are these that ye have one to another, as ye

walk, and are sad? And the one of them, whose name was
Cleopas, answering said unto him, Art thou only a stranger
in Jerusalem, and hast not known the things which are come
to pass there in these days? And he said unto them, What
things? And they said unto him, Concerning Jesus of Nazareth, which was a prophet mighty in deed and word before
God and all the people . . .

[Luke (KJV) 24:13–19]

As T. S. Eliot's *The Waste Land* concludes, the journey to Emmaus is compounded with echoes of the closing lines of *Song of Myself* and "When Lilacs Last in the Dooryard Bloom'd" (1865). Only
in his closing years did Eliot reconcile himself with Whitman. He
admitted that he found in the American bard something like a perfect fusion of form and content.

He may have discovered there also the ghost of a passion perhaps only once fulfilled. There was a Whitmanian comradeship between Eliot and Jean Verdenal, one link being Jules Laforgue, who
translated Whitman into French and wrote a kind of verse that stimulated the young Eliot to search for his own voice. Eliot records a
nostalgic moment in which he and Verdenal enjoyed a rendezvous
in the Luxembourg Gardens, each carrying a sprig of lilac, one of
Walt's favorite images of voice that he called the "tally."

Eliot is a daemonic poet haunted by ghosts. Many of them are
literary. Others are personal. Walt Whitman is so substantial a presence that he scarcely seems suited to the role of a ghost.

The literary mythology of the United States of America centers
upon Whitman just as in Britain its matrix is Shakespeare. I share
the common experience that every rereading of a major work by
Shakespeare is revelatory. Rereading Whitman, as I do several times
a week, I am always surprised. In recollection his largeness is constant. But the act of rereading him slowly and out loud uncovers difficulties and splendors beyond expectation:

I am the poet of the body
And I am the poet of the soul.

The pleasures of heaven are with me and the pains of hell are
     with me,

The first I graft and increase upon myself . . . . the latter I
    translate into a new tongue.

                         [*Song of Myself* (1855)]

What would it be to translate infernal pain into a new tongue?
Dante's *Inferno* is a brilliant nightmare on the verge of madness.
What should be the American evasion of eternal punishment?

I am the poet of the woman the same as the man,
And I say it is as great to be a woman as to be a man,
And I say there is nothing greater than the mother of men.

I once provoked an audience of scholars by remarking that Whitman was a kind of male lesbian. That may have its difficulties, but
to speak of Walt's erotic stance as "homosexual" is inadequate to the
vision of love in *Song of Myself*. Whitman is pansexual, excluding no
possible stance:

I chant a new chant of dilation or pride,
We have had ducking and deprecating about enough,
I show that size is only development.

Have you outstript the rest? Are you the President?
It is a trifle . . . . they will more than arrive there every one,
    and still pass on.

In Whitman's radical sense of democracy each of us is President.

I am he that walks with the tender and growing night;
I call to the earth and sea half-held by the night.

The immense power of this annunciation emanates from a
man-god.

Press close barebosomed night! Press close magnetic nourish-
    ing night!
Night of south winds! Night of the large few stars!
Still nodding night! Mad naked summer night!

Smile O voluptuous coolbreathed earth!
Earth of the slumbering and liquid trees!
Earth of departed sunset! Earth of the mountains misty-topt!
Earth of the vitreous pour of the full moon just tinged with
    blue!
Earth of shine and dark mottling the tide of the river!
Earth of the limpid gray of clouds brighter and clearer for my
    sake!
Far-swooping elbowed earth! Rich apple-blossomed earth!
Smile, for your lover comes!

The Psalms and the Song of Songs presaged Whitman as the divine new lover of the earth.

Prodigal! You have given me love! . . . therefore I to you give
    love!
O unspeakable passionate love!

Thruster holding me tight and that I hold tight!
We hurt each other as the bridegroom and the bride hurt each
    other.

The parable of the Prodigal Son, Luke 15:11–32, is exceeded by what certainly seems to be an incestuous embrace between father and son.

I laugh at what you call dissolution,
And I know the amplitude of time.

"Dissolution" takes its double sense of "dissolving" and "debauchery." Whitman knows the amplitude of time because he is one with the ocean waves and their oscillation. But above all he is one with himself:

Walt Whitman, an American, one of the roughs, a kosmos,
Disorderly fleshy and sensual . . . . eating drinking and breeding,
No sentimentalist . . . . no stander above men and women or
    apart from them . . . . no more modest than immodest.

That is mostly bravura. Walt Whitman is an American and perhaps a kosmos but, however he attired himself, he was not one of
the roughs. Nor was he a promiscuous, sensual breeder. Quite the
contrary. He mostly did not want to be touched. All that is swept
away as the deep voice of the daemon rises up from the soles of his
feet and proclaims human liberation:

> Unscrew the locks from the doors!
> Unscrew the doors themselves from their jambs!
>
> Whoever degrades another degrades me . . . . and whatever is
>   done or said returns at last to me,
> And whatever I do or say I also return.
>
> Through me the afflatus surging and surging . . . . through me
>   the current and index.
>
> I speak the password primeval . . . . I give the sign of democracy;
> By God! I will accept nothing which all cannot have their
>   counterpart of on the same terms.

That remains a more radical democracy than we are ever likely
to inhabit. Whitman here is in the direct line of Amos and Micah,
prophets protesting on behalf of the poor and the exploited.

> Through me many long dumb voices,
> Voices of the interminable generations of slaves,
> Voices of prostitutes and of deformed persons,
> Voices of the diseased and despairing, and of thieves and
>   dwarfs,
> Voices of cycles of preparation and accretion,
> And of the threads that connect the stars—and of wombs, and
>   of the fatherstuff,
> And of the rights of them the others are down upon,
> Of the trivial and flat and foolish and despised,
> Of fog in the air and beetles rolling balls of dung.
>
> Through me forbidden voices,
> Voices of sexes and lusts . . . . voices veiled, and I remove the veil,
> Voices indecent by me clarified and transfigured.

Nine repetitions of "voices" come at us in just twelve lines as Whitman becomes the trumpet of all those kept dumb for too long by reason, nature, and society.

I do not press my finger across my mouth,
I keep as delicate around the bowels as around the head and
    heart,
Copulation is no more rank to me than death is.
I believe in the flesh and the appetites,
Seeing hearing and feeling are miracles, and each part and tag
    of me is a miracle.

Divine am I inside and out, and I make holy whatever I touch
    or am touched from;
The scent of these arm-pits is aroma finer than prayer,
This head is more than churches or bibles or creeds.

If I worship any particular thing it shall be some of the spread
    of my body;
Translucent mould of me it shall be you,
Shaded ledges and rests, firm masculine coulter, it shall be you,

Whatever goes to the tilth of me it shall be you,
You my rich blood, your milky stream pale strippings of my
    life;
Breast that presses against other breasts it shall be you,
My brain it shall be your occult convolutions,
Root of washed sweet-flag, timorous pond-snipe, nest of
    guarded duplicate eggs, it shall be you,
Mixed tussled hay of head and beard and brawn it shall be you,
Trickling sap of maple, fibre of manly wheat, it shall be you;
Sun so generous it shall be you,
Vapors lighting and shading my face it shall be you,
You sweaty brooks and dews it shall be you,
Winds whose soft-tickling genitals rub against me it shall be you,
Broad muscular fields, branches of liveoak, loving lounger in
    my winding paths, it shall be you,
Hands I have taken, face I have kissed, mortal I have ever
    touched, it shall be you.

I dote on myself . . . . there is that lot of me, and all so luscious,
Each moment and whatever happens thrills me with joy.

I cannot tell how my ankles bend . . . . nor whence the cause of
    my faintest wish,
Nor the cause of the friendship I emit . . . . nor the cause of the
    friendship I take again.

To walk up my stoop is unaccountable . . . . I pause to consider
    if it really be,
That I eat and drink is spectacle enough for the great authors
    and schools,
A morning-glory at my window satisfies me more than the
    metaphysics of books.

To behold the daybreak!
The little light fades the immense and diaphanous shadows,
The air tastes good to my palate.

Hefts of the moving world at innocent gambols, silently rising,
    freshly exuding,
Scooting obliquely high and low.

Something I cannot see puts upward libidinous prongs,
Seas of bright juice suffuse heaven.

The earth by the sky staid with . . . . the daily close of their
    junction,
The heaved challenge from the east that moment over my head,
The mocking taunt, See then whether you shall be master!

Unlike his disciple Stevens, Whitman can be agonistic toward
the sun. Most certainly the sun is aggressive in regard to the American Bard. Challenged, the sun mocks the only poet who could respond by chanting:

Dazzling and tremendous how quick the sun-rise would kill me,
If I could not now and always send sun-rise out of me.

In earlier days I would compare this declaration to Captain
Ahab's: "I'd strike the sun if it insulted me." Yet Ahab, like Melville,

is Gnostic. Whitman loves the creation and considers it in no way less excellent than it has ever been. For him, there was never more inception than there is now.

Whitman had an English admirer: Anne Gilchrist, the widow of Alexander Gilchrist, William Blake's first biographer. William Michael Rossetti, the brother of Dante Gabriel Rossetti and Christina Rossetti, both of whom he survived to edit, was a friend of Swinburne, and they shared an enthusiasm for Whitman (Swinburne later swerved from this, but by then he was hopelessly alcoholic). The first appearance of Whitman's poetry in England was in a volume edited by William Michael Rossetti, though unfortunately it was mangled by censorship.

Anne Gilchrist fell in love with the image of Whitman in his poetry. She frightened him a bit with passionate love letters and came to the United States hoping to marry him. It worked out as a lasting close friendship.

Whitman achieved an inadequate sense of William Blake despite Anne Gilchrist and Swinburne, whose book on Blake (1868) concluded with a comparison of Blake and Whitman that stressed their affinities. That did not please Whitman, who insisted that his vision was coherent while Blake's was not. And yet at the heart of the cosmos there is a rhythm shared by both poet-prophets.

Etymologically, rhythm is "flow," going back to the Greek *rhuthmos*. The late Angus Fletcher remains indispensable for apprehending Walt Whitman's reconciliation of Lucretian atomism and what is now called "wave theory."

Ebb and flow. Fletcher read Whitman as an instance of an iconography of waves:

Thematic approaches to poetic effect are always bound to mislead, or else lead us away from the poetics of the poem in question. The trouble here with thinking simply in terms of the iconography of waves is that it does nothing to explain how the poem comes into being as a powerful poetic form; it merely shows the allegory of the poem, its use in this case of the symbols of the undulant. But Whitman in his way, and my other descriptive poets in their ways, write less *about* waves of life than they actually write *in waves*. Arguing that

Whitman manages this undulant effect by means of his lists would be true, as long as we understand that the lists themselves are not catalogues, as they always violate categorical order. Their systematic-looking orders are subversively dismembered, as much as possible, until finally these lists are not lists at all, rather, they are phrasal processions of thoughts.

Their expressive, ceremonial mode is dependent upon a well-known classical figure of speech, anaphora. Anaphora is a device of organizational decorum that produces the sense of ritual, procession, or when let loose produces an opposed sense of onrushing elemental force. Anaphora reinforces belief in a ritualized spell binding poetic rhythm, whose force attains sometimes to religious ecstasy, as in the mystical poems of the seventeenth-century Catholic poet, Richard Crashaw. The technique requires waves of segmented phrases whose repetition builds into pulsations rather than points and predications. Ritual rhythm—to what purpose, one must ask—is thus the almost inevitable anaphoric consequence.

[*A New Theory for American Poetry* (2009)]

Fletcher regarded John Clare, Whitman, John Ashbery as what he called *descriptive* poets. Another traditional term for what he means is the *picturesque*. Essentially Fletcher valorizes the *picturesque* over the Sublime, the horizontal over the vertical. Horizons, on which William Blake based his name for Urizen, god of the compasses, make me nervous. What happens to Walt Whitman as prophet if you totally surround us with his *environmental* poems, as Fletcher calls them? Can you prophesy by pulsations?

There can be various purposes for ritual rhythm. Hypnotic chants have been features of almost all known religions since ancient shamanism. Whitman as a secular Christ attempts not to convert you but to alter your sense of yourself and its relation to otherness. His own life became a parable of this alteration.

Walt Whitman, ministering angel of the understaffed and inadequate squalors called hospitals in our Civil War, ruined his health and his daemon or genius by his years of volunteer unpaid service to maimed and dying soldiers. With only occasional exceptions, his great poetry ends in 1865 with his threnody for Abraham Lincoln, "When Lilacs Last in the Dooryard Bloom'd." I am not an American historian, but Lincoln and Whitman seem to me the best we can show.

Yet for any poet, particularly an American, Whitman can be a troublesome father. Emily Dickinson, who refused to read him, approaches his eminence, but who else does? Rereading Whitman daily or chanting him silently to myself during the long nights, I can hardly believe how astonishingly wonderful it is:

Whoever you are, I fear you are walking the walks of dreams,
I fear those realities are to melt from under your feet and
    hands;
Even now, your features, joys, speech, house, trade, manners,
    troubles, follies, costume,
        crimes, dissipate away from you,
Your true soul and body appear before me,
They stand forth out of affairs—out of commerce,
        shops, law, science, work, farms, clothes, the
        house, medicine, print, buying, selling, eating,
        drinking, suffering, begetting, dying.

Whoever you are, now I place my hand upon you, that you be
    my poem,
I whisper with my lips close to your ear,
I have loved many women and men, but I love none better than
    you.

O I have been dilatory and dumb,
I should have made my way straight to you long ago,
I should have blabbed nothing but you, I should have chanted
    nothing but you.

I will leave all, and come and make the hymns of you;
None have understood you, but I understand you,
None have done justice to you, you have not done justice to
    yourself,
None but have found you imperfect, I only find no imperfec-
    tion in you,

None but would subordinate you, I only am he who
    will never consent to subordinate you,
I only am he who places over you no master, owner,
better, god, beyond what waits intrinsically in yourself.

Painters have painted their swarming groups, and the centre
    figure of all,
From the head of the centre figure spreading a nimbus of
    gold-colored light,
But I paint myriads of heads, but paint no head without its
    nimbus of
    gold-colored light,
From my hand, from the brain of every man and woman it
    streams,
    effulgently flowing forever.

O I could sing such grandeurs and glories about you!
You have not known what you are—you have slumbered
    upon yourself all your life,
Your eye-lids have been the same as closed most of the time,
What you have done returns already in mockeries,
Your thrift, knowledge, prayers, if they do not return
    in mockeries, what is their return?

The mockeries are not you,
Underneath them, and within them, I see you lurk,
I pursue you where none else has pursued you,

Silence, the desk, the flippant expression, the night,
    the accustomed routine, if these conceal you from
    others, or from yourself, they do not conceal you
    from me,
The shaved face, the unsteady eye, the impure complexion,
if these balk others, they do not balk me,
The pert apparel, the deformed attitude, drunkenness,
    greed, premature death, all these I part aside,
I track through your windings and turnings—I come
    upon you where you thought eye should never
    come upon you.

There is no endowment in man or woman that is not tallied in
    you,
There is no virtue, no beauty, in man or woman, but as good is
    in you,
No pluck, no endurance in others, but as good is in you,
No pleasure waiting for others, but an equal pleasure waits for you.

As for me, I give nothing to any one, except I give the like
    carefully to you,
I sing the songs of the glory of none, not God, sooner
    than I sing the songs of the glory of you.

Whoever you are, you are to hold your own at any hazard,
These shows of the east and west are tame compared to you,
These immense meadows, these interminable rivers
    —you are immense and interminable as they . . .
                [“Poem of You, Whoever You Are”]

This is from the 1856 Second Edition of *Leaves of Grass*, which
contained also a poem-of-poems that Whitman finally titled “Crossing Brooklyn Ferry.” I recite or read it and am exalted and abashed.
In certain moments of my youth I could have sustained this call to
what is best and oldest in myself, but at ninety I gently settle for
aesthetic satisfaction.

What a poor response that is to Whitman’s summons! He seeks
to break through my shell and open me again to more life. No other
poet has been this direct:

Whoever you are, now I place my hand upon you, that you
be my poem.

How does one apprehend this saving gesture? Whitman writes
his own death and resurrection in *Song of Myself*. He is the American Christos, the “anointed,” a translation of the Hebrew *mashiyach*
or *messiah*. His Gospel is healing. He is the son of Walter Whitman Sr., a carpenter and Hicksite Quaker.

At ninety I ponder the mystery of poetic incarnation. Walt
Whitman was the second of eight surviving children born to Louisa

Van Velsor and Walter Whitman. Why was he the anointed poet? Hart Crane was the only child of Clarence Crane and Grace Hart. Why did poetic incarnation exalt him? Wallace Stevens was one of five children of Margaretha Catharine Zeller and Garrett Barcalow Stevens. What concatenation of daemons joined together to bring forth the seer of *Notes toward a Supreme Fiction* and *The Auroras of Autumn?*

At any single time there are a plethora of poets who achieve esteem and then vanish forever. How many among us, meaning receptive auditors, could now identify poets who seemed, in my far-off youth, to be of importance: Joseph Auslander, J. V. Cunningham, Howard Nemerov, Theodore Weiss, Donald Davidson, Witter Bynner, John Gould Fletcher, Louis Simpson, Horace Gregory, Robert Hillyer, Stanley Kunitz, William Ellery Leonard, John Peale Bishop, Archibald MacLeish, Edna St. Vincent Millay, Muriel Rukeyser, Reed Whittemore, Howard Baker, Arthur Davison Ficke, and so many more? Millay, Rukeyser, and Baker each had one or two good poems. Going through my shelves and revisiting the others, I find only dismal imitations of precursors. The melancholy question is, who are the likely candidates for joining these in oblivion?

That returns me to the inexplicable genesis of poetic greatness in Walter Whitman Jr. Before 1850 his attempts at authorship were rather pathetic. In the six years 1850–1855 he underwent a transformation into something rich and strange.

Whitman's father and mother were followers of the radical Quaker evangelist Elias Hicks, who endeavored to restore the Society of Friends to the inwardness of George Fox and other founders in the seventeenth century. We might now call Hicks a Socialist since he denounced the market economy of the United States. Walt Whitman recalled instances from his childhood in which his parents took him to hear Hicks orate against state and state church. In his own old age Walt said of Hicks: "He is one of the prophets."

Hicks at his meetings encouraged individuals to rise up and testify to the workings of the Spirit moving within them. *Song of Myself* cannot be called a Quaker poem, yet it is frequently Hicksite:

> Swiftly arose and spread around me the peace and knowledge
>   that pass all the argument
>   of the earth;

And I know that the hand of God is the elderhand of my own,
And I know that the spirit of God is the brother of my own,
And that all the men ever born are also my brothers . . . .
  and the women my sisters and lovers,
And that a kelson of the creation is love,
And limitless are leaves stiff or drooping in the fields,
And brown ants in the little wells beneath them,
And mossy scabs of the wormfence, and heaped stones, and
  elder and mullen and pokeweed.

[*Song of Myself* (1855)]

Until those marvelous last three lines—Whitman at his most original—this could well be an eloquent Hicksite testifying in meeting. The two emphatic instances of "And I know that" pass on to "And that all," and "all" is magic for Walt. If "a kelson of the creation is love" holding the world together as a kelson does a ship, then once more we can contrast the two American titans. Ishmael speaks for Melville when he intones: "Though in many of its aspects this visible world seems formed in love, the invisible spheres were formed in fright."

Walt Whitman never read *Moby-Dick* (1851) and Melville refused to read Whitman. It is an adventure to do their reading for them. They are totally antithetical. Whitman knows that love is very difficult, but who can survive without it? Melville knows that love is impossible and he barely survives marriage and fatherhood. It remains unclear how much sexual experience Whitman enjoyed, except with himself, yet it seems likely that his eight-year relationship with the Confederate veteran Peter Doyle achieved some consummation.

Think of Walt Whitman and the phrase "the love of comrades" will engage you. There is a sadness here. He wanted his poems to be read by "rude uneducated people" but he is ineluctably difficult. I find him to be so cunning and so evasive that he can be as difficult as Hart Crane or John Ashbery. Poets like Gerard Manley Hopkins and Dylan Thomas present surface problems. You clear them up and sail on easily. There are rather too many Walt Whitmans, and they are all authentic denizens of his poems.

It is not that he is large and contains multitudes. Rather he is as huge as the North American continent and impossibly wants to

inhabit everybody. No single term will encompass Walt, but "shaman" may be the most useful. Scholars of shamanism frequently
disagree with one another. In my youth I considered Mircea Eliade
to be reliable, but he turns out to be rather dubious, perhaps reflecting his youthful attachment to the Romanian Iron Guard, a Fascist
organization.

There is no agreement on what "shaman" means. Its etymology
is in dispute. By now shamans abound as staples of counterculture,
whatever that still means. Every year or so one of my students becomes a convinced shaman with the aid of radical drugs. She or he
seems hardly changed as a student.

I cannot recall that Whitman, anywhere in his verse or prose,
employs the word "shaman." "Poet" and "orator" are his chosen
terms. Since he presents himself as a healer and as subject to visions,
he does seem a kind of shaman. But shamans go through illness,
madness, and death in order to achieve their powers. That is not
very Whitmanian.

Whitman was obsessed with health. He was indeed the wound-
dresser. A kind of ministering angel, he caught forever the poignance
of sacrifice for others:

I

An old man bending I come among new faces,
Years looking backward resuming in answer to children,
Come tell us old man, as from young men and maidens that
    love me,
(Arous'd and angry, I'd thought to beat the alarum, and urge
    relentless war,
But soon my fingers fail'd me, my face droop'd and I resign'd
    myself,
To sit by the wounded and soothe them, or silently watch the
    dead;)
Years hence of these scenes, of these furious passions, these
    chances,
Of unsurpass'd heroes, (was one side so brave? the other was
    equally brave;)
Now be witness again, paint the mightiest armies of earth,
Of those armies so rapid so wondrous what saw you to tell us?

What stays with you latest and deepest? of curious panics,
Of hard-fought engagements or sieges tremendous what
    deepest remains?

2
O maidens and young men I love and that love me,
What you ask of my days those the strangest and sudden your
    talking recalls,
Soldier alert I arrive after a long march cover'd with sweat and
    dust,
In the nick of time I come, plunge in the fight, loudly shout in
    the rush of successful charge,
Enter the captur'd works—yet lo, like a swift running river
    they fade,
Pass and are gone they fade—I dwell not on soldiers' perils or
    soldiers' joys,
(Both I remember well—many of the hardships, few the joys,
    yet I was content.)

But in silence, in dreams' projections,
While the world of gain and appearance and mirth goes on,
So soon what is over forgotten, and waves wash the imprints
    off the sand,
With hinged knees returning I enter the doors, (while for you
    up there,
Whoever you are, follow without noise and be of strong heart.)

Bearing the bandages, water and sponge,
Straight and swift to my wounded I go,
Where they lie on the ground after the battle brought in,
Where their priceless blood reddens the grass, the ground,
Or to the rows of the hospital tent, or under the roof'd
    hospital,
To the long rows of cots up and down each side I return,
To each and all one after another I draw near, not one do I
    miss,
An attendant follows holding a tray, he carries a refuse pail,
Soon to be fill'd with clotted rags and blood, emptied, and fill'd
    again.

I onward go, I stop,
With hinged knees and steady hand to dress wounds,
I am firm with each, the pangs are sharp yet unavoidable,
One turns to me his appealing eyes—poor boy! I never knew
    you,
Yet I think I could not refuse this moment to die for you, if
    that would save you.

3
On, on I go, (open doors of time! open hospital doors!)
The crush'd head I dress, (poor crazed hand tear not the
    bandage away,)
The neck of the cavalry-man with the bullet through and
    through I examine,
Hard the breathing rattles, quite glazed already the eye, yet
    life struggles hard,
(Come sweet death! be persuaded O beautiful death!
In mercy come quickly.)

From the stump of the arm, the amputated hand,
I undo the clotted lint, remove the slough, wash off the matter
    and blood,
Back on his pillow the soldier bends with curv'd neck and side
    falling head,
His eyes are closed, his face is pale, he dares not look on the
    bloody stump,
And has not yet look'd on it.

I dress a wound in the side, deep, deep,
But a day or two more, for see the frame all wasted and sinking,
And the yellow-blue countenance see.

I dress the perforated shoulder, the foot with the bullet-wound,
Cleanse the one with a gnawing and putrid gangrene, so
    sickening, so offensive,
While the attendant stands behind aside me holding the tray
    and pail.

I am faithful, I do not give out,
The fractur'd thigh, the knee, the wound in the abdomen,

These and more I dress with impassive hand, (yet deep in my
    breast a fire, a burning flame.)

4
Thus in silence in dreams' projections,
Returning, resuming, I thread my way through the hospitals,
The hurt and wounded I pacify with soothing hand,
I sit by the restless all the dark night, some are so young,
Some suffer so much, I recall the experience sweet and sad,
(Many a soldier's loving arms about this neck have cross'd and
    rested,
Many a soldier's kiss dwells on these bearded lips.)

"The Wound-Dresser" (1865; 1891–1892 version given here) is
far from Whitman at his best. He is overwhelmed by his experience
confronting the sufferings of others. But there is a grandeur in his
capacity for love and for an almost miraculous empathy. It is when
Whitman stands back from all the suffering that he sees what cannot be seen and reaches us where I might have thought we could not
be touched. Here is the brief poem "Reconciliation" from *Sequel to
Drum-Taps* (1865–1866):

Word over all, beautiful as the sky,
Beautiful that war and all its deeds of carnage, must in time be
    utterly lost,
That the hands of the sisters Death and Night incessantly softly
    wash again, and ever again, this soil'd world:
For my enemy is dead, a man divine as myself is dead,
I look where he lies white-faced and still in the coffin—I draw
    near,
Bend down and touch lightly with my lips the white face in the
    coffin.

It is the third line that transcends all expectation. The trope is
Homeric though not to be found in Homer. Many years ago I lectured in Valencia, where I returned when I toured Catalonia. My first
visit there was sponsored by the United States Information Service

sometime in the mid-1970s. Somehow Catalonia seemed the right place to lecture on Whitman, and I remember the audience as being very receptive. The next morning, I left the hotel and almost fell over my own feet in astonished joy. It was the orange blossom festival and the young women of Valencia were marching down the street with orange blossoms adorning their tresses, so that for a second I had the optical illusion that the trees had grown even more beautiful and were moving in cadence.

I had lectured on Whitman's *Drum-Taps* and compared them to some of the poems that came out of the defeated loyalist side of the war in which the Fascist Franco triumphed, thus ruining Spain, and Catalonia in particular, for more than a generation. I cannot locate the text of my lecture but I remember that much of it was on "Vigil Strange I Kept on the Field One Night" (1865):

> Vigil strange I kept on the field one night;
> When you my son and my comrade dropt at my side that day,
> One look I but gave which your dear eyes return'd with a
>   look I shall never forget,
> One touch of your hand to mine O boy, reach'd up as you
>   lay on the ground,
> Then onward I sped in the battle, the even-contested battle,
> Till late in the night reliev'd to the place at last again I made
>   my way,
> Found you in death so cold dear comrade, found your body son
>   of responding kisses, (never again on earth responding,)
> Bared your face in the starlight, curious the scene, cool blew
>   the moderate night-wind,
> Long there and then in vigil I stood, dimly around me the
>   battle-field spreading,
> Vigil wondrous and vigil sweet there in the fragrant silent
>   night,
> But not a tear fell, not even a long-drawn sigh, long, long
>   I gazed,
> Then on the earth partially reclining sat by your side leaning my
>   chin in my hands,
> Passing sweet hours, immortal and mystic hours with you
>   dearest comrade—not a tear, not a word,

Vigil of silence, love and death, vigil for you my son and my
soldier,
As onward silently stars aloft, eastward new ones upward stole,
Vigil final for you brave boy, (I could not save you, swift was
your death,
I faithfully loved you and cared for you living, I think we shall
surely meet again,)
Till at latest lingering of the night, indeed just as the dawn
appear'd,
My comrade I wrapt in his blanket, envelop'd well his form,
Folded the blanket well, tucking it carefully over head and
carefully under feet,
And there and then and bathed by the rising sun, my son in his
grave, in his rude-dug grave I deposited,
Ending my vigil strange with that, vigil of night and battle-
field dim,
Vigil for boy of responding kisses, (never again on earth
responding,)
Vigil for comrade swiftly slain, vigil I never forget, how as day
brighten'd,
I rose from the chill groun bloody stump,d and folded my
soldier well in his blanket,
And buried him where he fell.

The rhetorical power is so immense that it may take a while to
see how audacious an erotic poem this is. The surviving older soldier regards his lost lover as a son. We have no way of knowing
whether that is literally true. Palpably the poem's speaker, who keeps
vigil, confesses a sexual love for a boy "of responding kisses." The
poem is stark, natural if you share Whitman's premises, and a reminder that "vigil" originally meant "wakefulness."

In this twenty-six-line narrative and elegiac poem, the word
"vigil" is repeated thirteen times. The repetitions work as internal-
ized refrain, prompting the reader to wakefulness. I kept vigil many
years ago for my father and fifteen years later for my mother. Even
the loss of my four older siblings did not prompt me to renew the
ordeal of wakefulness. The Indo-European root of "vigil" is "strength,"
presumably of being.

Is Whitman always keeping watch for the dead and for those to come? Here is "Dirge for Two Veterans" (1865) from *Sequel to Drum-Taps:*

THE last sunbeam
Lightly falls from the finish'd Sabbath,
On the pavement here, and there beyond it is looking,
    Down a new-made double grave.

LO, the moon ascending,
Up from the east the silvery round moon,
Beautiful over the house-tops, ghastly, phantom moon,
    Immense and silent moon.

I see a sad procession,
And I hear the sound of coming full-key'd bugles,
All the channels of the city streets they're flooding,
    As with voices and with tears.

I hear the great drums pounding,
And the small drums steady whirring,
And every blow of the great convulsive drums,
    Strikes me through and through.

For the son is brought with the father,
(In the foremost ranks of the fierce assault they fell,
Two veterans son and father dropt together,
    And the double grave awaits them.)

Now nearer blow the bugles,
And the drums strike more convulsive,
And the daylight o'er the pavement quite has faded,
    And the strong dead-march enwraps me.

In the eastern sky up-buoying,
The sorrowful vast phantom moves illumin'd,
('Tis some mother's large transparent face,
    In heaven brighter growing.)

O strong dead-march you please me!
O moon immense with your silvery face you soothe me!

O my soldiers twain! O my veterans passing to burial!
    What I have I also give you.

    The moon gives you light,
And the bugles and the drums give you music,
And my heart, O my soldiers, my veterans,
    My heart gives you love.

This is not Walt Whitman at his most powerful. But can it be dismissed? It is pitched too high and sometimes awkwardly phrased. Whitman shows us how tensile is his gift at representing loss as universal and commonplace. He does this by achieving a dearth of meaning rather than the plenitude he longs for. He is an antiphon in himself.

Only major poets can enlist us in the quest for a dearth in meaning, for an ellipsis in figuration, for the high art of leaving things out. Whitman was a great artist in verse. His American peer Herman Melville manifests equal artistry in *Moby-Dick* (1851), published four years before the first *Leaves of Grass*.

A good text is now available of *Melville's Complete Poems*, edited by Hershel Parker (Library of America [2019]). Five hundred out of nine hundred pages of poetry are given to *Clarel: A Poem and Pilgrimage in the Holy Land* (1876). Admirers of *Clarel* remain only a few handfuls. The late Robert Penn Warren urged it upon me but I responded slowly. The poem is slow.

Some of Melville's shorter poems retain a fierce vitalism, as here in "The Maldive Shark" (1888):

About the Shark, phlegmatical one,
Pale sot of the Maldive sea,
The sleek little pilot-fish, azure and slim,
How alert in attendance be.
From his saw-pit of mouth, from his charnel of maw,
They have nothing of harm to dread,
But liquidly glide on his ghastly flank
Or before his Gorgonian head;
Or lurk in the port of serrated teeth
In white triple tiers of glittering gates,

And there find a haven when peril's abroad,
An asylum in jaws of the Fates!
They are friends; and friendly they guide him to prey,
Yet never partake of the treat—
Eyes and brains to the dotard lethargic and dull,
Pale ravener of horrible meat.

This would be worthy of an interchapter in *Moby-Dick.* The dotard
Shark yields in interest to the azure pilot-fish, who know precisely
what they are doing.

Except for Clarel, Melville's most ambitious poem is "After the
Pleasure Party" (1891):

LINES TRACED
UNDER AN IMAGE OF
AMOR THREATENING

Fear me, virgin whosoever
Taking pride from love exempt,
    Fear me, slighted. Never, never
Brave me, nor my fury tempt:
Downy wings, but wroth they beat
Tempest even in reason's seat.

AFTER THE PLEASURE PARTY.
Behind the house the upland falls
With many an odorous tree—
White marbles gleaming through green halls—
Terrace by terrace, down and down,
And meets the star-lit Mediterranean Sea.

    'Tis Paradise. In such an hour
Some pangs that rend might take release.
Nor less perturbed who keeps this bower
Of balm, nor finds balsamic peace?
From whom the passionate words in vent
After long revery's discontent?

    Tired of the homeless deep,
Look how their flight yon hurrying billows urge,

Hitherward but to reap
Passive repulse from the iron-bound verge!
Insensate, can they never know
'Tis mad to wreck the impulsion so?

    An art of memory is, they tell:
But to forget! forget the glade
Wherein Fate sprung Love's ambuscade,
To flout pale years of cloistral life
And flush me in this sensuous strife.
'Tis Vesta struck with Sappho's smart.
No fable her delirious leap:
With more of cause in desperate heart,
Myself could take it—but to sleep!

    Now first I feel, what all may ween,
That soon or late, if faded e'en,
One's sex asserts itself. Desire,
The dear desire through love to sway,
Is like the Geysers that aspire—
Through cold obstruction win their fervid way.
But baffled here—to take disdain,
To feel rule's instinct, yet not reign;
To dote, to come to this drear shame—
Hence the winged blaze that sweeps my soul
Like prairie-fires that spurn control,
Where withering weeds incense the flame.

    And kept I long heaven's watch for this,
Contemning love, for this, even this?
O terrace chill in Northern air,
O reaching ranging tube I placed
Against yon skies, and fable chased
Till, fool, I hailed for sister there
Starred Cassiopea in Golden Chair.
In dream I throned me, nor I saw
In cell the idiot crowned with straw.

    And yet, ah yet, scarce ill I reigned,
Through self-illusion self-sustained,

When now—enlightened, undeceived—
What gain I, barrenly bereaved!
Than this can be yet lower decline—
Envy and spleen, can these be mine?

    The peasant-girl demure that trod
Beside our wheels that climbed the way,
And bore along a blossoming rod
That looked the sceptre of May-Day—
On her—to fire this petty hell,
His softened glance how moistly fell!
The cheat! on briers her buds were strung;
And wiles peeped forth from mien how meek.
The innocent bare-foot! young, so young!
To girls, strong man's a novice weak.
To tell such beads! And more remain,
Sad rosary of belittling pain.

    When after lunch and sallies gay
Like the Decameron folk we lay
In sylvan groups; and I—let be!
O, dreams he, can he dream that one
Because not roseate feels no sun?
The plain lone bramble thrills with Spring
As much as vines that grapes shall bring.

    Me now fair studies charm no more.
Shall great thoughts writ, or high themes sung
Damask wan cheeks—unlock his arm
About some radiant ninny flung?
How glad with all my starry lore,
I'd buy the veriest wanton's rose
Would but my bee therein repose.

    Could I remake me! or set free
This sexless bound in sex, then plunge
Deeper than Sappho, in a lunge
Piercing Pan's paramount mystery!
For, Nature, in no shallow surge
Against thee either sex may urge,

Why hast thou made us but in halves—
Co-relatives? This makes us slaves.
If these co-relatives never meet
Self-hood itself seems incomplete.
And such the dicing of blind fate
Few matching halves here meet and mate.
What Cosmic jest or Anarch blunder
The human integral clove asunder
And shied the fractions through life's gate?

   Ye stars that long your votary knew
Rapt in her vigil, see me here!
Whither is gone the spell ye threw
When rose before me Cassiopea?
Usurped on by love's stronger reign—
But, lo, your very selves do wane:
Light breaks—truth breaks! Silvered no more,
But chilled by dawn that brings the gale
Shivers yon bramble above the vale,
And disillusion opens all the shore.

   One knows not if Urania yet
The pleasure-party may forget;
Or whether she lived down the strain
Of turbulent heart and rebel brain;
For Amor so resents a slight,
And hers had been such haught disdain,
He long may wreak his boyish spite,
And boy-like, little reck the pain.

   One knows not, no. But late in Rome
(For queens discrowned a congruous home)
Entering Albani's porch she stood
Fixed by an antique pagan stone
Colossal carved. No anchorite seer,
Not Thomas a Kempis, monk austere,
Religious more are in their tone;
Yet far, how far from Christian heart
That form august of heathen Art.

Swayed by its influence, long she stood,
Till surged emotion seething down,
She rallied and this mood she won:

    Languid in frame for me,
To-day by Mary's convent-shrine,
Touched by her picture's moving plea
In that poor nerveless hour of mine,
I mused—A wanderer still must grieve.
Half I resolved to kneel and believe,
Believe and submit, the veil take on.
But thee, arm'd Virgin! less benign,
Thee now I invoke, thou mightier one.
Helmeted woman—if such term
Befit thee, far from strife
Of that which makes the sexual feud
And clogs the aspirant life—
O self-reliant, strong and free,
Thou in whom power and peace unite,
Transcender! raise me up to thee,
Raise me and arm me!
                Fond appeal.
For never passion peace shall bring,
Nor Art inanimate for long
Inspire. Nothing may help or heal
While Amor incensed remembers wrong.
Vindictive, not himself he'll spare;
For scope to give his vengeance play
Himself he'll blaspheme and betray.

    Then for Urania, virgins everywhere,
O pray! Example take too, and have care.

I once, quite mistakenly, assumed that Urania was the formidable and unfortunate Margaret Fuller. She was in fact Maria Mitchell (1818–1889), the first prominent American woman astronomer. Nathaniel Hawthorne and his wife, Sophia, traveled in Italy with Maria Mitchell in 1858. Melville may have heard gossip that his Urania had a passionate attachment in Italy, although the identity of that admirer is unknown.

How can you say farewell to Walt Whitman, since at ninety I will not write on him again? D. H. Lawrence, after a spasm of fault-finding with Whitman, emerged into praise both accurate and prophetic:

> Whitman, the great poet, has meant so much to me. Whitman, the one man breaking a way ahead. Whitman, the one pioneer. And only Whitman. No English pioneers, no French. No European pioneer-poets. In Europe the would-be pioneers are mere innovators. The same in America. Ahead of Whitman, nothing. Ahead of all poets, pioneering into the wilderness of unopened life, Whitman. Beyond him, none. His wide, strange camp at the end of the great high-road. And lots of new little poets camping on Whitman's camping ground now. But none going really beyond. Because Whitman's camp is at the end of the road, and on the edge of a great precipice. Over the precipice, blue distances, and the blue hollow of the future. But there is no way down. It is a dead end.
>
> Pisgah. Pisgah sights. And Death. Whitman like a strange, modern, American Moses. Fearfully mistaken. And yet the great leader.
>
> [*Studies in Classic American Literature* (1923)]

It is curious that Wallace Stevens, a poet very different from Lawrence, chanted a Whitman who was both Moses and Aaron. Hart Crane invoked Whitman as the Angel of America. I once told Tony Kushner I was surprised that he did not do the same. And yet my question was mistaken, since whatever Kushner's aesthetic intention, his Angel paraphrases Whitman, while Kushner accurately remarks: "We are all children of *Song of Myself.*"

Walt's progeny was extensive: it commences with George Cabot Lodge and Kate Chopin and passes on to Ezra Pound, T. S. Eliot, Robinson Jeffers, Wallace Stevens, William Carlos Williams, John Brooks Wheelwright, Hart Crane, Allen Ginsberg, John Ashbery, A. R. Ammons, and Mark Strand.

Lawrence said that Whitman broke the new road. Gershom Scholem, a surprising student of Whitman, told me that *Leaves of Grass* broke the vessels and that Walt was an intuitive Kabbalist.

There is no end to Whitman. With Herman Melville, he is the most capacious of American writers. We have no Shakespeare, but we have *Moby-Dick* and *Leaves of Grass*.

CHAPTER ELEVEN

Robert Frost

Drink and Be Whole Again beyond Confusion

R ECALCITRANT AND RUGGED, SHAGGY and self-motivated, Robert Frost is subtle and deep, cunning beyond belief, with an enigmatic reserve always on the verge of shattering disclosure. He writes for two audiences, the first large and absorbing what it can. The second is only those he will admit to his secrets.

The Wordsworthian "Two Tramps in Mud Time" (1934) is an eminent way to begin reading and teaching Frost, whose ludic propensities emerge with his proper fondness for his own name: "Be glad of water, but don't forget / The lurking frost in the earth beneath . . ." (ll. 37–38).

From childhood on, I have gone about chanting "The Trial by Existence" (1915):

> Even the bravest that are slain
>> Shall not dissemble their surprise
> On waking to find valor reign,
>> Even as on earth, in paradise;
> And where they sought without the sword
>> Wide fields of asphodel fore'er,

To find that the utmost reward
    Of daring should be still to dare.

The light of heaven falls whole and white
    And is not shattered into dyes,
The light for ever is morning light;
    The hills are verdured pasture-wise;
The angel hosts with freshness go,
    And seek with laughter what to brave;—
And binding all is the hushed snow
    Of the far-distant breaking wave.

And from a cliff-top is proclaimed
    The gathering of the souls for birth,
The trial by existence named,
    The obscuration upon earth.
And the slant spirits trooping by
In streams and cross- and counter-streams
    Can but give ear to that sweet cry
For its suggestion of what dreams!

And the more loitering are turned
    To view once more the sacrifice
Of those who for some good discerned
    Will gladly give up paradise.
And a white shimmering concourse rolls
    Toward the throne to witness there
The speeding of devoted souls
    Which God makes his especial care.

And none are taken but who will,
    Having first heard the life read out
That opens earthward, good and ill,
    Beyond the shadow of a doubt;
And very beautifully God limns,
    And tenderly, life's little dream,
But naught extenuates or dims,
    Setting the thing that is supreme.

Nor is there wanting in the press
    Some spirit to stand simply forth,

Heroic in its nakedness,
  Against the uttermost of earth.
The tale of earth's unhonored things
  Sounds nobler there than 'neath the sun;
And the mind whirls and the heart sings,
  And a shout greets the daring one.

But always God speaks at the end:
  "One thought in agony of strife
The bravest would have by for friend,
  The memory that he chose the life;
But the pure fate to which you go
  Admits no memory of choice,
Or the woe were not earthly woe
  To which you give the assenting voice."

And so the choice must be again,
  But the last choice is still the same;
And the awe passes wonder then,
  And a hush falls for all acclaim.
And God has taken a flower of gold
  And broken it, and used therefrom
The mystic link to bind and hold
  Spirit to matter till death come.

'Tis of the essence of life here,
  Though we choose greatly, still to lack
The lasting memory at all clear,
  That life has for us on the wrack
Nothing but what we somehow chose;
  Thus are we wholly stripped of pride
In the pain that has but one close,
  Bearing it crushed and mystified.

The swing and verve of this do not conceal or lessen pride and
pain. Somehow we choose, though Frost cannot clarify what part
God plays or the identity of such a god. What Frost took from
Wordsworth is so tempered by Emerson that we are close to *The
Conduct of Life* (1860, 1876), the Sage of Concord's darker testament.

Once at Bread Loaf I heard Frost recite his sonnet "Design" (1922). He spoke without affect. He walked away. A showman was at work. Scary and elegant, this earns its antithetical power.

I do not recall Frost commenting anywhere on William Blake and yet "Design" seems to me a Song of Experience. Think of "The Sunflower." Frost is never more admirable in tone, diction, metric, and imagery. The spider is dimpled, fat, and white, a snowdrop, kindred to its dinner, the white moth. Everything is as it should be. A miniature Black Mass.

The sestet asks three questions. Are they rhetorical? Is some demiurge speaking the poem? Frost, a master at sonnets, brought together the horrible and the beautiful in the intricately layered "Design," with its final couplet, "What but design of darkness to appall?— / If design govern in a thing so small."

As an argument from design, this can seem a weighted song like those of William Blake and of Emily Dickinson. Frost's sonnets are dangerous even when celebratory, like "Never Again Would Birds' Song Be the Same" (1942), which ends, "Never again would birds' song be the same. / And to do that to birds was why she came."

Frost's lifelong love affair with his wife, Elinor White, was unceasing. Both of them were strong-willed and disagreed frequently. But they stayed together until her death at sixty-four, sustained by an authentic mutual sexual passion. Of their six children, only two survived Frost. I do not know another sonnet that takes its own thirteenth line as title: "Never again would birds' song be the same." The poem's speaker assimilates Adam to Robert Frost and so transforms Elinor into an American Eve. As such she survives for her husband in the soft eloquence of birds who have acquired an oversound from her.

The superb erotic sonnet "The Silken Tent" (1942) was one of Frost's tributes to Kay Morrison, an exuberant being who became the poet's secretary, muse, and mistress after the death of Elinor. Frost desperately needed Kay but had to share her with her husband, Ted, and with the Princeton scholar Lawrance Thompson, who became the poet's disaffected biographer. Evidently Kay Morrison also had intimate relations with Frost's friends and employees. After forty years of monogamous passion, he found this very difficult. There is a kind of wryness in this almost ecstatic vision of a woman who in-

sisted upon being very loosely bound to any particular man, so that
only when one of her "silken ties" goes taut is she "of the slightest
bondage made aware." The bondage and the slight tautness are
Frost's and not Kay Morrison's. A wise woman and good reader, she
must have understood the poem very well.

"The Wood-Pile" (1914) is one of the subtlest and most harrowing of Frost's poems:

> Out walking in the frozen swamp one gray day,
> I paused and said, "I will turn back from here.
> No, I will go on farther—and we shall see."
> The hard snow held me, save where now and then
> One foot went through. The view was all in lines
> Straight up and down of tall slim trees
> Too much alike to mark or name a place by
> So as to say for certain I was here
> Or somewhere else: I was just far from home.
> A small bird flew before me. He was careful
> To put a tree between us when he lighted,
> And say no word to tell me who he was
> Who was so foolish as to think what *he* thought.
> He thought that I was after him for a feather—
> The white one in his tail; like one who takes
> Everything said as personal to himself.
> One flight out sideways would have undeceived him.
> And then there was a pile of wood for which
> I forgot him and let his little fear
> Carry him off the way I might have gone,
> Without so much as wishing him good-night.
> He went behind it to make his last stand.
> It was a cord of maple, cut and split
> And piled—and measured, four by four by eight.
> And not another like it could I see.
> No runner tracks in this year's snow looped near it.
> And it was older sure than this year's cutting,
> Or even last year's or the year's before.
> The wood was gray and the bark warping off it
> And the pile somewhat sunken. Clematis

Had wound strings round and round it like a bundle.
What held it though on one side was a tree
Still growing, and on one a stake and prop,
These latter about to fall. I thought that only
Someone who lived in turning to fresh tasks
Could so forget his handiwork on which
He spent himself, the labor of his ax,
And leave it there far from a useful fireplace
To warm the frozen swamp as best it could
With the slow smokeless burning of decay.

Frost is far from home, his motivation hinted by "like one who
takes / Everything said as personal to himself."

The wood-pile *is* the poem. As such it does not represent a lost
aspect of life. Perhaps it is a life and a marriage only partly fulfilled,
though the forty years of Elinor White and Robert Frost surely were
a consummation.

Sometimes when I think of Frost I suddenly remember "The
Oven Bird" (1916):

There is a singer everyone has heard,
Loud, a mid-summer and a mid-wood bird,
Who makes the solid tree trunks sound again.
He says that leaves are old and that for flowers
Mid-summer is to spring as one to ten.
He says the early petal-fall is past
When pear and cherry bloom went down in showers
On sunny days a moment overcast;
And comes that other fall we name the fall.
He says the highway dust is over all.
The bird would cease and be as other birds
But that he knows in singing not to sing.
The question that he frames in all but words
Is what to make of a diminished thing.

This vociferous bird is very nearly Frost's emblem. He knows in
singing not to sing and his enterprise is to make what can be made
of a diminished thing.

I used to have frequent disagreements with my late friend Richard Poirier as to which were Frost's most important poems. Poirier, who died at eighty-four after falling in his apartment, was a considerable literary critic and the author of *Robert Frost: The Work of Knowing* (1965), perhaps the best of its kind on Frost. One of our contentions concerned the poem "Directive" (1946), which for me stands apart and above the rest of Frost. An affectionate acerbity marks the poet's strenuous directive. Frost wants the reader to be complicit on two levels: one commonplace, but the second, lower one hidden in the depths. He has hidden a broken goblet like the Grail in an old cedar tree and cast a spell "So the wrong ones can't find it, / So can't get saved, as Saint Mark says they mustn't" (ll. 58–59). The enigmatic first Gospel of Mark offers not salvation but dispersal:

That seeing they may see, and not perceive; and hearing they may hear, and not understand; lest at any time they should be converted, and their sins should be forgiven them.

[Mark (KJV) 4:12]

Very little in the Gospel of Mark can be easily comprehended. Its Jesus is always whirling about and cannot rest. He does not know precisely his own identity and keeps asking his blockhead disciples: But who do people say I am? Ruthlessly, only the devils and demons recognize Jesus. That is worth considerable meditation. Mark is the initial gospel, and its best news is that only the diabolic in you can know Jesus.

What is it in you that can know Robert Frost? "Directive" is addressed to the chosen few of Frost's readers who can follow inference and implication. And yet it is a missive or injunction he sends to himself at the age of sixty-nine. How far must you be lost in order to begin to find yourself? Elinor White Frost died in 1938 at sixty-five. Frost, a year younger, lived until 1963. In a dislocated way, "Directive" is not so much an elegy for Elinor as it is for the lost time of their early, failed mutual venture at farming. And yet it is so much more than that, being an argument with existence.

In Frost's bitter and funny poem "Provide, Provide" (1937), Abishag is a wryness in herself. Because of her beauty she is chosen to sleep next to the aged and impotent King David, so as to warm him to little purpose. Few lines even in Frost are so mordant as: "What worked for them might work for you." "Better to go down dignified," Frost writes, aided by "boughten friendship" (ll. 15, 19–20). Down you will go in any case and likely be forgotten. Purchased relationships are expensive, in more than financial ways, but to die dignified seems a human necessity. Frost, a classicist, plays upon the etymological meaning of "provide": get ready.

Robert Frost said that Emerson had written "the greatest Western poem yet," "Uriel" (1847):

> "Line in nature is not found;
> Unit and universe are round;
> In vain produced, all rays return;
> Evil will bless, and ice will burn."
> As Uriel spoke with piercing eye,
> A shudder ran round the sky;
> The stern old war-gods shook their heads;
> The seraphs frowned from myrtle-beds;
> Seemed to the holy festival
> The rash word boded ill to all;
> The balance-beam of Fate was bent;
> The bounds of good and ill were rent;
> Strong Hades could not keep his own,
> But all slid to confusion.
>
> [ll. 21–34]

Drink and be whole again beyond confusion was Frost's directive to himself and his right readers. The Angel Uriel, whose name means "fire of God," unsettled all things in heaven, earth, and Hades.

I have been reading and appreciating Robert Frost since I was about ten, nearly eighty years ago. Teaching him has been rewarding, and I always learn by trying to write about him. Yet he has never had the personal effect upon me of Wallace Stevens, Hart Crane, and John Ashbery. Quite possibly this is a question of temperament. If we have an American Wordsworth, it would be Frost. He is out far and in deep enough.

At Bread Loaf and elsewhere I encountered Frost perhaps a dozen times. He seemed to have come from some earlier world to which he could not return. Though he was always amiable I did not trust it and wanted to depart. Yet some of his poems have gone with me wherever I've gone. One is the sonnet "Putting in the Seed" (1920):

You come to fetch me from my work to-night
When supper's on the table, and we'll see
If I can leave off burying the white
Soft petals fallen from the apple tree.
(Soft petals, yes, but not so barren quite,
Mingled with these, smooth bean and wrinkled pea;)
And go along with you ere you lose sight
Of what you came for and become like me,
Slave to a springtime passion for the earth.
How Love burns through the Putting in the Seed
On through the watching for that early birth
When, just as the soil tarnishes with weed,
The sturdy seedling with arched body comes
Shouldering its way and shedding the earth crumbs.

The joy of this is that Frost transmutes his sonnet into a miniature Robert Browning monologue. Intense conjugal love between Elinor White and Robert Frost is conveyed with conviction and decorum. There is something wholesome beyond any ironical twists of metaphor in the wonderfully fused natural and human plantings and births.

A favorite since childhood is the somewhat Keatsian "After Apple-Picking" (1915):

My long two-pointed ladder's sticking through a tree
Toward heaven still,
And there's a barrel that I didn't fill
Beside it, and there may be two or three
Apples I didn't pick upon some bough.
But I am done with apple-picking now.
Essence of winter sleep is on the night,
The scent of apples: I am drowsing off.
I cannot rub the strangeness from my sight
I got from looking through a pane of glass
I skimmed this morning from the drinking trough

And held against the world of hoary grass.
It melted, and I let it fall and break.
But I was well
Upon my way to sleep before it fell,
And I could tell
What form my dreaming was about to take.
Magnified apples appear and disappear,
Stem end and blossom end,
And every fleck of russet showing clear.
My instep arch not only keeps the ache,
It keeps the pressure of a ladder-round.
I feel the ladder sway as the boughs bend.
And I keep hearing from the cellar bin
The rumbling sound
Of load on load of apples coming in.
For I have had too much
Of apple-picking: I am overtired
Of the great harvest I myself desired.
There were ten thousand thousand fruit to touch,
Cherish in hand, lift down, and not let fall.
For all
That struck the earth,
No matter if not bruised or spiked with stubble,
Went surely to the cider-apple heap
As of no worth.
One can see what will trouble
This sleep of mine, whatever sleep it is.
Were he not gone,
The woodchuck could say whether it's like his
Long sleep, as I describe its coming on,
Or just some human sleep.

One hears in this Keats, "And fill all fruit with ripeness to the core," and his source in *King Lear:* "Ripeness is all." Apple-picking becomes a synecdoche for the whole of human life: "I am overtired / Of the great harvest I myself desired." Not being woodchucks, we cannot hibernate, so the intense sleepiness portends the sleep of sleeps, death our death.

Frost's "Birches" (1915) enchants but rather deviously:

When I see birches bend to left and right
Across the lines of straighter darker trees,
I like to think some boy's been swinging them.
But swinging doesn't bend them down to stay
As ice-storms do. Often you must have seen them
Loaded with ice a sunny winter morning
After a rain. They click upon themselves
As the breeze rises, and turn many-colored
As the stir cracks and crazes their enamel.
Soon the sun's warmth makes them shed crystal shells
Shattering and avalanching on the snow-crust—
Such heaps of broken glass to sweep away
You'd think the inner dome of heaven had fallen.
They are dragged to the withered bracken by the load,
And they seem not to break; though once they are bowed
So low for long, they never right themselves:
You may see their trunks arching in the woods
Years afterwards, trailing their leaves on the ground
Like girls on hands and knees that throw their hair
Before them over their heads to dry in the sun.
But I was going to say when Truth broke in
With all her matter-of-fact about the ice-storm
I should prefer to have some boy bend them
As he went out and in to fetch the cows—
Some boy too far from town to learn baseball,
Whose only play was what he found himself,
Summer or winter, and could play alone.
One by one he subdued his father's trees
By riding them down over and over again
Until he took the stiffness out of them,
And not one but hung limp, not one was left
For him to conquer. He learned all there was
To learn about not launching out too soon
And so not carrying the tree away
Clear to the ground. He always kept his poise
To the top branches, climbing carefully

With the same pains you use to fill a cup
Up to the brim, and even above the brim.
Then he flung outward, feet first, with a swish,
Kicking his way down through the air to the ground.
So was I once myself a swinger of birches.
And so I dream of going back to be.
It's when I'm weary of considerations,
And life is too much like a pathless wood
Where your face burns and tickles with the cobwebs
Broken across it, and one eye is weeping
From a twig's having lashed across it open.
I'd like to get away from earth awhile
And then come back to it and begin over.
May no fate willfully misunderstand me
And half grant what I wish and snatch me away
Not to return. Earth's the right place for love:
I don't know where it's likely to go better.
I'd like to go by climbing a birch tree,
And climb black branches up a snow-white trunk
Toward heaven, till the tree could bear no more,
But dipped its top and set me down again.
That would be good both going and coming back.
One could do worse than be a swinger of birches.

You cannot admire a poem by Robert Frost for the wrong reasons. He tells you all reasons are wrong. Nothing in my own experience as a boy resonates with Frost's in "Birches." There were some elms and oaks in the Southeast Bronx but no birches that I recall. My more adventurous acquaintances—friends and enemies—climbed lampposts, but for me that would have been suicide.

I set aside what may be Frost's phallic pride at having subdued so many birches. I have not the slightest idea what Frost's religion was. He was classical pagan and not Christian. And he saw us darkly but with some accuracy. When I recite "Birches" to myself, I am stopped by the line:

You'd think the inner dome of heaven had fallen.

Perhaps for him it had. He may be thinking of life, like a dome of many-colored glass, staining the white radiance of eternity, since he loved Shelley.

Rather than leave Frost here with something weighty, I turn to his doggerel whose title disconcerts me: "Our Doom to Bloom" (1950, 1962), with its epigraph from Robinson Jeffers.

"The bud must bloom till blowsy blown / Its petals loosen and are strown": This is addressed to the Sybil at Cumae by an apprentice sybil at Rome. I'm not at all sure what Frost considered to be the "Surviving Book," mentioned in "Our Doom to Bloom." He did not mean the Bible and may have meant Homer or perhaps Virgil. The jollity is like hard iron.

CHAPTER TWELVE

Wallace Stevens

The Hum of Thoughts Evaded in the Mind

THE CONTEMPORARY RIVALS FOR Stevens did not include Robert Frost, whose mode was so radically different, but had to be William Carlos Williams, his amiable acquaintance, and T. S. Eliot, who became the English publisher of the Hartford seer. Eliot appears in Stevens's poetry not by name but as X, unlike Whitman and Shelley, who are praised as world-transformers.

Stevens nodded to Eliot's ascetic temperament but gave him little more. I have written about this extensively in *The Daemon Knows* and need not return to it here. Oddly all that Stevens and Eliot shared were Shelley and Whitman, but it took Eliot a lifetime to acknowledge his authentic precursors.

I have been teaching Stevens since 1955, the year after the poet's death. In 1977 I published *The Poems of Our Climate*, a large commentary on most of his poetry. I would hope that what I write now is more than a grace note, but there are poorer enterprises than that.

Stevens, throughout his poetic career, battled against his own reductiveness. He did not want to believe that the worst thing you could say about any particular phenomenon was the truth.

The Victorian prophet-critic John Ruskin formulated what he called the Pathetic Fallacy. This was the imputation of life to the object-world. Ruskin, sublimely inconsistent, also defined the poet as a man to whom things spoke.

Stevens's classic representation of this dilemma is the famous "The Snow Man" (1921), a poem of a single sentence doubling back upon itself:

> One must have a mind of winter
> To regard the frost and the boughs
> Of the pine-trees crusted with snow;
>
> And have been cold a long time
> To behold the junipers shagged with ice,
> The spruces rough in the distant glitter
>
> Of the January sun; and not to think
> Of any misery in the sound of the wind,
> In the sound of a few leaves,
>
> Which is the sound of the land
> Full of the same wind
> That is blowing in the same bare place
>
> For the listener, who listens in the snow,
> And, nothing himself, beholds
> Nothing that is not there and the nothing that is.

One senses the presence of Nietzsche, himself a Snow Man. There are other ghostly forms hovering: Emerson, Emily Dickinson, Thoreau, Whitman. Most palpable is Sigmund Freud, urging us to make friends with the necessity of dying.

Harmonium (1923) was Stevens's long-delayed first book of poems. It has been the fashion to characterize it as a volume in the mode of "The Snow Man." That seems wrong to me. "Stars at Tallapoosa" is more representative:

> The lines are straight and swift between the stars.
> The night is not the cradle that they cry,
> The criers, undulating the deep-oceaned phrase.
> The lines are much too dark and much too sharp.

The mind herein attains simplicity,
There is no moon, no single, silvered leaf.
The body is no body to be seen
But is an eye that studies its black lid.

Let these be your delight, secretive hunter,
Wading the sea-lines, moist and ever-mingling,
Mounting the earth-lines, long and lax, lethargic.
These lines are swift and fall without diverging.

The melon-flower nor dew nor web of either
Is like to these. But in yourself is like:
A sheaf of brilliant arrows flying straight,
Flying and falling straightway for their pleasure,

Their pleasure that is all bright-edged and cold;
Or, if not arrows, then the nimblest motions,
Making recoveries of young nakedness
And the lost vehemence the midnights hold.

This is a tribute to the most influential of American shore odes, Whitman's "Out of the Cradle Endlessly Rocking" (1860, 1871). We are located where Walt's spirit truly dwells: beach meets water; sea-drift slides into earth-lines into sea-lines; star-lines are also the lines underfoot, where a Jobean spirit waits to seize those studying the nostalgias of lost vehemence.

Harmonium was in the wake of *The Waste Land* and remained there for a generation. Stevens's major poems—the great sequences *Notes toward a Supreme Fiction, The Auroras of Autumn, An Ordinary Evening in New Haven* (1950)—were absorbed very slowly.

Here I revisit two crucial moments, the first in *Notes*, the second in *Auroras*. Motions of the mind finding what will suffice; movements mapping engagements of the challenged spirit; the body quickened and the mind in root.

I break into Canto 8 of the third part of *Notes*, where Stevens insists on a time "in which majesty is a mirror of the self: / I have not but I am and as I am, I am." I cannot think of a great poet, except for Stevens, so averse to employing the word "I." Rather desperately, he keeps saying "one." But in this sublime breakthrough all is reversed. Indeed Stevens all but identifies himself with Yahweh in the monosyllabic line: "I have not but I am and as I am, I am."

Stevens has invented a fiction: the Canon Aspirin. The Canon fulfills aspiration by dreaming he is a Miltonic angel in full flight. But then the Canon falls into imposing premature orders. Disengaging from his creature, Stevens instructs the angel to be silent and hear the luminous melody of proper sound.

Mounting to his own challenge, Stevens achieves the High Sublime through a knowing agon with Wordsworth and with Whitman. In *The Prelude*, Wordsworth insists that

> the power, which all
> Acknowledge when thus moved, which Nature thus
> To bodily sense exhibits, is the express
> Resemblance of that glorious faculty
> That higher minds bear with them as their own.
> This is the very spirit in which they deal
> With the whole compass of the universe:
> They from their native selves can send abroad
> Kindred mutations; for themselves create
> A like existence; and, whene'er it dawns
> Created for them, catch it, or are caught
> By its inevitable mastery,
> Like angels stopped upon the wing by sound
> Of harmony from Heaven's remotest spheres.
> . . .
> Such minds are truly from the Deity,
> For they are Powers; and hence the highest bliss
> That flesh can know is theirs—the consciousness
> Of Whom they are, habitually infused
> Through every image and through every thought,
> And all affections by communion raised
> From earth to heaven, from human to divine . . .
>   [1850 Prelude, 14.86–99, 112–118]

Wordsworth achieves a sublime sense of self with an ease Stevens cannot rival. Walt Whitman *is* that sublime sense with something beyond ease:

18

I will confront these shows of the day and night,
I will know if I am to be less than they,
I will see if I am not as majestic as they,
I will see if I am not as subtle and real as they,
I will see if I am to be less generous than they,
I will see if I have no meaning, while the houses and ships have
    meaning,
I will see if the fishes and birds are to be enough for themselves,
    and I am not to be enough for myself.
  . . .
I know now why the earth is gross, tantalizing, wicked, it is
    for my
       sake,
I take you specially to be mine, you terrible, rude forms.
["As I Sat Alone by Blue Ontario's Shore" (1881); emphasis
                                added]

"Majesty is a mirror of the self." With that massive affirmation Stevens joins Whitman. Stopping the angel on his wing acknowledges Wordsworth. But the joining is hesitant, the acknowledgment indirect. In the country of the giants, Stevens frequently fears he is a dwarf of disintegration.

In a sequence otherwise uneven—"Things of August" (1949)—Stevens suddenly ignites. "We'll give the week-end to wisdom, to Weisheit, the rabbi, / Lucidity of his city, joy of his nation," he writes. My friend Eleanor Cook has catalogued the colorful array of Stevens's rabbis in her books *Poetry, Word-Play and Word-War in Wallace Stevens* (1988) and *The Reader's Guide to Wallace Stevens* (2007). These lively fellows pop up frequently in Stevens and defy design. I begin to think they have some relation to Browning's exuberant Rabbi Ben Ezra and to the ultimate wisdom rabbi Sigmund Freud.

I realize again why I most treasure Stevens among all the poets who were my older contemporaries. In a letter he speaks of returning from a visit to New York City's art galleries and observes that the best part of the trip was sitting again in his kitchen drinking milk and eating cookies. Despite yearnings for transcendence, Stevens celebrates things as they are. But things as they are transmute on the Shelleyan azure guitar of the imagination:

> There were ghosts that returned to earth to hear his phrases,
> As he sat there reading, aloud, the great blue tabulae.
> They were those from the wilderness of stars that had ex-
>   pected more.
>
> There were those that returned to hear him read from the
>   poem of life,
> Of the pans above the stove, the pots on the table, the tulips
>   among them.
> They were those that would have wept to step barefoot into
>   reality,
>
> That would have wept and been happy, have shivered in the
>   frost
> And cried out to feel it again, have run fingers over leaves
> And against the most coiled thorn, have seized on what was
>   ugly
>
> And laughed, as he sat there reading, from out of the purple
>   tabulae,
> The outlines of being and its expressings, the syllables of its law:
> *Poesis, poesis*, the literal characters, the vatic lines,
>
> Which in those ears and in those thin, those spended hearts,
> Took on color, took on shape and the size of things as they are
> And spoke the feeling for them, which was what they had
>   lacked.

Stevens called this "Large Red Man Reading" (1950). In his heraldic mode proclaiming a possible ecstasy, the poem refreshes and enchants me. How much we are offered in these generous lines. And how little we need to give in return. At his rarest there is a breaking of the vessels in the poet who desired to call his collected poems *The Whole of Harmonium.*

"After the final no there comes a yes / And on that yes the future world depends," Stevens writes in "The Well-Dressed Man with a Beard" (1942). Evidently this poem meant a great deal to Stevens. His late poem "As You Leave the Room" chooses it as one of four that vindicate him, the others being "Someone Puts a Pineapple Together" (1951), "Examination of the Hero in a Time of War" (1942), and "Credences of Summer" (1947).

Stevens was given to qualifying his affirmations, yet they do make things firm even in the minimal mode, as here in "A Postcard from the Volcano" (1936):

> Children picking up our bones
> Will never know that these were once
> As quick as foxes on the hill;
>
> And that in autumn, when the grapes
> Made sharp air sharper by their smell
> These had a being, breathing frost;
>
> And least will guess that with our bones
> We left much more, left what still is
> The look of things, left what we felt
>
> At what we saw. The spring clouds blow
> Above the shuttered mansion-house,
> Beyond our gate and the windy sky
>
> Cries out a literate despair.
> We knew for long the mansion's look
> And what we said of it became
>
> A part of what it is . . . Children,
> Still weaving budded aureoles,
> Will speak our speech and never know,
>
> Will say of the mansion that it seems
> As if he that lived there left behind
> A spirit storming in blank walls,
>
> A dirty house in a gutted world,
> A tatter of shadows peaked to white,
> Smeared with the gold of the opulent sun.

"The look of things" is left behind by each of the dying generations at their song. Children unknowingly will *see* what each generation added to sight. And though the poem labors to accept reductiveness, it concludes with "the opulent sun" as painter smearing the dirt and tatters with gold.

Sometimes it is best to catch Stevens when he is off-guard, as in his quasi-sonnet "Autumn Refrain" from *Ideas of Order* (1935–1936), where he writes, "The skreak and skritter of evening gone / And grackles gone and sorrows of the sun. . . ." American poets favor the hermit thrush or the wood dove or sea birds. Stevens, who never visited Europe, even England, ruefully addresses himself to the "Ode to a Nightingale" and to its birdsong he will never hear. There are poems by Stevens that might have delighted Keats, but I do not think he would have cared for this one.

John Keats was mischievous and might have loved, as I do, Stevens's comic masterpiece "Mrs. Alfred Uruguay" (1940):

So what said the others and the sun went down
And, in the brown blues of evening, the lady said,
In the donkey's ear, "I fear that elegance
Must struggle like the rest." She climbed until
The moonlight in her lap, mewing her velvet,
And her dress were one and she said, "I have said no
To everything, in order to get at myself.
I have wiped away moonlight like mud. Your innocent ear
And I, if I rode naked, are what remain."

The moonlight crumbled to degenerate forms,
While she approached the real, upon her mountain,
With lofty darkness. The donkey was there to ride,
To hold by the ear, even though it wished for a bell,
Wished faithfully for a falsifying bell.
Neither the moonlight could change it. And for her,
To be, regardless of velvet, could never be more
Than to be, she could never differently be,
Her no and no made yes impossible.

Who was it passed her there on a horse all will,
What figure of capable imagination?

Whose horse clattered on the road on which she rose,
As it descended, blind to her velvet and
The moonlight? Was it a rider intent on the sun,
A youth, a lover with phosphorescent hair,
Dressed poorly, arrogant of his streaming forces,
Lost in an integration of the martyrs' bones,
Rushing from what was real; and capable?

The villages slept as the capable man went down,
Time swished on the village clocks and dreams were alive,
The enormous gongs gave edges to their sounds,
As the rider, no chevalere and poorly dressed,
Impatient of the bells and midnight forms,
Rode over the picket rocks, rode down the road,
And, capable, created in his mind,
Eventual victor, out of the martyrs' bones,
The ultimate elegance: the imagined land.

Stevens is grandly comic when it suits him. Mrs. Alfred Uruguay could emerge from Edith Wharton. The fantastic name plays upon T. S. Eliot's J. Alfred Prufrock and on the capital city of Uruguay, Montevideo. The velvet-clad Mrs. Uruguay is climbing the mount of vision. She fears that elegance must suffer like the rest, but it is her poor donkey who suffers for her. Her quest is undertaken in her usual attire: a velvet evening gown. An authentic reductionist who has denied everything in order to find herself, she dazzles us with a great emphasis: "I have wiped away moonlight like mud." Riding naked is out of the question. And yet she may find the real "with lofty darkness." It will not matter. Her being is set.

The poem's second half gives us her heroic antithesis: the figure of the youth as virile poet or the incarnation of the poetic character. Like similar poets in William Collins and Samuel Taylor Coleridge, he is indeed a figure of capable imagination, marked by luminous hair as he rushes down a mountain away from the reductive real. Three times the youth is called capable, partly in its older meaning of taking and holding. He will win at last and create in his own mind what Stevens beautifully calls "the ultimate elegance: the imagined land."

That elegance achieved definitive clarification in *Notes toward a Supreme Fiction*, with its image of the man in "slouching pantaloons" who will "confect / The final elegance." The Chaplinesque figure is to be the *materia poetica* from which the ephebe, or potential poet, is to make a final elegance, but the making is modified by confecting, thus clarifying that the poetic enterprise must eschew consolation or sanctification. One must begin with putting forward what is plain. This tricky endeavor is at the center of the difficult, reductive poem "A Rabbit as King of the Ghosts" (1937), "In which everything is meant for you / And nothing need be explained."

Stevens summed up his characteristic poetic argument and imagistic interplay in the poem "Puella Parvula" (1949):

Every thread of summer is at last unwoven.
By one caterpillar is great Africa devoured,
And Gibraltar is dissolved like spit in the wind.

But over the wind, over the legends of its roaring,
The elephant on the roof and its elephantine blaring,
The bloody lion in the yard at night or ready to spring

From the clouds in the midst of trembling trees
Making a great gnashing, over the water wallows
Of a vacant sea declaiming with wide throat,

Over all these the mighty imagination triumphs
Like a trumpet, and says in this season of memory,
When the leaves fall like things mournful of the past,

Keep quiet in the heart, O wild bitch. O mind
Gone wild, be what he tells you to be: Puella.
Write pax across the window pane. And then

Be still. The *summarium in excelsis* begins . . .
Flame, sound, fury composed . . . Hear what he says,
The dauntless master, as he starts the human tale.

The two opening tercets are in the mode of *Notes toward a Supreme Fiction*, where elephant and lion attempt to impose a First Idea. The next two tercets are another Stevensian recapitulation of the "Ode to the West Wind." Full resonance is achieved in the last two, where Whitman's "real me" or "me myself" is addressed initially as "wild bitch" but then modulates to a little girl, the interior paramour, writing a secular "peace" even as the poet, dauntless master, overcomes the flame, sound, fury, of the auroras and begins anew our story.

And yet there are anxieties. That "vacant sea declaiming with wide throat" is the Whitmanian mother summoning her castaways home. And the theological language is retained, however secularized.

Though Stevens can seem—to some readers—a difficult poet, many of the demanding poems and passages clear up quickly enough with some deep study. The single exception is the extraordinary "The Owl in the Sarcophagus" (1947), an elegy for Henry Church, patron of the arts and Stevens's closest friend.

The first canto of the elegy bestows upon us a sublimity and a dark mythology indebted to Walt Whitman. "Two forms move among the dead," Stevens writes, sleep, peace and the mother, "the forms of dark desire." If this were Yeats or D. H. Lawrence these forms would be unsurprising. In Whitman they appear in the most mysterious poem of the 1855 first edition, untitled but eventually to be known as "The Sleepers": "Peace is always beautiful, / The myth of heaven indicates peace and night," Whitman writes, and then,

> I too pass from the night;
> I stay awhile away O night, but I return to you again and love you;
> Why should I be afraid to trust myself to you?
> I am not afraid . . . . I have been well brought forward by you;
> I love the rich running day, but I do not desert her in whom
>   I lay so long;
> I know not how I came of you, and I know not where I go
>   with you . . . . but I know I came well and shall go well.
>
> I will stop only a time with the night . . . . and rise betimes.
>
> I will duly pass the day O my mother and duly return to you;
> Not you will yield forth the dawn again more surely than you will
>   yield forth me again,
> Not the womb yields the babe in its time more surely than I shall
>   be yielded from you in my time.
>
> [ll. 195–204]

Stevens says that his three forms do not move in the element of time but in a realm where "reality is prodigy." That is very close to the realm of Walt Whitman's phantasmagoric sleep chasings.

The difference between Whitman and Stevens is that the image of the mother is ambivalent in Whitman and only rarely negative in Stevens. The fourfold trope of Night, Death, the Mother, and the Sea is at the center of Whitman. The threefold triad of Sleep, Peace, and the Mother wavers in Stevens, where the mother is the muse as she is for Keats.

"Peace" in Stevens as in Whitman retains a finer edge from its etymology in the Indo-European *pak- ("to fasten, stick, place"). It is a fastening or holding in place, thus making a covenant. Like Whitman, Stevens believes that our lives have made a covenant with our deaths. Peace-after-death takes a stance as watchman for that covenant.

In the syllable between living and dying, memory or the mother cries, "Keep you, keep you," where "keep" returns to its etymological meaning of "guard" or "watch."

Stevens was not a man who opened himself to anyone else. His only friend was Henry Church. They were the same age, both of them social traditionalists and both dedicated aesthetes. Except for George Santayana, Church is Stevens's principal emblem of the possibility that imaginative apprehension might bring us to the frontier of a transcendence.

There is an authentic shock in Stevens in regard to the sudden loss of Church. He writes in "The Owl in the Sarcophagus" (Section 2), "One day / A man walked living among the forms of thought." It is unclear whether the man walking is Stevens or Church. I tend to agree now with my former student Charles Berger that it is likelier to be Stevens, "Releasing an abysmal melody, / A meeting, an emerging in the light, / A dazzle of remembrance and of sight." "Dazzle" probably means to be overcome by intense light. The word's etymological meaning is "vanish." If dying releases the song of the abyss, it is also a reunion, a light breaking through, remembrance and sight transcendentalized to the point of disappearance.

III

There he saw well the foldings in the height
Of sleep, the whiteness folded into less,
Like many robings, as moving masses are,

As a moving mountain is, moving through day
And night, colored from distances, central
Where luminous agitations come to rest,

In an ever-changing, calmest unity . . .

. . .

       Sleep realized
Was the whiteness that is the ultimate intellect,
A diamond jubilance beyond the fire,

That gives its power to the wild-ringed eye.
Then he breathed deeply the deep atmosphere
Of sleep, the accomplished, the fulfilling air.

Elegies have a way of mixing up the poet's own apprehension of mortality with his protagonist's vista. Refined as Henry Church's sensibilities may have been, they are unlikely to have taken on the Stevensian colors of the imagination: robings, moving mountains, jubilance of the weather, fire imprisoned in diamonds.

IV

There peace, the godolphin and fellow, estranged, estranged,
Hewn in their middle as the beam of leaves,
The prince of shither-shade and tinsel lights,

Stood flourishing the world. The brilliant height
And hollow of him by its brilliance calmed,
Its brightness burned the way good solace seethes.

This was peace after death, the brother of sleep,
The inhuman brother so much like, so near,
Yet vested in a foreign absolute . . .

. . .

This is that figure stationed at our end,
Always, in brilliance, fatal, final, formed
Out of our lives to keep us in our death,

To watch us in the summer of Cyclops
Underground, a king as candle by our beds
In a robe that is our glory as he guards.

High peace, as Charles Berger emphasizes, seems an ambivalent figure. The godolphin, a highly bred Arabian racehorse, is evidently the mount ridden by peace. Though peace after death wavers, ultimately it is our guardian, formed by generations of poets' imaginings. Its brilliance emanates from good solace, a comforting that endures. Berger, however, is disturbed, with some justice, because peace has stolen our robe and glory. He therefore sees this equivocal peace as a kind of warder, to keep the dead in their place. Otherwise, like Odysseus and his mariners, they will attempt an exodus from the cave of Cyclops, hoping for a return home. Berger's central insight cuts deeply into the difficult matrix of the poem:

> Though Stevens can foresee continuity between earthly and higher vision, speech cannot follow beyond the fire. He is not the first to make this observation, but to envision the truth of the end-point oneself means experiencing it anew. So Stevens suffers the wounding force of the muse-mothers disappearance into "silence," the obsolescence of our only true begettings. . . . If we are to survive, Stevens seems to be saying at the end of the vision proper in "The Owl in the Sarcophagus" (the end of canto V), we will survive in the refining and self-extinguishing fire of ultimate intellect.
>
> [*Forms of Farewell* (1985)]

As Berger knows, that fire was Shelley's before it was Yeats's and Stevens's. It is the burning fountain from which we came and to which we thirst to return.

V

But she that says good-by losing in self
The sense of self, rosed out of prestiges
Of rose, stood tall in self not symbol, quick

And potent, an influence felt instead of seen.

. . .

          she moved

With a sad splendor, beyond artifice,
Impassioned by the knowledge that she had,
There on the edges of oblivion.

O exhalation, O fling without a sleeve
And motion outward, reddened and resolved
From sight, in the silence that follows her last word—

Stevens, throughout his poetry, developed in many guises the
figure he called the Interior Paramour. Muse, mother, memory: it is by
stance, movement, gesture that she communicates her inwardness,
her knowledge. Her last word is "good-by," and we pass into the silence
that follows it, accompanied by "death's own supremest images, /
The pure perfections of parental space." Stevens concludes, "It is a
child that sings itself to sleep, / The mind, among the creatures that
it makes, / The people those by which it lives and dies" (Section 6).

This astonishing coda is a single sentence culminating in what
always seems to me Stevens's most poignant image: a child asleep in its
own life. Now ninety, at the other end of existence, I could not sleep
last night though I attempted my almost endless silent recitation of poems, including "The Owl in the Sarcophagus." But it would not work.
I miserably went downstairs at midnight and slept in a chair until five.

Still, Stevens comforts me now. Child, mind, and people at their
best sing themselves to sleep. Our minds make images of all the
people we cared for, departed or still here. By them we live and by
them we will die.

The most complex influence upon the poem stems from Whitman's "When Lilacs Last in the Dooryard Bloom'd":

Then with the knowledge of death as walking one side of me,
And the thought of death close-walking the other side of me,

And I in the middle as with companions, and as holding the
    hands of companions,
I fled forth to the hiding receiving night that talks not,
Down to the shores of the water, the path by the swamp in the
    dimness,
To the solemn shadowy cedars and ghostly pines so still.

[ll. 120–125]

To walk between knowing death and thinking of it, which is closer, is to be between the mother and the generations stitched by the imagination. Whitman himself *is* high peace as he flees down to the shores of America. In the imaginative space between the elegiac Whitman and Stevens at elegy, the "Owl in the Sarcophagus" seeks its place.

John Hollander died at eighty-four in 2013. It is difficult for me to write these final words about the closest friend I ever had. I met John when we were both thirteen, but we did not become friends until the summer of 1956 in Cambridge, Massachusetts. For the next fifty-seven years we were brothers.

John was an astonishingly erudite scholar-critic of all the arts. He was also, at his best, a permanent poet, though now rather neglected. W. H. Auden was a strong influence on the early Hollander but yielded to the influx of Wallace Stevens, who changed John's poetry until the end.

Rereading Hollander I am most moved by the sequence of 169 quasi-sonnets, thirteen lines each, titled *Powers of Thirteen* (1983). Arbitrarily I begin with 65:

Heroic Love danced on our stage awhile, in the dark
Of the days that shone and shook with Heroic Battle.
But that act was over by the time Sir John Failstiff mocked
Love: "Sock it to me—that's what half-mooning's all about,"
He chortled, brandishing a dirty sock. Even then
The slack-jawed face appealed to the bumpkin in the hay
Or in the back seat of the car, its wordless message
Flashed out "Have me, I'm hopeless" or blinked its "Now now
    now."
Now the dance is Love for All, love well lost for the world,

The risks taken are those of intimacy; love fell
A casualty of the unceremonial,
Laughed at by the wind in our heckling, red leaves, themselves
Gone the way of the whirled, fallen to mere easiness.

                                                              The Lovers

Hollander's erotic argument is sinuous, so much so that the reader
must struggle, phrase by phrase, to decipher the dark wit offered. One
can begin with Sir John Falstaff, presented as Failstiff or impotent
(I protested to John that while this was good unclean fun, it was
hardly fair to my hero). But male sexual failure rendered as hilarity
is crucial here. All for love, the Dryden emasculation of Shakespeare's *Antony and Cleopatra*, reduces to love for all. In his "A Prayer
for My Daughter" (1919), W. B. Yeats rhetorically asked:

How but in custom and in ceremony
Are innocence and beauty born?

                                                              [ll. 77–78]

The reader can wonder to what extent Hollander disagrees with
Yeats:

The risks taken are those of intimacy; love fell
A casualty of the unceremonial,

In "The Fall," *Powers of Thirteen*'s poem 66, Romulus, son of
Mars who founded Rome and destroyed his brother Remus, is the
master of "Arch / ceremonies, repositories of injustice." The paragon of erotic justice, Rosalind in *As You Like It*, charmingly says to
Celia, "From henceforth I will, coz, and devise sports. Let me
see—what think you of falling in love?" (Act 1, Scene 2). I recall an
exchange between John and me in which I wondered aloud at the
trope of "falling," and he replied: "Harold, it could hardly be *rising*
in love."

The two concluding stanzas of the sequence's last thirteener play
upon one of Hollander's favorite works: James Thurber's *The Thirteen Clocks* (1950). Thurber's fantasy centers upon the wicked duke
of Coffin Castle, an edifice freezing cold so that all its clocks are

frozen at ten of five. The duke has a superb niece (she is not in fact related to him), Saralinda. Her suitors are butchered one by one, but just before she turns twenty-one, the heroic Prince Zorn arrives disguised as a wandering minstrel named Xingu. A benign and mysterious creature called Golux offers to assist Zorn in securing the unfortunate princess.

The duke imposes an ordeal upon Zorn if he wishes to marry Saralinda. In just ninety-nine hours the prince must return with one thousand jewels and deliver them as all thirteen frozen clocks strike five.

The mission is accomplished when the passionate Saralinda somehow warms up the clocks. And all ends happily as it should, except for the duke.

Here is the ending of *Powers of Thirteen:*

This black gap between days is no place for us: should you
Creep into my bed then you would find me shuddering
As at the opening of a secret whose shadowed
Power unbroken lay in coupling day unto day.

I asked Hollander if Thurber had inspired *Powers of Thirteen*. He was uncharacteristically evasive.

Something altogether his own began to emerge in Hollander's *Powers of Thirteen*. To me, the apotheosis of that voice, still modified by Wallace Stevens, can be heard in what seems to me John's finest poem, "A Shadow of a Great Rock in a Weary Land" (2009). The title is from an astonishing passage Hollander cites: "And a man shall be as an hiding place from the wind, and a covert from the tempest; as rivers of water in a dry place, as the shadow of a great rock in a weary land" (Isaiah [KJV] 32:2).

The technical splendor of Hollander's quatrains, with Wilfred Owen's consonance or slant rhyme and closing perfect rhyme, accurately follows Owen's mode of the second slant rhyme pitched lower in vowel sound than the first.

Hollander's triumph here is in tone. It catches the United States, its readership, its encroachment of popular culture and divisive politics upon the academies, its descent into the inauthentic, its "political correctness" of 1999, the year of publication. Twenty years later, seven years after the poet's death, I hear the diminished music of our cognitive lapses and spiritual waverings more clearly than before.

In 1963, a third of a century before Hollander's poem, James Baldwin published his essay *The Fire Next Time*. At a dinner given for him by my friend R. W. B Lewis, I asked Baldwin about the title. He kindly corrected my ignorance by citing the song "Mary Don't You Weep":

> God gave Noah the rainbow sign
> "No more water but fire next time"
> Pharaoh's army got drownded
> O Mary don't you weep

John Hollander was at that dinner, which could be the seed of this poem of negative sublimity. Shadow and stone were linked in Hollander's imagination. This received a last flowering in the posthumously published monograph *The Substance of Shadow: A Darkening Trope in Poetic History*, edited by Kenneth Gross (2016).

The crux of Hollander's lament is one poignant line: "What can we still do well?" I ask myself that every day, and since I begin teaching the academic year 2019–2020 tomorrow, the question will be a touch more urgent.

A worn-out voice at eighty-nine, I will do as well as I can. I wasted time denouncing what I called the School of Resentment, and now time wastes me. Hollander said it better anyway in "A Shadow of a Great Rock in a Weary Land":

> Bewail with an outraged heart
> Infringements upon what
> Is our Divine Right Not
> To Have Our Feelings Hurt?
>
> Not even that—the airs
> And choruses of complaint
> Are poorly intoned, and faint:
> They fall on our own deaf ears.

Each two-quatrain pairing now commences with "not even that." Acedia, "the malady of monks," has its classical statement in

Dante's *Inferno*, Canto 7, ll. 121–124: "We sullen were / In the sweet air, by which the sun is gladdened, / Bearing within our-selves the sluggish reek; / Now we are sullen in this sable mire" (Longfellow translation).

If in any world to come, John and I meet again, I hope to tell him my admiration for the closing lines of his "Shadow of a Great Rock":

> That is the fire this time.
>
> The fire that brings to a boil
> A terror beyond all fears,
> A broth of soured tears
> Fills the horizon's bowl,
>
> Loud in such darkness, whether
> Soon to be burnt or drowned,
> Our dimmed noise and unsound
> Light will come together.

Negativity is a hard mode for metaphor. Here it persuades me. I fall back on the elegy by Catullus for his brother:

> Multas per gentes et multa per aequora Vectus
>   Advenio has miseras, frater, ad inferias,
> Ut te postremo donarem munere mortis
>   Et mutam nequiguam adloquerer cinerem,
> Quandoquidem fortuna mihi tete abstulit ipsum,
>   Heu miser indigne frater adempte mihi.
> Nunc tamen interea haec, prisco quae more parentum
>   Tradita sunt tristi munere ad inferias,
> Accipe fraterno multum mananta fletu
>   Atque in perpetuum, frater, ave atque vale.

Through many nations and through many seas borne, I come, brother, for these sad funeral rites, that I may give the last gifts to the dead, and may vainly speak to your silent ashes, since fortune has taken yourself away from me. Ah, poor brother, undeservedly snatched from me. But now receive these gifts, which have been handed down in the ancient

manner of ancestors, the sad gifts to the grave, drenched with
a brother's tears, and for ever, brother, hail and farewell.
                    [Translated by Leonard Smithers]

John loved this brief elegy by Catullus and liked to recite it to
me. He and I shared an admiration for Tennyson's amalgam of these
lines and another poem by Catullus.

Row us out from Desenzano, to your Sirmione row!
So they row'd, and there we landed—"O venusta Sirmio"
There to me through all the groves of olive in the summer glow,
There beneath the Roman ruin where the purple flowers grow,
Came that "Ave atque Vale" of the Poet's hopeless woe,
Tenderest of Roman poets nineteen-hundred years ago,
"Frater Ave atque Vale"—as we wandered to and fro
Gazing at the Lydian laughter of the Garda Lake below
        Sweet Catullus's all-but-island, olive-silvery Sirmio!
                    ["'Frater Ave Atque Vale'" (1883)]

Not being a poet, I cannot elegize John Hollander, and am glad
that Catullus and Tennyson provide my farewell to my brother.

In the presence of dying, nothing is stable. My close friend Holly
Stevens, the poet's only child, fiercely denied to me the reports that
her father converted to Roman Catholicism on his deathbed. In the
moment of dying I doubtless will return to the Orthodox Judaism
of my youth and will repeat the appropriate Hebrew prayers silently
to myself if I can no longer speak. I really cannot think of Wallace
Stevens, harmonious skeptic, assuming the guise of a Christian. It
would repudiate a lifetime's magnificence of accomplishment in
American poetry.

It is a delicate matter for me to adjudicate the vexed matter of
Stevens's transcendentalism. In the lucid late poem "A Clear Day and
No Memories" (1955), he writes,

Today the air is clear of everything.
It has no knowledge except of nothingness
And it flows over us without meanings,
As if none of us had ever been here before

And are not now: in this shallow spectacle,
This invisible activity, this sense.

"Shallow" is the troublesome word there. I wonder if Stevens, always alive to the history of words, intimated a suggestion of its origin, "shoal." I write this on Monday, April 1, in midafternoon of a very clear but windy day in New Haven. A medical visit for very minor surgery lasted from noon to two thirty. I stare outside and take the poem into myself. I think too much about the beloved dead and am happy to join Stevens in an air clear of everything. It would cleanse my spirit if it flowed over me without knowledge, without meanings. Perhaps it would have been good not to have been here before or to be absent now. The spectacle is of moving young people. One negates this visual activity and seeks an evasion of sense.

This mode of negative transcendence is the veritable Stevens. I have been reading him for more than three-quarters of a century, and now it scarcely seems like reading anymore. I am now perpetually on oxygen yet still have the sensation that I breathe the clear air of Stevens.

In the late brief intricate poem "A Child Asleep in Its Own Life" (1954), we are asked to so mix origin and end as to make us doubt the difference:

Among the old men that you know,
There is one, unnamed, that broods
On all the rest, in heavy thought.

They are nothing, except in the universe
Of that single mind. He regards them
Outwardly and knows them inwardly,

The sole emperor of what they are,
Distant, yet close enough to wake
The chords above your bed to-night.

The unnamed old man need not be Stevens but may as well be. Or, like the emperor of ice cream, he may be death. The child sleeps in his own life as the old cannot. What shall we make of the awakening of the chords? They may indicate the necessity of mortality but happily far away from the child.

At the other side of life, Stevens achieved another poetic triumph in his pre-elegy for George Santayana, "To an Old Philosopher in Rome." Even as Shelley chanted his own threnody in *Adonais*, so Stevens finds his own farewell in saluting a mentor. George Santayana, raised a Roman Catholic, made himself into a skeptic yet sought the company of a convent of Roman nuns as a place to die in. During his Harvard years, Stevens did not study with Santayana, but they became friends and engaged in a sonnet competition.

Here is the culmination in these nobly measured stanzas: Santayana's candle joins a "hovering excellence" and becomes "part only of that which / Fire is the symbol: the celestial possible." The Shelleyan fire for which all thirst is evaded in the hope of the celestial possible. Shelley can be an insidious influence, streaming in where least expected. Elizabeth Bishop has a lovely, brief early essay that celebrates Shelley:

> This summer I spent on Cape Cod surrounded by picturesque, shadow-haunted groves of scrub pine, desolate, sunbrilliant dunes, and bays whose intense blueness nubs the senses to anything but color. Such things are extremely conducive to the reading of poetry and, at first, I feasted upon all sorts of morsels from various anthologies, but finally ended up by devoting all of my reading time to Shelley. . . .
>
> I remember sailing late one evening this summer to an island far out in the bay. It was a bleak, deserted place— nothing but sand and gulls. We, the sailors of the camp I attended, planned to camp overnight there. During all the long sail out we read Shelley from a water-stained, paperbound copy. It was a cold, star-sharp night and I slept with the music of his lines echoing through my brain. Early in the morning we sat up to watch the sun rise. It began with faint, rosy figures reaching up to the east, and at last flamed a burning gold that glimmered across the water and stained the dunes and flying gulls with gilt. It seemed to me then that Shelley was a spirit of the sunrise—one of his own creatures of whom he says:

See where the child of Heaven with winged feet,
Runs down the slanted sunlight of the dawn.
                    ["In Appreciation of Shelley's Poems" (1927)]

In Stevens's late poem "The Course of a Particular," "The Ode to the West Wind" sweeps through, bestowing transcendence that cannot be denied. "Today the leaves cry, hanging on branches swept by wind," Stevens begins.

I have written several commentaries on this apotheosis of evasion. To avoid repetition, I will center here on the presence/absence of Shelley's kinetic "Ode." In my only conversation with Stevens we talked about Shelley. I regret I did not ask whether in the "Ode" the leaves cry out. Shyness confronting genial splendor could not manage it. I think though that he would have answered yes.

The word "cry" occurs eight times in this short poem. Leaves cry out three times. It is and is not the cry of the human. Leaves that do not transcend themselves do not cry out. At eighty-nine I feel the force of "One feels the life of that which gives life as it is." The final finding of the ear precedes death.

Perhaps there is an Elysium of great poets. One hardly envisions Wallace Stevens and Percy Bysshe Shelley becoming friendly shades. I assume personality somehow survives in the paradise of poets. Shelley, most acute of readers, might be charmed and amused by "The Course of a Particular."

The fiction of the leaves stems from Homer and Isaiah and winds its way through much of Western poetry, from Virgil through Dante to Milton to Shelley to Whitman to Stevens. It is an all but universal trope for mortality. But Shelley's "Ode" argues resurrection, a new birth. There is a final mystery in "The Course of a Particular." I cannot be certain whether the final finding of the ear needs to be read reductively.

Affirmation returns in the late lyric "The Planet on the Table" (1953), where Stevens writes, "Ariel was glad he had written his poems," the "makings of his self" and "no less makings of the sun."

The planet on the table is the lifelong labor of the poet Stevens. Following Shelley's love lyrics to Jane Williams, the poet assumes the identity of Ariel. In all his poetry—early, middle, late—Stevens identifies Walt Whitman with the sun. Again and again Stevens the poet is a man of sun. The lion of poetry sleeps in the sun. It could kill a man.

Yet always there is another Stevens. He is the scholar of one candle, as here in the late poem "A Quiet Normal Life" (1952): "There was no fury in transcendent forms. / But his actual candle blazed with artifice."

Stevens can be most poignant when he defends against his own transcendental drive. The snow man, old and solitary, satirizes himself in "A Quiet Normal Life," with its babbling crickets. Forms of beyond blaze in fury despite his denial, and his work as artificer is another blazon.

One of my habitual night pieces kept reciting itself during an insomniac interlude yesterday, "A Discovery of Thought" (1950):

> At the antipodes of poetry, dark winter,
> When the trees glitter with that which despoils them,
> Daylight evaporates, like a sound one hears in sickness.
>
> One is a child again. The gold beards of waterfalls
> Are dissolved as in an infancy of blue snow.
> It is an arbor against the wind, a pit in the mist,
>
> A trinkling in the parentage of the north,
> The cricket of summer forming itself out of ice.
> And always at this antipodes, of leaden loaves
>
> Held in the hands of blue men that are lead within,
> One thinks that it could be that the first word spoken,
> The desire for speech and meaning gallantly fulfilled,
>
> The gathering of the imbecile against his motes
> And the wry antipodes whirled round the world away—
> One thinks, when the houses of New England catch the first
>   sun,
>
> The first word would be of the susceptible being arrived,
> The immaculate disclosure of the secret no more
>   obscured.
> The sprawling of winter might suddenly stand erect,

Pronouncing its new life and ours, not autumn's prodigal returned,
But an antipodal, far-fetched creature, worthy of birth,
The true tone of the metal of winter in what it says:

The accent of deviation in the living thing
That is its life preserved, the effort to be born
Surviving being born, the event of life.

I have written a close commentary upon this in a book, *Wallace
Stevens: The Poems of Our Climate*. To avoid any repetition, even
in a finer tone, I will meditate here in something of the spirit of
Stevens.

Frequently after a Connecticut ice storm I think of the line:
"When the trees glitter with that which despoils them." That is one
of the discoveries of thought. Summer's cricket alludes to Keats's
sonnet "On the Grasshopper and Cricket" and thus shares in Keats's
affirmation: "The poetry of earth is never dead." As "A Discovery
of Thought" concludes, winter finds its true tone in the miracle of a
new life, a susceptibility or openness that may leap over spring and
become one of the credences of summer.

Stevens had a particular fondness for the sequence "Credences
of Summer." For once his Keatsian impulse to celebrate a natural
splendor was almost allowed to prevail. "The roses are heavy with a
weight / Of fragrance and the mind lays by its trouble," he writes in
"Credences," but then adds, "Now the mind lays by its trouble and
considers. / The fidgets of remembrance come to this" (Section 1).

The poet is sixty-eight and again says farewell to desire. Samuel
Beckett might have appreciated "the fidgets of remembrance." He
once anonymously reviewed Rilke (for the *Criterion* in 1934) and
said: "Such a turmoil of self-deception and naïf discontent gains
nothing in dignity from that prime article of the Rilkean faith, which
provides for the interchangeability of Rilke and God. He has the
fidgets, a disorder which may very well give rise, as it did with Rilke
on occasion, to poetry of a high order. But why call the fidgets God,
Ego, Orpheus and the rest?"

The question of Stevens's tone in "Credences of Summer" is difficult to resolve. I like best the formulation of my late friend Isabel
MacCaffrey:

Stevens has, therefore, established conditions of maximum difficulty in which to assert the imagination's power. Winter, "the nothing that is," cannot satisfy us for long, however scrupulously we submit to it; its perfect ineloquence invites the imagination's additions. But summer offers a rival rhetoric; its richness "must comfort the heart's core," its eloquence silences our speech.

That has true balance. Stevens aspires towards balance in the mode of Keats, but negative capability is an endowment, and not the object of quest. Keats and Stevens seem to me the two post-enlightenment poets easiest to assimilate to Freud's idea of reality-testing. Their mutual resistance to transcendental temptings steadies the reader. They live in a physical world in which evil, in or out of the self, is the simple result of being a natural woman or natural man. We live in a place that is not our own, and much more, not ourselves. Stevens adds: "And hard it is in spite of blazoned days."

["The Other Side of Silence: 'Credences of Summer' as an Example" (1969)]

"Let's see the very thing and nothing else," Stevens writes in Section 2 of "Credences," and a few lines later,

> fill the foliage with arrested peace,
> Joy of such permanence, right ignorance
> Of change still possible. Exile desire
> For what is not. This is the barrenness
> Of the fertile thing that can attain no more.

"Barrenness" is remarkably placed. The thing in itself is oxymoronic, fecund with emptiness. There is a center of arrested peace. Will it not dissolve?

In Section 3 of "Credences" Stevens invokes

> a tower more precious than the view beyond,
> A point of survey squatting like a throne,
> Axis of everything, green's apogee

And happiest folk-land, mostly marriage-hymns.
It is the mountain on which the tower stands,
It is the final mountain. Here the sun,
Sleepless, inhales his proper air, and rests.
This is the refuge that the end creates.
It is the old man standing on the tower,
Who reads no book. His ruddy ancientness
Absorbs the ruddy summer and is appeased,
By an understanding that fulfils his age,
By a feeling capable of nothing more.

Stevens had little regard for Eliot or Pound, and considerable affection for William Carlos Williams and Marianne Moore. He maintained mutual respect with Robert Frost, but it was a cool friendship. W. B. Yeats unsettled Stevens. Here the old man on the tower might appear to be Yeats, except that he reads no book. Also, this figure is more Shelleyan or even Keatsian in its sense of fulfillment.

Keats is much on Stevens's mind in the playful and powerful "Extracts from Addresses to the Academy of Fine Ideas." In Section 2 of "Extracts," the slightly mad academician invokes John Keats as the Secretary for Porcelain, doubtless remembering the Grecian Urn. "It is good death / That puts an end to evil death and dies," Stevens writes.

Evil death is out of phase; good death is timely. "Evil" has no tinge of moral judgment but again refers to the pain and suffering we experience in the world that only for a brief moment can be our own.

The classic statement of Keatsian humanism in Stevens is the final section of his wonderfully polemical "Esthétique du Mal":

XV
The greatest poverty is *not* to live
In a physical world, to feel that one's desire
Is too *difficult* to tell from despair. Perhaps,
After death, the non-physical people, in paradise,
Itself non-physical, may, by chance, observe
The green corn *gleaming* and experience
The minor of what we feel. The adventurer

In humanity has not conceived of a race
Completely physical in a physical world.
The green corn *gleams* and the metaphysicals
Lie sprawling in majors of the August heat,
The rotund emotions, paradise unknown.

This is the thesis *scrivened* in delight,
The reverberating psalm, the right chorale.
One might have thought of sight, but who *could* think
Of what it sees, for all the ill it sees?
Speech found the ear, for all the evil sound,
But the *dark italics* it could not propound.
And out of what one sees and hears and out
Of what one feels, who *could* have thought to make
So many selves, so many *sensuous* worlds
As if the air, the mid-day air, was swarming
With the metaphysical changes that occur,
Merely in living as and where we live.

The italics are mine and suggest the emphases I want when chanting the poem aloud. Surging into the optative mood, Stevens founds
his hope upon the minute particulars that make up what must change
to flesh out a metaphysics that can make space for natural thrivers.

In Section 4 of "Credences of Summer," Stevens describes Oley,
"A land too ripe for enigmas, too serene." Here Stevens is at his happiest. He grew up just ten miles from the Oley Valley, which centered upon the town of Oley. The "clairvoyant eye," mentioned here,
seems ambiguous. It ought to mean "seeing within surfaces" or even
"prophecy," but Stevens probably intends the etymological sense of
"seeing clearly." Oley has become what the Sufis called Hurqalya,
which Henry Corbin called "the earth of visions." It is an intermediate phase between our subject-object relationships and a restored
Pleroma, for Christians the harmony of heaven but for Gnostics the
world before the creation-fall.

Here is Section 5 of "Credences":

One day enriches a year. One woman makes
The rest look down. One man becomes a race,
Lofty like him, like him perpetual.

Or do the other days enrich the one?
And is the queen humble as she seems to be,
The charitable majesty of her whole kin?
The bristling soldier, weather-foxed, who looms
In the sunshine is a filial form and one
Of the land's children, easily born, its flesh,
Not fustian. The more than casual blue

Contains the year and other years and hymns
And people, without souvenir. The day
Enriches the year, not as embellishment.
Stripped of remembrance, it displays its strength—
The youth, the vital son, the heroic power.

Despite the self-questionings, veteran readers of Stevens will hear in this the gradually accumulating ecstasy of celebration. The day of epiphany surges until it enriches the year and then transmutes into the figure of the youth as virile poet, heroic power moving from poverty (imaginative need) into the only wealth, which is life.

In Section 6 of "Credences" Stevens writes, "The rock cannot be broken. It is the truth," and again, "It is the rock of summer, the extreme . . ." Stevens is so deeply interconnected that you need to be very limber in moving between his poems. His great image of the rock is elaborated in the major poem of that title, published as the centerpiece of a section called "The Rock" in his *Collected Poems* of 1954. Stevens, approaching seventy-five, thinks back to when he was a five-year-old in the house of his mother: "Absurd. The words spoken / Were not and are not. It is not to be believed."

I once wrote that "Absurd" and "It is not to be believed" are to be uttered in an incredulous tone. More than ever it seems to me a necessity in reading late Stevens to accommodate his tonal metamorphoses, as here, in Section 1 of "The Rock":

The meeting at noon at the edge of the field seems like

An invention, an embrace between one desperate clod
And another in a fantastic consciousness,
In a queer assertion of humanity:

A theorem proposed between the two—
Two figures in a nature of the sun,
In the sun's design of its own happiness,

As if nothingness contained a métier,
A vital assumption, an impermanence
In its permanent cold, an illusion so desired

That the green leaves came and covered the high rock,
That the lilacs came and bloomed, like a blindness cleaned,
Exclaiming bright sight, as it was satisfied,

In a birth of sight. The blooming and the musk
Were being alive, an incessant being alive,
A particular being, that gross universe.

The tone of irreality and disbelief, in reference to the first rendezvous between Elsie Moll and Wallace Stevens, is transformed a few lines later into "an illusion so desired," so deeply desired that its illusive or fictive nature is dispelled by the accents of ecstasy. Walt Whitman's lilacs, his central image of voice, the tally of his days and nights, bloom and with the green leaves change the high rock into a being alive.

During the many years of my close friendship with Holly Stevens, she brooded aloud frequently about her parents' marriage. It was a strange choice on the part of Wallace Stevens. A tall, broad man, rather heavy, he was twice Elsie's weight, seven years her senior, and she was twenty-three when they married.

Holly insisted that she was conceived on a Caribbean cruise Stevens and Elsie took. I found it a little incredible that Holly also insisted, quite fiercely and yet calmly, that this was the only complete consummation of the marriage. All things are possible. Stevens was superbly sane and self-contained. Elsie's mental health was precarious. I must add, against my friend Paul Mariani, that Holly insisted all accounts of a deathbed conversion to Roman Catholicism by her father were invidious and mistaken. Stevens lived and died an Epicurean hedonist and humanist, in the tradition of Walter Pater and Oscar Wilde. Here is Section 2 of "The Rock":

It is not enough to cover the rock with leaves.
We must be cured of it by a cure of the ground
Or a cure of ourselves, that is equal to a cure

Of the ground, a cure beyond forgetfulness.
And yet the leaves, if they broke into bud,
If they broke into bloom, if they bore fruit,

And if we ate the incipient colorings
Of their fresh culls might be a cure of the ground.
The fiction of the leaves is the icon

Of the poem, the figuration of blessedness,
And the icon is the man.

Since my childhood, this meditation has sustained my own solitary broodings. The fiction of the leaves begins with Homer and
Tanakh and may have concluded with Wallace Stevens. There is an
elaborate account of it in my brief book *The Breaking of the Vessels*
(1982). I have returned to it several times earlier in the present book
because poets have played upon this fiction in order to take arms
against a sea of troubles. When autumnal leaves are troped as possible human vanishings, that fiction has proved so strong it seems
universal: "The fiction of the leaves is the icon / Of the poem, the
figuration of blessedness, / And the icon is the man."

Remove "icon" from its Eastern Orthodox Christian context
and you can achieve a secular equivalent in the poem as a figuration
of the blessedness of more life, a man's life becoming more like a
poem.

What is it to seek a cure of the ground? Taking care of the
ground is now rightly an obsessive concern. But Stevens is not an
ecologist. He secularizes the Christian cure of souls. Had Wallace
Stevens and Walter Whitman Jr. ever met, it would have been a fi-
asco. And yet Stevens, despite his surfaces, is the most Whitmanian
of poets.

One reason this has been hard to see is that Whitman, for Ste-
vens, is only secondarily the celebratory chanter of *Song of Myself.*
The elegiac Whitman, of "Out of the Cradle Endlessly Rocking" and
"When Lilacs Last in the Dooryard Bloom'd," impacted as deeply on

Stevens as he did on Henry James, once James got over "that little atrocity"—as he called it—his review of *Drum-Taps* in 1865.

Henry James, like Edith Wharton and Emerson before them, found in Whitman what must be found: American poetry at its most original, most universal, most influential. Wallace Stevens, I think, was always rather startled and unsettled when his crucial poems were somewhat overdetermined by Whitman, more than by Keats or Wordsworth.

In Section 3 of "The Rock," Stevens chants,

The rock is the gray particular of man's life,
The stone from which he rises, up-and-ho,
The step to the bleaker depths of his descents . . .

The rock is the stem particular of the air,
The mirror of the planets, one by one,
But through man's eye, their silent rhapsodist,

Turquoise the rock, at odious evening bright
With redness that sticks fast to evil dreams;
The difficult rightness of half-risen day.

The rock is the habitation of the whole,
Its strength and measure, that which is near, point A
In a perspective that begins again

At B: the origin of the mango's rind.
It is the rock where tranquil must adduce
Its tranquil self, the main of things, the mind,

The starting point of the human and the end,
That in which space itself is contained, the gate
To the enclosure, day, the things illumined

By day, night and that which night illumines,
Night and its midnight-minting fragrances,
Night's hymn of the rock, as in a vivid sleep.

The favorite time of day for Wallace Stevens was first light, but before the sun had raised itself above the horizon. He speaks of this in his prose but also here in that precise line: "The difficult rightness of half-risen day."

In "The Man with the Blue Guitar" (Section 5), he had written, "There are no shadows in our sun," catching the same moment of day. Can that moment be construed as "the gate / To the enclosure, day"?

Visionary optics in Stevens can be confusing. Here they blend in "the origin of the mango's rind," mango a favorite fruit of the Hartford seer, rind being distraction. The final part of "The Rock" continues to make me restless. If the rock is the reductive gray particular of man's life, what kind of hymns of the night can it inspire? Sleep, however vivid, remains sleep unless night's hymn is composed by Walt Whitman, a magnificence already achieved in "The Sleepers":

> I stand in the dark with drooping eyes by the worst-suffering
>   and the most restless,
> I pass my hands soothingly to and fro a few inches from them,
> The restless sink in their beds, they fitfully sleep.
>
> Now I pierce the darkness, new beings appear,
> The earth recedes from me into the night,
> I saw that it was beautiful, and I see that what is not the earth
>   is beautiful.
>
> I go from bedside to bedside, I sleep close with the other
>   sleepers each in turn,
> I dream in my dream all the dreams of the other dreamers,
> And I become the other dreamers.
>
> I am a dance—play up there! the fit is whirling me fast!
>
> I am the ever-laughing—it is new moon and twilight,
> I see the hiding of douceurs, I see nimble ghosts whichever
>   way I look,
> Cache and cache again deep in the ground and sea, and where
>   it is neither ground nor sea.

This is from the untitled text of 1855, where its first line is "I wander all night in my vision." Note that Walt is not *at* a dance; he *is* the dance. "Douceurs" could be bribes or literal sweeteners. I think, though, that in Whitman it has erotic meaning. Since he becomes the other dreamers as well as their dreams, eros is relevant. Those ghosts are as nimble as Yeats's nymphs and satyrs, copulating in the foam.

Stevens's "The Rock" cannot compete with "The Sleepers," as Stevens knew. Like Paul Valéry in regard to Stéphane Mallarmé or Mallarmé confronting Victor Hugo, the point is to do what the forerunner had not done: to find a new way that will suffice.

"The Rock" has marvelous epiphanies but finishes less strongly. "Credences of Summer," sometimes uneven, gathers strength in its later cantos. The enterprise of "Credences of Summer" is the difficulty of singing in face of the object. Stevens learns that Wordsworthian truth but in his own manner. Presumably the proclamation is the poem demonstrating the world is larger in summer.

A trumpet cries in Section 8 of "Credences." Trumpets in Stevens tend to go back to the "Ode to the West Wind." But here the cry as clarion does not awaken a sleeping earth. In Section 9, Stevens writes, "The gardener's cat is dead, the gardener gone / And last year's garden grows salacious weeds."

This is the final reddening before celebration. Those "salacious weeds" are a riposte to the calamus or sweet-flag of Walt Whitman, though scarcely justified. In his final section, 10, Stevens pictures the "personae of summer":

> roseate characters,
> Free, for a moment, from malice and sudden cry,
> Complete in a completed scene, speaking
> Their parts as in a youthful happiness.

That total contentment modifies itself even as it is spoken. Youthful happiness is a precarious condition in high literature. It must change. Age, sadness, alienation, unsolved puzzles of being, cannot be contained complete in any completed scene. Stevens holds on to celebration, but on the border of a warning cry.

Much earlier, in *Ideas of Order*, Stevens included a strong admonitory poem, "How to Live. What to Do." It fascinates me and I wonder why he left it out of his *Collected Poems*. Sometimes it seems odd to me that after two-thirds of a century reading Stevens, I find myself repeating a poem I took too much for granted. Here is the first part, "All the Preludes to Felicity," of "The Pure Good of Theory," a four-part meditation in *Transport to Summer* (1945):

It is time that beats in the breast and it is time
That batters against the mind, silent and proud,
The mind that knows it is destroyed by time.

Time is a horse that runs in the heart, a horse
Without a rider on a road at night.
The mind sits listening and hears it pass.

It is someone walking rapidly in the street.
The reader by the window has finished his book
And tells the hour by the lateness of the sounds.

Even breathing is the beating of time, in kind:
A retardation of its battering,
A horse grotesquely taut, a walker like

A shadow in mid-earth . . . If we propose
A large-sculptured, platonic person, free from time,
And imagine for him the speech he cannot speak,

A form, then, protected from the battering, may
Mature: A capable being may replace
Dark horse and walker walking rapidly.

Felicity, ah! Time is the hooded enemy,
The inimical music, the enchantered space
In which the enchanted preludes have their place.

Stevens, a master of the ineluctable, has the unwisdom to battle time. In these twenty-one lines the word "time" beats seven times, an inward refrain like "vigil" in Whitman's *Drum-Taps* poem. Enchanted preludes are clear enough, but what does it mean to call space "enchantered"? Possibly Stevens is treating French and English as a single language so that space is bewitched. His poem proposes that a platonic person, invulnerable to time's battering, can mature into a figure of capable imagination.

Memory after ninety years is capricious; poems move on the horizons of my mind flickering. Today it is another late poem by Stevens, "The Dove in Spring" (1954), in which the dove makes "this
howling at one's ear, too far / For daylight and too near for sleep."
In the poetry of Stevens, the dove is the emblem of a male desire
that has outlived male potency.

There is a late experimental longish poem by Stevens: "The Sail
of Ulysses" (1954). It is spoken by a kind of American Transcendentalist Ulysses, more Emersonian than the long sequence of
transformations of Homer's Odysseus. Its Canto 5 intrigues my
meditations in my eighty-ninth year, with its promise that "we shall
have gone beyond the symbols" to "the true legend, / Like glitter
ascended into fire." There is a noble aggressivity in this declaration.

The final glory of Wallace Stevens was his death poem "Of Mere
Being" (1955). Here a "gold-feathered bird" sings in "the palm at the
end of the mind," which "stands on the edge of space." Stevens had
considerable and varied knowledge of many traditions. The palm
tree was almost sacred to him, though he might have demurred at
that notion. My favorite instance is his "Nomad Exquisite" (1923):

> As the immense dew of Florida
> Brings forth
> The big-finned palm
> And green vine angering for life,
>
> As the immense dew of Florida
> Brings forth hymn and hymn
> From the beholder,
> Beholding all these green sides
> And gold sides of green sides,
>
> And blessed mornings,
> Meet for the eye of the young alligator,
> And lightning colors
> So, in me, come flinging
> Forms, flames, and the flakes of flames.

Paul Valéry, in his poem "Palme" (1922), concludes by invoking
the tree as the image of a mind in meditation enlarged by its own
spiritual gifts:

Pareille à celui qui pense
Et dont l'âme se dispense
À s'accroître de ses dons!

[ll. 97–99]

William Blake in *Jerusalem* 23 locates the palm tree "upon the edge of Beulah," thus transforming an image of the entrance of Jesus into Jerusalem so that it stands at the edge of the abyss, where the dead souls are caught. I once thought that Stevens's "Of Mere Being" is a deliberate rival to Yeats's vision of a metal bird in his Byzantium, but that no longer persuades me.

"Mere" in the title plays upon the archaic meaning of "pure" and on the root that means "flickering." The "foreign song" plays upon the Latin word for "out of doors." Its root meaning is "doorway." If the bird is a phoenix, as I think it is, then the doorway opens to what is beyond the mind, perhaps transcending death. What matters is that the bird *sings*. The dying poet observes that its feathers *shine*. Stevens is among the happy because there is still weather for him and an intermission of renewed sun in the fire of the phoenix.

A mischievous note is sounded in "The bird's fire-fangled feathers dangle down," where the archaic "fangled" for "fashioned" is rhymed against the insouciant "dangled down."

Some years back I edited an anthology with commentary called *Till I End My Song: A Gathering of Last Poems* (2010). It did not attract a wide readership, but it familiarized me with the enormous range of distinguished last poems in English. The final vision of Wallace Stevens is utterly unlike any of the other poems I selected. It is mysterious, suggestive, perhaps evasive, and unforgettable. No single reading of it is possible. Yet I hear an augury of transcendence as though a doorway is about to open and a new threshold appear on the verge of the unapparent.

CHAPTER THIRTEEN

William Butler Yeats and D. H. Lawrence
Start with the Shadow

I RECALL WRITING MANY years ago that the poet-critic Allen Tate, with the authority of strong-minded misinformation, asserted that Yeats's Romanticism would be invented by his critics. Though I would not withdraw that statement, in old age and back in the hospital dictating this, I would say it more gently. Tate and I met on several occasions, maintained civility, and had stimulating conversations concerning Hart Crane, who had been very close to Tate and his first wife, Caroline Gordon.

William Butler Yeats himself insisted that William Blake and Percy Bysshe Shelley were his prime forerunners. He also extolled Walter Pater and William Morris as precursors.

Teaching Yeats to gifted undergraduate students in 2019 is a very different experience from what it was in the 1950s. It is now eighty years since Yeats died, and for my students he can seem as archaic as Edmund Spenser. Poems quarried from Yeats's private esoteric system, such as "The Second Coming" and "Byzantium," have a puzzling appeal for them, whereas personal reflections like "Adam's Curse" and "A Dialogue of Self and Soul" impact more swiftly and decisively:

I am content to follow to its source
Every event in action or in thought;
Measure the lot; forgive myself the lot!
When such as I cast out remorse
So great a sweetness flows into the breast
We must laugh and we must sing,
We are blest by everything,
Everything we look upon is blest.

[ll. 65–72]

This is the final stanza of the "Dialogue." Last week my discussion group and I worked through "The Second Coming," the two "Byzantium" poems, and the two songs from the play *The Resurrection* and concluded with "A Dialogue of Self and Soul." I was already feeling rather unwell and sensed I was laboring to guide discussion. The students were responsible and active but then came suddenly quite alive with the "Dialogue." They burst into discussion, and I was able to stay silent while we ran overtime. When the class was dissolved, many of them stayed to go on debating the poem.

I would hesitate to prefer aesthetically the "Dialogue" over the other poems, yet unquestionably it spoke to them more urgently than the more hieratic works of Yeats's personal religion-making. Perhaps if I were nineteen and not eighty-nine I too would respond to the urgency of casting out remorse.

Yeats was aware he followed Shelley and Nietzsche in dismissing remorse. For Shelley, famously, it was only "the dark idolatry of self." Nietzsche advised us to take just one step more and forgive ourselves everything through our own grace. The entire drama of fall and redemption will then be reenacted in our own souls.

There are more than two poets in Yeats, but a dialectical tension between soul or primary quester and self or antithetical sage seems to be at his center. "The Circus Animals' Desertion," composed 1937–1938, gloriously manifests his rebellion against his own mythologies. Its final stanza, which ends, "I must lie down where all the ladders start / In the foul rag and bone shop of the heart," is open to weak misreadings. Yeats does not *choose* to begin again with the heart, presumably in the Shakespearean sense of Hamlet's heart, matrix of an infinite consciousness. Yeats *must* fall back upon the heart, because he has failed his own mythologies. It is instructive that he charts his career with the narrative poem *The Wanderings of Oisin* (1889), the play *The Countess Cathleen* (1892), and the play *On Baile's Strand* (1903), where Cuchulain, in grief and desperation, fights the sea when he discovers he has slain his own son in battle.

Yeats's endless passion for Maud Gonne was unfulfilled and unfulfillable. He kept proposing marriage, and she rejected him except as a friend. In 1908 they finally spent the night together in Paris but again the Irish beauty chose to be the muse and not the mistress or wife of the archpoet. Instead she married the abusive gunman Major John MacBride, later executed by the British for his part in the Easter 1916 rebellion in Dublin. The marriage ended in separation. Maud Gonne never remarried, but Yeats in 1917 married Georgie Hyde-Lees, twenty-seven years younger than himself.

In an essay on Shelley, Yeats identified himself with two solitary beings, Prince Athanase and Ahasuerus the Wandering Jew. Athanase is the hero of an 1817 poetic fragment by Shelley:

His soul had wedded Wisdom, and her dower
Is love and justice, clothed in which he sate
Apart from men, as in a lonely tower,

Pitying the tumult of their dark estate—
           ["Prince Athanase," Fragment 1, ll. 31–34]

That lonely tower is everywhere in Yeats. So is the figure of an aged oracle dwelling in a cavern. Wisdom in Yeats is always antithetical, set against nature. William Blake's rejection of the natural man and woman is quite different from Shelley's stance, since Shelley hoped for an apotheosis in which nature could be refined without being abolished. Nietzsche allowed Yeats to absorb the contrary elements in Blake and Shelley, reinforcing the effect of Walter Pater's secularization of the epiphany.

Yeats was both a serious and an ironic occultist. Mrs. Yeats was his medium, and much of what went into the two versions of *A Vision* (1925, 1937) was filtered through her revelations. But Yeats's spooks told him they had come to bring him metaphors for poetry.

You might say that Yeats was prepared to believe and disbelieve absolutely everything. What mattered was the continuous stream of poetry.

There are great poets who possessed considerable cognitive power. Blake and Shelley are among them. Yeats aged into his desired persona as a wise old wicked man. Much of his thinking is best set aside. Contemplating the major European poets of the last century and a half, I wonder if I do not need to award Yeats the palm over the varied splendors of Paul Valéry, Georg Trakl, Giuseppe Ungaretti, Antonio Machado, Osip Mandelstam, and others. Invoking the poets of the Western Hemisphere, one would have to mention Robert Frost, Wallace Stevens, T. S. Eliot, Hart Crane, and, in Spanish, Octavio Paz, Pablo Neruda, Gabriela Mistral, and César Vallejo.

For some years now I have regarded one of Yeats's death poems, "Cuchulain Comforted," as his uncanniest masterpiece. Like Shelley in *The Triumph of Life* and Keats in *The Fall of Hyperion*, Yeats in his closing days turns to Dante for a vision of judgment. It may be that in this powerful modification of *terza rima*, Yeats makes peace with Wilfred Owen, the major English poet of World War I. Yeats had excluded Owen from the *Oxford Book of Modern Verse* by insisting that passive suffering was not a proper theme for poetry. But here Yeats with great skill adopts Owen's invention of pararhyme or consonance, in which there is a fall in pitch when you go from one incidence to another.

Yeats at the end dismembered the hero Cuchulain, here and in the play *The Death of Cuchulain*. Who could have expected that Cuchulain in the afterlife should find his place among convicted cowards? I have never known what to make of Yeats's observation that a man can show greater courage by entering the abyss of himself than engaging in a battle.

Cuchulain in this austere poem yields to passivity and joins the cowards in sewing shrouds. A man violent and famous, he now accepts anonymity and a communal activity: "They sang, but had nor human tunes nor words / . . . / They had changed their throats and had the throats of birds."

The Irish hero concludes in a metamorphosis whose aura is distinctly felt yet difficult to apprehend. I hear a note of triumph in that final line, as when Dante's Brunetto Latini seems to be among the victorious, even though he is condemned to the refiner's fire. There is something mysterious in "Cuchulain Comforted," something Yeats withheld from himself. In the play *The Death of Cuchulain*, something of the same troubling figuration achieves a lesser yet still pungent eloquence. Cuchulain sees floating on the water "the shape that I shall take when I am dead, / My soul's first shape," and proclaims, "I say it is about to sing" (ll. 178–179, 183). Proudly barbaric, this is Yeats's version of the death of the hero and of heroism. The Blind Man is about to decapitate the mortally wounded Cuchulain. What sense of recognition are we to gather from this event? Is any of this meaningful, or is this nihilism programmatic?

Late Yeats had his proto-Fascist moments but I do not think that this is one of them. Conor Cruise O'Brien once reaffirmed to me his conviction that Yeats was giving us an allegory of the death of Fascism. I deferred to O'Brien with his vast knowledge of Irish politics, but I remained unconvinced. In his final years the archpoet was satyric. He had an extended relationship with Margot Ruddock, an English actress, singer, and very minor poet, forty-two years his junior. Still, what does this matter? He was not a prophetic poet like Blake and Shelley. We do not go to him for wisdom. At its grandest his poetry seems to emanate not from a person but from the burning fountain that Shelley celebrated. How can any poem be more accomplished than "Long-Legged Fly" (1938)?

> That civilization may not sink
> Its great battle lost,
> Quiet the dog, tether the pony
> To a distant post.
> Our master Caesar is in the tent
> Where the maps are spread,
> His eyes fixed upon nothing,
> A hand under his head.
>
> Like a long-legged fly upon the stream
> His mind moves upon silence.
>
> That the topless towers be burnt
> And men recall that face,
> Move most gently if move you must

In this lonely place.
She thinks, part woman, three parts a child,
That nobody looks; her feet
Practice a tinker shuffle
Picked up on the street.

Like a long-legged fly upon the stream
Her mind moves upon silence.

That girls at puberty may find
The first Adam in their thought,
Shut the door of the Pope's Chapel,
Keep those children out.
There on that scaffolding reclines
Michael Angelo.
With no more sound than the mice make
His hand moves to and fro.

Like a long-legged fly upon the stream
His mind moves upon silence.

Julius Caesar, Helen of Troy, Michael Angelo: Are these linked arbitrarily? Caesar the military genius; Homer's Helen, the paragon of beauty (but here in the accents of Christopher Marlowe); Michael Angelo as what *A Vision* calls Creative Mind: what unites them is the movement of the mind upon silence. As an occultist Yeats followed Hermetic tradition in regarding silence as more unfallen than speech.

I scarcely know how to overpraise the metric and subtle art of the young Helen practicing a street dance covertly. The movement from "nobody looks" to "her feet" has an ineluctable grace:

She thinks, part woman, three parts a child,
That nobody looks; her feet
Practice a tinker shuffle
Picked up on the street.

Something of the same spirit but turned toward parody emerges in the delightful "News for the Delphic Oracle" (1938), with its golden codgers flashing "belly, shoulder, bum," while "nymphs and satyrs / Copulate in the foam" (ll. 34–36). Yeats mounts a jovial transumption upon Shelley's deliciously mocking, mythological lyric "Hymn of Pan," whose final stanza sets the tone:

> I sang of the dancing stars,
>   I sang of the daedal Earth,
> And of Heaven, and the giant wars,
>   And Love, and Death, and Birth—
>   And then I chang'd my pipings,
> Singing how down the vale of Maenalus
>   I pursu'd a maiden and clasp'd a reed.
> Gods and men, we are all deluded thus!
>   It breaks in our bosom and then we bleed.
> All wept, as I think both ye now would,
> If envy or age had not frozen your blood,
>   At the sorrow of my sweet pipings.

Yeats, deliberately coarser, happily joins his own satyriasis to that of the ancients. The sage Plotinus yawns himself into the general miasma of longing and lust. One feels the exuberance of the aged Yeats as he boisterously exults.

The two remarkable death poems by Yeats are "Cuchulain Comforted" and "Man and the Echo," in which the poet, sleepless, old, and ill, broods on all he has said and done. The Archpoet who hoped he had cast out remorse is afflicted by it in his final days. Though, this being Yeats, the instances are all self-enhancing. Poems and plays by Yeats did not instigate the Easter 1916 uprising. This may just be a personal reaction, but nothing else in Yeats seems more humane and wiser than these lines from "The Man and the Echo": "What do we know but that we face / One another in this place?" Since the other is but an echo, what is it that we know?

It may seem a leap to move from Yeats to the poetry of D. H. Lawrence. And yet who are the major poets in England after Thomas Hardy? Lawrence died at only forty-four but created something like a literary canon all his own. *The Rainbow* (1915) is his great achievement in the novel, followed by *Women in Love* (1922). It may be, though, that his shorter narrative fictions, widely varying in length, are as important. His travel writings (to call them that), polemics, critical studies contain permanent elements. But he means most to me as a poet. He went from the early influence of Shelley and of Thomas Hardy through a furious agon with Walt Whitman, which gave him an image of voice that became at last his own.

Lawrence distinctly was a prophetic poet urging us to renew our links with the cosmos. "Start with the sun," the dying Lawrence wrote at the end of *Apocalypse* (written 1929–1930), "and the rest will slowly, slowly happen." And yet the force of his best work depends upon the pathos of the oracle who has to be neglected. Begin with the death poems that center on the falling away from natural process and simultaneously affirm and reject that fading.

Sir Thomas Browne wrote in *Hydriotaphia* (1658) that "Life is a pure flame and we live by an invisible sun within us." Though he was raised a working-class Nonconformist Protestant, Lawrence, like Shelley, Hardy, Whitman, was anything but a Christian. Essentially his creed is vitalism, though it is very different from the energetics of Balzac or the godlike potency of Victor Hugo. It seems to me biblical in its range and intensity. The opening chapters of *The Rainbow* are a kind of Genesis and Ursula's apotheosis at the novel's conclusion is Lawrence's Revelation:

And the rainbow stood on the earth. She knew that the sordid people who crept hard-scaled and separate on the face of the world's corruption were living still, that the rainbow was arched in their blood and would quiver to life in their spirit, that they would cast off their horny covering of disintegration, that new, clean, naked bodies would issue to a new germination, to a new growth, rising to the light and the wind and the clean rain of heaven. She saw in the rainbow the earth's new architecture, the old, brittle corruption of houses and factories swept away, the world built up in a living fabric of Truth, fitting to the over-arching heaven.

At our best Lawrence sees us as "rising to the light and the wind and the clean rain of heaven." That is the spirit of his breakthrough volume of poems, *Look! We Have Come Through!* (1917). The crown of the volume is the Shelleyan "Song of a Man Who Has Come Through":

NOT I, not I, but the wind that blows through me!
A fine wind is blowing the new direction of Time.
If only I let it bear me, carry me, if only it carry me!
If only I am sensitive, subtle, oh, delicate, a winged gift!
If only, most lovely of all, I yield myself and am borrowed
By the fine, fine wind that takes its course through the chaos
     of the world
Like a fine, an exquisite chisel, a wedge-blade inserted;
If only I am keen and hard like the sheer tip of a wedge
Driven by invisible blows,
The rock will split, we shall come at the wonder, we shall find
     the Hesperides.

Oh, for the wonder that bubbles into my soul,
I would be a good fountain, a good well-head,
Would blur no whisper, spoil no expression.

What is the knocking?
What is the knocking at the door in the night?
It is somebody wants to do us harm.

No, no, it is the three strange angels.
Admit them, admit them.

I think I first read this poem as an undergraduate in the late 1940s and have a dim recollection of writing an essay comparing it to "Ode to the West Wind." Seventy years later I am puzzled, though with admiration, at Lawrence's compounding Shelley with the story of Lot in Sodom. Lawrence, like Whitman, is omnisexual. Whitman can seem a kind of male lesbian while Lawrence, permanently in love with his wife, Frieda, celebrated his passion for her with the image: "The rock will split, we shall come at the wonder, we shall find the Hesperides," an exalted description of anal intercourse. Lawrence evidently was so excitable that he invariably arrived too soon, as it were.

Women in Love concludes with Rupert Birkin (Lawrence) lamenting the death of Gerald Crich. There is an implication that Gerald could have been saved from Gudrun's fatal embrace, if the two men had entered into a kind of brotherhood with clear sexual implications, as in their extraordinary bout of naked wrestling.

Lot and the Angels of Destruction transform the poem from Shelley's trumpet of a prophecy into an intimation of what it costs to be a man who has come through. Three angels, one of them Yahweh himself, appear to Abraham, but only the two punishers go on to Sodom. When Lawrence ends, "Admit them, admit them," he chooses the destiny of Lot: to go into exile.

If you consider Lawrence on Freud you become baffled. He had trouble reading the words on the page and somehow convinced himself that Freud wished to sanction sexual permissiveness. Still there is justification for Lawrence's impatience. Freud sensibly wished us to settle for ordinary unhappiness. To Lawrence that was blasphemy against the living god who had to sustain us:

I
Now it is autumn and the falling fruit
and the long journey towards oblivion.

The apples falling like great drops of dew
to bruise themselves an exit from themselves.

And it is time to go, to bid farewell
to one's own self, and find an exit
from the fallen self.

II
Have you built your ship of death, O have you?
O build your ship of death, for you will need it.

The grim frost is at hand, when the apples will fall
thick, almost thundrous, on the hardened earth.

And death is on the air like a smell of ashes!
Ah! Can't you smell it?

And in the bruised body, the frightened soul
finds itself shrinking, wincing from the cold
that blows upon it through the orifices.

[ll. 1–16]

Writing about Lawrence's "The Ship of Death" on February 23, 2019, weary of my long confinement in the cardiac unit of the Yale

New Haven hospital, I find myself curiously heartened by that wonderful trope of the apples falling to bruise themselves an exit from themselves. I am not yet prepared to build *my* ship of death, though I may soon need it:

III
And can a man his own quietus make
with a bare bodkin?

With daggers, bodkins, bullets, man can make
a bruise or break of exit for his life;
but is that a quietus, O tell me, is it quietus?

Surely not so! for how could murder, even self-murder
ever a quietus make?

IV
O let us talk of quiet that we know,
that we can know, the deep and lovely quiet
of a strong heart at peace!

How can we this, our own quietus, make?

[ll. 17–27]

Lawrence's quibble derives from Hamlet's. It is singular that Shakespeare's tragedy of consciousness had parallel effects upon T. S. Eliot and on Lawrence. Eliot infamously called the play almost certainly an aesthetic failure. Lawrence, in better control, found the Prince to be a "creeping unclean thing" but went on to accurate praise of the great soliloquies: "For the soliloquies of Hamlet are as deep as the soul of man can go, in one direction, and as sincere as the Holy Spirit itself in their essence" (*Twilight in Italy* [1916]):

V
Build then the ship of death, for you must take
the longest journey, to oblivion.

And die the death, the long and painful death
that lies between the old self and the new.

Already our bodies are fallen, bruised, badly bruised,
already our souls are oozing through the exit
of the cruel bruise.

Already the dark and endless ocean of the end
is washing in through the breaches of our wounds,
Already the flood is upon us.

Oh build your ship of death, your little ark
and furnish it with food, with little cakes, and wine
for the dark flight down oblivion.
. . .

X
The flood subsides, and the body, like a worn sea-shell
emerges strange and lovely.
And the little ship wings home, faltering and lapsing
on the pink flood,
and the frail soul steps out, into the house again
filling the heart with peace.

Swings the heart renewed with peace
even of oblivion.

Oh build your ship of death. Oh build it!
for you will need it.
For the voyage of oblivion awaits you.

[ll. 28–40, 97–109]

The variations here are exercises in controlled pathos. Good readers differ on "The Ship of Death." For many it is too simplistic and repetitive in its urgings. It works for me, though it may not be Lawrence at his most accomplished. Eliot, driven to frenzy by Lawrence, dismissed him in an essay of 1927 as "demoniac, a natural and unsophisticated demoniac with a gospel." There is a great deal to be said in criticism of Lawrence, but it had better always commence in appreciation. The poetry of Eliot survives because it is demoniac in its origins. What persuaded Eliot that anything about Lawrence was unsophisticated, I cannot imagine.

In 1929 Lawrence composed "Bavarian Gentians." "Persephone herself is but a voice," he writes, "pierced with the passion of dense gloom, / among the splendor of torches of darkness, shedding darkness on the lost bride and groom."

Lawrence thought Walt Whitman was like an archaic Greek. What lilacs were to Whitman, gentians became to Lawrence, a signature flower, the image of voice that Whitman called the "tally." This marvelous poem has enhanced power and beauty for me as I meditate upon it in the hospital. Lawrence chants with a singular authority as he accepts the descent into Dis. He goes down as a voice and seems persuaded voice will not cease.

In 1999 John Hollander gave the Clark Lectures at Cambridge University. Kenneth Gross edited John's manuscript and published it under the title of *The Substance of Shadow: A Darkening Trope in Poetic History* (2016). Hollander mulls over every kind of shadow but in particular considers what Stevens in *The Auroras of Autumn* named "a great shadow's last embellishment." Stevens has departed, as have Lawrence, Eliot, Ashbery, but fresh splendors and the shadows they will cast may come.

Of all Lawrence's poems I am most troubled and exalted by his deathbed meditation "Shadows," where he pictures himself in the hands of the unknown God, "breaking me down to his own oblivion / to send me forth on a new morning, a new man." This makes inexorable demands upon a reader: How are we to understand the oblivion of a God himself unknown? Lawrence at his very end pushes back against the horizon. He desires to write the poem of resurrection, of shadows becoming fecund. Unlike Yeats, for whom the shadow is programmatic, Lawrence finds shadows both anthropomorphic and theomorphic. They have in them a touch of Emily Dickinson. When the "Seal Despair" comes in Dickinson's poem "There's a certain Slant of light," "the Landscape listens— / Shadows—hold their breath—." In "Byzantium" Yeats sings of shades more than man, more image than a shade, and of mouths that have no moisture and no breath, breathless mouths may summon. Dickinson's breath-holding shadows are Amherst realities, while Yeats's shades are occult. Lawrence's shadows mediate between Dickinson's and Yeats's; they are the lapses and renewals of the dark earth.

If we go back thirteen years from Lawrence dying to the young man of "Under the Oak" in *New Poems* (1916), I have some difficulty assimilating the aggressive lover to the visionary seer:

> You, if you were sensible,
> When I tell you the stars flash signals, each on dreadful,
> You would not turn and answer me
> "The night is wonderful."
>
> Even you, if you knew
> How this darkness soaks me through and through, and infuses
> Unholy fear in my essence, you would pause to distinguish
> What hurts from what amuses.
>
> For I tell you
> Beneath this powerful tree, my whole soul's fluid
> Oozes away from me as a sacrifice steam
> At the knife of a Druid.
>
> Again I tell you, I bleed, I am hound with withies,
> My life runs out.
> I tell you my blood runs out on the floor of this oak.
> Gout upon gout.
>
> Above me springs the blood-born mistletoe
> In the shady smoke.
> But who are you, twittering to and fro
> Beneath the oak?
>
> What thing better are you, what worse?
> What have you to do with the mysteries
> Of this ancient place, of my ancient curse?
> What place have you in my histories?

Ungracious, surging onward, Lawrence stands against what Blake called the Female Will, which would make him a Druid victim of a woman's passion. That pungent final stanza is addressed to every reader. I like juxtaposing "Under the Oak" with a proud section of Yeats's "Vacillation":

III

Get all the gold and silver that you can,
Satisfy ambition, animate
The trivial days and ram them with the sun,
And yet upon these maxims meditate:
All women dote upon an idle man
Although their children need a rich estate;
No man has ever lived that had enough
Of children's gratitude or woman's love.

No longer in Lethean foliage caught
Begin the preparation for your death
And from the fortieth winter by that thought
Test every work of intellect or faith,
And everything that your own hands have wrought
And call those works extravagance of breath
That are not suited for such men as come
proud, open-eyed and laughing to the tomb.

[ll. 19–34]

There is a debt to Ben Jonson in "ram them with the sun." Beautifully measuring and weighing his metric, Yeats makes a classic statement of his own refusal to die with any illusions. Stevens, in a kind of war poem, "Death of a Soldier" (1918), sets aside even the illusions as being no more than perfunctory. Death is absolute, Stevens says, "As in a season of autumn, / When the wind stops." In a season of autumn there can be no pretentions. The soldier is not Christ and he falls as autumn falls, movements of cloud and of wind. In Stevens, the mind is the great poem of winter.

Bringing together Lawrence, Yeats, and Stevens ought not to be exemplary of any common qualities they may seem to share. Probing them in the atmosphere of a rehabilitation process has to be disfiguring. What holds them together are three modes of mastery. In Lawrence it is chthonic. In Yeats it is occult. In Stevens it is massive acceptance of things as they are.

There is relatively little sense of human otherness in Lawrence, Yeats, and Stevens. Chaucer and Shakespeare have charted personality and its discontents for us. So have Montaigne and Cervantes.

Belated visionary poets from Blake and Shelley to Hart Crane and Geoffrey Hill struggle with nightmare:

> Weight him down, O side-stars, with the great weightings of
> the end.
> Seal him there. He looked in a glass of the earth and thought
> he lived in it.
> Now, he brings all that he saw into the earth, to the waiting
> parent.
> His crisp knowledge is devoured by her, beneath a dew.
>
> Weight him, weight, weight him with the sleepiness of the
> moon.
> It was only a glass because he looked in it. It was nothing he
> could be told.
> It was a language he spoke, because he must, yet did not know.
> It was a page he had found in the handbook of heartbreak.
>
> The black fugatos are strumming the blackness of black . . .
> The thick strings stutter the finial gutturals.
> He does not lie there remembering the blue-jay, say the jay.
> His grief is that his mother should feed on him, himself and
> what he saw,
>> In that distant chamber, a bearded queen, wicked in her
>>> dead light.

That is "Madame La Fleurie" by Wallace Stevens (1951). One might believe this is Baudelaire and not the poet of *Harmonium*. In Stevens the mother's face, the purpose of the poem, fills the room. That is Margaretha Catharine Zeller, benign mother of Stevens, his brothers, and his sister, who created for them and her husband, Garrett, a heaven-haven of a home. Madame La Fleurie is the devouring mother of her handbook of heartbreak.

As he developed into his final phase, Stevens surprised himself by coming to birth again as several very different poets. He began to take on the persona of Ulysses, neither Homeric nor Dantesque nor Joycean but an oracular shaman. Tennyson's Ulysses hovers, yet I hear the accents of what seems a personal gnosis emanating oddly from the secular Stevens, whose Ulysses, "read[ing] his own mind," proclaims, "As I know, I am and have / The right to be" ("The Sail of Ulysses," ll. 3–5). If knowing and being are one, then we join ourselves to Prince Hamlet. That is not the Tennysonian Ulysses who follows after Dante and Milton's Satan. But I wonder if it is not a critique by Stevens of the endless series of questing wanderers in Yeats?

There may be no better-known poem by Yeats than the very early "The Song of Wandering Aengus" (1899):

> I went out to the hazel wood,
> Because a fire was in my head,
> And cut and peeled a hazel wand,
> And hooked a berry to a thread;
> And when white moths were on the wing,
> And moth-like stars were flickering out,
> I dropped the berry in a stream
> And caught a little silver trout.
>
> When I had laid it on the floor
> I went to blow the fire a-flame,
> But something rustled on the floor,
> And someone called me by my name:
> It had become a glimmering girl
> With apple blossom in her hair
> Who called me by my name and ran
> And faded through the brightening air.
>
> Though I am old with wandering
> Through hollow lands and hilly lands,
> I will find out where she has gone,
> And kiss her lips and take her hands;
> And walk among long dappled grass,
> And pluck till time and times are done,
> The silver apples of the moon,
> The golden apples of the sun.

The common readers of poetry, and we still have some, have taken this song to themselves. It is simple but in no way simplistic. Yeats first published it in 1897 under the title of "Mad Song." It is sung here by the god of youth and poetry, who has grown old and deranged in his hopeless quest for the lost beloved. Yeats was a friend of William Morris, whom he called "the happiest of the poets," and the mode of Morris is perpetuated here. Sun and moon are transformed to fictions, the golden and silver apples that will be plucked only when the Hesperides are attained.

Yeats's critique of this ideology of quest was expressed most compellingly in the poem "Adam's Curse" (1904):

> We sat together at one summer's end,
> That beautiful mild woman, your close friend,
> And you and I, and talked of poetry.
> I said, "A line will take us hours maybe;
> Yet if it does not seem a moment's thought,
> Our stitching and unstitching has been naught.
> Better go down upon your marrow-bones
> And scrub a kitchen pavement, or break stones
> Like an old pauper, in all kinds of weather;
> For to articulate sweet sounds together
> Is to work harder than all these, and yet
> Be thought an idler by the noisy set
> Of bankers, schoolmasters, and clergymen
> The martyrs call the world."
>   And thereupon
> That beautiful mild woman for whose sake
> There's many a one shall find out all heartache
> On finding that her voice is sweet and low
> Replied, "To be born woman is to know—
> Although they do not talk of it at school—
> That we must labour to be beautiful."
> I said, "It's certain there is no fine thing
> Since Adam's fall but needs much labouring.
> There have been lovers who thought love should be
> So much compounded of high courtesy
> That they would sigh and quote with learned looks
> Precedents out of beautiful old books;
> Yet now it seems an idle trade enough."

We sat grown quiet at the name of love;
We saw the last embers of daylight die,
And in the trembling blue-green of the sky
A moon, worn as if it had been a shell
Washed by time's waters as they rose and fell
About the stars and broke in days and years.

I had a thought for no one's but your ears:
That you were beautiful, and that I strove
To love you in the old high way of love;
That it had all seemed happy, and yet we'd grown
As weary-hearted as that hollow moon.

I hear in this a legacy from Shelley's middle style. Yeats follows Shelley in taking as given a community of love, with its sophisticated common rhetoric, implicit code, and ethos of the likely defeat of love, but a defeat with dignity. This is Yeats in 1902, struggling with the perpetual frustration of his obsessive love for Maud Gonne. He wrote magnificently until the end in 1939, but I am uncertain if he ever excelled "Adam's Curse."

The poem is addressed to Maud Gonne and to her sister, here disguised as "your close friend." Summer ends, the poet and the two lovely women talk about poetry and, more implicitly, eros. Perhaps the crucial line is spoken by Maud's sister: "That we must labour to be beautiful."

"Adam's Curse" is labor. Poetry and the beauty of women are hard work. Baldassare Castiglione (1479–1528), in his *Book of the Courtier* (1528), was the guide to "the old high way of love." He coined the word *sprezzatura*, meaning both a throwaway quality in the art of love and a deliberate carelessness in poetry and painting.

Yeats is not lamenting yet once more Maud Gonne's refusal of his marriage proposals. The sorrow is the death of love. Exultation is thaumaturgic since the poem itself replaces lost passion with a magician's courtesy "to articulate sweet sounds together."

Etymologically, "vacillation" means an unsteady swaying, hardly suitable for heroes. Yeats, professedly not a Christian, vacillated continually on Jesus, whom he regarded both as another hero and as something more. In the play *The Resurrection*, particularly in its revised form (1931), Jesus is resurrected as any phantom might be in the context of the earlier version of *A Vision* (1925). Its first song (in Yeats's "Two Songs from a Play") tells us that Dionysus, begotten by Zeus upon Persephone, has suffered a *sparagmos* by the Titans. Athena, who is the staring virgin, tears out his beating heart and brings it to Zeus. After swallowing the heart, Zeus rebegets Dionysus upon Semele. The second song invokes the "Galilean turbulence" and "Odour of blood when Christ was slain."

The final Chorus of Shelley's *Hellas* overcomes Yeats's appropriation because its skepticism severely qualifies *The Resurrection*'s visionary ferocity.

"One who rose" must be Christ, yet Shelley values more the return of Saturn's Golden Age and the dominion of Love (presumably as prophesied by Diotima in Plato's *Symposium*, which Shelley had translated). The final stanza ("Oh cease! Must hate and death return?") yields to Shelley's own skepticism and his impending despair of life.

William Butler Yeats had the good fortune and the vital temperament to refuse any despair of his own quest. Here is "All Souls' Night," the epilogue to *A Vision*, and stationed also as the final poem in *The Tower* (1928):

MIDNIGHT has come, and the great Christ Church Bell
And may a lesser bell sound through the room;
And it is All Souls' Night,
And two long glasses brimmed with muscatel
Bubble upon the table. A ghost may come;
For it is a ghost's right,
His element is so fine
Being sharpened by his death,
To drink from the wine-breath
While our gross palates drink from the whole wine.

On All Souls' Night the dead traditionally can manifest themselves. Yeats the occultist believed everything that could be believed and so awaits his friends, departed mediums.

I need some mind that, if the cannon sound
From every quarter of the world, can stay

Wound in mind's pondering
As mummies in the mummy-cloth are wound;
Because I have a marvellous thing to say,
A certain marvellous thing
None but the living mock,
Though not for sober ear;
It may be all that hear
Should laugh and weep an hour upon the clock.

The marvelous thing is the system of *A Vision*, where everyone is
fated to be reborn, and then to die into the next cycle, and on and on.

Horton's the first I call. He loved strange thought
And knew that sweet extremity of pride
That's called platonic love,
And that to such a pitch of passion wrought
Nothing could bring him, when his lady died,
Anodyne for his love.
Words were but wasted breath;
One dear hope had he:
The inclemency
Of that or the next winter would be death.

Two thoughts were so mixed up I could not tell
Whether of her or God he thought the most,
But think that his mind's eye,
When upward turned, on one sole image fell;
And that a slight companionable ghost,
Wild with divinity,
Had so lit up the whole
Immense miraculous house
The Bible promised us,
It seemed a gold-fish swimming in a bowl.

W. T. Horton was a visionary artist much influenced by Aubrey
Beardsley. Yeats befriended him and sponsored him as a member of
the Hermetic Order of the Golden Dawn, occult followers of Madame Blavatsky. Poor Horton had a platonic passion for Amy Audrey

Locke, another mystical enthusiast, but she died young and much in Horton died with her. She is the "slight companionable ghost" of Horton's heaven.

> On Florence Emery I call the next,
> Who finding the first wrinkles on a face
> Admired and beautiful,
> And knowing that the future would be vexed
> With 'minished beauty, multiplied commonplace,
> Preferred to teach a school
> Away from neighbour or friend,
> Among dark skins, and there
> permit foul years to wear
> Hidden from eyesight to the unnoticed end.

> Before that end much had she ravelled out
> From a discourse in figurative speech
> By some learned Indian
> On the soul's journey. How it is whirled about,
> Wherever the orbit of the moon can reach,
> Until it plunge into the sun;
> And there, free and yet fast,
> Being both Chance and Choice,
> Forget its broken toys
> And sink into its own delight at last.

Florence Farr Emery was renowned as a beautiful actress on the London stage. After she and Yeats became lovers, Farr acted in many of Yeats's plays and gave recitations of his poems. But she was very strong-minded and went her own way. They remained friends and her letters to him from Ceylon inspired "All Souls' Night." She too was a Golden Dawn occultist but was passionately literal-minded, unlike Yeats:

> And I call up MacGregor from the grave,
> For in my first hard springtime we were friends.
> Although of late estranged.
> I thought him half a lunatic, half knave,

And told him so, but friendship never ends;
And what if mind seem changed,
And it seem changed with the mind,
When thoughts rise up unbid
On generous things that he did
And I grow half contented to be blind!

He had much industry at setting out,
Much boisterous courage, before loneliness
Had driven him crazed;
For meditations upon unknown thought
Make human intercourse grow less and less;
They are neither paid nor praised.
But he'd object to the host,
The glass because my glass;
A ghost-lover he was
And may have grown more arrogant being a ghost.

Samuel Liddell MacGregor Mathers, founding member of the
Golden Dawn, was a rather weird English occultist who persuaded
himself that he came from the MacGregor clan. That was pure myth
but did not prevent him from stalking about in full Highland rega-
lia, kilts and all:

But names are nothing. What matter who it be,
So that his elements have grown so fine
The fume of muscatel
Can give his sharpened palate ecstasy
No living man can drink from the whole wine.
I have mummy truths to tell
Whereat the living mock,
Though not for sober ear,
For maybe all that hear
Should laugh and weep an hour upon the clock.

Such thought—such thought have I that hold it tight
Till meditation master all its parts,
Nothing can stay my glance
Until that glance run in the world's despite

To where the damned have howled away their hearts,
And where the blessed dance;
Such thought, that in it bound
I need no other thing,
Wound in mind's wandering
As mummies in the mummy-cloth are wound.

The magnificence of gesture, metric, diction overcomes what could be judged sheer silliness. It remains true that most of mankind, from dawn of creation until our dusk of departure, believed and goes on believing in ghosts. I have encountered one or perhaps two, declined to accept my senses, and go on wondering. Sometimes, pondering Yeats, I wonder if we are all ghosts, as that is the contention of *A Vision*.

At ninety I find Yeats most artful when he is apparently simple. For some years now I have not been able write anything without remembering the second lyric in "A Woman Young and Old" (1926–1929):

If I make the lashes dark
And the eyes more bright
And the lips more scarlet,
Or ask if all be right
From mirror after mirror,
No vanity's displayed:
I'm looking for the face I had
Before the world was made.

What if I look upon a man
As though on my beloved,
And my blood be cold the while
And my heart unmoved?
Why should he think me cruel
Or that he is betrayed?
I'd have him love the thing that was
Before the world was made.

I ken no more elegant brief account of a Gnostic stance:

I'm looking for the face I had
Before the world was made.

The wit of a woman, disclaiming vanity as she enhances her beauty, imparts delight to the declaration that our faces were marred not by the Fall but by the Creation/Fall, botched by the Demiurge. I hear in this the variant: I'm listening for the voice I heard / Before the world was made. Forlorn, I myself listen. Silence never fell. How are we to interpret it?

Etymologically, silence is windlessness. Yet silence is spirit, *ruach*, or the breath of Yahweh. All mothering, all fathering, the original abyss was despoiled by the Demiurge. Silence lives, moves, has its being in the *Niphal*, spaced between action and passivity. Silence is in-between.

In the volume *The Winding Stair* (1933) Yeats includes the brief, grim poem "Death":

> Nor dread nor hope attend
> A dying animal
> A man awaits his end
> Dreading and hoping all;
> Many times he died,
> Many times rose again.
> A great man in his pride
> Confronting murderous men
> Casts derision upon
> Supersession of breath;
> He knows death to the bone—
> Man has created death.

This strong but self-contradictory fragment is an elegy for Kevin O'Higgins, founder of the police force of the Irish Free State, and a friend of Yeats. O'Higgins was assassinated by the IRA in 1927, at the age of thirty-five.

To say that man has created death is to emulate William Blake and the Shelley of *The Witch of Atlas*. If death, as in Yeats's *A Vision*, is unreal, then what happens to the praise of O'Higgins?

> A great man in his pride
> Confronting murderous men

Death is more persuasively confronted in "At Algeciras—A Meditation upon Death," composed in November 1928 and included in *The Winding Stair*. Yeats was recuperating from a severe illness in the sun at the largest Spanish port on the Bay of Gibraltar:

> The heron-billed pale cattle-birds
> That feed on some foul parasite
> Of the Moroccan flocks and herds
> Cross the narrow Straits to light
> In the rich midnight of the garden trees
> Till the dawn break upon those mingled seas.
>
> Often at evening when a boy
> Would I carry to a friend—
> Hoping more substantial joy
> Did an older mind commend—
> Not such as are in Newton's metaphor,
> But actual shells of Rosses' level shore.
>
> Greater glory in the sun,
> An evening chill upon the air,
> Bid imagination run
> Much on the Great Questioner;
> What He can question, what if questioned I
> Can with filling confidence reply.

The great questioner is death. Why is Yeats so confident that he possesses the adequate reply? His system tells him that man has invented death, a Shelleyan supposition. The subtle answer in is that marvelous line: "Greater glory in the sun . . ."

Glory has an aura of the radiance of God or Christ. Yeats, not a Christian, borrows it for his pagan purpose. The force of his diction and metric brushes argument aside. It is in the "Supernatural Songs" (1934) that Yeats propounds most clearly his religious stance.

Here is "Ribh Considers Christian Love Insufficient":

> Why should I seek for love or study it?
> It is of God and passes human wit.

I study hatred with great diligence,
For that's a passion in my own control,
A sort of besom that can clear the soul
Of everything that is not mind or sense.
Why do I hate man, woman Or event?
That is a light my jealous soul has sent.
From terror and deception freed it can
Discover impurities, can show at last
How soul may walk when all such things are past,
How soul could walk before such things began.
Then my delivered soul herself shall learn
A darker knowledge and in hatred turn
From every thought of God mankind has had.
Thought is a garment and the soul's a bride
That cannot in that trash and tinsel hide:
Hatred of God may bring the soul to God.
At stroke of midnight soul cannot endure
A bodily or mental furniture.
What can she take until her Master give!
Where can she look until He make the show!
What can she know until He bid her know!
How can she live till in her blood He live!

This is the most telling of the "Supernatural Songs." What shall
we make of Ribh saying, "Hatred of God may bring the soul to
God"? Devoted readers of Yeats learn that for him God and Death
are one. As a Gnostic formulation, that has cogency. For the Jews,
Christians, and Muslims, this is outrageous blasphemy. What is it
that Yeats attempts by this shock tactic?

Yeats powerfully enables his ferocity in one marvelous couplet:

Thought is a garment and the soul's a bride
That cannot in that trash and tinsel hide:

The naked soul has singular power to receive a God himself
free of all human formulations. The long tradition of Yeats's ancestors, who for generation after generation were Protestant ministers
in the United Church of Ireland, was broken by John Butler Yeats,

the poet's father, who became a raffish painter and relocated to New York City. William Butler Yeats and his brother, the painter Jack Butler Yeats, joined in their father's departure from an ebbing vocation.

In 1890 Yeats, with Ernest Rhys, founded the Rhymers' Club, whose members included Francis Thompson, Lionel Johnson, Lord Alfred Douglas, Ernest Dowson, Victor Plarr, Arthur Symons, and John Todhunter, among others. When they met in private homes rather than taverns, Oscar Wilde sometimes joined them.

Lionel Johnson, who came from an English military family, joined Yeats in the Celtic Revival. Yeats and Johnson were close friends, and when Yeats thought of the Tragic Generation, as he named it, Johnson, more than Dowson or Symons, was his exemplar. Johnson's struggle with his own homoeroticism made him an acute alcoholic and led to a fall that ended him at thirty-five.

In June 1891 he converted to Roman Catholicism and afterward was strictly devout. Yet he remained a disciple of Shelley, who perpetually denounced remorse and religion. His struggle with Shelley culminates in the best of his poems, "The Dark Angel" (1893):

DARK Angel, with thine aching lust
To rid the world of penitence:
Malicious Angel, who still dost
My soul such subtile violence!

Because of thee, no thought, no thing,
Abides for me undesecrate:
Dark Angel, ever on the wing,
Who never reachest me too late!

When music sounds, then changest thou
Its silvery to a sultry fire:
Nor will thine envious heart allow
Delight untortured by desire.
. . .
I fight thee, in the Holy Name!
Yet, what thou dost, is what God saith:
Tempter! should I escape thy flame,
Thou wilt have helped my soul from Death:

The second Death, that never dies,
That cannot die, when time is dead:
Live Death, wherein the lost soul cries,
Eternally uncomforted.

Dark Angel, with thine aching lust!
Of two defeats, of two despairs:
Less dread, a change to drifting dust,
Than thine eternity of cares.

Do what thou wilt, thou shalt not so,
Dark Angel! triumph over me:
Lonely, unto the Lone I go;
Divine, to the Divinity.

[ll. 1–12, 41–56]

The italicized lines translate Plotinus and add to the poem's burden. Somehow Johnson's Dark Angel is compounded of Shelley's battle against remorse, Johnson's homosexuality, and what Yeats would have called Johnson's daemon. The poem, now undervalued or neglected, is dense and dialectical in its spiritual argument.

Lionel Johnson was a Paterian aesthete and a mystical Roman Catholic. These are irreconcilable. All Johnson could do was to choose between two defeats, two despairs: an aesthetic investment in annihilation or the death of the soul in sin.

Ribh's dark wisdom develops to a point affirmed in Yeats's famous poem "Among School Children" (1926):

I

I walk through the long schoolroom questioning;
A kind old nun in a white hood replies;
The children learn to cipher and to sing,
To study reading-books and history,
To cut and sew, be neat in everything
In the best modern way—the children's eyes
In momentary wonder stare upon
A sixty-year-old smiling public man.

II

I dream of a Ledaean body, bent
Above a sinking fire, a tale that she
Told of a harsh reproof, or trivial event
That changed some childish day to tragedy—
Told, and it seemed that our two natures blent
Into a sphere from youthful sympathy,
Or else, to alter Plato's parable,
Into the yolk and white of the one shell.

III

And thinking of that fit of grief or rage
I look upon one child or t'other there
And wonder if she stood so at that age—
For even daughters of the swan can share
Something of every paddler's heritage—
And had that colour upon cheek or hair,
And thereupon my heart is driven wild:
She stands before me as a living child.

IV

Her present image floats into the mind—
Did Quattrocento finger fashion it
Hollow of cheek as though it drank the wind
And took a mess of shadows for its meat?
And I though never of Ledaean kind
Had pretty plumage once—enough of that,
Better to smile on all that smile, and show
There is a comfortable kind of old scarecrow.

V

What youthful mother, a shape upon her lap
Honey of generation had betrayed,
And that must sleep, shriek, struggle to escape
As recollection or the drug decide,
Would think her son, did she but see that shape
With sixty or more winters on its head,

A compensation for the pang of his birth,
Or the uncertainty of his setting forth?

VI

Plato thought nature but a spume that plays
Upon a ghostly paradigm of things;
Solider Aristotle played the taws
Upon the bottom of a king of kings;
World-famous golden-thighed Pythagoras
Fingered upon a fiddle-stick or strings
What a star sang and careless Muses heard:
Old clothes upon old sticks to scare a bird.

VII

Both nuns and mothers worship images,
But those the candles light are not as those
That animate a mother's reveries,
But keep a marble or a bronze repose.
And yet they too break hearts—O Presences
That passion, piety or affection knows,
And that all heavenly glory symbolise—
O self-born mockers of man's enterprise;

VIII

Labour is blossoming or dancing where
The body is not bruised to pleasure soul,
Nor beauty born out of its own despair,
Nor blear-eyed wisdom out of midnight oil.
O chestnut tree, great rooted blossomer,
Are you the leaf, the blossom or the bole?
O body swayed to music, O brightening glance,
How can we know the dancer from the dance?

More than ever I have a mixed response. I think the best answer to the culminating question is: not without a loss of power. It moves me that Yeats wants to evade his own dualisms—Neoplatonic, Hermetist, Gnostic—though he knows he cannot do so.

The poem is another lament for Maud Gonne and for Yeats himself. Though Yeats insisted he cared little for Wordsworth, the poem's action is the surrender of power to knowledge, the heart of Wordsworth. Yeats addresses his masters from Plato and Plotinus onward and partly rejects them in the hope of the human enterprise for an enduring love:

> —O Presences
> That passion, piety or affection knows,
> And that all heavenly glory symbolise—
> O self-born mockers of man's enterprise;

It is difficult to resist Yeats when he fully states his capacity to hold on both to the present and to the personal past, as in the final stanzas of Part 2 of "The Tower." Here Yeats, "old lecher with a love on every wind," remembers being lured "into the labyrinth of another's being" (ll. 105, 112) and turning aside from this labyrinth out of pride, cowardice, silly over-subtlety, or conscience.

This is Yeats at sixty-three, a wild old wicked man, as he liked to call himself. All of us—women and men alike—in old age find the imagination dwelling upon fulfilled or lost loves. It may not be true that for all of us, as for Yeats, otherness is always a labyrinth. And yet it is. If achieved love is templar, then the perplexing road to get there will be labyrinthine, and pragmatically most of our erotic relationships will take place on the threshold between assurance and perplexity.

Yeats celebrates loss rather than laments it. Pride, timidity, agenbite of inwit, supposed conscience: these are cast aside as the devastations of memory bring finish to the light of day.

Is loss the central tonality of poetry? I think now that William Blake took the name Los for his maker with a hammer from the Old Norse *los*, which referred to the breakup of an army. Sometimes I wish Milton had entitled his epic *Lost*. I recall also the twentieth-century Yiddish poet H. Leivick: "A song means filling a jug and then breaking the jug. In the language of the Kabbalah we might call it: *broken vessels.*"

Yeats liked to use the verb "breaking" as though it also meant "making." There is never more than a thin partition in Yeats between the esoteric and the public. It was his daemonic gift to exploit that edge.

I have come full circle from nine to ninety in my enthusiasm for some of Yeats's early poems, including "The Madness of King Goll" (1887):

> I sat on cushioned otter-skin:
> My word was law from Ith to Emain,
> And shook at Inver Amergin
> The hearts of the world-troubling seamen,
> And drove tumult and war away
> From girl and boy and man and beast;
> The fields grew fatter day by day,
> The wild fowl of the air increased;
> And every ancient Ollave said,
> While he bent down his fading head.
> "He drives away the Northern cold."
> They will not hush, the leaves a-flutter round me, the beech
>   leaves old.

Ollaves were highly esteemed priestly judges, and here they credit the king with curbing winter. The wonderful refrain picks up a mounting madness as the poem proceeds:

> I sat and mused and drank sweet wine;
> A herdsman came from inland valleys,
> Crying, the pirates drove his swine
> To fill their dark-beaked hollow galleys.
> I called my battle-breaking men
> And my loud brazen battle-cars
> From rolling vale and rivery glen;
> And under the blinking of the stars
> Fell on the pirates by the deep,
> And hurled them in the gulph of sleep:
> These hands won many a torque of gold.
> They will not hush, the leaves a-flutter round me, the beech
>   leaves old.

But slowly, as I shouting slew
And trampled in the bubbling mire,
In my most secret spirit grew
A whirling and a wandering fire:
I stood: keen stars above me shone,
Around me shone keen eyes of men:
I laughed aloud and hurried on
By rocky shore and rushy fen;
I laughed because birds fluttered by,
And starlight gleamed, and clouds flew high,
And rushes waved and waters rolled.
They will not hush, the leaves a-flutter round me, the beech
    leaves old.

King Goll, warrior and ruler, suddenly is caught up in a secular epiphany. The whirling, wandering fire pursued by the Shelleyan poet in *Alastor* grows within the king's spirit. He understands little but drives on with birds, clouds, waving rushes, and rolling water, but above all with the aged beech leaves fluttering around him and augmenting his madness.

And now I wander in the woods
When summer gluts the golden bees,
Or in autumnal solitudes
Arise the leopard-coloured trees;
Or when along the wintry strands
The cormorants shiver on their rocks;
I wander on, and wave my hands,
And sing, and shake my heavy locks.
The grey wolf knows me; by one ear
I lead along the woodland deer;
The hares run by me growing bold.
They will not hush, the leaves a-flutter round me, the beech
    leaves old.

Goll sings in harmony with all that passes and is one with nature. But the refrain beats again ominously.

I came upon a little town
That slumbered in the harvest moon,
And passed a-tiptoe up and down,
Murmuring, to a fitful tune,
How I have followed, night and day,
A tramping of tremendous feet,
And saw where this old tympan lay
Deserted on a doorway seat,
And bore it to the woods with me;
Of some inhuman misery
Our married voices wildly trolled.
They will not hush, the leaves a-flutter round me, the beech
    leaves old.

A tympan is an archaic drum. Against the percussive beat Goll trolls or ululates a monody. It has to be for himself as his madness augments.

I sang how, when day's toil is done,
Orchil shakes out her long dark hair
That hides away the dying sun
And sheds faint odours through the air:
When my hand passed from wire to wire
It quenched, with sound like falling dew
The whirling and the wandering fire;
But lift a mournful ulalu,
For the kind wires are torn and still,
And I must wander wood and hill
Through summer's heat and winter's cold.
They will not hush, the leaves a-flutter round me, the beech
    leaves old.

Orchil is thought to have been a Saxon goddess who lived in a giant underground cavern with two looms. A great weaver, she spun life up through the grass with one hand, but with the other she wove death outward and downward through the earth. The weaving's sound is perpetual and we know it as time. She weaves what poets want to call beauty and fix eternally, but inwardly she is metamorphic.

Yeats was an incessant reviser of his own poetry. Increasingly I tend to prefer the original versions, but "The Madness of King Goll" acquired a kind of eloquent lacquer in its final form. There are touches of William Morris and of Dante Gabriel Rossetti in the poem, but it has a weight and universality that those admirable poets sometimes lack.

Poems by Yeats sometimes can seem so universal that one is surprised that he wrote it. Perhaps the most famous is "The Lake Isle of Innisfree" (1888), written when the poet was twenty-three and residing in London, where he missed the uninhabited isle so close in his childhood. Yeats compared this lyric to Thoreau's *Walden*, rather surprising for this elaborate Celtic keening:

> I will arise and go now, and go to Innisfree,
> And a small cabin build there, of clay and wattles made:
> Nine bean-rows will I have there, a hive for the honey-bee;
> And live alone in the bee-loud glade.
>
> And I shall have some peace there, for peace comes dropping slow,
> Dropping from the veils of the morning to where the cricket
>   sings;
> There midnight's all a glimmer, and noon a purple glow,
> And evening full of the linnet's wings.
>
> I will arise and go now, for always night and day
> I hear lake water lapping with low sounds by the shore;
> While I stand on the roadway, or on the pavements grey,
> I hear it in the deep heart's core.

This makes a considerable contrast with Yeats's official death poem for himself, "Under Ben Bulben" (initially he titled it "My Convictions"):

I

>   Swear by what the Sages spoke
> Round the Mareotic Lake
> That the Witch of Atlas knew,
> Spoke and set the cocks a-crow

Swear by those horsemen, by those women,
Complexion and form prove superhuman,
That pale, long visaged company
That airs an immortality
Completeness of their passions won;
Now they ride the wintry dawn
Where Ben Bulben sets the scene.

. . .

III
You that Mitchel's prayer have heard
"Send war in our time, O Lord!"
Know that when all words are said
And a man is fighting mad,
Something drops from eyes long blind
He completes his partial mind,
For an instant stands at ease,
Laughs aloud, his heart at peace,
Even the wisest man grows tense
With some sort of violence
Before he can accomplish fate
Know his work or choose his mate.

[ll. 1–11, 25–36]

John Mitchel (1815–1875) was an Irish revolutionary exiled to Tasmania. He escaped to the United States, where he devoted himself to advancing the cause of black slavery, and lost two sons fighting for the Confederacy. Eventually, he returned to England and was elected to the House of Commons, but as a felon could not be seated. Yeats vigorously endorses the prayer: "Send war in our time, O Lord!"

IV
. . .
Quattrocento put in paint,
On backgrounds for a God or Saint,
Gardens where a soul's at ease;
Where everything that meets the eye

Flowers and grass and cloudless sky
Resemble forms that are, or seem
When sleepers wake and yet still dream,
And when it's vanished still declare,
With only bed and bedstead there,
That Heavens had opened.
. . .

V
Irish poets learn your trade
Sing whatever is well made,
Scorn the sort now growing up
All out of shape from toe to top,
Their unremembering hearts and heads
Base-born products of base beds . . .

[ll. 53–63, 69–74]

This farrago has been much admired, by W. H. Auden in particular. Much of it is of a badness not to be believed. And yet the Shelleyan element in the poem partly saves it, where it deliberately alludes to *The Witch of Atlas*:

LVIII.
By Moeris and the Mareotid lakes,
    Strewn with faint blooms like bridal chamber floors,
Where naked boys bridling tame water-snakes,
    Or charioteering ghastly alligators,
Had left on the sweet waters mighty wakes
    Of those huge forms—within the brazen doors
Of the great Labyrinth slept both boy and beast,
Tired with the pomp of their Osirian feast.

LIX.
And where within the surface of the river
    The shadows of the massy temples lie,
And never are erased—but tremble ever
    Like things which every cloud can doom to die,
Through lotus-paven canals, and wheresoever

The works of man pierced that serenest sky
With tombs, and towers, and fanes, 'twas her delight
To wander in the shadow of the night.

. . .

LXX.

For on the night when they were buried, she
    Restored the embalmers' ruining, and shook
The light out of the funeral lamps, to be
    A mimic day within that deathly nook;
And she unwound the woven imagery
    Of second childhood's swaddling bands, and took
The coffin, its last cradle, from its niche,
And threw it with contempt into a ditch.

. . .

LXXV.

The soldiers dreamed that they were blacksmiths, and
    Walked out of quarters in somnambulism;
Round the red anvils you might see them stand
    Like Cyclopses in Vulcan's sooty abysm,
Beating their swords to ploughshares;—in a band
    The jailors sent those of the liberal schism
Free through the streets of Memphis, much, I wis,
To the annoyance of king Amasis.

. . .

LXXVIII.

These were the pranks she played among the cities
    Of mortal men, and what she did to Sprites
And Gods, entangling them in her sweet ditties
    To do her will, and show their subtle sleights,
I will declare another time; for it is
    A tale more fit for the weird winter nights
Than for these garish summer days, when we
Scarcely believe much more than we can see.

                    [ll. 505–520, 601–608, 641–648, 665–672]

Shelley's urbane, almost tender ironies are alien to Yeats. Yet however he tried, he could not get Shelley out of his ear or mind. The great poem "Byzantium" is quarried from these stanzas of *The Witch of Atlas*. Yeats divided himself from Shelley politically, socially, in every mode of ideology, yet the daemon in Yeats, as he acknowledged, was Shelley.

CHAPTER FOURTEEN

Hart Crane

The Unknown God

I N THE ACTS OF the Apostles, St. Paul, who had been Saul of
Tarsus, addresses the citizens of Athens:

Then Paul stood in the midst of Mars' street, and said, Ye
men of Athens, I perceive that in all things ye are too superstitious. For as I passed by, and beheld your devotions,
I found an altar wherein was written, UNTO THE UNKNOWN
GOD. Whom ye then ignorantly worship, him show I unto
you. God that made the world, and all things that are therein,
seeing that he is Lord of heaven and earth, dwelleth not in
temples made with hands.

[Acts (Geneva Bible) 17:22–24]

Hart Crane, hymning Brooklyn Bridge, invoked an unknown
god:

O harp and altar, of the fury fused,
(How could mere toil align thy choiring strings!)
Terrific threshold of the prophet's pledge,
Prayer of pariah, and the lover's cry,—

Again the traffic lights that skim thy swift
Unfractioned idiom, immaculate sigh of stars,
Beading thy path—condense eternity:
And we have seen night lifted in thine arms.

Under thy shadow by the piers I waited;
Only in darkness is thy shadow clear.
The City's fiery parcels all undone,
Already snow submerges an iron year . . .

O Sleepless as the river under thee,
Vaulting the sea, the prairies' dreaming sod,
Unto us lowliest sometime sweep, descend
And of the curveship lend a myth to God.

["Proem: To Brooklyn Bridge,"
from *The Bridge* (1930), ll. 29–44]

The bridge is both an Aeolian harp and an altar. Michelangelo's *Pietà* informs the magnificent "And we have seen night lifted in thine arms." Something of the aura of the dark night of the soul, as in St. John of the Cross, enters "Only in darkness is thy shadow clear." Hart Crane coins the word "curveship" for the Bridge's leap to lend a myth to God, who badly needs another one. Unchurched and desperate, believing only in the next poem if he can write it, Walt Whitman's most eloquent heir calls down a god unknown.

Hart Crane was an autodidact who left high school without finishing his junior year. But he seems to have read everything and to have remembered what could nurture his art. He is a religious poet totally unchurched. And yet his spiritual temperament allies him to the poignant triad of Luis de León, Teresa de Avila, and Juan de la Cruz. All of them had Jewish converso ancestry and suffered many sorrows and vicissitudes, partly on that account. When I recite Hart Crane and Juan de la Cruz in sequence, I experience a sense of continuity:

Under thy shadow by the piers I waited;
Only in darkness is thy shadow clear.
The City's fiery parcels all undone,
Already snow submerges an iron year . . .

En una noche obscura,
con ansias en amores imflamada,
¡oh dichosa uentura!
sali sin ser notada,
estando ya mi casa sosegada.

A escuras y segura,
por la secreta escala disfraçada,
¡oh dichosa uentura!
a escuras y ençelada,
estando ya mi casa sosegada.

Upon an obscure night
Fevered with love in love's anxiety
(O hapless-happy plight!),
I went, none seeing me,
Forth from my house where all things be.

By night, secure from sight,
And by the secret stair, disguisedly,
(O hapless-happy plight!)
By night, and privily,
Forth from my house where all things quiet be.

                                    [Translated by Arthur Symons]

When Hart Crane incants, *"Under thy shadow by the piers I waited,"* he joins Juan de la Cruz in the Dark Night of the Soul. Binding the American pariah and the converso mystic together are the strains of the Song of Solomon:

> By night on my bed I sought him whom my soul loveth: I sought him, but I found him not. I will rise now, and go about the city in the streets, and in the broad ways I will seek him whom my soul loveth: I sought him, but I found him not.
>
>   [Song of Solomon (KJV) 3:1–2]

"I sought him, but I found him not": that is the burden of Hart Crane's life and of his poetry. Of all American poets, Walt Whitman and Emily Dickinson stand apart. Their inescapable descendants include Robert Frost, Wallace Stevens, William Carlos

Williams, Marianne Moore, and Thomas Stearns Eliot, and a later group: Elizabeth Bishop, John Ashbery, A. R. Ammons, and James Merrill. None of these, not even Whitman or Dickinson, had as pure a gift as Hart Crane. Unfortunately, he drowned himself at the age of thirty-two, and so could not give full measure. Yet the best of his poems—the lyrics and meditations of *White Buildings* (1926), the epic *The Bridge*, and the death ode "The Broken Tower" (1932)—are uniquely fiery zones of American romanticism, deserving comparison with Shelley and with Keats.

I teach Hart Crane for at least two discussion meetings every year. It has to be acknowledged that he is a difficult poet, but it delights me that my students are so adept at overcoming the initial problems of his impacted density.

Crane spoke of his work as manifesting "the logic of metaphor" (letter to Harriet Monroe, October 1926). He is a great abuser and extender of trope. I frequently begin with one of his most purgatorial poems, difficult and radiant, "Possessions" (1923):

Witness now this trust! the rain
That steals softly direction
And the key, ready to hand—sifting
One moment in sacrifice (the direst)
Through a thousand nights the flesh
Assaults outright for bolts that linger
Hidden,—O undirected as the sky
That through its black foam has no eyes
For this fixed stone of lust . . .

Accumulate such moments to an hour:
Account the total of this trembling tabulation.
I know the screen, the distant flying taps
And stabbing medley that sways—
And the mercy, feminine, that stays
As though prepared.

And I, entering, take up the stone
As quiet as you can make a man . . .
In Bleecker Street, still trenchant in a void,
Wounded by apprehensions out of speech,

I hold it up against a disk of light—
I, turning, turning on smoked forking spires,
The city's stubborn lives, desires.

Tossed on these horns, who bleeding dies,
Lack all but piteous admissions to be spilt
Upon the page whose blind sum finally burns
Record of rage and partial appetites.
The pure possession, the inclusive cloud
Whose heart is fire shall come,—the white wind rase
All but bright stones wherein our smiling plays.

When I was young I could make little of this poem, enthusiastic
as I was for Crane. Endless rereadings clarified and purged away the
difficulties. The poet, driven by desperate lust, cruises the streets of
Greenwich Village and hopes for relief through any homoerotic encounter he can manage.

One of the images tightening "Possessions" is the stone. In the
final line of the first stanza it appears as "this fixed stone of lust." In
the opening line of the third stanza, we are enjoined: "take up the
stone." Hart Crane, unchurched but intensely spiritual, relies upon
the Book of Revelation for the greatly transformed "bright stones"
of the poem's final line. He intends us to remember:

> He that hath an ear, let him hear what the Spirit saith unto
> the churches; To him that overcometh will I give to eat of the
> hidden manna, and will give him a white stone, and in the
> stone a new name written, which no man knoweth saving he
> that receiveth it.
>
> [Revelation (KJV) 2:17]

Why does Hart Crane use the plural in the title "Possessions"?
I begin to think that the second "possession" would be the new name
that the poet hopes to receive.

The opening irony of "Possessions" is "Witness now this
trust!" Is the reader called upon to certify a covenant? Certainly
Crane does not trust in Revelation. I recall writing that the stone
becomes his image of voice, his version of the Whitmanian tally,

since it counts up nights of undirected lust and counts down to self-immolation.

Meticulously Crane heaps up nouns and verbs of counting: "sifting," "a thousand nights," "accumulate," "account the total," "tabulation," "medley," "blind sum," and "record."

Whitman's tally was an image of voice. Crane transumes this into the voice of an image. An omnivorous reader, he knew from Plato and from Walter Pater's *Plato and Platonism* (1893) that the Greek daemon appeared as an image, in contrast to the prophetic daemon of the Bible, which was a voice.

All of the voices and images of "Possessions" are gathered into one negative tally or image of wounded and bleeding voice: Crane's frightening depiction of being roasted on the spit of the whirling skyscrapers of the city:

> I, turning, turning on smoked forking spires,
> The city's stubborn lives, desires.
> Tossed on these horns, who bleeding dies . . .

Crane is gored as on the horns of a bull until the bleeding is transumed into the writing of the poem, "Possessions": "piteous admissions to be spilt / Upon the page." The "blind sum" catches fire and the white wind burns away everything but a newness.

I always find it moving when Crane puns upon his own name so as to suggest a playful and limited redemption:

> The pure possession, the inclusive cloud
> Whose heart is fire shall come,—the white wind rase
> All but bright stones wherein our smiling plays.

Several of my departed friends requested that Crane's "At Melville's Tomb" (1925) be recited as part of their final farewell. By "tomb" the poem means the ocean as well as Melville's writings:

> Often beneath the wave, wide from this ledge
> The dice of drowned men's bones he saw bequeath
> An embassy. Their numbers as he watched,
> Beat on the dusty shore and were obscured.

"Their numbers" are "the dice" into which the drowned mariners have been reduced. "Calyx" is the vortex or whirlpool of the sinking *Pequod* but also a cornucopia. The Greek "calyx" is the flower's outer whorl, but also a chalice for drinking wine. Melville bequeaths the embassy of engulfment as Hamlet in some sense did.

> And wrecks passed without sound of bells,
> The calyx of death's bounty giving back
> A scattered chapter, livid hieroglyph,
> The portent wound in corridors of shells.

John T. Irwin, in his book *American Hieroglyphics* (1980) and in his equally vast commentary on Hart Crane, *Hart Crane's Poetry* (2011), contributes much to our seeing that all of *Moby-Dick* is a hieroglyph: Captain Ahab; Queequeg the Harpooner; the inscrutable White Whale; Ishmael the Platonist; Fedallah the Parsi Harpooner; overwhelmingly, the book itself; all need unpacking.

> Then in the circuit calm of one vast coil,
> Its lashings charmed and malice reconciled,
> Frosted eyes there were that lifted altars;
> And silent answers crept across the stars.

We are still very much in *Moby-Dick*, where Ahab is caught up in a coil and confronts the White Whale face-to-face in their final combat.

> Compass, quadrant and sextant contrive
> No farther tides . . . High in the azure steeps
> Monody shall not wake the mariner.
> This fabulous shadow only the sea keeps.

Ahab discards all his navigational aids and ends beyond monody or lament. Whatever bargain he has struck, through Fedallah or directly with the clear spirit of clear fire, he is removed from the realm of earth, where at best he would be a shadow. Only the sea keeps him, in the archaic sense of taking care of his fabulistic, more authentic shadow.

When I was a boy, my favorite poem by Hart Crane was "Voyages" II (1925):

> —And yet this great wink of eternity,
> Of rimless floods, unfettered leewardings,
> Samite sheeted and processioned where
> Her undinal vast belly moonward bends,
> Laughing the wrapt inflections of our love;

> Take this Sea, whose diapason knells
> On scrolls of silver snowy sentences,
> The sceptred terror of whose sessions rends
> As her demeanors motion well or ill,
> All but the pieties of lovers' hands.

By "diapason" Crane implies a full compass. The Sea is a royal court that decrees a tearing apart of the lovers.

> And onward, as bells off San Salvador
> Salute the crocus lustres of the stars,
> In these poinsettia meadows of her tides,—
> Adagios of islands, O my Prodigal,
> Complete the dark confessions her veins spell.

Emil Opffer, Crane's sailor lover, had told him that you could hear the bells of a sunken city tolling as you sailed the Caribbean. Earth, stars, tides come together in the melded imagery of this stanza.

> Mark how her turning shoulders wind the hours,
> And hasten while her penniless rich palms
> Pass superscription of bent foam and wave,—
> Hasten, while they are true,—sleep, death, desire,
> Close round one instant in one floating flower.

The Caribbean becomes a watch winding the hours. The two floating lovers close round in a water flower that follows a William Blake illustration.

Bind us in time, O Seasons clear, and awe.
O minstrel galleons of Carib fire,
Bequeath us to no earthly shore until
Is answered in the vortex of our grave
The seal's wide spindrift gaze toward paradise.

The binding here is a covenant of love, while those minstrel galleons suggest the fireships the English used against the Spanish Armada. William Blake's conceptual image of the vortex, a whirlpool reflecting a triumph of vision over mortality, is enhanced by the Melvillean baby seals whose gaze is spindrift, meaning wind spray or cresting waves blown by the wind. Crane preferred "the seal's wide findrinny," where that Old Irish word refers to white bronze, but his friends overruled him.

The sequence of six "Voyages" monumentalizes the great passion of Hart Crane's life, his relationship with the Danish-American merchant seaman Emil Opffer. It meant far more to Crane than to Opffer. Much later in life Opffer, who had married conventionally and gone back to Denmark, was asked about his memories of Crane. Evidently he had none.

"Voyages" incants the heights of ecstatic fulfillment—"I have seen the Word made flesh"—and the inevitable departure of Emil Opffer. The word "voyages" stems ultimately from the Latin "provisions for a journey." Crane was aware of the poetic voyages of Baudelaire and of Rimbaud but turns to the Shelley of *Alastor* and of Asia's voyage in *Prometheus Unbound*.

Formally, the "Voyages" sequence begins in a little poem very different from the massively orchestrated five lyrics that will follow it. "Voyages" (I) (1921) starts, "Above the fresh ruffles of the surf / Bright striped urchins flay each other with sand." Crane may be remembering Wordsworth's "Intimations" ode:

Hence in a season of calm weather
Though inland far we be,
Our Souls have sight of that immortal sea
Which brought us hither,
Can in a moment travel thither,

And see the Children sport upon the shore,
And hear the mighty waters rolling evermore.

It makes a kind of sense to say of Hart Crane that he was the poet of the Caribbean. His few happy memories of childhood came from sojourns on the Isle of Pines (near Cuba). The intense word-consciousness that marks his mature style, as in "Voyages" II, to some extent rises from his ambition to represent the total experience of homoerotic rapture in a new register, beyond any other depictions.

Herman Melville, both in *Moby-Dick* and in the shorter fiction, provided Crane with diction for "Voyages." The chapter "The Spirit-Spout" of *Moby-Dick* memorably tells us "all the waves rolled by like scrolls of silver; and, by their soft, suffusing seethings, made what seems a silvery silence." There is something Tennysonian in "samite sheeted and processioned," yet Crane darkens it by speaking of the Caribbean's "undinal vast belly," with its reference to *Undine* (1811), a short novel by Friedrich de la Motte Fouqué. Undines were female spirits of the water who sought to seduce men to steal their souls.

Crane, for whom Walt Whitman was a constant presence, shied away from the great fourfold image of night, death, the mother, and the sea. His inward self knew better, as here in a wonderful fragment:

The sea raised up a campanile . . . The wind I heard
Of brine partaking, whirling into shower
Of column that breakers sheared in shower
Back into bosom,—me—her, into natal power . . .
[ca. 1926–1927]

It may be that a little poem or fragment, with its suggestion of Emily Dickinson, was the last thing Crane composed:

To Conquer Variety
I have seen my ghost broken
My body blessed
And Eden
Scraped from my mother's breast

When the charge was spoken
Love dispossessed
And the seal broken. . . .

                                                    [ca. 1931–1932]

Hart Crane meditated upon every word he used. He would
have known that "variety" originally meant "change in fortune." Approaching suicide, the conquest of ill fortune seemed impossible.
He knew it went back to the sundering of his parents' marriage and
to his fixation upon his devouring mother.

Broken ghost and blessed (wounded) body abrogate a minimal
Eden. "Scraped" takes its etymological meaning of scratching with
the fingernails, as though the infant Crane (an only child) both
fought and welcomed the mother's nurture. The charge is guilt in
Kafka's sense: it is never to be doubted. Dispossessed Eros is weighted
down by the homosexual chagrin of the poem "Possessions." I use
"chagrin" in Crane's spirit, since it meant "rough skin" in its origins.

The broken seal does not seem to fit the text in Revelation. It is
not a sign but veritably urges death by water to break the hold of the
mother. "Voyages" II accepts the mother because it must yet set
against her the pieties of lovers' hands, Opffer's joined to Crane's.

There are several Hart Cranes. The ecstatic lyricist with his high
Pindaric sweep uttering apostrophes is only one of them. He is also
a poet of exquisite reverie, as here in "Repose of Rivers," composed
in 1926 and added to *White Buildings*:

The willows carried a slow sound,
A sarabande the wind mowed on the mead.
I could never remember
That seething, steady leveling of the marshes
Till age had brought me to the sea.

Do we hear the voice of the river or of the poet? We do hear the
voice of Herman Melville in Chapter 58 of *Moby-Dick*, describing
right whales feasting on brit, tiny crustaceans:

As morning mowers, who side by side slowly and seethingly
advance their scythes through the long wet grass of marshy

meads; even so these monsters swam, making a strange, grassy, cutting sound.

Many of us, wandering in Andalusia, have delighted in seeing a sarabande danced. It is slow, stately, and in triple time.

Flags, weeds. And remembrance of steep alcoves
Where cypresses shared the noon's
Tyranny; they drew me into hades almost.
And mammoth turtles climbing sulphur dreams
Yielded, while sun-silt rippled them
Asunder . . .

How much I would have bartered! the black gorge
And all the singular nestings in the hills
Where beavers learn stitch and tooth.
The pond I entered once and quickly fled—
I remember now its singing willow rim.

And finally, in that memory all things nurse;
After the city that I finally passed
With scalding unguents spread and smoking darts
The monsoon cut across the delta
At gulf gates . . . There, beyond the dykes

I heard wind flaking sapphire, like this summer,
And willows could not hold more steady sound.

Those mammoth male turtles, destroyed by coition, stem from Melville's tale "The Encantadas" (1854) and perhaps from D. H. Lawrence's tortoise poems. The Oedipal trespass, from which the boy Crane flees, contrasts to Whitman's willing merger with the sea as mother in the "Lilacs" elegy. Crane's homoerotic initiation in New Orleans is pungently expressed in "With scalding unguents spread and smoking darts." The final citation of the willows implies a resolution of mitigated self-acceptance if not quite of peace.

Hart Crane rocks back and forth between elegy and celebration but at his strongest melds them together, as here in his poignant "Praise for an Urn" (1922), a monody for his friend the painter William Sommer:

It was a kind and northern face
That mingled in such exile guise
The everlasting eyes of Pierrot
And, of Gargantua, the laughter.

His thoughts, delivered to me
From the white coverlet and pillow,
I see now, were inheritances—
Delicate riders of the storm.

The slant moon on the slanting hill
Once moved us toward presentiments
Of what the dead keep, living still,
And such assessments of the soul

As, perched in the crematory lobby,
The insistent clock commented on,
Touching as well upon our praise
Of glories proper to the time.

Still, having in mind gold hair,
I cannot see that broken brow
And miss the dry sound of bees
Stretching across a lucid space.

Scatter these well-meant idioms
Into the smoky spring that fills
The suburbs, where they will be lost.
They are no trophies of the sun.

Crane's authentic love for the lost painter is subdued until the
final two stanzas. It is acutely subtle to convey a particular quality
of the lost friend by the image of "dry sound of bees / Stretching
across a lucid space." Sommer's essential being is caught up in
that reflective paradigm, where "lucid" is used as though it meant
"shining."

Undertones of Shelley and of Blake enter the final quatrain. The
"scatter my words among mankind" of "The Ode to the West Wind"
is severely qualified by Crane's self-deprecating "well-meant idioms."
Even more striking is the use of Keats's "Ode on Melancholy":

Turning to poison while the bee-mouth sips:
Ay, in the very temple of Delight
   Veil'd Melancholy has her sovran shrine,
     Though seen of none save him whose strenuous tongue
  Can burst Joy's grape against his palate fine;
His soul shalt taste the sadness of her might,
   And be among her cloudy trophies hung.

"They are no trophies of the sun" plays against these "cloudy trophies" in what will be the temple of the sun in an allied passage in Keats's *The Fall of Hyperion*.

From boyhood on, I have been haunted by Crane's lyric "Passage" (1925). Is there a more American hope than "I was promised an improved infancy"? Crane, whose intellect was extraordinarily keen, rightly traced his own tragedy to unhappy family beginnings.

Where the cedar leaf divides the sky
I heard the sea.
In sapphire arenas of the hills
I was promised an improved infancy.

Sulking, sanctioning the sun,
My memory I left in a ravine,—
Casual louse that tissues the buck-wheat,
Aprons rocks, congregates pears
In moonlit bushels
And wakens alleys with a hidden cough.

Dangerously the summer burned
(I had joined the entrainments of the wind).
The shadows of boulders lengthened my back:
In the bronze gongs of my cheeks
The rain dried without odour.

"It is not long, it is not long;
See where the red and black
Vine-stanchioned valleys—": but the wind
Died speaking through the ages that you know
And bug, chimney-sooted heart of man!

So was I turned about and back, much as your smoke
Compiles a too well-known biography.

The evening was a spear in the ravine
That throve through very oak. And had I walked
The dozen particular decimals of time?
Touching an opening laurel, I found
A thief beneath, my stolen book in hand.

"Why are you back here-smiling an iron coffin?"
"To argue with the laurel," I replied:
"Am justified in transience, fleeing
Under the constant wonder of your eyes—."

He closed the book. And from the Ptolemies
Sand troughed us in a glittering abyss.
A serpent swam a vertex to the sun
—On unpaced beaches leaned its tongue and drummed.
What fountains did I hear? What icy speeches?
Memory, committed to the page, had broke.

Wordsworth's "Intimations" ode is the clear source for hearing
the sea though one is far inland. Describing the hills as bright blue
possibly marks them as the realm of azure aspiration, as in some
French Symbolists, Shelley, and Wallace Stevens.

John T. Irwin, Hart Crane's most comprehensive critic, eluci-
dates "Passage" in the Nietzschean mode by relating it to the very
complex lyric "Lachrymae Christi" (1924). Lachrymae Christi, "tears
of Christ," remains a highly drinkable wine, but the poem is one of
those rare complexities I have never liked:

Whitely, while benzine
Rinsings from the moon
Dissolve all but the windows of the mills
(Inside the sure machinery
Is still
And curdled only where a sill
Sluices its one unyielding smile)

Immaculate venom binds
The fox's teeth, and swart
Thorns freshen on the year's
First blood. From flanks unfended,
Twanged red perfidies of spring
Are trillion on the hill.

And the nights opening
Chant pyramids,—
Anoint with innocence,—recall
To music and retrieve what perjuries
Had galvanized the eyes.

While chime
Beneath and all around
Distilling clemencies,—worms'
Inaudible whistle, tunneling
Not penitence
But song, as these
Perpetual fountains, vines,—

Thy Nazarene and tinder eyes.

(Let sphinxes from the ripe
Borage of death have cleared my tongue
Once again; vermin and rod
No longer bind. Some sentient cloud
Of tears flocks through the tendoned loam:
Betrayed stones slowly speak.)

Names peeling from Thine eyes
And their undimming lattices of flame,
Spell out in palm and pain
Compulsion of the year, O Nazarene.

Lean long from sable, slender boughs,
Unstanched and luminous. And as the nights
Strike from Thee perfect spheres,
Lift up in lilac-emerald breath the grail
Of earth again—

Thy face
From charred and riven stakes, O
Dionysus, Thy
Unmangled target smile.

I have the odd sensation that D. H. Lawrence wrote this poem.
Crane's genius for impacted rhetoric gets away from him here. You
can unpack this, but that will not confer upon it the aesthetic splendor that Crane gives at his best. His originality and gift for cognition are present but, for me at least, they do not give pleasure. I
happily return to "Passage," where Crane's antithetical struggle with
memories both personal and literary provides the drama of a revision of Walt Whitman's grand self-elegy "As I Ebb'd with the Ocean
of Life" (1860):

1

As I ebb'd with the ocean of life,
As I wended the shores I know,
As I walk'd where the ripples continually wash you Paumanok,
Where they rustle up hoarse and sibilant,
Where the fierce old mother endlessly cries for her castaways,
I musing late in the autumn day, gazing off southward,
Held by this electric self out of the pride of which I utter poems,
Was seiz'd by the spirit that trails in the lines underfoot,
The rim, the sediment that stands for all the water and all the
        land of the globe.

Fascinated, my eyes reverting from the south, dropt, to follow
        those slender windrows,
Chaff, straw, splinters of wood, weeds, and the sea-gluten,
Scum, scales from shining rocks, leaves of salt-lettuce, left by
        the tide,
Miles walking, the sound of breaking waves the other side of me,
Paumanok there and then as I thought the old thought of
        likenesses,
These you presented to me you fish-shaped island,
As I wended the shores I know,
As I walk'd with that electric self seeking types.

2

As I wend to the shores I know not,
As I list to the dirge, the voices of men and women wreck'd,
As I inhale the impalpable breezes that set in upon me,
As the ocean so mysterious rolls toward me closer and closer,
I too but signify at the utmost a little wash'd-up drift,
A few sands and dead leaves to gather,
Gather, and merge myself as part of the sands and drift.

O baffled, balk'd, bent to the very earth,
Oppress'd with myself that I have dared to open my mouth,
Aware now that amid all that blab whose echoes recoil upon
     me I have not once had the least
     idea who or what I am,
But that before all my arrogant poems the real Me stands yet
     untouch'd, untold,
     altogether unreach'd,
Withdrawn far, mocking me with mock-congratulatory signs
     and bows,
With peals of distant ironical laughter at every word I have written,
Pointing in silence to these songs, and then to the sand beneath.

I perceive I have not really understood any thing, not a single
     object, and that no man ever can,
Nature here in sight of the sea taking advantage of me to dart
     upon me and sting me,
Because I have dared to open my mouth to sing at all.
                                        [1891–1892 version]

Crane was perhaps too courageous in having his "Passage" confront so directly Whitman at his most awesome. The debt is clearest when Walt, *Leaves of Grass* in his hand, is confronted by his Real
Me with mockery. Crane, acute in self-knowledge, in search of the
laurel of poetic incarnation, finds a thief, with book in hand evidently
stolen from Whitman:

Pointing in silence to these songs, and then to the sand beneath.

Touching an opening laurel, I found
A thief beneath, my stolen book in hand.

One of Hart Crane's deepest strengths is to hold himself open to so many forerunners and yet to make himself seem earlier and they belated. Crane's immediate precursors included Eliot and Whitman, only apparently antitheses. But his lineage is larger: Christopher Marlowe, Shakespeare, Milton, Blake, Wordsworth, Shelley, and Keats are a cavalcade leading on to Crane. Rimbaud was a vital example. The American ancestors in addition to Whitman are Melville, Dickinson, Emerson, Stevens, and, going back earlier, William Cullen Bryant.

On the surface Crane's poetry can seem quite traditional. He writes in closed forms, accustomed metrics, clarified diction. What makes him initially difficult, marvelously original, and strangely disturbing is his radical revision of rhetoric. He turns rhetoric into a story of negation, evasion, and extravagance. By raising word-consciousness to its vertex and maintaining that rhetoricity all through his high invocations, he broke the new road as surely as Whitman had done before him.

The common reader need not trouble herself with the formal names of Hart Crane's tropes, but recognizing them can help clear away apparent difficulties. Alphabetically I might list these as anacoluthon, catachresis, chiasmus, crossing, irony, negation and negativity, and, most important, transumption.

Anacoluthon simply reverses grammatical sequence so that expectation can be confounded. You could call catachresis a malapropism or mistake of one word for another. Chiasmus reiterates words or cognitions but in reverse order.

Metalepsis or transumption thus becomes a total, final act of taking up a poetic stance in relation to anteriority, particularly to the anteriority of poetic language, which means primarily the loved and feared poems of the precursors. Properly accomplished, this stance figuratively produces the illusion of having fathered one's own fathers, which is the greatest illusion, the one that Vico called "divination," or that we could call poetic immorality.

Though Edelman and other informed scholars have doubted Crane's acquaintance with classical rhetoric, the poet's close friend Kenneth Burke told me that in their conversations he had given Crane an education in rhetoric.

From my childhood on I have heard Hart Crane's *The Bridge* (1930) slandered as "a splendid failure." More than ever I wonder what these critics could have meant by "failure." Though I prefer reading and teaching *The Bridge* in its 1926 version, and in the order of its composition, in whatever text, the poem dwarfs most rivals.

I have meditated upon "Proem: To Brooklyn Bridge" in part but need now to see it complete:

> *How many dawns, chill from his rippling rest*
> *The seagull's wings shall dip and pivot him,*
> *Shedding white rings of tumult, building high*
> *Over the chained bay waters Liberty—*
>
> [ll. 1–4]

The verbal interplay of this opening quatrain comprises an impact of assonance and internal rhyme, compact even for Crane: chill, rippling, wings, dip, pivot, white rings. Joining white wings to tumult is High Romantic synesthesia as in Shelley and Keats. That the harbor waters are chained suggests William Blake's Thames, chartered or bound between its banks.

> *Then, with inviolate curve, forsake our eyes*
> *As apparitional as sails that cross*
> *Some page of figures to be filed away;*
> *—Till elevators drop us from our day . . .*
>
> [ll. 5–8]

Up and down are as equivocal for Crane as they were for Blake. He revised "—Till elevators drop us from our day" "And elevators heave us to our day."

> *I think of cinemas, panoramic sleights*
> *With multitudes bent toward some flashing scene*
> *Never disclosed, but hastened to again,*
> *Foretold to other eyes on the same screen*
>
> [ll. 9–12]

Even as a boy or when young, I was never happy inside a cinema. Crane taught me that I was in Plato's cave, shut off from the true light.

And Thee, across the harbor, silver-paced
As though the sun took step of thee, yet left
Some motion ever unspent in thy stride,—
Implicitly thy freedom staying thee!

[ll. 13–16]

Crane is thinking of Blake:

Ah Sun-flower! weary of time,
Who countest the steps of the Sun:
Seeking after that sweet golden clime
Where the travellers journey is done.

Where the Youth pined away with desire,
And the pale Virgin shrouded in snow:
Arise from their graves and aspire,
Where my Sun-flower wishes to go.

The Bridge is not a heliotrope; it holds power in reserve.

Out of some subway scuttle, cell or loft
A bedlamite speeds to thy parapets,
Tilting there momently, shrill shirt ballooning,
A jest falls from the speechless caravan.

[ll. 17–20]

The mad suicide is applauded as he goes on to join William Cullen Bryant's endless caravan in "Thanatopsis" (1817).

Down Wall, from girder into street noon leaks,
A rip-tooth of the sky's acetylene;
All afternoon the cloud-flown derricks turn . . .
Thy cables breathe the North Atlantic still.

[ll. 21–24]

Rendering acetylene as a trope for sunlight is consonant with the vitalism of the stanza in which the Bridge is seen as alive, breathing in and out the winds stirring the North Atlantic.

And obscure as that heaven of the Jews,
Thy guerdon . . . Accolade thou dost bestow
Of anonymity time cannot raise:
Vibrant reprieve and pardon thou dost show.

O harp and altar, of the fury fused,
(How could mere toil align thy choiring strings!)
Terrific threshold of the prophet's pledge,
Prayer of pariah, and the lover's cry,—

[ll. 25–32]

Crane was a constant Bible reader searching for tropes. He knew that there was no Judaic afterlife except for Sheol in the Tanakh. The Bridge is now a god conferring the gift of oblivion, vibrant reprieve, and pardon for the poet's desire to leave a lasting name. Blake's Tyger may be in the background of the fusing fury that renders the Bridge both giant Aeolian harp and altar of the unknown god. On the threshold between temple and labyrinth, the poet-prophet pledges his vocation, but for us this is now pariah's prayer and lover's cry of loss.

Again the traffic lights that skim thy swift
Unfractioned idiom, immaculate sigh of stars,
Beading thy path—condense eternity:
And we have seen night lifted in thine arms.

Under thy shadow by the piers I waited;
Only in darkness is thy shadow clear.
The City's fiery parcels all undone,
Already snow submerges an iron year . . .

O Sleepless as the river under thee,
Vaulting the sea, the prairies' dreaming sod,
Unto us lowliest sometime sweep, descend
And of the curveship lend a myth to God.

[ll. 33–44]

These three quatrains are complex since they move from a Pietà (Jesus lifted in the arms of Mary) to an evocation of shadow as dark night of the soul, and onto the remarkable metaphor of the skyscraper's lights going on in the evening, across the bay. They are like carefully wrapped Christmas presents undone into segments looking up, yet they are demonic since snow submerges a year not of precious metal but of hard iron.

Then comes the closing salutation to the Sleepless Bridge vaulting the North Atlantic in one direction and Whitman's America in the other. The prayer is humble: sweep, descend, lend, and of the Bridge's curveship give a story back to a god who needs it badly.

The seagull at dawn rises from rest on the waves and synesthetically sheds a tumult of ringed whiteness, another white skyscraper to enhance the book's title, *White Buildings*.

What does it mean to call a curve inviolate? In the final line of the "Proem," the Bridge is implored to lend a myth to God "of the curveship." It is the curve, the leap, the vaulting, the sweep, the descent built into Brooklyn Bridge by John A. Roebling (1806–1869) that captured Crane.

There are a myriad of visions and raptures that inform Hart Crane's joyous obsession with Brooklyn Bridge. The strongest is his memory of walking across the bridge with Emil Opffer at the vertex of their erotic relationship:

> And I have been able to give freedom and life which was acknowledged in the ecstasy of walking hand in hand across the most beautiful bridge of the world, the cables enclosing us and pulling us upward in such a dance as I have never walked and never can walk with another.
> [Letter to Waldo Frank, April 21, 1924]

The bridge, as Kenneth Burke suggested, is the only bride Crane would ever possess. It will become one song, one bridge of fire, and a propulsion forward and upward:

> The bridge in becoming a ship, a world, a woman, a tremendous harp (as it does finally) seems to really have a career. I have attempted to induce the same feelings of elation, etc.— like being carried forward and upward simultaneously—both in imagery, rhythm and repetition, that one experiences in walking across my beloved Brooklyn Bridge.
> [Letter to Waldo Frank, January 18, 1926]

Two of the difficult strengths that have marred the reception of *The Bridge* are its originality of diverse forms and its negative sublimity. Walt Whitman's "Crossing Brooklyn Ferry" (1856) has the same relation to Crane's brief epic as Brooklyn Ferry has to the Brooklyn Bridge that replaced it, except that even Crane has not the amplitude and glory of Walt at his most poignant.

Crane's poetry is rarely discussed in regard to its fiery affect and its Virgilian longing for the farther shore, even as it voyages out into a star world brought down to earth and sea. So far as I know, Crane's Latin was rudimentary or nonexistent, but he read the *Aeneid* in translation with some care, hoping to employ it as a model.

Critics personally friendly to Crane, such as Allen Tate and Yvor Winters, attacked *The Bridge* for what they judged to be epic pretentions. Crane sensibly responded by granting that the epic hero was no longer possible. And yet the poet-voyager of *The Bridge* is indeed what Tate finally granted: the poet as hero. Alas that this should be an Orphic poet who will be torn in pieces and then sing on after he has drowned and his sundered world has broken to pieces.

I begin to see that Crane was a new kind of poet even as the biblical King David was a new kind of man. Rimbaud, under the shadows of Victor Hugo and of Baudelaire, burned with this kind of newness. Crane, shadowed by Whitman and Eliot, even more radically broke the vessels of creation.

Though Crane professed to compose *The Bridge* as an answer to *The Waste Land*, Walt Whitman, who sang as the Answerer, is the Sharer in the epic quest. Crane was so deep a reader that I think he anticipated our later realizations of the extent to which Eliot's masterwork was a revision of Whitman, and particularly of "When Lilacs Last in the Dooryard Bloom'd."

One of the mysteries of Crane is his rejection of Whitmanian form while embracing the content, and his rejection of Eliotic argument while emulating Eliot in form and indeed surpassing him toward even more elaborate closed forms. Crane's blank verse, when he chooses it, is perhaps more Marlovian than Shakespearean. His lyric practice follows William Blake, Shelley, Keats, though sometimes you can hear John Donne.

The most unsettled aspect of Crane's poetry is its palpable spirituality, its yearning for transcendence. Crane did not believe in the

Incarnation or in Resurrection. When he exalts the Word, he follows Emily Dickinson in her "Beloved Philology." It is impossible to think of him as a Roman Catholic devotional poet, and yet something profound in him might have been redeemed by such an identity.

A rigorous consideration of Crane must address his relation to the ancient religion of Orphism. When my students wish to write essays on him, I urge them to read *The Greeks and the Irrational* (1951) by E. R. Dodds. Crane was a kind of Platonist, but the kind is difficult to define. Perhaps it could be termed a Platonic Orphism founded upon traces of that religion in the *Dialogues*.

Orphic myth is grotesque. Zeus contains the entire cosmos after he devours Phanes, child of the world-egg and so seed of all substance. In consequence the universe is the body of Zeus. This goes beyond pantheism and is curiously similar to Hermeticism and later to Kabbalah.

The darkest aspect of Orphism is the sparagmos of Dionysus or Zagreus by the Titans. The heart of Dionysus is safely carried to Zeus, who then obliterates the Titans with lightning. It is from their ashes that humanity rises. So we have a Titanic guilt that needs to be expiated. The rending apart of Orpheus by the Maenads brings the story closer to the origin and fatality of poetic vocation.

Crane read extensively in Walter Pater and in Nietzsche. Both influenced him in bringing together Dionysus and Orpheus. John Irwin thinks that Jessie Weston's *From Ritual to Romance* (1920), acknowledged by T. S. Eliot in his notes to *The Waste Land*, also had an effect on Crane. Weston's book has always seemed to me dubious. It argues that Arthurian legend and the quest for the Holy Grail goes back to a Christian Gnostic text.

If you wish to formulate Hart Crane's quest as a poet, it may be best to think of it as an Orphic journey downward and outward in search of a lost Eurydice. The identity of that longed-for bride is multiform: Is it an improved version of the rather dreadful mother Grace Hart Crane? Is it the woman neither found nor findable, the American Eve, goddess of our Evening Land? Is it Walt Whitman's America that never was nor could be, a nation of comrades and of poets? Or is it Brooklyn Bridge itself, vaulting arc reaching after transcendence?

Pragmatically the bride is the poem itself, not so much the text as the relational event of its composition. Crane always staked his life on the next poem. If it could be achieved, he could continue to live. He went to his death believing his gift had departed since bad communications convinced him that his magnificent death ode "The Broken Tower" had found no response.

I have always been puzzled and saddened by Crane's suicide. It seems incredible that a poet who had just composed "The Broken Tower" should despair of his potential. Though highly volatile, Hart Crane relied upon a quietism at his still center, as here:

> —visible wings of silence sown
> In azure circles, widening as they dip
>
> The matrix of the heart . . .

Let us contextualize these tropes in Crane's sublime death ode, "The Broken Tower":

> The bell-rope that gathers God at dawn
> Dispatches me as though I dropped down the knell
> Of a spent day—to wander the cathedral lawn
> From pit to crucifix, feet chill on steps from hell.
>
> Have you not heard, have you not seen that corps
> Of shadows in the tower, whose shoulders sway
> Antiphonal carillons launched before
> The stars are caught and hived in the sun's ray?
>
> The bells, I say, the bells break down their tower;
> And swing I know not where. Their tongues engrave
> Membrane through marrow, my long-scattered score
> Of broken intervals . . . And I, their sexton slave!
>
> Oval encyclicals in canyons heaping
> The impasse high with choir. Banked voices slain!
> Pagodas, campaniles with reveilles out leaping—
> O terraced echoes prostrate on the plain! . . .
>
> And so it was I entered the broken world
> To trace the visionary company of love, its voice

An instant in the wind (I know not whither hurled)
But not for long to hold each desperate choice.

My word I poured. But was it cognate, scored
Of that tribunal monarch of the air
Whose thigh embronzes earth, strikes crystal Word
In wounds pledged once to hope—cleft to despair?

The steep encroachments of my blood left me
No answer (could blood hold such a lofty tower
As flings the question true?)—or is it she
Whose sweet mortality stirs latent power?—

And through whose pulse I hear, counting the strokes
My veins recall and add, revived and sure
The angelus of wars my chest evokes:
What I hold healed, original now, and pure . . .

And builds, within, a tower that is not stone
(Not stone can jacket heaven)—but slip
Of pebbles,—visible wings of silence sown
In azure circles, widening as they dip

The matrix of the heart, lift down the eye
That shrines the quiet lake and swells a tower . . .
The commodious, tall decorum of that sky
Unseals her earth, and lifts love in its shower.

All of Crane's truncated poetic career is packed together in these ten quatrains. They are his alpha and omega, his starting point of the human and its end. The poem earns its audacious allusion to *Paradiso* 14, lines 25–27:

Qual si lamenta perché qui si moia
per viver colà sù, non vide quive
lo refrigerio de l'etterna ploia.

Whoso lamenteth him that here we die
    That we may live above, has never there
    Seen the refreshment of the eternal rain.
                    [Translated by H. W. Longfellow]

To Saint Thomas and to Beatrice this comes readily: they have witnessed this shower that is the water of life. How persuaded is Dante? But Crane, despite all his transcendental yearnings, had no faith in immortality, resurrection, redemption. Whitman naturalized these speculations but Crane could not. Going on ninety, I wonder if the enigma of Crane's spirituality can ever be resolved.

"Prayer of pariah" is one of Hart Crane's blazons. Had he returned to the United States in 1932, with the Great Depression afflicting so many, he would have lived the life of an outcast: a difficult poet, alcoholic, homoerotic, without income, homeless, a burden for his remaining friends. He had confronted all that before and found the strength to go on living and writing. Why did he pass so wrongful a final judgment upon himself?

There is deep unease underlying all of the last letters he wrote his friends from Mexico. But it is a malaise just this side of breakage. The poems are the best of Hart Crane, and I would think that, read deeply, they might uncover his Orphic drive beyond the pleasure principle.

The occultism of W. B. Yeats and, in a different register, of D. H. Lawrence, somehow does not prepare me for my wonderment at Crane's interest in the writings of the crank esotericist P. D. Ouspensky. Changing the relation between space and time is a dominant desire in Crane's poetry, where it follows William Blake rather than cosmological charlatanry.

Something of the authentic permanence of Hart Crane's poetry is inextricably wound up with the image of "bridging." Etymologically the word goes back to "a beam" or "a log." There is a cosmos separating the necessary *materia* and the vast implications of bridging. Crane's Brooklyn Bridge binds past and future together. It is harp, altar, ship, vision of the voyage, American Eve to American Adam, substance of things hoped for, evidence of things not seen, the poem above all, seeking fulfillment of Walt Whitman's prophecy while fighting against the perfection of death in Eliot's *The Waste Land*.

The burden of *The Bridge* has been judged too heavy for Hart Crane to sustain. When I was young the organized lament of R. P. Blackmur, Allen Tate, Yvor Winters, Edmund Wilson, and their followers was that Crane's epic was a "failure." Granted that such weak reading could afflict anyone, and that this was somewhat less

misguided than T. S. Eliot's pronunciamento that *Hamlet* was most
certainly an aesthetic failure, I have been made forever wary of my
own negative judgments.

I tend to think of major works in conjunction with one another.
William Carlos Williams's *Paterson* Book 1 was not published until
1946, but its crucial passages were written in 1926, when most of
The Bridge was composed. Faulkner's *As I Lay Dying* (1930) came to
our bard of negation in just six weeks in 1929. After his magnificent
advent in *Harmonium* (1923), Stevens was increasingly stifled and
did not emerge again until 1931, after which he enjoyed a quarter
century of fresh creation. I admire *Paterson* Book 1 but cannot set it
alongside *The Bridge* and *As I Lay Dying*. Williams proclaims new
realities, but his strength in representation fuses the heroic naturalism of John Keats with the American Lucretianism of Walt Whitman. Hart Crane and Faulkner at his most original persuade us of
new thresholds, new anatomies in the days we suffer and yet we are
spared.

Angus Fletcher located the threshold of sublime literature between temple and labyrinth. There is no American temple: there
seems only labyrinth. Whitman, following Emerson, takes his stance
on a threshold to the beyond. Hart Crane is more singular:

> I wanted you, nameless Woman of the South,
> No wraith, but utterly—as still more alone
> The Southern Cross takes night
> And lifts her girdles from her, one by one—
> High, cool,
>   wide from the slowly smoldering fire
> Of lower heavens,—
>   vaporous scars!
>
> Eve! Magdalene!
>   or Mary, you?
>
> Whatever call—falls vainly on the wave.
> O simian Venus, homeless Eve,
> Unwedded, stumbling gardenless to grieve
> Windswept guitars on lonely decks forever;
> Finally to answer all within one grave!

And this long wake of phosphor,
                    iridescent
Furrow of all our travel—trailed derision!
Eyes crumble at its kiss. Its long-drawn spell
Incites a yell. Slid on that backward vision
The mind is churned to spittle, whispering hell.

I wanted you . . . The embers of the Cross
Climbed by aslant and huddling aromatically.
It is blood to remember; it is fire
To stammer back . . . It is
God—your namelessness. And the wash—

All night the water combed you with black
Insolence. You crept out simmering, accomplished.
Water rattled that stinging coil, your
Rehearsed hair—docile, alas, from many arms.
Yes, Eve—wraith of my unloved seed!

The Cross, a phantom, buckled—dropped below the dawn.
Light drowned the lithic trillions of your spawn.

This is "Southern Cross" from the "Three Songs" canto of *The
Bridge*. The one time I met Tennessee Williams he recited the poem
from memory. The Southern Cross is a four-star constellation visible in the Southern Hemisphere. Here it is the blazon of a totally
dead Christianity but also of a fiercely desired woman.

The constellation begins as a trio of Eve, Magdalene, and Mary
the Virgin Mother. Crane insists this is "no wraith," but by the conclusion of the poem Eve is "wraith of my unloved seed" and the
Cross only an apparition in the dark.

The Southern Cross is threshold between the void and the bride,
between lost Atlantis or lost America and the Bridge seen as beacon
from the abode where the eternal are. The fire for which all thirst
smolders slowly and the Cross is reduced to embers. Shelley's embers from an unextinguished hearth have climbed to the ebbing fil-
ament of a temple.

High, cool,
     wide from the slowly smoldering fire

Of lower heavens,—
               vaporous scars!

    . . . The embers of the Cross
Climbed by aslant and huddling aromatically.
It is blood to remember; it is fire
To stammer back . . .

"Southern Cross" is hardly a poem of religious nostalgia. What
then is it? Hart Crane scarcely secularizes his perpetual use of religious imagery. Because he is not a Christian, we cannot call his work
"devotional." In the late sheaf of poems he considered publishing as
a volume to be called *Key West*, there is a strong, neglected meditation: "A Name for All" (1926):

Moonmoth and grasshopper that flee our page
And still wing on, untarnished of the name
We pinion to your bodies to assuage
Our envy of your freedom—we must maim

Because we are usurpers, and chagrined—
And take the wing and scar it in the hand.
Names we have, even, to clap on the wind;
But we must die, as you, to understand.

I dreamed that all men dropped their names, and sang
As only they can praise, who build their days
With fin and hoof, with wing and sweetened fang
Struck free and holy in one Name always.

I do not associate Hart Crane with St. Francis of Assisi and yet
these quatrains are Franciscan in spirit. We are usurpers. Even the
winds have suffered our namings. The third quatrain opens up to
redemptive vision but only when we have joined ourselves to all that
lives that is not human.

Sometime around 1926, Crane wrote an anguished poem, "A
Postscript":

Friendship agony! words came to me
at last shyly. My only final friends—

the wren and thrush, made solid print for me
across dawn's broken arc. No; yes . . . or were they
the audible ransom, ensign of my faith
towards something far, now farther than ever away?

Remember the lavender of that dawn, lilies,
their ribbon miles, beside the railroad ties
as one nears New Orleans, sweet trenches by the train
after the western desert, and the later cattle country;
and other gratuities, like porters, jokes, roses . . .

Dawn's broken arc! the noon's more furbished room!
Yet seldom was there faith in the heart's right kindness.
There were tickets and alarm clocks. There were counters
     and schedules;
and a paralytic woman on an island of the Indies,
Antillean fingers counting my pulse, my love forever.

I find this eloquent in its torment, but would I know this was Hart Crane had it not been among his papers? "Dawn's broken arc" is repeated with more urgency the second time. Crane's violent behavior during his frequent intoxications alienated many of his friends. His great year of creation, 1926, came out of a solitary existence on the Isle of Pines, where Sally Simpson cooked for him and looked after him as best she could. This postscript is his loving tribute to her.

Yet it is more than that. Crane longs for the farther shore, lavender dawn approaching New Orleans, pulsations of an artery in which a poet's work is done. The broken arc ends the curveship that might have lent a gift to God. The vision of a lifetime recedes far into the unapparent.

Everything that could go wrong with Crane's life transpired. But that forgets *The Bridge*, "Voyages," the other major lyrics and meditations of *White Buildings*, and "The Broken Tower." W. B. Yeats remarked that the intellect of man must choose between perfection of the life and perfection of the work. "Perfect" means to complete. Orphic sacrifice at thirty-two, Crane completed neither. His life vacillated between agony and a sense of glory. His work, though truncated, comes closest to Whitman in touching the American Sublime.

Here in a letter to the critic Yvor Winters, distinctly an enemy of Emerson, Whitman, and the American Sublime, Crane muses on the poetry of William Carlos Williams and then suggestively remarks on Walt Whitman's strength:

> There is no doubt of the charm of almost all of W's work. I except the "Paterson" and "Struggle of Wings" lately published in the *Dial*. I think them both highly disorganized. But in most of Williams' work I feel the kind of observations and emotions being "made" which seem to me too casual, however delightfully phrased, to be especially interesting. I feel much the same about most of Whitman. But with Whitman there is a steady current—under or overtone—that scarcely ever forsakes him. And a rhythm that almost constantly bespeaks the ineffable "word" that he has to speak. This "tone," assertion, or whatever—emerges through all the paradoxes and contradictions in his work. It doesn't try to be logical. It is an "operation" of some universal law which he apprehends but which cannot be expressed in any one attitude or formula. One either grasps it or one doesn't. When it comes out in a thing like the first "paragraph" of "Out of the Cradle Endlessly Rocking" it is overwhelming. The man is both distant and near:
>
>> This is the far-off depth and height reflecting my own face;
>> This is the thoughtful merge of myself, and the outlet again.
>
> [March 19, 1927]

Crane quotes, perhaps from memory, two grand lines from Section 19, *Song of Myself.* I once told John Ashbery that his vision of his own face reflected not in the water but in the worn stone floor of his bridge ("Wet Casements" [1977]) went back to this moment in Whitman. As was customary, John smiled and was silent.

Crane's insight is useful: Walt Whitman is both distant and near. What other poet ever could have written: "I place my hand upon you that you may be my poem" ("To You")? And yet Walt will always be out ahead of us or beneath our boot soles. He tells us: "Encompass worlds but never try to encompass me" (*Song of Myself*).

There is no particular intimacy between Hart Crane and his adept reader. Crane is a poet of apostrophe. He invokes Brooklyn Bridge, Whitman, the Caribbean Sea, Faustus and Helen, the American past, and the North Atlantic. Since I was a child I have been entranced by one apostrophe in particular:

> O Thou steeled Cognizance whose leap commits
> The agile precincts of the lark's return;
> Within whose lariat sweep encinctured sing
> In single chrysalis the many twain,—
> Of stars Thou art the stitch and stallion glow
> And like an organ, Thou, with sound of doom—
> Sight, sound and flesh Thou leadest from time's realm
> As love strikes clear direction for the helm.
>   ["Atlantis," from *The Bridge*, ll. 57–64]

"Cognizance" is both awareness and the heraldic emblem of the Bridge's vaulting of covenant between past and future. The etymological edge of "commits" is trust in that covenant, while here "precincts" is a way toward "encinctured" from the same root, meaning "encircling." "The lark's return" alludes to Shelley's "To a Skylark." Shelley's skylark flies so high that we cannot see him. We hear his song as though it were disembodied. In some ways the lark's return establishes a covenant between Shelley and Crane. And yet, this binds together two skeptical idealists who understood that the means of love and love were irreconcilable. The "lariat sweep" and "stallion glow" tell us the stars are those of the constellation Pegasus, winged horse of poetry.

Sustaining a note of rapture is immensely difficult. After Shakespeare and Christopher Marlowe, Richard Crashaw and Henry Vaughan, Christopher Smart and William Blake, Shelley and Keats, Gerard Manley Hopkins and Christina Rossetti, Whitman and Hart Crane are the masters. Sometimes Wallace Stevens will grant us this quiet ecstasy but it is infrequent in him.

I turn to Samuel Greenberg, who died at twenty-three in Manhattan of tuberculosis and thus abandoned in manuscript some

remarkable Emersonian poems and fragments. Here is Greenberg's "Conduct" (ca. 1916):

> By a peninsula the painter sat and
> Sketched the uneven valley groves.
> The apostle gave alms to the
> Meek. The volcano burst
> In fusive sulphur and hurled
> Rocks and ore into the air—
> Heaven's sudden change at
> The drawing tempestuous,
> Darkening shade of dense clouded hues.
> The wanderer soon chose
> His spot of rest; they bore the
> Chosen hero upon their shoulders,
> Whom they strangely admired, as
> The beach-tide summer of people desired.

Hart Crane deliberately utilized Greenberg's poem in his own
"Emblems of Conduct" (1924):

> By a peninsula the wanderer sat and sketched
> The uneven valley graves. While the apostle gave
> Alms to the meek the volcano burst
> With sulphur and aureate rocks . . .
> For joy rides in stupendous coverings
> Luring the living into spiritual gates.
>
> Orators follow the universe
> And radio the complete laws to the people.
> The apostle conveys thought through discipline.
> Bowls and cups fill historians with adorations,—
> Dull lips commemorating spiritual gates.
>
> The wanderer later chose this spot of rest
> Where marble clouds support the sea
> And where was finally borne a chosen hero.
> By that time summer and smoke were past.
> Dolphins still played, arching the horizons,
> But only to build memories of spiritual gates.

Greenberg must have read Emerson's severe late collection of essays *The Conduct of Life*. I remarked once to John Ashbery that the final four lines of Greenberg's "Conduct" sounded to me as though they had been plagiarized from Ashbery. As was very rare, John assented.

It is very peculiar that Crane's use of Greenberg should be regarded as plagiarism. "Conduct" is a good poem. "Emblems of Conduct" is rather more than that. "Spiritual gates," the last line of all three stanzas, is Crane's. In Angus Fletcher's formulation, Hart Crane is lost in the labyrinth and must find spiritual gates to reach the temple.

"Summer and smoke," which gave Tennessee Williams the title for a 1948 play, is also curiously characteristic of Crane. His summers all too frequently went up in smoke. The crux of the poem arrives in its most Cranean lines:

Dolphins still played, arching the horizons,
But only to build memories of spiritual gates.

One ought to remember in using the word "crux" that it goes back to a cross. Similarly, when Crane writes, "arching the horizons," he is thinking of the root in "archer" or "archery" going back to the Latin *arcus*. Dolphins can be playful and helpful; they are the most benign of whales. Crane probably knew that they went back to a Greek word for "womb." How can they arch horizons? Only, according to Crane, by augmenting our memories of lost gates to the spirit. It is as though they are miniature bridges between drowning men and transcendence.

The reverse comes in "The Wine Menagerie" (1925–1926), where there is only internal drowning. I have never enjoyed this powerful and original poem. It rehearses the bitter drama of a barroom quarrel between Hart Crane's parents, Clarence and Grace. They were a hopelessly incompatible couple who had married just two months after meeting. Grace Hart, the poet's mother, was mentally unstable and her unimaginative husband could not deal with her. Married in 1898, they had several separations and divorced in 1917.

Hart Crane called this "the curse of sundered parentage." He became much too close to his mother, who was an ongoing disaster for him. Homosexuality, as we have learned, is quite as normal as heterosexuality. John Irwin and others have adopted Freudian explanations for Crane's erotic orientation, but Freud was just wrong. One of Crane's many misfortunes was to have been born, lived, and died in a society that could not accept homoeroticism. Walt Whitman, endlessly and beautifully evasive, gave offense in his day not for the autoeroticism, incestuous suggestions, and homosexuality of his work but for the poems celebrating the sexual relations between men and women. These are not necessarily among his best.

The crux—in every sense—of the poem is a famous quatrain:

> New thresholds, new anatomies! Wine talons
> Build freedom up about me and distill
> This competence—to travel in a tear
> Sparkling alone, within another's will.
>
> [ll. 29–32]

Crane seems to have used as his text for William Blake a large Modern Library volume purporting to contain all of Blake and John Donne, rather an unlikely pairing. His quatrain deliberately alludes to one by Blake in an undistinguished poem, "The Grey Monk," in the Pickering Manuscript (ca. 1801–1803):

> "For a tear is an intellectual thing,
> And a sigh is the sword of an Angel King,
> And the bitter groan of the martyr's woe
> Is an arrow from the Almighty's bow."
>
> [ll. 53–56]

In that great cry, "New thresholds, new anatomies!" Crane asserts his own identity and separates from calamitous parents. Nietzsche remarked that if you did not have a good father, it is necessary to invent one. Hart Crane found authentic fatherhood in Walt Whitman. He thus avoided the evasive escapades of Ezra Pound, T. S. Eliot, William Carlos Williams, and Wallace Stevens and presaged the worldwide acceptance of Whitman by Russian, Polish, German, Spanish, Portuguese, and Latin American poets, among others.

Major figures like Federico Garcia Lorca, Fernando Pessoa, Pablo Neruda, Octavio Paz, and Jorge Luis Borges all identified themselves as children of Whitman.

Ritual rhythm characterizes both Whitman and Crane. Anaphora is the rhetorical mode of Hart Crane's processional poetry, particularly "The River" and "The Dance" cantos of *The Bridge*. Procession means forward movement, but in Christian theology it signifies the Holy Spirit in the act of emanation.

Emanation, in its long cavalcade from Plotinus and the Gnostics through Kabbalah and other theosophies, can be said to have reached apotheosis in William Blake, where the image is personified as Jerusalem the Emanation or Bride of Albion. Each of the Four Zoas or Sons of Albion has his separate Emanation. Their strife, jealousies, and final reconciliation constitute Blake's story or myth of deliverance.

The Bridge is many poems in one: epic, panoramic, processional, above all moving onward in what Emerson called the optative mood:

> Our American literature and spiritual history are, we confess, in the optative mood; but whoso knows these seething brains, these admirable radicals, these unsocial worshippers, these talkers who talk the sun and the moon away, will believe that this heresy cannot pass away without leaving its mark.
>
> ["The Transcendentalist" (1842)]

Hart Crane's spiritual yearnings were too extreme for us to call them transcendental. Ruach ha Kodesh, biblical Hebrew for "the Holy Spirit" or "breath of Yahweh," is the prime trope of the processional mode. Shelley in the "Ode to the West Wind" and the final seventeen stanzas of *Adonais* became the classic instance of a secularized Holy Spirit.

At dawn today of an unseasonable May 10, I was half-asleep in bed and brooding on Hart Crane. A great line of Sir Walter Raleigh came into my head:

> The broken monuments of my great desires

After a few moments I remembered three quatrains from his
"The 11th: and last booke of the Ocean to Scinthia":

The blossumes fallen, the sapp gon from the tree,
The broken monuments of my great desires,
From thes so lost what may th' affections bee,
What heat in Cynders of extinguisht fiers?

Lost in the mudd of thos high flowinge streames
Which through more fayrer fields ther courses bend,
Slayne with sealf thoughts, amasde in fearfull dreams,
Woes withourt date, discumforts without end,

From frutfull trees I gather withred leues
And glean the broken eares with misers hands,
Who sumetyme did inioy the weighty sheves
I seeke faire floures amidd the brinish sand

[ll. 13–24]

Ralegh utters a processional lament for his loss of favor with
Queen Elizabeth. Those who still find Hart Crane and *The Bridge*
to be failures, however "splendid," do not much trouble me, but I sorrow that Crane, in his final moments, may have seen only the broken monuments of his great desires.

William Cullen Bryant (1794–1878) was considered by Walt Whitman to be the major American poet before the advent of *Leaves of Grass*
(1855). I cannot recall any mention of Bryant by Hart Crane, but both
"To a Waterfowl" and "Thanatopsis" were lodged in his consciousness.
The "Proem" makes meaningful contrast with "To a Waterfowl":

Whither, 'midst falling dew,
While glow the heavens with the last steps of day,
Far, through their rosy depths, dost thou pursue
Thy solitary way?
. . .
There is a Power, whose care
Teaches thy way along that pathless coast,—
The desert and illimitable air
Lone wandering, but not lost.

All day thy wings have fanned,
At that far height, the cold thin atmosphere;
Yet stoop not, weary, to the welcome land,
Though the dark night is near.

[ll. 1–4, 13–20]

Bryant became a Jacksonian Democrat and then a Free Soiler
and finally a Lincoln Republican. As a journalist and editor he fought
for abolition and the rights of workingmen. His tonalities are simple
but sonorous. Something in their reverberation caught Crane's ear,
particularly the close of Bryant's stately death march "Thanatopsis":

So live, that when thy summons comes to join
The innumerable caravan, which moves
To that mysterious realm, where each shall take
His chamber in the silent halls of death,
Thou go not, like the quarry-slave at night,
Scourged to his dungeon, but, sustained and soothed
By an unfaltering trust, approach thy grave,
Like one who wraps the drapery of his couch
About him, and lies down to pleasant dreams.

[ll. 73–81]

The suicide in "Proem: To Brooklyn Bridge" is troped as "A jest
falls from the speechless caravan." Falling and rising, lifting down
and up, gazing upward and downward: these movements are dialectical in Hart Crane's poetry. In the inscriptions on his illustrations
to Dante (1824–1827), William Blake wrote:

This is Upside Down When viewd from Hells Gate
[Written in reverse direction:] But right When Viewd from
    Purgatory after they have passed the Center
In Equivocal Worlds Up & Down are Equivocal
    [on design no. 101, diagram of the nine circles of Hell]

Crane, Blake's deep reader, heaped upon himself the task of writing an American brief epic in the bad years 1926–1930, when an
inflated market detonated and the Great Depression began. He could
have said of his America: In Equivocal Worlds Up & Down are

Equivocal. And yet his central trope is vaulting or leaping; what he comes to comprehend is that the descent always beckons.

One of the most dramatic moments in Hart Crane's poetry comes in "The River" canto of *The Bridge*. It is when the poem moves from the accidental death of the legendary Dan Midland, primordial hobo, to the stately quatrains of the Mississippi flowing down to the Gulf:

> I could believe he joked at heaven's gate—
> Dan Midland—jolted from the cold brake-beam.
>
> Down, down—born pioneers in time's despite,
> Grimed tributaries to an ancient flow—
> They win no frontier by their wayward plight,
> But drift in stillness, as from Jordan's brow.
>
> You will not hear it as the sea; even stone
> Is not more hushed by gravity . . . But slow,
> As loth to take more tribute—sliding prone
> Like one whose eyes were buried long ago
>
> The River, spreading, flows—and spends your dream.
> What are you, lost within this tideless spell?
> You are your father's father, and the stream—
> A liquid theme that floating niggers swell.
>
> [ll. 111–124]

Crane employs "niggers" to indicate that these are lynched blacks whose corpses have been dumped in the river.

Many years ago I briefly discussed Hart Crane over the transatlantic telephone with Geoffrey Hill, the formidable English poet who died four years ago at the age of eighty-four. He had chosen me to write an introduction to what would be the first American volume of his verse, and I agreed because I had long admired it. He did not like the introduction and insisted on revisions. I offered to withdraw it. He refused. To relieve the tension, we talked about Hart Crane and I quoted a fragment that fascinates me:

> Thou canst read nothing except through appetite
> And here we join eyes in that sanctity

Where brother passes brother without sight,
But finally knows conviviality . . .

Go then, unto thy turning and thy blame.
Seek bliss then, brother, in my moment's shame.
All this that balks delivery through words
Shall come to you through wounds prescribed by swords:

That hate is but the vengeance of a long caress,
And fame is pivotal to shame with every sun
That rises on eternity's long willingness . . .
So sleep, dear brother, in my fame, my shame undone.

Hill said he would look into the poem. We then returned to our more or less amiable dispute. It was never quite resolved, but the introduction remained in the book. I finally met Hill for just a few minutes in the green room of the 92nd Street Y in Manhattan when I introduced his reading of portions from his new long poem *The Triumph of Love*. Since I had a class at Yale the next morning, I had to leave as soon as I had finished my improvised remarks. Years later I read his very ambivalent poem on Hart Crane:

Super-ego crash-meshed idiot-savant.
And what have you.
This has to be the show-stopper. Stay put.
Slumming for rum and rumba, dumb Rimbaud,
he the sortilegist, visionary on parole,
floor-walker watching space, the candy man,
artiste of neon, traffic's orator,
gaunt cantilevers engined by the dawn
of prophecy. A sight to see itself:
he, swinger with the saints in mission belfries,
broken and randy zooming on the toll,
love-death by elocution a close thing.
Publish his name, exile's remittancer,
prodigal who reclaimed us brought to book.
　　["Improvisations for Hart Crane: thou canst read nothing
　　　　　　except through appetite" (2004), ll. 1–14]

This is certainly not Geoffrey Hill at his dark best, yet I like it better each time I read it. The ambivalence tempers itself by admiration breaking in. William Empson once said to me that Hart Crane had become a kind of guide for him as a poet, because Crane demonstrated that poetry had become "a mug's game." Hill links himself to Crane in the poem's closing lines:

> What derelicts
> we must have been, ripped off by infancy.
> Thou canst grasp nothing except through appetite.
>
> [ll. 40–42]

"Appetite" in Crane's fragment is homoerotic lust. Hill shrewdly transposes to heterosexual lust and implies that in, and for, a poet, desire is death, as Shakespeare phrased it in a sonnet. Hill and Crane both were derelicts, fragments of an abandoned ship. Crane longed for "an improved infancy"; Hill debits infancy itself as culprit.

During the last week I have been reading back and forth in *The Book of Baruch by the Gnostic Justin* (2019), Hill's posthumous book. I am absorbed but keep wondering what I am reading. It is a sequence of 276 "poems," a kind of rant, rap, rag, rage for broken hierarchies. Hill quarrels with Hill, which can be very interesting, and with everyone else except a favored few.

I am not a scholar of the Gnostic religion (heresy, if you prefer), but I am a lifelong student of this ancient and still ongoing mode of spirituality. My mentors have included several friends who are profound scholars of this phenomenon: Hans Jonas, Bentley Layton, Moshe Idel, and the sublime Gershom Scholem.

Certain poets can be described accurately as Gnostics: William Blake (though very much in his own way), Shelley (again highly individualized), Thomas Lovell Beddoes, Victor Hugo, Nerval, Rimbaud, perhaps even Baudelaire, Edgar Allen Poe, Herman Melville, aspects of Emerson, William Butler Yeats, a tendency in Robert Frost, and something strangely new in Hart Crane. Until now I would not have thought of Geoffrey Hill in that mixed company:

59

By gnosis I mean both what it ought to have been and what it is, to tell the truth.

O it is an all youth! is a true gnosis: the body first no obstacle to the erotic soul but its oracle.

"True gnosis is moved by self-loss to redeemed stasis." False gnosis never changes but in agents, and is demeaned.

Widely applauded honours and prizes are false gnosis. So is "the World rejoices."

As for cost: refuse to be drawn on—by mere euphony, I suggest—to suppose our love remains.

Hill is accurate in seeing that Gnosticism makes creation and fall the same event. In some way I do not yet understand, he expanded gnosis well beyond any foreshadowings by others. Gnosis distinguishes between self or *pneuma* (breath), and soul or *psyche*. The self is an unfallen seed within us, while the soul belongs to the Demiurge, the false God who made and mangled this world. The stranger or alien God wanders the outer spaces, waiting for the self to awaken and make the journey to it.

Spiritually as well as poetically, Geoffrey Hill is too vital for a true reader to pass by. We do not yet have perspective upon him, but he may be a legitimate successor to a sublime tradition of English poets: Shakespeare, Milton, Blake, Shelley, Wordsworth, Hardy, and D. H. Lawrence. Hill makes an eighth: they do not so much live in him as he lives in them.

It is not yet clear whether, like Blake and Lawrence, Hill is an English *nabi:* in the ultimate line of Amos or Micah. As man and poet he had problems with otherness. His evident ferocity, marked by that marvelous scowl, could have been a reaction formation to his apparent bipolarity.

As Hill raps on, comparing himself to rap masters, there are saving moments of tributes to dead poets, Robert Desnos and Keith Douglas among them. Those are auspicious choices: more ambivalent are Gottfried Benn, Bertolt Brecht, and Ezra Pound.

Best of all, there are sudden outbursts of insight:

174

The canon is a chain letter to which you must commit; there is
    a curse on it like
    a cast rune.
To come up with a good line is like briefly discovering that
    you are sane.
What survives of spirit is method; or method withstood; which
    indeed has the
    greater merit.

Each of those three lines from *The Book of Baruch* is a perspicuous apothegm. A lifetime of sublime poetic labor stands behind them. Geoffrey Hill earned them. The bleak resonance of Geoffrey Hill when he enjoys full freedom as a poet haunts my ear. To bear witness, despite oneself, to a beyond that will never answer is a comfort only if you could write this poem or one as permanent.

Perhaps Hill wanted to be more of a Gnostic than he was. He may be one of the strangest and least persuaded devotional poets in the language, but then I think of Samuel Johnson's distrust of devotional verse:

> Pleasure and terror are indeed the genuine sources of poetry; but poetical pleasure must be such as human imagination can at least conceive, and poetical terror such as human strength and fortitude may combat. The good and evil of Eternity are too ponderous for the wings of wit; the mind sinks under them in passive helplessness, content with calm belief and humble adoration.

This is from *The Life of Milton* (1779), which, together with *The Life of Pope*, is the glory of *The Lives of the Poets*. Johnson's own belief was intense and hardly calm, though his adoration issues from humility. I think everyone would agree that the major devotional poet in the English language remains George Herbert, who startles me afresh each time I read him:

> Having been tenant long to a rich Lord,
>   Not thriving, I resolved to be bold,

And make a suit unto him, to afford
A new small-rented lease, and cancel the old.

In heaven at his manor I him sought;
    They told me there that he was lately gone
    About some land, which he had dearly bought
Long since on earth, to take possession.

I straight returned, and knowing his great birth,
    Sought him accordingly in great resorts;
    In cities, theaters, gardens, parks, and courts;
At length I heard a ragged noise and mirth

    Of theeves and murderers; there I him espied,
    Who straight, *Your suit is granted*, said, and died.
                    ["Redemption" (1633)]

Shakespeare, in Sonnet 125, hovers in Herbert's poem:

Were't aught to me I bore the canopy,
With my extern the outward honouring,
Or laid great bases for eternity,
Which proves more short than waste or ruining;
Have I not seen dwellers on form and favour
Lose all, and more, by paying too much rent,
For compound sweet forgoing simple savour,
Pitiful thrivers, in their gazing spent?
No;—let me be obsequious in thy heart,
And take thou my oblation, poor but free,
Which is not mix'd with seconds, knows no art,
But mutual render, only me for thee.
    Hence, thou suborn'd informer! a true soul,
    When most impeach'd, stands least in thy control.

Those "pitiful thrivers" paying too much rent anticipate Herbert's "not thriving" and seeking "a new small-rented lease." Magnificently worldly and erotic, Shakespeare's sonnet is a universe apart, but with sublime subtlety George Herbert appropriates it for the Augustinian project of redemption.

I had never read anything by Caroline Gordon (1895–1981) until yesterday, when I ventured on *The Malefactors* (1956). Gordon was married twice to the poet-critic Allen Tate (1925–1945; 1946–1959). Tate died in 1979 at eighty, having been born in the same year as his close friend Hart Crane. I dined with Tate several times at the homes of mutual friends: Holly Stevens and also Eleanor Clark and Robert Penn Warren. We had some difficulties but found common ground on Hart Crane.

The Malefactors is a *roman à clef* in which Tate appears as Tom Clairborne and the deceased Hart Crane is called Horne Watts. Gordon portrays herself with the same skill at delineation that she brings to Tate and Crane.

Gordon and Tate converted to Roman Catholicism, and *The Malefactors* is tendentiously a call to those not yet enlightened. As such, I found it both irritating and strangely captivating. Its portrait of Hart Crane, to whom Gordon was devoted, has a spectral intensity and an open generosity that makes the dead poet the cynosure of the novel.

Several good poets have suggested that Hart Crane was the Shelley of his age. I find that true. Shelley and Crane are religious poets but not devotional, because their god is beyond reach, beyond hope or hopelessness, beyond history, beyond personality, though remaining as the possibility of a person. Shelley wanted to believe that we could become our own gods. Even Crane could not be that exalted. But then Shelley was a committed political revolutionary. Crane had no politics.

His letters show that, for him, there was only the next poem, whether in progress or projected. He cultivated no protection against poetic failure. Totally vulnerable, he was open to the skies and to the daemon who held him in an antithetical embrace.

Contrary to some critics and to himself, when most hopeful, he entertained Whitman's American Dream without believing in it. Self-reliance at its farthest stretch is reliance on the god within. Emerson once wrote: "The daemons lurk and are dumb." If they refuse to speak, self-reliance is vastated.

Can you make a useful distinction between devotional poetry and the religious poetry of Shelley and Hart Crane? The two most

inventive and valuable devotional poets in the English language are
John Donne and his disciple George Herbert. They do not trans-
gress. It may be that religious poetry stepping away from traditional
Christianity has no choice but to invest in fables of vanished dreams.
If you want a better god, you must search for her in broken stories
and fragmentary poems.

Calling down a god traditionally was named "theurgy." It began
in Neoplatonism and in the Hermetic tradition. Many strands of it
persist into our own time. I find it best clarified by the Israeli scholar
of Kabbalah Moshe Idel, who speaks of it in *Kabbalah* (1988) as three
operations:

1. Augmenting a god to increase the divine energy
2. Drawing down a god to bring the god closer to our needs
3. World-propping, to sustain the divine cosmological order

It would seem to me that none of these is appropriate for devotional verse. John Donne and George Herbert would have been
transgressive in either of the first two procedures. I am a little puzzled as to whether their boldness did not involve them in the third.
Still, contrast them with the Hermetic poet Henry Vaughan, much
influenced by George Herbert, but also by his twin brother, Thomas
Vaughan, who was an esoteric philosopher. A trace of Hermetism
can be heard in the magnificent "The World" (1650):

I saw Eternity the other night,
Like a great ring of pure and endless light,
All calm, as it was bright;
And round beneath it, Time in hours, days, years,
Driv'n by the spheres
Like a vast shadow mov'd; in which the world
And all her train were hurl'd.
The doting lover in his quaintest strain
Did there complain;
Near him, his lute, his fancy, and his flights,
Wit's sour delights,
With gloves, and knots, the silly snares of pleasure,

. Yet his dear treasure
All scatter'd lay, while he his eyes did pour
Upon a flow'r.

[ll. 1–15]

I find it difficult to describe what might be called the exuberant restraint of "The World." In a sense, the poem is at work on world-propping. Eternity, totally unlike Dante's *Paradiso*, is peopled by the same foibles and silly obsessions as obtain here. When the singer urges true light, the whisper achieves authority: the great ring of pure and endless light is for the Bride of Jesus, the Church Thomas Vaughan serves, and which probably should have been the existence of Henry Vaughan, noted physician.

These days, virtually all friends deceased, one of my night-chantings of Henry Vaughan is more poignant:

They are all gone into the world of light!
And I alone sit ling'ring here;
Their very memory is fair and bright,
And my sad thoughts doth clear.

It glows and glitters in my cloudy breast,
Like stars upon some gloomy grove,
Or those faint beams in which this hill is drest,
After the sun's remove.

I see them walking in an air of glory,
Whose light doth trample on my days:
My days, which are at best but dull and hoary,
Mere glimmering and decays.

[1655, ll. 1–12]

Vaulting back to Hart Crane, one appreciates an element of theurgy in his vision of Brooklyn Bridge, and Neoplatonism in his use of the lost continent Atlantis. Though he placed it last in his ordering of the complete *Bridge*, "Atlantis" was the first canto to be composed:

Through the bound cable strands, the arching path
Upward, veering with light, the flight of strings,—

Taut miles of shuttling moonlight syncopate
The whispered rush, telepathy of wires.
Up the index of night, granite and steel—
Transparent meshes—fleckless the gleaming staves—
Sibylline voices flicker, waveringly stream
As though a god were issue of the strings. . . .

[ll. 1–8]

Crane persisted in rewriting "Atlantis," particularly the opening octaves. In this final version, he walks Brooklyn Bridge at night,
dazzled by sight and hearing as we are by this stanza's high rhetoricity. Always chant Crane aloud very slowly. More than almost any
other poet he positions every syllable. And he writes American English as Shelley and Tennyson wrote their language, as though the
quantity of every vowel sound could be stressed. Assonance is constant: strands and arching, flights and strings, taut and shuttling, sibylline and flicker, issue and strings. Internal rhyme is frequent, as is
delayed meaning. Here we move upward through the bridge's cables
to the music of a giant Aeolian harp, up as if reading an index, the
sibylline oracle beginning to flicker, as though the Bridge as harp
gives birth to a god.

And through that cordage, threading with its call
One arc synoptic of all tides below—
Their labyrinthine mouths of history
Pouring reply as though all ships at sea
Complighted in one vibrant breath made cry,—
"Make thy love sure—to weave whose song we ply!"
—From black embankments, moveless soundings
    hailed,
So seven oceans answer from their dream.

[ll. 9–16]

Hart Crane remade the language for himself. "Complighted"
would seem to mean sharing a common plight, whether as potential
shipwreck or human divorce. The epigraph to "Atlantis" is from Plato's *Symposium:* "Music is then the knowledge of that which relates
to love in harmony and system."

And on, obliquely up bright carrier bars
New octaves trestle the twin monoliths
Beyond whose frosted capes the moon bequeaths
Two worlds of sleep (O arching strands of song!)—
Onward and up the crystal-flooded aisle
White tempest nets file upward, upward ring
With silver terraces the humming spars,
The loft of vision, palladium helm of stars.

[ll.17–24]

Crane's extensive use of the constellations, the zodiac in particular, has been massively documented by John T. Irwin. Humming
is a subtle trope for poetic voice in Whitman and in Stevens. So long
as Athena served as its palladium, Troy stood. When the judgment
of the gods went against it, the goddess abandoned the loft of vision
and the stars were bereft of their major helmswoman.

Sheerly the eyes, like seagulls stung with rime—
Slit and propelled by glistening fins of light—
Pick biting way up towering looms that press
Sidelong with flight of blade on tendon blade
—Tomorrows into yesteryear—and link
What cipher-script of time no traveller reads
But who, through smoking pyres of love and death,
Searches the timeless laugh of mythic spears.

[ll. 25–32]

Crane's eyes have an affinity with the seagull that opened the
proem "To Brooklyn Bridge." Rime—aside from its work in
poetry—is fog coldly condensing on the surfaces of both poet's
and seagull's eyes. Looking upward at the Bridge, Crane's eyes
suffer division yet are still propelled by the towers at night, as
though Brooklyn Bridge, like Moby Dick, had glistening fins of
light. The towers, following Melville, are seen as giant looms of
time. The cipher-script, a poem like the *Aeneid*, renders Crane as
poet-quester into a new Aeneas. The smoking pyres of a deathly
eros are Dido's.

Like hails, farewells—up planet-sequined heights
Some trillion whispering hammers glimmer Tyre:
Serenely, sharply up the long anvil cry
Of inchling aeons silence rivets Troy.
And you, aloft there—Jason! hesting Shout!
Still wrapping harness to the swarming air!
Silvery the rushing wake, surpassing call,
Beams yelling Aeolus! splintered in the straits!

[ll. 33–40]

The hail and farewell greeting take one, as epic must, to heights
great enough that planets become decorations. Tyre is one of the
great literary lost cities, though not on the scale of Troy. Since Brooklyn Bridge for Crane is both a resounding Aeolian harp and a ship
in midvoyage, it is an exciting vault when he summons Jason, the
helm of the Argonauts. Jason, though in command of many heroes,
including Heracles and Orpheus, is serving as the lookout and shouts
out the words of warning. Aeolus, god of the winds, arrives as swarming air, silvery wake, the sunbeams themselves yelling his dangerous proclivity to splinter the *Argo* in the straits.

From gulfs unfolding, terrible of drums,
Tall Vision-of-the-Voyage, tensely spare—
Bridge, lifting night to cycloramic crest
Of deepest day—O Choir, translating time
Into what multitudinous Verb the suns
And synergy of waters ever fuse, recast
In myriad syllables,—Psalm of Cathay!
O Love, thy white, pervasive Paradigm . . . !

[ll. 41–48]

Vision-of-the-Voyage names Brooklyn Bridge as a clipper ship.
The Bridge, seen from above, raises nights to a cyclorama frequently
visible in cities of the nineteenth century as outdoor spectacles with
musical accompaniment. The dawn comes up as a psalm of Cathay,
the beautiful mistake of Columbus as to his goal. For Hart Crane
this cycloramic dawn is the white Paradigm, now set as the standard

of love by Diotima, the wise prophetess of the *Symposium*, who may
indeed have been an actual personage.

> We left the haven hanging in the night
> Sheened harbor lanterns backward fled the keel.
> Pacific here at time's end, bearing corn,—
> Eyes stammer through the pangs of dust and steel.
> And still the circular, indubitable frieze
> Of heaven's meditation, yoking wave
> To kneeling wave, one song devoutly binds—
> The vernal strophe chimes from deathless strings!
>
> [ll. 49–56]

The one song that binds devoutly might be the words of Jesus
to the Apostles:

> And I will give unto thee the keys of the kingdom of heaven:
> and whatsoever thou shalt bind on earth shall be bound in
> heaven: and whatsoever thou shalt loose on earth shall be
> loosed in heaven.
>
> [Matthew (KJV) 16:19]

Crane may have taken it for the salient trope of binding/loos-
ening, for that is the dominant motif of this octave. The night voyage out begins backward with the softly shining harbor lanterns.
There is a play on "Pacific," ocean and mode, oddly associated with
the corn the Old World found in the New. This could be Columbus
again, Crane's and Whitman's, seeking an elusive Cathay. With brilliant abuse of metaphor, Crane converts all his verbs to bindings/
loosenings: hanging, fled, bearing, stammer, yoking, binds, chimes.
Invoking the zodiac as the "circular, indubitable frieze / Of heaven's
meditation," Crane lances back to Donne among his precursors.

> O Thou steeled Cognizance whose leap commits
> The agile precincts of the lark's return;
> Within whose lariat sweep encinctured sing
> In single chrysalis the many twain,—
> Of stars Thou art the stitch and stallion glow

And like an organ, Thou, with sound of doom—
Sight, sound and flesh Thou leadest from time's realm
As love strikes clear direction for the helm.

[ll. 57–64]

This has been always, for me, the octave of octaves, since my childhood. Above and beyond the Bridge in the night sky, Crane beholds the constellation Pegasus, hence the lariat sweep and the encinctured (circled with a belt). We are entering a sequence of octaves that take part of their impetus from Shelley's *Adonais* and, at the start, from Shelley's "To a Skylark":

Hail to thee, blithe Spirit!
   Bird thou never wert,
That from Heaven, or near it,
   Pourest thy full heart
In profuse strains of unpremeditated art.

[ll. 1–5]

The skylark is out of sight. Its song is unsponsored, free. Poet and bird are disunited but not estranged. The implicit identity between Shelley and skylark is already in play. Moonlight and rainbow cannot provide the similitudes Shelley needs. "What is most like thee?" is unanswerable.

Like a Poet hidden
   In the light of thought,
Singing hymns unbidden,
   Till the world is wrought
To sympathy with hopes and fears it heeded not

[ll. 36–40]

An impatient reader might say Shelley does not know when to stop. Aesthetically, politically, erotically, he never did learn to stop. There is also the question of hyperbole: Does the bird's song surpass all that ever was joyous, clear, fresh? If he is not to lose us, Shelley must mount to the high sublime:

Teach us, Sprite or Bird,
    What sweet thoughts are thine:
I have never heard
    Praise of love or wine
That panted forth a flood of rapture so divine.

    Chorus Hymeneal,
        Or triumphal chant,
Match'd with thine would be all
    But an empty vaunt,
A thing wherein we feel there is some hidden want.

                              [ll. 61–70]

A skeptical or annoyed reader might want to protest that Shelley tries to exalt cause on the basis of effect. Again challenged, the poet surges on:

We look before and after,
    And pine for what is not:
Our sincerest laughter
    With some pain is fraught;
Our sweetest songs are those that tell of saddest thought.

    Yet if we could scorn
        Hate, and pride, and fear;
If we were things born
    Not to shed a tear,
I know not how thy joy we ever should come near.

    Better than all measures
        Of delightful sound,
Better than all treasures
    That in books are found,
Thy skill to poet were, thou scorner of the ground!

    Teach me half the gladness
        That thy brain must know,
Such harmonious madness
    From my lips would flow
The world should listen then, as I am listening now.

                            [ll. 86–105]

Shelley, a poet of the highest decorum, closes with humane modesty. Why quote much of the lyric to illustrate Crane's "whose leap commits / The agile precincts of the lark's return"? Aside from my fondness for "To a Skylark," now a neglected radiance, the lyric's poetics are remarkably close to Hart Crane's "poetics of metaphor":

> Swift peal of secular light, intrinsic Myth
> Whose fell unshadow is death's utter wound,—
> O River-throated—iridescently upborne
> Through the bright drench and fabric of our veins;
> With white escarpments swinging into light,
> Sustained in tears the cities are endowed
> And justified conclamant with ripe fields
> Revolving through their harvests in sweet torment.
>
> [ll. 65–72]

How should we read "fell unshadow"? Synesthetically the Bridge peals secular light, itself an intrinsic myth whose severe or pernicious dispelling of shadow is no more, no less than the absolute wound of our death. But that is delayed or mitigated in the rich vocables of our voices throated by the River: think of your veins as flooded fabric, swinging into the Bridge's light with cliffs rendered white. That prodigious vaulting of thought justifies the image of cities sustained by their weeping, and so enriched and justified, crying out all together. The ripe fields revolving through the oxymoronic intensities of their harvests are Keatsian.

> Forever Deity's glittering Pledge, O Thou
> Whose canticle fresh chemistry assigns
> To wrapt inception and beatitude,—
> Always through blinding cables, to our joy,
> Of thy white seizure springs the prophecy:
> Always through spiring cordage, pyramids
> Of silver sequel, Deity's young name
> Kinetic of white choiring wings . . . ascends.
>
> [ll. 73–80]

"Wrapt" is Crane's portmanteau word for both rapt and wrapped. Solomon's Song of Songs, called also Canticle of Canticles, is the spousal verse Crane renews in his epithalamion for his bride, the Bridge. The Shelleyan intensity, sparked by *Adonais*, gives us Brooklyn Bridge as an epiphany of God, but which God? "Spiring cordage" can be read as the peaked ropes and cords of the Bridge as a ship, but is that adequate for the structure's cables ablaze with light? The pyramids flank the Bridge almost as parents, and the ascension of "Deity's young name" makes us wonder, whose birth is this?

> Migrations that must needs void memory,
> Inventions that cobblestone the heart,—
> Unspeakable Thou Bridge to Thee, O Love.
> Thy pardon for this history, whitest Flower,
> O Answerer of all,—Anemone,—
> Now while thy petals spend the suns about us, hold—
> (O Thou whose radiance doth inherit me)
> Atlantis,—hold thy floating singer late!
>
> [ll. 81–88]

Crane likes to pun on his name with "heart" for "Hart." Seeing himself as Walt Whitman's true son, he turns his Atlantis rhapsody into a celebratory elegy for the poet who wrote "Song of the Answerer." Addressed here as "Love," Whitman is asked to pardon *The Bridge*, and to protect Crane, even as the white Anemone or wind-flower becomes evidence for the raising of lost Atlantis, up from the waves. Walt is the wind-flower and gives his radiance to his heir. The floating singer is Orpheus, transmembered by the Bassarids who throw his severed head into the river, where it continues to sing.

> So to thine Everpresence, beyond time,
> Like spears ensanguined of one tolling star
> That bleeds infinity—the orphic strings,
> Sidereal phalanxes, leap and converge:
> —One Song, one Bridge of Fire! Is it Cathay,
> Now pity steeps the grass and rainbows ring
> The serpent with the eagle in the leaves . . . ?
> Whispers antiphonal in azure swing.
>
> [ll. 89–96]

Whitman, like Keats in Shelley's *Adonais*, is transported beyond time:

> I am borne darkly, fearfully, afar;
> Whilst, burning through the inmost veil of Heaven,
> The soul of Adonais, like a star,
> Beacons from the abode where the Eternal are.
>   [*Adonais* LV, ll. 492–495]

The Orphic strings fulfill Emerson's prophecy for the Orphic poet in America. "—One Song, one Bridge of Fire!" is the *consummatum est* of an American Pentecost. There is a return to Crane's Columbus from the "Ave Maria" canto of *The Bridge*, and to Walt Whitman's broken Columbus as well. Whether Cathay is delusion or fulfillment cannot be told. The ancient trope of the serpent and the eagle at strife, central to Byron, Shelley, D. H. Lawrence, and Hart Crane, may achieve a rainbow harmony. But all that is question. The final affirmation is Whitmanian. "The sea, / Delaying not, hurrying not, / Whisper'd me through the night," Whitman writes in "Out of the Cradle Endlessly Rocking" (ll. 165–167), and he calls a poem of 1868 "Whispers of Heavenly Death," later the title for a section of *Leaves of Grass*. The antiphons swing between the Bridge's two towers in a dawn song of azure, color of the sublime in Shelley and in the French symbolists.

By all accounts Crane was a superb incanter of his own poems. Unfortunately, he was never recorded. When I teach Crane I ask the students to chant him out loud with all the verve they possess. Like Christopher Marlowe, John Donne, Richard Crashaw, Milton, Shelley, and Walt Whitman, Crane is a poet for the ear. The ecstasies of "The River" canto of *The Bridge*, "Atlantis," "The Broken Tower," "Voyages" have to take over your whole being until you are the poem.

Hart Crane was a poet's poet. In Great Britain that could be Edmund Spenser or the Shakespeare of the songs and sonnets. There have been fallings away, yet we abide in the America of Emerson and Whitman. Our authentic poets are going to be Orphic even against their will.

Crane knowingly was Orphic. He does not resort to the myth as overtly and as frequently as John Ashbery did. Alas, he incarnated the myth and found his only Eurydice in the Bridge.

For some readers, poets have become, in their work as in life, a new mythology. The lives of Dante, Chaucer, Molière, Cervantes, Montaigne, Shakespeare (though we know nothing of his inwardness), Milton, Goethe, Victor Hugo, Baudelaire, Pushkin, Lord Byron, Shelley, and Walt Whitman now constitute an inevitable form of literary legend. Hart Crane has become the poet of the American myth, as Whitman was before him.

CHAPTER FIFTEEN

Sigismund Schlomo Freud

Speculation and Wisdom

L UDWIG WITTGENSTEIN DISMISSED FREUD as "a powerful mythology." The Austrian Jewish philosopher remarked that Freud had not even presented a theory but
only a speculation. I see no reason to dispute Wittgenstein
on Freud as opposed to Wittgenstein on Shakespeare. Like David
Hume, Wittgenstein was annoyed by Shakespeare. He seemed incapable of reading the foremost English poet.

Sigmund Freud was born on May 6, 1859, and died on September 23, 1939. Today is October 12, 2019; it is more than a century
and a half since he was born and eighty years since his departure. If
there is a consensus on Freud, it is that he was the major literary essayist since Montaigne. I reread him as I do Montaigne or Cervantes
or Shakespeare.

Freud's great hope was that his work would make some contribution to biology. That was a delusion. His new science, psychoanalysis, or the talking cure, cured few if any. And yet the power of
mind manifested in his essays is almost unmatchable. His inventiveness is Shakespearean, even though, as with Montaigne, his principal guise is Freud the solitary brooder.

An experiential thinker, Freud the Pilgrim is closer to Chaucer the Pilgrim than to Dante the Pilgrim. He is closest to Prince Hamlet, who may be the son of the assassinated King Hamlet, or just as likely the child of incest between Gertrude and the assassin-king Claudius. Hamlet does not know; we do not know; Freud and Shakespeare may not have known.

What I think we do know is that Freud had a Hamlet complex and not an Oedipal fixation. Sophocles did not induce any anxieties in Freud. *Angst vor etwas*, "anxious expectations": that is Freud's deep mode.

In the summer of 1967, on my thirty-seventh birthday, I composed an anxious dithyramb, *The Covering Cherub or Poetic Influence*. After considerable revision, it emerged in January 1973 as *The Anxiety of Influence*.

I considered the little book to be Nietzschean and Kierkegaardian. Most reviewers called it Freudian. The strong effect of Anna Freud's *The Ego and the Mechanisms of Defense* (1936) pervades such of my books as *A Map of Misreading*, *Poetry and Repression* (1976), and *Agon* (1982). Defense in Freud is aggressive. Like classical rhetoric, it wards off, makes discoveries, and can be very dangerous indeed.

The late Philip Rieff thought that Freud was the first completely irreligious moralist, but he thus forgot Goethe and Montaigne, where Socrates is a presence and Jesus an absence. Sixty years ago, Rieff could write about Freud as a dominant figure in our culture; that dominance has vanished. Freud, who wanted to be a third with Copernicus and Darwin, became a third with Montaigne and Goethe. His dwindling psychoanalytical societies will vanish in less than another generation. The phrase "the literary Freud" will become a redundancy and will sound as odd as "the literary Montaigne" or "the literary Goethe." Science (or scientism) was Freud's defense against anti-Semitism: psychoanalysis was not to be categorized as "the Jewish science," as it became for the disturbed Jung, a mock-Gnostic closer to the original Faust than to Simon Magus. Freud, a magnificent personality, does not resemble Goethe's colorless Faust, but was considerably less impish than Goethe and Goethe's Mephistopheles. Though frustrated crews of current resenters stigmatize Freud as a charlatan, they do him violence, he being so majestic. The sage of Vienna, who intended to become no less than a new Moses, replacing Judaism by psychoanalysis, became instead a new Prospero, but one who would not break his staff or drown his book.

Freud delighted in calling himself a conquistador or, failing that, a Hannibal, Semitic enemy of Rome, or a Cromwell, throwing over an established church. In his exile, he went to London, not Jerusalem, believing that Palestine always would be the cradle of fresh superstitions. I am delighted by Freud's *The Future of an Illusion* (1927), though it may be his weakest book, if only because I relish the image of T. S. Eliot, respectable anti-Semite, reading it in a fury. Freud too would have been delighted. *Moses and Monotheism* (1939), Freud's novel, makes fairly explicit the identity between the history of Jewish religion and that of the life of the New Moses, Solomon Freud (to give him his Hebrew name, which suited him far better than the Wagnerian Sigmund). Freud's pragmatic motto, in regard both to Catholics and to normative Jews, might well have been: "Outrage, outrage, always give them outrage." T. S. Eliot indeed was outraged, but then even a far less gifted Jew than Freud would have been enough for Eliot to deplore. The only Jewish genius who pleased Eliot was Christopher Marlowe's Barabas, the Jew of Malta, who dies in boiling oil, though to be just to the abominable Eliot, one should mention his fondness for Groucho Marx.

In retrospect, Freud's most surprising achievement was his all but complete capture of intellectual authority in what remained the Age of Einstein and of Marx. I had some disagreements with the late Hannah Arendt but happily acknowledged her best book, *Between Past and Future* (1961), which clarified my understanding of authority. As Arendt shows, the concept is neither Greek nor Hebrew but Roman, and the test for it is to "augment the foundations." As a usurper of authority, Freud resembled Julius Caesar and then Augustus Caesar.

Freud's Eros is never freedom, because it is a repetition, a transference of authority from past to present. The inventor of psychoanalysis had an obsession with Moses: a virtual identification. For three weeks in 1913, Freud sat in the church of San Pietro in Vincoli, Rome, to admire and brood upon Michelangelo's extraordinary statue of Moses. For Freud, it was his own portrait worked out by Michelangelo four hundred years in advance.

Though Freud regarded religion as a destructive illusion, and equated Christianity with anti-Semitism, his relation to normative Judaism was vexed. He insisted that Moses had been an Egyptian, and not a Hebrew. Monotheism was an Egyptian invention, and the dark truth was that the Hebrews had murdered Moses and divided his body among them. This is the pattern Freud had set forth in his *Totem and Taboo* (1913), in which a horde of enemy brothers execute and devour their father, who had monopolized the women, keeping them for himself at the expense of the horde.

This is all Freudian myth. It has no relation to history but provides an ultimate foundation for psychoanalysis, in which the totem father is the analyst, and the rebels against him are his disciples and patients.

Why did Freud always hold on to his Jewishness? I will have to make a wide sweep even to begin answering that tenacious question.

There is no analysis of the phenomenon of masochism that matches Freud's in range, perplexed cunning, and culled human nature. Freud's idea of masochism relates this exile of the drive to an unconscious sense of temporal loss, rather than to the unconscious sense of guilt. Literary representations of masochistic experience frequently emphasize a curious conviction of timelessness that comes upon tormentor and victim alike. More naive accounts frequently cite a paradoxical feeling of freedom, which seems to be the particular delusion of the victimized partner. Freud doubtless would relate such illusions of temporal freedom to the renewed childishness of masochistic experience, a regression hardly in the service of the ego. But there may be another kind of contamination of the drive with a defense also, one in which the drive encounters not regression but an isolating substitution, in which time is replaced by the masochist's body, and by the area around the anus in particular. Isolation is the Freudian defense that burns away context, and is a defense difficult to activate in normal sexual intercourse. When masochism dominates, isolation is magically enhanced, in a way consonant with Freud's description of isolation in obsessional neuroses. Writing two years after the paper on the economic problem in masochism, in the great book of 1926, *Inhibitions, Symptoms and Anxiety*, Freud described again what he had observed first in the "Rat Man" case, the defense that interposes an interval and so disrupts temporality. In the midst of a felt unpleasantness, active or passive, the obsessional neurotic creates a time span in which nothing further must happen, during which nothing is perceived and nothing is accomplished. Affect and associations alike fade away, and a magical compulsion concentrates the ego so as to remove it from all possibilities of contact with others or otherness. The perversion of masochism is not, for Freud, an obsessional neurosis, but a vicissitude of the drive. And yet the defense of isolation, when it and the drive contaminate one another, is indistinguishable from erotogenic masochism. I venture that the thinking burned away by the isolating aspect of masochism is the thinking of temporality, the sense of loss and belatedness that an obsession with time brings about.

Freud's concepts of memory, time, history are essentially Jewish. I recall reviewing Yosef Hayim Yerushalmi's *Zakhor: Jewish History and Jewish Memory* (1982) and then expanding my remarks into an introduction to a later version of his book (1996).

Yerushalmi argues that Jewish memory, the Oral Tradition represented by Mishna and the two Talmuds, and Jewish historiography cannot be reconciled. Freud lurks always in Yerushalmi's reticences. I would go beyond Yerushalmi in concluding that *Moses and Monotheism* is a meditation upon Freud's Jewishness. Uneasy as he was, Freud compelled himself to recognize that psychoanalysis, after all, was precisely "a Jewish science," one that is as much a reaction to European anti-Semitism as was Theodor Herzl's *The Jewish State* (1895). Herzl's remains reside in Jerusalem on the mountain named for him. Freud's ashes are contained in an ancient Greek krater painted with Dionysian interludes. It had been a gift from Princess Bonaparte and adorned his lost Viennese study. Now it rests in a North London columbarium.

I last stood on Mount Herzl in 1980 on my fiftieth birthday. I think it was sometime in the early 1990s that I last visited Freud's remains. Herzl was one kind of hero: he died at forty-four of a heart attack. Freud, indubitable hero of the modern intellect, died at eighty-three of morphine administered to relieve the horrible pains of his jaw cancer. I am moved positively but abstractly by Herzl; profoundly but ambivalently by Freud.

In the middle of the journey (1965) I experienced endless depression. For a year and a half, I entered analysis with the late

Dr. Theodore Lidz (1910–2001), a shrewd and humane practitioner. Dr. Lidz terminated the relationship by gently telling me I was paying him so that he could endure endless lectures on the right way of reading Freud. My wife and I went abroad to London, where my depression continued.

Close to the lower deeps, I phoned the analyst Masud Raza Khan, whose name Dr. Lidz had given me. At our first session, Masud Khan told me I had to keep in mind that he was a much, much more intelligent man than I was. I did not know how to react. He then started to criticize my physical appearance, particularly my uncombed hair. When I said I had a tendency not to comb it, he proffered me a comb and urged me to use it.

Masud Khan then handed me a copy of a book I had written on Shelley. He had annotated it rather thoroughly and explained that a book by him on Shelley would have been much better. By then I just wanted to get away and left abruptly, not intending to return. When I reached the house I was renting with my wife, a message was waiting from him appointing an hour for the next day. I duly attended.

Our second session seemed uncontrollable from the start. He indulged himself in an anti-Semitic rant, pointing out that he was an Aryan and I was not. I then had to listen to his life story. Again I left abruptly, but the farce played out for one more day.

At the third session, which was very brief, Khan denounced Freud, insinuated that his own teacher Winnicott was sexually impotent, and told me he was irresistible to all women. I left, and did not return. In a week or so I received a ghastly bill, which I paid just to exorcise the madman.

Why tell this story? Khan died in 1989 at the age of sixty-five, in what seems to have been a very bad condition. Since I am now eighty-nine, I hold no grudge but wonder what Sigmund Freud would have thought of Masud Khan. Freud was a literary ironist and would have shrugged it off with wit and compassion.

I return to the question of Freud's Jewish identity.

In the *New Introductory Lectures on Psychoanalysis* (1933), Freud boldly admitted that "the theory of the drives is, so to speak, our mythology." Drives (or "instincts," in Strachey's language in the Standard Edition) represent somatic demands upon the psyche. Bodily demands upon the soul are difficult to distinguish from psychic demands upon the body. Demands made across the frontier between inwardness and outwardness are conceptually peculiar, yet are crucial always for Freud, whose prideful dualism is more at war with outwardness than is generally recognized. Frontier concepts therefore have a hidden importance in Freud's work. I want to examine two of them here: the status of the drives and their ambiguous relation to the mechanisms of defense; and the even more difficult notion of the bodily ego, with its baffling relation to the nonrepressive defenses of introjection and projection. Partly I want to clarify these border speculations, if I can, but I am only an amateur student of psychoanalysis and so can make no contribution to it. But I am a professional student of literary interpretation, and I suspect that psychoanalysis and criticism alike are belated versions neither of philosophy nor of religion but of certain ancient modes of speculation, Hebraic and Hellenic. Frontier speculation marks both the Hebrew prophets and the Greek sages, whether pre-Socratics or later Neoplatonists. To ask either psychoanalysts or critics to become prophets and sages may be absurd, but a prophet or sage in our time is unlikely to become either a philosopher or one of the religious.

Psychoanalysis, as a speculation, is itself an interpretation, rather than a method of interpretation. Freud, in his later phases, found his prime precursor in Empedocles; I will show that he could have found another true forerunner in Jeremiah. Exploring Freud's dualism by way of his frontier concepts, we might come upon just what it is about interpretation that survives the extinction of particular meanings, or even the evanescence of the object.

But what exactly is the Freudian drive, if it is a bodily demand that makes every mental response inadequate? Nothing mythological could sustain that question, and so I go back to Freud's own authority, in the *New Introductory Lectures:* "The theory of the drives is, so to speak, our mythology. Drives are mythical entities, magnificent in their indefiniteness." "Magnificent in their indefiniteness" is a marvelous formula, and not so humorous as it sounds. We are incessantly pushed and pressured by a shadowy splendor, which we recognize only through the tensions supposedly caused by its force. Aside from these tensions, all that we know about the drive is its nonlocation. It is neither in the body nor in the mind, but on the frontier between the outward and the inward. Yet that beautifully locates our tensions, which are neither bodily nor psychic but hovering on or near those ghostly demarcations, as our circumference flows in or out. Drive becomes the guarantee that the narcissistic omnipotence of thought is an illusion, but also that the universe of sense, the body, has only a wavering power over the mind. I am suggesting that the ambiguous status of the drive is at once the key to and the defense of Freud's kind of dualism, a dualism neither Pauline nor Cartesian, neither Platonic nor Hegelian. Rather, it is precisely a speculative dualism, and though it may seek to be Empedoclean, I would locate it, after all, in prophetic and normative tradition—that is to say, in Jewish thought and sensibility. Few questions of spiritual or intellectual history are as vexed as the Jewishness of Freud. It mystified Freud, more than he knew, and we go on weakly misreading it. We ought to judge it in relation to Freud's profound and unstated assumptions: convictions about time, memory, hierarchy, rationality, ethics, morality, and continuity, and above all, ambivalence toward the self and toward others.

Jewish dualism is neither the split between body and soul, nor the abyss between subject and object. Rather it is the ceaseless agon within the self not only against all outward injustice but also against what might be called the injustice of outwardness or, more simply, the way things are. The Nevi'im or prophets inherit the Torah's skeptical inwardness, a spirit that drove Abraham upon his original journey, and that fostered the Second Commandment's rejection of all outward appearances. What appears to be most original in Elijah and in all his descendants down through Malachi is the exaltation of skeptical inwardness as the true mode of preparing to receive the God-word. When a prophet says, "The God-word was to me," everything turns upon the meaning of that "me." It is not meaning but rather will that gets started when Yahweh speaks. Meaning is there already in the prophetic "me," which as an ego is far closer to what we might call "the psychoanalytic ego" than to "the Romantic ego" of nineteenth- and twentieth-century Western philosophy and literature. The Romantic ego is the product of, and the protest against, a double split in consciousness, between adverting mind and its object in nature, and between the mind and the body it inhabits. But the psychoanalytic ego is indeed what Freud calls "the bodily ego"; as he says: "The Ego is first and foremost a bodily Ego." What this rather profoundly means is that the ego frames itself on the paradigm of the human body, so that all the processes of the ego frame themselves also upon the paradigm of the body's processes. Human sexual activity and human cognition alike thus model themselves upon the processes of eating, or excreting, of the stimulation of the genitalia. The consequence is that sexual intercourse and thinking can be assimilated to one another, and to the specific locations of mouth, anus, genitals. To visualize the ego as a body is to admit the image that pictures the ego physically ingesting the object of the drive, the image of introjection or swallowing up the object. In *The Ego and the Id* (1923), Freud told us that the bodily ego "is not merely a surface entity, but is itself the projection of a surface." Freud's remark, as he apparently recognized, is quite difficult, and he evidently authorized an explanatory footnote in the English translation of 1927, which, however, does not appear in any of the German editions. The footnote reminds us that the ego ultimately derives from bodily sensations, particularly sensations springing from the surface of the body. Is the bodily ego then a mental projection of the body's surface? Where would the frontier between body and psyche be in such a projection? Like the Freudian concept of the drive, the notion of the bodily ego seems to lie precisely upon the frontier between the mental and the physical. Presumably, we can know neither the body nor the bodily ego; we can know only the drives and the defenses. Freud implies that the drives and the bodily ego alike are constructed ambivalently—that is to say, from their origins they are dualistic. In both, the borders between the psychical and the somatic are forever in dispute.

I want to go back a long way in finding a similar vision of ambivalence. Freud, of course, was willing to go back to Empedocles and Heraclitus. I think Freud was closer even to Jeremiah, doubtless unknowingly. Ancient Jewish dualism does not oppose body to spirit, or nature to mind, but rather sets outwardness against inwardness. Jeremiah, rather than Freud, is the initial discoverer of the bodily ego, of an untraceable border between selfhood and the somatic. For the Romantic Ego, whether in Hegel or Emerson, the body is part of the Not-Me. But for Freud, as for Jeremiah, the body is uneasily part of the Me, and not part of the external world. The drive, which excites from within, and so menaces the ego, is a somatic demand upon the psyche, and is very different from an external excitation of any kind.

When Freud speaks of the psyche's "surface," he means perception and consciousness, and he founds this meaning upon what we commonly try to mean when we speak of the "surface" of the body.

Freud could speak of the bodily ego or the drives or even the defense of introjection as frontier concepts only because his image of the ego was that of the body, of a living organism. A body can be attacked and penetrated from without; it has a demarcation that needs defense, and can be defended. The bodily ego could as well have been called the egoistic body, because Freud's crucial metaphor is that of inwardness itself. "Inwardness" is the true name of the bodily ego. The defensive disorderings of the drive, or the vicissitudes of instinct, are figures of outwardness, or of what the prophet Jeremiah might have called "the injustice of outwardness."

In Chapter 20 of Jeremiah, the prophet laments to God that God has enticed him, and has overcome him, so as to make Jeremiah a mockery. But if Jeremiah seeks to speak no more in God's name,

> Then there is in my heart as it were a burning fire
> Shut up in my bones,
> And I weary myself to hold it in, but cannot.
>   [Jeremiah (JPS) 20:9]

The burning fire or inwardness drives outward, in a movement that culminates in the magnificence of Chapter 31, where God speaks of the days coming when he will make a new covenant with the house of Israel, in which all outwardness will be abolished: "I will put My law in their inward parts, and in their heart will I write it." Call this the ancient Jewish negation of the outward, since it is a new perspective upon the genesis of the ego. Indeed, it is a privileged perspective that has no relation to the external world. The drive out from inwardness, from the Freudian id, takes the ego as its object; it does not generate the ego. Doubtless, a strict psychoanalytic reading of Jeremiah would say that he is manic and stretches his own ego until it introjects God, or the ego ideal, whereas earlier, Jeremiah had been depressive and melancholic, projecting his own ego out of self-hatred and self-abandonment. But such clinical judgment, whether accurate or not, is less vital than the striking similarity between Jeremiah's negative dualism and Freud's. Both erase the frontier between psyche and body and in its place install a narcissistic ambivalence. The difficult concept of the bodily ego, in which an imaginary object is introjected as though it were real, is uncannily similar to the prophetic concept of the placing of the law in our inward parts. Surely we have underestimated the conceptual difficulties of the bodily ego. How, after all, can a thought become an object, when the bodily ego has introjected it? How can the law be inscribed upon our inward parts?

The answer has to depend on the meaning of "drive." Here is its crucial use in "Drives and Their Vicissitudes" (1915):

> A drive appears to us as a borderland concept between the mental and the physical, being both the mental representative of the stimuli emanating from within the organism and penetrating to the mind, and at the same time a measure of the demand made upon the energy of the latter in consequence of its connection with the body.

Stimuli emerge from within us and then penetrate our minds in the form of a representation, and that representation is what Freud calls "the drive." But are we not again in the same dilemma we confronted in Freud's concept of the bodily ego? There, an imaginary object was introjected, which means that a thought can become an object, which is admirable science fiction, but hardly biology. Here, the drive can be known only through its psychical envoy, the ambassador that penetrates our mind. But what then is the drive? It is an entity always in exile, always wandering through one vicissitude or another, unavailable to consciousness except through those vicissitudes, which means that each vicissitude necessarily is psychical rather than physical. Since the vicissitudes sometimes can be characterized either as defenses or as perversions, we have the further puzzle that defenses and perversions, and sadomasochism in particular, join the drive and the bodily ego as frontier concepts. But I have been discussing the Freud of the first theory of the mind, the Freud who did not yet have the vision of the death drive. What happens to frontier concepts in the new theory of the drive, the theory of aggression and sadomasochism set forth from 1919 to 1924?

Since the mind had been mapped anew, the perpetually strange frontier concept of the drive had to be thought through again also.

In particular, the darkest wandering or exile of the drive, into the labyrinths of sadomasochism, required a chronicle from 1919 onward that was very different from what had been written in 1915, the year of the metapsychological papers. Narcissism was the concept whose development had precipitated Freud's self-revision, but I amend this now by emphasizing that the precise stimulus from intellectual change was the insight that narcissism, when severely wounded, transformed itself into aggressivity, both against the self and against others. Aggressivity, however, is one of those human qualities whose analysis Freud seems to have usurped forever, so that a non-Freudian vision of aggressivity, while possible, might be rather uninteresting. That raises again a problem this discourse hopes to help resolve: How are we to understand those Freudian speculations that have been able to exclude nearly all possible rivals, so that the Freudian theories have assumed the status of necessary postulates if thinking about the human is to prolong itself?

Is the drive still such an idea? In *An Outline of Psychoanalysis* (1940), his final formulation, Freud is no more or less overtly mythological in positing the drive than he was in the paper of 1915, "Drives and Their Vicissitudes." Twenty-five continuous years of revisionism did not alter Freud's fundamental fiction of the drive, though it thoroughly reoriented the drives from the dualism between self-preservation and erotic union, to the dualism between the erotic and deathly strife. Freud openly rejoiced, early and late, in the indefiniteness of his notion of drive, realizing as he did that the magnificence of the conception lay in its frontier nature, always hovering between the mind and the body. No response, psychic or somatic, can be adequate to the demands of the drive, for if the drive represents what the body demands of the mind (as Freud thought), the converse is curiously true also. The fantasies of defense, activated by the drive, come to represent initially what the mind demands of the body, which is that it cease the full force of its demands. Shall we say that defense can appear to be the mind's drive against the body, just as the drive proper can seem the body's defense against the mind? The drive, as Freud emphasized, is a constant force, to which I seek to add that defense is no less constant a force. Like Plato, St. Paul, and Descartes, Freud is indeed one of the greatest of Western dualists, not only accepting but in a way celebrating the mind/

body division, making of it indeed a larger human issue than it is construed to be by philosophers. The exile of the drive into sado-masochism is the most dramatic Freudian story of just how the civil wars of the mind are modified by the endless wars between mind and body.

But what then happens to the proper and doubtless necessary Freudian distinction between the perversion of drive and the compulsive defense characteristic of obsession? I am venturing yet again the speculation that the border concept of the drive and the more empirical idea of defense have a more peculiar relation to one another in Freud's work than he himself realized. Their mutual contamination of one another constitutes Freud's implicit theory of temporality, in which time becomes the medium of exchange between the opposed dualities of body and mind. If drive is the somatic demand upon the mind, and so the body's prime defense against whatever in and about the mind is most antithetical to body, then defense may be the mind's drive against whatever that is bodily that is inimical to mind. Each duality reads the other as time and so as change, and so at last as death. In such a vision the body and the mind never can be friends, and the necessity for conceptualizing a death drive becomes overwhelming. I recall observing elsewhere that the superego, rather than the ego, let alone the id, is in some sense the most Jewish of the psychic agencies. Others have ventured that repression is in a complex way a peculiarly Jewish notion, related as it is to the programmatic sorrows of Jewish memory. I conclude this meditation, though, by venturing that Freud's most profound Jewishness, voluntary and involuntary, was his consuming passion for interpretation, a passion that led him into the wilderness of his frontier concepts. The psychical representative of the drive, not in the individual consciousness but in human history, allegorically or ironically considered, is the image of a wandering exile, propelled onward in time by all the vicissitudes of injustice and outwardness, all the bodily oppressiveness that is inflicted upon the representatives of interpretation itself, as they make their way along the frontiers between mind and body, known and unknown, past and future.

The fundamental building block of Freud's enterprise is the primary process. Freud expounded a version of the primary process in Chapter 7 of his masterwork, *The Interpretation of Dreams* (1900), but his classic account of it is in the essay of 1911, "Formulations on the Two Principles of Mental Functioning." There the primary process is spoken of as yielding to the secondary process when the person abandons the pleasure principle and yields to the reality principle, a surrender that postpones pleasure only in order to render its eventuality more certain.

The secondary process thus begins with a binding of psychic energy, which subsequently moves in a more systematic fashion. Investments in ideas and images are stabilized, with pleasure deferred, in order to make possible trial runs of thought as so many path-breakings toward a more constant pleasure. So described, the secondary process also has its links to the cognitive workings of poetry, as to all other cognitions whatsoever.

Prior to any pleasure, including that of creativity, Freud posits the "narcissistic scar," accurately described by a British Freudian critic, the late Ann Wordsworth, as the "infant's tragic and inevitable first failure in sexual love" (in a 1977 review of my *Figures of Capable Imagination*). Parallel to this notion of the narcissistic scar is Freud's speculative discovery that there are early dreams whose purpose is not hallucinatory wish fulfillment. Rather they are attempts to master a stimulus retroactively by first developing the anxiety. This is certainly a creation, though it is the *creation of an anxiety*, and so cannot be considered a sublimation of any kind. Freud's own circuitous path-breaking of thought connects this creation of an anxiety to the function of repetition-compulsion, which turns out, in the boldest of all Freud's tropes, to be a regressive return to a death instinct.

It is a curious truth that figurative meaning or Eros is "more conspicuous and accessible to study" than literal meaning or the death drive, as Freud argues in *The Ego and the Id*. If my analogy holds at all, then sadism and masochism are over-literalizations of meaning, failures in Eros and so in the possibilities of figurative language. Or perhaps we might speak of a "regressional libido," a fall into metonymizing, as being due to a loss of faith in the mind's capacity to accept the burden of figuration. Sexual "union" is, after all, nothing but figurative, since the joining involved is merely a yoking in act and not in essence. The act, in what we want to call normal sexuality, is a figuration for the unattainable essence. Sadomasochism, as a furious literalism, denies the figurative representation of essence by act.

The Freudian *Verneinung* involves the formulation of a previously repressed feeling, desire, or thought, which returns into consciousness only by being affectively disowned, so that defense continues. To carry the truth into the light while still denying it means that one introjects the truth cognitively, while projecting it emotionally. Few insights, even in Freud, are so profound as this vision of negation, for no other theoretical statement at once succeeds as well in tracing the epistemological faculty convincingly to so primitive an origin, or accounts nearly so well for the path by which thought sometimes can be liberated from its sexual past. Since the ego is always a bodily ego, the defenses of swallowing up and spitting out, though fantasies, still acknowledge cognitively the ultimate authority of the fact.

That Freud, more passionately even than the poets, shared in this figurative promise we know from many passages in his works, but never more revealingly than from some belated remarks that he added to an interleaved copy of the 1904 edition of *The Psychopathology of Everyday Life:*

> Rage, anger, and consequently a murderous impulse is the source of superstition in obsessional neurotics: a sadistic component, which is attached to love and is therefore directed against the loved person and repressed precisely because of this link and because of its intensity. —My own superstition has its roots in suppressed ambition (immortality) and in my case takes the place of that anxiety about death which springs from the normal uncertainty of life.

Against the literalism and repetition of the death drive, Freud sets, so early on, the high figuration of his poetic will to an immortality. Perhaps that may seem someday the truest definition of the Freudian Eros: the will's revenge against time's "it was" is to be carried out by the mind's drive to surpass all earlier achievements. Only the strongest of the poets, and Sigmund Freud, are capable of so luminous a vision of Eros.

If I apprehend Freud accurately, he tells us that religion and high literature are manifestations of our longing for the authority of the murdered and usurped father. We are condemned to love authority even when it has withdrawn its love from us. I think this is a large instance of Freud's negation of Shakespeare's enormous influence upon him.

Returning to Freud, after years of avoidance, troubles me deeply. I have learned to accept that my own work on influence, both literary and religious, is hopelessly misunderstood. I have also learned that this does not matter at all. Only time allows judiciousness. Comprehension will come when I myself am gone. What does trouble me is my increasing realization that, unknowingly, I have been using Milton, and some other great poets, as a screen for Freud. His relationship to all of Western tradition, down to Darwin and to Nietzsche, is very close to the scenario I have sketched of the strong poet accepting the contingency of precursors and then overcoming it by a powerful misprision or misreading. It is Freud who began anew on a *tabula rasa* of speculation. He endeavored to retell all our stories of the self. His historical place is with the major imaginative writers of the twentieth century: Proust, Joyce, Kafka, and Beckett, and poets including Georg Trakl, Paul Valéry, Yeats, Ungaretti, Stevens, and D. H. Lawrence.

It is sublimely outrageous that the pragmatic consequence, now largely archaic, of Freud's total usurpation of tradition was the psychoanalytic encounter between analyst and patient, based as it was on the hidden pattern of *Totem and Taboo*, in which the totem is the analyst and the taboo the transference, an artificial Eros that soon enough became real enough. An imaginary neurosis was induced and then "cured" by the magic of transference. It returns me to the grand remark of Karl Kraus: "Psychoanalysis is itself that disease of which it purports to be the cure."

But that is ancient music. What continues to matter is the persistence of Freud's vision of the predicament of being human. His pragmatic defense was the unassailable credo that his patients could be transformed from a condition of hysterical misery to one of ordinary unhappiness.

But that also is sour wit and wilts away. What remains is a tragic secular humanism, massively quarried out of Shakespeare. The book we know as *Civilization and Its Discontents* (1930) should have the title *The Uneasiness in Civilization* or, even better, *Our Discomfort with*

Culture. Whenever I ask myself the impossible question, "What is most important that I have learned from reading Shakespeare?" I tend to answer that Shakespeare's darkest insight is that each of us is his or her own worst enemy. Freud appropriated this, with what degree of awareness I do not know. He is the prophet of what happens when we turn aggressivity against the self.

Is there in fact a universal death drive beyond the pleasure principle? History, Shakespeare, and our contemporary world would all seem to support Freud's argument that the strife of Eros and Thanatos is incessant. And yet that is hardly an argument, whether we encounter it in Empedocles or in Freud.

Freud's favorite among all of Shakespeare's plays was *Macbeth*. It is startling that he identified himself with a brutal murderer of children and yet he seems to have understood implicitly that Macbeth incarnated Shakespeare's own proleptic imagination just as Hamlet represented the capaciousness of Shakespeare's skeptical intellect. In some uncanny way Freud associated Shakespeare with Moses: neither was what he seemed to be. Shakespeare was an actor who had plagiarized all the plays from the Earl of Oxford. Moses was an Egyptian killed by the Jews.

I think that Freud was anxious about Shakespeare because he had learned anxiety from the plays, even as he had learned narcissism, ambivalence, and schism in the self. We might begin always by celebrating Freud as a great reader. For almost all of us, Shakespeare is a bounty, a treasure house of language and insight, and a cornucopia of men and women. We receive from him, and the richness costs us only the effort to absorb what is so much beyond us. But Freud was a great original, a fountain burning with its own fire. He would accept his cure only from himself. What then was he to do with Shakespeare?

Freud's interpretations of various plays range from the preposterous to the acute. To believe that the tragedy of Lear and Cordelia is founded on a repressed incestuous relation is very odd. Was Freud confusing himself with Lear, and Cordelia with Anna Freud, his favorite child? *Hamlet*, intricate and difficult, was reduced to the Oedipus complex. What play was Freud reading? Gertrude may be a sexual magnet, but Prince Hamlet does not share the lust for her that dominated King Hamlet and the usurper King Claudius. As she dies, Gertrude cries out, "O my dear Hamlet!" to which the dying Prince responds, "Wretched Queen, adieu!" That reads to me as, "So much for you!"

Probably Freud is at his best on *The Merchant of Venice*, but where is Shylock? In my own view, Shylock is one of those personalities who got away from Shakespeare, a group including Falstaff, Hamlet, Edgar, Caliban, and Barnardine (*Measure for Measure*). It may be that Shylock was intended to overgo Barabas in Christopher Marlowe's *The Jew of Malta*. We were to find him a comic menace. Shakespearean personalities overflow all bounds and go where they will.

Some years ago that splendid actor Al Pacino played Shylock in New York City and took issue with my argument that the Jew was intended to be a comic villain. Pacino played Shylock as the hero and explained that he had particular insight into the role because he was a Sicilian, and the Sicilians were the Jews of Italy.

Sometime in the later 1970s when I was teaching in Bologna, I flew down to Palermo to lecture there on Walt Whitman. I visited some abandoned synagogues in the city, and their emptiness depressed me. Palermo seemed very grim, and I was glad to fly back to Bologna the next day. It was like returning to Italy.

Freud, like Goethe, loved Rome. Both associated the city with sexual release. Though both toured Venice, I have always wondered why Freud did not meditate upon Shylock and Othello when he was in place.

Goethe spoke and wrote about Shakespeare with considerably more insight than Freud manifested. I go on learning when I ponder Goethe's remark that Shakespeare's best effect upon the reader is to hinder understanding.

For Goethe, Shakespeare was endless. For Freud, Shakespeare was both liberation and blockage. The conquistador in Freud required an originality that Shakespeare both inspired and shadowed.

You do not diminish Freud by comparing him to Montaigne. But it is questionable how well he can survive what I have learned to call a Shakespearean reading. Freud's psyche is capacious, but the mind of Shakespeare is capaciousness itself.

CHAPTER SIXTEEN

Dante/Center and
Shakespeare/Circumference

THIS BOOK HAD ITS beginning in a cavalcade of illnesses
and accidents, so that much of it was dictated to generous assistants in hospitals and rehabilitation centers.
Happily, it is ending a few months after my eighty-ninth
birthday, and I seem so far to be holding together. I am rather superstitious, and three charming ladies of Gypsy descent—in Wales,
Jerusalem, and Los Angeles, each ten years apart—read my palm
and granted me eighty-nine years, three months, and eleven days.
Once that cheered me, but I have no intention of departing on
October 22, 2019, though I will be particularly careful that day.

How can I assert coherence for a reverie that begins with Shakespeare and concludes with Dante, and also encompasses such poets
as Geoffrey Hill and John Hollander, and others who were alive during my own lifetime and are now no more? The only living poet
discussed here is Jay Wright, in my judgment the best American poet
still standing after the losses of Elizabeth Bishop, May Swenson,
James Merrill, A. R. Ammons, William Merwin, and the luminous
John Ashbery.

Why, in 2020, should a literate reader turn to a relatively advanced study of the traditional sequence of major poets in Britain

and the United States? Initially there may seem something archaic in such an enterprise. Shakespeare, who is of all times and still ahead of our time, is the clear exception. He makes us archaic. Perhaps Walt Whitman is also exempt from the taint of the archaic. He tells us there was never any more inception than there is now. Wallace Stevens has Walt chant: "Nothing is final. No man shall see the end."

A teacher of how to read poetry, I am not a poet and not Samuel Johnson, my hero of criticism. After wasting many years in mimic warfare against the tides of fashion, I have given up polemic. But as a lifelong lover of William Blake, I will not cease from mental fight.

This book ends by contrasting Dante and Shakespeare. My understanding of Dante began to clarify after I taught several semesters in Bologna and Rome. Until then my Italian was self-taught, relying on a thorough undergraduate education in Latin. Hearing Italian spoken and having to do my best speaking it, I returned to Dante during several days I suffered lecturing to the Florentines, who seemed to me the least friendly people in Italy. Still, that helped accustom me to the factionalism that tormented Dante's life, and to which he himself contributed.

Setting aside the ancients, the two indispensable European poets have to be Dante and Shakespeare, who was agile at evading theology. But Dante not only is proudly indebted to the Fathers from Augustine through Aquinas; he also is an original theologian and, in my perhaps insufficiently informed judgment, frequently heretical. I follow Ernst Robert Curtius in wondering whether the intrusion of Beatrice into the scheme of Christian salvation is not a private gnosis.

Like other secular readers I am most at home in *Purgatorio. Inferno*, with all its magnificence, seems scarcely sane. *Paradiso*, now that I am very old, is a preoccupation. I am uncertain if I will ever fully apprehend it, yet I need to continue my quest to feel less alienated in and by it. I always think of my old friend John Freccero, whom I have not seen in many years. I believe he lives in Florence and hope that he is well, since he is exactly a year younger than I am.

All of Freccero's commentaries on Dante challenge me and frequently compel me to dissent, though his knowledge of Dante is far deeper than mine. Here is an instance of agon between us:

The passage from the events of Dante's life to the words and images he uses to signify them is one that we cannot make. This is why it is impossible to guess at the identity of the *Donna Pietra*, just as it is impossible to see in the Medusa some event of the poet's life. We must be content with words on words, the double focus on poetic expression, beyond which it would take an act of faith equal to Dante's to go; beyond which, indeed, there is no Dante we can ever know.

The address to the reader is thus not a stage direction, but an exhortation to conversion, a command to await the celestial messenger so that we, like the pilgrim, may "trapassare dentro." Beneath the veil of Moses, we behold the light of the Gospel; beneath the veil of Dante's verse, the *dottrina* is derived from that, or it is nothing at all.

["Medusa: The Letter and the Spirit" (1972)]

But if his verse is only a veil, then it is *secondary* to the language of the Gospel. Is that truly Dante's stance? Are his poetics "an exhortation to conversion"? I yield to John Freccero in most respects, yet here I hold my ground. As much as Milton, Dante refused to be less than *first* or earliest. As Freccero says, the *Commedia* does not imitate Scripture. It is a third Scripture and thus a companion to Joachim of Flora, whose apocalyptic Everlasting Gospel impressed Dante as a true voice of prophecy.

Long ago I argued, against the school of Erich Auerbach, Charles S. Singleton, and John Freccero (and his many disciples), that the Christian trope of *figura* was suspect both as to ideology and as to the actual relationship between texts. I do not want to repeat what I set forth at length in my Charles Eliot Norton Lectures, published as *Ruin the Sacred Truths* (1989). Here I wish to give only the pith of the matter.

Christianity won a permanent victory when it reduced Tanakh, or the Hebrew Bible, to "the Old Testament." The New Testament supposedly fulfilled and canceled what I think we might call "the Original Testament." Moses died and was buried in an unmarked grave by Yahweh himself. The Jesus of what I think of as the "Belated Testament" dies on the cross, a Roman instrument of torture. Though he was the greatest of the prophets, Moses lived and died as a man. Jesus, in the Christian revelation, is both God and man from birth to death.

In figural interpretation, Joshua, the lieutenant of Moses, is fulfilled in Jesus, since they share the same name, Yeshua. Any port in a storm. This seems to me merely fantastic, but the *figura* school of Auerbach/Singleton/Freccero finally capsizes, despite its continued American ascendancy, in its own phantasmagoria.

Dante presents himself as fulfilling Virgil. Since the text of Lucretius was unknown to Dante and his contemporaries, we have the oddity that Virgil, who endlessly imitates his fellow Epicurean Lucretius, is seen by Dante as a believer in an orderly and rational cosmos. Dante was a great reader, but what was he reading? Everything that matters most in the *Aeneid* is drenched in pain and in the consciousness of more pain to come. Virgil's gods are unreasonable, violent, and, in the instance of Juno, absolutely vicious. Dante tames the *Aeneid*. Unreasonably Dante places his own mentor Brunetto Latini as a supposed sodomite (for which there is no evidence) in Hell. Virgil, who was homoerotic, is seen as a harbinger of Christian revelation.

In life and in literature no person or text fulfills another. I do not regard that as a happy sentence, but it may well be the truth. Paul de Man delighted in saying to me: "The trouble with you, Harold, is that you do not believe in the truth." For Paul, all was irony, and death was the truth. On its own grounds, his stance was unassailable. Most of our experience is ironical and we must all die.

But not all experience reduces to irony, and we all want to live as joyously as we can, until we must wander off. And yet we are not Dante or Petrarch or Chaucer or Milton. They were titanic agonists, though Chaucer's comic powers saved him, at least until the end, from the anxieties of exalting invention over faith. Dante was both an original theologian and a shatteringly original poet-prophet. He knew instinctively that theologians could be as agonistic as poets, and he exemplifies both projects.

As a poet, Dante's agon was with his best friend, Guido Cavalcanti. At one time Dante regarded Cavalcanti as a mentor. Eventually they broke politically, theologically, even poetically. Cavalcanti, a great lyric poet, was a freethinker who cast aside the Christian revelation, and also a realistic psychologist of eros for whom love reduced to illness.

Cavalcanti does not appear in the *Commedia*, but in Canto 10, *Inferno*, his father, politically placed by Dante in Hell, wonders plaintively why Dante and not Guido is the Pilgrim guided by Virgil. Also in Hell is the great Farinata, Guido's father-in-law, who is sublimely haughty: "As if of Hell he had a great disdain."

Half a century ago I frequently encountered my friend John Freccero on the Yale campus in the early-morning fog. He loomed up in a black overcoat, and I would cry out to him cheerfully:

Ed el mi disse: "Volgiti! Che fai?
Vedi là Farinata che s'è dritto:
da la cintola in sù tutto 'l vedrai."

Io avea già il mio viso nel suo fitto;
ed el s'ergea col petto e con la fronte
com' avesse l'inferno a gran dispitto.

—

And unto me he said: "Turn thee; what dost thou?
    Behold there Farinata who has risen;
    From the waist upwards wholly shalt thou see him."

I had already fixed mine eyes on his,
    And he uprose erect with breast and front
    E'en as if Hell he had in great despite.
                            [Inferno 10.31–36, translated
                                    by H. W. Longfellow]

It is with affection and admiration for Freccero that I dispute his final observation on the *Paradiso:*

The dialectic between the human soul and God was for Dante never to be dissolved into its two polarities, as it was later in the Renaissance. Just as individuality could not be totally absorbed into divinity, so God could not be completely reduced to the proportions of the human soul. The dialectic was maintained by synthesis, the Incarnation, which

is to say that the final image maintains its coherence only by
the grace of the vision that precedes it.

[“The Final Image: *Paradiso* XXXIII, 144” (1964)]

Lucid, accomplished, accurate: Why should I find this inadequate? This *is* Dante’s theology, both traditional and individual.
But is the Incarnation in itself a severe poem? Consider the closing
lines of *Paradiso*:

A l’alta fantasia qui mancò possa;
ma già volgeva il mio disio e ’l *velle*,
sì come rota ch’igualmente è mossa,

l’amor che move il sole e l’altre stelle.

———

Here vigour failed the lofty fantasy:
    But now was turning my desire and will,
    Even as a wheel that equally is moved,

The Love which moves the sun and the other stars.
[*Paradiso* 33.142–145, translated by H. W. Longfellow]

That wheel is Ezekiel’s, taken up in Revelation, and greatly transformed in Dante’s Triumphal Chariot of the Church in *Purgatorio*:

e vidi le fiammelle andar davante,
lasciando dietro a sé l’aere dipinto,
e di tratti pennelli avean sembiante;

sì che lì sopra rimanea distinto
di sette liste, tutte in quei colori
onde fa l’arco il Sole e Delia il cinto.

Questi ostendali in dietro eran maggiori
che la mia vista; e, quanto a mio avviso,
diece passi distavan quei di fori.

Sotto così bel ciel com’ io diviso,
ventiquattro seniori, a due a due,
coronati venien di fiordaliso.

Tutti cantavan: "*Benedicta* tue
ne le figlie d'Adamo, e benedette
sieno in etterno le bellezze tue!."

Poscia che i fiori e l'altre fresche erbette
a rimpetto di me da l'altra sponda
libere fuor da quelle genti elette,

sì come luce luce in ciel seconda,
vennero appresso lor quattro animali,
coronati ciascun di verde fronda.

Ognuno era pennuto di sei ali;
le penne piene d'occhi; e li occhi d'Argo,
se fosser vivi, sarebber cotali.

A descriver lor forme più non spargo
rime, lettor; ch'altra spesa mi strigne,
tanto ch'a questa non posso esser largo;

ma leggi Ezechïel, che li dipigne
come li vide da la fredda parte
venir con vento e con nube e con igne;

e quali i troverai ne le sue carte,
tali eran quivi, salvo ch'a le penne
Giovanni è meco e da lui si diparte.

———

And I beheld the flamelets onward go,
   Leaving behind themselves the air depicted,
   And they of trailing pennons had the semblance,

So that it overhead remained distinct
   With sevenfold lists, all of them of the colours
   Whence the sun's bow is made, and Delia's girdle.

These standards to the rearward longer were
   Than was my sight; and, as it seemed to me,
   Ten paces were the outermost apart.

Under so fair a heaven as I describe
  The four and twenty Elders, two by two,
  Came on incoronate with flower-de-luce.

They all of them were singing: "Blessed thou
  Among the daughters of Adam art, and blessed
  For evermore shall be thy loveliness."

After the flowers and other tender grasses
  In front of me upon the other margin
  Were disencumbered of that race elect,

Even as in heaven star followeth after star,
  There came close after them four animals,
  Incoronate each one with verdant leaf.

Plumed with six wings was every one of them,
  The plumage full of eyes; the eyes of Argus
  If they were living would be such as these.

Reader! to trace their forms no more I waste
  My rhymes; for other spendings press me so,
  That I in this cannot be prodigal.

But read Ezekiel, who depicteth them
  As he beheld them from the region cold
  Coming with cloud, with whirlwind, and with fire;

And such as thou shalt find them in his pages,
  Such were they here; saving that in their plumage
  John is with me, and differeth from him.
      [*Purgatorio* 29.73–105, translated by H. W. Longfellow]

Ma'aseh Merkabah, "the work of the chariot," was a forbidden subject, except for mature initiates, in Talmud and in Kabbalah. Dante, rather pugnaciously, says that Saint John the Divine is with him in differing from Ezekiel. I think there is a problem here. By his own testimony Dante could not read Hebrew (*Paradiso*, Canto 12, l. 73), though there are Hebrew words in the *Commedia.* One of Dante's good friends was the Hebrew poet Immanuel ben Solomon, who was inspired by the *Commedia* to write his *Tofet ve-'eden,* "Hell and Eden."

Dante read Ezekiel in the Vulgate, Saint Jerome's translation of the Hebrew Bible and the New Testament. Myself an amateur yet passionate student of the "work of the chariot," I carefully read Ezekiel's Hebrew and the Vulgate side by side when I wrote *The Shadow of a Great Rock: A Literary Appreciation of the King James Bible* (2011). I would not say the Vulgate falls short, but it lacks the awesome shock Ezekiel brings to his vision:

> And the likeness of the firmament upon the heads of the living creature was as the colour of the terrible crystal, stretched forth over their heads above.
>
> And under the firmament were their wings straight, the one toward the other: every one had two, which covered on this side, and every one had two, which covered on that side, their bodies.
>
> And when they went, I heard the noise of their wings, like the noise of great waters, as the voice of the Almighty, the voice of speech, as the noise of an host: when they stood, they let down their wings.
>
> And there was a voice from the firmament that was over their heads, when they stood, and had let down their wings.
>
> And above the firmament that was over their heads was the likeness of a throne, as the appearance of a sapphire stone: and upon the likeness of the throne was the likeness as the appearance of a man above upon it.
>
> And I saw as the colour of amber, as the appearance of fire round about within it, from the appearance of his loins even upward, and from the appearance of his loins even downward, I saw as it were the appearance of fire, and it had brightness round about.
>
> As the appearance of the bow that is in the cloud in the day of rain, so was the appearance of the brightness round about. This was the appearance of the likeness of the glory of the Lord. And when I saw it, I fell upon my face, and I heard a voice of one that spake.
>
> [Ezekiel (KJV) 1:22–28]

Ezekiel's Hebrew is quite difficult: it moves in spasms and can seem manic. Herbert Marks, in his Norton Bible, and Moshe Greenberg, in his two Anchor Yale Bible volumes, are the best aids I have discovered for deciphering Ezekiel's language.

Marks emphasizes that the Yahweh of Ezekiel is a God who has exiled himself. I would add that Yahweh—like the text of Ezekiel, the prophet himself, Jerusalem—has broken apart. Kabbalah was to call this "the Breaking of the Vessels." Yahweh's *ruach*, his fiery breath, arrives as a whirlwind from the north and shatters prophet, prophecy, and the holy city of Jerusalem, where Ezekiel had served as a priest but without access to the bare Holy of Holies, to be entered only by the High Priest on the Day of Atonement. There and then he would speak out loud the YHWH, forbidden name of Israel's God.

Ezekiel and his fellow elite are exiles in Babylon. Yahweh rides his chariot with asomatous awesomeness, described by the word *hashmal*, rendered "amber" in the KJV. The translation is inadequate, though I cannot suggest another one other than "electricity," the meaning of *hashmal* in current Hebrew. We use the word "amber" for a kind of yellow resin, and that seems absurd for describing God.

The Second Commandment strictly forbids visual representation:

Thou shalt not make unto thee any graven image, or any likeness of any thing that is in heaven above, or that is in the earth beneath, or that is in the water under the earth.

[Exodus (KJV) 20:4]

And yet the J writer depicts Yahweh making a figurine out of the red clay and breathing divine breath into it, thus creating Adam as a living being. J's Yahweh is both mischievous and sublime. He likes to investigate things for himself, brings down the Tower of Babel, picnics on roast veal with Abraham at Mamre, attempts to murder Moses when that reluctant prophet makes a night encampment in the Negev, and participates in the ultimate barbecue, silently facing Moses and seventy elders of Israel in the theophany on Mount Sinai:

Then went up Moses, and Aaron, Nadab, and Abihu, and seventy of the elders of Israel.

And they saw the God of Israel: and there was under his feet as it were a paved work of a sapphire stone, and as it were the body of heaven in his clearness.

And upon the nobles of the children of Israel he laid not his hand: also they saw God, and did eat and drink.

[Exodus (KJV) 24:9–11]

Seventy-four Israelites stare at Yahweh. He is not described except as an aerial clarity, presumably blue like the sapphire beneath him. Despite the Second Commandment, Tanakh gives us two memorable images of God. Ezekiel's chariot is one and follows in the wake of Isaiah's vision in the Temple:

In the year that king Uzziah died I saw also the Lord sitting upon a throne, high and lifted up, and his train filled the temple.

Above it stood the seraphims: each one had six wings; with twain he covered his face, and with twain he covered his feet, and with twain he did fly.

And one cried unto another, and said, Holy, holy, holy, is the Lord of hosts: the whole earth is full of his glory.

And the posts of the door moved at the voice of him that cried, and the house was filled with smoke.

Then said I, Woe is me! for I am undone; because I am a man of unclean lips, and I dwell in the midst of a people of unclean lips: for mine eyes have seen the King, the Lord of hosts.

Then flew one of the seraphims unto me, having a live coal in his hand, which he had taken with the tongs from off the altar:

And he laid it upon my mouth, and said, Lo, this hath touched thy lips; and thine iniquity is taken away, and thy sin purged.

Also I heard the voice of the Lord, saying, Whom shall I send, and who will go for us? Then said I, Here am I; send me.

[Isaiah (KJV) 6:1–8]

Ezekiel develops the enthroned Yahweh by images of dynamism, so as to show us God in motion, hastening to ends beyond our expectations. But then Ezekiel was an exile. Isaiah of Jerusalem was a diplomat, laboring to preserve kingdom and city. His Yahweh is stationed in the Temple as though immovable. What has Dante done with Isaiah's throne of Yahweh and with Ezekiel's chariot of Yahweh in exile?

Tosto che ne la vista mi percosse
L'alta virtù che già m'avea trafitto
prima ch'io fuor di püerizia fosse,

volsimi a la sinistra col respitto
col quale il fantolin corre a la mamma
quando ha paura o quando elli è afflitto,

per dicere a Virgilio: "Men che dramma
di sangue m'è rimaso che non tremi:
conosco i segni de l'antica fiamma."

Ma Virgilio n'avea lasciati scemi
di sé, Virgilio dolcissimo patre,
Virgilio a cui per mia salute die'mi;

né quantunque perdeo l'antica matre,
valse a le guance nette di rugiada,
che, lagrimando, non tornasser atre.

"Dante, perché Virgilio se ne vada,
non pianger anco, non piangere ancora;
ché pianger ti conven per altra spada."

Quasi ammiraglio che in poppa e in prora
viene a veder la gente che ministra
per li altri legni, e a ben far l'incora;

in su la sponda del carro sinistra,
quando mi volsi al suon del nome mio,
che di necessità qui si registra,

vidi la donna che pria m'appario
velata sotto l'angelica festa,
drizzar li occhi ver' me di qua dal rio.

Tutto che 'l vel che le scendea di testa,
cerchiato de le fronde di Minerva,
non la lasciasse parer manifesta,

regalmente ne l'atto ancor proterva
continüò come colui che dice
e 'l più caldo parlar dietro reserva:

"Guardaci ben! Ben son, ben son Beatrice.
Come degnasti d'accedere al monte?
non sapei tu che qui è l'uom felice?"

Li occhi mi cadder giù nel chiaro fonte;
ma veggendomi in esso, i trassi a l'erba,
tanta vergogna mi gravò la fronte.

Così la madre al figlio par superba,
com' ella parve a me; perché d'amaro
sente il sapor de la pietade acerba.

Ella si tacque; e li angeli cantaro
di sùbito *In te, Domine, speravi*;
ma oltre *"pedes meos"* non passaro.

Sì come neve tra le vive travi
per lo dosso d'Italia si congela,
soffiata e stretta da li venti schiavi,

poi, liquefatta, in sé stessa trapela,
pur che la terra che perde ombra spiri,
sì che par foco fonder la candela;

così fui sanza lagrime e sospiri
anzi 'l cantar di quei che notan sempre
dietro a le note de li etterni giri;

ma poi che 'ntesi ne le dolci tempre
lor compatire a me, par che se detto
avesser: "Donna, perché sì lo stempre?,"

lo gel che m'era intorno al cor ristretto,
spirito e acqua fessi, e con angoscia
de la bocca e de li occhi uscì del petto.

Ella, pur ferma in su la detta coscia
del carro stando, a le sustanze pie
volse le sue parole così poscia:

"Voi vigilate ne l'etterno die,
sì che notte né sonno a voi non fura
passo che faccia il secol per sue vie;

onde la mia risposta è con più cura
che m'intenda colui che di là piagne,
perché sia colpa e duol d'una misura.

Non pur per ovra de le rote magne,
che drizzan ciascun seme ad alcun fine
secondo che le stelle son compagne,

ma per larghezza di grazie divine,
che sì alti vapori hanno a lor piova,
che nostre viste là non van vicine,

questi fu tal ne la sua vita nova
virtüalmente, ch'ogne abito destro
fatto averebbe in lui mirabil prova.

Ma tanto più maligno e più silvestro
si fa 'l terren col mal seme e non cólto,
quant' elli ha più di buon vigor terrestro.

Alcun tempo il sostenni col mio volto:
mostrando li occhi giovanetti a lui,
meco il menava in dritta parte vòlto.

Sì tosto come in su la soglia fui
di mia seconda etade e mutai vita,
questi si tolse a me, e diessi altrui."

—

As soon as on my vision smote the power
    Sublime, that had already pierced me through
    Ere from my boyhood I had yet come forth,

To the left hand I turned with that reliance
    With which the little child runs to his mother,
    When he has fear, or when he is afflicted,

To say unto Virgilius: "Not a drachm
   Of blood remains in me, that does not tremble;
   I know the traces of the ancient flame."

But us Virgilius of himself deprived
   Had left, Virgilius, sweetest of all fathers,
   Virgilius, to whom I for safety gave me:

Nor whatsoever lost the ancient mother
   Availed my cheeks now purified from dew,
   That weeping they should not again be darkened.

"Dante, because Virgilius has departed
   Do not weep yet, do not weep yet awhile;
   For by another sword thou need'st must weep."

E'en as an admiral, who on poop and prow
   Comes to behold the people that are working
   In other ships, and cheers them to well-doing,

Upon the left hand border of the car,
   When at the sound I turned of my own name,
   Which of necessity is here recorded,

I saw the Lady, who erewhile appeared
   Veiled underneath the angelic festival,
   Direct her eyes to me across the river.

Although the veil, that from her head descended,
   Encircled with the foliage of Minerva,
   Did not permit her to appear distinctly,

In attitude still royally majestic
   Continued she, like unto one who speaks,
   And keeps his warmest utterance in reserve:

"Look at me well; in sooth I'm Beatrice!
   How didst thou deign to come unto the Mountain?
   Didst thou not know that man is happy here?"

Mine eyes fell downward into the clear fountain,
   But, seeing myself therein, I sought the grass,
   So great a shame did weigh my forehead down.

As to the son the mother seems superb,
    So she appeared to me; for somewhat bitter
    Tasteth the savour of severe compassion.

Silent became she, and the Angels sang
    Suddenly, "*In te, Domine, speravi*":
    But beyond "*pedes meos*" did not pass.

Even as the snow among the living rafters
    Upon the back of Italy congeals,
    Blown on and drifted by Sclavonian winds,

And then, dissolving, trickles through itself
    Whene'er the land that loses shadow breathes,
    So that it seems a fire that melts a taper;

E'en thus was I without a tear or sigh,
    Before the song of those who sing for ever
    After the music of the eternal spheres.

But when I heard in their sweet melodies
    Compassion for me, more than had they said,
    "O wherefore, lady, dost thou thus upbraid him?"

The ice, that was about my heart congealed,
    To air and water changed, and in my anguish
    Through mouth and eyes came gushing from my breast.

She, on the right-hand border of the car
    Still firmly standing, to those holy beings
    Thus her discourse directed afterwards:

"Ye keep your watch in the eternal day,
    So that nor night nor sleep can steal from you
    One step the ages make upon their path;

Therefore my answer is with greater care,
    That he may hear me who is weeping yonder,
    So that the sin and dole be of one measure.

Not only by the work of those great wheels,
    That destine every seed unto some end,
    According as the stars are in conjunction,

But by the largess of celestial graces,
    Which have such lofty vapours for their rain
    That near to them our sight approaches not,

Such had this man become in his new life
    Potentially, that every righteous habit
    Would have made admirable proof in him;

But so much more malignant and more savage
    Becomes the land untilled and with bad seed,
    The more good earthly vigour it possesses.

Some time did I sustain him with my look;
    Revealing unto him my youthful eyes,
    I led him with me turned in the right way.

As soon as ever of my second age
    I was upon the threshold and changed life,
    Himself from me he took and gave to others."
      [*Purgatorio* 30.40–126, translated by H. W. Longfellow]

What Charles Williams called "the figure of Beatrice" forever will remain the glory and enigma of the *Commedia*. Is she a highly original myth invented by Dante? Is she Dante's muse? Since she is installed by Dante into a position of all but the highest honor in the project of salvation, why is she not as much a heresy as Gnosticism was and is?

Admirable in his ruthlessly audacious enshrinement of a Florentine young woman he had scarcely known, and who had gently mocked him, Dante almost succeeded in forcing his own vision of love upon Christendom.

It is Beatrice, not Yahweh or Jesus or the Virgin Mother, who rides the Triumphal Chariot of the Church. Virgil fades away and Beatrice becomes the guide to Paradise. But who or what is she? Dante tells us that she was sent to save him by a rather obscure Saint Lucia, at the command of an unnamed, even higher lady, evidently not Mary the mother of Jesus. There is a mystery in this that has much to do with Dante's exalted place as prophet of a new Christian empire.

With marvelous artistic control, Dante conjures up his heroic Crusader ancestor Cacciaguida to prophesy both his descendant's suffering and ultimate glory:

Qual si partio Ipolito d'Atene
per la spietata e perfida noverca,
tal di Fiorenza partir ti convene.

Questo si vuole e questo già si cerca,
e tosto verrà fatto a chi ciò pensa
là dove Cristo tutto dì si merca.

La colpa seguirà la parte offensa
in grido, come suol; ma la vendetta
fia testimonio al ver che la dispensa.

Tu lascerai ogne cosa diletta
più caramente; e questo è quello strale
che l'arco de lo essilio pria saetta.

Tu proverai sì come sa di sale
lo pane altrui, e come è duro calle
lo scendere e 'l salir per l'altrui scale.

—

As forth from Athens went Hippolytus,
    By reason of his step-dame false and cruel,
    So thou from Florence must perforce depart.

Already this is willed, and this is sought for;
    And soon it shall be done by him who thinks it,
    Where every day the Christ is bought and sold.

The blame shall follow the offended party
    In outcry as is usual; but the vengeance
    Shall witness to the truth that doth dispense it.

Thou shalt abandon everything beloved
    Most tenderly, and this the arrow is
    Which first the bow of banishment shoots forth.

Thou shalt have proof how savoureth of salt
  The bread of others, and how hard a road
  he going down and up another's stairs.
      [*Paradiso* 17.46–60, translated by H. W. Longfellow]

In Canto 15 Cacciaguida tells Dante,

Tu credi che a me tuo pensier mei
da quel ch'è primo, così come raia
da l'un, se si conosce, il cinque e 'l sei;

—

Thou think'st the truth; because the small and great
  Of this existence look into the mirror
  Wherein, before thou think'st, thy thought thou showest.
      [*Paradiso* 15.61–63, translated by H. W. Longfellow]

That is to say that, even as a child, Dante incarnated what would be the truth of his life and work. The life, bitter; the work, perfection. From brokenness to completion is the path of the poem. Dante thought that for his life to be complete, he had to live to the age of eighty-one, nine nines. Alas, he died at fifty-six, evidently of malaria.

Jesus dies at thirty-three. Dante believed that had Jesus lived until eighty-one, he would have merged with God in this life and not the next one. Similarly, Dante hoped that at eighty-one he would know everything and perhaps also resurrect without dying.

The *Commedia* is beyond argument, even though Dante insists upon arguing. Vico thought that if Dante had cast out theology, he would have surpassed Homer. Italian scholars, to this day, favor a less theological reading of the *Commedia* than Anglo-American exegetes practice.

T. S. Eliot once expressed a preference for Dante over Shakespeare because the Florentine poet depended upon a coherent view of time and eternity, while Shakespeare improvised wildly. We can doubt that Eliot believed himself. His poetry strives to be Dantesque yet is thronged by Shakespearean echoes and allusions.

James Joyce emulated both Shakespeare and Dante. He loved Dante and rather resented Shakespeare. But when asked to state a preference, he said it had to be the "Englishman," because Shakespeare was richer. With his Paterian feeling for the finer edge of words, Joyce may have been thinking of the etymological meaning: strong or powerful.

Shakespeare never read Dante. Chaucer, Spenser, Milton, Blake, Shelley, Byron, Keats (in the Cary translation), and most major poets after them are changed by Dante. Italian poets from Petrarch through Leopardi to Ungaretti have flourished in his shadow.

The notion of how Dante would have reacted to Shakespeare, or the English dramatist to the Florentine visionary, would need the late Anthony Burgess to develop in the mode brilliantly evidenced in his late short story "A Meeting in Valladolid," where a gentle and patient Shakespeare encounters a surly and exasperated Cervantes.

I have Shakespeare all but committed to memory, while the *Commedia* is still strange to me, no matter how many times I read through it. In my exhausted midnights, when I think about the two poets in visual images, the effect is like the shock of comparing Caravaggio to Giotto.

Except for their shared eminence, Dante and Shakespeare seem to me antithetical. William Butler Yeats would have agreed. Dante was more crucial for him than Shakespeare. In *A Vision* Shakespeare is stationed with Balzac and also with Napoleon (!) in Phase 20, The Concrete Man. Though Yeats calls Shakespeare "the greatest of modern poets," one senses a certain detachment in the Anglo-Irish Archpoet.

In comparison Dante dominates Yeats's own Phase 17, The Daimonic Man. This phase also contains Shelley and Landor, both of whom are portrayed as violently excitable, and who thus come short of the Unity of Being that Yeats shares with Dante:

Yet Dante, having attained, as poet, to Unity of Being, as poet saw all things set in order, had an intellect that served the *Mask* alone, that compelled even those things that opposed it to serve, and was content to see both good and evil.

This puzzling assertion makes me realize again that Yeats's Dante comes to him from the pre-Raphaelite poets and painters, headed by Dante Gabriel Rossetti. Their Dante is not ours. The hard-edged phantasmagoria presented as nature by the pre-Raphaelites is not there in the *Commedia*. Dante Gabriel Rossetti brilliantly translated the magnificent stony sestina of Dante, the second of his *Rime petrose* (1296):

> To the dim light and the large circle of shade
> I have clomb, and to the whitening of the hills,
> There where we see no color in the grass.
> Natheless my longing loses not its green,
> It has so taken root in the hard stone
> Which talks and hears as though it were a lady.
>
> Utterly frozen is this youthful lady,
> Even as the snow that lies within the shade;
> For she is no more moved than is the stone
> By the sweet season which makes warm the hills
> And alters them afresh from white to green
> Covering their sides again with flowers and grass.
>
> When on her hair she sets a crown of grass
> The thought has no more room for other lady,
> Because she weaves the yellow with the green
> So well that Love sits down there in the shade,—
> Love who has shut me in among low hills
> Faster than between walls of granite-stone.
>
> She is more bright than is a precious stone;
> The wound she gives may not be healed with grass:
> I therefore have fled far o'er plains and hills
> For refuge from so dangerous a lady;
> But from her sunshine nothing can give shade,–
> Not any hill, nor wall, nor summer-green.
>
> A while ago, I saw her dressed in green,—
> So fair, she might have wakened in a stone
> This love which I do feel even for her shade;

And therefore, as one woos a graceful lady,
I wooed her in a field that was all grass
Girdled about with very lofty hills.

Yet shall the streams turn back and climb the hills
Before Love's flame in this damp wood and green
Burn, as it burns within a youthful lady,
For my sake, who would sleep away in stone
My life, or feed like beasts upon the grass,
Only to see her garments cast a shade.

How dark soe'er the hills throw out their shade,
Under her summer green the beautiful lady
Covers it, like a stone cover'd in grass.

I wonder how self-abnegation could be more severe than this:

        who would sleep away in stone
My life, or feed like beasts upon the grass,
Only to see her garments cast a shade.

In *On the Genealogy of Morals* (1887), Nietzsche subjected Dante to a hammer blow:

> Dante, it seems to me, made a gross mistake when, with frightful ingenuity, he placed the inscription above the gate to his hell, "Me too eternal love created." Above the door of the Christian paradise and its "eternal blessedness" the inscription "Me too eternal *hate* created" would certainly be more appropriate—granting a truth to be appropriate above the entrance to a falsehood!
> [Translated by William Hausemann]

Had someone, whether of a rival faction or of a family seeking revenge, knifed Dante after finishing only *Inferno*, what would we think of him now? I was never really hurt by *Inferno* until I had taught several terms in Bologna and Rome and began to have a better sense of the language when I read Dante in his own vernacular. It hurt dreadfully and gave me nightmares until I went on to read deeply the actual text of *Purgatorio* and *Paradiso*. I wondered if I was unique in this regard, but was greatly cheered when I read Robert Pogue Harrison's review of a Dante biography:

> When violence enters its cycles of reciprocity, when it spreads like a contagion out of all proportion, it turns into a form of mimetic insanity, drawing everyone, including God, into its vortex. Because Dante scholars operate on the assumption that their author is always in full control of his poem, they tend to blind themselves to all the indications that Dante— the author as well as his character—is starting to lose his mind at the end of *Inferno*.
>
> ["Dante: He Went Mad in His Hell," 2016]

Harrison, an acute and erudite scholar-critic, goes on to the passage where Dante actually urges genocide against the entire city of Genoa. *Purgatorio* saved its poet from madness, though no professional Dante scholar whom I know or have read would admit that. It has long been recognized that Chaucer the Pilgrim in the *Tales of Canterbury* is an amiable satire on the darker figure Dante the Pilgrim. Chaucer was a grand plagiarist, particularly from Boccaccio, but was happy to loot Dante as well.

Dante the Pilgrim and Dante the poet manifest rather different personalities until they come together in the encounter with the crusading ancestor Cacciaguida in *Paradiso*. Necessarily they are the only personalities in *Commedia* capable of change. Individuals both of *Inferno* and of *Paradiso* are fixed forever in their finality. *Purgatorio* allows only the single change of refining.

> The encounters do not take place in this life, where men are always met with in a state of contingency that manifests only a part of their essence, and where the very intensity of life in the most vital moments makes self-awareness difficult and renders a true encounter almost impossible. Nor do they take place in a hereafter where what is most personal in the personality is effaced by the shadows of death and nothing remains but a feeble, veiled, or indifferent recollection of life. No, the souls of Dante's other world are not dead men, they

are the truly living; though the concrete data of their lives and the atmosphere of their personalities are drawn from their former existences on earth, they manifest them here with a completeness, a concentration, an actuality, which they seldom achieved during their term on earth and as-suredly never revealed to anyone else. And so it is that Dante finds them; surprise, astonishment, joy, or horror grips both parties to the meeting, for the dweller in the Other World as he is shown there is also deeply moved by an encounter with one of the living; the mere fact of seeing and recognizing one another reaches into the deepest foun-dations of human feeling and creates images of unparalleled poetic force and richness.

This is Erich Auerbach's acute observation from his *Dante: Poet of the Secular World* (1929). I would not so much desire to question this as to worry the word "personalities." An unchanging fiction can-not be a personality. Hamlet, Cleopatra, Iago, Macbeth, Falstaff, and Lear incessantly undergo metamorphic transmutations that can bewilder and captivate us. Francesca, Ugolino, Farinata, Ulysses, Matelda, and Beatrice above all are finalities.

Nicholas of Cusa (1401–1464) famously repeated the Hermetic Corpus in his dictum "God is an infinite circle whose center is ev-erywhere and whose circumference is nowhere." Dante centers the Incarnation everywhere. That is his power and his achievement. Shakespeare pragmatically evades the Incarnation, and the circum-ference of his plays cannot be located, for always they move beyond.

Have Dante and Shakespeare anything in common? I find it a shock when I read *King Lear* and then open the *Paradiso*. It is not just the difference between a pagan play directed at a Christian au-dience and a highly personalized inward epic that transmembers the Catholic scheme of salvation by inserting Beatrice. As E. R. Cur-tius says:

To choose as guide in a poetic vision of the otherworld a loved woman who has been thus exalted is still within the bounds of Christian philosophy and faith. But Dante goes much further than this. He gives Beatrice a place in the objective process of salvation. Her function is thought of as not only for himself but also for all believers. Thus, on his own authority, he introduces into the Christian revelation an element which disrupts the doctrine of the church. This is either heresy—or myth.

[*European Literature and the Latin Middle Ages* (1948)]

You have to be deaf to reject the *Commedia*. Every literary Catholic I have ever known has kept it close as warrant and resource. Beatrice may have been heresy, but that is no longer relevant. If myth is gossip grown old, she is no longer myth.

John Milton's muse was the Spirit that moved upon the waters and brought forth creation. Dante's muse replaces Ezekiel's Yahweh and St. John the Divine's Christ, by riding like a sunburst upon the Triumphal Chariot of the Church.

The American theological exegetes are careful to distinguish between Beatrice and Christ. Was Dante equally careful? His poem says that every believer must follow him in accepting the mediation of Beatrice. And yet he limits her: in the presence of God she contemplates the One without understanding. Confronting the dazzling light of Revelation, Dante more than comprehends the Divine Love that moves the cosmic wheel of creation.

William Blake's study of Dante's countenance brings out all the familiar features: large staring eyes, long nose, jutting jaw, air of imperiousness. The man Dante was formidable: relentless, unforgiving, agonistic. We know very little about Shakespeare's personality, and the portraits are inadequate. And yet we have the testimony of Ben Jonson and others. Unlike Jonson or Christopher Marlowe, Shakespeare had the good sense to go the other way when violence threatened. A peaceful, quiet man (when sober), he avoided court politics, religious disputes, and family strife (by staying away from Stratford) and maintained a kind of detachment toward even his own amorous adventures.

God is not a character in Shakespeare's theater. There is a parodistic interlude in *Cymbeline* where Jupiter appears as a travesty of epiphanies. Dante concludes his poem by *seeing* "three in one and one in three." Displayed as lights and colors, they are the Triune God.

Dante does not say that he sees God face-to-face. His vision is geometric, incandescent, steady. He thus avoids what will be John Milton's error. The God of *Paradise Lost* is an angry schoolmaster and also an affronted monarch.

William Blake venerated both Dante and Milton and made wonderful illustrations for their poetry. Necessarily he had disagreements with each. The conclusion of *Paradiso* and the opening of St. John's Gospel are opposed by the final lines of Blake's "Auguries of Innocence":

We are led to Believe a Lie
When we see not Thro the Eye
Which was Born in a Night to perish in a Night
When the Soul Slept in Beams of Light
God Appears & God is Light
To those poor Souls who dwell in Night
But does a Human Form Display
To those who Dwell in Realms of day

Jewish tradition, particularly as Kabbalah, sometimes visualized Yahweh as a titanic human being. The divine features were troped in the Sh'iur Qomah, a fragmentary text forever in dispute. It seems to be part of the Merkabah tradition that descends from Ezekiel. During the later 1970s I had several stimulating conversations with the late Saul Lieberman (1898–1983), an articulate, learned, and passionate scholar and an advocate of Conservative Judaism. Lieberman had the insight that the Yahweh of the Sh'iur Qomah was a youthful warrior, possibly like the figure who appears to Joshua at Jericho.

At ninety I feel a longing for the Orthodox Judaism of my childhood home. It is difficult to believe that I will find my way back to it. Yet I share with it and with all of Judaic tradition a firm belief that Yahweh has a human shape and face. William Blake clearly felt the same. Dante would have regarded that as grotesque heresy, except that Jesus was both God and man.

Years ago I spent much time with the late George Plimpton (1927–2003), who edited the *Paris Review* and was a fireworks enthusiast. Several times my wife and I accompanied George and his wife to the Fourth of July fireworks display, presided over by George. I have never liked fireworks, though my wife does. Is my aversion quasi-theological? Dante is so harsh that frequently he renders me defensive. That too is a tribute to his rhetorical power. Yet whatever God is, she cannot be a light show.

The Hebrew Bible does not so much give us an anthropomorphic God as it does theomorphic men and women. Dante's Beatrice is a theomorphic woman. He implies that she lived as an angel before she was reborn as the Florentine Beatrice. After her earthly death she is transformed into a being above that of the angels.

Simon Magus, regarded by the Church Fathers as the inaugural Gnostic, came out of Samaria as a disciple of John the Baptist. It seems dubious that he was a Gnostic, but everything about him is dubious. Legend had him go to Tyre, where he picked up a whore named Helen and named her the Lost Thought of God. He proceeded to Rome, where he performed miracles, including levitation. Christian writings cheerfully recorded his demise as taking place in a levitation contest with St. Peter, out of which Simon came tumbling down. When he came to Rome, Simon took the cognomen of Faustus, "the favored one," and so became the father of the Faust legend.

If you stand back from the *Commedia*, you can see it as the antitype to Simon/Faust. The whore Helen, hailed by Simon as the reincarnation of Helen of Troy, is the demonic antithesis to the figure of Beatrice.

I continue to be frightened by *Inferno*. *Purgatorio* challenges anything except Shakespeare. *Paradiso* becomes an obsession as I age and will be my study until the end. What will always baffle me is Beatrice. The most crucial figures in the *Commedia* are the fourfold of Dante the Pilgrim, Dante the poet, Virgil, and Beatrice. Triumphantly the first two merge at the end of *Purgatorio*. Virgil vanishes, his place and function taken over by Beatrice.

The Blessing is for me a vital question. Jacob outwits Esau and wrongly secures it. Wrestling all night with one of the Elohim, who may well be the Angel of Death, Jacob holds him off and wins the new name Israel. As patriarch he awards the Blessing to Judah. The precise meaning of the Hebrew Blessing can be ascertained, but there are difficulties. For me it means more life into a time without boundaries.

Beatrice—in name, function, apotheosis—constitutes Dante's blessing. She guides him to the truth of the Incarnation. Whether he is awakened to more life is hardly a question for Dante scholars. But a poem is a poem before all else. It is a fiction of duration and not truth. Singleton states that the fiction of the *Commedia* is that it is *not* a fiction.

Wallace Stevens, secular seer of the Supreme Fiction, which is poetry, speaks for me in his *Adagia* (1930–1955):

> The final belief is to believe in a fiction, which you know to be a fiction, there being nothing else. The exquisite truth is to know that it is a fiction and that you believe in it willingly.

Stevens was a great poet, whose work helps keep me alive, but of course he was not Dante, who would not have agreed either with Singleton or with Stevens. As much as Joachim of Flora, Dante had a Third Testament to uncover. For him the *Commedia* was as much the truth as the New Testament. I have spent many weary hours reading the Greek New Testament and have had little aesthetic reward. Almost all of it is very badly written. In my view the *Commedia* more than eclipses the Gospels and Paul. But then I am an aesthete.

What shall a secular reader make of the figure of Beatrice? In 1961 I purchased Charles Williams's book of that title, read it with mixed feelings, and have rarely returned to it since. Sixty years ago I went through a phase of reading everything by Charles Williams. W. H. Auden had recommended *The Descent of the Dove: A Short History of the Holy Spirit* (1939), and I read it through several times with considerable unease. Williams was a fantasist; I tried several of his "religious thrillers" (T. S. Eliot) and was unhappy. *Shadows of Ecstasy* (1933) moved me to some fury. I did develop a curious taste for Williams's Arthurian torso of long, tangled poems, but then I like odd poems.

Charles Williams was an editor and writer and was not ordained, but he could hardly be described as secular. He had worked out a doctrine he called "co-inherence" that asserted all human love reflected the God/man of Jesus Christ. Here he is in his book *The Figure of Beatrice: A Study in Dante* (1943):

What seems to us the terrible phrase of Beatrice when she says to Virgil himself "I am made such that your misery does not touch me" (II, 92) means a division which has to be endured. . . . Virgil is poetry, and the greatest of European poets knew the limitation of poetry. Poetry may be as "spiritual" as its rash devotees are in the habit of calling it. In so far as it is "spiritual" it is of the nature of those visions and locutions from which the wise are warned to be detached. Poetry cannot possess charity; it cannot be humble. It is therefore justly presented in Virgil, who precisely lacked baptism; that is, by the theological decision of the time, the capacity for infinite charity and infinite humility. So of Virgil as philosophy, and Virgil as human learning; nay, of Virgil as the Institution itself. It is a part of the poem that Virgil should lack grace; did he not, he would be too like Beatrice herself. The *Aeneid* has *pietas* and not *caritas;* so must its author have here.

I can see why Auden cheered this on. To me it seems inadequate. Must a poet or any one of us accept the Incarnation in order to manifest *caritas* for the insulted and injured, for victims and outcasts, for the miserable and impoverished? To say of Virgil that the limit of his love was *pietas*, reverence for ancestors and country, is to defraud him of his Epicurean firmness in a disorderly universe, merciless and violent, with a monstrous goddess Juno, who presides over nightmare.

It comes down to this: Is there any interpreter who can speak for Dante? Anglo-American modern Dante scholarship follows Charles S. Singleton, whose most eminent student remains John Freccero. My distrust of Singleton was reinforced by reading *Dante's Journey of Sanctification* (1990) by Antonio C. Mastrobuono and *Dissent and Philosophy in the Middle Ages: Dante and His Precursors* (2002) by Ernest L. Fortin, AA. Readings of Dante, even if they follow the Allegory of the Theologians, may well be mistaken. I think of the earlier Auerbach and of Bruno Nardi, who prompted Peter Dronke's remarkable *Dante and Medieval Latin Traditions* (1986).

Mastrobuono was a caustic critic of Singleton and Freccero, and I am not happy with his misguided dismissal of Freccero. But he seems accurate to me when he argues, in regard to Singleton, that

Singleton's thesis of the *Comedy* is based on an erroneous interpretation of St. Thomas, and that [instead] Dante's journey under Virgil's guidance through Inferno and Purgatory
is an effect of (not a preparation for) sanctifying grace, which
Dante has already received before entering the world beyond.

The difference is of some importance since Virgil also would
have an enhanced status on this view. Much more temperate,
Ernest L. Fortin seems to me persuasive:

It would seem from this that Dante's allegory is reducible to
neither the allegory of the poet nor the allegory of the theologian, but that in what it has that is most distinctive it represents a third type of allegory that could be called
philosophical allegory. At least this is what Dante's first in-
terpreters thought. Boccaccio notes in this connection that
Dante was distinguished from the other poets of his time by
the extent of his knowledge both in natural philosophy and
in moral philosophy. His work is not that of a poet *tout court*,
but of a philosophical poet who, thanks to his extraordinary
gifts of expression, has the advantage over the philosopher
of making himself understood by all.

That at least aids in ridding us of my own black beast in Dante
criticism: the Allegory of the Theologians. I need scholarly support
here since I am far away from what I know best, and delight in the
immensely learned Peter Dronke:

So too, Nardi was able to argue, on the basis of his incom-
parable detailed knowledge of medieval thought, that the notion of sustained allegorical, moral and mystical reading of
the *Commedia* was *historically* inappropriate, that "any attempt
to extract from Dante's poems the hidden sense which Jewish and Christian theologians were wont to extract from the
Bible is simply an attempt at cabbalistics." And yet—so the
objection runs—was it not precisely this kind of reading that
Dante himself had espoused, in the letter in which he dedicated the *Paradiso* to his patron Cangrande? Where in 1944

Nardi spoke of a "grave and justifiable doubt" about whether Dante wrote that exposition, in his later work on the question he concluded, with a wealth of observations, many of which have been neither countered nor superseded, that the expository text which follows the dedication—the seeming foundation-stone for the systematic allegorizing of the *Commedia*—could not be attributed to Dante himself.

Perhaps I should blame myself for piling on authorities, and so I give a voice to John Freccero at his uppermost clarity:

> We shall see that the "allegory of the poets" may be interpreted broadly to mean all of the figures and tropes a poet must employ in order to express his intended meaning. Because the meaning is intended, theologians sometimes referred to this kind of allegory as "allegory of the letter." Like the fictive narrations mentioned in Augustine, it is to be found in the Bible, as well as in secular literature. Beyond this kind of allegory, however, there is another kind, not in the writer's control, called the "allegory of theologians," which appears only in the Bible and was thought to be divinely inspired. From a modern, naturalistic point of view, it might be said that the allegory of theologians was sometimes a way of interpreting a text in spite of the author's intended meaning, as a way of superimposing a Christian significance anachronistically on an Old Testament text. The significance might also be referred to as the "allegory of the spirit," or simply, the spiritual sense.
>
> ["Allegory and Autobiography" (2007)]

"Anachronistically" is the key word there. The sly Freccero, prince of foxes, has it both ways. Loyally he follows his teacher Singleton. Intellectually he follows Freccero, who sees that the relation between Hebrew Bible and New Testament is agonistic, and who knows that Dante is always agonistic, whether against all previous poets (Virgil included) or against Scripture.

It may be that Dante's most anxious agon was with Guido Cavalcanti, his best friend and almost a mentor. Cavalcanti is one of the permanent Italian poets, but he had the misfortune of Dante as direct contemporary, and the advent of Petrarch in the next generation.

Cavalcanti's most remarkable poem, "Donna me prega," states his essential stance: the soul is mortal and needs to be renovated by love, but love alas is an illness that passes.

There is some dispute as to Cavalcanti's intellectual affiliations, yet I find it pointless. Dante's best friend and rival had an original mind, not of course of Dante's perspicuity and salience. Petrarch, a far larger poet than Cavalcanti, is less self-generating, since his whole career turns upon fending off Dante. For Cavalcanti, desire is death, as it was for Shakespeare. I turn here to the impressive scholar Teodolinda Barolini in her book *Dante's Poets* (1984):

> The second stanza of "Donna me prega" offers a definition of love that begins by saying that love resides "dove sta memora," that is, in the sensitive rather than intellective soul, and then proceeds to assign the origin of love to Mars, the planet of anger and violent irrational feelings. In the following stanza, the poet again stresses love's connection with that faculty of the soul that is "non razionale, —ma che sente" ("not rational, but which feels" [31]); once more, then, love is assigned to the seat of the passions, the sensitive soul, which corresponds to the body rather than to the intellect. The effects of such an association are apparent in the next verses:
>
> > for di salute—giudicar mantene,
> > ché la 'ntenzione—per ragione—vale:
> > discerne male—in cui è vizio amico.
> > Di sua Potenza segue spesso morte
>
> Thus love infects reason and judgment and, in the strikingly simple verse that falls at the poem's mathematical center (not including the *congedo*), love is explicitly aligned with death: "Di sua Potenza segue spesso morte . . ." Since love cancels the light of reason, it inevitably leads to spiritual death; the association between love and darkness is made not only in the second stanza, where love is said to originate in a dark-

ness ("scuritate") that comes from Mars, but again in the closing verses of the last stanza, where the earlier "scuritate" is echoed by the phrase "'n mezzo scuro": "For di colore, d'essere diviso, / assiso—'n mezzo scuro, luce rade" ("Without color, cut off from being, love dwells in a dark place, and puts out the light" [67–68]). Love's alignment with death and the dark powers is thus complete; it not only comes from darkness, but it dwells in darkness, and destroys the light.

For Dante his love of Beatrice is salvation. Dante had the tact not to assign Guido Cavalcanti to a particular location in the *Inferno*, but we can assume he lodges there in one exasperation or another. The "first friends" had parted politically, spiritually, and quite specifically on Dante's apotheosis of Beatrice. Cavalcanti died in 1300, possibly of malaria, on his way home after exile from Florence. Dante is believed to have begun writing *Inferno* in 1308.

As I struggle to apprehend Dante more accurately, I begin to appreciate his authentic gusto. Francesca endlessly tells her pathetic story. Paolo weeps and weeps. Dante the Pilgrim faints. At least Francesca, a strong woman, keeps going. Cavalcanti hovers. Dark passion dilates the woman's sense of being. It reduces men.

I begin by observing my discomfort with Dante for damning Francesca and her poor Paolo. What is their sin? Adultery. Boccaccio says of Dante that he was noted for his venery. In an age when most aristocratic marriages were political, adultery became the norm. Troubadour poetry is founded upon it.

I venture that the supposed sin of Francesca and Paolo might better be called a literalizing of romance reading or the crossing of art by experience. Francesca falls in love with her husband's brother Paolo. She has no love for her husband; nor does Dante; nor do we. The cuckolded husband murders both his wife and his brother. You might say that their sin is the victimization visited upon them. Francesca narrates. Paolo weeps. Dante faints. Why?

Petrarch, inferior to Dante as poet and as thinker, is one of us; Dante is not. For Dante there is or ought to be a universal world order, presided over by an emperor, who will set limits upon even a reformed papacy. Self-development, whether poetic or erotic, has to be sublimated. Love of one's own muse, Beatrice, is sublimated to the love of God. The pride of authorship burns freely but for the sake of Heaven.

The intense spirituality of the *Commedia* transcends even Dante's own theologizings. There are insoluble mysteries in the poem. What was Dante's precise relation to the Everlasting Gospel of Joachim de Flora? Joachim is placed high in *Paradiso*. Cacciaguida, Dante's heroic ancestor, prophesies a glorious role for the poet in the revival of Italy. Alas, Dante lived long enough to see his hopes thwarted. The Holy Roman Emperor Henry VII of Luxembourg died suddenly, a year after subduing Florence, and that made it impossible to return to Florence on terms honorable enough for him to accept. Dante died in exile but with the comfort of having finished the *Commedia*.

It is difficult for a contemporary visitor to Florence to achieve a true sense of the city during the age of Dante. Florentines hated and butchered one another. Dante was liberal in populating Hell with his enemies and Heaven with his patrons. I feel uncomfortable that the poet-prophet of Divine Love, creator of the more than angelic Beatrice, should be so unrestrained as to indulge his private and political hatreds. But that is Dante. He is beyond all moralizings. The *Commedia* is the strongest and strictest literary work of the West except for the total panoply of all Shakespeare. Without Dante as the center, European literature might not hold together.

Dante's God is not available to me, nor is his Beatrice. Shakespeare, the circumference beyond which Western literature cannot voyage, does not offer us his God or his muse.

It seems just to observe that Dante, like Augustine, wishes to save us. Shakespeare is leagues away from being so intrusive. He is the least tendentious of all great writers. You will derive wisdom from him, though he does not intend you to do so. He does not teach, moralize, or edify.

I find more wisdom in Koheleth and Job than I do in the *Commedia*. And yet it may be that a great unwisdom ultimately is better for us than the emptiness of truth. The blessing of more life can become an unwisdom. I hate that sentence I have just written. What then would remain?

Why do we smile with joy when someone brings a baby into the house? Hope floods in and with it trepidation. Shelley and Yeats were capable of casting out remorse. Hamlet, returning from the sea, massively makes himself free of his former obsessions. The rest is silence.

Dante, poet and man, is obsessive. This is particularly true in the Latin meaning of the word: besiege or be besieged. Shakespeare's protagonists sometimes are obsessive or besieged. Yet they can and do change. Leontes emerges from his madness. Prospero acknowledges Caliban, this thing of darkness, as his own. Falstaff dies, plucking at flowers and singing the twenty-third Psalm.

Dante or Shakespeare? We need not choose. Who are we to choose? They choose us or pass us by. When I think of Dante the man, I think of his pride. Originally it meant courage. At twenty-four he fought with courage as a cavalryman in the Battle of Campaldino (June 11, 1289). He showed even more courage when he entered into the abyss of himself and thus conceived the *Commedia*.

We know much more about Dante than we do about Shakespeare. Who, meditating on Shakespeare, would think first of the poet-dramatist's pride? Ben Jonson proclaimed his own pride, even in such theatrical failures as *Catiline His Conspiracy* (1611) and *Sejanus His Fall* (1603). We have nothing to tell us how Shakespeare regarded his own achievement. Can you compose *Hamlet, Othello, King Lear, Macbeth, Antony and Cleopatra* without rejoicing in them? Perhaps it is better we not know.

There is always surmise. Dante changes his scholars. Shakespeare changes most, if not all, of us. Shakespeare, always Ovidian, *is* change. In the *Commedia* only Dante changes. An unchanging fiction does not give pleasure. Dante overcame this by composing an autobiography of the inward self. Freccero rightly finds precedence in the *Confessions* of Augustine. Virgil was Augustine's model. That can seem odd in 2020, but we now underread Virgil. The plangency of his images of voice, whether Dido's or Turnus's or even Aeneas's, is the undertone of his troubled and highly self-conscious secondary epic. All is suffering.

Dante does not seem to have wondered why an imperial epic gave its sympathy to the losers—Dido, Turnus, Camilla—as much as to Aeneas, the victor. There is a legend that the dying Virgil requested the *Aeneid* be destroyed, perhaps because he regarded it as unfinished. It may be that he had lost faith in the Emperor Augustus.

Some aspects of the *Commedia* mean little to most of us: the messianic possibility of Henry of Luxembourg; the Church's depravity under Pope Boniface; the cruelty of the dominant faction in Florence. But then the fervent declarations of royal patriotism in Shakespeare also resonate as hollow. You can shrug them off as they come. You cannot do the same with Dante. Prophets make us uncomfortable if they do their job. Dante is a master at rendering the secular reader uncomfortable indeed.

He is too strong to be argued with. Either become his partisan or yield up reading the poem. If his argument were to be regarded as his glory, you could read him only as you read Augustine or Freud, accepting tendentiousness as the price of brilliance. But Dante is the poet of his language and in some ways needs to be read as we read Chaucer and Shakespeare. He sings a center, a song of the answerer, and demands piety of his reader.

This is and is not limitation. One of his greatest gifts is to flesh out belief until it becomes a passion. I once told John Freccero that his best essay was "Manfred's Wounds and the Poetics of the *Purgatorio*," where he writes, "In God's book, Manfred's brow is clear":

> God's book has no marks that are subject to misinterpretation; Manfred's wounds, however, might have been taken as signs of his damnation when read from a purely human perspective, without benefit of their radiant smile.

[1983]

It is a kind of textual miracle that Dante intimates we need not read from a merely human perspective, but can read as Augustine did, transmuting man's book into God's. Pragmatically we have to read the *Commedia* as though it were God's book. Still, even the strongest of books—be it Tanakh, Homer, Chaucer, Shakespeare, Cervantes, or Montaigne—cannot become God's book without political and spiritual imposition. Dante walks a fine line. The *Commedia* is and is not Scripture. Dante insists he tells the truth. Certainly he tells *his* truth with a completeness and vividness almost unmatched in literature, "almost" because there is Shakespeare.

T. S. Eliot once wrote, in *The Sacred Wood* (1928), that he preferred Dante to Shakespeare "because it seems to me to illustrate a saner attitude towards the mystery of life." As an observation this is not literary criticism but religious polemic.

I rather doubt that Shakespeare took up attitudes toward that ghastly phrase "the mystery of life." He was not interested in solving our problems. Rather he showed that each of us was her or his own problematic malformation of truth too elusive to be possessed.

Do I derive as much pleasure from Beatrice as I do from Cleopatra? Who turns me more: Dante the Pilgrim or Hamlet the Black Prince? Perhaps if I could go back to Bologna and to Rome, and live there again as a teacher, I might recite Dante to myself on sleepless nights as I now recite Shakespeare. But my globe has shrunk to my house in New Haven.

Dante had universal ambitions. His poem offered us all salvation through Beatrice, which is to say, through his poem. An ambition so vast could not be fulfilled.

We know nothing of Shakespeare's ambitions, which is just as well. The tragedy *King Lear* offers us nothing, but its vision of love's destructiveness, particularly in families, takes away from us our final illusions as pitiful thrivers.

As an ancient Emersonian, I would like to choose the center, but I live at the circumference, edged by nothingness. For me Shakespeare is saner, Dante more remote than Homer or the Yahwist. William Empson found *Paradise Lost* to be barbaric unless you accepted the notion that his God intended to abdicate. The *Commedia* moves from the barbaric *Inferno* through the captivating *Purgatorio* and on to the divine mysteries of *Paradiso*.

The unidentified prophet known as Malachi ("my messenger") gave us the great image on which *Purgatorio* is founded—the refiner's fire:

Behold, I will send my messenger, and he shall prepare the way before me: and the Lord, whom ye seek, shall suddenly come to his temple, even the messenger of the covenant, whom ye delight in: behold, he shall come, saith the Lord of hosts.

But who may abide the day of his coming? and who shall stand when he appeareth? for he is like a refiner's fire, and like fullers' soap:

And he shall sit as a refiner and purifier of silver: and he shall purify the sons of Levi, and purge them as gold and silver, that they may offer unto the Lord an offering in righteousness.

[Malachi (KJV) 3:1–3]

Employ this as a touchstone and contrast *Paradiso* and *King Lear.* Which is more "like a refiner's fire"? Righteousness fares badly in *King Lear.* Albany, Kent, and Edgar remain, but Albany is worn out by the struggle between guilt at fighting Cordelia and his British loyalty defending against the French. Kent is wholly spent and desires only to join Lear in death, that he may go on serving his king. Edgar, condemned to a throne he does not want, anticipates a violent and unhappy reign that will end with his own early death. It is true that the monsters Edmund, Goneril, Regan, Cornwall, and Oswald have been obliterated, but so have Lear, Cordelia, Gloucester, and the vanished Fool. I would not call that "a refiner's fire." It is a purely destructive flame that leaves nothing.

Righteousness, we are asked to believe, is fulfilled in *Paradiso.* But everything is so arbitrary that some skepticism is provoked. Ripheus, loyal always to Aeneas, is saved, whereas Virgil is not, because Dante fantasizes that Ripheus somehow accepted Christ before he died. Statius, a really bad poet but one for whom Dante had some admiration, reaches the Earthly Paradise because of his supposed (and nonexistent) conversion. Saladin, the great Kurdish leader who defended the Muslims during the Crusades, is given an honorable place in Limbo with the heroes of Greece and Troy. And above all there is Beatrice, the personal muse glorified beyond glory. Who is the refiner and whose is the fire?

I cannot be the only reader of Dante who prefers Matelda to Beatrice. Dante's daemon or genius is embodied in Beatrice, but something wary and even more original in his creative mind gave us Matelda. Percy Bysshe Shelley and his wife, Mary Godwin Shelley, reacted with passion to Matelda. Shelley translated most of the great passage in which Matelda gathers flowers and sings of love. Mary Shelley wrote a curious novella, *Mathilda* (1819–1820), which is alas not very good, but her husband's version of Dante is the best in the language, unless you want to assign that position to *The Triumph of Life*.

Matelda is another Eve in an earthly paradise, but Matelda cannot fall. We and Dante and Shelley fall in love with her because a beautiful young woman singing of love as she gathers flowers is irresistible. She seems fully human, though she cannot be, and unlike Beatrice, she does not scold. With Matelda, we are implicitly invited to set aside the apparatus of salvation in the poem, and since that includes Beatrice, something in Dante is recoiling from the allegory of the theologians.

Matelda improves upon Proserpina, and her real parallel is Shakespeare's Perdita in *The Winter's Tale*, who gathers and distributes flowers, and offers herself to Florizel without quite realizing her abandon.

I suppose that if there is a Beatrice in Shakespeare, it might be the ambivalent Portia of *The Merchant of Venice*. But then I do not like Portia, a fault in me, and I think that Dante the man was very lucky that the actual Beatrice mocked him.

Not being a Dante scholar, I observe that some of the best of them, such as Auerbach, were Jews. Despite *The Merchant of Venice*, which I think should be played as an anti-Semitic romantic comedy, I am at home in Shakespeare. Down to the end I will feel foreign, out-of-doors in Dante, since the Incarnation is to me a bad poem.

The relation of poetry to belief has vexed me for too many decades. The Cross was a Roman instrument of torture. Telling me to take up the Cross is to request that I join the weary cycle of all my ancestors, who suffered Roman brutality and then underwent the long martyrdom imposed upon them by official Christianity. Fortunately the *Commedia* is not an act of faith. No one has been burned because of it.

Is it, as John Freccero insists, the triumph of a poetics of conversion? That is to read it as if Augustine had composed it. Perhaps his soul joined Dante's. Still, Dante chose Virgil and not Augustine as his guide, a choice that might have been congenial to Augustine, for whom Virgil was poetry.

Whatever his theological, political, and philosophical interests may have been, Dante was a poet, a prince of poetry outshining even

Petrarch and Spenser. He lights up for me when he is compared to
Virgil or to Cavalcanti; to Chaucer, or to Shakespeare; to Milton,
or to Leopardi. If you wish, you can read him side by side with
Augustine or with Aquinas, but then you are likelier to go astray
than with Virgil or Shakespeare. It depends who you are or what
you want.

There are not many readers who are at ease with *Inferno*. Dante
seems at once in control and hopelessly out of it. A Muslim reader,
confronted by Dante's Muhammad, has to become furious. Dante
rather weirdly takes Muhammad to be a Christian heretic, but there
he follows a European blunder:

> Già veggia, per mezzul perdere o lulla,
> com' io vidi un, così non si pertugia,
> rotto dal mento infin dove si trulla.
>
> Tra le gambe pendevan le minugia;
> la corata pareva e 'l tristo sacco
> che merda fa di quel che si trangugia.
>
> Mentre che tutto in lui veder m'attacco,
> guardommi e con le man s'aperse il petto,
> dicendo: "Or vedi com' io mi dilacco!
>
> vedi come storpiato è Mäometto!
> Dinanzi a me sen va piangendo Alì,
> fesso nel volto dal mento al ciuffetto.
>
> E tutti li altri che tu vedi qui,
> seminator di scandalo e di scisma
> fuor vivi, e però son fessi così."

———

> A cask by losing centre-piece or cant
>   Was never shattered so, as I saw one
>   Rent from the chin to where one breaketh wind.
>
> Between his legs were hanging down his entrails;
>   His heart was visible, and the dismal sack
>   That maketh excrement of what is eaten.

While I was all absorbed in seeing him,
>   He looked at me, and opened with his hands
>   His bosom, saying: "See now how I rend me;

How mutilated, see, is Mahomet;
>   In front of me doth Ali weeping go,
>   Cleft in the face from forelock unto chin;

And all the others whom thou here beholdest,
>   Disseminators of scandal and of schism
>   While living were, and therefore are cleft thus."
>   [*Inferno* 28.22–36, translated by H. W. Longfellow]

Poor Ali, sainted martyr of the Shi'a, has his head split open, while his father-in-law, Muhammad, is torn apart from top to bottom. If you are still sane, this certainly is unacceptable. Again I follow Robert Pogue Harrison in wondering what was happening to Dante's consciousness as he completed *Inferno*.

We can only surmise the ways in which Shakespeare's invention of Falstaff, Hamlet, Iago, Lear, and Cleopatra changed him. In fourteen months of incessant composition, Shakespeare wrote *Othello* and *King Lear*, revised them, and without a break went on to *Macbeth* and then cut loose into the wider world of *Antony and Cleopatra*. This seems inconceivable to me, yet it happened. Intuition is a poor guide to how different Shakespeare was after this furnace had come up at last.

But *Purgatorio* and then *Paradiso* reinvented Dante. The poet of *Inferno* implicitly feels guilt at not avenging a kinsman, since Florentine vendettas were a question of family honor. The grotesque horrors of *Inferno* are purged from Dante by his composing of the *Purgatorio*. Dante the Pilgrim is a different person after again encountering Beatrice and is even more subtly transformed by the vision of Matelda gathering flowers and singing.

Poets as various as James Merrill and Jay Wright have told me that Dante taught them how to be changed by conceiving and carrying through large-scale epics (I would say romances). Hart Crane in his desperation turned increasingly to Dante. Eliot and Pound had broken that path, though I suspect as a screen shielding them from Whitman.

Can we attempt to read Dante as Shakespeare might have read him? (Evidently he never did.) I think I have reached the point where I can read Christopher Marlowe or even Ben Jonson through Shakespearean optics. I have tried to do that with Chaucer and the Geneva Bible, but that is too difficult for me. Dante challenges me so strongly that all I want to do is somehow keep up with *Purgatorio* and overcome my aversion to *Paradiso*.

After many decades I can teach *Hamlet* and *King Lear* well enough to hope that I do not mislead my students. I could never teach Dante. My reactions, negative and positive, are very strong, but I have no faith in their rightness.

T. S. Eliot once said with regard to Shakespeare that one could only hope to be wrong in a new way. My only hope in apprehending Dante is indeed to be wrong in a way of my own. These nights I dream episodes from *Purgatorio*. Even with the best guidance available I cannot find my way in *Paradiso*. Salvation is too alien a concept.

And yet the *Commedia* is so large and generous in scope that questions like salvation, redemption, and conversion can be set aside by a secular reader. Dante teaches far more than even Augustine. The author of *The City of God* and the *Confessions* teaches you how to read and how to remember. Dante teaches you how and what to see.

I would hesitate to say Dante teaches how to accept God's love. But you cannot set a bourn to his teaching. E. R. Curtius quoted the poet Stefan George as saying that the *Commedia* was the book and school of the ages. Stefan George translated Dante and Shakespeare and took as his Beatrice a young man who died early, whom he named Maximin.

What can it mean to accept or reject God's love? Theological answers are profuse, but for me they answer nothing. If God's love is a poem, nothing more or less, what can it mean to reject a poem? I cannot accept or reject the *Commedia*. Yet there is coherence either way. It would be meaningless to accept or reject *Hamlet* or *King Lear*.

I come back to Singleton's bold statement that the fiction of the *Commedia* is that it is not a fiction. What if we were to contrast this with Don Quixote's overbold proclamation that his knight-errancy is not a fiction, which he combines with the confident stance: I know perfectly well who I am and who I may be if I choose. The Knight of the Sorrowful Countenance wins the face-off with ease. Perhaps Cervantes is psychologically and metaphysically more strongly grounded than the exiled poet of Florence. How far had Dante gone in working through the moral psychology of sin?

Our word "sin" is related to the Latin for "guilty." For the ancient Athenians sin was *hamartia*, throwing wide of the mark. The Hebrews associated guilt or sin with missing the golden center of a target but hitting nearby.

One admires Dante for not explicitly placing Guido Cavalcanti in Hell, though his denial of God, Beatrice, and salvific love merits damnation. Most of my friends, dead and living, are or will be there, as I will. Should that make a difference to the human dimension in reading a poem?

This is a poem unlike any other. Unless you are obsessed with Christian theology, you are probably not what Dante would have wanted in a reader. Despite his venery, Dante was not what you would call a loving man. The younger Dante, before he wrote *Purgatorio*, might be termed a great bad man. You might want to call Augustine that since, as soon as he converted, he rejected what we would call his common-law wife. Yet who would dare pass moral judgment upon so foundational a mind and spirit? And who among us is qualified to moralize against anyone else, let alone one of the world's two or three major poets?

Reading the *Commedia* in 2019 is a difficult act of mounting up a steep place or going out on a precipice until you find you are isolated, wanting to scramble down or back but needing help. It is an instance of what Ludwig Binswanger, the Swiss psychiatrist and phenomenologist, called *Verstiegenheit*, wittily translated by Jacob Needleman as "extravagance," *extra-vagans* (wandering beyond limits).

Even Dante's most eminent scholars do not greatly help my scramblings. Walt Whitman, withdrawing from his powerful press of self, lamented: "I went myself to the headland . . . my own hands carried me there" (*Song of Myself*, 1855 version). Reading Shakespeare I am never isolated. Great critics—Samuel Johnson, William Hazlitt, A. C. Bradley—are there to help me. Wrestling with Dante has to be a lonely enterprise. Why?

Dante creates the companions of his journey. His Virgil is not Virgil. His Beatrice never was nor could have been except in the

Commedia. His Pilgrim is not the man Dante, and the poet in the poem could not have written it. It is not Beatrice but Dante who is the miracle. The word "miracle" goes back to an Indo-European root meaning to be astonished or to smile.

To be wounded by wonder is a Shakespearean trope.

To incarnate wonder is a miracle and is Dante's central trope.

Augustine teaches reading as a contemplative act. When Dante evokes a heaven of lights flowing within one another and finds therein the mystery of the Incarnation, he is true both to Augustine and to himself. His difficulties, necessarily insoluble, stem from what I have to call the poem of the Trinity. I have tried to disentangle that complex web in Chapter 9, pp. 96–109, of a book, *Jesus and Yahweh: The Names Divine* (2005). I don't want to repeat that here and think I can achieve more clarity than I did before.

Every theological construct of the Trinity is a tangle of metaphors. I would have to call the Trinity a bad but historically successful poem. It makes little sense yet myriads of people have died for it or because of it.

The Trinity reduces the outrageous Yahweh to a tamed God the Father. Yeshua of Nazareth, who seems to mean all things to all women and men, is transmuted into Jesus Christ the martyred Son of God. A third person, the Holy Ghost, is also reduced from the Holy Spirit that moved upon the waters and brought forth dry land.

This three-in-one has undergone subtle convolutions and controversies. Sabellius held that the Father was his own Son. Arius made the Son subordinate to the Father. Both Sabellius and Arius were repudiated. Athanasius, whose views eventually triumphed, argued that the Father and the Son were two persons but one substance.

The Cappadocian Fathers, subtlest of the subtle, shrewdly relied upon Plato in their choreographing of the intricate dance of persons and substances. They persuade me of their rigor and inventiveness, but cannot persuade me that even a diminished Yahweh and Yeshua are an indivisible entity, one that also has space for the Holy Ghost.

Their champion, the late theological scholar Jaroslav Pelikan, expounds them with gusto:

The congruence of Cappadocian Trinitarianism, this "chief dogma," with Cappadocian apologetics, was summarized in their repeated claim that the orthodox doctrine of the Trinity was located "between the two conceptions" of Hellenism and Judaism, by "invalidating both ways of thinking, while accepting the useful components of each." Gregory of Nyssa put this claim boldly: "the Jewish dogma is destroyed by the acceptance of the Logos and by belief in the Spirit, while the polytheistic error of the Greek school is made to vanish by the unity of the [divine] nature abrogating this imagination of plurality." In sum, therefore, "Of the Jewish conception, let the unity of the [divine] nature stand; and of the Hellenic, only the distinction as to the *hypostases*, the remedy against a profane view being thus applied, as required on either side." This apologetic symmetry permitted him to assert: "It is as if the number of the Three were a remedy in the case of those who are in error as to the One, and the assertion of the unity for those whose beliefs are dispersed among a number of divinities."

[*Christianity and Classical Culture* (1993)]

Dante on the Trinity is the knowing heir of the Cappadocian Fathers and of his other authorities from Augustine to Aquinas. And yet the fireworks display is altogether his own. Heaven's smiles are not our smiles, and Dante is too individual to represent our poor selves. Would we be able to sustain the love that moves the sun and the other stars? Dante, man *and* poet, sees and is seen by the incarnate love, which needed him for its full revelation:

Ne la profonda e chiara sussistenza
de l'alto lume parvermi tre giri
di tre colori e d'una contenenza;

e l'un da l'altro come iri da iri
parea reflesso, e 'l terzo parea foco
che quinci e quindi igualmente si spiri.

Oh quanto è corto il dire e come fioco
al mio concetto! e questo, a quel ch'i' vidi,
è tanto, che non basta a dicer "poco."

O luce etterna che sola in te sidi,
sola t'intendi, e da te intelletta
e intendente te ami e arridi!

Quella circulazion che sì concetta
pareva in te come lume reflesso,
da li occhi miei alquanto circunspetta,

dentro da sé, del suo colore stesso,
mi parve pinta de la nostra effige:
per che 'l mio viso in lei tutto era messo.

Qual è 'l geomètra che tutto s'affige
per misurar lo cerchio, e non ritrova,
pensando, quel principio ond' elli indige,

tal era io a quella vista nova:
veder voleva come si convenne
l'imago al cerchio e come vi s'indova;

ma non eran da ciò le proprie penne:
se non che la mia mente fu percossa
da un fulgore in che sua voglia venne.

A l'alta fantasia qui mancò possa;
ma già volgeva il mio disio e 'l velle,
sì come rota ch'igualmente è mossa,

l'amor che move il sole e l'altre stelle.

———

Within the deep and luminous subsistence
   Of the High Light appeared to me three circles,
   Of threefold colour and of one dimension,

And by the second seemed the first reflected
   As Iris is by Iris, and the third
   Seemed fire that equally from both is breathed.

O how all speech is feeble and falls short
   Of my conceit, and this to what I saw
   Is such, 'tis not enough to call it little!

O Light Eterne, sole in thyself that dwellest,
 Sole knowest thyself, and, known unto thyself
 And knowing, lovest and smilest on thyself!

That circulation, which being thus conceived
 Appeared in thee as a reflected light,
 When somewhat contemplated by mine eyes,

Within itself, of its own very colour
 Seemed to me painted with our effigy,
 Wherefore my sight was all absorbed therein.

As the geometrician, who endeavours
 To square the circle, and discovers not,
 By taking thought, the principle he wants,

Even such was I at that new apparition;
 I wished to see how the image to the circle
 Conformed itself, and how it there finds place;

But my own wings were not enough for this,
 Had it not been that then my mind there smote
 A flash of lightning, wherein came its wish.

Here vigour failed the lofty fantasy:
 But now was turning my desire and will,
 Even as a wheel that equally is moved,

The Love which moves the sun and the other stars.
  [*Paradiso* 33.115–145, translated by H. W. Longfellow]

I have just read through *Dante: The Story of His Life*, by Marco Santagata (2013), translated by Richard Dixon (2016). It is a strong yet rather unpleasant biography. The tone is bothersome, but I have not read the Italian original. From several perspectives, Dante's life was grim. In his own stance Dante resembles Milton. They are prideful, totally dedicated, self-knowing geniuses of language, each with immense learning. Both were determined to be the poet, the prophet, the liberator: of Florence and much of central Italy, or of the British Isles. Each saw himself as the possessor of religious truth and so of all truth that mattered.

Dante and Milton alike had severe, even savage personalities. The Florentine showed courage on the field of battle. The Londoner would not risk himself, but then gradually became blind and even more determined to compose *Paradise Lost* before he died. Dante was sentenced to be burned at the stake in Florence, and went into exile, joined there by his wife, three sons, and a daughter.

He lived under the patronage of Cangrande I della Scala, ruler of Verona, who was pleased to have the great poet and scholar at his court. The same relationship was played out during Dante's final years at Ravenna.

The difference between Dante and Milton is Shakespeare. Freedom from an overwhelming vernacular precursor liberated Dante. That did not prevent him from experiencing anxieties in regard to Brunetto Latini and Guido Cavalcanti.

Though Milton could never exorcise Shakespeare, and so was blocked from creating stage dramas, still he received the grand figure of Satan by way of the tragic protagonists Hamlet, Iago, Edmund, and Macbeth.

It is difficult to determine the existence of what we call personality before Shakespeare, Cervantes, and Montaigne. Who in the *Commedia*, besides Dante the Pilgrim, possesses such inwardness that she or he can change by self-otherseeing or self-overhearing? No one among them can see herself as though she is someone else, or be startled by overhearing something alien to the self.

Perhaps the simplest test for establishing personality in literature is already endemic among readers. Who does not have the experience of reading a new novel or story and finding that the characters seem only to be names on a page? One can have this trouble even with very good writers such as Edith Wharton, John Galsworthy, or Iris Murdoch. I read each new novel by Murdoch with a kind of delight as they came out. They have lost their freshness and I have trouble rereading them. I keep asking who is who, why do they all lust after one another, and what keeps them from merging into a few repetitive types. All this is a sorrow, as Murdoch was a very intelligent writer and set herself the standard of matching Shakespeare.

My late friend Angus Fletcher spoke of a "crisis of scale" in the current literary scene. Without deep educations, readers are helpless in the difficult work of absorbing Dante's *Commedia*. Shakespeare may seem simpler but he is not. No one else in Western literature, not even Dante, is so great a master at the art of leaving things out, or ellipsis. You learn to read Shakespeare for his silences, his unanswered questions, the refusal of his protagonists to listen to what anyone else is saying. While death in Shakespeare is absolute and frequently without memorial, he abounds in ghosts. I think he believed in them as I do and as most people throughout the ages have done.

Dante has no need or use for ghosts. Your spirit being immortal, you must pass eternity either in suffering, or in purgation, or in the bliss of the redeemed. The immortality of the soul is only a flickering illumination in Shakespeare. He does not want to instruct you in any overt manner, and he keenly apprehends that our problems are insoluble. If our little life is rounded with a sleep, there is not much to add, except to so expand consciousness beyond to yet another inwardness.

It seems accurate to say that Dante converted himself to believe fervently in his version of the Catholic God. It is improbable that Shakespeare died either a devout Protestant or a Catholic. Negative capability finding an apotheosis in nihilism may be the best description of his final stance.

The *Commedia* is spacious enough to give us Matelda. That refined version of pastoral would be at home in *The Winter's Tale* except that Perdita's earthly paradise is crowned by a Maying.

Dante chose and was rewarded by a center of centers. Shakespeare chose and gloriously widened a circumference of circumferences. Some of the greatest poets are reconcilable with one another: Lucretius with Virgil, Spenser with Milton, Schiller with Goethe, Victor Hugo with Victor Hugo. Some are so idiosyncratic that no reconciliation with forerunners is possible: William Blake, Wordsworth, Shelley, Walt Whitman, Emily Dickinson, and even W. B. Yeats, who pretended affinities where there were none, and denied them when they were real.

Setting aside the Scriptures—Tanakh, the New Testament, the Holy Qur'an—the Western world's giant forms are Homer, Plato, Dante, and Shakespeare, and, in prose, Montaigne, Cervantes, Proust, and Joyce. Montaigne keeps God at a safe distance, though he professes Catholicism. So does Cervantes, though the ironies of existing in a country going mad make it difficult to know how politic that was. Proust was baptized but took care to bury his Jewish mother, love of his life, with the ancient ceremonies of her people. Joyce too was baptized but hated Christianity for what he called its "hangman god."

Dante remains unique. He has made it all but impossible to disentangle his poetic inventiveness from his inventive theology.

One of Shakespeare's many paradoxes is that he is too large to be unique. Or is it that he has made it difficult for anyone after him to be unique?

Early this morning I devoted some hours to rereading Dante and Shakespeare in alternation, mostly juxtaposing *Paradiso* and *King Lear*. This became spiritually confusing because the two poems are incompatible. By this I mean that Beatrice and Lear are antithetical to one another. You cannot apprehend a literary cosmos containing both.

There is no single perspective we can take upon Shakespearean representation. I am always a little puzzled at scholars so adamant they apply an Augustinian grid to *Commedia*. Sometimes I enjoy the fantasy of Augustine reading Dante in heaven. Would he endure it rather than growl: "back to Virgil"?

Augustine's Christ, as Peter Brown tells us, is rather different from Dante's:

> Above all, the Christianity of the fourth century would have been presented to such a boy as a form of "True Wisdom." The Christ of the popular imagination was not a suffering Saviour. There are no crucifixes in the fourth century. He was, rather, "the Great Word of God, the Wisdom of God." On the sarcophagi of the age, He is always shown as a Teacher, teaching His Wisdom to a coterie of budding philosophers. For a cultivated man, the essence of Christianity consisted in just this. Christ, as the "Wisdom of God," had established a monopoly in Wisdom.
>
> [*Augustine of Hippo* (1967)]

Certainly for Dante, Christ was and was not a Teacher. The Incarnation itself is the Truth. And yet Dante was Augustinian enough to regard Incarnation as the Wisdom of God.

John Freccero wrote a classic essay contrasting the poetics of Petrarch and his precursor, Dante, "The Fig Tree and the Laurel" (1975):

> Petrarch's prodigious originality . . . is that he was entirely self-conscious about the principles of which his predecessors were only dimly aware. By transforming the Augustinian analysis of sin into a new esthetic, he made self-alienation in life the mark of self-creation in literature and so established a literary tradition which has yet to be exhausted.

That enhancement of self-creation can be traced from Edmund Spenser through Shakespeare, Ben Jonson, John Donne, and Milton on to Romanticism in British and American poetry, perhaps culminating in Yeats, D. H. Lawrence, Wallace Stevens, and Hart Crane. Dante, despite his effect on Spenser, Milton, Yeats, and others (one thinks of Seamus Heaney), stands apart.

But why? Dante manifested surprising anxiety in regard to relatively minor precursor poets. But instead of self-creation he chose Beatrice the heavenly muse, in effect created her. There are no limits to this audacious creation. Without her, Dante cannot be converted or redeemed. That remains startling enough. But he makes her part of the machinery of salvation: to reach Christ or God, Dante's reader must turn to Beatrice.

After an initial agon with Christopher Marlowe, Shakespeare was remarkably free of even his formidable contemporary Ben Jonson. Perhaps fortunately, Jonson had troubles freeing himself from Shakespeare. The agon gave us *Bartholomew Fair* (1614). This is an indescribable stage work, fantastic yet homely, with wild laughter and bitter satire. Shakespeare is unlikely to have read it, though he may have seen it performed in one of his rare returns to London from his Stratford sanctuary.

Something about *Bartholomew Fair* breaks all limits. The play is almost Joycean. Ben Jonson identified himself with Cicero, though with reservations. Dante places Cicero in the Limbo of virtuous pre-Christians, in the odd company of Saladin the Kurdish defender of Muslim Jerusalem. It is very much a mixed bag, and the air seems to have gone out of Limbo. Dante does give you a vigorous Harrowing of Hell in which Christ snatches up his more virtuous ancestors, from Adam and Abraham on to Jacob/Israel, his sons, his beloved Rachel, and on to King David.

In a vivid Dantesque fantasy, Ripheus, whose place in Virgil was to die as a defender of justice and be unrewarded by the gods for it, is stationed in the sixth circle of Heaven. The beloved Virgil ends with the pagans, but remains the poet's guide through *Inferno* and *Purgatorio*. Unlike the proudly irrational Yeats, who pops poets in and out of the various categories of *A Vision*, Dante's assignments are sometimes reasonable, though what has reason to do with the *Commedia*? Following Aquinas, Dante might have said everything. Set aside philosophy and faith and a certain Dante will still be there.

But why set them aside? Dante thought his way through to a vision of Beatrice anointing him as poet and prophet. Everything turns upon that vision. It does not persuade me. But the paradox is that the *Commedia*, like Homer and Shakespeare, is so abundant that persuasion becomes secondary.

Credits

Hart Crane, "To Brooklyn Bridge," "Possessions," "At Melville's Tomb," "Voyages II," "The Sea Raised Up . . . ," "To Conquer Variety," "Repose of Rivers," "Passage," "Lachrymae Christi," "The Broken Tower," "Southern Cross," "A Name for All," "A Postscript," "Atlantis," "Emblems of Conduct," "The Wine Menagerie," "The River," "Thou Canst Read Nothing . . . ," from *The Complete Poems of Hart Crane*, by Hart Crane, edited by Marc Simon. Copyright 1933, 1958, 1966 by Liveright Publishing Corporation. Copyright © 1986 by Marc Simon. Used by permission of Liveright Publishing Corporation.

Samuel Greenberg, "Conduct," by Samuel Greenberg, from *Poems by Samuel Greenberg*, edited by Harold Holden and Jack McManis, © 1947, 1975 by Harold Holden and Jack McManis. Reprinted by permission of Henry Holt and Company. All rights reserved.

Geoffrey Hill, *The Book of Baruch by the Gnostic Justin*, by Geoffrey Hill, pp. 26, 92. © 2019 by Oxford University Press. Reproduced with permission of the Licensor through PLSclear.

Geoffrey Hill, "Improvisations for Hart Crane," from *Without Title*, by Geoffrey Hill. First published in the United Kingdom in 2006 by the Penguin Group. © 2006 by Geoffrey Hill. Reproduced with permission of the literary estate of Geoffrey Hill. All rights reserved.

John Hollander, "A Shadow of a Great Rock in a Weary Land," from *Figurehead: And Other Poems*, by John Hollander, copyright © 1999 by John Hollander. Used by permission of Alfred A. Knopf, an imprint of the Knopf Doubleday Publishing Group, a division of Penguin Random House LLC. All rights reserved. Used by permission of Natalie Charkow Hollander.

John Hollander, "The Lovers," from *Powers of Thirteen, Poems*, by John Hollander, published by Atheneum, 1983. Used by permission of Natalie Charkow Hollander.

D. H. Lawrence, "The Ship of Death," from *The Complete Poems of D. H. Lawrence*, by D. H. Lawrence, edited by Vivian de Sola Pinto & F. Warren

Index

Abrams, M. H., 124

Ackroyd, Peter, works by: *Milton in America*, 39

Adam and Eve, 48, 49, 55, 71, 73, 95, 96, 104–108, 412

Aeolian harp, 210, 264, 501, 521, 549, 551

Aeschylus, 202, 240, 257

African mythology, 32–34

Aiken, Conrad, 351

allegory, 131, 321; Allegory of the Theologians, 605–607

Ammons, A. R., 70, 407, 503, 577

anacoluthon, 518

anaphora, 388, 537

anti-Semitism. *See* Judaism and Jews

aporias, 20

Apuleius, works by: *The Metamorphoses (The Golden Ass)*, 329

Aquinas, Thomas, 616, 628

Arendt, Hannah, 561

Aristotle, 264

Arius, 620

Arnold, Matthew: Bradley and, 161; Browning and, 351, 352; Shelley and, 185

Ashbery, John: Crane and, 558; as descriptive poet, 388; as difficult poet, 393; effect of reading, 416; on Greenberg's poetry, 535; as playwright, 70; in poetic lineage, 503, 577; Whitman and, 407; works by: "Self-Portrait in a Convex Mirror," 193; "Wet Casements," 532

Athanase, 462

Athanasius, 620

Auden, W. H., 196–197, 437, 497, 604, 605

Auerbach, Erich, 579, 580, 605, 615; works by: *Dante: Poet of the Secular World*, 599–600

Augustine: Blake and, 138; contemplative act of reading and, 620; conversion of, 619; Dante and, 610, 612, 615, 616, 618, 626; Herbert and, 545; Virgil as model of, 611; works by: *The City of God*, 618; *Confessions*, 611, 618

Auslander, Joseph, 392

azure (sublime color): Browning and, 311; Crane and, 506, 514, 525, 526, 557; Melville and, 401, 402; Shelley and, 209, 217, 222, 223, 232, 253, 265, 427, 514; Stevens and, 514; Whitman and, 296, 556

Babbitt, Irving, 25

Bacon, Francis, 53, 133

Baker, Howard, 392

Baldwin, James, works by: *The Fire Next Time*, 440

Barfield, Owen, 124

Barolini, Teodolinda, works by: *Dante's Poets*, 608–609

Bate, Walter Jackson, 124, 320, 323; works by: *John Keats*, 321

Baudelaire, Charles, 212, 475, 508, 523, 542, 558

Beardsley, Aubrey, 480

Beckett, Samuel, 62, 447, 574

Beddoes, Thomas Lovell: Gnosticism and, 542; as Shelley's disciple, 220, 350; works by: *Death's Jest-Book*, 205, 268, 327

Bellow, Saul, 56

Benjamin, Walter, 213–214

Benn, Gottfried, 543

Berger, Charles, 433, 435; works by: *Forms of Farewell*, 435

Bergin, Thomas Goddard, 18

Berkeley, George, works by: *Of the Principles of Human Knowledge*, 194

Bernhard, Thomas, 62

Bible: Anchor Yale Bible, 586; Geneva Bible, 84–85, 106, 618; King James Version, 585–587; Norton Bible, 586; Shakespeare and, 146, 194; Vulgate (Jerome), 135, 585. *See also* Hebrew Bible; New Testament; scriptural citations

Bielik-Robson, Agata, 7

Binswanger, Ludwig, 619

Bishop, Elizabeth, 503, 577; works by: "In Appreciation of Shelley's Poems," 444–445

Bishop, John Peale, 392

Bishop, Morchard, works by: *Blake's Hayley*, 150, 151

Blackmur, Richard P., 29, 527

Blake, William: aims of, 83; Albion in, 123, 126, 142; in the Ancients with Palmer, Calvert, and Richmond, 133; as apocalyptic humanist and social rebel, 123; audience of his epics, 154; Augustine and, 138; Butler and, 69; Byron and, 293, 295; Chaucer and, 111, 124; on consciousness, 142; Crane and, 507–508, 512, 518–521, 523, 527, 533, 536, 539; criticizing his rivals, 133; Dante and, 124, 596, 601, 602; death and, 484; on delight, 11; as difficult poet, 33, 121; Drayton and, 113; Dryden and, 123; engravings as main livelihood for, 151; at Felpham village, 148–149; on "the Female Will," 57, 111, 151–152, 156, 157, 473; on freedom, 48, 139; Freud and, 133, 138; Frost and, 412; Frye on, 122; Hebrew Bible and, 65, 122; Hill and, 125, 543; on Human Form Divine, 48, 57, 87, 139; identification with poets of Sensibility and the Sublime, 121; on Idiot Questioner, 4–5, 158; as illustrator for Dante, 539; as illustrator for Young's *Night-Thoughts*, 127; imagination and, 123–124, 463; "In Equivocal Worlds Up & Down are Equivocal," 89; as intellectual satirist, 112; irony of, 151–152; Jesus and, 146; Jones and, 153–154; Kabbalah and, 122; Keats and, 322; Lawrence and, 144, 473; Melville and, 192; metric used by, 113; Milton and, 18, 42–43, 46–47, 50, 56, 61, 69, 103, 112, 124, 126, 131, 146–158, 602; mythmaking by, 130; narrative continuity in epics of, 125; nature and, 155–156; Neoplatonism and, 122, 124, 126, 139, 145, 155; nightmare and, 475; Plato and, 139; in poetic lineage,

116, 124, 146; poverty of, 151, 153;
Protestant Christianity and dissent
of, 69, 122, 146, 154; sadomasochism
in, 152; Satan in, 45, 137; as sect of
one, 107, 122, 146, 347, 625; Shakespeare and, 90, 124; Shelley and,
119, 215–217, 222, 227, 240; Spectre
of Urthona in, 126, 130, 140–143,
145, 167–168; Spenser and, 124;
Stevens and, 59; Swift and, 133;
Tharmas in, 126, 133–135; on
time, 296; transcendence and, 139;
truth-telling and, 99; Vision in,
139; Whitman and, 387; wife of
(Catherine), 152; wife of (Mary),
39; the will and, 146; Wordsworth
and, 131–132; Yeats and, 141, 206,
208, 460, 462, 464
Blake, William, works by: *Apology for
His Catalogue*, 150; "Auguries of
Innocence," 602; *The Four Zoas*,
123–127, 135–136, 148, 154, 168;
The Gates of Paradise (artwork), 133;
The Ghost of Abel, 293; "The Grey
Monk," 536; *Jerusalem*, 99, 103,
121, 124, 125, 131, 140, 142–143,
154, 459; "Jerusalem", 113–114;
"The Laocoön," 64, 136–137;
letter to Reverend John Trusler
(August 23, 1799), 127; *Life of
Cowper* (artwork), 149; *The Marriage of Heaven and Hell*, 42, 100,
121, 137, 154–155; *Milton*, 4, 69, 99,
110–111, 112, 124, 125, 146–158;
"Ninth the Ninth," 129; *Songs of
Innocence*, 135; *Songs of Innocence and
Experience*, 167; "The Sunflower,"
412, 520; "To Nobodaddy," 56, 63,
76, 198; *Vala*, 126, 255; *Visions of
the Daughters of Albion*, 156
Blavatsky, Madame, 480
Bloom, Harold: afterlife visions of,
441, 445, 619; Auden, meeting
with, 196–197; Baldwin, meeting
with, 440; Bate, meeting with, 320;
Blake, teaching of, 110; Browning,
teaching of, 333; Charles Eliot
Norton Lectures, 579; Crane,
teaching of, 503, 519, 557; Dante,
teaching of, 618; Dante's *Inferno*
as frightening to, 603; de Bolla
on rhetoric of, 289; depression
and psychoanalysis of, 563–564;
dissertation of, 185, 230–231; as
Emersonian, 9, 380, 613; Empson,
meeting with, 59, 542; as Epicurean,
366; Erdman's friendship with, 153;
family of, 76; fireworks and, 603;
Florence trip while teaching in
Italy, 578; flowers, love of, 10;
Freccero vs., 579, 581–582; Frost,
meeting with, 412, 416–417; Frye,
meeting with, 122, 204; ghosts,
belief in, 375, 625; Hartman's
friendship with, 58, 90; Hill's
friendship with, 25, 540–541;
Hollander's friendship with,
437–442; honorary degree from
University of Coimbra (Portugal),
61; hospital stays and health of,
28, 348, 436, 443, 460, 469–470,
472, 577; immortality and desire
to go on living, 8, 192, 625; Incarnation and, 615; insights and
wisdom of age, realizations from,
121, 123, 125, 131, 133, 138–139, 141,
144, 154, 166, 173, 177–178, 190,
192, 246, 283, 309, 331, 344–345,
369–370, 440, 447, 451, 456–457,
459, 460, 468, 483, 491, 528, 574,
609, 618, 620; Inverness College
lecture, 2; in Jerusalem, 563;
Johnson as model for reading, 2;
as Kierkegaardian, 560; Knight,
meeting with, 227; MacNeice,
meeting with, 334; naming Wright
as best living American poet, 31,
577; as Nietzschean, 560; nodding

Bloom, Harold (continued)
off in old age, 21; Orthodox
Judaism of his youth, 8, 442,
602; outliving friends, family, and
contemporary poets, 1, 25, 30, 90,
124, 152, 375, 378, 548, 577; Plimpton, meeting with, 602–603; poetic
incarnation and, 391–392; Poirier's
friendship with, 415; postcolonial
discourse as tiresome to, 345; pre-
dicted death of, 577; Ransom,
meeting with, 152–153; reading
Dante in original language, 598;
reading's salubrious effects, 1–3,
133, 158; religious views of, 145;
rereading Whitman weekly, 381;
Shakespeare, teaching of, 4, 22,
111, 276, 575, 618; Shelley, teaching
of, 196–197; Stevens, meeting
with, 445; Stevens, teaching of,
422; Stevens, treasured effect of
reading, 416, 426–427, 443; Tate,
meeting with, 460, 546; teachers
and mentors of, 137–138, 185–186,
231, 334–335; teaching in Bologna
and Rome, 181, 224, 576, 578,
598, 613; teaching's role in life
of, 108–109, 111, 578; Tennyson,
teaching of, 367; on time as remedy
to his work's being misunderstood,
574; truth, failure to believe authors
provide, 19–20, 121, 138, 276,
580; in Valencia, Spain, 397–398;
Vico, acknowledging debt to, 15;
Williams, meeting with, 529;
on Yahweh, 602; at Yale English
Department, 186; Yates, conversations with, 461
Bloom, Harold, works by: *Agon*, 122,
560; *The Anatomy of Influence*, 39;
The Anxiety of Influence, 14–15, 59,
138, 275, 289, 560; *Artforum* review
of Walter Benjamin's correspondence, 214–215; *Blake's Apocalypse*,
123; "Blake's *Jerusalem*: The Bard
of Sensibility and the Form of
Prophecy," 140; "The Breaking
of Form," 193–194; *The Breaking of
the Vessels*, 453; *The Complete Poetry
and Prose of William Blake* (critical
commentary), 89, 100, 123, 141,
153; *The Covering Cherub or Poetic
Influence*, 560; *The Daemon Knows*,
112, 422; *Deconstruction and
Criticism*, 193; *Figures of Capable
Imagination*, 572; *Jesus and Yahweh:
The Names Divine*, 620; *Kabbalah and
Criticism*, 16; *Macbeth: A Dagger of
the Mind*, 65; *A Map of Misreading*,
14–15, 53, 97, 132, 275, 289, 560;
The Poems of Our Climate, 422;
Poetry and Repression, 560; *Possessed
by Memory*, 7; *Romanticism and
Consciousness: Essays in Criticism* (ed.),
124–125; *Ruin the Sacred Truths*, 579;
*The Shadow of a Great Rock: A Liter-
ary Appreciation of the King James
Bible*, 585; *Shelley's Mythmaking*,
227, 230; *Till I End My Song: A
Gathering of Last Poems* (ed.), 459;
Transference and Authority (not pub-
lished), 132; "The Uses of Poetry,"
14; *The Visionary Company*, 222;
*Wallace Stevens: The Poems of Our
Climate*, 447; *Yeats*, 207–208, 227
Boccaccio, 48, 100, 206, 227, 599, 609
Boehme, Jacob, 69, 124
Boniface VIII (pope), 612
Borges, Jorge Luis, 56, 537
Boswell, James, 2, 128
Bounty, mutiny on, 295
Bradley, A. C., 161, 327, 619
Brawne, Fanny, 104, 325
Breaking of the Vessels, 427, 453, 586
Brecht, Bertolt, 543
Bridges, Robert, 301–302
Bromwich, David, 175, 322; works by:
Hazlitt, 327–328

Brontë, Charlotte, works by: *Jane Eyre*, 372

Brontë, Emily, works by: *Wuthering Heights*, 372

Brooklyn Bridge, Crane's obsession with, 522–523, 527, 548–551, 555–556

Brooklyn Ferry, Whitman's poem on, 391, 523

Brooks, Cleanth, 138, 186

Brown, Peter, works by: *Augustine of Hippo*, 626

Browne, Thomas, 76; works by: *Hydriotaphia*, 467

Browning, Elizabeth Barrett: spiritualism of, 351; works by: *Aurora Leigh*, 354

Browning, Robert: Arnold and, 351, 352; audience of, 333; characterization of, 334, 344; Chaucer and, 348; diction and rhymes of, 339, 342; excessive length of, 351; Frost and, 417; Hopkins and, 333, 339; Judaism and, 342–344; Keats and, 311, 350; MacNeice and, 334; religion and, 342–343, 348, 351; Shakespearean influence on, 345; Shelley and, 111–112, 346–348, 350; Tennyson and, 367; transcendence and, 347; Yeats and, 355

Browning, Robert, works by: "Andrea del Sarto," 333; *Asolando: Fancies and Facts*, 354–355; "By the Fire-Side," 354; "Caliban upon Setebos," 333, 344–347; "Childe Roland to the Dark Tower Came," 201, 333, 344–345, 348–351; "Cleon," 351–354; "Fra Lippo Lippi," 333; "The Heretic's Tragedy," 335–339; "Holy-Cross Day," 339–342; "Mr. Sludge: 'The Medium,'" 351; "Popularity," 310–311; "Rabbi Ben Ezra," 343–344, 426; *The Ring and the Book*, 335; "Saul," 344; *A Toccata of Galuppi's*, 334

Bruno, Giordano, 373, 377–378

Bryant, William Cullen: Crane and, 518, 520, 538; political and social positions of, 539; works by: "Thanatopsis," 520, 538, 539; "To a Waterfowl," 538–539

Buddha, 155

Bunyan, John: Beulah as earthly paradise for, 156–157; Shelley and, 216; tradition of Protestant dissent and, 146

Burckhardt, Jacob, 63–64

Burgess, Anthony, works by: "A Meeting in Valladolid," 596

Burke, Kenneth, 289, 518, 522

Burns, Robert, 148

Burton, Robert, works by: *The Anatomy of Melancholy*, 74, 321

Butler, Samuel, 76, 112

Bynner, Witter, 392

Byron, Lord (George Gordon): Blake and, 293, 295; Clare and, 180; Dante and, 596; death of, 256, 296; disagreeing with Shelley about Hamlet, 181–182; Keats and, 312, 325; as nihilist, 295; relationship with Claire Clairmont, 244; religious fervor of, 180; reputation of, 558; reverence of, following his death, 296; sadomasochism in, 181; self-exaltation of, 160, 181; serpent and eagle trope and, 557; Shelley and, 180–182, 240, 254, 272, 290, 294, 295, 318, 349; Southey and, 290

Byron, Lord (George Gordon), works by: *Cain, a Mystery*, 292–293, 295, 327; *Don Juan*, 294; *The Island*, 295; *Manfred*, 295, 327; *The Vision of Judgment*, 289–291

Callimachus, 24

Calvert, Edward, 133, 155

Cappadocian Fathers, 620–621
Castiglione, Baldassare, works by: *Book of the Courtier*, 478
catachresis, 518
Cathars, 192
Catholicism and Catholics: *Commedia* and, 601; crucifixion converting Jewish God to, 63; Dante and, 625; Freud and, 561; Gordon's and Tate's conversion to, 546; Johnson and, 487; Montaigne and, 625; Stevens and, 442, 452; Wimsatt and, 138
Catullus, 441–442; works by: "'Frater Ave Atque Vale,'" 442
Cavalcanti, Guido, 100, 580–581, 607–609, 616, 619, 624
censorship, 61, 300, 387
Cervantes, Miguel de: Dante compared with, 619; as giant of Western literature, 625–626; as God's book, 612; as literary legend, 558, 559; personality of protagonists in, 474, 624; sustenance of reading, 11; as truth-teller, 121, 138
Chalandritsanos, Lukas, 296
Charles I (king of England), 70
Charles II (king of England), 82
Chartist movement, 183, 190, 219
Chatterton, Thomas, 121, 125, 252, 350
Chaucer, Geoffrey: Blake and, 111, 124; Browning and, 348; comic powers of, 580; Dante and, 100, 596, 599, 612, 616; Geneva Bible and, 618; as God's book, 612; Milton and, 53, 91, 108; personality in, 474; in poetic lineage, 3, 9, 212; reputation of, 69, 558; role of author in *Canterbury Tales*, 152; satire on Dante in *Tales of Canterbury*, 599; Shakespeare and, 146, 194; Spenser and, 69; truth and, 121; women portrayed by, 156

Chesterton, Gilbert Keith, 335, 351
chiasmus, 518
Chopin, Kate, 407
Christ: Augustine and, 626; Blake and, 146, 459; as both man and God, 580, 602; crucifixion, 63, 87–88; Dante and, 595, 602, 626; disagreements over who and what he was, 56; in Gospel of Mark, 415; Huxley and, 155; Milton and, 47, 120; pagan prophecy of coming of, 260–261; Pietà image, 521; Shelley and, 216, 479; Trinity, role of, 620; Whitman and, 380–381, 388, 391; Wilde on, 56. *See also* Incarnation
Christian, Fletcher, 295
Christianity and Christians: Blake and, 122, 143, 146; Browning and, 348; Crane and, 529–530; *figura* trope, 579–580; harmony of heaven and, 450; Milton and, 48, 88, 107, 121; Mithraism displaced by, 273; redemption and, 316; Shakespeare and, 107, 625; Shelley and, 318–319; as speculation and mythology, 7; Stevens and, 442; tradition of Protestant dissent, 146; Trinity and, 620–621; Virgil as harbinger of Christian revelation, 580; Yeats and, 485–486
Church, Henry, 432–433
Cicero, 627
Clare, John, 180, 388; works by: "Badger," 165–166; "Song: Secret Love," 166–167
Clarendon. *See* Hyde, Edward
Clark, Eleanor, 546
classical mythology: Apollo, 63, 217, 242, 243, 256, 361; Athena, 479, 550; Cupid and Psyche, 331–332; Dionysius, 27, 63, 259, 479, 516, 524; Heracles, 34, 204, 551; Jason and the Argonauts, 551; Juno, 580; Romulus and Remus, 438; Sybil at

Cumae, 421; Tiresias, 86; Ulysses
(Odysseus) figure, 131, 258, 357–359,
362, 435, 458, 475–476; Venus, 331;
Zeus, 92, 202, 359, 479, 524. *See also*
Homer; Orpheus

Cobban, Alfred, 124

Cohen, Joshua, 62

Coleridge, Samuel Taylor: Donne and,
186; Hume and, 40; imagination
and, 170; Milton and, 39–40, 58,
71; Pater and, 40; Shakespeare
and, 58, 107–108; Shelley and, 283;
Stevens and, 430; Wordsworth and,
57–58, 161

Coleridge, Samuel Taylor, works by:
"Christabel," 58; "Kubla Khan,"
58, 283, 286; "On Donne's Poetry,"
186; "The Rime of the Ancient
Mariner," 58; *Table Talk*, 71; "To
William Wordsworth," 57

Collins, William, 430

Columbus figure, 551–552, 557

Cook, Eleanor, 81, 426; works by:
*Poetry, Word-Play and Word-War
in Wallace Stevens*, 426; *The Reader's
Guide to Wallace Stevens*, 426

Corbin, Henry, 450

Coverdale, Myles, 65

Cowper, William, 121, 149

Crane, Hart: anacoluthon and, 518;
Ashbery and, 558; audience of, 533;
azure color and, 506, 514, 525, 526,
557; biblical influence on, 521; Blake
and, 507–508, 512, 518–521, 523,
527, 533, 536, 539; Brooklyn Bridge
obsession of, 522–523, 527, 548–551,
555–556; Bryant and, 518, 520, 538;
Caribbean and, 509; catachresis and,
518; chiasmus and, 518; Columbus
and, 551–552, 557; compared to
other American poets, 503, 558;
criticism and defense of *The Bridge*,
523, 527, 538; Dante and, 526, 617;
dialectical aspect of, 539; Dickinson and, 509, 518, 524; diction and
metric of, 518, 519, 523, 549, 557;
as difficult poet, 33, 393, 503, 518,
527; Donne and, 523, 536, 552;
education of, 501, 518, 523; effect
of reading, 416; Eliot and, 518, 523,
524, 536, 617; Emersonian vision
of, 111, 518; family background
of, 392, 513, 535, 542; Gnosticism
and, 542; God in, 501; Greenberg,
Crane's possible plagiarism of,
534–535; homoerotic urges of, 504,
510, 536, 542; Hopkins and, 299,
533; on Isle of Pines, 509, 531; John
of the Cross (Juan de la Crux) and,
501–502; Keats and, 503, 512–513,
518, 519, 523, 533, 555; lament for
loss of his friend Sommer, 511–512;
Lawrence and, 511, 516; Marlowe
and, 518, 523, 533; Melville and,
505–506, 509, 510, 518, 550; Milton
and, 518; mother (Grace Hart
Crane) and, 510, 511, 524, 535;
multiple personalities of, 510–511;
Nietzsche and, 524; nightmare and,
475; Opffer as lover of, 507–508,
510, 522; as Orphic poet, 523–524;
Pater and, 524; Plato and, 505, 519,
524; in poetic lineage, 463, 518,
627; poetics of metaphor and, 503,
555; pun on his own name for
"heart," 556; religion and, 501,
523–524, 527, 529–530, 546;
reputation of, 558; rhyme and, 549;
rhythm and, 537; as sect of one,
528; self-knowledge and, 516–517;
serpent and eagle trope and, 557;
shadow and, 521; Shakespeare and,
518, 533; Shelley and, 59, 264, 351,
503, 512, 518, 519, 523, 529, 533,
546, 555; as Shelley of his age, 546;
Stevens and, 518, 536; stone image
in, 504; suicide of, 503, 510, 525,
527; Tate and, 146, 460, 546;

Crane, Hart (continued)
    transcendence and, 523–524, 535,
    537; transumption in, 518; Virgil
    and, 523, 550; Whitman and,
    407, 501, 504–505, 509, 516–518,
    522, 523, 527, 531–533, 536, 546,
    556–558; Wordsworth and, 508,
    514, 518; Wright and, 35
Crane, Hart, works by: "Atlantis,"
    533, 548–553, 555–556, 557; "At
    Melville's Tomb," 505–506; "Ave
    Maria," 557; *The Bridge*, 111, 296,
    501, 503, 518–519, 523, 527–529,
    531, 533, 537–538, 540, 548, 557;
    "The Broken Tower," 503, 525–526,
    531, 557; "The Dance," 537;
    "Emblems of Conduct," 534–535;
    Key West, 530; "Lachrymae Christi,"
    514–516; letter to Harriet Monroe
    (October 1926), 503; letter to Waldo
    Frank (April 21, 1924), 522; letter
    to Waldo Frank (January 18,
    1926), 522; letter to Yvor Winters
    (March 19, 1927), 532; "A Name
    for All," 530; "Passage," 513–514,
    516–517; "Possessions," 503–505;
    "A Postscript," 530–531; "Praise
    for an Urn," 511–512; "Proem:
    To Brooklyn Bridge," 500–501,
    519–522, 538, 539, 550; "Repose of
    Rivers," 510–511; "The River,"
    537, 540, 557; "Southern Cross,"
    529–530; "Summer and Smoke,"
    535; "Thou canst read nothing
    except through appetite" (frag-
    ment), 540–541; "To Conquer
    Vanity," 509–510; *Voyages*, 59, 531,
    557; "Voyages I," 508; "Voyages
    II," 507–508, 509, 510; *White
    Buildings*, 503, 510, 522, 531; "The
    Wine Menagerie," 535–536
Crashaw, Richard, 388, 533, 557
Crawford, Robert, 202
Cromwell, Oliver, 60–61, 146

crucifixion, 63, 87–88
Cunningham, J. V., 392
Curtius, Ernst Robert, 109, 578, 618;
    works by: *European Literature and
    the Latin Middle Ages*, 55, 600–601

Damon, S. Foster, works by: *William
    Blake, His Philosophy and Symbols*, 144
Dante Alighieri: ability of reader to
    know, 613; accessibility of, 612;
    agonistic approach of, 607; ambi-
    tions of, 83, 613; Beatrice in *Com-
    media* and, 198, 527, 578, 593,
    600–601, 603–605, 609–610,
    613–615, 617–620, 627, 628; Blake
    and, 124; Bloom feeling incapable
    of teaching, 618; Cacciaguida and,
    594–595, 599, 610; Cavalcanti and,
    580–581, 616, 619; Chaucer and,
    100, 596, 599, 612, 616; courage
    and pride of, 611, 624; Crane and,
    526, 617; death of, 595; devil in,
    294; Eliot and, 24, 112, 187, 595,
    612; enemies assigned to Hell and
    patrons to Heaven, 610; in exile,
    624; Ezekiel and, 588; on freedom,
    48; on God, 40, 602; Homer and,
    628; inability to read Hebrew, 584;
    Isaiah and, 588; Jewish scholars on,
    615; Keats and, 596; Limbo created
    by, 627; Matelda in *Purgatorio*,
    187–188, 614–615, 625; Milton
    and, 50–52, 91, 99–100, 101, 602,
    623–624; on mode of structure, 50;
    Muhammad in *Inferno*, 616–617;
    muse of, 601; Nietzsche and, 598;
    personality of protagonists, 611,
    614; poetic imagination in, 4, 580;
    in poetic lineage, 3, 116, 212, 445,
    596, 610, 625, 627; reputation of,
    69, 558, 578, 619; rhetorical power
    of, 603; righteousness in *Paradiso*,
    614; role of author in *Commedia*,

152; Rossetti and, 309; Shakespeare compared to, 578, 596, 611, 614, 626; Shelley and, 18–19, 187–189, 209, 216, 223, 240, 246, 254, 273, 281, 288, 596, 614–615; Singleton as foremost scholar of, 605–606; Tennyson and, 357, 359; as theologian, 578, 580, 607, 609–610, 626; Trinity and, 621; truth in, 604, 612; Unity of Being and, 596; Virgil and, 580, 593, 603, 607, 615, 616, 619, 628; Yeats and, 463–464

Dante Alighieri, works by: *Commedia*, 69, 100, 268, 281, 579, 581, 584, 593, 595, 596, 597, 599, 601, 604, 610–615, 618, 624, 628; *Inferno*, 51, 278, 281, 382, 441, 464–465, 578, 581, 598, 599, 603, 606, 609, 613, 616–617, 628; *Paradiso*, 187, 526–527, 548, 578, 582–584, 594–595, 599, 600–601, 603, 614, 617, 618, 621–623, 626; *Purgatorio*, 117–118, 187–188, 578, 582–584, 588–593, 599, 603, 613, 617, 618, 619, 628; *Rime petrose*, 597–598

Darwin, Charles, 560, 574

David (biblical king), 415–416, 523, 628

Davidson, Donald, 392

Davie, Donald, 218

death: adequacy of (Meredith), 307; Bloom's pondering of, 470; desire as death (Shakespeare and Cavalcanti), 542, 608; emperor of ice cream as (Stevens), 443; evil death vs. good death (Stevens), 449; Freud on, 423; funeral readings of Crane's "At Melville's Tomb," 505; God and death as one (Yeats), 486; last poems of distinguished English poets, 459; Lawrence's death poems, 467; life as covenant with (Stevens and Whitman), 433; as man's creation (Blake and Shelley), 484–485; passing of youth and necessity of

dying (Keats), 313–318; peace after death (Stevens), 433, 435; randomness of (de Man), 192; recall of the dead in phantasmagoria (Tennyson), 375; reunion offered by (Stevens), 433; Shakespeare's use of ghosts, 74, 625; Shelley vs. Keats vs. Stevens on, 315–316; soul sleep as (Christina Rossetti), 304; as truth (de Man), 19–20, 580; vigil for the dying (Whitman), 398–400; what dying generation leaves behind (Stevens), 429; Yeats's death poems, 463–464, 466, 484–485

death drive, 254, 569, 571–573, 575

death-in-life, 268, 276

de Bolla, Peter, works by: *Harold Bloom: Towards Historical Rhetorics*, 289

deep reading, 1, 158, 193, 322, 527, 598–599, 624–625

de Man, Paul: Bloom's disputes with, 19–20, 122, 194; critique of *The Anxiety of Influence*, 14, 288–289; death of, 124, 192; deconstructive gospel and, 194; irony of, 15; Keats and, 297; as Nazi collaborator, 192, 274–275; Shelley and, 19–20, 190–192, 211–212, 267–268, 274; truth, belief in, 19–20, 276, 580; works by: "Shelley Disfigured," 190–191, 267–268

Derrida, Jacques, 122, 193

Descartes, René, 570

Desnos, Robert, 543

DeVane, William Clyde, 334–335

Dewey, Meredith, 230

Dickinson, Emily: Crane and, 509, 518, 524; Frost and, 412; Keats and, 299; in poetic lineage, 502; as sect of one, 107, 122, 347, 502, 625; shadows and, 472; Shelley and, 244–246; Stevens and, 423; Whitman and, 389; works by: "There's a certain Slant of light," 472

Dobranski, Stephen B., 39
Dodds, E. R., works by: *The Greeks and the Irrational*, 524
Dolben, Digby, 299
Donne, John: Coleridge and, 186; Crane and, 523, 536, 552; as devotional poet, 547; Herbert and, 547; Hermetic tradition and, 378; in poetic lineage, 627; as poet meant to be heard, 557; Shelley and, 186–187; word creation by, 95–96; works by: "A Noctural upon St. Lucy's Day," 186
Dostoevsky, Fyodor, 69; works by: *Crime and Punishment*, 56
Douglas, Keith, 543
Doyle, Peter, 393
Drayton, Michael, works by: *The Muses Elizium*, 113; *Poly-Olbion*, 113
Dronke, Peter, works by: *Dante and Medieval Latin Traditions*, 605, 606–607
Dryden, John: Blake and, 123; on Milton considering Spenser his original, 90; Shakespeare and, 438
Dryden, John, works by: "Farewell, ungrateful traitor," 311; *The State of Innocence*, 49

Eaton, Daniel Isaac, 101
Ebionites, 143
Eckhart, Meister, 69, 139, 155
Edelman, Lee, 518
Edwards, Richard, 127
elegy: Catullus and, 441–442; Crane and, 511, 556; Eliot and, 23–24; Frost and, 415; Keats and, 315; Shelley and, 218, 248–254; Stevens and, 234, 432–433, 437, 444; Whitman and, 24, 26, 437, 511; Yeats and, 484. *See also* threnody
Eliade, Mircea, 394
Elijah, 566

Eliot, T. S.: anti-Semitism of, 561; Bloom on poetic achievement of, 112; Crane and, 518, 523, 524, 536, 617; Dante and, 24, 112, 187, 595, 612; as dogmatist, 12–13; Freud and, 561; imagination and, 145; Lawrence and, 12, 471; literary judgments of, 12, 24, 471; on literary precursors, 197; on mankind's inability to bear reality, 109; personality of, 112; in poetic lineage, 463, 503; Schwartz and, 25; Shakespeare and, 24, 197, 470, 528, 595, 612, 618; Shelley and, 13, 25, 185, 187, 197, 201, 227, 351, 422; Stevens and, 422, 449; Tate and, 146; Tennyson and, 372; Whitman and, 26–27, 197, 201, 381, 407, 422, 523; Wimsatt and, 138; Wright and, 35; Yale English Department's regard for, 186; Yeats and, 25
Eliot, T. S., works by: *After Strange Gods*, 12; *Burnt Norton*, 24; *The Cocktail Party*, 204; *The Dry Salvages*, 24; *East Coker*, 24; *Four Quartets*, 24; *Little Gidding*, 24, 26–27, 197, 201; "The Love Song of J. Alfred Prufrock," 204, 430; *The Sacred Wood*, 612–613; *Sweeney Agonistes*, 204; "Sweeney Erect," 201; *The Waste Land*, 22–26, 86, 197, 381, 424, 523, 524, 527
Eliot, Valerie, 22
Elizabeth I (queen of England), 69, 538
Emerson, Ralph Waldo: Bloom as Emersonian, 9, 380, 613; Crane and, 111, 518; Frost and, 411, 416; Gnosticism and, 542; Orphic poet in America and, 557; Romantic ego and, 567; on self-reliance, 546; Shakespeare and, 5; Shelley and, 226; Stevens and, 423; Whitman and, 111, 380, 454, 528; Winters as

critic of, 532; Wordsworth and, 161, 175

Emerson, Ralph Waldo, works by: *The Conduct of Life*, 411, 535; *Journals*, 106; *Nature*, 175; "The Poet," 9, 20; "The Transcendentalist," 537; "Uriel," 416

Emery, Florence Farr, 481

Empedocles, 565–567, 575

Empson, William, 45, 542, 613; works by: *Milton's God*, 59–60

Engels, Friedrich, 219

Epicurus and Epicureanism, 1, 151, 261, 278, 365–367, 452, 580

Erdman, David V., 123, 130, 133, 153; *The Complete Poetry and Prose of William Blake* (ed.), 123, 141, 153

Eros, 216, 254, 510, 561, 572–574

Euripides, works by: *Alcestis*, 204

Fascism, 464

Faulkner, William, works by: *As I Lay Dying*, 528

feminism, 152, 155–156

Ficke, Arthur Davison, 392

fiction: accepting as truth, 99, 604; cause and effect as, 288; Dante's *Commedia* as, 604; as final belief, 255; "of the leaves," 50, 209, 445, 453

Fisch, Max Harold, 18

Fitzgerald, Edward, works by: *Rubaiyat of Omar Khayyam*, 298–299, 367

Flaubert, Gustave, 69

Flesch, William, 104

Fletcher, Angus, 15, 58–59, 92, 131, 289, 528, 535, 624

Fletcher, Angus, works by: *Colors of the Mind*, 2, 59; *King Henry VIII*, 69; *A New Theory for American Poetry*, 387–388

Fletcher, John Gould, 392

Florence, Italy, 578, 610, 612, 617

Foot, Michael, 184

Ford, Andrew, works by: *Homer and the Poetry of the Past*, 9

Fortin, Ernest L., works by: *Dissent and Philosophy in the Middle Ages: Dante and His Precursors*, 605–606

Fouqué, Friedrich de la Motte, works by: *Undine*, 509

Fowler, Alastair, 52, 75, 76

Fox, George, 392

Francis of Assisi, St., 530

Franco-Heideggerian textualism, 3

Freccero, John, 578, 581–582, 605, 611, 615; works by: "Allegory and Autobiography," 607; "The Fig Tree and the Laurel," 627; "The Final Image: *Paradiso* XXXIII, 144," 581–582; "Manfred's Wounds and the Poetics of the Purgatorio," 612; "Medusa: The Letter and the Spirit," 578–579

freedom: Kant and, 9; Milton's *Areopagitica* and, 60–61; of poetry, 9; of publication, 101; of readers, 11

French Revolution, 100–101, 148, 175

French Symbolists, 514, 557

Freud, Anna, 575; works by: *The Ego and the Mechanisms of Defense*, 132, 560

Freud, Sigmund: anti-Semitism and, 560, 562–563; ashes of, resting place of, 563; birth and death of, 559; Blake and, 133, 138; Bloom compared to, 16, 560; bodily ego and, 566–569, 573; choosing London for his exile, 561; creation of anxiety and, 572; death drive and, 569, 573; as dominant cultural figure, 560; on drives, 564–571; dualism of, 565–571; on dying, 423; Eliot and, 561; Empedocles and, 565–567, 575; Eros and, 561, 572–574; as essayist, 132, 559; frontier or border concepts in, 565,

Freud, Sigmund (continued)
568–569; Goethe and, 560; Herzl
compared to, 563; on homoeroticism, 536; intellectual authority of,
561, 612; inwardness and, 565–568;
Jeremiah and, 565, 567–569; Joyce
and, 574; Judaism of, 132, 562–563,
564, 566; Jung and, 560; Keats
and, 448; Lawrence and, 469, 574;
masochism and, 562–563, 572; on
memory, 176; Milton and, 105;
Moses as obsession of, 561, 575;
narcissism and, 105, 566, 569,
570, 572; Nietzsche and, 132, 574;
primary process and, 571–572;
Proust and, 574; psychoanalysis's
roots and benefits, 69, 559, 562–563;
"Rat Man" case, 562; Reality Principle and, 132, 572; on religion as
longing for authority of murdered
father, 573–574; Rome and, 576;
sadomasochism and, 570, 572–573;
secular humanism of, 574; Shakespeare and, 574–576; Shelley and,
279; Stevens and, 426, 448, 574;
tabula rasa of speculation and, 574;
temporality and, 571; transference
and, 574; Venice and, 576; *Verneinung* and, 573; the will and, 146;
Wittgenstein on, 7, 132, 559; on
"work of mourning," 254; Yeats
and, 574
Freud, Sigmund, works by: *Beyond the
Pleasure Principle*, 132; *Civilization
and Its Discontents*, 574–575; "Drives
and Their Vicissitudes," 569–570;
The Ego and the Id, 567, 572; "Formulations on the Two Principles
of Mental Functioning," 572; *The
Future of an Illusion*, 561; *Inhibitions, Symptoms and Anxiety*, 132,
562–563; *The Interpretation of
Dreams*, 571; *Moses and Monotheism*,
561, 563; *New Introductory Lectures
on Psychoanalysis*, 564–565; *An

Outline of Psychoanalysis*, 570; *The
Psychopathology of Everyday Life*,
573; *Studies in Hysteria*, 132;
Totem and Taboo, 562, 574; *The
Uncanny*, 132
Frost, Robert: Adam and Eve in, 412;
audience of, 409, 415; Blake and,
412; Bloom meeting with, 416–417;
Browning and, 417; children's
deaths prior to his own, 412;
Dickinson and, 412; Emerson
and, 411, 416; existence and, 415;
Gnosticism and, 542; Homer and,
421; Keats and, 417–418; marriage
to Elinor White, 412, 414, 417; in
poetic lineage, 463, 502; relationship with Kay Morrison, 412–413;
religion and, 420–421; Stevens and,
422, 449; Virgil and, 421; Wordsworth and, 411, 416
Frost, Robert, works by: "After
Apple-Picking," 417–418; "Birches,"
419–421; "Design," 412; "Direc-
tive," 415; "Never Again Would
Birds' Song Be the Same," 412;
"Our Doom to Bloom," 421;
"The Oven Bird," 414; "Provide,
Provide," 415–416; "Putting in the
Seed," 417; "The Silken Tent,"
412; "The Trial by Existence,"
409–411; "Two Tramps in Mud
Time," 409; "The Wood-Pile,"
413–414
Fry, Christopher: libretto for *Paradise
Lost* opera, 50
Frye, Northrop, 25, 122, 124, 125, 131,
143–146, 204, 208
Frye, Northrop, works by: "Antique
Drum," 204; "Blake's Introduction
to Experience," 144; *Fearful
Symmetry*, 143–144, 145–146;
"The Keys to the Gates," 127;
A Study of English Romanticism,
205
Fuller, Margaret, 406

Galsworthy, John, 624

gender: Blake on "the Female Will," 57, 111, 151–152, 156, 157, 473; Chaucer's portrayal of women, 156; Dante's Beatrice as theomorphic woman, 603; feminism, 152, 155–156; Milton on women, 75, 96

George, Stefan, 618

Gifford, Emma Lavinia, 12

Gigante, Denise, 315

Gilchrist, Alexander, 387

Gilchrist, Anne, 387

Ginsberg, Allen, 407

Gnosticism: Beddoes and, 542; Blake and, 122, 123, 124, 139, 141, 145, 542; Bloom and, 542; Crane and, 542; Frost and, 542; Hill and, 542–544; Holy Grail and, 524; Hugo and, 542; Melville and, 386–387, 542; Shelley and, 243, 250, 255, 542; Simon Magus and, 603; Stevens and, 450, 475; Yeats and, 486, 490, 542

God: acceptance or rejection of God's love, 618; Blake's image of, 602; breath of Yahweh as Holy Spirit, 537; in Browning, 347; in Crane, 501; in Ezekiel, 117; in Frost, 411; images in Hebrew Bible (Tanakh), 587; as Jewish joke, 62; Milton on Yahweh as consuming fire, 60; in Milton's *Paradise Lost*, 39–40, 45–46, 49, 56, 63, 75, 90, 145, 217, 602; Montaigne and, 625; in Rilke, 447; in Saramago's *Gospel*, 62–63; Shakespeare and, 40, 601, 612; Trinity role of, 620; Yahweh of J writer, 586, 613; Yahweh of J writer vs. Elohim of Priestly writer, 40, 61; in Yeats, 486

Godwin, William, 93, 278; works by: *Enquiry Concerning Political Justice*, 184

Goethe, Johann Wolfgang von: as final representative of classic tradition, 58; Freud and, 560; irony of, 151; in poetic lineage, 3, 69, 212; reputation of, 558; Rome and, 576; Schiller with, 625; Shakespeare and, 576; Shelley and, 240

Gogarty, Oliver St. John, 131

Golden Dawn (followers of Madame Blavatsky), 480–482

Gonne, Maud, 462, 478, 491

Gordon, Caroline, works by: *The Malefactors*, 546

Gorgias, 212

Graves, Robert, works by: *Wife to Mr. Milton*, 39

Gray, Thomas, 121; works by: *The Progress of Poesy*, 114

Greenberg, Moshe, 586

Greenberg, Samuel, works by: "Conduct," 533–535

Gregory, Horace, 392

Gross, Kenneth, 54, 66, 67, 97, 344, 440, 472

the grotesque, 335, 338, 370, 524, 617

Hallam, Arthur Henry, 359, 373, 375, 377

Hardy, Thomas: Eliot and, 12; first marriage to Emma Lavinia Gifford, 12; Hill and, 543; Lawrence and, 467; in poetic lineage, 466; Shelley and, 11, 350

Hardy, Thomas, works by: *Jude the Obscure*, 17; "Neutral Tones," 12; *Tess of the d'Urbervilles*, 17; "We Are Getting to the End," 11

harmony: of heaven, 450; rainbow, 557

Harrison, Robert Pogue, 599, 617

Harrison, Thomas, 122

Hart, David Bentley, 85, 123, 143, 153–154; works by: "The Lost Modernist," 153; *That All Shall Be Saved*, 6

Hartman, Geoffrey, 58, 99, 124, 161, 164, 168, 193, 325; works by: *The Fate of Reading*, 89–90; "The Romance of Nature and the Negative Way," 125; *Wordsworth's Poetry: 1787–1814*, 161

Hausemann, William, 598

Hawthorne, Nathaniel: Shelley and, 248; travel with Maria Mitchell, 406; works by: "Dr. Heidegger's Experiment," 248

Hawthorne, Sophia, 406

Hayden, Robert, 37

Hayley, William, 148–151; works by: *The Triumphs of Temper*, 149

Hazlitt, William, 19, 29, 71, 109, 200–201, 297, 322, 323, 327, 619

Heaney, Seamus, 627

Hebrew Bible (Tanakh): in agonistic relationship to New Testament, 607; breath of Yahweh as Holy Spirit, 537; Christianity reducing to Old Testament, 579; Crane and, 521; "fiction of the leaves" and, 453; as God's book, 612; human nature and, 65; images of God in, 587; immortality and, 8; Milton's *Paradise Lost* and, 99; prophets and, 566; Second Commandment, 566, 586, 587; Talmud on proper way to read, 11; theomorphic people in, 603; truth telling of Yahwist, 121; Yahweh of J writer vs. Elohim of Priestly writer, 40; Yahweh on his choice of when to be present, 72; Yahweh's name used by Ezekiel, 586. *See also* scriptural citations

Hegel, Georg Wilhelm Friedrich: Romantic ego and, 567; Shakespeare and, 65; works by: *The Spirit of Christianity and Its Fate*, 64

Heidegger, Martin, 19

Henry VII of Luxembourg (Holy Roman Emperor), 610, 612

Henry VIII (king of England), 69

Heraclitus, 567

Herbert, George: as devotional poet, 112, 544–545, 547; Donne and, 547; Hermetic tradition and, 378; Shakespeare and, 545; works by: "Redemption," 544–545

Hermetic Corpus, 75–76, 145, 377–378, 465, 490, 524, 547, 600

Herzl, Theodor, 563

Hesiod, 126, 135

Hicks, Elias, 392–393

Hill, Christopher, 48

Hill, Geoffrey: Blake and, 125, 543; Bloom's introduction to his poetry volume, 540–541; on Crane, 540–542; as difficult poet, 33; Gnosticism and, 542–544; Lawrence and, 543; Milton and, 543; nightmare and, 475; in poetic lineage, 543; as sect of one, 122

Hill, Geoffrey, works by: *The Book of Baruch by the Gnostic Justin*, 542–544; "Improvisations for Hart Crane," 541–542; *The Triumph of Love*, 25, 541

Hilles, Frederick W., 133

Hillyer, Robert, 392

Hodgart, Matthew, 185

Hollander, John: admiration of, 441; in anthology *Romanticism and Consciousness: Essays in Criticism*, 124; Catullus and, 442; Clark Lectures (Cambridge University 1999) by, 472; death of and farewell to, 437, 442; eroticism and humor of, 438; "figure of interpretive allusion" and, 267; influences on, 437; Milton and, 81; shadow and stone in, 440, 472; Stevens and, 437, 439; Thurber and, 438–439; transumption and, 92; trope and, 275, 289; Yeats and, 438

Hollander, John, works by: "The Fall," 438; *The Figure of Echo*, 15; *The Lovers*, 438; *Powers of Thirteen*,

437–439; "Romantic Verse Form
and the Metrical Contract," 125;
"A Shadow of a Great Rock in
a Weary Land," 439–441; *The
Substance of Shadow: A Darkening
Trope in Poetic History*, 440, 472;
The Untuning of the Sky, 264

Hollander, Robert, works by: "Milton's
Elusive Response to Dante's *Comedy*
in *Paradise Lost*," 100

Holmes, Richard, works by: *Shelley: The
Pursuit*, 180–181

Holy Spirit, 106, 537, 620

Homer: ability of reader to know, 613;
Dante and, 628; "fiction of the
leaves" and, 453; freedom of, 9;
Frost and, 421; as God's book, 612;
irony of, 151; Milton and, 50–52;
Plato and, 99; in poetic lineage,
212, 367, 445, 625; Shelley and,
209; truth and, 121; Vico and, 18;
Whitman and, 397; Wright and, 35

Homer, works by: *Iliad*, 51, 99;
Odyssey, 281, 458

homosexuality and homoeroticism,
23, 220, 377, 382, 487, 488, 504,
509–511, 527, 536, 542, 580

Hopkins, Gerard Manley: Browning
and, 333, 339; Crane and, 299, 533;
death of, 299–300; as devotional
poet, 112; humanism of, 300; Keats
and, 299, 300, 370; Pater and, 300;
reputation of, 302–303; Rossetti
and, 303; spiritual anguish of, 302;
Tennyson and, 370; Whitman and,
300, 302, 370, 393

Hopkins, Gerard Manley, works by:
letter to R. W. Dixon (October 12,
1881), 333; letter to Robert Bridges
(October 1882), 302; "That Nature
Is a Heraclitean Fire and of the
Comfort of the Resurrection,"
300–301; "To R.B.," 302–303

Horace, 48, 90, 392

Horton, W. T., 480–481

House, Humphry, 124

Hugo, Victor: Gnosticism and, 542;
Lawrence and, 467; Mallarmé and,
456; in poetic lineage, 3, 212, 523;
reconcilable with himself, 625;
reputation of, 69, 558; self-image
of, 83

human nature, 24, 64–65, 112, 144,
196, 230, 355, 562

Hume, David, 40, 207, 282–283, 559

Hunt, Leigh, 187, 297, 319

Huxley, Aldous, 155

Huxley, Thomas Henry, 11

Hyde, Edward (First Earl of Clarendon), 81; works by: *The History of
the Rebellion*, 82

Hyde-Lees, Georgie, 462

hyperbole, 13, 29, 153, 289, 316, 553

Ibn Ezra, Abraham, 342

Idel, Moshe, 542; works by: *Kabbalah*,
547

imagination: influence of creative
imagination, 145; Milton and, 49,
54; Stevens and, 457; Wordsworth
and, 164

Immanuel ben Solomon, 584

immortality: compared to resurrection and redemption, 316; Crane
and, 527; Dante and, 625; Freud
and, 573; Judaism and, 8; Keats
and, 316; literary criticism and, 8;
longing and, 8; Plato and, 139, 316;
Shelley and, 219, 255

Incarnation: Browning and, 348, 351;
Dante and, 604, 605, 615, 626;
Ebionites rejecting, 143; Frye on,
144–145, 146; Milton and, 47–48;
Shakespeare evading, 3, 24

irony, 15, 20, 151, 193–194, 212, 267,
275, 281, 289, 518

Irwin, John T., 514, 524, 536, 550;
works by: *American Hieroglyphics*,
506; *Hart Crane's Poetry*, 506

Jacob and Esau, 603
James the Just, 143
James, Henry, 454; works by: *The Bostonians*, 246
James, William, 146
Jeffers, Robinson, 407, 421
Jerome, St., 367, 585
Jesus. *See* Christ
Jews. *See* Judaism and Jews
Joachim of Flora, 579, 604, 610
John of the Cross, St., 7, 112, 155, 501–502
John the Divine, St., 584, 601
Johnson, Lionel, 350–351, 487; works by: "The Dark Angel," 487–488
Johnson, Samuel: Bate on, 320; Bloom's role model in reading, 2; compared to Dante, 619; compared to Hazlitt, 327; defense of Alexander Pope, 367; distrust of devotional verse, 544; as hero of Bloom, 578; on Milton's *Paradise Lost*, 106–107; Shakespeare and, 5, 21; on Young's *Night-Thoughts*, 128
Johnson, Samuel, works by: *The Life of Milton*, 544; *The Life of Pope*, 544; *The Lives of the Poets*, 544
Jonas, Hans, 542
Jones, David, 153–154; works by: *The Anathemata*, 154; *In Parenthesis*, 153, 154; *The Tribune's Visitation*, 154
Jonson, Ben: Milton and, 54; in poetic lineage, 627; Shakespeare and, 601, 618, 627; soliloquy and, 71; word creation by, 95–96; Yeats's metric debt to, 474
Jonson, Ben, works by: *Bartholomew Fair*, 627; *Catiline His Conspiracy*, 611; *Sejanus His Fall*, 611
Joshua (biblical figure), 377, 580, 602
Joyce, James: as creator of literary art, 83; Dante and, 596; Freud and, 574; as giant of Western literature, 625; Pater and, 596; religious views of,

626; Schwartz and, 25; sense of humor of, 62; Shakespeare and, 596; works by: *Finnegans Wake*, 154; *Ulysses*, 131
Juan de la Cruz. *See* John of the Cross, St.
Judaism and Jews: anti-Semitism, 560, 562–563, 564, 615; Bate's death and, 320; Bloom's background in Orthodox Judaism, 8, 442, 602; Browning and, 342; converso Catholics, 501; covenant with Yahweh, 99; Dante scholars, Jews among, 615; dualism in, 566; Freud and, 132, 561–562, 564; God as Jewish joke, 62; Hebrew Blessing, meaning of, 603; immortality and, 8; Jewish gnostics, 214; Jewish memory and the Oral Tradition, 563, 571; life exalted over death by, 132; Macbeth and, 64–65; Merkabah tradition and Ezekiel, 80, 117, 120, 123, 160, 273, 584, 602; Palermo's abandoned synagogues, 576; Proust's mother accorded Jewish funeral, 626; redemption and, 316; repression and, 571; speculation and mythology in relation to, 7, 565; Spinoza excommunicated by, 373; Stevens's mentions of rabbis, 426; superego and, 571; Trinity's effect on, 621. *See also* Hebrew Bible (Tanakh); Kabbalah
Julius, Anthony, works by: *T. S. Eliot, Anti Semitism and Literary Form*, 112
Jung, Carl: Blake and, 139; Freud and, 560

Kabbalah, 122, 123, 124, 145, 214, 408, 524, 537, 547, 584, 586, 602
Kafka, Franz, 62, 510, 574
Kant, Immanuel, 9, 279

Keats, George (brother of John Keats), 315

Keats, John: Blake and, 322; Browning and, 311, 350; Byron and, 312, 325; Crane and, 503, 512–513, 518, 519, 523, 533, 555; Dante and, 596; death of, 248; de Man on, 297; family background of, 324; Freud and, 448; Frost and, 417–418; heroic naturalism of, 528; humanism of, 201, 300, 449; immortality and, 255; Meredith and, 308; Milton and, 132, 159, 297, 299, 317; mother figure in, 433; Negative Capability and, 312, 323, 329; Pater and, 300; playwrighting as desire of, 327; in poetic lineage, 297, 299, 316, 332; religion and, 300, 316; Rossetti and, 299, 308–309; sexual love and, 331; Shakespearean influence on, 104, 160, 297, 299, 312, 321–322, 327–328; Shelley and, 239–240, 248–253, 254, 317, 322, 325, 370; Stevens and, 29, 297, 299, 324, 429, 447–449; Tennyson and, 299, 316, 371; unconsummated love for Fanny Brawne, 104, 325; Wordsworth and, 104, 161, 297, 299, 325, 328; working-class background of, 322

Keats, John, works by: *Endymion*, 160, 205, 297, 311, 377; *The Fall of Hyperion*, 87, 104, 297, 312, 321, 323–325, 377, 463, 513; "Hymn to Pan," 160; *Hyperion*, 104, 297, 312, 318, 325, 377; "In drear nighted December," 311–312; *Lamia*, 325; letter to Benjamin Bailey (November 22, 1817), 104; letter to his brothers (December 22, 1817), 312, 322–323; "Ode on a Grecian Urn," 298, 449; "Ode on Melancholy," 319–321, 512–513; "Ode to a Nightingale," 86–87, 159–160, 313–318, 429; "Ode to Psyche," 329–332; "On Sitting Down to Read King Lear Once Again," 22; "On the Grasshopper and Cricket," 447; "Sleep and Poetry," 160; "This living hand" (fragment), 332; "To Autumn," 21, 325–327, 418; "Written in Disgust of Vulgar Superstition," 318–319

Keats, Tom (brother of John Keats), 315

Kermode, Frank, 28, 67; works by: "Adam Unparadised," 45; *Wallace Stevens*, 57

Kernan, Alvin, 124

Kerrigan, William, 90

Khan, Masud Raza, 564

Kierkegaard, Søren, 72, 560; works by: *The Sickness unto Death*, 140

Kincaid, James R., works by: *Annoying the Victorians*, 369–370

Knight, G. Wilson, works by: *The Starlit Dome*, 227

Kraus, Karl, 574

Kunitz, Stanley, 392

Kushner, Tony, 407

Kyd, Thomas, 23

Laforgue, Jules, 197, 381

Landolfi, Tommaso, works by: "Gogol's Wife," 224

Landor, Walter Savage, 348

Latini, Brunetto, 580, 624

Lau, Beth, works by: *Keats's Paradise Lost*, 160

Law, William, 155

Lawrence, D. H.: biblical range of writing of, 467–469; Blake and, 144, 473; Crane and, 511, 516; deathbed meditation of, 472; Eliot and, 12, 471; Freud and, 469, 574; Hardy and, 467; Hill and, 543; Hugo and, 467; lack of human

Lawrence, D. H. (continued)
otherness in, 474; marriage to
Frieda, 468; novel form and, 4,
466; as omnisexual, 468; in poetic
lineage, 466–467, 627; as prophetic
poet, 467, 474; religion and, 467,
527; as sect of one, 122, 468;
serpent and eagle trope and, 557;
shadow and, 472; Shakespeare and,
470; Shelley and, 351, 467–468;
sun and, 467; tortoise poems of,
511; travel writings and, 466–467;
vitalism of, 467; Whitman and,
407, 408, 467, 472
Lawrence, D. H., works by: *Apocalypse*,
467; "Bavarian Gentians," 472; *Look!
We Have Come Through!*, 467; *New
Poems*, 473; *The Rainbow*, 466, 467;
"Shadows," 472; "The Ship of
Death," 469–471; "Song of a Man
Who Has Come Through,"
467–469; *Studies in Classic
American Literature*, 407–408;
Twilight in Italy, 470; "Under the
Oak," 473; *Women in Love*, 466, 468
Lawrence, Frieda, 468
Layton, Bentley, 542
Leavis, F. R., 185
Le Guin, Ursula K., 89
Leivick, H., 491
Leonard, William Ellery, 392
Leopardi, Giacomo, 212, 596, 616
Levin, Harry, 56
Lewis, C. S., 39, 43
Lewis, R. W. B., 440
Lidz, Theodore, 564
Lieberman, Saul, 602
Lincoln, Abraham, 302, 389
Locke, John, 133, 155
Lodge, George Cabot, 407
Lorca, Federico Garcia, 537
love: acceptance or rejection of God's
love, 618; ambivalence and, 17;
Christian love, 69, 485–486; free

love and Shelley, 112, 182, 212, 245,
261, 346; Melville and, 393; sexual
love in Keats, 331; Shelley, love
and means of love in, 246–247, 267;
Tennyson and, 373; Whitman
and, 393
Lucan, 90, 252
Lucretius, 4, 196; Dante and, 580;
Epicureanism and, 1, 151, 366–367,
580; Shelley and, 205, 240; Tennyson and, 362–367; Virgil and, 261,
625; Whitman and, 528
Luis de León, 501

MacBride, John, 462
MacCaffrey, Isabel, works by: "The
Other Side of Silence: 'Credences
of Summer' as an Example,"
447–448
Machado, Antonio, 463
MacLeish, Archibald, 392
MacNeice, Louis, 334; works by:
"Bagpipe Music," 334
Macpherson, James, 125
Macpherson, Jay, works by: *The Spirit
of Solitude: Conventions and Continu-
ities in Late Romance*, 199–200
Maeonides, 86
Maimonides, Moses, 273
Malcolm X, 100
Mallarmé, Stéphane, 456
Mammon, 97, 322
Mandelstam, Osip, 463
Mann, Thomas, 62
Mariani, Paul, 452
Marks, Herbert, 76, 586
Marlowe, Christopher: Crane and, 518,
523, 533; Milton and, 55; Milton's
Satan and, 99–100; in poetic lin-
eage, 9; as poet meant to be heard,
557; Shakespeare and, 146, 194,
601, 618, 627; soliloquy and, 71;
Yeats and, 465

Marlowe, Christopher, works by: *Doctor Faustus*, 55–56, 99–100; *The Jew of Malta*, 561, 576

Marvell, Andrew, 378

Marx, Eleanor, works by: "Shelley and Socialism," 184

Marx, Karl, works by: *The Eighteenth Brumaire of Louis Bonaparte*, 184

Marxism, 48, 62, 153, 175, 183, 219

"Mary Don't You Weep" (African American spiritual), 440

Mastrobuono, Antonio C., works by: *Dante's Journey of Sanctification*, 605–606

Mathers, Samuel Liddell MacGregor, 482

McGann, Jerome, 240

Melville, Herman: Blake and, 192; casting of Maria Mitchell as Urania in "After the Pleasure Party," 407–408; Crane and, 505–506, 509, 510, 518, 550; Gnosticism of, 386–387, 542; influence of and centrality to American literature, 401, 408; love and, 393; as sect of one, 107, 122; Shelley and, 191–192; Whitman and, 393

Melville, Herman, works by: "After the Pleasure Party," 402–406; *Clarel: A Poem and Pilgrimage in the Holy Land*, 401; "The Encantadas," 511; "Fragments from a Lost Gnostic Poem of the Twelfth Century," 191; "The Maldive Shark," 401–402; *Moby-Dick*, 393, 401, 408, 505–506, 509, 510–511; "Shelley's Vision," 191

memory, 55, 170, 175–176, 312, 436, 458, 563

Meredith, George, 303, 305–308; works by: "A Ballad of Past Meridian," 306–307; *The Egoist*, 305; "Lucifer in Starlight," 307–308; *Modern Love*, 305–306

Merrill, James, 70, 503, 577, 617

Merwin, William (W. S.), 70, 316, 577

metalepsis, 20, 82, 275, 518

metaphor, 2, 97, 212, 441, 462, 503, 555. *See also* tropes, systems of

Michelangelo, 501, 561

Midland, Dan, 540

Miles, Josephine, 124

Millay, Edna St. Vincent, 392

Miller, J. Hillis, 15

Milton, John: Adam in *Paradise Lost*, 49, 52, 55, 93, 96, 103–104; admiration of Bloom for, 91; ambitions of, 83–84; anti-papism of, 64; Arianism of, 47; Blake and, 18, 42–43, 50, 56, 61, 69, 103, 112, 124, 126, 131, 146–158, 602; blindness and, 52, 66–67, 71, 74, 76, 86, 624; Chaucer and, 53, 91, 108; as Christian humanist, 48–49, 64; Coleridge and, 39–40, 58, 71; Crane and, 518; Cromwell and, 60–61; Dante and, 50–52, 91, 99–100, 101, 596, 602, 616, 623–624; death and, 27, 45; Eve in *Paradise Lost*, 48–50, 55, 61, 70–71, 73, 86, 88–90, 96, 102, 104–106; expressiveness through Shakespearean personalities, 38, 49, 55, 69, 71, 82, 88, 90, 94; family background of, 90; fears of, 92; first wife (Mary Powell) and, 39; on freedom, 48; God in *Paradise Lost*, 39–40, 45–46, 49, 56, 63, 75, 90, 145, 217, 602; Gospel of John and, 84–85; Hebraic influence on, 65, 76; Hill and, 543; Holy Spirit as muse of, 106; on human face divine, 87; Jonson and, 54; Keats and, 132, 159, 297, 299, 317; knowledge of Hebrew and ability to read Old Testament in original, 65; on the Light vs. Logos, 84–85; linguistic mastery of and word creation by, 95; Malcolm X and,

Milton, John (continued)
100; Marlowe and, 55, 99–100;
melancholy and, 74; on Messiah,
42–43; monism of, 69; muse of,
601; Nietzsche and, 97; Ovid and,
90, 97; personality missing from
protagonists of, 61, 108; poetic
ambition of, 218; in poetic lineage,
3, 116, 146, 445; poetic mind's
influence upon his indwelling spirit,
101, 105, 107; poetic ranking of,
212, 558; as poet meant to be heard,
557; popularity of, 154; pride of
and limits of his work, 101–102,
108; relationship to Shakespeare,
5–6, 38, 46, 49–55, 61, 69–72, 77,
82, 90, 92–93, 96–97, 107–108, 624;
Satan in *Paradise Lost*, 6, 11, 38,
42–50, 58, 61, 63, 70–74, 75, 80, 82,
93, 97, 99–103, 108, 293–294, 308,
359, 624; as sect of one, 122, 347;
Shelley and, 44, 107, 132, 209, 223,
240, 252, 254, 273, 293; soliloquy
in *Paradise Lost*, 73, 105; on the
Son, 46–48, 56, 87–88, 90, 119;
Spenser and, 625; Tennyson and,
359; tradition of Protestant dissent
and, 146; transumption and, 49–53,
55, 61, 84, 92, 97, 120, 194; on
universe of death, 11; "unruly
allusion" in, 92, 96, 97; Vico and,
18; Virgil and, 50–53, 90, 97; on
women, 75, 96; Wordsworth and,
46, 132, 159, 163, 170, 172
Milton, John, works by: *Areopagitica*,
60–61; *Eikonoklastes*, 82; "Il Penseroso," 74, 172; "L'Allegro," 70;
Lycidas, 60, 83–84, 92, 218, 248,
274; *Of Education*, 47–48; *On Shakespeare*, 53–54, 70; *Paradise Lost*,
5–6, 18, 38–56, 68, 70, 74–75, 81,
84, 86–88, 90–91, 93–95, 98–99,
102–103, 106–107, 119–120, 172–173,
189, 202, 206, 207, 268, 359, 602,

613, 624; *Paradise Regained*, 110;
"The Passion," 80–81; *Samson
Agonistes*, 65–67, 70, 88; "To
Shakespeare," 80
Milton, Mary Powell, 39
Mistral, Gabriela, 463
Mitchel, John, 496
Mitchell, Maria, 406
Mithraism, 273
Molière, 558
Moll, Elsie, 452
Monk, Samuel, 124
Montaigne, Michel de, 279, 576, 612;
God and religion in, 560, 625; as
literary legend, 558, 559; personal-
ity in, 474, 624; Shakespeare and,
24; truth and, 121, 138–139
Moore, Marianne, 449, 503
Morris, William, 303, 460, 477, 495
Morrison, Kay, 412–413
Morse, William Inglis, 133
Moses, 561, 575, 579–580, 586
mother figures: Crane and, 510, 511;
Eliot and, 197; Keats and, 302, 324;
Schopenhauer and, 17; Shelley
(Mary) and, 93; Shelley (Percy
Bysshe) and, 198; Stevens and,
432, 433, 475; Whitman and,
432, 433, 511
Muggleton, Ludowicke, 106
Muhammad, 616–617
Murdoch, Iris, 624
Murry, John Middleton, works by:
William Blake, 144
Myth of Memory, 170
mythology: African, 32–34; Freud as,
559; poets as, 558; Saxon, 494. *See
also* classical mythology

Náhuatl poetry, 34–35
narcissism, 11, 105, 216, 566, 569, 570,
572
Nardi, Bruno, 605–607

nature: Blake and, 155–156; Dante and, 597; Keats and, 370; lilacs in Whitman and, 10, 27, 472; Shelley and, 199, 493; Wordsworth and, 164–165, 170; Yeats and, 462

Needleman, Jacob, 619

Nemerov, Howard, 392

Neoplatonism, 122, 124, 126, 139, 145, 155, 215, 251, 490, 548, 565

Neruda, Pablo, 463, 537

New Critical school, 3

New Testament: Blake and, 123, 136; Milton's *Paradise Lost* and, 99; Prodigal Son parable, 383; replacing Old Testament, 579. *See also* scriptural citations

Newton, Isaac, 133

Nicholas of Cusa, 75, 76, 600

Nietzsche, Friedrich Wilhelm: Bloom's writing as Nitezschean, 560; Burckhardt and, 63; choosing between Nietzsche and Pauline thought, 7; Crane and, 524; Dante and, 598; on father figure, 536; Freud and, 132, 574; on Hamlet, 71; Milton and, 97; pain in relation to aesthetic delight and, 4; perspective on existence and the world, 110; poetic thinking and wisdom and, 6, 17, 299; Rorty and, 16; Schopenhauer and, 17; Shakespeare and, 5, 16; Stevens and, 58–59, 423; truth and, 16; the will and, 146; Yeats and, 141, 461, 462

Nietzsche, Friedrich Wilhelm, works by: *On the Genealogy of Morals*, 49, 598; *Twilight of the Idols*, 288; *The Will to Power*, 17–18, 96

nihilism, 16, 287, 295, 464, 625

Nuttall, A. D., 48, 107

O'Brien, Conor Cruise, 464

O'Connor, Flannery, 204

Odysseus. *See* classical mythology; Homer

Oedipal transgression, 511, 560, 575

O'Higgins, Kevin, 484

Old Testament. *See* Hebrew Bible (Tanakh)

Opffer, Emil, 507–508, 510, 522

Orpheus, 27, 126, 139, 209, 243; Crane as Orphic poet, 523–524, 527, 531, 551, 556–558; Orphic song, 225–226, 258

Ouspensky, P. D., 527

Ovid: Milton and, 90, 97; Shakespeare and, 71, 146, 194, 611; Shelley and, 240

Owen, Wilfred, 299, 439, 463

Pacino, Al, 576

Palmer, Samuel, 133, 155

palm trees, imagery of, 458–459

parabasis, 275

Paracelsus, 124

Parker, Hershel (ed.): *Melville's Complete Poems*, 401

Pascal, Blaise, 24

Pater, Walter: Coleridge and, 40; Crane and, 524; Hopkins and, 300; Joyce and, 596; Keats and, 300; Stevens and, 298, 452; Yeats and, 141, 460, 462

Pater, Walter, works by: "A Fragment on *Measure for Measure*," 77; *Plato and Platonism*, 505

Pathetic Fallacy, 423

pathos, 103, 108, 267–268, 275–276, 467, 471

Paul, Saint, 7, 143, 211, 500, 570

Paz, Octavio, 463, 537

Peacock, Thomas Love, 204, 306

Pelikan, Jaroslav, works by: *Christianity and Classical Culture*, 620–621

Percival, Milton, works by: *Blake's Circle of Destiny*, 144 personality development: Cervantes and, 474, 624; Keats and, 325, 327; Milton lacking, 61, 108; Montaigne and, 624; Shakespeare and, 3, 9–10, 49, 53, 71, 77, 96, 108, 474, 600–601, 611, 624; shortcomings even in good writers, 624

perspectivism, 96–97, 110

Pessoa, Fernando, 537

Peter, Saint, 603

Peterloo Massacre, 183

Petrarch: Dante and, 69, 118, 309, 596, 608, 609, 616, 627; in poetic lineage, 69, 116, 608; Rossetti and, 309; Shelley and, 273; works by: *The Triumph of Love*, 118–119

Phillips, Rowan Ricardo, works by: "An Excuse for Mayhem," 293

Philo Judaeus, 123

Phineus, 86

picturesque, 127, 388, 444

Pierce, John, works by: "The Shifting Characterization of Tharmas and Enitharmon," 133–134

Pindar, 212

Pitt the Younger, William, 100–101

Plato: Blake and, 139; Cappadocian Fathers and, 620; Crane and, 505, 519, 524; Diotima in *Symposium*, 479, 552; dualism of, 570; Emerson and, 175; Homer and, 99; immortality and, 139, 316; in poetic lineage, 625; Shelley and, 205, 206, 240, 246, 288; Socratic irony and, 212; at start of argument between philosophy and poetry, 96; Vico and, 18; Yeats and, 491

Plato, works by: *Dialogues*, 524; *Phaedo*, 8; *Symposium*, 479, 549, 552; *Timaeus*, 227

pleasure principle, 102, 132, 254, 527, 572, 575

Plimpton, George, 602–603

Plotinus, 139, 249, 488, 491, 537

Poe, Edgar Allen, 542

poetic thinking, 2–3, 6; Blake's cognitive power, 463; as cognitive rhetoric, 15; Crane and, 546; Freud's secondary process and, 572; hard work of (Yeats), 478; last poems of distinguished English poets, 459; loss and, 491; poetry as more than language, 20–21; Shelley's cognitive power, 463; Stevens's poetic argument, 431, 453; Yeats's occultism and, 462–463. *See also* Hermetic Corpus

poetic voice, humming as, 550

Poirier, Richard, works by: *Robert Frost: The Work of Knowing*, 415

Pope, Alexander, 367

Pottle, Frederick A., 124, 186, 205, 231

Pound, Ezra, 23, 25, 407, 449, 536, 543, 617; works by: *Cantos*, 154

pre-Raphaelite poets, 303, 597

Price, Martin, 124; works by: "The Standard of Energy," 125; *To the Palace of Wisdom*, 125

Prometheus, 38, 44, 93

Protestantism. *See* Christianity and Christians

Proust, Marcel: Freud and, 574; as giant of Western literature, 83, 625; religious roots of, 626; truth and, 138

Pulos, C. E., works by: *The Deep Truth: A Study of Shelley's Skepticism*, 207

Puttenham, George, 82

Quakers, 392

Quint, David, works by: *Inside Paradise Lost*, 48–49, 87–88

Raleigh, Walter, 537; works by: "The 11th: and last booke of the Ocean to Scinthia," 538

Ransom, John Crowe, 152; works by:
"Survey of Literature," 152–153
rapture: Crane and, 509, 522, 533;
Shelley and, 213; Wordsworth
and, 170
reading: Augustine's contemplative act
of reading, 620; deep reading, 1,
158, 193, 322, 527, 598–599,
624–625; delight as part of, 11;
devouring books, 2; difficulty of
reading certain poets, 33, 121, 393,
432, 503, 518, 527; poets meant to
be read aloud, 557; sustenance
from, 1–3, 1–3, 11, 133, 158;
treasured effect of reading Wallace
Stevens, 416, 426–427, 443
redemption: compared to immortality
and resurrection, 316; Crane and,
527; Hamlet and, 16; Herbert and,
544–545; literary criticism and,
6–8; Milton and, 46, 59; Shelley
and, 219, 222–223, 255
religion: Browning and, 342–343, 348,
351; Crane and, 501, 523–524, 527,
529–530, 546; Freud's view of
religion as longing for authority of
murdered father, 573–574; Frost
and, 420–421; Herbert as devotional poet, 544–545; Keats and,
300, 316; Montaigne and, 625;
poetry's relation to, 615, 625–626;
religious truths, expression of, 7;
Shakespeare's lack of, 3, 107;
Shelley and, 180, 192, 273–274,
318–319, 546; spiritualism, 351;
Stevens and, 442, 452, 475–476;
Tennyson and, 373; theurgy and,
547–548; Whitman and, 392; Yeats
and, 461, 478, 485. See also Catholicism and Catholics; Christianity
and Christians; Judaism and Jews
remorse, 181, 276, 461, 487–488, 611
resurrection: compared to immortality and redemption, 316; Crane

and, 527; Lawrence and, 472;
literary criticism and, 8; Shelley
and, 253; Yeats and, 478–479
rhyme: Browning and, 339, 342;
Crane and, 519, 549; Hollander
and, 439; Owen and, 439, 463
Rhymers' Club, 487
Rhys, Ernest, 487
rhythm: in American poetry, 387–388;
Blake and, 387; Crane and, 537;
ritual, 388, 537; Whitman and,
387–388, 532, 537
Richardson, Samuel, works by:
Clarissa, 275
Richmond, George, 133
Rieff, Philip, 560
Rilke, Rainer Maria, 447
Rimbaud, Arthur, 264, 508, 518, 523,
542
Roebling, John A., 522
Rogers, John, works by: "The Secret
of *Samson Agonistes*," 67
Romanticism: Crane and, 503, 519;
Eliot and, 13; Keats and, 327;
Romantic ego, 566, 567; self-
creation and, 627; Shelley and, 268;
Yeats and, 460
Rorty, Richard, works by: *Contingency,
Irony, and Solidarity*, 16–17
Rossetti, Christina, 112, 533; works
by: "Passing away, saith the World,
passing away," 303–304; "Up-Hill,"
304
Rossetti, Dante Gabriel: Hopkins
and, 303; Keats and, 299, 308–309;
Yeats and, 495, 597
Rossetti, William Michael (ed.):
Selected Poems of Walt Whitman,
300, 387
Rossiter, William, 77
Roth, Philip, 62
Rousseau, Jean-Jacques: Shelley and,
240, 268, 274, 276, 278, 282; works
by: *Julie, or The New Héloïse*, 274, 275

Ruddock, Margot, 464
Rukeyser, Muriel, 392
Rumrich, John P., 39
Ruskin, John, 423

Sabellius, 620
sadomasochism, 152, 181, 570, 572–573
Saladin, 614, 627
Sand, George, 377–378; works by: *La Comtesse de Rudolstadt*, 377; *Consuelo*, 377
Sanskrit, 23
Santagata, Marco, works by: *Dante: The Story of His Life*, 623
Santayana, George: Stevens and, 235, 433, 444; works by: *Interpretations of Poetry and Religion*, 107
Sappho, 359
Saramago, José, 61; works by: *The Gospel According to Jesus Christ*, 61–62
Satan: in Blake, 45, 137; in Milton's *Paradise Lost*, 6, 11, 38, 42–50, 58, 61, 63, 70–74, 75, 80, 82, 93, 97, 99–103, 108, 293–294, 308, 359, 624; in Shelley, 45; in Stevens, 49
satire, 112, 133, 204, 306, 446, 599, 627
Saussure, Ferdinand de, 20
Savage, Richard, 2
Schiller, Friedrich, 69, 625
Schlegel, Friedrich, 15
Scholem, Gershom, 8, 213, 214, 408, 542
School of Resentment, 440
Schopenhauer, Arthur, 17, 132, 146
Schwartz, Delmore, 25
Scofield, John, 131–132
scriptural citations: Genesis, 27–28, 76, 84; Genesis 1:26, 214; Genesis 39:2, 105; Exodus 20:4, 586; Exodus 24, 117; Exodus 24:9–11, 586–587; Exodus 40, 117; Deuteronomy 4:24, 60; Judges 5, 66, 120; Judges 13–16, 65; Job, 5, 47, 50, 56, 110, 137, 208, 210, 610; Job 9:4, 8–9, 52; Psalms, 383; Psalm 18, 117; Psalm 23, 611; Psalm 50:21, 346; Proverbs 8:25–30, 91–92; Proverbs 20:27, 106; Ecclesiastes, 221; Ecclesiastes 1:18, 105; Song of Solomon (Song of Songs), 303, 304, 383, 555; Song of Solomon 3:1–2, 502; Isaiah, 135, 211, 445; Isaiah 6, 117; Isaiah 6:1–8, 114–115, 587; Isaiah 32:2, 439; Isaiah 34:4, 50–52; Isaiah 62:4, 156; Isaiah 64:8, 344; Jeremiah, 565, 567–569; Jeremiah 18:2–6, 344; Jeremiah 20:9, 568; Jeremiah 31, 568; Ezekiel, 117, 124, 140, 223, 273, 582, 585, 588; Ezekiel 1:1–13, 116; Ezekiel 1:22–28, 585; Ezekiel 14:12–15, 135; Ezekiel 28:14–16, 134; Ezekiel 48:35, 121; Joel 3:14, 123; Amos, 211, 384; Amos 5:8, 53; Micah, 211, 384; Zechariah 9:13, 64; Malachi, 566, 613; Malachi 3:1–3, 613–614; Matthew 5:13–14, 102; Matthew 16:19, 552; Matthew 27:51, 255; Mark, 61, 120, 145, 146; Mark 4:12, 415; Luke 15:11–32, 383; Luke 24:13–19, 380–381; John, 84–85, 145; Acts 17:22–24, 500; I Corinthians 15:52, 211; Ephesians 6:12, 125–126; Hebrews 12:29, 60; Revelation, 223, 582, 601; Revelation 2:17, 504; Revelation 4, 123; Revelation 4:6–9, 116
Segal, Charles, 366–367
Sellwood, Emily, 373
Sewall, Richard, 244
Shakespeare, William: on art as nature, 355; Bible and, 146, 194; Blake and, 90, 124; Browning and, 345; Chaucer and, 146, 194; Coleridge and, 58, 107–108; Crane and, 518, 533; creation of presence

by, 3, 10; creative imagination and, 145–146; Dante compared to, 578, 596, 611, 612, 614, 616, 626; desire as death in, 542, 608; Drayton and, 113; Dryden and, 438; Eliot and, 24, 197, 470, 528, 595, 612, 618; Emerson and, 5; foreign language knowledge of, 95; freedom of, 9; Freud and, 574–576; ghosts in, 625; God and, 40, 601, 612; Goethe and, 576; Hegel on, 65; Herbert and, 545; Hill and, 543; inability of readers to know, 111, 576, 601, 610, 613, 617; influence of, 5, 21, 82, 90; Johnson and, 5, 21; Jonson and, 601, 618, 627; Joyce and, 596; Keats and, 104, 160, 297, 299, 312, 321–322, 327–328; Lawrence and, 470; Marlowe and, 146, 194, 601, 618, 627; Milton and, 5–6, 38, 46, 49–55, 61, 69–72, 77, 82, 90, 92–93, 96–97, 107–108, 624; Montaigne and, 24; Nietzsche and, 5, 16; original role in literature, 5, 90, 194, 578, 625; Ovid and, 71, 146, 194, 611; paradise in, 101; personality of protagonists in, 3, 9–10, 53, 77, 96, 108, 474, 600, 611, 624; poetic imagination in, 4, 101–102; religion's absence in, 3, 107; on remembering to forget, 176; as replacement for God, 110; reputation of, 69, 212, 557, 558, 578, 625; Shelley and, 249–250, 261, 282; silence and, 92, 625; soliloquy and, 71–73, 470; songs in plays of, 179; transumption and, 194; truth and, 121, 138–139; vocabulary of, 95; what we learn by reading, 3, 575, 613, 619; Whitman compared to, 90, 381; the will and, 146; Wittgenstein's deprecation of, 21, 559; word creation by, 95; "wounded by wonder" as Shakespearean trope, 620; Yeats and, 461, 596

Shakespeare, William, works by: *All's Well That Ends Well*, 77; *Antony and Cleopatra*, 101, 257, 317, 328, 438, 617; *As You Like It*, 331–332, 438; *Coriolanus*, 66–67, 197; *Cymbeline*, 40, 601; *Hamlet*, 5, 6, 16, 28, 46, 49, 50, 58–59, 61, 70–74, 82, 88–89, 93, 94, 95, 101, 108, 147–148, 181–182, 197, 276, 282, 297, 312, 317, 321–322, 461, 470, 476, 506, 528, 560, 575–576, 611, 618; *Henry IV*, 101, 194; *Henry VIII*, 69; *King Lear*, 3–4, 5, 22, 58, 63, 65, 71, 95, 101, 104, 326–327, 350, 418, 575, 600, 613–614, 617–618, 626; *Macbeth*, 33, 49, 50, 58, 61, 65, 70, 71, 89, 95, 101, 249, 312, 575, 617; *Measure for Measure*, 21, 76–80, 95, 367, 371, 576; *Merchant of Venice*, 65, 576, 615; *A Midsummer Night's Dream*, 97; *Othello*, 4, 49, 50, 58, 61, 63, 70, 75, 95, 101, 617; *Richard III*, 63, 70; *Romeo and Juliet*, 189–190; Sonnet 125, 545; *The Tempest*, 101, 334, 345–346, 611; *Troilus and Cressida*, 77, 95, 96; *The Winter's Tale*, 377, 611, 615, 625

shamanism, 36, 139, 394

Shankara, 155

Shaw, Bernard, 350; works by: *Man and Superman*, 211

Shell, Marc, works by: *The End of Kinship*, 76–77

Shelley, Mary Godwin: Dante and, 614; Milton's *Paradise Lost* and, 93; Shelley's *The Witch of Atlas* and, 227, 233

Shelley, Mary Godwin, works by: *Frankenstein*, 93; *Mathilda*, 614; *Midas* (with Percy Bysshe Shelley), 241

Shelley, Percy Bysshe: as Ariel, 261–262, 264, 346, 445; Arnold and, 185; Athanase as hero of

Shelley, Percy Bysshe (continued)
poetic fragment by, 462; atheism
of, 180, 273; audience of, 295; azure
(sublime color) and, 209, 217, 222,
223, 232, 253, 265, 427, 514; Beddoes
as disciple of, 220, 350; Bishop and,
444–445; Blake and, 119, 215–217,
222, 227, 240; Browning and,
111–112, 346–348, 350; Butler and,
69; Byron and, 180–182, 240,
254, 272, 290, 294, 295, 318, 349;
Coleridge and, 283; Crane and, 59,
264, 351, 503, 512, 518, 519, 523,
529, 533, 546, 555; criticisms of,
185–186, 196–197, 201; Dante and,
18–19, 187–189, 209, 216, 223,
240, 246, 254, 273, 281, 288, 596,
614–615; death, acceptance of, 219,
220–221; death of, 296; de Man on,
19–20, 190–192, 211–212, 267–268,
274; dialectical aspect of, 219,
226–227, 240; disagreeing with
Byron about Hamlet, 181–182;
Donne and, 186–187; elegy and,
218, 248–254; Eliot and, 13, 25,
185, 187, 197, 201, 227, 351, 422;
Emerson and, 226; family background of, 198; free love and, 112,
182, 212, 245, 261, 346; Freud and,
279; Gnosticism and, 243, 250,
255, 542; hallucinations of, 181,
204, 250; Hardy and, 11, 350;
Hawthorne and, 248; Hill and,
543; Homer and, 209; imagination
and, 463; immortality and, 219, 255;
influence of, 184, 201, 350–351;
irreplaceability of, 111; Johnson
(Lionel) and, 487; Keats and,
239–240, 248–253, 254, 317, 322,
325, 370; Keats's death as subject
of Adonais, 248–256, 557; Lawrence
and, 351, 467–468; love and means
of love in, 246–247, 267; Lucretius
and, 205, 240; Mammon or

principle of self and, 322; marriage
to Harriet Westbrook (first wife),
182, 272; marriage to Mary Shelley
(second wife), 272; in Mary Shelley's
Frankenstein, 93; Melville and,
191–192; Milton and, 44, 107, 132,
209, 223, 240, 252, 254, 273, 293;
Neoplatonism and, 215; nightmare
and, 475; as nihilist, 295; Ovid and,
240; Petrarch and, 273; Plato and,
205, 206, 240, 246, 288; poetic
ranking and in poetic lineage, 116,
201, 212, 240, 254, 273, 445, 558;
as poet meant to be heard, 557;
redemption and, 219, 222–223, 255;
relationship with Claire Clairmont, 244, 272; relationship with
Jane Williams, 195, 241, 261,
265, 272, 346, 445; religion and,
180, 192, 273–274, 318–319, 546;
remorse and, 461, 488, 610–611;
responsibility for suicides of his
first wife and his second wife's
sister, 182, 272; Rousseau and, 240,
268, 274, 276, 278, 282; on Satan,
45; self-exaltation of, 160, 276, 294;
self-knowledge of, 212–213; serpent
and eagle trope and, 557; Shakespeare and, 249–250, 261, 282; as
social agitator, 190, 209, 240, 318,
546; Times of London on death of,
45; transcendence and, 217, 289,
316; transumption and, 240, 240,
267, 267, 289, 289; urbanity of, 218,
251, 499; Virgil and, 209; Wordsworth and, 147–148, 215, 218, 240,
250, 252, 254, 268, 281, 284–285,
289; Yeats and, 25, 141, 183, 189,
206–208, 227, 233, 234, 238–239,
259–260, 267, 270, 287, 297, 350,
435, 460–462, 464, 478–479, 493,
497, 499
Shelley, Percy Bysshe, works by:
Adonais, 24, 187, 194, 241, 248–256,

274, 282, 295, 317–318, 377, 444, 537, 553, 556, 557; *Alastor*, 24, 185, 189, 198–199, 204, 216, 272, 295, 377, 493, 508; *The Cenci*, 198, 295, 327; *The Daemon of the World*, 190; *A Defence of Poetry*, 38, 44, 195–196; *Epipsychidion*, 241, 243–246, 377; "Essay on the Devil and Devils," 45; *Hellas*, 241, 256–259, 479; *Homeric Hymn to Mercury*, 229; "Hymn of Pan," 466; "Hymn to Intellectual Beauty," 283, 287–288, 289; *Julian and Maddalo*, 295, 349; letter to Leigh Hunt (December 1819), 282; "A Letter to Lord Ellenborough," 101; *Letter to Maria Gisborne*, 218, 273–274; "Lines Written in the Bay of Lerici," 265–266; *Lines Written in the Euganean Hills*, 295; *The Mask of Anarchy*, 183, 318; *Midas* (with Mary Shelley), 241–242; "Mont Blanc," 229, 283–288; "Ode to the West Wind," 185, 194, 208–210, 255, 315–316, 431, 445, 456, 468, 512, 537; "On the Devil and Devils," 293; *Peter Bell the Third*, 147; *Posthumous Poems*, 200–201; "Prince Athanase," 462; *Prometheus Unbound*, 44, 48, 180, 182–183, 186, 189, 198, 202–208, 211, 213, 215–217, 219–226, 246, 251, 279, 287, 325, 346, 508; *Queen Mab*, 183, 189–190, 219, 223, 285, 295; *The Revolt of Islam*, 181; "To a Skylark," 178, 533, 553–555; "To Byron," 294; *The Triumph of Life*, 19, 74, 119, 182, 183, 190, 192–195, 201, 206, 212, 241, 247, 261, 267–282, 295, 325, 463, 615; *The Wandering Jew*, 256, 462; *The Witch of Atlas*, 194, 195, 201, 225, 227–239, 484, 497–499; "With a Guitar. To Jane," 195, 261–264

Sidney, Philip, 252

silence: Browning and, 347; Shakespeare and, 92, 625; Stevens and, 436, 448; usefulness in teaching, 11; Yeats and, 465, 484
Simon Magus, 603
Simpson, Louis, 392
Singleton, Charles S., 579, 580, 604, 605–606, 607, 618
Smart, Christopher, 350, 533
Smithers, Leonard, 442
Socrates, 139, 264, 317
soliloquy, 71–72; in Milton's *Paradise Lost*, 73, 105; in Shakespeare's *Hamlet*, 72–73, 470
Sommer, William, 511–512
Sophocles, 212, 560
Southey, Robert, works by: *Vision of Judgement*, 289–290
Spain, 397–398
Spenser, Edmund: Blake and, 124; Chaucer and, 69; Dante and, 596, 616; Drayton and, 113; Dryden and, 90; Keats and, 299; Milton and, 625; poetic ranking of, 212, 557, 627; Shelley and, 216, 269, 273
Spenser, Edmund, works by: *The Faerie Queene*, 154, 256, 269; *Fowre Hymnes*, 289
Spinoza, Baruch, 373
Statius, 614
Stevens, Garrett Barcalow, 475
Stevens, Holly, 442, 452, 546
Stevens, Wallace: acceptance of things as they are, 474; aesthetic of, 298; Blake and, 59; Canon Aspirin and, 425; Coleridge and, 430; Crane and, 518, 536; on death of Satan, 49; Dickinson and, 423; as difficult poet, 432; elegy for Henry Church by, 432–433; Eliot and, 422, 449; Emerson and, 423; family background of, 392; on "fiction of the leaves," 50, 453; Freud and, 426, 448, 574; Frost and, 422, 449;

Stevens, Wallace (continued)
Gnosticism and, 450, 475; High
Sublime and, 425; Hollander and,
437, 439; humming as trope for
poetic voice, 550; humor of, 430;
on indwelling spirit, 105; Interior
Paramour and, 10, 105, 370, 432,
436; Japanese flower arrangement
and, 297; Keats and, 29, 297, 299,
429, 447–449; on Keats's *The Fall
of Hyperion*, 324; lack of human
otherness in, 474; mother figure
and, 432, 433, 475; Nietzsche and,
58–59, 423; Pater and, 298, 452;
pleasure as essential element of
poetry for, 41; in poetic lineage,
445, 463, 502, 627; presence of self
in his poems, 424–425; religion
and, 442, 452, 475–476; rock
imagery in, 451, 454–456; Santayana and, 234–235, 433, 444; shadow
in, 472; Shelley and, 29, 195, 210,
234–235, 243, 255, 351, 427, 431,
435, 444–445; silence and, 436,
448; on sleep and phantasmagoric
forms, 432–433; Tennyson and,
370; tone of, 447, 451–452; transcendence and, 427, 442–448,
458–459; transumption and, 82;
treasured effect of reading, 416,
426–427, 443; visionary optics in,
455; Whitman and, 10, 29, 386,
407, 423, 425–426, 432–433,
436–437, 453, 456, 578; Wordsworth and, 28–29, 425, 456; Yeats
and, 298, 449, 459, 476
Stevens, Wallace, works by: *Adagia*,
604; "All the Preludes to Felicity,"
457; "As You Leave the Room,"
428; *The Auroras of Autumn*, 27,
111, 324, 392, 424, 472; "Autumn
Refrain," 429; "A Child Asleep in
Its Own Life," 443; "A Clear Day
and No Memories," 442–443;

Collected Poems, 451, 456; *The
Comedian as the Letter C*, 23, 27;
"The Course of a Particular,"
315–316, 445; "Credences of
Summer," 428, 447–451, 456;
"Death of a Soldier," 474; "A
Discovery of Thought," 446–447;
"The Dove in Spring," 458; "Esthé-
tique du Mal," 87, 449–450;
"Examination of the Hero in a
Time of War," 428; "Extracts from
Addresses to the Academy of Fine
Ideas," 297–298, 449; "Final
Soliloquy of the Interior Par-
amour," 105, 370; *Harmonium*, 27,
423–424, 427, 475, 528; "How to
Live. What to Do.," 456; "The Idea
of Order at Key West," 28–29, 57;
Ideas of Order, 429, 456; "The Im-
perfect Paradise," 299; "It Must
Give Pleasure," 243; "Large Red
Man Reading," 427; "Madame La
Fleurie," 475; "The Man with the
Blue Guitar," 455; *Mr. Burnshaw
and the Statue*, 195; "Mrs. Alfred
Uruguay," 429–430; "Nomad
Exquisite," 458; *Notes toward a
Supreme Fiction*, 27, 210, 243, 392,
424–425, 426, 431; "Of Mere
Being," 458–459; *An Ordinary
Evening in New Haven*, 27, 424;
"The Owl in the Sarcophagus,"
432–437; "The Planet on the
Table," 445; "The Pleasures of
Merely Circulating," 73; "The
Poems of Our Climate," 58,
298–299; "A Postcard from the
Volcano," 428–429; "Puella
Parvula," 431–432; "The Pure
Good of Theory," 457; "A Quiet
Normal Life," 446; "A Rabbit
as King of the Ghosts," 431;
"The Rock," 451–453, 454–456;
"The Sail of Ulysses," 458, 476;

"The Snow Man," 423; "Someone Puts a Pineapple Together," 428; "Stars at Tallapoosa," 423–424; "Sunday Morning," 370; "Things of August," 426; "To an Old Philosopher in Rome," 234–235, 444; *Transport to Summer*, 457; "The Well-Dressed Man with a Beard," 428

Stickney, Trumbull, 29; works by: "Mnemosyne," 29–30; "On Some Shells Found Inland," 31

Strand, Mark, 70, 407

the Sublime: aporias and, 20; Blake and, 121, 127; Crane and the American Sublime, 531; Emerson and, 175; Fletcher on, 388; Freud and, 132; humanistic Sublime, 88; questioning of, 5; Shelley's quest for, 343; Stevens's High Sublime, 425; Whitman and the American Sublime, 531–532; Wordsworth and, 161, 172, 425

Swenson, May, 577

Swift, Jonathan: Blake and, 133; works by: *A Tale of a Tub*, 133

Swinburne, Algernon Charles, 303, 350, 367, 387; works by: *Poems and Ballads*, 366

Symons, Arthur, 502

Talmud, 11, 563, 584

Tanakh. *See* Hebrew Bible

Tanner, John, works by: *Revolutionist's Handbook*, 211

Taoism, 89

Tarphon, Rabbi, 7

Tasso, Torquato, 294, 349–350

Tate, Allen, 25, 29, 146, 460, 523, 527, 546

Taylor, Thomas, works by: *The Mystical Initiations, or Hymns of Orpheus*, 126

Tennyson, Alfred (Lord): Browning, Robert and, 367; Catullus and, 442; Dante and, 357, 359; death in, 375, 378; diction and cadence of, 359, 361; Eliot and, 372; Hopkins and, 370; Keats and, 299, 316, 371; love in, 373; Lucretius and, 362–367; marriage to Emily Sellwood, 373; Milton and, 359; perfect poem by ("Mariana"), 367; religion and, 373; Stevens and, 370; Virgil and, 359; Wordsworth and, 370, 375, 377

Tennyson, Alfred (Lord), works by: "Crossing the Bar," 378; *Idylls of the King*, 316; *In Memoriam A.H.H.*, 316, 373–377; "Lucretius," 362–367; "Mariana," 367–373; "Tithonus," 356, 359–362; "Ulysses," 356–359, 362

Teresa de Avila, 501

textualism, 3, 131, 133

Thamyris, 86

Thelwall, John, 101

theurgy, 547–548

thinking: Milton's Satan and, 46, 49, 71; Shakespeare and, 24; as suffering, 49. *See also* poetic thinking

Thomas, Dylan, 393

Thompson, Lawrance, 412

Thomson, James, works by: *The City of Dreadful Night*, 201–202

Thoreau, Henry David, 423, 495; works by: *Walden*, 495

threnody, 10, 315, 389, 444

Thurber, James, works by: *The Thirteen Clocks*, 438–439

Tolstoy, Leo: reputation of, 69; truth and, 121, 138; Wordsworth and, 178

Tolstoy, Leo, works by: *The Cossacks*, 178; *Hadji Murad*, 178; *War and Peace*, 178

Tourneur, Cyril, 208

Trakl, Georg, 463, 574

transcendence: Blake and, 139;
Browning and, 347; Crane and,
523–524, 535, 537; poetry providing, 111; Shelley and, 217, 289, 316;
Stevens and, 427, 442–448, 458–459
transumption: Crane and, 518;
Hollander and, 92; Milton and,
49–53, 55, 61, 84, 92, 97, 120, 194;
pathos and, 275; Puttenham on, 82;
Shakespeare and, 194; Shelley and,
240, 267, 289; trope of, 15, 20–23,
53, 240
tropes, systems of, 15; aporias and, 20;
Crane and, 503, 518; de Man and,
20; fiction of the leaves, 445; Freud
and, 132; Hollander and, 275, 289;
humming for poetic voice, 550;
pathos and, 275–276; revision and,
20; serpent (snake) and eagle,
294–295, 557
Trotsky, Leon, 184–185
truth: Blake and, 121; Bloom's failure
to believe in, according to de Man,
19–20, 276, 580; Dante and, 612;
death as, 276; fiction accepted as,
99; Incarnation as basis of, 144,
626; list of few writers who tell the
whole truth, 121, 138; poetic truth,
15; poetry not intended to be, 604;
Shelley and, 221, 276; Stevens and,
422
Tucker, Herbert F., works by:
"Dramatic Monologue and the
Overhearing of Lyric," 2–3, 347
Tyndale, William, 65, 84–85, 105

Ungaretti, Giuseppe, 463, 574, 596
University of Coimbra (Portugal), 61
Untersteiner, Mario, works by: The
Sophists, 212

Valéry, Paul, 19, 267, 456, 463, 574;
works by: "Palme," 458–459

Vallejo, César, 463
Vallon, Annette, 148
Van den Berg, J. H., 124; works by: The
Changing Nature of Man, 328–329
Vane, Henry, 146
Vaughan, Henry, 378, 533; works by:
"The World," 547–548
Vaughan, Thomas, 547, 548
Vendler, Helen, 175
Verdenal, Jean, 23, 24, 26, 381
Vico, Giambattista: Dante and, 595;
on divination or poetic immorality,
518; on human freedom, 9; on
poetic wisdom, 17, 18; Yeats and,
329; works by: The New Science,
6–7, 14–15, 18
Victorian poets, 335, 370
Virgil: Augustine and, 611; Crane
and, 523, 550; Dante and, 580, 593,
603, 607, 615, 616, 619, 628; death
wish to destroy Aeneid, 611;
Epicureanism and, 580, 605; Frost
and, 421; homoeroticism of, 580;
irony of, 151; Lucretius and, 261,
625; Milton and, 50–53, 90, 97;
in poetic lineage, 3, 212, 445;
providing pagan prophecy of
coming of Christ, 260–261;
Shelley and, 209; Tennyson and,
359; Williams describing Virgil's
role in Dante, 605
Virgil, works by: Aeneid, 51–53, 151,
523, 550, 580, 605, 611; Fourth
Eclogue, 260
Viviani, Teresa, 206, 244

Wallis, Henry, works by: The Death of
Chatterton, 306
Warner, William, 123; works by:
Albion's England, 113
Warren, Robert Penn, 401, 546
Watson, Caroline, 152
Webster, John, 208; works by: The
White Devil, 93–94

Weil, Simone, 65
Weiskel, Thomas, works by: *The Romantic Sublime*, 88, 108
Weiss, Theodore, 392
Weston, Jessie, works by: *From Ritual to Romance*, 524
Wharton, Edith, 430, 454, 624
Wheelwright, John Brooks, 407
Whitman, Walt: as Answerer, 393, 556; audience and, 393; azure color and, 296, 556; Blake and, 387; Christ figure and, 380–381, 388, 391; Columbus and, 552, 557; Crane and, 407, 501, 504–505, 509, 516–518, 522, 523, 527, 531–533, 536, 546, 556–558; creativity coming from within self, 312; Dante and, 619; as descriptive poet, 388; difficulty of reading, 393; Emersonian vision of, 111, 380, 454, 528; eroticism of, 300, 384, 399, 456, 536; family background of, 391–392; freedom and, 9–10; health and healing powers of, 388, 394–397; Homeric influences on, 397; homosexuality and, 382, 536; Hopkins and, 299; humming as trope for poetic voice, 550; immediacy with his readers, 380, 391; influence of and centrality to American literature, 197, 381, 392, 401, 407, 408, 445, 502, 509, 536–537, 558, 578; Laforgue translating into French, 197, 381; Lawrence and, 407, 408, 467, 472; love and, 393; Melville and, 393; multiple selves in his writing, 393–394; at one with himself, 383; Orphic poet in America and, 557; pansexuality of, 382, 468; as poet meant to be heard, 557; relationship with Anne Gilchrist, 387; religion of, 392; reputation of, 302, 389, 558; rhythm of, 387–388, 537; as sect of one, 107, 122, 502; Shakespeare and, 90, 381; Spanish writers influenced by, 537; Stevens and, 10, 29, 386, 407, 423, 425–426, 432–433, 436–437, 453, 456, 578; sun and, 386; Tennyson and, 370, 375, 377; Winters as critic of, 532
Whitman, Walt, works by: "As I Ebb'd with the Ocean of Life," 516–517; "As I Sat Alone by Blue Ontario's Shore," 426; "Crossing Brooklyn Ferry," 391, 523; "Dirge for Two Veterans," 400–401; *Drum-Taps*, 454, 457; *Leaves of Grass*, 83, 296, 301, 380, 391, 408, 517, 557; "Out of the Cradle Endlessly Rocking," 29, 424, 453, 557; "Poem of You, Whoever You Are," 389–391; "Reconciliation," 397; *Sequel to Drum-Taps*, 397, 398, 400; "The Sleepers," 301, 432–433, 455–456; *Song of Myself*, 111, 379–380, 381–383, 384–387, 391, 392–393, 407, 453, 532–533, 619; "To You," 380, 389, 391, 532; "Vigil Strange I Kept on the Field One Night," 398–399; "When Lilacs Last in the Dooryard Bloom'd," 10, 23, 26–27, 197, 381, 389, 436–437, 452, 453, 511, 523; "Whispers of Heavenly Death," 557; "The Wound-Dresser," 394–397
Whittemore, Reed, 392
Wilbur, Richard, 70
Wilde, Oscar, 56, 452, 487; works by: *De Profundis*, 56
Williams, Charles, 593, 604; works by: *The Descent of the Dove: A Short History of the Holy Spirit*, 604–605; *The Figure of Beatrice: A Study in Dante*, 604–605; *Shadows of Ecstasy*, 604
Williams, Jane, 195, 241, 261, 265, 272, 346, 445
Williams, Tennessee, 529; works by: *Summer and Smoke*, 535

Williams, William Carlos, 299, 407, 422, 449, 502–503, 532, 536; works by: *Paterson 1*, 528, 532

Wilson, Edmund, 527

Wimsatt, William K., 14–15, 124, 137–138; works by: *Hateful Contraries*, 137–138

Winnicott, Donald, 564

Winters, Yvor, 523, 527, 532

Wittgenstein, Ludwig, 7, 8, 17, 21, 71, 95–96, 132, 559

women. *See* gender

Wordsworth, Ann, 572

Wordsworth, William: affair with Annette Vallon, 148, 175; aims of, 83; as Anglican, 168; Bible and, 163; Blake and, 131–132; Coleridge and, 57–58, 161; Crane and, 508, 514, 518; Emerson and, 161, 175; as first modern poet, 58, 109; in French Revolution, 148, 175; Frost and, 411, 416; Hartman and, 161; Hill and, 543; imagination and, 170; Keats and, 104, 161, 297, 299, 325, 328; marriage to Mary Hutchinson, 175; memory and, 170, 176; Milton and, 46, 132, 159, 163, 170, 172; nature and, 164–165, 170; in poetic lineage, 3, 125; poetic ranking of, 212; as sect of one, 625; sense of self in tension with outward scene in, 328; Shakespeare and, 163; Shelley and, 147–148, 215, 218, 240, 250, 252, 254, 268, 281, 284–285, 289; on "spots of time," 57; Stevens and, 28–29, 425, 456; the Sublime and, 161, 172, 425; unlovable, 58; Yeats and, 491

Wordsworth, William, works by: *The Borderers*, 327; *Ecclesiastical Sonnets*, 168–169; *The Excursion*, 161; *Home at Grasmere*, 161–163; "It is a beauteous Evening, calm and free," 176; "Michael," 169; "Ode: Intimations of Immortality," 169, 174–175, 179, 215, 283, 288, 328, 375, 508–509, 514; "The Old Cumberland Beggar," 169, 177–178; *Peter Bell*, 147; *The Prelude*, 31, 57–58, 159, 169, 425; *Prospectus*, 161–163; "Resolution and Independence," 169; "The Solitary Reaper," 28; *Sonnets upon the Punishment of Death*, 169; "The Tale of Margaret," 169; "Tintern Abbey," 169, 171–176, 288; "To a Cuckoo," 178, 179

Wright, Jay, 31–37, 577, 617; works by: "The Albuquerque Graveyard," 32; "The Cradle Logic of Autumn," 33; "Desire's Persistence," 34–36; *The Homecoming Singer*, 31–32

Wylie, Elinor, 351

Yahwist (Torah writer), 63, 95, 121, 613

Yale English Department, 186

Yates, Frances, 378

Yeats, Jack Butler (brother of William Butler Yeats), 487

Yeats, John Butler (father of William Butler Yeats), 487

Yeats, William Butler: audience of, 476; Blake and, 141, 206, 208, 460, 462, 464; "breaking" and "making" in, 491–492; Browning and, 355; Byzantium poems of, 227, 238, 239, 350, 459, 461; in Celtic Revival, 487; choice between perfection of work and perfection of life and, 531; classical allusions in, 465; Cuchulain plays by, 73, 462, 463–464; Dante and, 463–464, 596; death poems of, 463–464, 466, 484–485, 495–496; diction and metric of, 474, 483; Eliot and, 25; evasion of dualisms in, 490; Fascism and, 464; Freud and, 574; Gnosticism and, 486,

490, 542; God in, 486; Horton and, 480–481; on imagination, 2; Jonson and, 474; Keats and, 329; lack of human otherness in, 474; love and, 478, 491; Marlowe and, 465; marriage to Georgie Hyde-Lees, 462; Morris and, 477, 495; Nietzsche and, 141, 461, 462; occultism of, 462–463, 465, 472, 474, 479, 527; Owen and, 463; Pater and, 141, 460, 462; Plato and, 491; in poetic lineage, 460, 491, 627; relationship with Florence Farr Emery, 481; relationship with Margot Ruddock, 464; relationship with Maud Gonne, 462, 478, 491; religion and, 461, 478, 485; remorse and, 461, 466, 488, 610–611; revising his own poetry, 495; in Rhymers' Club, 487; Rossetti and, 495, 597; satyriasis of, 464, 466, 491; as sect of one, 625; shadow and, 472; Shakespeare and, 461, 596; Shelley and, 25, 141, 183, 189, 206–208, 227, 233, 234, 238–239, 259–260, 267, 270, 287, 297, 350, 435, 460–462, 464, 478–479, 493, 497, 499; soul vs. self as tension in, 461–462; Stevens and, 298, 449, 459, 476; Thoreau and, 495; Unity of Being and, 596; Vico and, 329; wisdom in, 462, 464; Wordsworth and, 491

Yeats, William Butler, works by: "Adam's Curse," 460, 477–478; "All Souls' Night," 479–483; "Among School Children," 488–491; "At Algeciras—A Meditation upon Death," 485; *At the Hawk's Well*, 73; "Blood and the Moon," 208; "Byzantium," 460, 461, 472, 499; "The Circus Animals' Desertion," 141, 461–462; *The Countess Cathleen*, 462; "Cuchulain Comforted," 73,

141, 237, 463–464, 466; "Cuchulain's Fight with the Sea," 73; "Death," 484; *The Death of Cuchulain*, 73, 463–464; "A Dialogue of Self and Soul," 460–461; "The Lake Isle of Innisfree," 495; "Long-Legged Fly," 464–465; "The Madness of King Goll," 492–495; "Mad Song," 476–477; "Man and the Echo," 141, 466; "My Convictions," 495–496; "News for the Delphic Oracle," 465–466; *On Baile's Strand*, 462; *The Only Jealousy of Emer*, 73; *Oxford Book of Modern Verse* (ed.), 463; "The Philosophy of Shelley's Poetry," 206–207; "Prayer for My Daughter," 438; "Prometheus Unbound," 207; *The Resurrection*, 259–260, 461, 478–479; "Ribh Considers Christian Love Insufficient," 485–486, 488; "The Second Coming," 183, 460, 461; "The Song of Wandering Aengus," 476–477; "Supernatural Songs," 485–486; "The Tower," 491; *The Tower*, 479; "Two Songs from a Play," 259–260, 479; "Under Ben Bulben," 237, 495–496; "Vacillation," 473–474; *A Vision*, 238, 462, 465, 479, 480, 483, 484, 596, 628; *The Wanderings of Oisin*, 462; *The Winding Stair*, 484, 485; "A Woman Young and Old," 483–484

Yerushalmi, Yosef Hayim, works by: *Zakhor: Jewish History and Jewish Memory*, 563

Young, Edward, works by: *Night-Thoughts*, 127–129

Zeller, Margaretha Catharine, 475
Zoroastrianism, 8, 204